China Academic Library

This book series collects, organizes and presents the master pieces in contemporary China studies. Titles in this series include those by Chinese authors who studied and worked abroad during early times whose works were originally in English and had already made great impacts in the Western world, such as Hu Shi, Fei Xiaotong and others; as well as works by more recent authors, Chinese and non-Chinese, that are of critical intellectual importance in introducing and understanding the transformation of the modern Chinese society. A wide variety of topics are covered by the series, from philosophy, economics, and history to law, cultural geography and regional politics. This series is a key English language resource for researchers and students in China studies and related subjects, as well as for general interest readers. The book series is a cooperation project between Springer and Foreign Language Teaching and Research Press of China.

More information about this series at http://www.springer.com/series/11562

Zhenmin Wang

Relationship Between the Chinese Central Authorities and Regional Governments of Hong Kong and Macao: A Legal Perspective

外语教学与研究出版社
FOREIGN LANGUAGE TEACHING AND RESEARCH PRESS

 Springer

Zhenmin Wang
School of Law
Tsinghua University
Beijing, China

Sponsored by Chinese Fund for the Humanities and Social Sciences (本书获中华社会科学基金资助)

ISSN 2195-1853   ISSN 2195-1861   (electronic)
China Academic Library
ISBN 978-981-13-2320-1   ISBN 978-981-13-2322-5   (eBook)
https://doi.org/10.1007/978-981-13-2322-5

Jointly published with Foreign Language Teaching and Research Publishing Co., Ltd, Beijing, China

The print edition is not for sale in Chinese mainland. Customers from Chinese mainland please order the print book from: Foreign Language Teaching and Research Publishing Co., Ltd.

Library of Congress Control Number: 2018952897

This Springer imprint is published by the registered company Springer Nature Singapore Pte Ltd.
The registered company address is: 152 Beach Road, #21-01/04 Gateway East, Singapore 189721, Singapore

Preface

Several years ago, Mr. Wu Hao of Beijing's Foreign Language Teaching and Research Press (FLTRP) suggested an English version of my 《中央与特别行政区关系——一种法治结构的解析》 (*Relationship Between the Chinese Central Authorities and Regional Governments of Hong Kong and Macao: A Legal Perspective* (Tsinghua University Press, 2002)), to be jointly published by FLTRP and Springer Group among the English series of "FLTRP-Springer China Academic Library." After years' effort, the translation finally came to an end. Before its publication, Mr. Wu asked me to write the preface anew, expounding the academic pursuit of this research and general design of its results, along with the content, structure, and inner logic of the book. As the author, it is my compelling duty to do that without doubt.

This book originates in my doctoral dissertation. From 1992 to 1995, I studied for a doctor's degree in the Law School of Renmin University of China under the tutorship of the famed constitutionalist Xu Chongde, specializing in the relationship between the Central Authorities and Special Administrative Regions under the Basic Law of Hong Kong Special Administrative Region. A member of the draft committee both of the 1982 Chinese Constitution and the Basic Laws of Hong Kong and Macao Special Administrative Regions, Prof. Xu, is undoubtedly an authority in this respect. For the purpose of this dissertation, I spent about two years studying and researching in the Law School of Hong Kong University, which greatly enlarged the content of my dissertation. Upon graduation in 1995, I taught Constitution in Tsinghua University. As the most active field of the Chinese Constitution, the Basic Law of Hong Kong Special Administrative Region becomes naturally a key point in Constitution teaching and research. Taking into consideration the real practice since Hong Kong's return to China, I revised and amended the dissertation, which turned out to be the 2002 publication by Tsinghua University. Quite unexpectedly, the book soon became a key reference book for the research of issues related to Hong Kong and "one country, two systems," as well as a must for the teaching and research of the Basic Law. For years, it has been the only monograph on the relationship between Chinese Central Authorities and Regional Governments of Hong Kong and Macao. As the book has already been sold out for long, Tsinghua University Press and I often received calls inquiring where to get it. To satisfy this demand, Joint Publishing HK published the book in 2014 in the original complex form of Chinese. At the end of the following year, I was transferred to the Liaison Office of the Central People's Government in the Hong Kong Special Administrative Region. The two years were spent on handling major issues on the relationship between the Central Authorities and HKSAR, which broadly updated my knowledge.

It is indeed much beyond my expectation that so many years after its publication, the book is still often been referred to and widely quoted. Given the changes and development over the decades, I should have revised and amended the book before having it translated into English. But the Press decided to have an English edition of the original text without revision. As I see it, they hope to present to their English readers a genuine picture of "one country, two systems" as well as its original design.

People nowadays often say "do not forget your original intention." So what is my original intention of writing this book? I think it is to discuss China's unique way of administrating Hong Kong and Macao under "one country, two systems." Obviously, Hong Kong and Macao is by no means a common issue. Innovative mind is needed so as to realize a win-win or even multi-win situation. I believe that in dealing with the relationship between the Central Authorities and the SARs, China has mainly drawn references in two aspects. One is its administration of the frontier area, especially the special system for the minority nationalities. As a matter of fact, throughout the dynasties there have always been special places requiring special treatment and enjoying policies and systems similar to *jimi fuzhou* that are at once hard and soft. Although it is not the direct source of "one country, two systems," there runs the same vain within the two in spirit. The other is the treatment of similar issues in modern and contemporary Western countries. As the saying goes, every family has a skeleton in the cupboard. Every country, be it under a unitary or federal system, has more or less special issues like China's special administrative regions. To name just a few, Scotland and Northern Ireland in Great Britain, Québec in Canada, Louisiana and Indigenous Indianans in America, Catalonia in Spain, and Crimea between Russia and Ukraine. Although there are lots of differences in details, the basic logic and thinking behind them are similar. In the vast cosmos, humankind is quite alone. Despite their hostile stances, it is all too natural that countries learn from each other. After all, in the foreseeable future, we cannot whatsoever learn from other planets. Therefore, it is no wonder if China takes inspiration from other nations so far as its "one country, two systems" is concerned.

This being said though, we should acknowledge that China's "peaceful unification and one country, two systems" is neither a simple replica of *jimi fuzhou* in history nor a direct transplant of a Western country's mode. It is a special program developed by China in its creative administration of Hong Kong and Macao Special Administrative Regions based on their respective situations. An intellectual property completely owned by China, it embodies typical Chinese wisdom and sets up a good example for other nations to learn. From that, we can also have a glimpse of the supernormal strategic thinking, solid strategic confidence, and excellent politic art of Chinese people when dealing with difficulties. An American historian once told me that the US always attempts to teach China how to do things, little thinking that it has lived for 200 years only, whereas China has five thousand years' civilization to boast already! So how did China manage to survive and come all this way when there had been no America, not to mention American's guidance? A lot of problems mankind face today have already been met with and solved by China. Therefore, Chinese people have a better say as far as administration is concerned. Neither advice nor guidance is needed from the Americans. Chinese people will always have the wisdom to tide over hardships both for itself and the world at large.

The purpose of this book is to discuss the unique logic and mode of China's administration of its special administrative regions under the "one country, two systems" policy from a legal perspective. Chapter 1 discusses a theoretic issue. According to the traditional science of constitutional law, the criterion for state structure is chiefly the power division between national government (central government or federal government) and local government (local government or state government). Specifically, if the power of the local government surpasses that of the national government, it is a federal state. If the other way around is the case, then it is a unitary one. But the case in China is that under a unitary system, special administration regions enjoy much more power than states under a federal system. Therefore, to judge a country is under a unitary system or a federal one, and the criterion is not the allocation of power alone. We should see who the power giver is, and who the power receiver. Although China's special administrative regions have much more power than a federal state in America, the power is given by the central government instead of inborn. Therefore, China under "one country, two systems" is still a unitary country.

Chapter 2 discusses the historical development of state structure in China, focusing on special local establishments in the past so as to locate special administration system in history and seek linkage.

Chapters 3 and 4 discuss the formation, connotation, and legalization of "one country, two systems," the legal status of special administrative regions, and the influence of such establishments on China's state structure.

The following six chapters are the core of this book, which discuss the basic principles governing the relationship between the Central Government and Special Administrative Regions, factors affecting the relationship between the two, and analyze in detail the rights and responsibilities of the Central Government and Special Administrative Regions, respectively. In addition, there are discussions on the management of several relative relationships, including departments, provinces, autonomous regions, and municipalities under the Central Government with Special Administrative Regions, and the relationship among Special Administrative Regions. After these follows a combing of organizational setting concerning the relationship between the Central Government and Special Administrative Regions, their working principles and systems. Finally, there is a study on typical cases happened during the first five years since Hong Kong's return in 1997.

After a systematic study on the relationship between the Central Government and Special Administrative Regions, I find that the key to its management is the rule of law, and the key to the rule of law is the constitutional review. Accordingly, the last chapter discusses the constitutional review system in China, the constitutional review (judicial review) in Special Administrative Regions under the "one country, two systems" policy, the role of the rule of law in maintaining national unification, and two methods of maintaining national unification. The process of the rule of law in China is directly related to the process of its national unification. The further a country goes in the rule of law, the firmer it is in unity, and the less likelihood its division. Therefore, my suggestion is to speed up the process of the rule of law on the one hand, and make better use of the rule of law so far as the relationship between the Central Government and Special Administrative Regions is concerned.

Over the past 20 years, there have been unending arguments as follows: How much power do Special Administrative Regions enjoy under the "one country, two systems" policy? Where is the limit of the high-degree autonomy? Under what circumstances will there be a "central intervention"? With these in mind, I once made an "experiment." Several years ago, an American legist asked me about the division of power between the Central Authorities and Special Administrative Regions under "one country, two systems," and the relationship between "one country" and "two systems." Deliberately, I spoke only of "two systems" without mentioning "one country"; I listed all kinds of autonomy Hong Kong SAR enjoys in accordance with the Basic Law, including executive, legislative and independent judicial power, independent power of execution, prosecution, jurisdiction, and adjudication, independent tax system, independent membership in such international organizations as WTO and International Olympic Committee, independent Customs and Exit–Entry, and the right to issue money which is allowed to a sovereign country only. I listed all the high degree of autonomy as stated in Chaps. 5 and 6 of the Basic Law, while omitting the right of the Central Authorities on purpose. I wondered how this American scholar would react. Out of my expectation, however, he burst out: If that is the case, what is the relationship between Hong Kong and China? Hong Kong is obviously an independent politic entity!"

Then, I told him the rights of the Central Authorities as stipulated in the Basic Law. In addition to the right to foreign affairs and defence which are familiar to all, the Central Authorities have the right to establish special administrative regions and stipulate major systems for them (including the right to determine the development of politic system in Hong Kong), and the right to appoint the Chief Executive and the principal officials of the executive authorities of the Hong Kong Special Administrative Region. The Chief Executive is accountable and shall report duty to the Central People's Government who has the right to issue directives to it. If the Standing Committee of the National People's Congress, after consulting the Committee for the Basic Law of the Hong Kong Special Administrative Region under it, considers that any law enacted by the legislature of the Region is not in conformity with the provisions of the Basic Law regarding affairs within the responsibility of the Central Authorities or regarding the relationship between the Central Authorities and the Region, the Standing Committee may return the law in question. Any law thus returned shall immediately be invalidated. The Standing Committee of the National People's Congress may add to or delete from the list of laws in Annex III after consulting its Committee for the Basic Law of the Hong Kong Special Administrative Region and the government of the Region. The power of interpretation of the Basic Law shall be vested in the Standing Committee of the National People's Congress, and so shall be the power of its amendment. Most important of all, all the autonomy enjoyed by HK SAR are vested by the Central Government in accordance with the Basic Law, in other words, the Central Government has the "right to give right." All these rights as a whole are called "general control power." This power, as stipulated in the Basic Law, is a natural result now that China resumes its sovereignty over Hong Kong. It was until then that my American listener understood the real meaning of "one country, two systems," and that the relationship between the Central Government and Hong Kong SAR is by no means what some Hong Kong people described, that is, the complete picture, origin, and truth of the "one country, two systems" policy.

Therefore, if we continue to stress only "two systems" and the high degree of autonomy, to the neglect of "one country" and the rights of the Central Government in accordance with the Basic Law, there will arise a wrong impression that "Hong Kong is an independent political entity" and even that "Hong Kong can be independent." I always wonder how on earth that a 20-year-old person in Hong Kong gets the idea that Hong Kong can be independent? Where does an idea as absurd as that come from? Now I have the answer. It is because for long we only speak of "two systems" without the least mentioning of "one country," and that irresponsibly, we tell them about "two systems" and "a high degree of autonomy," dishonestly omitting "one country" and the rights of the Central Government. In consequence, they can not have a whole picture of the "one country, two systems" policy and the Basic Law, nor do they know that the original intention of the "one country, two systems" policy is for the unification of China. That is why whenever the Central Government exercises its right in accordance with the Law, chances are it is distorted as "an intervention" or "western district ruling Hong Kong." We should honestly tell the truth of "one country, two systems" to the young generation in Hong Kong, letting them know not only "two systems" and the high degree of autonomy vested to Hong Kong, but also "one country" and the rights and responsibilities of the Central Government. We should let them know not only their rights in accordance with the Law, but also their responsibilities and obligations to the country and society in accordance with the Law. "One country, two systems" is neither what one imagines nor what a senior authority describes. Its true and complete picture is elaborated in the Chinese Constitution and the Basic Law, and it is that edition which all should comply with.

The past two decades have proved the success of the "one country, two systems" policy both in theory and practice. But we have to confess that throughout history and across the world, "one country, one system" is the norm. Even the European Union today adopts a unified system in many cases. For instance, more than 20 countries adopt the same exit–entry system. The reason is that humankind tends to pursue convenience both in work and life, the more convenient, the better, not the other way around. In point of fact, "one country, two systems" has incurred a lot of inconveniences. I often hear people in the Chinese mainland complaining: After Hong Kong's return to China in 1997, it becomes even more inconvenient going to Hong Kong than to Britain or the US! There goes a true funny story. A girl in the Chinese mainland married an English man. They planned a tour of Hong Kong via Beijing. The Englishman needed no visa procedures but a plane ticket. But a Hong Kong visa was required of the Chinese girl which she failed to get. And their plan miscarried! In utter astonishment the husband asked: "Has Hong Kong returned to China or not? Does Hong Kong belong to Britain or China? Why as an Englishman I can come and go to Hong Kong freely, while a Chinese should have so much trouble?" He tried in vain to get an answer.

I also had a similar experience. About ten years ago, a Canadian professor attended a conference in Hong Kong. After that, I invited him to another conference in Beijing. But he was detained in Hong Kong airport when checking, because he had no Chinese visa! Greatly annoyed, he called me in the airport: "Has Hong Kong returned to China or not? If I have arrived in Hong Kong, am I not in China already?" I said yes to his answer, but as for why a person going to the Chinese mainland from Hong Kong has to apply for a Chinese visa, whereas the same person going to America from Hawaii need no American visa, my explanation was the policy of "one country, two systems." My Canadian friend retorted: "What 'one country, two systems' has to do with me?" It was until then that I realized the majority of people in the world do not know "one country, two systems." What they know is that Hong Kong has returned to China, taking it for granted that going to Hong Kong is like going to Beijing or Shanghai. No other visa is needed. Quite obviously, "one country, two systems" is inconvenient both to our foreign friends and us, and the world at large do not know nor understand it.

Since Hong Kong's return to China, the Central Government has proposed quite a few well-intended measures favorable to Hong Kong, which, unfortunately, were either demonized or defiled by some people in Hong Kong. For instance, the Central Government has been long working hard for the earliest realization of general election in Hong Kong. The general election plan in 2014 was not a "perfect" general election in western style, but it signaled a good beginning. Quite unexpectedly, however, the opposition party in Hong Kong vetoed it, which was extremely irrational and unwise. In consequence, democracy in Hong Kong suffered a lot, and Hong Kong missed the opportunity of general election. Another example is that about ten years ago, the Central Government, at the invitation of Hong Kong SAR, agreed to extend the high-speed rail to Hong Kong. When it was almost completed, the opposition party opposed to the idea of "co-location of immigration and customs" at the terminal of West Kowloon, which would otherwise benefit all people. Especially after the failure of national security legislation in Hong Kong in 2003, Hong Kong has been weak in maintaining national security. As a result, local radicals sprang up, and some went so far as to raise the banner of "Hong Kong's independence." In various names, Hong Kong Independence organizations continuously challenged the bottom line of the country, and the red line of "one country." These are the things I could not have foreseen when I was writing this book. People will think that as time goes by, the relationship between the Chinese mainland and Hong Kong SAR will be closer and closer, instead of the opposite.

Now that the good-will "one country, two systems" has incurred so many troubles, and the cost for its operation is so high, why then in his speech at the 20th anniversary of Hong Kong's return on July 1, 2017, President Xi Jinping still reiterated the unswerving implementation of "one country, two systems," and promised to continue doing things in strict accordance with "one country, two systems" and the Basic Law? As I see it, it is not only because of the "50-years" commitment, but more because of its original intention. The practice of "one country, two systems" in Hong Kong SAR is in conformity with China's strategic benefit.

Some friends ask me whether I am worried about today's disorder in Hong Kong SAR, especially the Occupy Turmoil in 2014, civil unrest in Mong Kok, public insult of China at parliament member's inauguration, independence spreading on campus, and other inconceivable affairs that are irrational and quite abnormal. Should these things happen in other countries, there will be serious punishment. But in Hong Kong they were just let pass. My friend was very anxious and worried. I comforted him that China has enough wisdom, confidence, patience, composure, and capacity to solve these problems. However, they riot, Hong Kong can not run away. In recent years, there has been a similar case like the 79-day illegal occupation in Hong Kong in 2014. The result irrevocably was a hard fight and great loss of life. But it was peacefully settled in Hong Kong by a piece of prohibition from the court. Therein lay the strategic composure and wisdom of the Chinese people. Time and trend will always stand by the side of righteousness. We will not sway with the flag of the opposition party. Despite the continuous wind and tide over the twenty years, the increasingly close cooperation and exchange between Hong Kong SAR and the Chinese mainland cannot be stopped. The peaceful development of China and the complete rejuvenation of Chinese nation cannot be stopped. In the vast chessboard of history, it is all too natural that Hong Kong makes some troubles. But that will not change the general trend of development both in China and the world. Therefore, we will as ever forge ahead, clinging to our original intention.

I would like to give my sincere gratitude to Wang Huimin, chief translator of this book. We got to know each other through Wu Hao, and exchanged views on many details in the process of translation. His understanding of Chinese and Western culture and proficiency in both Chinese and English languages deeply impressed me. How woeful that he departed last year! Here, I express my deepest respect and grievance to him. My heartfelt thanks also go to the late Professors Huang Yulin and Xu Chongde. Both have generously helped me throughout my research.

I am also indebted to Prof. Raymond Wacks in the Law School of Hong Kong University who invited me to his University and provided all kinds of conveniences. Professor Chen Hongyi, then Dean of the Law School of Hong Kong University, Prof. Yash Ghai, and many other friends in the field of law in Hong Kong and Macao who have offered to help, my gratitude also owes to them.

Leaders and colleagues at Tsinghua University assisted me a lot during my 20-year stay from 1995 to 2015. I am thankful to them all.

Lastly, I am especially obliged to Wu Hao for his enormous effort in the translation and final publication of this book. Without his encouragement and promotion, the English edition of this book would be impossible.

Beijing, China   Zhenmin Wang
March 2018

Contents

Chapter 1
The State Structure (Nation–Region Relationship) in Constitutional Law

1.1 The Status of the State Structure Theory in Constitutional Law

It is often said that a constitution is a nation's basic law, that it stipulates the nation's basic political, economic, and legal systems, that it embodies the institutionalization and legalization of the democratic system, and that it manifests the balance of power amongst the nation's social classes.[1] Put in clear and simple terms, constitutions may be explained as the law that defines peoples' political relationships and political acts, that they are a country's "fundamental law," and that they are the law that regulates democratic governance. Constitutions resolve the question of how human beings' democratic governance is to be conducted, i.e., how democratic governance in which the multitudes participate is to be legalized and institutionalized so that it proceeds in a well-ordered manner. The constitutions of capitalist countries are designed to resolve the question of legalizing and institutionalizing capitalist democracy, whereas socialist constitutions are designed to resolve the question of how to use laws to ensure socialist democracy. Constitutions are evidently the most important among a nation's diverse laws due to their intense political and fundamental nature. In modern societies, the form of democratic governance chosen and the sort of constitution enacted often determine the destiny of a state and nation.

A constitution generally stipulates a nation's democratic governance in three respects. The first, and also the most important respect, is that it must first of all stipulate the relationship between the people and the state in a country, or in other words, to whom does the state belong, by which people is it owned, what powers and rights do the people enjoy, and what powers does the state wield (via the government). This is the "state system" issue often referred to in political science and constitutional law. Up to the present, state systems have consisted in the main of

---

[1] Wu Jialin. *Constitutional Law*. Beijing: Qunzhong Press, 1983, p. 46.

© Foreign Language Teaching and Research Publishing Co., Ltd and Springer Nature Singapore Pte Ltd. 2019
Z. Wang, *Relationship Between the Chinese Central Authorities and Regional Governments of Hong Kong and Macao: A Legal Perspective*, China Academic Library, https://doi.org/10.1007/978-981-13-2322-5_1

two varieties. One of these is the monarchy, where all powers of the state belong to the ruler, the ruling household and the state are integrated as a single entity, the state is the private property of the ruler and his expanded household, the powers of the ruler are unlimited, and the people are merely the ruler's subjects and have no powers or rights of any kind. The other state system is the democratic system. Under this system, all powers and rights of the state belong to the people, the state pertains to the multitudes, only the people's power is unlimited, the power enjoyed by the state is conferred to it by the people, and for which reason the government is limited government. Since the constitution is a product of the institutionalization and legalization of democracy, there is, strictly speaking, no constitution to speak of under a monarchy.[2]

Article 1 of China's Constitution stipulates that China is "a socialist state under the people's democratic dictatorship led by the working class and based on the alliance of workers and peasants." Article 2 stipulates that "all power in the People's Republic of China belongs to the people." Chapter Two specifically stipulates the fundamental rights the people should enjoy and the duties they should fulfill with regard to the state, that is, China's state system, or in other words, the relationship between the state and the people as defined in China's Constitution.

Two, having obtained certain powers from the people, the state must set up various state institutions and distribute those powers for implementation by different state structures. The second task or mission of a constitution is to stipulate the various state powers exercised by the different state institutions in a lateral sense, mainly by conducting a division of duties and work among such state institutions as the legislative, executive, and judicial organs, that is, the so-called "state system" issue. The way a country sets up its own state institutions, the way it allocates state powers among its various state institutions, and how these powers are deployed to best effect—all of these must be consistent with its own political, economic, historical, geographical and social circumstances and may not be done in a willful or arbitrary manner. The question of science exists here as well. Those who design and draft constitutions must also be scientists, and must handle political system issues with a conscientious and scientific attitude. For example, such matters as preventing graft and corruption among government officials by means of government institutions and how to set up government institutions in order to improve the efficiency and effects of government work are first and foremost scientific issues, not simply political issues.

There have always been a great many ways of differentiating the types of political systems. Some Western capitalist states divide state powers, set up state institutions, and adopt a presidential system in line with the principle of "separation of exec-

---

[2]Scholars hold different views as to whether constitutions may or may not exist under a monarchical system. For example, Britain, as the place of origin of the modern constitution, has consistently retained its monarchical form, yet we cannot claim that Britain lacks a constitution or doubt that a substantive democracy (a capitalist democracy, of course) exists in Britain. True, Britain's is an unwritten constitution, but an unwritten constitution is nonetheless a constitution. Hence, even from the perspective of Britain's case, the statement that constitutions are the institutionalization and legalization of democracy is not wrong. Britain would certainly not have developed a constitution had it clung to its traditional, "classical" monarchy.

utive, legislative and judicial powers." Others implement a parliamentary political
system in line with the principle of "parliamentary sovereignty." China's Constitution, on its part, stipulates that China's fundamental political system is the national
people's congress system, similar to the parliamentary system practiced by states
that implement "parliamentary sovereignty."

Three, having obtained certain powers from the people, it is not enough for the
state to conduct a lateral division of these powers for implementation by various state
institutions; the state must also conduct a vertical division and set up various levels
of government from the top downward or vice versa, and have government structures
at different levels exercise the diverse state powers, that is, the constitution's third
important mission. In other words, it should vertically stipulate the relations between
the state as a whole and its component parts as well as define how the divisions
between the national and regional governments should be fashioned and what kind
of local government systems to adopt. Or, in the common parlance: How the limits
of authority are to be defined between the central and local authorities. Such is the
issue of the state structure and local government systems in terms of constitutional
law. There are broadly two main systems in this respect—the federal system and
the unitary system. China implements the unitary system, and that is the subject
discussed in the present book.

The three aspects listed above constitute the basic framework and basic substance
of a constitution. A constitution effectuates its regulation of socio-political relations
by stipulating the relations of the people and the state and by defining the state's
lateral and vertical powers and functions. Those are the foci of constitutional law,
which researches such matters as how to regulate the relationship between the people
and the state as well as the relationships among diverse departments and between
the central and local authorities. See the following diagram:

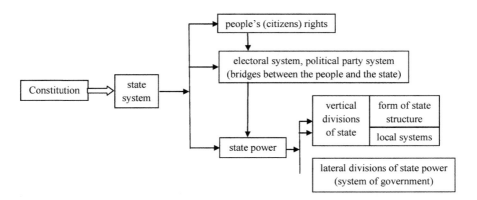

We see from the above diagram that state structure occupies a most important
position in the constitution as a whole and in constitutional law since it directly concerns the unity or splitting [division] of the state and it concerns the very survival of
the state, that is, a matter of real significance for today's China as well. It should be

noted that China's constitutional law quarters had never differentiated between the concepts "state structure" and "local government." China's scholars had conducted a great deal of research on local government, but these were mainly studies on local state power systems below the provincial level, such as issues of municipal and county establishments and village and county governments. Very little research was done on state power at the provincial level, or in other words on the regulation of relationships of the central authorities with the provinces, autonomous regions and directly administered municipalities, or on major changes in the state structure subsequent to the implementation of Reform and Opening Up to the Outside.[3] Traditionally, the relationship between the central authorities and provincial-level governance was only mentioned in passing when discussing local systems and was rarely accorded in-depth research as an independent issue.[4]

In view of this circumstance, I call on China's scholars of constitutional law in particular to pay attention to China's state structure, or in other words, to the relationship of the central authorities with provincial-level governance (including that of provinces, ethnic minority autonomous regions, and special administrative regions), conduct in-depth and detailed studies in this respect, and thereby serve the great cause of national unity and the needs of developing a socialist market economy and democratic rule by law. This book chooses one aspect of this major issue—i.e., the relationship between the central authorities and the special administrative regions—for conducting a monographic study.

1.2   Basic Theories of the State Structure

1.2.1   State Governance by Means of Regions

Human beings are social creatures who naturally form certain types of social organizations and who make a living and seek progress by means of collective strengths. Single and isolated individuals cannot exist in the world. The great Greek philosopher Aristotle once said: "Man is an animal whose nature it is to live in a polis (city). Man is by nature a political animal."[5] However, the forms of man's social organizations have differed throughout the different stages of society's development. In primitive society, man's social organizations were formed in line with natural consan-

---

[3]In various Chinese writings on constitutional law, the concepts "state structures" and "local government systems" were seldom differentiated and often mutually inclusive. The two concepts ought to be differentiated and their various connotations and denotations specified so as to standardize the concepts of constitutional law and make them more scientific as well as to highlight the importance of state structures.

[4]In the textbook *The Chinese Constitution* edited by Xu Chongde for China's institutions of higher learning, Xu presented these two issues in independent chapters and expounded both in great detail. See Xu Chongde. *The Chinese Constitution*. Beijing: China Renmin University Press, 1989.

[5]Translation from H. D. F. Kitto. *The Greeks*. New York: Penguin, 1951, 1957.

guineous relationships rather than being divided by area of inhabitation. Everything was aligned in accordance with blood lines; there were no signs of anything "man-made." But later on, exploitation and social classes arose in the wake of advances in the forces of production. An entirely new, hitherto unknown, and immense human social organization emerged—the state. Compared with the primitive clan, the state, besides serving as a tool for class domination and class oppression, also embodied a very important difference, i.e., in its internal structure. The state no longer exercised self-organization according to the ties of consanguinity as was done in the primitive clan, but structured itself in accordance with people's different areas of inhabitation. When discussing the origins of the state, Engels noted: "As distinct from the old gentile order, the state, first, divides its subjects according to territory."[6] And, "This organization of citizens according to locality is a feature common to all states."[7]

Indeed, all states, whether in ancient or modern times or in China or abroad, have separated and governed their citizens by regions, irrespective of the size of their territories or populations. No ruler, regardless of his or her eminence, greatness, or prestige, has ever been able to control every locality and every citizen in his or her domains, and has always had to "divide and rule" while retaining some important powers for his or her own personal enforcement. First of all, a state in its entirety needs an authoritative national (central) government to act as a unified representative of the state both internally and externally. Second, the state is divided into large regions, and limits of authority between the unified national (central) government and the various large regions are well defined, thereby forming the structures of diverse kinds of states and determining whether a state implements the unitary system or a federal system. After that, the large regions are divided into increasingly lower tiers of governance, right down to the lowest grassroots administrative regions. And then corresponding local governments are set up by various means and methods in the various tiers of administrative regions based on their different circumstances, thereby forming local systems with different characteristics. This produces a pyramid-like structure that may be graphically illustrated as follows:

---

[6]Friedrich Engels. *The Origin of Family, Private Property and State*. pp. 752–753.
[7]Translation from H. D. F. Kitto. *The Greeks*. New York: Penguin, 1951, 1957.

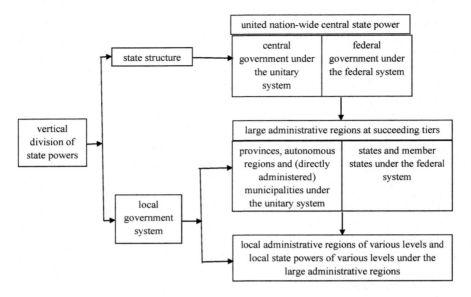

From this graph, we can see how a state is governed by means of dividing it into regions. We can also see the differences and relations between the state structure and local government systems and their positions in the constitution as a whole.

1.2.2 General Factors that Affect State Structures

Based on the above analyses, by "state structure" is meant the vertical structures within a state. That involves studies of which major components comprise the state as a whole, and the relationships of these components with the state as a whole. In other words, what forms does the state adopt to regulate the mutual relationships between the entire state and its components; how does the state conduct divisions of power between nationwide and local political powers, which are original powers and which are derived powers among the powers of the national government (either central government or federal government) and those of the local governments (meaning the provinces, states, and districts) in a state's vertical division of powers, and to whom do the residual powers go?

The choice of state structure by a country's ruling class is by no means haphazard; it is governed and limited by a series of factors—economic, cultural, historical, ethnic, religious, linguistic, geographical, military, and so forth. When the rulers give consideration to this issue, their first concern is of course that their choice must favor the consolidation of their rule and strengthen their vested political interests. In no country does one find exceptions. Also, the decision-makers must also give consideration to the most vigorous ways of promoting the state's economic and cultural development; and they must also take into consideration their country's historical traditions, the people's political conventions and aspirations, and their level of acknowledgement of the unified authority. Ethnic and religious factors, too, have always been most important. If a state comprises many ethnic groups with highly disparate religious beliefs and even with very different languages, it must give full consideration to these factors when determining its state structure. National defense and security must of course be a matter of concern for the decision-makers. And one thing is quite clear: unless there are special reasons, every country in the sense of an integrated state must have a unified national defense setup and normally does not disperse its military command powers to the localities. When defining the relations between the state as a whole and its parts, consideration must be given to choices that favor the safeguarding of the country's security. Geography is also an important aspect. Experts in political geography point out that the strength of modern nations stems from the territories in which they have settled down and exist.[8] The division into large administrative regions and the extent of the powers enjoyed by the localities is to a certain degree related to the topography and configuration of their lands. Insulated regions may form self-enclosed systems because "the mountains are high and the emperor is far away," and the powers they enjoy are greater because of their difficulty of access to the "higher-ups." Conversely, local governments that "lie at the feet of the Son of Heaven" and whose every move is in the purview of the "higher-ups" dare not make full or ample use of their power even if given substantial powers.

The state's highest decision-makers can decide the state structure their country adopts only after giving ample and comprehensive consideration to the various factors described above. From the perspective of the history of constitutions, the forming of the state structure of all countries is a "natural" historical process which rulers cannot alter by issuing arbitrary orders, although rulers may make adjustments to the structure so that it is more conducive to consolidating their rule.

1.3 Three Major Models of State Structure

The state structure issue is, in substance, a question of which level of government should best be used for implementing a country's sovereignty and powers. By "sovereignty" is meant a country's highest and ultimate political authority, both internal and external. By calling a government a "sovereign government," we mean that this government is legally and politically independent of all other governments, and that it may make decisions independently. Based on this understanding, we may in the main identify three kinds of state structures, i.e., the confederal system, the federal system, and the unitary system.

Many world states with extensive territories have adopted the federal system, as, for example the United States, Russia, Canada, Australia, India, and Germany. Some

---

[8]Geoffrey Parker. *Western Geopolitical Thought in the Twentieth Century.* London: Croom Helm, 1985.

small countries, such as Switzerland, also implement a federal system. Other countries, such as France, Britain, Italy, Sweden, and Japan as well as China, implement the unitary system. Generally speaking, federal systems are more suitable for countries with large areas and complex ethnic make-ups, whereas unitary systems are best for small countries and countries with single ethnic group.

1.3.1   The Concepts of the Three Major State Structures

The state structures adopted by various countries in the world may well be characterized as manifold and multifarious. Confederations, federations, and unitary systems are merely the three main forms.

1.3.1.1   The Confederal System

Confederations are loose coalitions formed for certain political and economic purposes by states that possess independent sovereignty and constitutes one form of national alliance. Although confederations are formed on the basis of certain legal documents, they do not have a unified "nationwide" constitution in the strict sense of the word, nor do they have a nationwide general government or a unified nationality (citizenship) or unified finances. Nor do they possess the main attributes of a state; they are more like a closely linked international organization, and for that reason are not comparable with, and are qualitatively different from, the unitary and federal systems. It may be said that confederations are quasi-states that bear some of the characteristics of states, and are in general a form or process of transition toward "complete states." However, whether they are able to become truly unified "complete states" depends on a variety of complex factors.

One example of the confederal system often cited by academics is the "North American Confederation" prior to the formal establishment of today's United States of America, i.e., the "United States of America" from 1781 to 1789 established on the basis of the Articles of Confederation that entered into force in 1781.[9] At the very outset, the Articles clearly stipulated: "Each state retains its sovereignty, freedom, and independence, and every power, jurisdiction and right…," and the states "enter into a league of friendship" only for the sake of "their common defense, the security of their liberties, and their mutual and general welfare…." It is evident that each of the states retained its form as a country and possessed independent sovereignty. The confederal government was not vested with the highest and final powers of decision-making; it was merely a coordinating institution, or it provided a forum for meetings attended by the various member states and had some power to exhort and advise the

---

[9]The United States of America (U.S.A. or U.S. for short, or colloquially "The States"). From its name, it is evident that the United States of America was new country (nation) composed of a number of states.

various states, and was therefore called a "league of friendship." This "league" was formally replaced by what was substantially a "joint-stock company" in 1789.

1.3.1.2 The Federal System

The "federal system" refers to a new state in the complete sense, formed by a number of states or political entities for certain political and economic purposes, the member states of which each retains its own form and a number of powers, and only "delegate" powers related to sovereignty and national defense to the federation for execution thereof. The delimitation of powers between the federal government and the governments of the member states is clearly defined in writing in a constitution, while "residual powers" are retained by the member states or the people. In states with a federal system, there exists a unified, federation-wide constitution as well as a central government and legislative institutions and a judicial system. At the same time, each member state also retains its own constitution, central government, legislative institutions, and judicial system.

The U.S.A. is a typical federal system state. As well as the federal government having it own constitution and its own central government and congress and federal laws, its 50 member states too all have their own constitutions, central governments, congresses, and laws, and the federal government is not empowered to intervene in the everyday administration by governments of the member states. Hence, there are altogether 51 constitutions, 51 central governments, and 51 sets of laws in the United States as a whole. This is a typical federal system. Although there are states within the nation-state under the federal system, externally the federal government exercises the nation's sovereignty in a unified manner and has only one voice on the international stage. The federal government in fact serves as the commonly shared ministry of foreign affairs and ministry of national defense for all of its member-state governments.

The true essence of the federal system rests in "balancing," i.e., striking a balance between the national interests of the country as a whole and the local interests of each member state and preventing any party from "aggrandizing" its own powers. In terms of the composition of the two chambers of Congress, each state, regardless of its size, has two seats in the Senate, and their main function is to represent the local interests of the states. In the House of Representatives, the seats are apportioned according to the number of people in each state. There are a total of 435 congressional electoral districts throughout the country; congressmen are directly voted for and elected by each electoral district, respectively, and their main function is to represent the interests of the country as a whole. Hence, the U.S. Congress is a venue that regulates national interests and local interests, a place where various forces openly and legally contend and engage in "all-out competition and rivalry," and which, in essence, constitutes a "political free market." While ensuring the interests of each state, an important function of the federal Congress is also to safeguard the unity and interests of the country as a whole and seek to balance national interests and local interests at the constitutional level. The U.S. Supreme Court is the highest institution in the United States for resolving disputes on the limits of federal authority and member-state authority. Among its nine Justices, there are always a few who tend more toward protecting national interests and others who lean toward protecting state and local interests, and although their views are at times sharply opposed, they must work together to reach certain compromises. The outcome of such compromises is to afford a certain degree of satisfaction to the interests of each side, but not complete satisfaction. This is a sort of dynamic balance. Regardless of how intense the disputes between the two sides may be, neither is apt to resort to force of arms, and the country will not be reduced to a situation of schisms.

Special note should be taken of the fact that under the American federal system, the federation and all of the states have their own parallel and independent government systems to carry out the duties devolved on them by the Constitution. It is true that the governments of all states and localities have their own complete sets of institutions to enforce state laws and local laws and to safeguard state interests and local interests. However, the federal government's administrative, judicial, and legislative duties are not fulfilled through the states' or local government institutions; the federal government has its own independent institutions that are strewn throughout the country and take charge of federal matters. The U.S. national government, or in other words the federal government, of course has its own set of institutions in the U.S. capital Washington D.C. In addition to these, all of the legislative, judicial, and administrative departments of the central federal government have their own branch offices in each state to directly carry out their constitutional duties and answer directly to the people. Members of the federal Congress set up offices in their own electoral districts which in fact exercise the function of soliciting local public opinion. These offices may be regarded as the federal Congress's "information and intelligence centers" and as "centers for disseminating general knowledge of law among the populace." As regards the federal court system, the federal government, in addition to establishing a federal Supreme Court, has also set up 13 federal appellate courts throughout the country, also known as federal intermediate courts. Each of these courts has jurisdiction over three or more states. Further down are established 94 federal district courts. These federal courts are responsible for handling appeals related to federal affairs. Meanwhile, each state has also set up its own court system, each with different appellations. The court systems in the states are responsible for legal actions within the states. The various departments of the federal administrative system also have their own independent working bodies which come in direct contact with the populace and exercise the administrative duties conferred on the federal government by the Constitution; they do not perform their duties through the various state governments or local governments. This is one aspect of the federal system of which we previously had insufficient understanding.

As to why things are done in this way, I believe the main reason is that all state governments and local governments in the United States are produced through direct elections by the local people instead of being appointed by the federal government. This results in the state governments and local governments being critically dependent on the likes of dislikes of the voters, being responsible to "those below" rather than to "those above," and evincing no need to report on their work to Washington

D.C. In the absence of a strong controlling and balancing mechanism, this circum-stance would very likely evolve as "self-aggrandizement" and separatist tendencies among local governments, and even schisms in the nation. To prevent the emergence of local separatism or even schisms in the nation under the circumstances of exercis-ing the federal system and a high degree of local autonomy, the U.S. Constitution, in addition to stipulating that military and diplomatic affairs must be handled in a unified manner and that the various states may not form external alliances (i.e., may not unilaterally declare independence), has, in terms of the institutional system, also established an entire set of federal government institutions to protect nationwide interests and the nation's unity. Wherever the Constitution stipulates that matters come under the responsibility and jurisdiction of the federal authorities, the federal government is sure to set up its own institutions and put them in charge, and does not lightly entrust these to the member states or local governments. In the view of the founders of the United States, allowing locally elected local officials to exercise federal government duties, safeguard nationwide interests and "defer to the overall situation" was a no-no, as that would have been tantamount to "asking a tiger to give up its skin."

Moreover, the U.S. federal government and the governments of each member state do not necessarily pertain to the same political party, each of which has problems of ingratiating itself with voters, contending for votes, and being reelected. Hence, when the federal government wishes to do some good deed—as for instance when GOP President George W. Bush implemented a tax reduction policy after taking office in January 2001—it of course took the benefits of the tax reduction directly to each voter. The federal treasury sent letters directly to the voters through its offices in various localities to inform them about tax-reimbursement matters. It thus gave voters the sense that the Bush government was as good as its word, in the hope that they would vote for Bush again four years later. The federal government naturally opted to do this good deed by itself rather than "bother" a Democrat state governor with "helping with" and "sharing in" that political career move. Of course, if anything bad happens, such as the electric power crisis that took place in Democratic Party-ruled California in 2001, the federal government and state governments make clear distinctions between the responsibilities that each should bear, and thereby avoid any blurring of responsibilities between the federal and local governments and between the political parties as well as prevent any mutual attributing of credits or responsibilities. Hence, the federal government insists on spreading its own branch institutions all over the country for the sake of maintaining contact with the populace and handling national affairs that fall under federal jurisdiction. There is good reason to do so.

1.3.1.3   The Unitary System

The unitary system, also known as the centralized system, refers to a state or nation that is composed of a number of ordinary local regions that do not possess the right to self-determination and in which state power is in the main concentrated in institutions of central authority. In terms of the theory of constitutional law, the local governments are merely agencies of the central government and represent the central government in the implementation of state power in their own localities. Major decision-making powers are held by the central authorities; the local governments often only have the power to implement and to make suggestions, and this power is conferred on them by the central authorities. They themselves possess no "inherent" powers. There is, in the nation as a whole, only one constitution and only one central government, and moreover only one nationally unified legislative organ and one judicial system. All localities must accept the central authorities' unified leadership; they have no independent powers separate from those of the central authorities. The central government exercises unified state power, both internally and externally, and qualifies as the sole principal under international law. Such is the unitary system in the traditional and strict sense of the term.

It should be noted, however, that numerous local self-government units usually exist in countries under the unitary system even though these countries emphasize centralism, and many localities enjoy certain freedoms. Based on ethnic and historical reasons, and the better to safeguard national unity and ethnic solidarity or for other specially designated purposes, the central government empowers people within certain areas to elect their own representative institutions and local governments and to autonomously administer local affairs in their own localities, generally without interference from the central government. The powers enjoyed by these autonomous localities are conferred by the central authorities and are derived rather than original. Hence, the powers of autonomous localities may at times be quite considerable, yet are nevertheless limited. And most importantly, the autonomous localities have no powers of self-determination, and they may not unilaterally secede from the central government and declare independence.

1.3.2   The Differences Between the Three Kinds of State Structure

There are many differences between the three state structures—confederate, federal, and unitary. However, the most basic differences are two.

1.3.2.1   The Foci of the Powers They Establish Differ

Theoretically, the confederal system means that the member states or member countries of a "nation-state" are political entities that possess independent sovereignty, and the nationwide confederal system merely exercises limited political powers permitted by the populace and by each member organization. The focus of state power as a whole rests on the "localities." Under the unitary system, state sovereignty rests entirely on implementation by the central government, each regional government is completely dependent on the central government, the ultimate powers of decision for all matters rest with the central authorities, and the focus of state power is also on the central authorities. The federal system, on the other hand, finds itself between the confederal and the unitary systems in terms of the distribution of state powers. National sovereignty is shared between the national federal government and the various member-state governments and leans slightly toward the member-state governments. On certain matters, the national government is supreme and the member-state governments must bow to the national government. But on certain other matters, the member-state governments are supreme and the national government must defer to the ultimate powers as exercised by the member-state governments on such matters.

A prominent characteristic of the federal system is that it allows the existence of various independent power centers, national powers are amply dispersed among the various levels of government nationwide, and the level of government that should best exercise these powers is determined by the nature of the matter in question. As an American scholar has stated that the basic political fact of federalism is that it creates separate, self-sustaining centers of power, prestige, and profit.[10] Under such a system, political personalities obtain their powers from their respective localities and regions, and they work to fulfill the interests of their own localities.

For example, on May 24, 2001, James Jeffords, a GOP senator from Vermont in the U.S. Federal Senate, disagreed with some new Republican policies and decided to leave the Republican Party to become an independent senator, and thereafter sided with the Democratic Party when casting votes. His decision altered the Senate's "political ecology," upset the 50-50 balance of power between the Democratic and Republican parties, and turned the Democrats into the majority party in the Senate with a one-vote lead. For Senator Jeffords, making such a big decision first of all required the approval or acknowledgement of voters in his own state, and so he made a special trip from Washington back to Vermont to announce this major decision to voters in his home state and explain to them why he was doing what he did. Since the voters had elected him to the Senate on the strength of his Republican background and stand, he of course had to provide his voters with a clear explanation for why he was about to change his party affiliation and political viewpoints. He himself was clearly aware that his powers came from the voters and that he represented the interests of his home state in the Senate.

Under the federal system, the powers of the federal authorities and member states are clearly defined by a written constitution. Yet overlaps and conflicts may still exist between the powers of the federal national government and those of regional governments, and numerous contradictions may arise between them. In the United States, for example, administration of highways and welfare projects fall mainly within the powers and responsibilities of state governments, despite the fact that these projects may be using federal government funds. Education, public security, and land administration, on the other hand, are chiefly the functions of local government, or in other words fall within the authority of cities, counties, and special

---

[10]Truman D. B. "Federalism and the Party System." In MacMahon Arthur, ed., *Federalism: Mature and Emergent.* New York: Russell, 1955, p. 123.

regions instead of mainly within the duties of the federal or state governments. In such matters as a good many social welfare projects, the management of all inter-state highways, all measures for improving municipal administration, providing job opportunities for the unemployed, improving the quality of water, and even military conscription (for the National Guard), the national government, has not been able to exercise as many powers as it would wish. It can only use such means as regulations, grants, plans, argumentation, and even cajolery to try and get the various state and local governments to consciously manage these endeavors in line with the targets of the national government. Of course, under the federal system, the member-state governments and local governments must also fully respect the federal government's exercise of powers in regard to matters that fall within the jurisdiction of the fed-eral government. However, in countries which implement the unitary system, as for example France, such matters as welfare, education, highways, public order, and land-use all come under the authority of the national government, and the situation is much more simple.

The foci of power as devised and established under the three kinds of state structure may be diagrammed as follows:

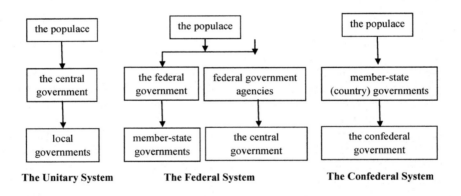

1.3.2.2   Differences of "Individuality" Under Constitutions and International Laws

No matter what kind of state structure they adopt, all countries have, in addition to a national government, a number of regional government entities such as states, prefectures, provinces, territories, districts, cities, counties, townships, villages, and the like. However, the legal status of the various state structures differs. In terms of constitutional status, only the next largest regional governments (state, prefectural, and provincial) under the confederal system possess independent legal status and are independent constitutional "legal persons" [legal entities]; the confederal government itself is not an independent constitutional "legal person," and its power capacity and conduct capability in terms of the constitution and international law are subject to strict limitations.

There is, of course, only one single independent constitutional "legal person" under the unitary system as well, but contrary to the confederal system, the unitary system's national central government is the sole independent "legal person" in terms of the constitution and international laws and, strictly speaking, no regional governments are independent "legal persons" in terms of international laws. Nor do they possess constitutional power capacities or conduct capabilities. They are merely expansions and extensions of the central government, and merely local "representatives" of the central government for carrying out central government administration in the localities. Since that is the case, the outcomes of such representation are borne by the consigner [of the representative status], and all responsibilities in terms of the constitution and international laws are borne by the central government. In other words, "he who wields power bears responsibility." Theoretically speaking, in countries where the unitary system is practiced, local and regional governments may be altered and even dismantled by the national government since they have no independent constitutional status, nor do they possess independent decision-making powers as regards any key governmental matter.

The federal system, on the other hand, devises and establishes two sets of constitutional "individualities." The national government and the regional governments at the next level are both independent "legal persons" in constitutional terms. Both have their own independent constitutional "individualities" and may not be unilaterally annulled or canceled by the other party. Both act independently within the limits of the power capacities established for them by the constitution, and independently bear legal responsibilities. On some matters (but certainly not on all matters), the national government has the power of final decision and, at least on some other matters, the local governments have the power of final decision and their independent existences are accorded special protections by the national constitution.[11] Hence, although every country may have a few regional local governments, not all of these countries practice the federal system. That depends on whether these regional local governments are able to exist independently of the national government, and whether they can independently exercise decision-making powers on at least a few matters, regardless of the preferences of the national government.

Under the federal system, the special protections for the independent legal "individualities" of the regional governments come chiefly from national constitutions. A national constitution is the outcome of equal negotiations by all parties; it is not forced by one party on other parties, and this ensures that all parties consciously respect and abide by that constitution. The national constitution clearly and specifically differentiates between the powers enjoyed by the national government and regional governments, respectively; and no sooner do conflicts arise between the two sides on the division of powers than adjudications are produced by independent, publicly trusted, and authoritative judicial agencies. The conflicts are not resolved by

---

[11]Riker William H. "Federalism," In F. I. Greenstein and N. W. Polsby, eds., *Handbook of Political Science*. Reading, Mass, Addison-Wesley, 1975 (5), p. 101.

the central government per se.[12] If revisions are to be made to the division-of-powers setup or even to the existence of the regional governments or the federal government, the constitution must be revised, which can only be done if both sides approve of and acknowledge the revisions. Hence, the national constitution is the protector of not only the people's rights but also of the powers of the national government, and it provides strong and reassuring guarantees for the regional governments' independent existence and exercise of powers.

Of course, special protections for the independent constitutional "individualities" of these regional governments also stem from a country's cultural traditions, concepts of governance, ethnic customs, civil composition, and the actual distribution of political powers in society. In the United States, the various states did not evolve into subsidiaries of the Washington government over the last two hundred or more years due merely to the existence of a commonly accepted and acknowledged national constitution, but also because of the staunch and steadfast attitude of America's citizens with regard to local self-governance. This is manifested in particular in the populace's direct elections of U.S. federal and state bi-cameral representatives and numerous administrative personnel who answer to their respective states and are not controlled by Washington.

Some American states are very small. For instance, the smallest state Rhode Island has an area of only 1545 square miles and 990,000 people. Yet, its independent existence is immune to change. Neither the federal government nor any of its large neighboring states or cities has any intention of converting it into a city under some state or a district of some large city, that is, because it (Rhode Island) was formed by history and is moreover one of the very first founding states that initiated the establishment of the U.S. federation, and despite the fact that it has always been quite passive and inactive. Another example is the city of Dallas in the state of Texas—a world-famous metropolis with an area of more than 420 square miles, a population of 1,050,000, and one of the ten largest municipal areas in the United States. But astonishingly, inside such a big city there is also a very small "mini-city" that boasts an area of merely 624 acres and a population of roughly 15,000 and is surrounded on all four sides by the city of Dallas. Despite the tiny size of this city, it sports a very big name—Universal City. It is said that pilots from many countries came here during the Second World War for training at the local U.S. air force base and, due to the presence of a large number persons from other countries, this spot seemed to have become a "universal locale" and was thereupon named Universal City. What counts is not the size of the city, but the fact that no affiliation whatsoever exists between Dallas and Universal City. Each of the two has its own independent governance institutions and management systems, and each is directly responsible to its inhabitants and the state government. Such is the current situation in the United

---

[12] An important content of constitutional law courses at American law schools is the adjudication of disputes over limits of authority by the U.S. Supreme Court. Although the Supreme Court is an institution of the federal government, it is independent in terms of its organization and finances. When it rules on disputes over limits of authority between the federal government and various state governments, it does not show partiality toward the federal government, nor, of course, toward the state governments.

States which goes for a diversified type of unity, respects local, and self-determined independence, and does not lightly make changes to local governments.

I believe that if this were in China, any "universal city" would have long since been converted into a district of Dallas, or maybe not even a district. And Rhode Island as a state would have long ended up as a sample of historical nomenclature. There used to be on Hong Kong's Kowloon Peninsula a neighborhood known as the Kowloon Walled City. In past years, when the Qing Government leased Kowloon to the British, it kept this small location under China's jurisdiction as a convenience for taking care of local Chinese residents. Hence, for many years, there existed in British administered Hong Kong a small enclave which legally remained under China's jurisdiction and where the Qing government even stationed some officials. Regrettably, the Chinese and British governments agreed in the 1980s, prior to Hong Kong's return to China, to do away with this neighborhood and convert it into a locality under the Hong Kong government's unified jurisdiction, purportedly to facilitate management and reduce illegal emigration and crime. Actually, there is no reason why the neighborhood could not have been retained and converted into a "special district" within that special administrative region. So long as it was properly managed, it might have become a unique tourist attraction and generated no small economic benefits. It is evident that China and the United States adhere to entirely different concepts of government and theories about local self-governance.

1.3.3 Differentiating Between the Standards of Different State Structures

Since the difference between the confederal structure and the unitary and federal structures is self-evident, the crux rests in the difference between the unitary and federal systems. Traditionally, the way to determine whether a country pertains to the unitary or the federal system has been to examine the extent of the powers enjoyed by local governments. It was generally believed that where local or regional governments wielded sizable powers the system was federal and vice versa. However, this criterion is at times inaccurate. Under some circumstances, a number of local self-governing regions may enjoy greater powers than states under the federal system. For example, the Hong Kong and Macao special administrative regions (SARs) in China enjoy substantial powers of self-governance, which in certain respects—such as issuing their own currencies and exercising independent border controls—are even greater than the powers of U.S. states. However, these powers are conferred on them by China's central government and for that reason the existence of these SARs does not change the nature of China's unitary state system. A rational differentiation of the two-state structures depends in the main on two standards, which are as follows:

First, the nature of the powers of the local and regional governments, and their jurisdiction over "residual powers." Where the powers of the local and regional governments are conferred on them by the national (central) government and are acquired or derived and not original, and where the regional governments are subordinate to the national government and the powers of the national government are primary, orthodox, and pre-existing as compared to those of the local governments—under such circumstances, no matter how great the powers enjoyed by the local or regional governments, the country or nation pertains to the unitary system. And under such circumstances, "residual powers" are naturally kept by the national government if laws do not stipulate who should exercise them. In fact, one might say the issue of "residual laws" does not even exist in unitary-system countries. Since "all" powers pertain to the national government and the powers of the local and regional governments are conferred by the national government, there can be no issue of "powers of indefinite jurisdiction," and all powers, including "residual powers," belong to the national government. Under the unitary system, there is only the "delegation of powers," no "division of powers."

Conversely, where the local and regional governments came into existence prior to the national government, where the powers they enjoy and the powers enjoyed by the central government originate directly from the people, where the two are parallel and both are directly responsible to the people within their respective powers of office stipulated by a constitution, and where the relationship between the two sides is parallel and clearly one of "division-of-powers" and no absolute superior/subordinate affiliations are present, the structure is federal. Under these circumstances, when "residual powers" emerge and the constitution does not clearly stipulate who should exercise them, such "residual powers" pertain in principle to the populace or to local and regional governments. Moreover, only circumstances such as these can give rise to the issue of "residual powers." Under the federal system, a very clear and concrete constitution is usually formulated to explicitly stipulate the extents of authority of the federal government and the various states as well as the solutions to be complied with when disputes arise. For instance, the U.S. constitution uses the method of citing precedents to explicitly detail the powers enjoyed by the federal government and the various state governments. That constitution also provides that powers not explicitly granted to the federal government, nor prohibited by it to the states, are reserved for and retained by the states or the people (10th Amendment). The American historian Samuel Eliot Morison (1887–1976) incisively revealed the characteristics of the U.S. federal system. He stated, the central government is the highest government within its own domain, but that domain is specified and limited… All states are mutually equal and similarly the highest within their specified domains; they are certainly not subordinate entities in the legal sense.[13] This profound statement shows that not only are all states under the federal system equal among themselves, but that all state governments are also equal with the federal government; that all are simply doing what the law stipulates they should do and that no subordinate relationships exist. The "central government" concept we usually talk about does not exist there. Hence, when we mention "local governments" in the United States, we normally refer to local (county), city, and township governments under the state governments and not state governments relative to the federal government.

---

[13]Morrison S. E. *The Growth of the American Republic*. London: Oxford University Press, 1980.

It should be noted that there has always been a very big misapprehension in China's constitutional law circles with regard to the division of state powers under the federal system. It is believed that under the federal system, the powers of local and regional governments are original, dominant, and primary relative to those of national governments, whereas those of national (central) governments are conferred on them by the local and regional governments and for that reason are derived, minor and secondary, and that the national governments' legal existence depends on voluntary impartment of powers by the local and regional governments. In other words, it is believed that national governments are a creation of and by local and regional governments. That, however, is not the case. Under the federal system, national federal governments and their component state governments have both been directly created and set up by the people. It is not that people in various states first created various state governments, after which these state governments created federal governments and then conferred certain powers on the latter. Federal governments are not the people's "grandsons"; they too are the people's "sons." There is merely an age difference between federal and state governments, no generational gap. Otherwise put, federal governments are the people's "younger sons," whereas state governments may be called the people's "elder sons" and were born a bit earlier.

The second standard for judging what constitutes a unitary system and what constitutes a federal system is whether local governments have "self-determined powers of organization," i.e., whether local and regional governments have the authority to choose their own form of government, decide their own system of governance, and formulate their own fundamental constitution-type laws. If the local and regional governments do have such powers, the system is federal. Conversely, if the constitution does not allow local and regional governments to formulate their own organizational laws at will, or does not allow local and regional governments to determine the forms of their own political-power organizations, the system is unitary.[14] For example, all states in the United States are empowered to formulate their own state constitutions and choose their own political systems. But China's two special administrative regions—Hong Kong and Macao—do not have the right to decide their political-power system or formulate their own "Basic Laws"; these must be stipulated by a central government organ—the National People's Congress. Hence, China is a state that practices the unitary system.

There are also academics who maintain that another standard for adjudging unitary and federal systems is whether the local or regional entities are empowered to collectively participate in government and political affairs. Under the federal system, the people of various states may elect representatives in the name of individual citizens to form a lower house (also called House of Representatives or House of Commons) of the federal parliament (Congress, Legislative Assembly, Diet, etc.) and directly exercise powers, and may also elect representatives under a state's collective name to form an upper house (also called Senate, Council of States, Rajya Sabha, House of Lords, etc.) of the federal parliament and indirectly exercise the powers of their state. Under the unitary system, the people have only the first power but not the

---

[14] Wu Jialin, *Constitutional Jurisprudence*. Beijing: Qunzhong Press, 1983, p. 246.

second power, because the national or central government is created by the people whereas the local governments are created by the national or central government.[15]

Under both the unitary and federal systems, the national government (central government, federal government) usually exercises the following powers: diplomatic powers (including exchanges of emissaries and conclusion of treaties with foreign countries), national defense powers (including the powers to command national military forces, declare war and make peace), the powers to issue currency, establish weights and measures, manage the postal service, administer interregional communications, stipulate the immigration and nationality (citizenship) systems, levy certain taxes, stipulate customs taxes and trade systems, safeguard intellectual rights, conduct litigation related to the above matters, and serve as arbiter when disputes arise between and among the above components. The powers of local and regional governments vary in accordance with the circumstances of each country.

1.4   New Developments of State Structures in the World Today

Since the late 1980s, substantial changes have taken place in both the theory and practice of state structures worldwide. The most obvious change was the breakup of the Soviet Union as the most massive federalist state in human history, to be replaced by a new Commonwealth of Independent States. West Germany ingested five East German states in its federalist model, to once again turn Germany into a European nation of crucial import. An alliance of European nations is growing in momentum, and a new European Union which seeks to unify political, economic, diplomatic, and military affairs has increasingly taken shape and is well on the way to acting as a counterweight to the United States on the other side of the Atlantic Ocean. Meanwhile, countries in Asia, Africa, South America, and Oceania are also adjusting their internal structures and attempting to set up certain forms of alliance in order to seek opportunities and greater space for development and better safeguard national security amid the acute competition for survival in the international macro-environment.

Changes, too, have taken place in China. In the wake of the deepening of China's Reform and Opening Up, China has injected many new contents into its own unitary system. Apart from expanding the powers of self-determination of ordinary localities, an important change is the setting up of two special administrative regions (SARs) after China resumed its exercise of sovereignty over Hong Kong and Macao. These SARs enjoy a "high degree of autonomy" according to the SARs' Basic Laws, and China has also committed itself to granting even greater autonomous powers to an eventual Taiwan Special Administrative Region. This is bringing many major changes to the content and form of China's unitary system and has enormously enriched the state structure theory of China's studies on constitutional law. These rapid changes

---

[15]Wu Jialin. *Constitutional Jurisprudence*. Beijing: Qunzhong Press, 1983, p. 247.

in state structures throughout the world have raised many new and arduous topics of research for academics in constitutional law and provide excellent opportunities for advancing the study of constitutional law. We ought to give deep thought to the forms and types of countries which mankind needs in the twenty-first century.

Actually, the crux of the type of state structure a country exercises rests in its substance and not in its name. What it is called is of no importance. Take, for example, the United States. The founding fathers who fashioned the state structure of United States had no idea what was meant by federal or confederal or unitary systems, and even less could they make any clear differentiation between these scientific concepts. The "confederation" or "federation" that many people spoke of in those days in fact meant one and the same thing. And even as regards the division of sovereign rights, they had no very clear intent of having these rights specifically shared between the federal and state governments. That matter, one should say, was summed up and then elevated to the height of scientific principle by later generations. People's sole concern at the time was to create a new system—one that could ensure inviolability for the people's basic rights and freedoms, respect for the states' rights, the existence of a fairly strong national government and, more importantly, a system accepted by the majority of the states. So long as these objectives were attained, any system would do and anything could be discussed. Its appellation was of little import; it might be called a "confederation" or a "federation." Even calling it a "unitary system" would do, since its name was merely a symbol, and the important thing was that it would solve actual problems and be accepted by all concerned. In fact, the U.S. founding fathers assimilated the strong points of both the federal and unitary systems and thereby devised a new and unique state structure, although they themselves were not aware of it.

Hence, giving definitions to different state structures and analyzing and adjudging the standards for different state structures held little significance for those founding fathers and for persons who drafted the constitution. Those matters have been of some inspiration to later generations and for new states and new constitutions of later times. However, latercomers should make certain to avoid being so bound by theories as to "trim their feet to fit the shoes," or in other words, one-sidedly pursue a certain kind of state structure, sacrifice the substance for the sake of the terminology, and impair the content to satisfy the form. In the final analysis, the tree of life is forever verdant and vibrant, and theories always lag behind realities. Politicians of all countries must proceed from the actualities and circumstances of their own countries and devise state structures suited to their own countries. They must dare to innovate and, like the American founding fathers, courageously conceive, boldly envisage, and innovatively plan their country's structural system. Should the theories summed up by scholars of constitutional law unfortunately become obstructions or hindrances to innovations by the practitioners of governance, we scholars would be guilty of a monumental crime. In which case, one would best do without constitutional law and scholars of constitutional law.

Chapter 2
The Historical Evolution of State Structures in China

When exploring the relationship between the central authorities and the Special Administrative Regions in China, it is necessary to first examine the historical development of China's state structure and, in particular, the historical circumstances of the establishment of special localities and territories. This will furnish historical references for dealing with the relations between the central authorities and the Special Administrative Regions.

2.1 State Structures in Ancient Times

China's ancient history is a narrative of the sorrows and joys and separations and reunions of the Chinese nation, of what was recognized as the general trend that unification was bound to emerge after prolonged division, and division after prolonged unification. A comprehensive survey of more than two-thousand-year-old history of China's feudal dynasties shows that unification has constituted the mainstream and divisions have been no more than diversions that unification has brought strength while divisions have hurt all involved and that well-devised unifications are bound to invigorate the nation whereas poorly executed unifications inevitably cause the nation to go into decline. Correct handling of the relations between the entire nation and its component parts is an important subject that all rulers in ancient and recent times as well as in China and abroad have been, and are today, obliged to ponder and examine.

© Foreign Language Teaching and Research Publishing Co., Ltd and Springer Nature
Singapore Pte Ltd. 2019
Z. Wang, *Relationship Between the Chinese Central Authorities and Regional
Governments of Hong Kong and Macao: A Legal Perspective*, China Academic
Library, https://doi.org/10.1007/978-981-13-2322-5_2

2.1.1 Prior to the Qin Dynasty

China's first dynasty—the Xia, set up in the twenty first century B.C.—was established by means of annexing and subjugating nearby tribes. It is said that "Yu [of Xia] convoked the tribal leaders at Tushan, all of whom brought tributes of jade or silk."[1] This indicates the way in which the Xia ruled the other tribes. Yu of Xia's division of the Central Kingdom into nine *Zhou* (an ancient administrative division—Tr.) also denotes the extent of its territories. The rule of the Xia monarchy over local feudal chieftains consisted in "relying on armed might to force allegiance from them and compel them to pay tribute."[2] Nevertheless, "The tribes that acknowledged allegiance to the monarchy continued to maintain a certain degree of autonomy. They frequently annexed or fought each other, and usually did so with no interference from the ruling monarchy so long as they submitted timely tributes to the monarchy—including tributes paid by the tribes they annexed. At times, the monarchy also granted them special levy-exacting powers of their own. Theirs was a process of highly dispersed yet gradually centralized amalgamation."[3]

By the time of the Shang Dynasty, the local dukes and princes had become *"wai fu,"* or "ministers from foreign states" of the Shang monarch and consisted mainly of the categories named *hou, dian, nan, wei, bang* and *bo*. All of those in the first four categories "were relatively independent political entities, which the Shang monarch dispatched to the country's outer regions to engage in armed defense as well as in economic activities such as land reclamation or cultivation of wasteland and animal husbandry; they were assigned armed personnel and laborers, held onto their lands on a fairly permanent basis, and could pass their status to their descendants." All became what they were as a result of "conferrals of titles from the Shang royal court," and were, therefore, absolutely subservient to the Shang court, which wielded full sovereignty over them.[4] The last two categories—*bang* and *bo*—were also subordinate to the Shang kings, but were more independent. They too were conferred their titles by the royal court and remained under its control. However, they were rulers of independent states that existed side by side with the Shang, and their relationships with the Shang were those of vassal states with a suzerain state. This alliance of states might also be called a "quasi-federation," the relations in which were more or less similar to today's British Commonwealth of Nations and its member countries.

In the Zhou era, the Zhou dynasty was set up by "a small state in the west of China which took over 'the lands under heaven' from the Shang." However, "perturbed by its own military deficiency and unable to hold in check the tribal peoples in the eastern part of the country, it resorted to extensive conferrals of titles and lands to persons with both the same and different surnames as well as to the descendants of ancient royalty in the east, so that these might serve as a 'protective screen' for

---

[1] *Discourses of the States, or, Guoyu: State of Lu.*

[2] Wei Qingyuan. *The History of China's Political Systems.* Beijing: China Renmin University Press, 1989, p. 42.

[3] Ibid., p. 43.

[4] Ibid., p. 46.

its own people."[5] These persons—dukes and princes—maintained a nominal fealty to the King of Zhou but were intensely independent. They could set up their own bureaucratic systems, levy taxes, and form their own armies within their borders. This system of conferring titles was quite evidently a sagacious strategy for the central authorities of the small and weak Zhou Dynasty. The Zhou was, in fact, a sort of military and political alliance and, in the years when the Zhou central authorities were stronger than the smaller and feebler dukes and princes, somewhat resembled a present-day federation.

The years from 770 B.C. to A.D. 221 are known in China's history as the Spring and Autumn and Warring States Period. In the final years of the Zhou Dynasty, the various dukes and princes gradually developed became increasingly powerful, and ultimately broke away from the Zhou monarchy to set up states in the sense of both independence and political integrity. These newly independent states each exercised their own authority, were not bound by affiliations, and never tired of fighting and mounting expeditions against each other. The larger and stronger ultimately swallowed up the smaller and weaker, leaving seven large states to hold sway over the "lands under Heaven." These were the states of Qin, Qi, Yan, Chu, Han, Zhao, and Wei, known in history as "the seven powers of the Warring States period." The historical mission of establishing a unified state was ultimately fulfilled in the year 221 B.C. by the State of Qin situated in the western part of China.

2.1.2 Qin Unifies Six States to Initiate China's "Great National Unity"

King Yingzheng of the state of Qin became the "First Emperor" of China, used armed force to "terminate the six (other) kings and unify the whole country," and set up a highly centralized form of government, a feat that produced a fundamental effect on the subsequent two thousand and more years of Chinese society. One might well say that the Chinese nation was still in its infancy during the Xia, Shang, Zhou, and even the Spring and Autumn and Warring States periods that the national character and the nation's customs and habits were as yet unformed, and that those "inherent" elements, therefore, exerted little influence on China's later generations (referring mainly to political traditions and political institutions). The establishment of the Qin Dynasty, however, was of epoch-making significance, and had a decisive influence on the hereditary political genes of the Chinese nation and even on the forming of the national character, or ethos. For example, the Qin had relied on armed force and punitive expeditions to subjugate the six other states. Yet, why didn't it employ such means as negotiations and get the seven states to sit down and jointly discuss the setting up of a "federal" state headed by the Qin and similar to the Zhou Dynasty's system of enfeoffment? Or—taking things a step further—why didn't it do like the 13 states in North America some two thousand years later and hold equal negotiations

---

[5]Zhao Xianxian. *Zhou Dynasty Society: Differentiation and Analysis.* Beijing: People's Publishing House, 1980, p. 114.

of the kind that founded the "United States of America"? Why was it that the unifier of the six states was the extremely backward Qin in the western hinterland instead of the Zhao, Wei (卫), Wei (魏), Qi or Chu, which were located in the Central Plains or along the seaboard and large rivers? We, of course, cannot make unfounded assumptions about history, nor should we be overcritical of the ancients. However, the nature and profundity of the effects that this era in history has had on the political culture and political ethos of our nation as well as on the subsequent pattern of social development are well worth studying.

The following things are clear. First, that whatever changes took place thereafter in the lands of the Chinese nation—whether dynastic permutations, or invasions by alien peoples, or national disintegrations, or three-way partitions of the country with each part dominated by a different entity—the country has ultimately moved toward unity. In the two thousand two hundred-plus years from 221 B.C. to the present, the quest for national unity has consistently taken a mainstream position, and unity has always figured as the orientation of popular sentiment and the general trend of events. These have long since been internalized as the political ethos and the political culture and tradition of the Chinese nation, penetrated the bones of every Chinese, and become rooted in the nation's political genes. For thousands of years, the Chinese have always sought to set up a state of "Grand Unity," with the emphasis on both "grandness" and "unity" as well as on territorial integrity. "The Chinese subconsciously believe that only under such circumstances is their country normal and acceptable, and believe (unity) to be a lofty cause most worthy of pursuit. And conversely, that the worst thing for a country is to be mired in secessions, separatist rule, partitions or localism; that such circumstances are abnormal and temporary, and unity must be quickly restored."[6]

Almost all of the pre-Qin sages maintained in their theories that there should be a one-and-only sovereign to rule the "land under Heaven." Almost all called, from different aspects, for setting up a government of centralized power and requested "the establishing of one supreme authority." That was the pre-Qin sages' summation of the course of historical development during the Spring and Autumn and Warring States period. Although their foci of attention and bases for argumentation differed, their conclusions were highly consistent in the conviction that unity should replace chaos and that centralization of power should supersede the simultaneous existence of numerous warlords, failing which stability and prosperity would be unattainable. These conclusions swept away the ideological hindrances to the Qin's implementation of centralization of power.[7] In fact, the sages and scholars of that time were at one on the issue of partition and unification. All were "integrationists," none were "separatists" or "partitionists." All stood for centralization of power, none stood for local self-government—not to mention "federalism." This, to a great extent, determined that the vast lands of East Asia could only give rise to a unified large state that

---

[6]Wang Zhenmin. "One Country, Two Systems: Its Historical Position, Present Operation and Future Development," Australia, LAWASIA Comparative Constitutional Law Newsletter, 1995 (1), p. 6.
[7]Wei Qingyuan. *History of China's Political Systems*. Beijing: China Renmin University Press, 1989, p. 42.

they could not give rise to numerous peacefully coexisting smaller states like those on the lands of Western Europe, despite the more or less equal areas of these two swaths of land.[8]

Two, in terms of the political system implemented nationwide, the Chinese have aspired for uniformity, for absolute unanimity with the central government. When each succeeding dynasty had unified the entire country, it at once set up a highly centralized system of governance that did not allow the localities any self-governance, or even flexibility, or any measures of accommodation. "Ever since the Qin Dynasty founded the system whereby '**all localities in the country were converted into prefectures or counties and all decrees were issued by one authority**,' seldom did the enfeoffment system reemerge in China, local separatist regimes frequently failed to win popular support, advances took place with extreme difficulty, and the entire country remained basically under the control of a single emperor. Meanwhile, local officials were no more than officials directly appointed by the imperial court and 'neurons' in the feudal monarchs' neural networks; they did no more than transmit instructions about specific controls, and essentially had no decision-making powers to speak of."[9] Thus, China established, from the top down, a high centralized and uniform system which prevailed over prolonged periods of time.

If we combine points one and two above and if we translate this traditional political concept into modern parlance, one gets "one country with one kind of system," which means implementing "one country one system" and setting up a state with a highly unified and unitary system nationwide—a principle which the development of China's governance has consistently adhered to ever since 221 B.C. when China's first feudal imperial dynasty unified the entire country.[10] The precise meaning of "Grand Unity" is to strive for territorial integrity and unity as well as institutional uniformity in the state. These constitute the core content of China's traditional political culture.

Three, armed force was employed as the method for realizing national unification, and examples of bringing about national unification by means of peaceful negotiation are scarce, even nonexistent. It is apparent that the factors of compromise and making concessions are completely absent in China's traditional political culture, which is entirely lacking in the "win-win" spirit of constructive negotiations and concessions for the sake of obtaining advances for both parties. The ancient Chinese were wont to use armed force to fight to the bitter end, as is time and again evidenced by post-Qin history. Is there, in this way of achieving unification, some sort of "genetic" relationship with the method for setting itself up adopted by the Qin—the first large dynasty in China?

---

[8]There is only one state or country on China's territory of approximately 9.6 million square kilometers (land area) whereas there are as many as 44 countries in the entirety of Europe which covers a total area of 10.16 million square kilometers (including islands). Source of data: China Yearbook editorial department's *China Yearbook 1994.*

[9]Wang Zhenmin. "Rebuild Our Country's Social Control Systems," submitted at the Second National Legal System Seminar in September 1988, carried by Gong Xiangrui ed. *The Ideal and the Reality of Constitutional Government.* Beijing: China Personnel Press, 1995.

[10]Wang Zhenmin. "One Country, Two Systems: Its Historical Position, Present Operation and Future Development," Australia, LAWASIA Comparative Constitutional Law Newsletter, 1995 (5), p. 6.

To sum up the above points, we may recap the post-Qin spirit of Chinese political culture in two phrases, i.e., Unification by armed force, and one system for one state. These words summarize the developmental history of the feudal state structure that lasted more than two thousand years in China. We must, of course, recognize that the Qin's unification of six states and its establishment of a state power of nationwide unity conformed to the regularities of social advance and the wishes of the people of all of China's states in those days, and was of major significance for social progress. That is especially true when we see how the European countries are moving today toward a unified state and have formed a unified European currency, how they are implementing joint European diplomatic and security policies, harmonizing the internal and judicial affairs of each country, setting up unified armed forces, and so forth, all of which the Chinese had already achieved more than two millennia ago. By then, China had already unified its currency, its system of weights and measures, and its spoken and written language. It already had a unified military, unified government, and judicial systems, and even unified political thought, and it had a unified time standard. Today, when we travel over the vast expanses of China's territory, we do not need to speak many different languages, convert currencies, or make time adjustments (even though China stretches across five time zones). We should be grateful to our ancestors for the benefits brought by unifying the country so long ago.[11]

Let us now specifically probe the course of this unique historical development.

2.1.3 The State Structures of the Qin, Han, Wei, Jin, and Northern and Southern Dynasties

After King Yingzheng of Qin crushed the six other eastern states and established his sole authority in 221 B.C., Chinese history has witnessed in succession the simultaneous existences of the two Hans (the Eastern and Western Han dynasties), the three Kingdoms (the Wei, Shuhan, and Wu kingdoms), the two Jins (the Eastern and Western Jin dynasties) and the Northern and Southern Dynasties, right up to the time when the Sui Dynasty once again unified the entire nation in A.D. 589. This may be regarded as a single historical entity. During those eight hundred-odd years, China experienced situations of long-term unity as well as splits and separatist rules. China's territories underwent constant expansion in this period. By the time of the Han dynasty, these territories extended to Liaodong and Donglang in the east, Jiaozhi and Rinan in the south, Bashu in the south, and Damo (the big desert) in the north, all of which were designated as prefectures and counties by the Han (206 B.C.–A.D. 220) imperial court and directly administered by the central authorities. The Han

---

[11]Americans traveling in China are often surprised that China has only one time zone even though it stretches several thousand *li* from east to west and that there is no need to make time adjustments. In the United States, one must constantly make time adjustments as one travels from the eastern to the central and then the western parts of the country.

imperial court also set up a Western Region Frontier Command which exercised overall control over the states in the Western Region. This vast region has been the earliest homeland of the Chinese nation, a land on which the Chinese have lived and procreated generation after generation.

In terms of state structure, the *jun* (i.e., prefecture) and *xian* (i.e., county) system established and constantly ameliorated in that period deserves special mention as it had a profound influence on later generations. Actually, counties had already been set up in the border areas by the states of Qin, Jin, and Chu way back in Spring and Autumn times (770–476 B.C.), after which prefectures were also set up. However, when the Qin unified the entire country, it drew lessons from the states-within-a-state situation and the lawlessness and disorder brought on by the Zhou Dynasty's enfeoffment system, and widely disseminated the county and prefectural system. The Qin initially set up 36 prefectures and later increased these to 40 or more. Prefectural mayors (*shou*), lieutenants (*wei*), and supervisors (*jian*) were set up in the prefectures, and county magistrates and *zhangli* ("senior aides") installed in the counties—all of them appointed directly by, and directly responsible to, the central authorities, and directly controlled by the emperor. Prefectural government organizations were patterned on and set up as counterparts to, central government organizations. They answered to the central authorities and at the same time exercised the function of supervising the counties under their jurisdiction. These local officials were known as "*chaoting mingguan*" (i.e., high-ranking officials who were appointed by the emperor, acted as his spokespersons, and could bypass their immediate leadership to send up reports without being constrained by legal or administrative procedures.) They were, in fact, the emperor's eyes and ears stationed throughout the country, albeit they had no autonomous powers. It was said: "The Qin replaced fiefdoms with prefectures and counties and, fearing that the latter would assume excessive powers, appointed in each prefecture a mayor, a supervisor and a lieutenant, over whom there were no other rulers."[12] The forming of the prefectural and county system indeed effectively prevented local separatism and enhanced the centralization of powers. And for that reason, the prefecture-and-county system served all dynasties as their main institutional mechanism for controlling the localities up to and until the middle period of the Sui Dynasty (581–618). Substantial changes later took place in the prefectural setup, but the county setup has been preserved ever since.

The Han Dynasty, while continuing the Qin system, reinstated states (feudatories), practiced this system in tandem with the prefectures and counties, placed them under the administration of dukes, princes, and kings, and accorded them semi-independent status. By the time of the Eastern Han (25–220), *zhou* (州) [an ancient administrative division—Tr.] became the highest organization of local administration, their highest officials being *ci shi* (governors) and *zhou mu* (prefects). They often maintained armies, defied central government orders, and set up separatist regimes. During the Wei (220–265), Jin (265–420), and Northern and Southern Dynasties (420–589), measures were frequently taken to convert the *zhou* into *jun* in order to prevent

---

[12] *The Book of Han*, vol. 19 (Part One), "Table of Nobility Ranks and Government Offices," Wang Mingsheng "Supplementary Notes."

external authority from overriding the authority of the imperial court and to restrict the expansion of local forces. In this period, *dao* (道) [administrative entities equivalent to prefectures—Tr.] were set up in regions where ethnic minorities lived in compact communities.

In terms of special local organizational systems, the Han imperial court began to dispatch garrison troops to open up wasteland and establish frontier commands in the Western Region for the purpose of guarding against incursions by the Huns, to ensure unimpeded and secure communications to Central and Western Asia, and protect normal economic and trade exchanges. However, the Han imperial court did so only to guarantee that its vassal states lived in peace and harmony with each other and to protect normal trade and cultural contacts; not to conquer or control these regions nor to demand that the Western Regions' political and economic systems be patterned on those in China's inland areas. This differs somewhat in nature from the United States' current practice of stationing massive garrisons in other countries. The Han imperial court's purpose in stationing forces in those places was relatively simple, and it had no ambitions of acting as "world police."

In sum, starting with the Qin Dynasty, China's feudal dynasties set up a highly compact network extending from prefectures level-by-level down to the villages and the grassroots for controlling the localities, with the emperor situated at the central pivot and subsidiaries extending to all corners of the country. The Han dynasty implemented a system in which states (feudatories) and prefectures existed in tandem. However, these "states within the state" frequently stood up against the central authorities, and the Han imperial court was compelled to whittle down the feudatories and place them under unified central control, causing them to exist in name only and depriving them of independent political powers. This method of ruling was time and again used as a model by all succeeding dynasties.

2.1.4   The State Structures of the Sui, Tang, the Five Dynasties, and Ten Kingdoms Period, and the Song

After hundreds of years of division and separatist regimes, the Sui imperial dynasty reunified the entire country in A.D. 589, and China's feudal society reached the zenith of its power and splendor. In the subsequent 698 years, China experienced the reign of the Tang imperial dynasty, followed by the successive rises of the Liang, Tang, Jin, Han, and Zhou dynasties, and then the separatist rules of ten states including the Wu and Shu. Not much later, however, the country was basically reunified again by the Song imperial dynasty (960–1279). In those years, the lands of China continued to expand. During the heyday of the Tang Dynasty (618–907), "its lands extended to Andong in the east, Anxi in the west, Rinan in the south and Shanyufu in the north, attaining the magnificence of the Han Dynasty in the south and north, though less so in the east and more so in the west."[13] The Tang was, in those days, an empire with the most extensive territories in the world.

During the Sui and Tang periods, the rulers further adopted a series of measures and methods for consolidating the system of centralism, strengthening their control over the localities and forestalling the emergence of local schisms. In the Sui and early Tang, three kinds of local administrative regions—*fu, jun* and *zhou*—were set up under the central government. *Fu* were set up around the capital cities and in important regions, whereas *duhufu* (frontier commands) were established in major remote and border districts. The status of the *fu* was superior to those of the *zhou* or *jun*. In A.D. 636, the emperor Tang Taizong divided the country into ten *dao* (道) in line with the regions' topographical features; in A.D. 733 the emperor Tang Xuanzong increased these to 15 *dao* and stationed permanent *caifangshi* (inspectors) and *guanchashi* (supervisors), with the result that the *dao* gradually evolved into local administrative entities of a higher status than the *zhou*. The Song Dynasty carried forward this system of demarcating administrative regions, but also set up the *lu* (路)—which became the highest-ranking local administrative region and of which a maximum of 26 existed at one point in time. Set up under the *lu* were *fu, zhou, jun,* and *jian*.

While modifications took place in this period in the organizational system of local administration, changes were also made to the local officials' previous powers of appointing aides and assistants; all local officials entering the official hierarchy thereafter were directly appointed by the central authorities. This, on the one hand, was aimed at securing control over the localities by means of controlling local personnel appointments/dismissals and, on the other, was designed to enhance the local senior administrative officials' affinity and cohesion with the central authorities and inculcate feelings of attachment and gratitude, thereby orienting their sense of responsibility upward rather than vice versa.

The Tang Dynasty *dao*, which were concurrently in charge of supervisory and military affairs and being of a highly autonomous character, very soon evolved into increasingly separatist entities of local governance. The chief administrative officers in these *dao* were their *jiedushi* (military commanders), who should originally have been in charge of military governance only; civil affairs were to be administered by *guanchashi* (supervisors). But in reality, the *jiedushi* assumed concurrent responsibility for military and ordnance, finances, and taxation and civil administration—in fact, everything. Although all *dao* had ministers for *du zhi* (budgeting), *ying tian* (farmland management), *zhao tao* (general administration), and *ji lue* (logistics and planning), in most cases these responsibilities were one and all taken over by the *jiedushi*. In this way, all powers—military, governmental, and civil—were concentrated in the person of the *jiedushi*, who became no different from an emperor. That ultimately led to the emergence of rival principalities and separatist regimes and to divisions and splits in the country. It became evident that when a local official held too many positions simultaneously, there was a very strong likelihood of his becoming too powerful and laying forcible claim to entire swaths of territory.

---

[13] *The New Book of Tang.* vol. 37, Geography I.

The practice of sending garrison troops to open up wasteland and establish frontier commands in remote border regions had started in the Han Dynasty. The Tang Dynasty set up a total of six large frontier commands in ethnic minority border regions, namely in Shanyu, Anbei, Beiting, Andong, Anxi, and Annan. Those at Anxi and Beiting had jurisdiction over the Western Region, those at Anbei and Shanyu had jurisdiction over the northern border, the one at Andong governed China's northeast, and the one at Annan had jurisdiction over the southern border. *Jimi fuzhou* was not set up under these frontier commands, which were special local setups different from those in the inland regions.

In A.D. 630, when Tang Taizong pacified the Tujue [a Turkic ethnic group in Western China—Tr.], *jimi fuzhou* was set up in the Tujue's land of origin. Tang Taizong appointed the Tujue's original chieftains as hereditary military governors and *zhizhou* (imperially appointed prefects) and allowed these localities to retain their original powers of political self-governance and thereby become semi-independent local administrative entities. Subsequently, the Tang also set up a total of more than eight hundred *jimi fuzhou* in other ethnic minority tribal societies, and thereby effectively pacified these remote frontier regions. The establishment of *duhufu* (frontier commands) played a major role in strengthening ethnic unity, safeguarding the country's unity, and promoting the common development of all nationalities.

Owing to the vastness of the territories of ancient China and the lack of modern means of communication, control over the border areas was at all times a major problem which sometimes necessitated the devising of special means and methods. For instance, many of the original rulers in these localities were allowed to retain all that was traditionally theirs, so long as they exhibited a semblance of fealty. Sometimes the emperor did not stint at marrying off one of his daughters to a local potentate and offering marital connections and monarchical alliances in exchange for peace in the border areas. "In Lhasa, the capital of the Tibet Autonomous Region, the statue of the Tang Princess Wen Cheng, who married the Tubo tsampo, king of Tibet, in 641, is still enshrined and worshiped in the Potala Palace. The Tang-Tubo Alliance Monument marking the meeting for this purpose between Tang and Tubo erected in 823 still stands in the square in front of the Jokhang Monastery."[14] These provided strong guarantees at that time for peace in the border regions and also laid the foundations for national unity in later years.

After the Tang, splits emerged once more in China. The various existing states fought endlessly among themselves until the Song Dynasty basically unified entire country in A.D. 960. Once the Song imperial court was established, it immediately rescinded the *jiedushi*'s military powers and placed the *fu, zhou, jun,* and *jian* under the direct control of the central authorities. It also decreed that documents approved and issued by a chief official should be perused by, deliberated, and jointly drafted with his deputy, in a deliberate move to bring about mutual supervision and checks between chiefs and secondary officials and to prevent concentration of powers. In A.D. 997, the Song added a new level of administration called the *lu*, which answered

---

[14]News Office of the State Council. "White Paper 1992: Tibet—Its Ownership and Human Rights Situation," Beijing, 1992.

directly to the central authorities and had departments of military and civil affairs, judicial and criminal affairs, finances and transportation and logistics, neither of which was controlled by or subordinate to another, and all of which were directly responsible only to the central authorities. In this way, military, civil, governmental, judicial, fiscal, and personal affairs were not subordinate one to another but came directly under the jurisdiction of the corresponding departments of the central authorities. There were only vertical leadership relations between high and low but no horizontal relations among local leadership. While this effectively concentrated power in the hands of the central authorities and prevented arrogations of power by local officials, it also created such problems as a lack of specific responsibilities, redundancies, and low work efficiency among officials.

2.1.5   State Structures of the Liao, Xia, Jin, Yuan, Ming, and Qing Dynasties

Ethnic minorities in Chinese history also set up regimes in remote border regions. In the later period of China's feudal society, due to the corruptness and incompetence of the Han people's imperial courts the northern ethnic minorities no longer swore fealty to the Han people's regimes in the south, but instead constantly mounted military attacks against them; some even took over the Central Plains and dominated the entire country. Among the five dynasties in the latter half of China's past history—the Liao, Xia, Jin, Yuan, Ming, and Qing—only the Ming was a regime of the Han people, all others were ethnic minority regimes. The Yuan and Qing actually unified the entire country, with the Qing governing the whole of China for as long as 276 years. It is obvious that ethnic minorities have played an important role in the historical development of the unified Chinese nation.

The Liao (A.D. 916–1125), Western Xia (A.D. 1038–1227), Jin (A.D. 1115–1234), and the Song (A.D. 960–1279) dynasties were in fact four dynasties that existed more or less simultaneously, and were independent regimes which fought each other endlessly and rarely coexisted in peace. That period was, of course, also one of the Han people merging and developing in a big way together with border-region ethnic minorities. All previous historical accounts have described the Song imperial court as the principal and orthodox player in this period in China's past history. This era in history does, in fact, resemble the Three Kingdoms period, but only in that the previous period consisted of a confrontation among three states whereas four dynasties held sway in the latter. The difference is that the Wei, Shu, and Wu of the Three Kingdoms Period were all set up by Han people, whereas among the later four dynasties—i.e., the Liao, Xia, Jin, and Song—only the Song was a Han people's regime; all others were regimes set up by ethnic minorities in northeastern and northwestern China. Hence, accounts of the latter era in history should tell about all four dynasties, and it may well be said that the Chinese nation was once again mired in a situation rife with splits and divisions due to the simultaneous emergence

of diverse groups of warlords. Those four dynasties were unable to negotiate the
setting up of a large unified state similar to a "federation." Governed as they were
by an intense "Grand Unity" ideology, they could only conceive of reclaiming "lost
territories" through relentless warfare and of reestablishing a vast unified empire of
centralized power by means of armed force. Ancient China's feudal dynasties have
had the most perfected "self-regenerating" mechanism in all countries in the world.[15]
That explains why the repeated confrontations among various states in Chinese history have ultimately ended with the reestablishment of a large unified country of
centralized power rather than the emergence of a "federal" state. This sort of outcome—of grand reunion and grand unity—is what the Chinese have craved and
aspired for and what has constituted their highest value in life. Moreover, such grand
unifications of the nation have also been consummated inwardly from the outside by
ethnic minority peoples in the border regions as well. Genghis Khan, monarch of the
Yuan Mongols, swept the length and breadth of China with unparalleled momentum
and pursued the young emperors of the Song Dynasty until they ended up in Hong
Kong and had nowhere else to go. The Yuan reunified China in the year 1279.[16]

The Yuan Dynasty's central government established a *zhongshusheng* (central secretariat) as the highest state administrative organ directly responsible to the emperor.
It administered six ministries responsible for various affairs of governance—officials' appointments, civil affairs, rites, military affairs, punishments, and works. In
terms of local institutions, the Yuan, for the purpose of strengthening controls over
the localities, stationed in each locality a secretariat, called a *xingzhong shusheng*
(an executive secretariat), to directly handle local affairs. These executive secretariats
were in effect the central government's agencies. This method of subsuming local
governments under the central government's overall system and turning them into
agencies and extensions of the central government is one of those used by governments of centralized powers for strengthening control over the localities and has
been an important characteristic of traditional unitary-system governments. Executive secretariats were called for short "*xingsheng*" or "*sheng*" [a designation that has
since been rendered in English as "province"—Tr.]. These administrative divisions
were gradually and permanently adopted in China as the highest local administrative
regions, and remain as such to this day.

The Yuan Dynasty set up 11 *xingsheng*, or provinces, nationwide—i.e., Henan,
Jiangzhe, Jiangxi, Huguang, Shaanxi, Sichuan, Liaoyang, Gansu, Yunnan, Lingbei,
and Zhengdong, and thereby established jurisdiction over vast lands described as
extending north to the Yin Mountains, west to the Flowing Sands, east throughout the
Liaozuo Region and south across the Seas.[17] This was another major development
in China's system of local organization subsequent to the devising of the county
system by the Qin, and it holds an important place in the history of the construction

---

[15]Wei Qingyuan. *History of China's Political Systems*. Beijing: China Renmin University Press,
1989, p. 42.

[16]Yuan Bangjian. *A Brief History of Hong Kong*. Hong Kong: Chung Lew Publishing Co., Ltd.,
1993, p. 38.

[17]*The History of Yuan*. vol. 58, "Geographical Treatises."

of China's local institutions. Setting up provinces effectively prevented splits in China and consolidated the unity of the nation. After the Yuan dynasty, the Ming and Qing dynasties carried on this system, and from then on very few instances have appeared in China of local separatist regimes so ubiquitous in China's history. The Yuan Dynasty also set up *anfu shisi* (appeasement departments) and *anwei shisi* (conciliation departments) in ethnic minority regions and remote border regions. These were under the jurisdiction of the central *xuanzheng* council [a department in charge of Buddhist affairs nationwide and regional military and political matters in Tibet—Tr.] and maintained certain contacts with the provincial authorities.

By the time of the Ming and Qing dynasties, China's feudal society was approaching its last days. However, as far as its system and techniques of feudal rule were concerned, it had attained a high degree of proficiency, and the feudal system of centralized power was at the zenith of its development. The reach of China's territories also attained its highest point during the early years of the Qing Dynasty (1644–1911). By the mid-eighteenth century, the Qing's territories extended to the northern bank of Lake Balkhash in Central Asia, included the Tannu Uriankhai region in the northwest, encompassed areas beyond the Gobi Desert in the north, reached the Sakhalin Islands in the east, and stretched across the sea to the Xisha and Nansha Islands in the south. This, at the time, was the world's largest empire.

To control these vast territories, the Ming and Qing rulers on the one hand further enhanced the already high degree of centralization and strove as far as possible to concentrate the powers of each province under the central authorities. But they also had to exercise some division of powers due to the sheer size of the country, so as to make it easier for the regional high commissioners to effectively exercise their function of ruling over the populace. For this purpose, the Ming and Qing rulers made constant adjustments to the organizational systems in the provinces.

The Ming Dynasty, in its first years, continued to practice the Yuan provincial system. However, the Ming central authorities sensed a potential threat in the growing powers of the provinces, and in 1376 issued a decree which annulled the *xingsheng* (administrative commissioner) system, converted all of the *xingsheng* into *chengxuan* (literally: "receive-and-announce") administrative entities, substantially cut down the number of institutions and officials in the local *buzheng shisi* (administrative secretariats), and turned these into administrative departments that "received decrees from above and announced them to the lower levels" and that ceased to be local power institutions in command of the provinces' important military and political affairs. Zhu Yuanzhang [the first Ming emperor—Tr.] divided the provinces' military and political powers into five parts, and had three departments—the *chengxuan* (civil administrative) department, a *tixingancha* (judicial and prosecution) department, and a *duzhihuishi* (military command) division—take charge of civil, prosecutorial, and military administration. Where major problems were encountered, these "three departments" would consult and together submit a memorial to the emperor for final decision. This deprived any single department of the power to monopolize decisions over matters of overall significance. This sort of "separation of the five powers" placed particular emphasis on exercising constraints and supervision among departments in the localities, and while this measure placed effective controls on the local authorities and made it impossible for them to aggrandize their powers, it also stifled local initiative and vitality.

After the Qing Dynasty set up its political power, it modified the system of local governance by affirming, improving, and developing the method of having *zongdu* (governors-general) and *xunfu* (roving imperial inspectors) control and regulate provincial affairs. Generally speaking, one governor-general was established over every two or three provinces to serve as the highest local official. The duties of a governor-general were to "**govern and administer the army and civilians, exercise overall management over military and civil affairs, examine and recommend officials, and maintain order in border regions.**"[18] In this way, a system of governors-general and imperial inspectors taking joint charge at the provincial level was established. That system made it very hard for any locality to devise a separatist local regime, and thereby effectively strengthened the Qing central government's control over the provinces. Although this gave the governors-general and imperial inspectors great powers, no instances of local governments assuming excessive powers or resisting the central government arose, and the relations of the central authorities with the provinces remained stable over a long period of time. This, from yet another aspect, indicates that China's feudal society had, over two thousand-some years of development, reached full maturity and that its methods had attained perfection. Hence, a state of relative harmony and stability existed in the relations of the central authorities with the localities.

In its border regions, the Qing government formed a special system of local administrators or administrations such as *jiangjun* (general's office), *dutong* (commander-in-chief's office) and *dachen* (minister's office). Specifically, the Qing set up *jiangjun* in Chengjing, Jilin, Heilongjiang, and Suiyuan city; the Ulyastai General's Office (the Permanent Deputy General of the Left), the Khovd Minister counsellor's Office and the Kulun Executive Minister' Office were installed in Khalkha, Mongolia; such local organizational administrations as the Chahar Banner Command and the Jehol Banner Command were also set up among the Mongol peoples south of the Gobi Desert; a Resident Minister was installed in Tibet; an Imperial Censor and the Taiwan *fu* were installed in Taiwan; while the Tusi [hereditary headman—Tr.] and subsequently the *tongguan* systems were installed in the ethnic minority regions of the Southwest. It is evident that the Qing government effectively maintained national unity by establishing different special local organizations in light of the different circumstances in different border regions. In the Qing Dynasty's later years, Xinjiang was turned into a province, replacing the Ili Military Administration. After that, the Khovd Minister counsellor was annulled and replaced by the Altai Executive Minister. The General's Offices of Shengjing, Jilin, and Heilongjiang were all superseded by the provincial system. Taiwan *fu* was also redesignated as Taiwan Province.

---

[18]*Draft History of Qing*. vol. 116, "The Official System III."

2.1.6 Changes After 1840

After the year 1840, China's society gradually evolved from an unalloyed feudal society into a semi-feudal, semi-colonial society. As this change took place in the nature of Chinese society, the Qing Dynasty was compelled to make corresponding changes in its ways and methods of ruling the country. The following changes took place, as reflected in the relationship of state institutions—or in other words, the central authorities—with the general run of provincial-level localities:

First, constant increases in the powers of the localities. Due to the needs of suppressing peasant uprisings and resisting foreign incursions, the Qing imperial court had to put greater reliance on the governors-general and imperial inspectors in the localities and invest substantial powers in them to expedite the processing of urgent matters. That, of course, consolidated the rule of the feudal dynasty, but it also generated opportunities for the localities to expand their powers and set up separatist regimes. This state of affairs reached its highest point when, after the Reform Movement of 1898, the southeastern provinces refused to execute orders from the Qing government and balked at dispatching troops to assist the Yihetuan Movement (i.e., the Boxers) in resisting foreign powers. Even when the Eight-Power Allied Forces occupied Beijing, the dukes and princes in southeast China either sat tight or openly opposed the imperial court by implementing "mutual protections in the Southeast" or "Chinese-foreign mutual protections." It was evident that the dukes and princes in those localities had already joined the imperialist powers in promoting Westernization endeavors. Such a situation, in the last years of dynastic rule, indeed, placed the highest rulers in a dilemma: In order to fight and extinguish "conflagrations" they had to surrender certain powers to the local princes and dukes, yet they feared the latter would thereby become too powerful and defy the imperial court. That situation was an inexorable vicious circle—a thorny political problem all rulers of all ages face when they go into decline.

The second change was the imperialist powers' invasions of the sanctuaries of monarchical power, which led to a series of new developments in the relations between China's central authorities and localities. Armed conflicts almost beyond count were taking place between China and foreign countries in modern times, and virtually all resulted in defeat for China, as the manifold records of indemnities and ceded territories can testify. China's territorial integrity was coming under grave threat. After Hong Kong was ceded to Britain in the wake of the First Opium War, the Qing government successively gave up large swaths of its mountains and rivers to Russia and Japan and other foreign powers, which resulted in the Qing government's forfeiting its ability to rule these localities. After the Boxer wars, the Western powers one after the other marked out "spheres of influence" in China, exercised administrative, judicial, and other powers in these spheres of influence, and collaborated with local forces in gradually forming regional entities of military power to counter the imperial court. The Western imperialists also did their level best to promote the growth and independence of local forces and to place these permanently under their control. Such were the intentions of the British when they meddled in Tibet and the

Russians who intervened in Xinjiang and Mongolia. Their abiding hope was that China would break up; that this huge Eastern dragon would fall apart to facilitate their divide-and-rule ambitions.

The third change consisted of the adjustments to central and local relations made by the Qing government when faced with the crises described above and prodded by reformers. In July 1907, the Qing government approved a memorial to the emperor entitled "Memorial on the Circumstances of the Revision of the Bureaucracy System in Each Province." The Directorate defined the bureaucratic establishment of the localities according to the principles of judicial independence and local self-government; it stipulated that governors-general be appointed to assume jurisdiction over local diplomatic and military affairs in one or several provinces and that imperial inspectors be established in provinces to take overall charge of local administration.[19] Thereafter, local self-government initiatives spread nationwide. Numerous provinces set up self-government bureaus drew up self-government statutes and made plans for exercising local self-government. One might well say that had there been a period of relative peace and stability, the Qing government might have gradually implemented local self-government and voluntarily granted ample powers to the localities, which would have had the effect of ensuring national unity and promoting local development. Regrettably, it was already too late for that, and the collapse of the Qing Dynasty had become a historical inevitability.

2.1.7   Historical Summation

As we sum up the history of China's state structure in the two thousand-plus years of the development of China's feudal society, we may draw the following conclusions:

One, the quest for national unification and territorial integrity has been the most basic political creed of the Chinese nation and the mainstream of China's historical development. In more than two millennia, no matter how fragmented the lands of China became, the country ultimately moved toward reunification. That has been an objective regularity of China's historical development.

Two, as regards the method used toward that end, unity as well as dynastic changes and substitutions were generally brought about by armed force, and all national unifications in past years may be summed up as taking one of the following courses: First, when a feudal dynasty had become hopelessly corrupt and inept in its last stages, a backward ethnic minority tribe in some border region would begin to encroach on the Central Plains by dint of its courage and fighting skills, ultimately conquering the entire country, overthrowing the former imperial dynasty and setting up a new dynasty. This was the case when the Zhou Dynasty vanquished the Shang (c. eleventh century B.C.), the Qin defeated the six other states (221 B.C.), the Northern Wei unified the northern part of China (439), the Yuan unified the whole country (1279) and

---

[19]Xin Xiangyang et al. *Princes of the Big States*. Beijing: China Social Sciences Publishing House, 1995, p. 205.

the Qing overthrew the Ming Dynasty (1644). The other circumstance would take place when a dynasty in its final years was threatened from the bottom upward by peasant rebellions that ultimately brought about dynastic changes. These two circumstances sometimes occurred alternatively, sometimes simultaneously. Almost never in China's ancient history did regime changes take place smoothly and peaceably by means of "elitist revolutions" of the Western type. Moreover, China's dynastic changes merely replaced a single personage; i.e., a ruler or emperor for a better one; they were never able to change over to a better system. And since the change of government was effected by means of armed force, the newly established dynasty was a regime of centralized power. There was no possibility of a democratic federalist state being set up by means of peaceful negotiation.

Three, all of the Chinese imperial dynasties of past years pursued a policy of "one country one system" in their areas of effective jurisdiction, and except in the case of feudatory vassal states or distant border regions, institutional uniformity from the central authorities to the localities was basically required nation-wide, and the existence of special regimes was on the whole forbidden.

Four, due to the reasons cited above, local forces frequently registered rapid growth in the last phases of monarchical dynasties. Confronted with diverse crises, the central dynastic authorities were compelled to confer more powers to the local authorities for the sake of "putting out conflagrations," but they feared the local authorities might aggrandize these powers and start up a separatist trend. This difficult choice has been one that no feudal emperor, however, astute, and no feudal dynastic government has been able to evade. It was also a ticklish political problem for which no feudal political theory or feudal "ruling methodology" was able to find a fundamental solution.

Five, due to the feudal rulers' fatally flawed concept of their domains being their own family property and their predilection for implementing "rule of man," no clear-cut methodology existed for successions to the throne and, as a result, kings and emperors, after choosing a crown prince, more often than not set up their remaining sons as princes and dukes in various parts of their domains. This brought about a situation of splits and hegemonies among rulers in the country and fallings-out between brothers during contentions for the throne. And the victors would again begin to "decimate the feudatories" and start up a new round of massacres, causing enormous damage to the lives and property of the ordinary people.

Six, during virtually every dynasty, a number of special local administrative regions were set up in distant border regions for the sake of pacifying the ethnic minority peoples there, and fairly substantial powers were conferred on these regions. Their rulers were even allowed to declare themselves kings or emperors and establish a sort of suzerainty or dependency with the central dynastic government. In some cases, political marriages were concluded to pacify these regions.

People who explore the long flow of Chinese history or roam the extensive lands of contemporary China are struck by the broad reach of ancient China's territories and the splendor of its ancient civilization. Envision those founding emperors of the Han, Qin, Tang and Song dynasties as well as the subsequent ethnic minority emperors who unified the nation by entering and taking over the Central Plains—those proud and powerful and illustrious Sons of Heaven who succeeded in bringing together all corners of this country, in commanding the loyalty of officials and subjects of diverse nationalities spread over thousands of miles, in maintaining the country's unity, and in exercising effective governance over this immense nation despite the vastness of the lands of China and its complex ethnic composition, and doing this at a time when there were no telephones, no fax machines, no Internet, and no trains or automobiles or airplanes! That was truly a marvel in the political history of mankind. Yet, they found no final solution to the problem of the "periodicity of history."

2.2   The State Structure from the 1911 Revolution to 1949

The Qing Dynasty time and again refused to institute reforms and took a perfunctory and even dismissive attitude toward constitutional reform and modernization. It ultimately reached a point of no return amid the mighty torrent of bourgeois revolution. This event differed from the various dynastic changes in China's past history in that it marked a fundamental change of regime. Previous changes had merely consisted of dynastic replacements in which the new and the old dynasties were of the same nature. This time, however, the regime set up was a dictatorship of the bourgeoisie, and a republic replaced the feudal autocracy. Hence, there were numerous fundamental differences between the old and new regimes in terms of state structure.

2.2.1   The Beiyang [Northern Warlords] Government from 1912 to 1928

The most notable feature of the relationship between the central and local authorities in this period was the nominal existence of a nationwide central government but the reality that the country existed in a state of incessant fighting among separatist warlord regimes and that the regions under effective administration by the central government were severely curtailed. After the 1911 Revolution broke out, a great many provinces immediately declared independence and dissociated themselves from the Qing central government. These independent provinces subsequently sent out representatives to discuss the matter of forming a nationally unified central state power, drew up a "Program for Establishing a Provisional Government of the Republic of China" and elected Dr. Sun Yat-sen to serve as president of the provisional government.[20] That period in history very much resembled the get-together of representatives of the 13 founding states of the United States of America to formulate a constitution, elect a president and set up a nationally unified federal regime. However, the period's later developments failed to live up to the original intentions.

---

[20] Shi Bolin and Deng Xiaoping. *Evolution and Development of China's Political Structure in Recent and Modern Times*. Zhengzhou: Henan People's Publishing House, 1991, p. 30.

After obtaining political power through fraud and deception, Yuan Shikai seized the opportunity to restore the imperial system on the one hand and, on the other, subdued the various warlord factions. Taking "suppression of the Second Revolution" as his excuse, he unified the southern provinces by armed force and put an end to the revolutionary factions' hopes for regional autonomy. Yuan Shikai, then seized the chance to take back the powers to appoint officials and administer finances in the various provinces. Military powers were also recouped by the central authorities. Yuan Shikai's perverse actions that ultimately led him to commit the fatal error of naming himself emperor; he himself was forever repudiated by history and he became a person condemned for all time. There were in this period a number of academics who stood for abating the powers of the central authorities and setting up a federal state, but as compared to the force of arms they attempted to surmount, their arguments proved to be much too flimsy and feeble.

After Yuan Shikai's death, a nationally unified central political power to all intents and purposes no longer existed, China became bogged down in a situation of chaotic fighting among warlords, normal relations between the central and local authorities were replaced by armed separatist regimes, and the "central government" concept was purely nominal and had become a mere instrument or toy in the hands of the warlords.

Mention should be made of the movement for local self-government, also called the Federalist Movement that emerged in the 1920s. Hunan and Zhejiang drew up provincial constitutions stipulating that their respective provinces were autonomous provinces of the Republic of China. Under Sun Yat-sen, Guangdong Province also carried out a campaign for self-government. Theoreticians, too, vigorously promoted this matter and for a while, the federalist campaign, federalism, and slogans touting the "Chinese Federalist Republic" were very much in vogue nation-wide. Yet, none of these gained any purchase. The situation of chaotic, separatist warlord infighting continued up to 1928 when the Chinese Nationalist Party (Kuomintang) reestablished a national "unity" which lasted until the year 1949.

Here, we must mention Sun Yat-sen's thought of equalism. He developed this way of thinking after he had studied China's historical experience and lessons. In other words, he retained the strong points of the unitary system and also drew upon the advantages of the federalist system in order to prevent excessive concentration of powers by the central authorities as well as avert separatism by local authorities. Based on these considerations, he devised criteria for central/local division of powers, i.e., divisions should be based on the nature of the powers. All matters that are common to the nation as a whole should be under the administration of the central authorities, and those that vary according to local conditions should be administered by the local authorities. There shall be no bias toward the centralized system of power or toward localized division of power. Hence, that is one reason why the central administration should be much less active than the local administrations. It is also a reason why the central administration should be oriented more toward external affairs than local administrations. And that is also why the central administration should be mostly in charge of political affairs while local administrations should be more in charge of vocational affairs. That, too, is why military and diplomatic matters are best assigned to the central authorities whereas matters of education and health are best assigned to the local authorities.[21]

As regards local self-governance, Sun Yat-sen stated in "Local Autonomy Practices" that the purpose of implementing local self-governance was to implement the principles of Nationalism and the People's Livelihood. And, organizations of local self-governance are not merely political organizations; they are also economic organizations. In Sun Yat-sen's view, local self-governance must be based on the constitution and be conferred by the state; it must be implemented within given regions; its membership must embrace all people within the respective regions; it must implement direct civil powers; and its purpose is to seek the well-being of the populace as a whole. As an economic organization, it must strive for the financial benefits of the local populace. Counties are entities of local self-governance, while provinces are situated between the central and county authorities for the purposes of liaison. The province is responsible to the central authorities and handles matters assigned by the central authorities on the one hand and, on the other, monitors the implementation of local self-governance at the lower levels. In this way the initiative and zeal of the localities is given full rein, the unity of the state and the authority of the central authorities are upheld, and the long-term stability of the political situation is maintained.

Sun Yat-sen's theories with regard to local self-governance and to the relations between the central and local authorities were quite abundant and differed substantially from the theories of governance prevalent in China's feudal society. Some of his theories displayed profound insights which are still inspirational today.

2.2.2 The Period of Kuomintang Rule from 1928 to 1949

When the Beiyang warlords withdrew from the stage of history, the newly arisen Kuomintang warlords were similarly riddled with cliques and factions that lorded it over their own localities and made no concessions to one another. China in effect remained in a state of disintegration. Eventually, in 1928, the Chiang Kai-shek faction, by means of a strategic combination of alliances and assaults, of political machinations and military actions, forced China's three northeastern provinces to come to heel and pledge fealty to Chiang Kai-shek's Kuomintang Government. National unification was accomplished.

---

[21]Xin Xiangyang et al. *Princes of the Big States*. Beijing: China Social Sciences Publishing House, 1995, p. 214.

However, wars continued unabated in China during this period, and it was impossible for relations between the central and local authorities to remain normal. A national assembly convened on May 5, 1931 adopted the Republic of China Government during Training about the Law, in which Chapter Six on the "Limits of Authority of the Central and Local Authorities" stipulated that the system of equalism should be applied to the limits of authority of the central and local authorities. However, it contained few clear-cut specifics, was in fact quite vague and ambiguous, and masked the fact that Chiang Kai-shek was implementing a personal and dictatorial autocracy. In November 1964, the National Constituent Assembly adopted the "Constitution of the Republic of China" which made a special point of stipulating and assigning the limits of power of the central and local authorities. Once again employing the principle of equalism, these stipulations used the method of separately listing the powers of the central and local authorities. The powers legislated and implemented by the central authorities" covered foreign affairs and matters of a nationally uniform nature (such as national defense, central finances, state taxes, the currency system, weights, and measures, etc.). Next came (no close quote!) matters legislated and implemented by the central authorities or matters handed over to the provinces and counties for implementation, as for instance general rules for provincial and county self-governance, the education system, the police system and so forth, altogether more than 20 items. The provinces could also formulate separate regulations for these items provided the regulations did not come in conflict with national laws. Last, came the limits of powers for provinces and counties, divided as limits for provincial matters and limits for county matters, all of which had to do with local matters. The said constitution also stipulated "should matters occur that are not set forth in the Constitution, those that are of a nationally uniform nature shall come under the central authorities, those that are of a province-wide uniform nature shall come under the provincial authorities, and those that are of a county-wide uniform nature shall come under the county. And should controversies arise, these shall be resolved by the Legislative Yuan. It must be said that the stipulations in this constitution regarding the relations between the central and local authorities were fairly comprehensive. However, this constitution had regressed considerably as compared to the earlier one, and no sign remained of the former stipulation that the province was the highest entity of local self-government or that it could enact a provincial constitution. Thus, the provisions of that constitution continued to be focused on strengthening centralized powers. In the overall, China experienced no substantive unification during those 21 years under Kuomintang rule, and the state of central/local relations remained highly abnormal.

It should be noted that it was during the Kuomintang rule that China witnessed the emergence of the Red Special Areas (Border Areas) that played such an important role in China's historical development. From 1927 to 1930, ten large "base areas" which covered more than 300 counties in ten or so provinces and disposed of a military force of a hundred thousand men took shape under the leadership of the Chinese Communist Party. These special areas implemented political and economic policies radically different from those in the Kuomintang-controlled areas. They had their own complete systems of state political power, and in January 1934 created the first nationwide Red political power in China—the Central Worker-Peasant Democratic Government of the Chinese Soviet Republic. When the War of Resistance against Japan broke out and the Kuomintang and Communist Party entered into a cooperative effort to fight Japan, the Chinese Communist Party agreed to rename its Worker-Peasant Government and call it the Special District Government of the Republic of China. The Red Army was also renamed the National Revolutionary Army and placed under the command of the Military Commission of the Nanjing Central Government. In February 1937, the Shaanxi-Gansu-Ningxia Revolutionary Base was renamed the Shaanxi-Gansu-Ningxia Special Area, and then again renamed a "border area," and in September set up its border-region government. This was a unique form of political power: Relative to the Nationalist Government it was a top-level local political power, but within its own area of jurisdiction it possessed full powers and was in effect the central government. It was in these "special areas" that the people's government of the New China was conceived and grew to maturity.

Two regions or areas existed in the China of this period—the "Red" and the "White"—each of which practiced its own social system and way of life. This, in its implications, very much resembled "one country, two systems."

2.3 Evolution of the State Structure in New China

In 1949, the Chinese Communist Party basically unified the Chinese mainland by means of armed struggle, and on October 1 formally founded the People's Republic of China. Having brought an end to the warlords' separatist wars and the social chaos that had begun in the final years of the Qing Dynasty and lasted several decades, China entered an entirely new era in history and embarked on a period of socialist revolution and construction.

2.3.1 The State Structure in the First Years of the New China

In the first years after the founding of the New China, it was not possible to immediately set up normal local governments nationwide since warfare had not yet ended in the country as a whole and circumstances differed in the various localities. In accordance with the provisions of the Common Program, all newly liberated areas were placed under military control, or under provisional local military control commissions which were appointed either by the Central People's Government or by frontline military authorities and which acted as local governments. Then, step-by-step transitions led to the establishment of regular local governments. This procedure was, of course, inapplicable to Hong Kong and Macao despite similarities in some of the circumstances.

As regards the state structure, six Greater Administrative Regions—the Northeast, North China, East China, South Central, Southwest, and Northwest regions—were inserted between the central and the provincial authorities, and central bureaus were established in each of the Greater Administrative Regions to represent the CPC Central Committee. Administrative institutions were set up in all of the Greater Administrative Regions except for the North China region. The administrative institution in the North China region was called a "people's government," whereas those in the Northeast, East China, South Central, Southwest and Northwest regions were referred to as "military commissions." All were appointed and generated by the Central People's Government. These Greater Administrative Regions constituted the highest level of local government, and they exercised leadership on behalf of the Central People's Government over the governments of the provinces, municipalities and autonomous regions under their jurisdiction.[22] The functions and duties of these Greater Administrative Regions—depending on the circumstances of the region in question—consisted of healing the wounds of war, setting up a new social order, building up the people's political power, launching various social reform campaigns and movements, rehabilitating the national economy and engaging in various other kinds of work.[23] It is evident that the Greater Administrative Regions possessed a fair amount of independence and were institutions to which relatively broad powers had been devolved. However, their orientation and setups were those of temporary and transitional local-level governments, and their purpose was to prepare for the formal establishment of regular local governments in all localities.

The various Greater Administrative Regions (military commissions) were assigned one chairman plus number of vice-chairmen and committee members by the Central People's Government, and were in general subdivided into departments of finance, civil affairs, public security, justice, commerce, culture, and education as well as committees for ethnic affairs and public supervision. All departments and commissions were each assigned a chief or director and a number of deputy chiefs or deputy directors. China's state structure would seem to be quite similar to the federal system when seen from their respective nomenclatures, but of course, China's Greater Administrative Regions were fundamentally different from states under the federal system. The basic circumstances of each Greater Administrative Region are shown in the following table[24]:

---

[22] General Rules for the Organization of the People's Governments of the Greater Administrative Regions, Article 3, December 1949.

[23] He Guoqiang. *Local Governments in Contemporary China*. Guangzhou: Guangdong Higher Education Press, 1944, p. 74.

[24] He Guoqiang. *Local Governments in Contemporary China*. Guangzhou: Guangdong Higher Education Press, 1944, p. 75.

Name of Greater Administrative Region	Provinces, municipalities, districts, and areas administered	Location of the Greater Administrative Region's government
North China Greater Administrative Region (two municipalities, one province)	Beijing Municipality, Tianjin Municipality, Hebei Province, Chaha'er Province, Suiyuan Province, Pingyuan Province	
Northeast Greater Administrative Region (seven municipalities, six provinces)	Shenyang Municipality, Changchun Municipality, Ha'erbin Municipality, Lüshun-Dalian Municipality, Anshan Municipality, Fushun Municipality, Benxi Municipality, Liaoning Province, Liaoxi Province, Jilin Province, Songjiang Province, Heilongjiang Province, Rehe Province	Shenyang Municipality
East China Greater Administrative Region (two municipalities, four districts, three provinces)	Shanghai Municipality, Nanjing Municipality, Subei District, Sunan District, Wannan District, Wanbei District, Shandong Province, Zhejiang Province, Fujian Province	Shanghai Municipality
Central South Greater Administrative Region (two municipalities, six provinces)	Wuhan Municipality, Guangzhou Municipality, Henan Province, Hubei Province, Hunan Province, Jiangxi Province, Guangdong Province, Guangxi Province	Wuhan Municipality
Northwest Greater Administrative Region (one municipality, five provinces)	Xi'an Municipality, Shaanxi Province, Gansu Province, Qinghai Province, Ningxia Province, Xinjiang Province	Xi'an Municipality
Southwest Greater Administrative Region (one municipality, four districts, three provinces, one area)	Chongqing Municipality, Chuandong District, Chuanxi District, Chuannan District, Chuanbei District, Xikang Province, Yunnan Province, Guizhou Province, Xizang (Tibet) Area	Chongqing Municipality

Notes
1. There were then altogether 15 municipalities, 23 provinces, 8 districts and 1 area nationwide
2. In the North China region, provinces and municipalities were directly under central government administration; there was no Greater Administrative Region
3. "District (区)" stands for "prefectural district (行署区)." These were in substance local governments set up to suit the circumstances of the older and newer liberated areas and were equivalent to provincial-level institutions. All provincial-level prefectural districts were canceled in 1952 when the provinces of Jiangsu, Anhui, and Sichuan were reinstated
4. Xizang (Tibet) had always been called an "area." It became an autonomous region in September, 1966

In reality, the North China Region People's Government was established before the year 1949, and since the Central People's Government was located within the North China Region after the founding of the People's Republic, all provinces and municipalities in the North China region fell under the direct jurisdiction of the Central People's Government. Meanwhile, because the Central People's Government had set up a special North China Affairs Department to attend those duties, the North China region had no Greater Region government. It was only in November 1952 when the Greater Region people's governments (military commissions) were one and all converted into administrative commissions that an administrative commission was set up in the North China Region and the Central Government's North China Affairs Department was simultaneously canceled.

The setting up of Greater Administrative Regions suited the actual circumstances of the times as it enabled the localities to adopt diverse policies in light of their own situations and had a major effect on healing the wounds of war, restoring social order and developing the economy. However, the Greater Administrative Regions setup eventually proved to be quite inconvenient when China began in 1953 to implement its first five-year plan for national economic and social development—inconvenient because the five-year plan was drafted on a national scale because many of its large projects straddled provinces and even the Greater Administrative Regions because the domestic and international situation called for all-round consideration and arrangements for China as a whole, and because manpower and material resources had to be assembled for huge endeavors. In November 1952, it was decided to strengthen the central authorities' unified leadership by converting all of the Greater Administrative Regions (military commissions) into administrative commissions, and the CPC Central Committee, in its Decision on Changing the Structure and Duties of the Governments of the Greater Administrative Region, explicitly pointed out: "Large-scale, planned economic and cultural construction will be commencing next year. Under the new situation, the central authorities' leadership over various items of work should be more concentrated and unified than at any previous time, and the central institutions should be greatly strengthened." This decision fundamentally altered the previous method placing provinces under the leadership of the Greater Administrative Regions, which were now serving as agencies of the Central people's government instead of as organs of local political power. This marked a fundamental change in the nature of the Greater Administrative Regions.

After the Gao Gang-Rao Shushi Incident took place in the Northeast Greater Administrative Region, the Party Center formally decided in June 1954 to cancel the Greater Administrative Region setup and have the central authorities exercise direct leadership over the various provinces, districts, and municipalities. It also further annulled some of the localities' self-governing powers. This system was defined in the constitution drafted in 1954.

The administrative system based on a high degree of centralized power inevitably fettered the initiative of the localities and affected economic development. Hence, the unitary system of centralized vertical leadership triggered a great deal of dissatisfaction among the various provinces. After doing a series of investigation and studies, Mao Zedong delivered a speech on the "Ten Great Relationships" to an expanded meeting of the CPC Central Political Bureau on April 25, 1956. Regarding the relationship between the central and local authorities, Mao Zedong put forward a number of guiding principles of a long-term nature, the core content of which was "a country like ours should give play to the initiative of both the central and local authorities," and that certain powers of economic administration should be devolved to the local authorities. The Party's Eighth Congress convened in September 1956 again stressed the necessity of "appropriately adjusting the extents of administrative power of the central and local authorities." In 1959, however, it became necessary to once again emphasize that "the whole nation must coordinate its moves as in a single game of chess," that the central authorities had to exercise appropriate centralization of powers. This campaign to recentralize powers and oppose decentralism lasted until the eve of the Cultural Revolution.

During the Cultural Revolution, centralization of powers was once again castigated as **"direct and exclusive control of enterprises by the ministry concerned"** and relationships between the central and local authorities were extremely abnormal. After the "Gang of Four" was deposed, and especially in the wake of the Third Plenary Session of the CPC Eleventh Central Committee [December 18–22, 1978] efforts to dispel chaos and restore order were implemented nationwide and all undertakings gradually returned to normal.

When summing up the history of the relationship between new China's central and local authorities after 1949, we find that those relationships underwent several major ups and downs; that powers were released and retracted by turns, sometimes being highly centralized and sometimes extremely decentralized. Powers that needed to be centralized could not be centralized, and those that should not have been centralized stayed with the central authorities. Conversely, powers that ought to have been released were not sent down, while those that should not have been released were taken over by the localities. There was a great deal of randomness. All were in a state of chaos, devoid of any rhyme or reason or of any strict legal or institutional guarantees. Deng Xiaoping was clearly aware of the situation. On October 4, 1979, when he gave a talk on "Some Opinions about Economic Work" and answered the question of whether there was too much or too little centralization at the time, he said: "As I see it, there is neither sufficient centralization nor sufficient decentralization… Some [powers] should be released and given over to the localities, so that the localities may have somewhat more power over financial affairs and more room for maneuver. That should be the overall policy. However, there are also cases of insufficient centralization." Hence, starting in the early 1980s, the state on the one hand gradually straightened out the relations between the central authorities and localities according the principles and spirit of Reform and Opening Up and conducted a rational division of powers between the central and local authorities and, on the other, gave full attention to institutionalizing and legalizing the results of reforms. It strove to avoid the erstwhile practice of simplistically taking over and releasing powers, and instead solve the problem in terms of institutions and structures.

2.3.2 *The State Structure as Stipulated by the Current Constitution*

The new Constitution approved by the Fifth Session of the Fifth People's Congress of China in 1982 sums up historical experiences and lessons and affirms the new fruits of the policy of Reform and Opening Up. In terms of state structure and handling the relations between the central authorities and localities, this Constitution stipulates the following basic principles.

First of all, the Constitution affirms that China is a country with a unitary system. Actually, when looking through the Constitution, in none of its articles does one see the term "unitary system," and one could well say the Constitution does not specify the form of state structure implemented in China. China's scholars of constitutional law frequently cite the statement that "the People's Republic of China is a unitary multinational state created jointly by the people of all its nationalities" written in the Preamble of the 1982 Constitution as the basis for claiming that China implements the unitary system and possesses a unitary system rather than a federal or confederal system. In reality, however, that statement does not suffice to denote the form of China's state structure because any country in the sense of an integrated state is unitary, and many countries are also multinational. The United States and Russia are both unitary countries and are made up of great many ethnic groups. We cannot say that these countries are not unitary, or that countries under the federal system are not unitary. However, I do not doubt that China's Constitution stipulates a unitary state system, or that China indeed practices a unitary system. There are ample grounds for that premise in the Constitution. Those grounds are not the aforementioned statement in the Preamble, but rather articles in the Constitution that define the powers of state institutions. Studies of a country's state structure require specific examination of the powers actually wielded by the country's national government and local governments. It is in this sense that I consider China to be a country with unitary state system.

There are several reasons for China's implementing the unitary state system. First, historically, China has exercised a unitary state system ever since the Qin Dynasty. A second reason is the distribution of ethnic groups. The ethnic Hans who make up 92% of the national population is spread out all over China, and while the 55 other ethnic peoples are fewer in number, they too are distributed over the whole country and cannot be brought together to form independent national states. Three, the diverse ethnic groups have formed profound friendly relations during their struggles against imperialism and feudalism in contemporary times. Four, historical experience has shown that ethnic schisms benefit no one and that all national groups can achieve common prosperity and common advances only if they come together to form a united country with a unitary state system. Five, the construction of a modern society calls for the setting up of a state with a unitary system, as only that will enable people to draw on others' strong points, work in unity and help one another. And six, Marxists have always maintained that the proletariat, after gaining state power, should in principle work toward setting up a united country with a unitary state structure; they, in general, do not recommend setting up a federalist system, and regard doing so only as an exception under special historical conditions in order to avoid national splits.[25] Moreover, setting up a unitary state structure does not preclude the possibility of some localities adopting special systems and measures in light of special local circumstances since the unitary state structure can also be quite versatile and inclusive.

The Constitution also stipulates specific principles for handling the relations between the central authorities and the localities. Article 3 of the Constitution provides: "The state organs of the People's Republic of China apply the principle of democratic centralism." And: "The division of functions and powers between the central and local state organs is guided by the principle of giving full scope to the initiative and enthusiasm of the local authorities under the unified leadership of the central authorities." This makes it clear that when handling the relations between the central authorities and the localities, the unified authority of the central authorities must first be upheld, as this is required by the unitary state system; and second, full attention is accorded to giving free rein to the initiative, enthusiasm, and creativeness of the local authorities, and to giving the latter due powers of self-governance.[26]

Based on the above principles, China has, in terms of the setup of administrative regions, established three major regions of local administration under the central government, i.e., provinces, directly administered municipalities and autonomous regions. In terms of the leadership structure, China has in reality adopted the form of local self-government, since in accordance with the Constitution and the Local Organization Law all provincial governors, mayors of directly administered municipalities and chairmen of autonomous region governments are elected and generated by the people's congresses at their respective levels. That is to say, the people of these localities have the right to organize their own governments—which is an important characteristic of local self-government. If the requirements of centralized power were strictly observed, senior local administrative officials should be appointed by the central government and the localities would not be empowered to organize their own governments. Hence, if looked at from the perspective of the Constitution and its provisions, it is evident that the organizational form of local self-government has been adopted for local political power under China's unitary state system.[27] And if

---

[25]Xu Chongde. *The Constitution of China*. Beijing: China Renmin University Press, 1989, pp. 158–163.

[26]As stated earlier, since China implements centralization of powers and a unitary state system, all powers in China should theoretically be wielded by the central authorities. Thus, the issue of so-called "division of powers" should not exist between the central and local authorities, and the sole issue should be how much power the central authorities "confer" on the local authorities. Accordingly, some scholars are against using the term "division of powers" for describing the power relationship between the central and local authorities in China, and maintain that the "division of powers" issue exists only under the federal system. However, since the term "division of functions and powers" is explicitly used in Article 3 of the Chinese Constitution, I feel there is nothing wrong in using the term "division of powers" to describe the relations between the central and local authorities in China, especially for convenience's sake in academic investigations.

[27]This has never been acknowledged by Chinese constitutional law circles. When the relations of provinces and directly administered municipalities with the central authorities are discussed, these relations are often sweepingly described as pertaining to the unitary system, and no deeper

seen from the way local governments are elected as stipulated in the Constitution, provincial-level governments are relatively independent of the central government.

Yet, the division of powers between central and local institutions, as provided for in the Constitution, manifests clear centralization-of-powers characteristics. Article 89, item (4) of the Constitution specifies the functions and powers of the State Council as: "to exercise unified leadership over the work of local organs of state administration at various levels throughout the country, and to formulate the detailed division of functions and powers between the Central Government and the organs of state administration of provinces, autonomous regions, and municipalities directly under the Central government; "and item (14) specifies: "…to alter and annul inappropriate orders, directives and regulations issued by local organs of state administration at various levels." Similar contents are present in item (8) of Article 67 of the Constitution which stipulates the functions of the National People's Congress, i.e., "…to annul those local regulations or decisions of the organs of state power of provinces, autonomous regions, and municipalities directly under the Central Government that contravene the Constitution, the law or the administrative rules and regulations." Article 108 of the Constitution stipulates: "Local people's governments at and above the county level direct the work of their subordinate departments and of people's governments at lower levels, and have the power to alter or annul inappropriate decisions of their subordinate departments and of the people's governments at lower levels." Article 110 stipulates: "… Local people's governments at various levels are responsible for and report on their work to the state administrative organs at the next higher level. Local people's governments at various levels throughout the country are state administrative organs under the unified leadership of the State Council and are subordinate to it." All these bear typical characteristics of centralization of powers under a unitary system and most clearly show that the relations between higher and lower levels of government in China are relations between the leaders and the led. This is despite the reality that the composition of China's local governments is a form of local self-government and that local administrative leaders and local governments are generated by means of local elections and need not be appointed by the Central Government.

Hence, it would appear from the setup of China's provinces and directly administered municipalities as stipulated by the Constitution that these have been configured as a form of self-government but that the powers they exercise bear obvious characteristics of centralization. China's scholars call this "the dual leadership system." In other words, local governments are subject to leadership by local state power insti-

---

analysis is made of the provinces' or the directly administered municipalities' mode of organization, which is, in fact, a sort of local self-government. The people's congresses of provinces and directly administered municipalities are elected and generated by the local people, and the local people's governments and people's courts at those levels are elected and generated by the people's congresses at the same level and need not be submitted to the Central People's Government or the Supreme People's Court for approval and appointment. The sole exceptions are the chief procurators of the provincial-level people's procuratorates who, after being elected by the people's congresses at that level, must be reported to the chief procurator of the Supreme People's Procuratorate, and then submitted to the National People's Congress Standing Committee for approval.

tutions at their own level and to direct leadership by the Central Government. This is a socialist unitary system with Chinese characteristics.

According to the stipulations of the Constitution, also set up—in addition to the provinces and directly administered municipalities throughout the country—are national autonomous areas of the same level as the provinces and directly administered municipalities. The term "national autonomous areas" refers to national self-governing localities set up on the premise of guaranteeing the country's unity in areas where ethnic minorities live in concentrated communities. These national autonomous areas establish organs of self-government and exercise the powers of autonomy so that the ethnic minority peoples that implement regional autonomy may conduct self-determined administration of affairs of a local nature within their own ethnic group. In addition to enjoying the powers of provincial-level local government, the national autonomous regions also enjoy a series of special rights. Nevertheless, the self-government exercised in China's ethnic regions is regional self-government, not ethnic self-government.

Another important stipulation on the state structure made in the 1982 Constitution concerns the setup of special administrative regions. Article 31 of the Constitution stipulates that the state may establish special administrative regions when necessary and that the systems to be instituted in the special administrative regions are to be determined by the National People's Congress in the light of specific conditions. This is a special stipulation made to meet the needs of national unification as well as a special provision in the Constitution. It will be discussed in detail in subsequent chapters of this book.

In sum, the 1982 Constitution to all intents and purposes affirmed China's unitary state structure, and at the same time paid attention to devising new stipulations in light of the characteristics of the new era. More than a decade has elapsed now since the formulation of the 1982 Constitution. Relations between China's central authorities and the localities have in general been fairly sound over these years, and have lived up to the principle of "mobilizing the enthusiasm of both." However, we must also see that the relations between the two have experienced big ups and downs. Sometimes government streamlining has led to powers being released to the lower levels. At other times, powers have had to be recentralized, but each recentralization has had the effect of stifling the localities. Yet, no sooner were powers released again than macro controls were lost. It is evident that the relations of the central authorities with the various provinces, directly administered municipalities and autonomous regions have yet to be fully standardized, institutionalized, and legalized. There are still no divisions of power of a systemic character, and the extent of the divisions hinge largely on chance or occasion. The relations between the central authorities and the localities should henceforth move toward legalization and institutionalization.

2.3.3 Stipulations in the Legislation Law on the Extent of Central/Local Division of Power

As noted in the foregoing text, an important issue in the division of powers between the central authorities and localities is that the provisions in the Constitution lack clarity and operability and give rise to much confusion in actual work, as matters which ought to be controlled by central legislation are left untended by the central authorities while other matters which the central authorities have no business controlling remain under tight central control. The Legislative Law passed on March 15, 2000 by the Third Session of the Ninth National People's Congress attempted to bring about breakthroughs in terms of the division of legislative powers. However, the problem is essentially a constitutional issue, and there is little hope of resolving a constitutional issue of such magnitude by way of ordinary legislation when the Constitution per se does not clearly define the division of powers between the central and local authorities. Yet, the Legislative Law does contain some new ideas in this respect, and it has made efforts within its capabilities toward defining the division of powers between the central and local authorities.

Principles for the division of powers between the central and local authorities may be discerned among the legislative principles stipulated in the Legislative Law. The Law provides that legislation is to abide by the basic principles of the Constitution and uphold the "one center and two basic points" principle. It provides that legislation should proceed in accordance with statutory extents of authority and procedures; proceed from the interests of the country as a whole and uphold the unity and dignity of the socialist legal system; that legislation should manifest the will of the people, carry forward socialist democracy, and ensure the people's participation in legislative activities through multiple channels; that legislation should proceed from realities and scientifically and rationally define the rights and duties of citizens, legal persons, and other organizations as well as the powers and responsibilities of state organs. Thus, it is evident that China's legislation must first and foremost give consideration to "the interests of the country as a whole," which is to say that priority should be given to safeguarding the powers of the central authorities who represent "the interests of the country as a whole." Legislation is also to promote democracy, and it should scientifically and rationally define the division of state powers, including that between the central and local authorities, which is to say that division of state powers should be "scientific and rational" and that one should not cling one-sidedly to the view that the bigger the central authorities' powers the better or that all matters are best legislated by the central authorities.

Article 7 of the Legislation Law stipulates that the National People's Congress and the NPC Standing Committee exercise the legislative powers of the State. As regards the division of powers between the National People's Congress and its Standing Committee, the said Law reiterates the stipulations in the Constitution, i.e., that the National People's Congress enacts and amends basic laws governing such matters as criminal offenses, civil affairs, and the State organs. It stipulates that the NPC Standing Committee enacts and amends laws other than those to be enacted by the National People's Congress, and when the National People's Congress is not in session, it may partially supplement and amend laws enacted by the National People's Congress but not in contradiction to the basic principles of those laws.

Article 8 of the Legislation Law regulates matters that can only be governed by law. That, in fact, has been the first time in the New China that matters governed by the Central Government are defined by law. These include: (1) affairs concerning State sovereignty; (2) the formation, organization, and the functions and powers of the people's congresses, the people's governments, the people's courts and the people's procuratorates at all levels; (3) the system of regional national autonomy, the system of special administrative regions, the system of self-government of people at the grassroots level; (4) criminal offenses and their punishment; (5) mandatory measures and penalties involving deprivation of citizens of their political rights or restriction of the freedom of their person; (6) requisitions of non-State-owned property; (7) the basic civil system; (8) the basic economic system and the basic systems of finance, taxation, customs and banking and foreign trade; (9) the systems of litigation and foreign trade; and (10) other affairs on which laws must be made by the National People's Congress or its Standing Committee. Matters other than these are to be governed by local legislation.

No matter how big the flaws of the Legislation Law, that Law should be seen as a worthy attempt to produce a fairly clear definition of the powers of the central authorities and localities from the perspective of legislative powers. Due, however, to the fact that relations between the central and local authorities are essentially a constitutional issue that must be resolved in and by the Constitution, it would be difficult to fundamentally resolve that issue from the perspective of legislative powers and by relying on legislation alone. That will have to wait for further amendments to the Constitution which thoroughly solve the power relationship issue between the central authorities and the localities.

Research in the historical development of China' state structure has furnished historical references and background materials on using "one country, two systems" to solve issues of national unity and for correctly handling the relations between the central authorities and the special administrative regions.

Chapter 3
The Genesis and Operations of "One Country, Two Systems" Policy

"One country two systems" is the theoretical basis for China's establishment of the Special Administrative Regions (SARs) and serves as the basic guiding thought for handling relations between the central authorities and the SARs. It is therefore necessary to conduct some explorations into the "one country, two systems" theory.

3.1 The Origins of the Hong Kong, Macao, and Taiwan Issues

The People's Republic of China was formally established on October 1, 1949. After its founding, the country was faced with two major issues: Restoring and building up the national economy, and continuing to complete the great cause of unifying China.[1] As regards the second task, all that remained after the peaceful liberation of Tibet was the effective incorporation of Hong Kong, Macao, and Taiwan in the territory of the People's Republic of China.[2] Thus, one of the major historical tasks

---

[1] In 1949, when the People's Republic of China was founded, large areas in Central South, West, and East China remained under the control of the Kuomintang armies, and military operations there continued up to October, 1951.

[2] On May 23, 1951, the Central People's Government and the Local Government of Tibet signed the "Agreement of the Central People's Government and the Local Government of Tibet on Measures for the Peaceful Liberation of Tibet." The Agreement provided that the Tibetan people would unite and drive imperialist aggressor forces out of Tibet; that the local government of Tibet would actively assist the People's Liberation Army in entering Tibet and consolidating China's national defenses; that Tibet would exercise national regional autonomy; that the central authorities would not alter Tibet's existing political system or the established status, functions, and powers of the Dalai Lama and the Panchen Ngerdeni and that officials of all ranks would hold office as usual; that the policy of religious freedom would be carried out and the religious beliefs, customs, and habits of the Tibetan people would be respected; that the spoken and written language and school education of

© Foreign Language Teaching and Research Publishing Co., Ltd and Springer Nature Singapore Pte Ltd. 2019
Z. Wang, *Relationship Between the Chinese Central Authorities and Regional Governments of Hong Kong and Macao: A Legal Perspective*, China Academic Library, https://doi.org/10.1007/978-981-13-2322-5_3

still confronting the government and people of the New China was the resolution of the Hong Kong, Macao, and Taiwan issues and the thorough completion of the great mission of unifying the nation. However, it was not until the end of the 1970s, after China had smashed the Gang of Four, ended the "Cultural Revolution," restored order after years of chaos, and weathered changes in the domestic and international political macro-environment, that the Chinese government and people put national unification back on the agenda and decided to complete this task—a matter which had remained unresolved over several generations and had long been listed as one of the major tasks China would accomplish in the 1980s.[3]

3.1.1 Hong Kong

Located on Pearl River Estuary on the southern coast of China's Guangdong Province, situated on the eastern side of Lingdinyang where it borders on the South China Sea, and forming an important communications hub where the Pearl River enters the sea, Hong Kong is an extremely vital port city in the eastern part of the Eurasian continent and on the western coast of the Pacific Ocean. The area usually referred to as Hong Kong includes Hong Kong Island, Kowloon Peninsula, the New Territories, and the territorial waters of some two hundred large and small islands. The Hong Kong region covers an area of 1,084 sq km. Of this, Hong Kong Island accounts for 75.6 km^2, the Kowloon Peninsula (including Stonecutters [Ang Chuan] Island) 11.1 km^2, the New Territories region (including 235 large and small islands) 975.1 km^2, plus another 20 or more square kilometers acquired by means of land reclamation from the sea.[4] Hong Kong's population at the end of 1995 stood at about 6.3 million, making Hong Kong one of the most densely populated regions in the world.[5]

Hong Kong has been China's territory since ancient times. In 214 B.C., the First Emperor of Qin sent troops southward to pacify the regions south of the Yangtze

---

the Tibetan people as well as Tibetan agriculture, livestock raising, industry, and commerce would be developed step by step and the livelihood of the people improved; and that the Central People's Government would exercise centralized management of Tibet's foreign affairs. The Agreement also clearly stipulated that the central authorities would not exercise any compulsion with regard to various reforms in Tibet and that the local government of Tibet would conduct reforms of its own accord. On October 26 the same year, the People's Liberation Army with support from the Tibetan people entered and took up station in Lhasa without incident, and the Chinese Communist Party finally reunified the Chinese mainland. See White Paper 1992 of the Information Office of the State Council of the People's Republic of China: Tibet—Its Ownership and Human Rights Situation.

[3] The Three Major Events of the 1980s: (a) Opposing hegemonism in world affairs and safeguarding world peace; (b) bringing Taiwan back to the motherland and reunifying the nation; and (c) intensifying the four modernizations. *Selected Works of Deng Xiaoping.* Vol. 2, 2nd printing, Beijing: People's Publishing House, 1993, pp. 239–241.

[4] See *Hong Kong Yearbook* (English edition), published by the government of Hong Kong, 1995. Hong Kong's area in 2001 was 1098 km^2, thanks to the reclamation of land from the sea.

[5] Beijing, *Legal Daily*, 1996-03-03. By the end of June 2000, Hong Kong's population had reached 6.78 million.

River, and incorporated the Lingnan area [i.e., today's Guangdong and Guangxi provinces] in his territories. "Thereafter the Lingnan region, including Hong Kong, remained under the jurisdiction of the Central Government of China without inter-ruption, until the time Britain invaded Hong Kong."[6] The Qin Dynasty set up three prefectures—Nanhai, Guilin, and Xiangjun—in Guangdong, and Hong Kong per-tained to Fanyu County in Nanhai Prefecture. The Han Dynasty set up a salt tax agency in Fanyu. In the Three Kingdoms period.

Hong Kong belonged to the Dongwan Prefecture of the Kingdom of Wu. In the Eastern Jin period, it remained under the jurisdiction of Dongwan Prefecture, the governing body of which was situated in Bao'an County, or today's Nantou City in Shenzhen which was also the site of the Fanyu Salt Tax Agency. This situation lasted until the tenth year (A.D. 590) of the founding emperor of the Sui Dynasty when Dongwan Prefecture was revoked and Bao'an County came under Guangzhou, though Hong Kong was still administered by Bao'an County. By the Tang Dynasty, a heavily garrisoned frontier command was established at Bao'an. Tuen Men [an earlier name for Hong Kong—Tr.] had become an important hub for sea communications and a military stronghold for coastal defense. Hong Kong's economy registered fairly significant development in the Song Dynasty.

In the last years of the Southern Song Dynasty, the dynasty's imperial court at one time took refuge here, and it was here that Yuan forces ultimately vanquished the Song army and unified China. In A.D. 1573, the Ming Dynasty set up Xin'an County (in addition to Dongwan County) under the jurisdiction of Guangzhou for the sake of strengthening coastal defense. Thereafter, Hong Kong remained under the jurisdiction of Xin'an County until it was invaded by the British in 1841. According to historical records, Hong Kong had approximately five thousand residents before being occupied by Britain.[7]

With the discovery of the American continent and the opening up of distant sea routes, the European countries began to cast covetous eyes on this ancient land in Asia. Hong Kong drew the most attention because of its unique location. From 1514, when the first Portuguese commercial vessel came here, up to 1661, colonialists from Portugal, Spain, and the Netherlands arrived one after the other in the hope of seizing a piece of land, but all were driven away. Britain, too, had always wished to hold direct talks with China's central government on establishing trade relations and wanted to take over an island as a base of operations. As far back as in 1583 and 1596, British Queen Elizabeth had twice sent out missives to the emperor of China, but neither of these reached their destination.[8] In 1635, the British ship HMS London first reached China's Macao. Thereafter, direct trade relations commenced between China and Britain, but conflicts kept arising. As Britain was anxious to

---

[6] Yuan Bangjian. *A Brief History of Hong Kong*. Hong Kong: Chung Lew Press Co., Ltd., 1993, p. 25.

[7] Wang Wenxiang. *Hong Kong and Macao Manual*. Beijing: China Prospect Publishing House, 1991, p. 4.

[8] Zhang Tiedong. "The First Contacts between China and Britain," carried in *Historical Research*, 1985 (5).

open China's gates, it dispatched its first diplomatic corps to China on December 21, 1787. Led by Charles Allan Cathcart who had held a military position in Bengal, the delegation started out on the HMS Vestal but the delegation came to grief during the trip.[9] On September 26, 1792, the King of Britain sent another embassy to China headed by Lord Macartney. The embassy succeeded in securing an audience with the Qianlong Emperor in the name of offering him birthday congratulations, but it failed to achieve its purpose of opening lines of commerce with China, and its request for a piece of land was sternly rejected by the Qianlong Emperor. That was the first official delegation from the West to reach China in recent times.[10]

On August 29, 1842, after the Opium War, the Qing government was compelled to sign its first unequal treaty—the Treaty of Nanking, which among other things ceded Hong Kong Island to Britain. In 1858, Britain and France launched the Second Opium War and among other things burned down the Yuanmingyuan—the old Summer Palace. The Qing government was forced to sign with Britain and France the Convention of Beijing, Article 6 of which stipulated that the district of Kowloon in East Guangdong would be ceded in perpetuity to the British monarch and be incorporated within the borders of British occupied Hong Kong. Thereafter the southern end of the Kowloon Peninsula was also seized by the British. After the Sino-Japanese War of 1895, the Western powers went on a frenzied spree of carving up China, and Britain took advantage of the situation to coerce the Qing government into signing the "Second Convention Between Great Britain and China Respecting an Extension of Hong Kong Territory" whereby parts of the Kowloon Peninsula south of the Shenzhen River and north of Boundary Street were leased to Britain for a term of ninety-nine years. The areas were grouped under the common denominator "New Territories," and from then on Britain occupied the entire region of Hong Kong.[11]

In 1949, after the founding of the People's Republic of China, the new government did not act immediately to recover Hong Kong. And it was only toward the end of the 1970s, when the ninety-nine-year lease of the "New Territories" would expire in June 1997 that the British side began to take the matter seriously. With a view to extending their control over Hong Kong, they brought up the "1997 issue" on their own initiative.[12] However, their adversary now was no longer the corrupt and decadent Qing imperial court, but a strong People's Republic of China, and Hong Kong's future found itself once more at a crucial turning point.

---

[9]Zhu Yong. *China's Reluctance to Open Its Doors*. Nanchang: Jiangxi People's Publishing House, 1989, pp. 155–162.

[10]George Staunton. *An Authentic Account of an Embassy from the King of Great Britain to the Emperor of China*. Hong Kong: Joint Publishing (Hong Kong) Company, Ltd., 1994.

[11]Yu Shenwu and Liu Cunkuan. *Hong Kong in the 19th Century*. Hong Kong: Unicorn Books Ltd., 1994, p. 111.

[12]Huang Wenfang. *The Course and Practice of China's Decision to Restore Its Sovereignty over Hong Kong*. Hong Kong Baptist University, p. 4.

3.1.2 Macao

Macao is located on the western bank of the mouth of the Pearl River next to the South China Sea. It is approximately 150 km south of Guangzhou and at a distance of about 60 km from Hong Kong. With a total area of 23.8 km^2, it includes the Macao Peninsula and two small islands and has a population of about 370 thousand (1992).[13] Despite its small size and population, it has a highly unique historical background and international status.

In ancient times, Macao was known by such names as Hao Jing, Hao Jiang, Hai Jing, Jing Hu, and Hao Jing Ao [Putonghua pronunciation—Tr.]. Prior to the Ming Dynasty, it was a little-known piece of frontier wasteland under the jurisdiction of Hong Kong County. The young emperors of the Southern Song court once sought refuge here. In 1513, Portuguese colonialists—among the first to come to China—cast anchor in the vicinity of Lingding Island and at one time reached Tuen Men (as Hong Kong was once called). They subsequently attempted to land on the Chinese coast a few times but each time were repelled. During the [Ming Dynasty's] Zhengde reign (1506–1521), the Guangzhou authorities gave permission for foreign merchants to engage in commerce in a coastal district called Dian Bai. In 1529, after the Guangdong Border Commissioner had requested the lifting of maritime bans, Macao gradually developed into a location for Chinese-foreign trade. In the 32nd year of the Ming Dynasty's Jiajing reign (1553), the Portuguese applied for a piece of land, citing the excuse that one their ships had run aground and sunk in the sea nearby and the tributes it bore were wet and had to be spread out to dry. They also bribed a marine transport official in Guangdong who let them land in Macao. In 1557, the Portuguese began to settle down in Macao, and set up a stronghold by erecting buildings and constructing forts in the coastal Nanwan district of Macao. Macao was formally opened up as a port for foreign trade and gradually became the largest center for entrepot trade in the Far East. It also developed into a center used by the West for disseminating culture and religion in China.[14] By the year 1621, Macao's population had increased to twenty thousand or more. Macao's economy and culture was registering sustained development and manifested a healthy momentum.

In the tenth year of the Wanli reign (1582) of the Ming Dynasty, the Portuguese government concluded with China a land lease pact which stipulated that the Portuguese would pay Xiangshan County a yearly land rental of 500 taels of silver. In 1632, Portugal sent D. Francisco Mascarenhas to serve as the first governor-general of Macao. However, Macao's local administrative affairs and judiciary were largely controlled by the Chinese government right up to the mid-nineteenth century, whereas the Portuguese there engaged mainly in ordinary commercial activities.[15]

---

[13] Yang Yunzhong. *Macao and Macao's Basic Law*. Macao: Macao Foundation, 1994, pp. 39–40. By September 2000, Macao's total population had reached 440,000.

[14] Yang Yunzhong. *Macao and Modern Economic Growth*. Macao: Macao Foundation, 1992, pp. 5–20.

[15] Mi Jian. *Legislations of Macao*. Macao: Macao Foundation, 1994, pp. 1–3.

The Qing Manchu government continued to implement the Ming Dynasty's laws and policies in Macao, and in the 24th year of the Kangxi reign (1685) expanded Macao's customs administrative division *guanbu xingtai*, one of China's four largest customs offices at the time. After the Opium Wars, Macao's status began to decline when the British carved away and occupied Hong Kong and turned it into a free port. In 1849, the Portuguese forcibly took over Wanghai (Portuguese: Mong-Hà) Village and forbade the continued existence of China's customs and tax offices, in consequence of which China's officials were compelled to withdraw from Macao. From then on, the Portuguese occupied the entire Macao Peninsula, seized Macao's powers of legislation and administration, extended Macao's boundaries, and levied taxes on its inhabitants. Later, the Macanese authorities also occupied two small islands and exercised control over them by setting up an "Island Town Council." Henceforth, Portugal occupied the entire Macao region and began to implement actual and overall control over it. And so, in the course of these dubious and obscure circumstances, China lost control over Macao.[16]

In 1862, when the Macanese Governor-general went to Beijing to discuss a treaty with the Qing government, the latter broached the subject of regaining possession Macao. The two sides agreed after negotiations that the Qing Government could continue to maintain a *yamen* in Macao, but it would not be allowed to collect land taxes or other levies. When exchanging the documents, the Portuguese side made *sub-rosa* changes to the contents stating that the Macao region would become independent from China's Guangdong Province. This was rejected by the Qing court. In December 1887, the two sides signed a Treaty of Amity and Commerce, and confirmed that "Portugal will exercise perpetual occupation and government over Macao," but at the same time stated that Portugal was not to "cede Macao to any other country" without China's agreement. Several subsequent proposals by the Portuguese government and the Macanese authorities to extend the scope of control were rejected.[17] In the seventeenth century, the King of Portugal conferred on Macao the appellation "City of the Name of God in China, There is none more loyal" and subsequently listed Macao as one of that country's overseas provinces. In April 1928, the Chinese government sent a note the Portuguese government proposing the abrogation of the Treaty of Amity and Commerce, but to no avail. During the Second World War, the Japanese occupied Hong Kong and Zhong Shan but not Macao. Macao's status declined even further after the war and only turned for the better in the 1960s thanks to the rise of Hong Kong. In 1974, after the April 25th Revolution in Portugal, the new Portuguese government declared renunciation of colonialism and acknowledged that Macao was Chinese territory under Portuguese administration. Portugal passed a new constitution in 1976 permitting Macao to exercise internal sovereignty, published Articles of Association of Macao (Estatuto Orgânico de Macau), and set

---

[16]Wang Wenxiang. *Hong Kong and Macao Manual.* Beijing: China Prospect Publishing House, 1991.

[17]See footnote 16.

up a legislative assembly for Macao.[18] China and Portugal established diplomatic relations on February 8, 1979, and exchanges between the two increased day by day. Subsequent to the resolution of the Hong Kong issue, the Macao issue, and the return of Macanese sovereignty to China was also placed on the agendas of the Chinese and Portuguese governments.

3.1.3 Taiwan

The Taiwan region includes Taiwan Island, the Penghu Islands as well as the Lan Yu (Orchid Island), Lü Dao (Green Island), Pengjia Islet, Diaoyu Island, Chiwei Island, and other islands and islets totaling 36,600 km^2. Taiwan itself covers an area of 35,800 km^2 and is China's largest island. As of the end of 2000, Taiwan's overall population numbered 22,280,000.

Taiwan has been an inseparable part of China since ancient times. In old Chinese books and documentation, it was called Dao Yi, and then called Yi Zhou during the Han and Jin Dynasties and Northern and Southern Dynasties. In the mid-twelfth century A.D., the Song Dynasty had already dispatched garrison troops to guard the Penghu Islands (Pescadores) and put these under the administration of Jinjiang County of Fujian Province's Quanzhou Prefecture. The Yuan Dynasty set up the inspection department *xunjiansi* in Penghu to administer the islands; this department was later abolished. In the latter years of the sixteenth century, the Ming Dynasty reinstated the *xunjiansi* which had been abolished for a period of time and dispatched more military forces to Penghu to guard against aggression by foreigners. From 1624 to 1661 (the fourth year of the Ming Dynasty Tianqi reign to the 18th year of the Qing Shunzhi reign), Taiwan was occupied by Dutch and Spanish colonialists. In 1662 (the first year of the Qing Kangxi reign), the national hero Zheng Chenggong (Koxinga) led his forces in a campaign to eject the Dutch colonialists entrenched in Taiwan and set up the Chengtian *fu* (later renamed Taiwan *fu*). Thereafter the Qing government constantly expanded its administrative institutions in Taiwan and strengthened governance over the island. In 1684, it established the *fen xuntaixia bingbeidao* (Taiwan-Xiamen Military Defense Circuit) as well as the Taiwan *fu* which was placed under the jurisdiction of Fujian Province and which consisted of three counties—Taiwan county (today Tainan), Fengshan county (today Kaohsiung) and Chulo county (today Chiayi). In 1714, the Qing government sent personnel to draw maps of Taiwan and collate distances within Taiwan's borders. In 1721, a *xunshi Taiwan jianchayushi* (an office of imperial supervisor of inspecting Taiwan) was newly instituted, and the Taiwan-Xiamen Military Defense Circuit was redesignated the *fen xuntaixia dao* (the Taiwan-Xiamen patrol command). Added a little while later were the Zhanghua County and the Danshui *ting* (a department under provincial authorities). In 1727, the Joint Taiwan-Xiamen Inspection Command was again redesignated as the Taiwan-

---

[18]Yang Yunzhong. *Macao and the Growth of the Modern Economy*. Macao: Macao Economic Association, 1992, pp. 5–20.

Xiamen patrol command, a Penghu *ting* was newly instituted, and "Taiwan" became the region's official name. In 1875, Taiwan was officially nominated as a unitary province, and Liu Mingchuan was appointed as its first provincial governor. Taiwan had jurisdiction over three *fu,* one *zhou,* and a total of 11 counties and 5 *ting.*

Taiwan was forcibly annexed by Japan when the Qing government was compelled to sign the Maguan Treaty [Treaty of Shimonoseki] in the wake of the 1895 Sino-Japanese War. At the end of the Second World War and after China's victory in the War of Resistance against Japanese aggression, Japan gave the Taiwan region back to China pursuant to the 1943 Cairo Declaration and the 1945 Potsdam Proclamation. The then Chinese Nationalist Government and the Japanese government held a formal ceremony for the handover of Taiwan which thereupon reverted to China. In 1949, Chiang Kai-shek's Nationalist Government was defeated during the tempestuous tide of the People's War of Liberation. It fled from the Chinese mainland and took over Taiwan, using it as a stronghold for continued resistance against the Chinese people. Subsequent to the debacle of the Kuomintang in Taiwan's elections in 2000, the Democratic Progressive Party assumed power and a separatist trend in Taiwan increasingly gained ground. Meanwhile, other countries concerned have time and again done their best to interfere in China's internal affairs and turn Taiwan into an independent state. Such is the Taiwan issue which confronts China today. The entire problem is quite evidently one left over from China's 1947–1949 civil war, and it stands to reason that the Taiwan issue pertains to China's internal affairs.

So those are the Hong Kong, Macao, and Taiwan issues left to us by history as well as the historical reasons for China's implementing "one country, two systems" and setting up special administrative regions.

3.2   Various Formulas for China's Reunification

3.2.1   The Differences and Similarities of the Hong Kong and Macao Issues

Hong Kong, Macao, and Taiwan are all located on China's southeastern seaboard; they are situated on the foremost front of East-West contacts and exchanges and have all along taken the lead in setting new trends and practices. They have boldly confronted the world and borne the brunt of all external impacts; they must acknowledge the presence of the vast land behind them and have carried along its thousands of years of history and cultural traditions. For the broad expanses of the Chinese hinterland, these regions have served as windows for perceiving and comprehending the "outside" world; where the rest of the world is concerned, these regions have served as keys for understanding this mysterious Eastern nation and unlocking China's gates. For a considerable period of time, they were the only legal channels that linked China with the world. Faced with influences and incursions from the West, the people here were shaken and amazed by the splendors of the outside world and at the same distressed by the poverty and backwardness of their motherland. Over several hundred years, they processed the various Western civilizations that "drifted in" from overseas, introduced these to their compatriots on the loess lands of China, and brought to their native lands substantial amounts of foreign capital and advanced production techniques. They also processed and packaged knowledge of the 5000-old civilization of their homeland for the edification of "blue-eyed foreigners" and disseminated it in all corners of the world. Every step forward by China in recent and modern times has been closely connected with these regions, as have been all of the world's understandings of China. Hence, the regions may be quite aptly described as "bridges," "links," "intermediaries" and "windows." Their "outpost" status gave them convenient and priority access to advanced civilizations on the one hand, yet on the other exposed them to both internal and external pressures. Whatever the case, these Chinese-populated regions eventually gained universally acknowledged achievements and released immense vitality during the advance toward modernization.

However, these regions experienced prolonged separations from their parent body, kinsmen were kept apart, and the nation could not be unified. In recent times, Hong Kong and Macao were reduced to foreign occupancies and subjected to de facto colonialist occupations and jurisdictions. China could no longer exercise sovereignty over them. Moreover, soon after Taiwan broke away from Japanese colonial rule and returned to the motherland in 1945, it was taken over by the Kuomintang clique in 1949 and to this day remains separated from the mainland. Hence, the histories of these regions share certain commonalities in that they pertained to the problem of China's reunification, yet they differed as regards their basic character.

On the Hong Kong and Macao issues, the New China consistently refused to recognize the unequal treaties signed by the Qing government in the last couple of centuries under coercion by the Western powers. Hence, the three so-called Sino-British treaties on the occupation and leasing of Hong Kong were invalid and the Hong Kong region could not be regarded as a colony. The same applied to the Macao region. Both these regions are Chinese territories that were seized by foreigners, and the independence issue did not apply to them. China consistently stood firm on this principle when handling specific matters concerned. An example is when the Supreme Court handled a case involving Hong Kong notarizations in December 1965. Based on Document (65) *Ling Yi Fa Zi* No. 913 issued by the Consular Department of the Foreign Ministry which had already explicitly prohibited the use of the term "colony of Hong Kong" in notarized documents, the Supreme Court required that the term "colony" be deleted before relevant documents could be delivered to the Foreign Ministry's consular department for the handling of notarization matters.[19]

Agencies within China too had always separately handled matters involving Hong Kong and Macao and those involving foreign affairs. Despite the Foreign Ministry's having departments for handling Hong Kong and Macao affairs in terms of its institutional setup and division of duties, the ministry was chiefly in charge of the two regions' international affairs, and entire responsibility for the regions' overall affairs

[19]"Letter Prohibiting the Use of the Term 'Colony' on Notarized Documents," Supreme People's Court, December 5, 1965.

was borne by the Hong Kong and Macao Affairs Office which had been set up by the State Council and was of the same level as the Foreign Ministry. Agencies in China have never regarded Chinese compatriots in Hong Kong and Macao as "foreigners." As the Supreme People's Court clearly pointed out in 1958 in an official reply to questions raised by the Guizhou Province High People's Court, Chinese compatriots residing in Hong Kong and Macao were not to be regarded as Overseas Chinese. If they wish to return to and settle down on the mainland, all they had to do is take their Hong Kong or Macao residence certificates (such as ID and residence cards) and obtain a home-going letter of recommendation from an inland frontier inspection station, and then apply for residence registration at their destination. No other procedures were required.[20]

In this connection, after the New China's seat in the United Nations was restored on March 8, 1972, Huang Hua, China's permanent representative at the United Nations, immediately wrote a letter to the chairman of the United Nation Special Committee on Decolonization, pointing out: "Hong Kong and Macao are the results of a series of unequal treaties forced on China by imperialism. Hong Kong and Macao are part of the Chinese territories occupied by the British and Portuguese authorities, and resolving the Hong Kong and Macao issues are matters that pertain entirely within the scope of China's sovereignty, and in no way fall with the scope of what are usually referred to as "colonies." Hence, they should not be entered in the list of colonial regions to which the Anti-colonial Declaration is applicable. As concerns the Hong Kong and Macao issues, the Chinese government has always advocated resolving them when the conditions are ripe and in an appropriate way. Before these are resolved, the current state shall be maintained." On June 15, the United Nations Special Committee on Decolonization passed a resolution accepting China's position and decided to propose to the United Nations General Assembly that Hong Kong and Macao be deleted from the abovementioned list of colonies. On November 8, the twenty-seventh session of the UN General Assembly approved this proposal put forward by the Special Committee on Decolonization.[21]

Hence, the Hong Kong and Macao issues were in reality a matter of China's exercising its national sovereignty, or in other words, a matter of foreign colonialists terminating their rule and a sovereign nation reinstating its exercise of sovereignty over occupied regions. This in turn involved the matter of relations between countries and the matter of unequal treaties. The most important thing about the Hong Kong issue was for China and Britain to reach agreement on transferring sovereignty over Hong Kong, i.e., for Britain to transfer sovereignty over Hong Kong to China and for China to restore its exercise of sovereignty over Hong Kong. The same applied to Macao. The matter of first importance was to terminate the several hundred years of Portuguese rule over Macao and have China restore its exercise of sovereignty over Macao. Sovereignty is a major issue of fundamental importance—one that allows of

[20]"Official Reply on Disallowing Chinese Compatriots in Hong Kong and Macao from Being Regarded as Overseas Chinese and Other Issues," Supreme People's Court, February 12, 1958.
[21]Lan Tian. *Research on Legal Issues of "One Country, Two Systems"* (Total Volume). Beijing: Law Press, 1997, p. 53.

acknowledgement only, not of negotiation. The sovereignty issue is also the basis for resolving all other issues. If China had not restored its exercise of sovereignty over the Hong Kong and Macao regions, there would have been no point in discussing other issues. Prior to the transfer of sovereignty, the Hong Kong and Macao issues were of course issues between China and Britain and between China and Portugal. However, after their sovereignty was transferred to China, Hong Kong and Macao matters became China's internal affairs and brooked of no interference from other countries.[22]

As stated earlier, the Taiwan issue was from the very outset an outcome of China's civil war, and from the very outset a matter of China's internal affairs. It falls within the scope of China's sovereignty and no foreign country or international organization has any right to interfere. After the founding of the Chinese People's Republic in 1949, the government of the Chinese People's Republic became the sole legal government that could represent the Chinese people.[23] In 1971, the New China recovered its seat in the United Nations, formally replacing the Kuomintang government. The United Nations formally acknowledged the government of the People's Republic of China as China's sole legal government, "restored all rights of the People's Republic of China in the organizations of the United Nations" and "evicted Chiang Kai-shek's representative," all of which further confirmed, enhanced, and consolidated China's status in the world.[24] Thereafter the New China gradually brought about the normalization of Sino-U.S. and Sino-Japanese diplomatic relations and established formal diplomatic relations with an overwhelming majority of countries in the world. All countries which have established such relations with China acknowledge Taiwan as being an inseparable part of the Chinese People's Republic and the Taiwan issue as a matter of China's internal affairs which allows of no outside interference.[25]

3.2.2 Diverse Formulas for China's Reunification

People in various quarters put forward numerous formulas and ideas of all kinds—more than a hundred, by an incomplete count—on how to bring about the return of Hong Kong and Macao so as to fulfill the great cause of reunifying the nation, and devised various types of relations for China as a whole and its component parts. A few of the more representative are listed here.

1. The "Confederation" Model

---

[22]Deng Xiaoping. "Our Basic Stand on the Hong Kong Issue," carried in *Deng Xiaoping on the Hong Kong Issue*. Hong Kong: Joint Publishing (H.K) Co., Ltd., 1993, pp. 1–4.

[23]Wang Xiliang. *History of the People's Republic of China*. Xi'an: Shaanxi Normal University Press, 1990, p. 19.

[24]Wang Tieya. *International Law*. Beijing: Law Press, 1991, p. 377.

[25]Only 28 countries, chiefly in Central and South America and Africa, currently maintain diplomatic relations with the "Republic of China." All other countries have established formal diplomatic relations with the People's Republic of China.

As stated earlier, "confederation" refers, in constitutional law, to the formation of a loose association of states for some specific purpose by a number of fully sovereign independent states. The "central" institution of a confederation is generally a confederation congress or a member-state summit. Both, however, are institutions of a negotiating nature and not power institutions. They cannot issue orders to any member states and their decisions are effective only if acknowledged by the latter. Confederations possess certain legislative powers but no unified judiciaries or administrations, and in general also lack unified military forces and a unified citizenship. Member states retain complete sovereignty over internal and external matters, and may freely join or withdraw from the confederation. It is evident that a confederation is actually not a sovereign nation in the true sense of the term. More accurately, it is a sort of close-knit international organization. A fairly typical confederation in history is the North American Confederation of 1776–1789.

On the matter of China's unification, those who held to the confederation concept stood for the mainland and Taiwan together formulating a treaty of confederation through negotiations on an equal footing, and then forming a "Confederation of China" in which both parties were independent "states" with full sovereignty internally and externally, and both entitled to apply for UN membership, set up diplomatic relations with all other countries, and engage in equal competition in world society. The two would engage in several decades of peaceful competition under the confederation, and their peoples would eventually decide the direction the nation would take.[26] Not only would the mainland and Taiwan be included under the "Confederation of China," Hong Kong, Macao, and even Tibet could join it in the capacity of independent states since the confederal formulation would be fairly easy for these regions to accept. The proponents of this idea were mainly personages in Taiwan. Some within the Kuomintang also held to this view.

It can be seen that this viewpoint in reality consisted in first getting Taiwan, Macao, and even Tibet to become independent "states" with complete sovereignty, and then, in conjunction with other regions on the Chinese mainland, form a nominal "nation-state" devoid of all powers. The substance of this viewpoint was to have Taiwan first become an independent country and then have it negotiate the reunification issue with the Chinese People's Republic on an equal footing. Thus, it is clear that the "confederation" argument was in essence identical to the "two Chinas" and the "one China, one Taiwan" viewpoints, because it not only disregarded China's history and traditions, but also was theoretically untenable and unworkable in practical terms, and entirely unacceptable to the Chinese people. Moreover, neither Hong Kong, nor Macao, nor Tibet possessed the basic requirements for existing as "countries."

---

[26]Yang Jianxin. *One Country, Two Systems and the Future of Taiwan*. Beijing: Sino-culture Press, 1989, pp. 116–117.

Other similar viewpoints were articulated as the "two Germany's" model[27], the Singapore model[28], the "National League/National Association" model[29], the "multi-system state" model[30], the "one-house-two-rooms-each-with-its-own-key" model[31], the "one country two governments" model[32], and so forth. All of these models were, in essence, diverse variants of the "confederation doctrine." They were infeasible in either theory or practice, were bound to digress eventually into some mode of separatism, and thus failed to gain support from the Chinese people as a whole.

2. The "Federation" Model

Since the various "confederation" models were not feasible, the "federation" doctrine appeared by comparison to be more logical and reasonable, and relevant writings and works have abounded.

Discussions on the federal system cropped up in the Hong Kong press before China and Britain began to negotiate the Hong Kong issue and had proliferated since 1989.[33] Proponents maintained that China has long had a federal tradition. In their opinion, the so-called "great national unity" meant "universal harmony under heaven" and existed in the times of Yao, Shun, and Yu as clan alliances. The enfeoffment of dukes and princes during the Zhou Dynasty was also a form of federalism. "Lao Zi," they said, "had been of a mind to govern by means of *wuwei* [Daoist philosophical concept of 'doing nothing' or 'letting matters take their own course'—Tr.], and the system of centralized authority was completely non-existent."[34] Proponents of

---

[27] In 1972, East and West Germany signed a Basic Treaty in which both parties acknowledged each other as sovereign states and developed good neighbor relations on the basis of equality. Neither side relinquished the possibility of future reunification and both called each other "sovereign country" instead of "foreign country." This was a mutual de facto acknowledgement rather than an official international recognition. In 1976, Ray S. Cline, executive director of the Center for Strategic and International Studies at Georgetown University in the United States, promoted this doctrine which found support among some personages in Taiwan. See Yang Jianxin. *One Country, Two Systems and the Future of Taiwan.* Beijing: Sino-culture Press, 1989, pp. 120–121.

[28] Supporters of this theorem advocated Taiwan turning itself into a Singapore of the Far East, abandoning its (meaning the Kuomintang's) illusion of becoming the sole legitimate regime in the whole of China, and claiming sovereignty only over Taiwan and the Penghu Islands—territories under their actual control. This in fact meant turning Taiwan into an independent country. See Yang Jianxin. *One Country, Two Systems and the Future of Taiwan.* Beijing: Sino-culture Press, 1989, pp. 121–122.

[29] This was in reality another variant of the "Singapore model."

[30] Supporters of this theorem believed that the world could accept the simultaneous presence of the Chinese People's Republic and the "Republic of China." This did not mean recognizing two Chinas; it only meant admitting the existence of two opposing systems. Its substance was to seek international acknowledgement of the "Republic of China" in Taiwan. See Yang Jianxin. *One Country, Two Systems and the Future of Taiwan.* Beijing: Sino-culture Press, 1989, pp. 122–123.

[31] This theorem was a variation on "one country two governments."

[32] This was also a variation on "one country two governments."

[33] Lu Liji. "Compilation of Ten Years of Hong Kongers' Selected Writings on Federalism," carried in *Legal Words,* Renewed Edition, 1989(5), pp. 12–15.

[34] Huang Kangxian. "The Feasibility of Changing from a Confederation to a Federation," carried in *the Hong Kong Economic Journal Monthly*, overall issue no. 199, pp. 14–19.

the theorem also stated that although national unification was emphasized after the Qin Dynasty, "the prevailing mentality was one of *neisheng waiwang* (a learning both sound in theory and practice); in other words, the substance of Confucianism would be retained without excessive interference, division of powers and governance would be permitted to a certain extent, and the concept of 'grand unity' would be maintained primarily by means of literature, culture, ideology and racial identity." However, proponents of the theorem also believed "that which is long unified must divide" on account of regional disparities and devolutions of power, and also "that which is long divided must reunify" because the Chinese nation had already become an integral whole, a circumstance that would forever preserve China as an entity. Even during the Nationalist China era, they stated, all warlords of various separatist regimes shared a "central authority" concept. Proponents of the theorem drew the conclusion that diverse political structures had appeared in China at various times. Prior to the Zhou Dynasty, the country was a *lianti,* or "conjoined entity," which became an alliance under a generally acknowledged central authority during the Zhou. This, however, was reduced to a confederation in the Spring and Autumn period. After that, there had been countless unifications and divisions. "Even during periods of unification China had not succeeded in setting up a unitary government, since China's central authorities had, strictly speaking, only been capable at most times of setting up federal systems, and the policies of the central authorities had in reality been incapable of influencing the localities..."[35]

These theorists believe the way the New China resolved the Tibet issue was in reality a "covert implementation of the federal system,"[36] and that this method was changed only because the concept of socialism could not tolerate the existence of a federal system. They believe if reunification is to be realized today, the best way to do so would be to set up a federalist state, which might first emerge as, and then change over from, a confederation. Only a federal system, they maintain, would be capable of preserving Hong Kong's prosperity and stability, prevent a decline in Hong Kong's international status, and present Taiwan with a convincing and attractive option.[37]

Once the federalist theory emerged, it immediately stoked immense interest among not a few persons at home and abroad. Many feel the federal system might serve as good way to realize national reunification. In other words, it could bring about national reunification and at the same time retain the independence and autonomy of all concerned, and be beneficial for the country's long-term stability. The federal system, they maintain, is also best suited to China's circumstances as it fits in with such features as large populations, vast territories, and uneven development. Some persons also stand for drafting a "federal constitution" acceptable to the peoples of Chinese mainland, Taiwan, Hong Kong, and Macao, and for defining divisions of powers among member-state governments to form a Chinese "federal" government which Taiwan, Hong Kong, Macao, and all provinces in the interior could join with the status of equal states and together form a "Chinese Federation [Common-

---

[35]Ibid., pp. 14–19.

[36]See footnote 35.

[37]See footnote 35.

wealth]." They have also suggested that "one country, two systems" can only be realized under a federal system, since under a unitary political system, the powers of the SARs would be conferred on the SARs by the central authorities, which would not be equals with the SARs because they could at any time take back the powers they conferred on the latter. Conversely, under a federal system, the central authorities would be equals with the SARs. The localities' powers would be derived from the public will instead of being conferred by the central authorities, which therefore would be unable to "recall" those powers. Hence, the federal system would be more conducive than the unitary system to maintaining the "two systems."[38]

Studies are still being conducted abroad on the federal system. Some people have even written up a draft "constitution of the Chinese Federal Republic."[39] But these people have not grasped the true essence of the issue and that draft constitution abounds in emotional and idealistic elements. It shows no real comprehension of China's history and actualities or of China's national psyche, and no understanding of the scientific intensions of "one country, two systems," and is therefore not worth recommending.

3.   The Combined Confederal/Federal Model

Some scholars maintain China must not only solve issues of reunification—such as those of Hong Kong, Macao, and Taiwan—but also resolve the internal issues of relations between the central authorities and its provinces, directly administered municipalities, and autonomous regions. One of the main functions of federalism, they believe, is that of resolving the problem of "coming together" or "holding together."[40] Where China is concerned, both of these problems exist. In their view, the Hong Kong and Macao issues are those of "coming together," and the internal issue between the central authorities and localities is one of how to "hold" them "together." Resolving these different issues requires the use of different models. The confederal model could be used for resolving the Hong Kong, Macao, and Taiwan issues because it is likely to attract all parties into "coming together," whereas the federal model could be used to solve the internal issue of the central authorities' relations with the various provinces, directly administered municipalities, and autonomous regions since that model would be more likely to "hold" all sides "together."[41] Some scholars believe that no matter how suitable the unitary system was for China in past history, it is no longer capable of resolving the complex state structure problems that confront China today, and the federal system can obviously do a better job than the unitary system of forging a unified country and consolidating

---

[38] Yang Jianxin. *One Country, Two Systems and the Future of Taiwan*. Beijing: Sino-culture Press, 1989, pp. 115–116.

[39] Hong Kong, *Open Magazine*, 1994 (3).

[40] Linz Juna. "Democracy, Multinationalism and Federalism." Alfred Stepan. "Toward a New Comparative Analysis of Democracy and Federalism: Demos Constraining and Demos Enabling Federations." Papers presented at the International Political Science Association XVII World Congress, Seoul, August 17–22, 1997.

[41] Davis C M. "The Case of Chinese Federalism." Washington D.C.: *Journal of Democracy*, April 1999.

a nation's unity. Moreover, China's traditional political culture in reality does not absolutely reject confederalism or federalism. After China implemented the policy of Reform and Opening Up, its political, economic, and cultural development have laid certain foundations for a new confederalism and federalism. Hence the best solution, they say, is to adopt a combined confederal/federal model as this would resolve both the issue of national reunification and the internal issue of the central authorities' relations with the localities.

The two issues described above do indeed exist in China. However, it is highly questionable whether either the confederal or federal system is a must, and whether dismantling or reconfiguring the internal unitary system is a must. This proposition is in reality a medley of the aforementioned two proposals and has little feasibility.

4. The "One Country Three Systems" Model

Former Chinese leader Deng Xiaoping's original intention in "inventing" the "one country, two systems" was to resolve the Taiwan issue. However, "one country, two systems" has first been applied to the Hong Kong and Macao issues, which are different in nature from the Taiwan issue since Hong Kong and Macao were previously colonies (though the Chinese government has all along disagreed with this formulation) while Taiwan is in Chinese hands and currently not a colony. So how can a method devised for colonies be applied to the solution of the Taiwan issue? Is that not tantamount to regarding Taiwan as a colony?

The above argument is manifestly a misrepresentation and misreading of "one country, two systems." Yet it has indeed become an excuse for the Taiwanese side to negate "one country, two systems" and allege that it "diminishes" Taiwan's stature, disrespects Taiwan, and places the two sides on an unequal footing. Since that is the case, why not further develop "one country, two systems" into "one country three systems" which would clearly differentiate the Taiwan issue from the Hong Kong and Macao issues?

Some scholars abroad are quite enthusiastic about this proposition. Professor Joseph S. Nye, dean of Harvard University's Kennedy School of Government, maintains that the so-called "one country three systems" does not imply that Taiwan is a province of the People's Republic of China, but means that Taiwan should get better treatment than Hong Kong and Macao, and should possess a high degree of self-determination. For example, it should preserve a democratic and free enterprise system and retain the symbolic concept of "One China." This would not mean that either the Republic of China or the People's Republic of China should cease to exist, but that the two would keep their own designation, maintain the status quo, and coexist. [42]

Actually, Chinese mainland has already made it quite clear that "one country, two systems" has different connotations for Taiwan than it does for Hong Kong and Macao. Under "one country, two systems," Taiwan would of course enjoy more self-governance, and could even retain armed forces, enjoy greater freedom and rights of diplomatic intercourse, and enjoy better benefits. Nor would Taiwan be

---

[42] Taiwan, *China Times*. 2001-07-06, http://news.chinatimes.com/.

compelled to emulate Hong Kong or adopt the same capitalist system as in Hong Kong. Taiwan could keep all that is its own. In this sense, the formulation could well be "one country three systems" or even "one country four systems" since the systems in Hong Kong and Macao, too, are somewhat different. If "one country three systems" is to be understood from this perspective, and all that needs to be changed is one single word for the matter to be resolved, so be it, because the formulation adheres to the fundamental principle of "one China" and complies with the orientation of a united China. However, if "one China" is merely seen as a "nominal state," the formulation "one country, two systems" becomes highly questionable. China's reunification cannot be a merely "nominal" exercise; it must also have substantive content.

5. The Unitary System Model

Although quite a hubbub is being raised about the confederal, federal or other models, very few people in Chinese mainland approve of these concepts. Moreover, official quarters quite unequivocally adhere to the "one country, two systems" model, maintaining that other propositions do not fit in with realities and cannot be carried out. The overwhelming majority of Chinese mainlanders stand for respecting history and actualities, for complying with the thousands of years of Chinese tradition, and for using the unitary system model to solve the country's reunification issue. Most Chinese in Hong Kong and abroad also support this view.

Among the various views regarding the unitary system, all advocate implementing the system. But there are differences as concerns points of departure, emphases, and specific objectives—some quite considerable and even poles apart. Three of the most representative those are listed below—the "Three People's Principles unification of China" model, the "one country one system" model, and the "one country, two systems" model.

(1) The "Three People's Principles Unification of China" Model

This was the model formerly advocated by China's Kuomintang. The Three People's Principles was the bourgeois democratic revolution program originally put forward by Dr. Sun Yat-sen during the Democratic Revolution era and consisted of the principles of Nationalism, Democracy, and the People's Livelihood. The intent then was to overthrow the Manchu Qing feudal autocracy, protect civil rights, develop national capitalism, throw off imperialist enslavement, and ultimately set up a bourgeois democratic republic. This, toward the end of the nineteenth century and in the early twentieth century, was in a certain sense quite progressive as it limned the portrait of a bourgeois democratic republic. After suffering a number of major setbacks, however, Dr. Sun Yat-sen reinterpreted the Three People's Principles at the First National Congress of the Kuomintang in January 1924. He reformulated these principles as "alliance with Russia," "cooperation with the Communist Party," and "assistance to the workers and peasants." These new Three People's Principles had certain limitations, but even so, the Kuomintang ruling clique headed by Chiang Kai-shek scrapped them in practice after the death of Sun Yat-sen.[43]

In 1949, just after the Kuomintang government moved to Taiwan, it still insisted it would recover the Chinese mainland by armed force and reunite China by means of the Three People's Principles. In 1981, Chiang Ching-kuo once stated that resolving the China issue in reality meant extirpating the "Communist autocracy" on the mainland, replacing socialism with the Three People's Principles and thereby realizing the reunification of China. He also said that in reunifying the Chinese mainland, the "Nationalist Republic" would in the main be relying on the Three People's Principles rather than armed force. Sun Yun-suan, then "president of the Executive Yuan" of the Taiwan Authorities, also stated that unless the Chinese Communists proclaimed in real earnest that they were abandoning communism and its system, the Taiwan Authorities would not give up their principles and engage in any contacts or talks with the Chinese communists. He maintained that China's peaceful unification would be naturally and automatically achieved if the Three People's Principles and the Five Power Constitution devised by Father-of-the-Nation Sun Yat-sen were faithfully followed and "the state system, national flag and national anthem of the Republic of China" were respected.[44]

It is apparent that the Kuomintang clique advocated one China and, later, even advocated peaceful reunification and setting up a unified nationwide unitary political power. However, the "China" they advocated was the "Republic of China," and the unitary system they advocated was a unitary system under the "Republic of China," or in other words, a unitary "Republic of China" system that would comprise the mainland, Taiwan, Hong Kong, and Macao areas as well as nationwide unified implementation of the Three People's Principles. This might be summarized as "peaceful unification, and The Three People's Principles." However, despite some slight improvement, in that pursuance of peaceful reunification replaced their stated avowal to "gloriously recover the mainland (by armed force)," modern and contemporary history has long since shown that plans for a bourgeois republic are not feasible in China, and there is no basis for establishing a unitary system under a bourgeois republic.

2. The "One Country One System" Model

Among the diverse plans for realizing national unification and defining the relationship of the central authorities with the localities, there is also one voice which, although quite faint, should not be overlooked, i.e., the advocacy about the establishment—after the realization of national unification by either armed force or peaceful talks—of a unitary-system government that would be uniform nationwide and highly centralized, that would consider Taiwan, Hong Kong, and Macao as ordinary local administrative regions and accord them equal treatment, and that would not allow the exercise of special self-governing powers.

[43]Yang Jianxin. *One Country, Two Systems and the Future of Taiwan*. Beijing: Sino-culture Press, 1989, pp. 127–129.
[44]Ibid., pp. 127–129.

This view is a reflection among some Chinese of a conservative trend of thought on the issue of national reunification as well as a modern manifestation of the feudal Grand Unification thinking. This thinking ignores the special circumstances of the Taiwan, Hong Kong, and Macao regions and overlooks the major changes that have taken place in the current international situation. It also runs fundamentally counter to dialectical materialism and historical materialism and counter to the basic state policy of "one country, two systems." If this view were to be put into effect, it would not only cast a dark pall over the future of the Hong Kong, Macao, and Taiwan regions but might also torpedo the nation's cause of Reunification.

As far back as in the 1980s, Deng Xiaoping astutely noted: "Peaceful reunification has become the common aim of the Kuomintang and the Communist Party. The idea is not that one party should swallow up the other." After Taiwan's reunification with the mainland, Taiwan's "Different systems may be practised... We recognize that the local government of Taiwan may have its own separate set of policies for domestic affairs. And although, as a special administrative region, Taiwan will have a local government, it will differ from local governments of other provinces, municipalities and autonomous regions. Provided the national interests are not impaired, it will enjoy certain powers of its own that the others do not possess." And, "After reunification with the motherland, the Taiwan special administrative region will assume a unique character and may practise a social system different from that of the mainland."[45] In a different venue in the year 1984, while analyzing the origins of "one country, two systems," he pointed out: "In recent years, China has worked hard to overcome 'Left' mistakes and has formulated its policies concerning all fields of endeavor in line with the principle of proceeding from reality and seeking truth from facts. After five and a half years things are beginning to pick up. It is against this background that we have proposed to solve the Hong Kong and Taiwan problems by allowing two systems to coexist in one country."[46]

This clearly shows that "one country, two systems" is an outcome of the entire nation promoting ideological emancipation and repudiating ultra-Left thinking after the ousting of the Gang of Four; that it is a result of the policy of reform and opening up, and that it is a negation of the "one country one system" thinking. China adheres to "one country, two systems," not to "one country one system." If we reflect on this in connection with the campaign for ideological emancipation that started in China at the end of the 1970s and with the larger background of China's reform and opening-up, we may form a deeper and more comprehensive understanding of the fact that "one country, two systems" is both a negation of the "confederal theorem" and the "federal theorem" as well as a negation of "one country one system." There have also been some people in Taiwan who put forward similar propositions. One example is the "one country, two systems, separate existence, peaceful competition"

---

[45] *Deng Xiaoping on the Reunification of the Motherland.* Beijing: Unity Press, 1995, p. 18.

[46] *Selected Works of Deng Xiaoping* vol. 3. Beijing: People's Publishing House, 1993, p. 58.

model[47], but which differs from the "one country, two systems" initiated by Deng Xiaoping.

3. The "One Country, Two Systems" Model

As stated above, the "one country, two systems" model is the basic national policy for realizing national reunification and defining the relations between the central authorities and the special administrative regions, as initiated and developed by Deng Xiaoping after China's reform and opening up. It adheres to China's tradition of a unitary system and at the same time takes full account of the histories and actualities of Hong Kong, Macao, and Taiwan. It is the most feasible policy decision for completing the great cause of reunifying our country.

3.3   The Formation and Contents of the National "One Country, Two Systems" Policy

Historical materialism tells us that investigations of historical events, whatever their nature, require that we understand the events by placing them in the specific historical context of their era, that we seek the objective inevitability of their emergence and development in the major laws of social and historical development. The same applies to understanding the "one country two system" policy decision; we understand it by placing it in the historical context that gave rise to this policy decision, and only then can we understand the inevitability and validity of its debut. The New China's policy on national reunification has experienced a complex evolution.

3.3.1   The Evolution of the New China's Policies on Hong Kong, Macao, and Taiwan

The People's Republic of China was established in 1949, but the wars to unify the Chinese mainland basically concluded only in October 1951. By then, with the exception of Hong Kong, Macao, Taiwan, the Penghu [Pescadores] Islands, the Jinmen [Quemoy] Islands, and the Mazu [Matsu] Islands, the Chinese Communist Party had reunified all areas throughout China. For various reasons, the new government of China did not take immediate action with regard to the Hong Kong, Macao, and

---

[47] This theorem was initiated by Shen Chun-shan, former president of Tsinghua University in Taiwan. He advocated taking China's culture as a symbol of the sovereignty of a reunified China and, under the shared sovereignty of this symbol, allowing the existence of two regimes which could compete on an equal footing. This advocacy resembled the theorem "one country, two political entities." See Yang Jianxin. *One Country, Two Systems and the Future of Taiwan*. Beijing: Sino-culture Press, 1989, pp. 123–125.

Taiwan regions at that time but preserved their status quo. However, the Chinese people and government never ceased making efforts to realize the country's unification. China had to be reunified. Such was common desire of generations of Chinese.

3.3.1.1 Evolution of the Policy for Hong Kong and Macao

On September 29, 1949, the First Plenary Session of the Chinese People's Political Consultative Conference passed the Common Program which served at that time as a temporary constitution. Article 2 of the Program stipulated "The Central People's Government of the People's Government of China must undertake to wage the people's war of liberation to the very end, to liberate all the territory of China, and to achieve the unification of China." Article 55 of the Common Program stipulated: "The Central People's Government of the People's Government of China shall examine the treaties and agreements concluded between the Kuomintang and foreign governments, and shall recognize, abrogate, revise, or renegotiate them according to their respective contents."

After the founding of the New China, the principled stand of the Chinese government on the Hong Kong issue was that Hong Kong had been Chinese territory since ancient times; that China did not recognize any of the unequal treaties imposed on China by the imperialist powers, including the three unequal treaties on ceding Hong Kong Island and the Kowloon Peninsula and leasing the New Territories; and that the Chinese would resolve the issue of returning Hong Kong to China by conducting peaceful negotiations with the British government when the conditions became ripe.[48]

If sole consideration were given to the military aspect, the People's Liberation Army could very well have taken back the Hong Kong and Macao regions in one fell swoop in 1949. However, the Chinese Communists had already estimated that when the New China was established, the Western capitalist countries headed by the United States would carry out a blockade and siege of the New China. Under such circumstances, and based on long-term strategic considerations, maintaining the Hong Kong and Macao status quo would be more in China's interests—as was later proved by history. In the subsequent decades, the Hong Kong and Macao regions virtually became the New China's sole windows for foreign contacts and economic and trade exchanges with the outside world, and China's main source for earning foreign currency. They brought substantial economic benefits to China, and also served as a main channel for the New China's communications with the world. Hence, for an extended period of time China's policy with regard to Hong Kong and Macao was one of "long-term planning and making full use."[49]

---

[48]He Hongjing. *The Yesterday, Today and Tomorrow of Taiwan*. Beijing: World Affairs Press, 1994, p. 175.

[49]Huang Wenfang. *The Process of China's Decision to Resume the Exercise of Sovereignty over Hong Kong and Its Implementation*. Hong Kong: Hong Kong Baptist University, 1994, p. 34.

The Chinese government stated at the time that Hong Kong's status quo could be maintained under certain conditions. When the British governor of Hong Kong visited Beijing in 1955, Premier Zhou Enlai enunciated these terms: (a) Hong Kong was not to be used as a military base against the Chinese People's Republic; (b) No activities designed to damage the prestige of the Chinese People's Republic were to be conducted; (c) Personnel of the People's Republic of China in Hong Kong were to be protected; and (d) Hong Kong was not to be taken toward independence.

In 1963, the People's Daily carried an article stating that we had consistently stood for resolving a number of unresolved issues left over from history by peaceful negotiations when conditions became ripe, and that the status quo ought to be maintained before those issues were resolved. This applied, for example, to the issues of Hong Kong, Kowloon, and Macao.

In 1972, the Chinese government successfully requested that the UN Special Committee on Decolonization and the UN General Assembly strike Hong Kong and Macao from the list of colonial territories. This fundamentally eliminated the possibility of Hong Kong and Macao moving toward independence. Although the extreme "Left" trend of thought did affect Hong Kong and Macao during the Cultural Revolution, it is evident that the Chinese government's above-described policies on Hong Kong and Macao were basically continuous and underwent no fundamental changes.

3.3.1.2   Evolution of the Policy on Taiwan

Whereas China's policy for Hong Kong and Macao may be described as having been fairly stable, its Taiwan policy underwent some sharp reversals. In 1949, despite calls to "fight all the way to Taiwan and liberate the whole of China," the People's Liberation Army made no move to cross the Taiwan Strait. However, both banks of the Strait remained thereafter in an extended state of grave armed confrontation. The mainland conducted small-scale shelling of Jinmen and Mazu in 1954 and 1955 and initiated heavy bombardments in 1958. Taiwan, too, constantly stated its determination to fight back to the mainland and recover the entire country. Despite occasional expressions of peaceful intentions toward Taiwan, the New China continued to articulate its basic policy as "liberate Taiwan." Nor did it have any special institutions for Taiwan-oriented work prior to 1971.

In February 1972, U.S. President Richard Nixon visited China, opening the door to Sino-U.S. exchanges for politicians of the two countries, and China and the United States issued the Sino-U.S. Shanghai Communiqué. In it, China solemnly stated that the liberation of Taiwan was China's internal affair in which no country had the right to interfere, and stated its opposition to "two Chinas" or "one China and one Taiwan." Due to China's insistence, the United States started to gradually withdraw its armed forces from Taiwan in 1972. Sino-U.S. exchanges increased between 1971 and 1978, and the mainland also began to resume contacts with Taiwan.

In December 1978, the Third Plenary Session of the 11th Central Committee of the Chinese Communist Party determined the long- and short-term policies for peacefully reuniting with Taiwan, and decided to drop the "liberate Taiwan" formulation. In December 1976, China and the United States issued a joint communiqué on establishing diplomatic relations in which the U.S. recognized the government of the People's Republic of China as the sole legal government of China and acknowledged China's stand that "there is only one China, and Taiwan is a part of China." In 1979, the National People's Congress Standing Committee issued "Message to Compatriots in Taiwan" calling for peaceful reunification, negotiations between the two sides, and the establishment of "three exchanges" across the Taiwan Strait [i.e., travel, trade, and postal communications]. Thereafter, a fundamental change took place in the policy toward Taiwan as the concept "peaceful reunification, one country two system" took an official form. However, just when the United States established formal diplomatic relations with China, the U.S. Congress passed the Taiwan Relations Act in a bid to continue sticking its fingers in the pie of China's internal affairs. It was due to these complex factors that China, despite its efforts toward peaceful reunification, never committed itself to the use of peaceful means to reunify with Taiwan. This issue will be discussed in the coming sections.

3.3.2 The Forming of the "Peaceful Reunification, One Country, Two Systems" Concept

The Reform and Opening-Up that commenced in the late 1970s brought profound changes to all aspects of China's undertakings, and China made a series of adjustments to its internal and foreign affairs policies, including the policies on Hong Kong, Macao, and Taiwan. The "peaceful Reunification, one country, two systems" concept took shape on the matter of reunifying the country. That concept was the reflection of the spirit of Reform and Opening-Up on the issue of national reunification as well as a major component of China's entire strategy of Reform and Opening-Up. It was an important outcome of the liberation of the mind and the restoring of the ideological line of seeking truth from facts; it was also a result of countering extreme "Left" interference in China's united front work. Were it not for the implementation of the entire reform and opening-up strategy, the "one country, two systems" concept could not have come into being. As long as there is no change in the fundamental direction of Reform and Opening-Up, there will also be no change in the "one country, two systems" policy decision.

3.3.2.1 Resolving the Taiwan Issue: The Initial Purpose in Putting Forward "One Country, Two Systems"

On New Year's Day, 1979, the National People's Congress Standing Committee suddenly publicized "Message to Compatriots in Taiwan" announcing that the fundamental policy hereafter was to be the peaceful reunification of the motherland,

and announcing that on the matter of reunifying the country, the principles would be "respect for Taiwan's status quo and the opinions of people of all walks of life in Taiwan, adoption of reasonable policies and methods, and avoidance of any harm to the people of Taiwan."[50] That was the Chinese government's first clear-cut enunciation of its intention to strive for peaceful reunification and to respect Taiwan's status quo.

On January 30 the same year, when Deng Xiaoping visited the United States and was invited to address the U.S. Senate and House of Representatives, he stated: "We will cease using the phrase 'liberate Taiwan.' So long as Taiwan returns to the motherland, we will respect the realities and the current system there."[51] That was the first time a top Chinese leader openly stated to the world that the "liberate Taiwan" formulation would be discontinued. On many occasions thereafter he elaborated on this line of thinking and expressed his thoughts on peaceful reunification and respect for Taiwan's current circumstances and structure.

When meeting with Japanese Premier Ohira Masayoshi on December 6, 1979, Deng again noted: "Our terms as regards Taiwan are quite simple. To wit, Taiwan's system will not change, its way of life will not change, and Taiwan's civil relations with other countries will not change… As a local government, Taiwan may have its own forces, military forces. There will be only one condition, and that is Taiwan must be an inseparable part of China. As a local government of China, it will have full powers of autonomy."[52] The basic outline of "one country, two systems" had taken shape.

By this time, the basic spirit and principles of "one country, two systems" had developed to the point of appearing in fairly systemized written form. On September 30, 1981, Chairman Ye Jianying of the National People's Congress Standing Committee, in an interview with journalists of the Xinhua News Agency, elaborated nine specific principles for the peaceful reunification of the motherland. These were later known as "Ye's nine principles" and included the following: "After the country is reunified, Taiwan can enjoy a high degree of autonomy as a special administrative region and can retain its armed forces. The Central Government will not interfere with local affairs on Taiwan."; "Taiwan's current socio-economic system will remain unchanged, and will retain its way of life and its economic and cultural relations with foreign countries. There will be no encroachment on proprietary rights or on the lawful right of inheritance of private property, houses, land and enterprises, or on foreign investments"; "People in authority and representative persons from circles in Taiwan may take up posts of leadership in national political bodies and participate in running the state." And, "When Taiwan's local finances are in difficulty, the Central Government may offer subsidies as appropriate."[53] By that time, the policies for exercising "one country, two systems" and for setting special administrative regions

---

[50]Beijing. *People's Daily*, 1979-01-01.

[51]Beijing. *People's Daily*, 1979-02-01.

[52]*Deng Xiaoping on the Reunification of the Motherland*. Beijing: Unity Press, 1995, p. 8.

[53]Beijing *People's Daily*, 1981-10-01.

had basically taken shape, and a number of principles for handling the relations of the central authorities with the special administrative region had been put forward.

3.3.2.2   Raising the Hong Kong Issue and Exercising "One Country, Two Systems"

Although the "one country, two systems" concept had initially been proposed in connection with the Taiwan issue and the issue of reunifying the motherland, the policy was first practiced, developed, and perfected on the issue of resolving Hong Kong's return to the motherland.[54] The Hong Kong issue was in fact raised by Britain. According to the Convention between Great Britain and China Respecting an Extension of Hong Kong Territory which Britain had compelled China to sign on June 9, 1898, the term of Britain's lease of the New Territories was for 99 years, or in other words, the lease was to expire in 1997. Although the New China had never recognized this unequal treaty, Britain maintained that its rule in Hong Kong was based on the three abovementioned treaties concluded with the Qing government. In the late 1970s, the Britain's Hong Kong government faced the problem of seeing whether the New Territories' land lease could be extended beyond 1997; if it could not, Hong Kong could hardly be developed any further. That was the objective situation. However, Britain raised the problem mainly because it believed the situation then presented the best opportunity for doing so. China's "Cultural Revolution" had just concluded, and many internal issues had yet to be resolved. Hence, China might not be able to attend to the Hong Kong '97 issue if it were raised at this juncture and might agree to Britain extending its rule in Hong Kong beyond and after 1997. This was indeed a very big problem for China because after China had ascertained its policy of "long-term planning and making full use" in the 1950s, Hong Kong had been of enormous importance to the embargoed China both economically and politically. At one time, China's foreign currency earnings from Hong Kong accounted for more than 75% of its total foreign exchange.[55]

How should Hong Kong's '97 issue be handled? How should Hong Kong be recovered, and how should it be administered? Would chaos ensue? None were commonplace issues. Recovering Hong Kong would be easy, but China was uncertain about how to preserve its prosperity and stability. A prime excuse for Britain's request to extend its rule in Hong Kong was that Hong Kong could remain prosperous and stable only under British administration. The implication was that no sooner would Hong Kong revert to China's hands than it was doomed, that the Chinese were incapable of doing a good job of administering Hong Kong. Nor did most Hong Kong people evince much confidence in China, which had only just emerged from those "ten catastrophic years."

---

[54] Huang Wenfang. *The Process of China's Decision to Resume the Exercise of Sovereignty over Hong Kong and Its Implementation*. Hong Kong: Hong Kong Baptist University, 1997, p. 28.
[55] Ibid., p. 14.

According to the reminiscences of Director Lu Ping of the Hong Kong and Macao Office of the State Council back in the spring of 1979 when Deng Xiaoping met with Hong Kong Governor Crawford Murray MacLehose, Deng said that China was handling Hong Kong as a special issue. From the present century [the nineteenth century—Tr.] and for a substantial period of time in the next century, Hong Kong would be permitted to practice capitalism whereas the mainland would implement socialism. That was no random comment by Deng Xiaoping; it had been given careful consideration. Prior to the Sino-British negotiations, Deng Xiaoping had personally met with and listened to the opinions of 12 groups of Hong Kongers. He had sent people to Hong Kong to conduct wide-ranging investigations and research. He had also set up a special team to study the factors for Hong Kong's economic success, the conditions leading to Hong Kong's economic prosperity, and how these conditions might be preserved after 1997.[56]

In June 1984, when Deng Xiaoping met a group of business people visiting Beijing and the celebrity Chung Sze-yuen, he explained in detail the principles, standpoint, and specific concepts of "one country, two systems" with a fair amount of assurance.[57] In the three years from 1979 to 1982, after conscientious research and multiple argumentations, China finally made up its mind to recover Hong Kong in 1997 and decided to use the basic "one country, two systems" policy to first of all resolve the Hong Kong issue. That was a highly complex and, in a certain sense, painful process.[58] It manifested the considerable foresight and broad vision of China's leaders headed by Deng Xiaoping, their wisdom and resolution, and their faith in the Chinese people.

In July 1984, when Deng Xiaoping met with the then British Foreign Secretary Geoffrey Howe, he stressed that the "one country, two systems" concept was not formulated today. It has been in the making for several years now, ever since the Third Plenary Session of our Party's Eleventh Central Committee. The idea was first presented as a means of settling the Taiwan and Hong Kong questions. In view of the history of Hong Kong and Taiwan and of their present conditions, if there is no guaranteed that they will continue under the capitalist system, prosperity and stability cannot be maintained, and peaceful reunification of the motherland will be out of the question. He emphasized his conviction that the "one country, two systems" principle was feasible.[59] On September 24, 1982, when Deng Xiaoping met British Prime Minister Margaret Thatcher, he again specifically stated that China must recover Hong Kong in 1997 and would practice the "one country, two systems" method to resolve problems. He also pointed out that whether Hong Kong would be able to maintain its prosperity "depends fundamentally on applying policies suitable

---

[56]Hong Kong *Wen Hui Po*, 1995-03-23. Huang Wenfang. *The Process of China's Decision to Resume the Exercise of Sovereignty over Hong Kong and Its Implementation.* Hong Kong: Hong Kong Baptist University, 1997, p. 14.

[57]*Selected Works of Deng Xiaoping.* Beijing: People's Publishing House, 1993, vol. 3, pp. 58–61.

[58]Huang Wenfang. *The Process of China's Decision to Resume the Exercise of Sovereignty over Hong Kong and Its Implementation.* Hong Kong: Hong Kong Baptist University, 1997, p. 22.

[59]Deng Xiaoping. "Our Basic Position on the Question of Hong Kong," carried in *Deng Xiaoping on the Hong Kong Issue.* Hong Kong: Joint Publishing (H. K) Co., Ltd., 1993, pp. 9–10.

to Hong Kong, under Chinese administration after the recovery. Hong Kong's current political and economic systems and even most of its laws can remain in force. Of course, some of them will be modified. Hong Kong will continue under capitalism, and many systems currently in use that are suitable will be maintained."[60] With this, he in effect refuted the argument that Hong Kong could be prosperous and stable only under British administration. In many subsequent venues, he continued to expound the scientific concept of "one country, two systems."

We may well say that by that time, "one country, two systems" and the national policy of setting up special administrative regions had formally taken shape. The Chinese government successfully conducted peaceful negotiations with Britain on the basis of these concepts and resolved the Hong Kong issue. The satisfactory resolution of the Hong Kong issue by China and Britain was the first great instance of putting the "one country, two systems" concept into practice after its formation. On April 13, 1987, China and Portugal successfully resolved the Macao problem by means of the same guiding principle and concluded a Sino-Portuguese joint declaration on the Macao issue. China's National People's Congress then formulated the Basic Law for the Hong Kong and Macao special administrative zones In accordance with the Constitution and the "one country, two systems" principle. Thus, "one country, two systems" changed from a concept into a political reality.

3.3.3 The Scientific Connotations of "One Country, Two Systems"

"Two countries one system," as a completely new way of thinking and a policy decision used by the Chinese government to resolve the issue of national reunification, has its scientific connotations, which may be summed up as follows.

3.3.3.1 Striving for Peaceful Unification

In Chinese history, "the chief means for bringing about unification has been armed expansion, or by concluding 'before-the-city-gate' treaties under armed duress."[61] Earlier in this text, we have also seen that resolving national unification issues by means of military means was virtually elementary knowledge in the China of past times when people were apparently completely ignorant of the fact that national unification could also be attained by peaceful negotiation instead of by armed force. The spirit of peaceful compromise, tolerance and making concessions, too, was apparently nonexistent in China's traditional political culture, which was replete with the culture of you-die-so-that-I-may-live struggles. Either you died or I died. Peaceful coexistence was impossible. And for an extended period of time even after the

---

[60] *Selected Works of Deng Xiaoping*, vol. 3. Beijing: People's Publishing House, 1993, pp. 12–15.

[61] Ge Jianxiong. *Unification and Separation*. Beijing: SDX Joint Bookstore, 1994, p. 187.

founding of the New China, the China, the Chinese government regarded "liberate Taiwan" as the first option of the plan for national reunification. Clearly, "one country, two systems" is a departure from China's traditional political culture. That culture affirms the value of seeking national unification but now advocates using more versatile means on the issue of how the country is to be unified. It promotes peaceful negotiation as the first option for achieving unification and armed force as a substitute means when no alternative is available. It also advocates "the idea is not that one party should swallow up the other."[62] Allowing different systems and localities to coexist peacefully and replacing unification by armed force with peaceful unification is a principle of epoch-making significance in China's political history. Of course, China does not renounce the use of armed force. The purpose is to guard against intervention by hostile foreign forces and Taiwan's secession.

Deng Xiaoping once pointed out: "There are many disputes in the world, and we must find ways to solve them. Over the years I have been considering how those disputes could be solved by peaceful means, rather than by war... If war is to be averted, the only alternative is an approach like the one I have just mentioned, an approach the people will accept. It can help stabilize the situation, and for a long time too, and is harmful to neither side." He went on: "Is it possible to find new solutions for the many problems that cannot be solved by old ones? New problems should be solved by new means... Some of my remarks may not be precise or thoughtful enough. But we must rack our brains to find ways to stabilize the world situation." He hoped "you will have a better understanding of our proposal for the solution of the Hong Kong and Taiwan questions and make a study of it. Anyhow, we must find a way out of this impasse."[63] When Deng Xiaoping met British Prime Minister Margaret Thatcher on December 19, 1984, he also pointed out that the practical problem confronting China was how to settle the questions of Hong Kong and Taiwan. There were only two possible ways: one was peaceful, the other non-peaceful. The only peaceful solution to the Hong Kong and Taiwan question was the "one country, two systems" arrangement, not by imposing socialism on them.[64] Scholars researching "one country, two systems" failed in past years to pay sufficient attention to the major changes since the 1970s in China's methods for bringing about national reunification, and had not recognized the radically different results that could ensue from peaceful reunification or reunification by armed force.

"Peaceful reunification" is the most important premise for realizing "one country, two systems." If national reunification were brought about by war instead of by peaceful negotiations, the existence of any special or different systems would certainly be interdicted. It is quite evident that only "one country one system" would exist, not "one country, two systems." Hence, "peaceful reunification" is the due implication of "one country, two systems" and the premise for the implementation of "one country, two systems."

---

[62]*Selected Works of Deng Xiaoping*, vol. 3. Beijing: People's Publishing House, 1993, p. 30.

[63]*Selected Works of Deng Xiaoping*. Beijing: People's Publishing House, 1993, vol. 3, pp. 49–50.

[64]Ibid., pp. 101–102.

3.3.3.2 Connotations in Terms of Political Science

From the perspective of political science, "one country, two systems" is a manifestation of political tolerance. Ever since reform and opening-up, the spirit of toleration has gradually risen in China. This is expressed in two main aspects. First, in terms of economics: On the precondition of upholding the socialist system of public ownership, multiple economic elements are allowed to coexist, the development of privately run and foreign-funded enterprises is encouraged, and four special economic regions as well as a number of open cities have been set up in the coastal areas. This would definitely be forbidden under the traditional economic system. Second, in terms of the national reunification issue: On the precondition of implementing socialism in the country's principal areas, yet for the sake of bringing about the country's peaceful reunification, Hong Kong, Macao, and Taiwan are to be permitted to keep their respective capitalist institutions and ways of life unchanged after they have completed their reunification with China's mainland. "Special administration areas," i.e., special administrative regions will also be set up in these territories and are to be bestowed a high degree of autonomy by the Central Government. This means fundamentally discarding the traditional political concept that a country may implement only a unitary social system, or in other words "one country one system." It means deeming that different social systems may be simultaneously implemented in different regions of a unified country, and that these systems can peacefully coexist with one another. Specifically, this means that the socialist system and the capitalist system may exist simultaneously within a country and be tolerated and accepted by a unified central government.

Clearly, moving away from "one country one system" to the creation of "special economic areas" and "special administrative areas," and then to the finalization and implementation of the "one country, two systems" concept, is indeed a huge break from the traditional Chinese concept of a country and of unification.[65] In Deng Xiaoping's words, this "was considered a new formulation, one that had never been offered by our predecessors."[66]

3.3.3.3 The Scientific Implications of "One Country, Two Systems"

"One country" is fairly easy to understand. It stands for the People's Republic of China, and not the Republic of China. Internationally and domestically, only the People's Republic of China can represent all the people of China, and it is the sole legal government of China. "One country" calls for bringing about the reunification of Hong Kong, Macao, and Taiwan with Chinese mainland under its unified flag. There have of course been some changes to the implications of "one country," but the connotation that the mainland and Taiwan both pertain to one country remains

---

[65] Wang Zhenmin. "One Country, Two Systems: Its Historical Background, Present Operation and Future Development," LAWASIA, *Comparative Constitutional Law*, 1995 (1), Australia.

[66] *Selected Works of Deng Xiaoping*, vol. 3. Beijing: People's Publishing House, 1993, pp. 101–102.

unchanged. Also unchanged is the connotation that China must be reunified as one country. I will now discuss this matter.[67]

How "two systems" is to be understood is quite another matter. The precise meaning of "two systems" is that some special regions may implement "special policies and systems" within the unified China. Moreover, these "special policies and systems" may differ entirely from the mainland's policies and systems as well as be completely different one from the other. That is to say, under "one country, two systems," not only is the existence of one such set of "special policies and systems" permissible; also permissible is the simultaneous existence of two or even three sets of "special policies and systems" dissimilar from the mainland's mainstream policies and systems. The Hong Kong SAR implements its own set of capitalist institutions which bear Hong Kong characteristics; the Macao SAR implements capitalist institutions with its own characteristics and the Taiwan SAR would implement capitalist institutions also with its own characteristics. Since they pertain to different capitalist setups, these capitalist institutions are also different one from the other. The national "one country, two systems" policy does not mean unifying them by means of socialism, nor does it imply using one of these capitalist systems to unify all of them and render them uniform. If the contrary were true, it would be necessary, and sufficient, to formulate only a single unified SAR Basic Law; there would be no need to formulate two separate basic laws for Hong Kong and Macao, or even three SAR basic laws. Despite the differences between the specific capitalist systems of these regions, however, they all fall under the rubric of capitalism and differ in essence from the socialism on the mainland. The term "one country, two systems" refers to the possibility of both major systems—socialism and capitalism—existing in one country. As for the different patterns of the capitalist system in its different regions, these may differ in a thousand ways. In this sense, "one country, two systems" may well be characterized as "one country multiple systems," in that not only are socialism and capitalism permitted to coexist in one country; also permitted is the coexistence of capitalisms of different patterns and characteristics.

"One country, two systems" has won the support of all Chinese, and also gained approbation from friends abroad. Some scholars in other countries even believe the "one-country-two-systems" thinking "ushers in a new era for future political philosophy" and "is capable of opening up new vistas in the world of the future"[68] At the very least, its proposal and implementation pave the way for ultimately bringing about the country's Reunification, create political conditions for realizing the grand unity of the Chinese nation, turn schisms and humiliations into things of the past, and open up a new epoch of unity for the Chinese nation. More broadly, it establishes a model for realizing a country's Reunification, points out a direction for long-term peace and stability in human society, and thereby contributes to mankind's cause

---

[67]Qian Qichen. "Complete the Great Cause of Reunifying the Motherland As Soon As Possible and Bring About the Great Rejuvenation of the Chinese Nation—the Speech at the Forum of People of All Walks of Life in Beijing to Commemorate the Sixth Anniversary of Chairman Jiang Zemin's Important Address to Taiwan." Beijing: Xinhua News Agency, 2001-01-22.

[68]Ronald Liang. "On One Country, Two Systems." Hong Kong: *Ming Pao*, 1984-06-15.

of progress. As Deng Xiaoping said, today "there are a great many divisions in the world—divisions between the Chinese mainland and Taiwan, between North and South Korea… the way to solve these is 'one country, two kinds of system.' What will remain after that will be issues of peaceful competition, solutions for which shall be the peoples' choices—choices not of war but of peace." [69]

Britain, too, gave high appraisal to the use of "one country, two systems" to resolve the Hong Kong issue. Margaret Thatcher, the then Prime Minister of Britain, commended it as an "innovation of genius."[70] Richard Evans, head of the British delegation to the Sino-British negotiations, said: "The joint declaration embodies that highly imaginative concept —'one China, two kinds of systems' and proves that peaceful negotiation is the best way for resolving problems left by history."[71] British Foreign Secretary Geoffrey Howe, when discussing the Sino-British Draft Agreement, also commented: "1997 will not only mark the conclusion of an era in Hong Kong. More importantly it will mark the beginning of a new era." He maintained that the "one country, two systems" proposed by Deng Xiaoping was "a tentative plan with great foresight."[72] Javier Perez de Cuellar, then UN secretary general, highly evaluated that pioneering undertaking, saying: "When tensions and confrontations unfortunately overshadow many regions in the world, the success attained by the negotiations on Hong Kong's future will undoubtedly be regarded as an outstanding example of effective and quiet diplomacy in today's international relations."[73]

From the perspectives of political science and constitutional law, the proposition has greatly enriched the theories regarding the state, national unification, and national structure, and has advanced the state theory and national structure theory of political science. It bears significance as an epoch-making milestone in the history of China's political development. It endeavors to replace the tradition of unification by armed force with peaceful unification, replaces the tradition of "one country one system" with "one country, two systems" or even "multiple systems," replaces political intolerance with political tolerance and replaces insularity with openness, and has thereby initiated a new political trend and set a new political example. Hence, it is said the proposal and implementation of "one country, two systems" is of far-reaching historical and international significance.

"One country, two systems" possesses great vitality. As stated earlier, it is an organic component of the reform-and-opening-up strategy that was initiated in China in the 1970s, and it is an outcome of the campaign against "leftism." It will not change so long as the general orientation of Reform and Opening-Up remains unchanged. The Chinese government will certainly not carry out socialist reforms in Hong Kong after 1997 as it did in Shanghai in 1949. If that should happen, Hong Kong will

---

[69] Beijing, *Outlook Weekly*, 1985 (5).

[70] Cheng Linsheng. *A Study of Deng Xiaoping's "One Country, Two Systems" Thought.* Shenyang: Liaoning People's Publishing House, 1992, p. 138.

[71] Beijing, *People's Daily*, 1984-09-27, p. 1.

[72] Beijing, *People's Daily*, 1984-12-07, p. 1.

[73] Beijing, *Red Flag* (magazine), 1984 (20), p. 23.

lose the value of and justification for its existence. The same goes for Macao and Taiwan. The national reunification carried out today differs entirely from the previous socialist reform of the 1950s in that the capitalist systems in these regions will be kept unchanged.

Also, "one country, two systems" has been formulated by China's highest institutions of state power as well as embodied in China's Constitution as the Basic Law of Special Administrative Regions, and as such is inflexible and unchangeable. In constitutional law this is known as a "non-modifiable clause."

Moreover, "one country, two systems" has many times been proclaimed to the world community by China's top leaders as well as embodied in international treaties (i.e., two Joint Declarations) and archived at the United Nations. The Chinese government and people have always kept their word and will certainly stand by their commitments. The Chinese government will certainly demonstrate to the world's people that it is able and responsible, that the Chinese are definitely capable of properly handling their own affairs, that the Chinese are definitely capable of doing an even better job of administering their territories and thereby gain greater prestige for the Chinese nation. Hence "one country, two systems" is entirely feasible, reliable, and imbued with vitality. As long as the principles and spirit of "one country, two systems" are upheld, the relations between the central authorities and special administrative regions will be well handled.

The Chinese government has already successfully used the guiding principle of "peaceful reunification and one country, two systems" to resolve the Hong Kong and Macao issues. It strictly adheres to this basic state policy and to the two Basic Laws in handing issues arising between the central authorities and the special administrative regions. Practice will prove their scientific nature and rationality.

As regards Taiwan, the results of a public opinion poll released by the Taiwan authorities' Mainland Affairs Council in March 2001 show that after Taiwan Democratic Party leaders who support "Taiwan independence" took office in March 2000, the number of Taiwanese who supported "one country, two systems" not only did not decline, but increased. Only about 5% of ordinary people had supported "one country, two systems" in previous opinion polls, but the recent poll showed that supporters of "one country, two systems" had reached a new historic high, rising from 12.2 to 16.1%, the highest ever. The proportion of supporters of "maintaining the status quo and proceeding to reunification at a later date" increased to 21.4% from 19.1% in 2000. As regards the prioritization of diplomacy and cross-Strait relations, 36.5% placed importance on "developing cross-Strait relations," for the first time exceeding the 33% who believed in "developing Taiwan's relations with other countries" and the 22.5% who maintained the two were equally important.[74] It is apparent that more and more of the Taiwan public were acknowledging and accepting "one country, two systems."

In June 2001, four years after the transfer of sovereignty over Hong Kong to China, an opinion poll conducted by the polling center of Taiwan's United Daily News found that, where the "peaceful reunification and one country, two systems"

---

[74]Hong Kong, *Ming Pao*, 2001-04-06. Also see Guangzhou, *the Nanfang Daily*, 2001-04-04.

consistently advocated by the mainland was concerned, 33% of the public could accept reunification with the mainland under "one country, two systems." And as compared to all previous polls by the United Daily News, the "one country, two systems" acceptance rate for the first time exceeded 30%—ten percentage points higher than at the end of 1999 when Macao sovereignty was transferred. Meanwhile, the opposition rate was lower than in all previous polls, declining by eight percentage points. The year-2000 poll had found that only 15% of the public could consider moving to the mainland; the current poll found that 24% were willing to relocate and live in Chinese mainland if the opportunity presented itself, and 34% were willing to work on the mainland. Among persons willing to relocate to, or find jobs on, the mainland, acceptance of "one country, two systems" exceeded 48%—double the number of those who rejected "moving to the west." There was also a considerable boost in confidence in the mainland among the Taiwan public. On the question of which "country" politically represents the "one country, two systems," the poll found that although 44% of the public insisted that the "Republic of China" could best represent "China" politically, some 34% maintained that the "People's Republic of China" was the orthodox representative and 22% were noncommittal. In the long-term perspective, most people were optimistic about the possibility of peacefully terminating the cross-Strait impasse; 58% maintained the cross-Strait schism could be resolved by peaceful means and only 26% felt that doing so was impossible. This poll further proved that the principle of "peaceful reunification and one country, two systems" is gaining acceptance among the Taiwan public. It is believed that along with further reform and opening-up on the part of China's mainland, the "one country, two systems" arrangement will find increasing acceptance among the Taiwan public. This will further prove the scientific nature and rationality of the guiding principle of "one country, two systems."[75]

On July 12, 2001, when State Council Vice Premier Qian Qichen met with a delegation of the Taiwan New Party's Mainland Affairs Council, he further defined the basic principles of the policy of "one China, cross-Strait talks, and establishing the three exchanges as soon as possible," and also pointed out that during specific implementation of the "one country, two systems" policy, the mainland side would let Taiwan have more autonomous powers than Hong Kong and Macao. This would include seven aspects, the specific contents of which were: (a) "Taiwan shall continue to use the Taiwanese currency." The mainland would not interfere with Taiwan's financial and monetary policies. (b) "Taiwan shall continue to retain its armed forces." Taiwan would continue to have substantial powers of self-determination on defense matters, and the mainland would not send troops to Taiwan. This was a power not available to Hong Kong or Macao, and showed that Taiwan would possess greater powers of autonomy than Hong Kong and Macao. (c) "Taiwan shall be a separate tariff area." This indicated that Taiwan could, after cross-Strait reunification, retain its status as an independent customs tariff area, and that its position in relevant international organizations would not be affected. (d) "Taiwan shall continue to

[75]New York, *World Journal*, 2001-07-01. *People's Daily* Renminnet News, 2001-07-01, http://www.peopledaily.com.cn/.

retain its government structure." The mainland side would not interfere in Taiwan current government institutions (on condition that these did not violate the one-China principle), and various electoral activities in the Taiwan region would be conducted as previously. (e) "The mainland shall not take even a penny from Taiwan, and shall not transfer Taiwan's funds." (f) "The general public and entrepreneurs in Taiwan shall continue to maintain possession of their assets." Assets of all kinds in Taiwan, including foreign currency holdings, would not be affected by the reunification, and concerns among some people in Taiwan that "money will be taken away by the mainland" were unnecessary. And the last item, "Autonomy in personnel matters; the mainland shall not send any officials to Taiwan." Rumors that "the mainland will send high-ranking officials to take over Taiwan" after the implementation of "one country, two systems" are pure fabrications. The mainland will fully respect Taiwan's autonomous powers.

These are clear indications that the mainland will be quite open-minded in the "two systems" aspect as long as the Taiwan side acknowledges that the two shores (banks) of the Taiwan Strait constitute "one country." The high level of autonomy that Taiwan shall enjoy will "probably be of a kind that no region in any country has ever enjoyed."[76]

---

[76]Beijing, *Global Times*, 2001-07-17, p. 1.

Chapter 4
Legalization of "One Country, Two Systems" and Establishment of the SAR Organizational System

We can see from the preceding chapter that "one country with two systems" was first and foremost a political-science concept and its emergence inevitably raised many new problems concerning the Constitution. "One country with two systems" was the theoretical basis and the political premise for setting up the Special Administrative Regions (SARs), and the SARs setup could not have emerged if the "one country with two systems" plan had not been advanced. It was on the foundation of the "one country with two systems" plan that the Chinese Government formulated the specific policies concerning the SARs and stipulated the relationship between the Central Government and the SARs. Conversely, the "one country with two systems" concept had to get help from the setting up of the Special Administrative Regions for its realization and implementation.

That, however, was not yet sufficient. Space for the concept's survival had to be sought under China's existing constitutional structure, and a rational constitutional status had to be devised for it both legally and institutionally. In this chapter I intend to explore the relevant constitutional issues of "one country, two systems" and the legal foundation for setting up the SARs.

4.1 Constitutional Issues Related to "One Country, Two Systems"

The theory and practice of China's Constitution have come up against two major challenges since the inception of China's policy of Reform and Opening Up. One of these is the challenge posed by the development of the market economy which has brought profound changes to all aspects of China's politics, economics and culture, all of which have raised numerous new problems for the theory and practice of China's Constitution. In response to this challenge three revisions have been made

© Foreign Language Teaching and Research Publishing Co., Ltd and Springer Nature Singapore Pte Ltd. 2019
Z. Wang, *Relationship Between the Chinese Central Authorities and Regional Governments of Hong Kong and Macao: A Legal Perspective*, China Academic Library, https://doi.org/10.1007/978-981-13-2322-5_4

in recent years to China's Constitution.[1] The second major challenge consists of the constitutional problems created by the implementation of "one country, two systems" and for the fulfillment of the great cause of national reunification. These issues involve virtually all aspects of China's Constitution, from the political to the economic and cultural, and may well be described as multi-faceted. In response to this second challenge, China, in addition to stipulating Article 31 of the Constitution, has drawn up two special laws of a constitutional nature, i.e. the two Basic Laws of the Hong Kong and Macao SARs.[2] We will first conduct some explorations into the new problems raised for the theory and practice of China's Constitution by the formulation and implementation of "one China two systems."

4.1.1 Constitutional Issues Related to the "One China Two Systems" Concept

Many tough issues in terms of the Constitution were in fact encountered during the initial proposal of "one country two system" concept, during the negotiations by China with Britain and Portugal on the Hong Kong and Macao issues, and during the formulation of the two Basic Laws. The main constitutional problems may be summed up as follows:

4.1.1.1 The State System Problem

China's Constitution specifies that China's state system is a people's democratic dictatorship, that China's economy is to implement a socialist market-economy system and social public ownership, and that in the initial stage of socialism, China is to persist in the main in developing a public ownership system side by side with diverse forms of ownership as well as in practicing in the main a system of "to each according to his work" side by side with diverse forms of distribution. In the cultural aspect, the Constitution stipulates the implementation of a socialist spiritual civilization.[3] Based on the "one country, two systems" plan and the stipulations of the Basic Laws, the two SARs are to retain capitalist political, economic and cultural systems instead of implementing people's democratic dictatorship, socialist public ownership or a

---

[1]After the Constitution of China was approved in December, 1982, revisions were made to in on April 12, 1998, March 29, 1993 and March 15, 1999 respectively. Most of the revisions on these three occasions had to do with the economic system and economic policies.

[2]There have always been different opinions on how to determine the nature of the Basic Laws. Most academics maintain both are laws of a constitutional nature and fall in the category of basic laws. I, however, believe this does not suffice to describe the special nature of the two Basic Laws and think it more appropriate to characterize them as "special laws of a constitutional nature."

[3]Article 1, Article 2, Article 14 (revised) and Article 24 of the Constitution of the People's Republic of China.

socialist spiritual civilization.[4] These stipulations differed radically from the above-mentioned stipulations of China's Constitution. This was a new problem which had never come up before the New China's Constitution. The state system stipulated by China's Constitution had not changed, but if this problem were not resolved, some persons might raise the question of whether "one country, two systems" constituted a violation of the Constitution since it permits certain regions of a socialist country to implement capitalism—something which was absolutely forbidden by China's Constitution.

4.1.1.2 Citizens' Right and Duties

Chapter II of China's Constitution stipulates five major categories of basic rights enjoyed by China's citizens[5] and the duties that China's citizens must fulfill. The provisions of the Constitution in these respects are clearly incompatible with those of the SARs. For example, the Constitution contains no provisions on the freedom of movement [migration], but the Basic Laws stipulate that residents of the special administrative regions are free to move anywhere they wish.[6] The Constitution stipulates that both husband and wife are duty-bound to practice family planning, but SAR residents have the right to procreate at will.[7] The Constitution specifies that citizens have the duty to perform military service, but that is not required of SAR residents.[8] As regards the nationality issue, on the premise of adhering to the basic principles of the Constitution, China handles the nationality issues of SAR residents in a flexible manner. It is also evident that Chinese citizens among SAR residents are not only entitled to take part in the management of national affairs but also enjoy much broader rights and freedoms that those stipulated by the Constitution.[9] SAR residents naturally enjoy rights enjoyed by all residents in the interior regions, plus rights which the latter do not enjoy. However, SAR residents may be exempted of the duties that interior region inhabitants must fulfill in accordance with the Constitution. All of the above are circumstances never before encountered under China's Constitution. That is to say, it fully manifests the "one country, two systems" principle and spirit in terms of its citizens' rights and duties.

---

[4]Preamble and Article 5 of the Basic Law of the Hong Kong Special Administrative Region and the Basic Law of the Macao Special Administrative Region.

[5]I.e. political rights and freedoms, personal rights, the right of freedom of spirit, social and economic rights, and cultural and educational rights.

[6]Article 31 of the Basic Law of the Hong Kong Special Administrative Region and Article 33 of the Basic Law of the Macao Special Administrative Region.

[7]Article 49 of the Constitution of the People's Republic of China, Article 37 of the Basic Law of the Hong Kong Special Administrative Region, and Article 38 of the Basic Law of the Macao Special Administrative Region.

[8]Article 55 of the Constitution of the People's Republic of China.

[9]Article 21 of the Basic Law of the Hong Kong Special Administrative Region and of the Basic Law of the Macao Special Administrative Region.

4.1.1.3   System of Government

The system of government specified by China's Constitution is the people's congress system, which in form is somewhat similar to the British parliamentary system.[10] Under the people's congress system, administrative and judicial organs are both generated through elections by local people's congresses and are responsible and report to the latter on their work.[11] The people's congresses are generated by means of popular elections. The SARs, however, use neither of these systems, nor do they adopt replicas of the separation-of-powers or the parliamentary system of the West. According to the provisions of the Basic Laws, the SARs each have a chief officer, i.e. a chief executive officer who serves at the same time as chief of the SARs' administrative institutions. The relationships among the SARs' legislation, administration and judiciary are designed to ensure judiciary independence as well as ensure checks and balances and cooperation among the special regions' administrative and legislative institutions.[12] This means that a new type of governmental and organizational structure has emerged in China under the unified constitutional framework of the people's congress system.

4.1.1.4   Structural Form of the State

China has always implemented a unitary system and, historically, has basically adhered to the "one country, one system" principle. With the establishment of the SARs, a new and unique local government system has emerged at the provincial level. As compared to the general run of provincial local governments, the new system is "unique" in that the SARs practice capitalism whereas the general run of local governments practice socialism; in that the SARs enjoy a high degree of autonomy—an autonomy not only greater than that of the ordinary run of localities but also greater than the powers of states under the federal system; in that the SARs' relations with the Central Government have to be clearly defined by law; and in that the establishment of the SARs and the systems they implemented have to be determined by the highest organ of state power, i.e. the National People's Congress.[13]

---

[10]Cai Dingjian. *The People's Congress System of China*. Beijing: the Law Press, 1998, p. 27.

[11]Regarding the composition and systems of local state institutions in China's inland regions, reference may be made to Gan Zangchun. *Local Institutions of the People's Republic of China*. Taiyuan: Shanxi People's Publishing House, 1995; Wan Wenguo. *The Theory and Practice of Local People's Congresses*. Wuhan: Wuhan Press, 1990; Lu Tianhong and He Huahui. *Local Government Power and People's Deputies*. Beijing: The Qunzhong Press, 1985; Diao Tianding. *The Local State Institutions of China: A Study*. Beijing: The Qunzhong Press, 1985; Editorial Team of "Studies on Local Government Power," *Studies on Local Government Power*. Beijing: The Qunzhong Press, 1986.

[12]Xiao Weiyun. *One Country, Two Systems and Hong Kong's Basic Legal System*. Beijing: Peking University Press, 1990, pp. 171 and 225.

[13]Constitution of the People's Republic of China, Article 31 and Article 62.

Despite the fact that China has set up the SARS and that the latter enjoy unprecedented powers, the nature of China as country with a unitary system has not changed. China remains a country with a unitary system. The only difference is that its inclusiveness has broadened to become a unitary system that includes SARs which exercise the capitalist system. With the constant deepening of Reform and Opening Up, and in particular with the eventual implementation of "one country, two systems" in Taiwan and the ultimate fulfillment of the great cause of national reunification, China's state structure will undergo greater adjustments which will further improve and perfect the form of China's state structure.[14] This matter will be discussed later and in greater detail.

4.1.1.5 The Judicial Structure

The difference between the inland regions and the SARs in the judicial aspect is the greatest among all of the disparities between the two. As stipulated in China's Constitution, the judicial system consists of people's courts which constitute the State's judicial organs and which are generated by, responsible to, and report on their work to people's congresses. Higher-level people's courts supervise the judicial work of lower-level people's courts.[15] People's procuratorates are the State's organs of legal supervision, and are likewise generated by, responsible to, and report on their work to people's congresses. Higher-level people's procuratorates direct the work of lower-level people's procuratorates. The courts independently exercise their judicial powers in accordance with the provisions of the law, and the procuratorates exercise their procuratorial powers in accordance with provisions of the law; neither are subject to interference from administrative organs, public organizations or individuals. The people's courts, people's procuratorates and public security organs handle criminal cases and in doing so should practice division of work and responsibilities, mutual coordination, and mutual constraints.[16]

After they have been set up, the SARs each retain their own judicial systems and are not affected by the mainland's judicial system. Since they have their own courts of last instance, final judgments on all cases are not rendered by [China's] Supreme People's Court. There is no higher judicial institution over and above the SARs' courts of last instance or the Supreme People's Court. Hence, a situation of "one country, two types of judiciaries" has taken shape in China. The actualities of the last two or more years shows that the SAR's judicial systems not only continue to

---

[14]Regarding China's State structure and form, reference may be made to Dong Zhiwei. *On State Structures and Forms.* Wuhan: Wuhan University Press, 1997; Zhu Guanglei. *The Processes of Contemporary Government in China.* Tianjin: Tianjin People's Publishing House, 1997; and Lin Shangli. *The Relationships Between Governments within China.* Hangzhou: Zhejiang People's Publishing House, 1998.

[15]Constitution of the People's Republic of China, Article 3, Sect. 7.

[16]Constitution of the People's Republic of China, Article 135.

exist but are exerting a major influence on the judicial reform currently taking place in Chinese mainland, and serve as an important reference for the mainland's judicial reform.[17]

4.1.1.6   Regarding the Electoral System and the Political Party System

In accordance with the provisions of China's Constitution and relevant electoral laws, China practices concurrent systems of direct and indirect elections and of regional and occupational representation; it implements the principles of universal and equal suffrage and secret voting, and has statutory measures to ensure the normal conduct of elections.[18] The elections and electoral systems of the SARs, on the other hand, are highly complex, and different methods are used for different elections. However, one thing is certain: The SARs may adopt electoral systems different from those on Chinese mainland, and that brings greater diversity to China's electoral system as a whole.

In regard to the political party system, China implements a system of multi-party cooperation and political consultations under the leadership of the Communist party in line with the provisions of China's Constitution. The Communist Party of China is China's governing party. The eight other parties are not "out-of-office" parties and even less are they opposition parties; they are "participant parties." (i.e. parties participating in governance and state affairs alongside the ruling party). The Chinese People's Political Consultative Conference is an institution for political consultations formed by the Chinese Communist Party and other democratic parties, and is the principal model used for multi-party cooperation and political consultations.[19] There is no unified model for the political party systems adopted locally by the SARs, and the ones they do use are chosen and determined by the SARs per se in light of their specific circumstances.

4.2   Whether the Force of China's Constitution Extends to the Special Administrative Regions

That the force of China's Constitution covers the entirety of China's territory does not come into question. As stated earlier, however, a large share of the systems and principles stipulated in China's Constitution have not been implemented in the SARs after the latter's establishment. Examples are such principles as the socialist system, the people's democratic dictatorship state system, the national people's congress form of government, the peoples' judiciary system, the procuratorial system, provisions

---

[17]Regarding China's judiciary system, reference may be made to Xiong Xianjue. *On China's Judicial System: New Discussions*, Beijing, China Legal Publishing House, 1999.

[18]Zhu Fuhui. *Constitutional Law: New Edition.* Beijing: Law Press, 1998, p. 175.

[19]Xu Chongde. *The Constitution of China.* Beijing: China Renmin University Press, 1996, p. 371.

related to citizens' rights and duties, the system of democratic centralism and so forth, none of which are implemented in the SARs. Thus it would seem that the force of China's Constitution does not extend to the SARs.[20] In that case, does the force of China's Constitution extend, in the final analysis, to the SARs? And is the Constitution applicable to case handlings by the SARs' judicial organs?

Academic quarters hotly debate these questions. Some people maintain that the Constitution of the People's Republic of China is by nature a socialist type of constitution, that in accordance with the "one county two systems" spirit the SARs do not practice socialism, and therefore China's Constitution exerts no legal force on these regions.[21] Others disapprove of this view, and maintain that China's Constitution applies to the SARs as well. I agree with the latter opinion, for the following reasons:

For one thing, China's Constitution was ratified by China's highest organ of state power; it is the nation's basic law, and neither the Constitution itself nor any other law places any limits on the force of the Constitution. Hence the Constitution's overall scope of force naturally covers the entirety of China's territory. Since the SARs are inseparable components of China's territory, it is only natural that the force of the Constitution extends to those regions. The Constitution of the Chinese mainland is without doubt the constitution of all localities in China, including the SARs. Hence, from the overall perspective, the force of China's Constitution should extend to the SARs.[22] It must be noted that in a country with a unitary system like China's, there can only be one constitution nationwide, and it is not permissible for a local administrative district to possess any legal document marked as a "constitution." That is why the SARs' Basic Laws are called Basic Laws and not "constitutions." That is also why the basic and comprehensive local legal norms for each ethnic minority's local self-governance formulated by the ethnic (national) autonomous regions on China's mainland can only be called "rules for self-governance" and not "constitutions."

A constitution, as a country's fundamental law, not only prescribes a country's basic system and basic tasks; as an entity it also serves as an important symbol of the country's unity and sovereignty. When we discussed the structural forms of countries, we stated that a unified constitution is an important characteristic of a unitary-system state, and that only federal states have multiple constitutions. Thus in China, the presence nationwide of only one constitution is required by China's unitary-system state structure and is also an important manifestation of China's national unity and territorial sovereignty and integrity. An important reason for saying our country is not yet reunified is that the power of the PRC's legally constituted authority centered on its Constitution has yet to be extended to all regions in China. After China recovered its sovereignty over the Hong Kong and Macao regions and set up the SARs, the

---

[20]The task force on the Central/SAR Relationship under the Basic Law Advisory Commission of the Hong Kong Special Administrative Region, "Relationship between the Basic Law and the Constitution (Final Report)," 1987.

[21]Ibid.

[22]Xiao Weiyun. *One Country, Two Systems and Hong Kong's Basic Legal System.* Beijing: Peking University Press, 1990, pp. 86–94.

power of China's Constitution was of course extended to the SARs. China, as a united nation with a unitary system, might put some laws into effect in some regions only and not in others. However, the power of its Constitution which symbolizes the nation's unity and sovereignty must be extended over every inch of its land, and there can only be one constitution nationwide, just as China has only one national flag, one national emblem, one capital city and one national army. The Constitution is, without question, effective in the SARs since these regions are inseparable components of China as well as local administrative regions of the Chinese government. If we were to say that the Constitution of the Chinese nation has no force or effect in the SARs, then what would serve as "constitutions" in these regions? If we were to recognize the SARs' Basic Laws as their "constitutions," China would have not one but three or four concurrent "constitutions," and that would turn China into a federalist state rather than a unitary-system state, would it not?

Secondly, the force of the Constitution extends to the SARs not only because the Constitution is an important symbol of state sovereignty and unity, but also because a portion of its contents indeed have to do with the SARs or directly concern the latter, and serve as constitutional grounds for formulating the SARs' Basic Laws. Article 31 and paragraph 13 of Article 52 of the Constitution directly concern the SARs and are of course effective in these regions. The provisions of the Constitution with regard to China's highest organs of state power, state leaders, the state's highest administrative organs and the state's highest military institutions, the provisions with regard to the national flag, the national emblem and the capital city as well as other provisions with regard to national sovereignty, foreign diplomacy and national defense—all unquestionably apply to the SARs or should be acknowledged and respected by the SARs, which is to say that paragraphs one to four of Chap. 3 and this chapter of the Constitution basically apply to the SARs. Some other contents of the Constitution—such as those regarding the Four Cardinal Principles, the socialist system and local institutions of state power and local administrative institutions, the state judicial and procuratorial organs—are not appropriate for the SARs and have been revised or replaced in the relevant provisions of the SARs' Basic Laws. It is evident that the Chinese Constitution is in principle applicable to the SARs. As to each specific provision or stipulation, its applicability has been determined in accordance with the principle and spirit of the "one country, two systems" disposition.

Three, if we examine the constitutions of other countries in the world, we see that, other than containing provisions applicable nationwide, in all of them the formulation is permitted of special provisions which pinpoint and apply to the special circumstances only of some special regions, and that this does not negate the effectiveness of the constitutions *in toto* over those special localities. This is quite normal. The provisions of China's Constitution on ethnic regional autonomy apply uniquely to ethnic autonomous localities. Moreover, Article 31 of the Constitution is a special provision. One might say that the force (effectiveness) of the Constitution was first manifested in these special provisions and subsequently extended to the SARs via the formulation of the SARs' Basic Laws. These Basic Laws have had the effect of "digesting and absorbing" the Constitution and making it clear which of the Constitution's provisions should or should not be applied.[23] In this sense, China's Constitution plays its due role in the SARs principally by way of, and in the form of, the latter's special laws—the SARs' Basic Laws.

The SAR Basic Laws have been formulated on the basis of the Constitution and are in effect expansions and extensions of the contents of China's Constitution as well as organic components of the Constitution of the People's Republic of China. In China's legal system, the Constitution is the highest law; under it come the Basic Laws, and under these, ordinary laws. The SAR Basic Laws are situated below the Constitution and above ordinary laws, derive their force from the Constitution, and are second only in importance to the Constitution. If China's Constitution itself was without legal force in the special administrative regions, the effectiveness of the SAR's Basic Laws, too, would be void of foundation or support; those laws would be "rivers without sources" and "trees without trunks."[24] The Constitution's legal force in the special administrative regions is self-evident.

Hence, even though the SAR's Basic Law appendices and attachments do not indicate that China's Constitution is implemented in the special administrative regions as the national law, it goes without saying that the force of China's Constitution covers the SARs, just as Britain's constitution and constitution-type documents held sway there before the regions were returned to China. And precisely because the Constitution wields due force over the special regions, the Hong Kong SAR courts of law have frequently cited the provisions of China's Constitution in their verdicts, despite the fact that courts in Chinese mainland courts still may not cite Constitutional provisions in their verdicts. For example, the Hong Kong SAR Court of Final Appeal quoted Article 31, Article 57 and Article 58 of China's Constitution in its verdict on the case of Wu Jialing and Wu Dandan versus the Chief of the Immigration Affairs Department on January 29, 1999.[25]

It is apparent that such Constitutional issues involved a wide range of matters, and that a special "loophole" was accorded to the SARs in China's Constitution according to the needs of the "one country, two systems" concept, with the SARs' Basic Laws specifying and legalizing the arrangements toward that end. However the question remains of how to avoid possible future investigations of "one country, two systems" and the SARs' Basic Laws for violations of the Constitution. This matter will be explored below.

---

[23] Xiao Weiyun. *One Country, Two Systems and Hong Kong's Basic Legal System*. Beijing: Peking University Press, 1990, p. 95.

[24] With regard to the relation between the Chinese Constitution and the SAR Basic Law, reference may also be made to Wang Shuwen. *An Introduction to the Basic Law of the Special Administrative Region*. Beijing: CPC Central Committee Party School Press, 1997, pp. 79–95.

[25] Wu Jialing & Wu Dandan versus Chief of the Entry Affairs Department, Hong Kong SAR Court of Final Appeal, January 29, 1999. This sort of quoting is not performed according to the provisions on case hearings in China's Constitution, nor does it take China's Constitution as a legal basis for hearing any specific case; it simply explains the functions of China's legal system and state structure.

4.3   Constitutional and Legal Grounds for Establishing the Special Administrative Regions

4.3.1   "One Country, Two Systems" Takes Its Place in the Constitution

The first time the "special administrative zone" (SAR) concept appeared in a formal document of the Chinese government was in 1981, on the eve of China's National day celebrations, when Chairman Ye Jianying of the National People's Congress Standing Committee announced China's nine-point policy proposal for the liberation of Taiwan. Point Three in this document affirmed: "After the country is reunified, Taiwan can enjoy a high degree of autonomy as a special administrative region and may retain its armed forces. The Central Government will not interfere with local affairs in Taiwan." Because China's mainlanders had always been accustomed to dealing with matters in accordance with the policies of the Chinese Communist Party, some people maintained that since the "one country, two systems" approach was also a firm and unshakeable policy, the commitments related to the SARs were unalterable and there was no need for any legislative changes. In its handling of this issue, however, China was obviously more circumspect, and not only wanted to put it in the Constitution but also legislate the matter. This was not merely a matter of "international practice," but an expression of China's determination, i.e. that China indeed wished to proceed in that manner and permit the Hong Kong, Macao and Taiwan regions to keep their original systems unchanged after they were re-unified with China, since doing so conformed with China's interests as a whole.

Thus this matter was already a topic of discussion in 1980 when China had started to discuss a revision to its 1978 Constitution, notwithstanding the fact that the Hong Kong issue was only just being resolved, that the Macao issue was not yet on the agenda, and that the discussion was focused at that time only on the Taiwan issue. During the 1982 constitutional revision, consideration was already being given to the need for consitutionalizing and further elaborating the "one country, two systems" thinking and on establishing special administrative regions. Hence, when the new Constitution of the People's Republic of China was ratified by the Fifth Session of the Fifth National Congress on December 4, 1982, the "one country, two systems" political proposition was formally written into the Constitution as a flexible and farsighted provision. On this matter, Peng Zhen, the then Vice-Chairman of the Committee for Revision of the Constitution stated: On the eve of the National Day celebrations last year, Comrade Ye Jianying, Chairman of the National People's Congress Standing Committee pointed out in a speech that Taiwan, after realizing peaceful unification, may enjoy a high degree of autonomy as a special administrative region. This autonomy includes keeping Taiwan's current social and economic systems unchanged, keeping its way of life unchanged, keeping its economic and cultural relations with other countries unchanged and so forth. In consideration of the needs of these special circumstances, the revised draft of the Constitution stipulates: "The State shall set up special administrative regions when necessary. The system implemented within a special administrative region shall be stipulated by law by the National People's Congress in accordance with the specific circumstances." We will never equivocate as regards the principles of upholding our country's sovereignty, unity and territorial integrity. At the same time, we can also be very flexible in terms of specific policies and measures and can give ample consideration to the present circumstances in the Taiwan locality and to the wishes of the people and personages in all quarters in Taiwan. This is our basic standpoint for handling problems of this type.[26]

This provided constitutional grounds for implementing "one country, two systems," setting up a Taiwan special administrative region and implementing systems and policies different from those on the mainland after the unification of the mainland and Taiwan. In those days, first consideration was given to resolving the Taiwan issue when the "one country, two systems" proposal was broached and written into the Constitution. However there is no question but that these Constitutional provisions were also applicable to the Hong Kong and Macao issues. Moreover, "one country, two systems" was in fact first implemented in Hong Kong and Macao.

Although the State's highest organ of power had responded to the new problems and challenges posed to China's Constitution by the broaching and implementation of "one country, two systems," as far as the text of the Constitution per se was concerned, the presence of that special provision—Article 31—did not suffice to fundamentally resolve all of the problems confronting China's Constitution. Moreover, Article 31 of the Constitution was prescribed at a time when the country's administrative divisions were being specified and only stated that China might be adding a new form of local governance. No provision was made for this in the country's basic policies, nor did the formulation "one country, two systems" appear in the Constitution. Hence, the constitutional protections for "one country, two systems" were neither ample nor sufficient. I maintain that this opinion should be taken in consideration in future when further revisions are made to the Constitution, and that "one country, two systems" be written into the Constitution so that the concept may obtain more ample expression in, and more substantial constitutional protections from, the Constitution.

Such are the constitutional grounds for setting up special administrative regions in China. Other than in the Constitution, there are also grounds for this in specific laws, i.e. the two SAR Basic Laws.

4.3.2 Legal Grounds for Setting up Special Administrative Regions

At present, initiatives to implement "one country, two systems" and set up a SAR in Taiwan have gone no further than the wording of Article 31 in the Constitution. However they have proceeded in real earnest in Hong Kong and Macao, where

---

[26]Peng Zhen. "Report on the Draft Amendment to the Constitution of the People's Republic of China," November 25, 1982.

these are no longer mere constitutional issues but require further legalization. On December 19, 1984, China and Britain, after grueling negotiations, signed the "The Joint Declaration of the Government of the United Kingdom of Great Britain and Northern Ireland and the Government of the People's Republic of China on the Question of Hong Kong" (Sino-British Joint Declaration). In Article 3 paragraph 1 of this statement, the Chinese government announced that "Upholding national unity national unity and territorial integrity taking account of the history of Hong Kong and its realities, the People's of China has decided to establish, in accordance with the provisions of Article 31 of the Constitution of the People's Republic of China, a Hong Kong Special Administrative Region upon resuming the exercise of sovereignty over Hong Kong." On April 13, 1987, in the "Joint declaration of the Government of the People's Republic of China and the Government of the Republic of Portugal on the question of Macao"(Sino-Portugal Joint Declaration), the Chinese government similarly announced, "the People's Republic of China will establish a Macao Special Administrative Region of the People's Republic of China upon resuming the exercise of sovereignty over Macao."

Accordingly, the 3rd Session of the Sixth National People's Congress decided on April 10, 1985 to set up a Hong Kong Special Administrative Region Basic Law Drafting Committee in order to formulate a basic law in the nature of a "constitution" for implementing "one country, two systems" and setting up the SAR. After drafting work that lasted nearly five years, the 3rd Session of the Seventh National People's Congress (NPC) approved the Basic Law of the Hong Kong Special Administrative of the People's Republic of China on April 4, 1990. This was the direct legal basis for establishing the Hong Kong Special Administrative Region. The NPC also passed the "Decision on Setting up the Hong Kong Special Administrative Region," which, among other things, stipulated that "the Hong Kong Special Administrative Region shall be set up starting on July 1, 1997," and also stipulated the areas under the Hong Kong SAR's jurisdiction would "include Hong Kong Island, the Kowloon Peninsula, and the islands and nearby maritime areas." A map of the administrative territories of the HK SAR was published separately by the State Council. These may be seen as an order issued by the highest organ of state power on setting up the Hong Kong Special Administrative Region. That meeting also approved other legal documents on setting up the Hong Kong SAR.

Due to the Hong Kong British government's repeated violations of the Joint Statement and its uncooperative attitude, the 1st Session of the Eighth NPC decided in March 1993 to accept a proposal by the delegation of Guangdong Province to set up the "Preliminary Working Committee of the Hong Kong Special Administrative Region Preparatory Committee" in order to start up initial work for establishing the SAR. Two years later, in December 1995, the Eighth NPC decided to formally establish the Hong Kong Special Administrative Region Preparatory Committee. On January 26, 1996 the establishment of the Hong Kong Special Administrative Region Preparatory Committee of the People's Republic of China was formally announced in Beijing and the work of preparing for the SAR henceforth went into full swing. On July 1, 1997 sovereignty over Hong Kong was restored to the Chinese Government and the Hong Kong SAR was formally set up the same day.

Subsequent to the signing of the Sino-Portuguese joint statement on the Macao issue, the Macao Special Administrative Region Basic Law Drafting Committee was formally established and began working on September 5, 1988. After more than four years of drafting, the 1st Session of the Eighth NPC formally ratified the People's Republic of China Macao Special Administrative Region Basic Law on March 31, 1993. This served as the "mini-constitution" of the Macao SAR. The same meeting also passed the Resolution on the Establishment of the Macao Special Administrative Region which stipulated that Macao would become a SAR after it was returned to China and that it would implement "one country, two systems, governance over Macao by Macanese, and a high degree of self-governance." The NPC Macao Special Administrative Region Preparatory Committee was established on May 5, 1998, and preparatory work on the SAR was formally launched. Pursuant to the provisions of the Sino-Portuguese Joint Statement, Macao was returned on schedule on December 20, 1999 and the Macao Special Administrative Region of the People's Republic of China was established on the same day.

The People's Republic of China Hong Kong Special Administrative Region Basic Law and the People's Republic of China Macao Special Administrative Region Basic Law were the concrete and legal manifestations of "one country, two systems" as well as the direct legal grounds for setting up the special administrative regions.

If the Taiwan issue is to be resolved in accordance with the "peaceful unification and one country, two systems" guiding principle, the eventual establishment of the Taiwan SAR will take place basically in line with the above procedure. Of course the Taiwan issue is unique in a good many ways, and the implementation of "one country, two systems" in Taiwan may also evince many new characteristics.

It is clear that the establishment in China of the Special Administrative Regions has been determined by the highest organs of state power, that the Basic Laws were formulated for the respective SARs in accordance with the "one country, two systems" concept and their specific circumstances, that preparatory work for the regions was conducted on the basis of these Basic Laws, and that the SARs were formally established when the conditions became ripe. First put forward in the late 1970s and early 1980s, and having undergone years of legal upgrading and elaboration, the "one country, two systems" guiding principle and policy has now entered the phase of formal implementation.

4.4   The Legal Status of the Special Administrative Regions

4.4.1   The Institution of China's Provincial-Level Governments

In Chap. 2 we have already explored the institution of China's current state structure. In accordance with the provisions of Article 30 and Article 31 of the Constitution,

China's present administrative areas basically fall into the four levels shown as follows:

The first level is the central government structure, i.e. China's national government, equivalent to the federal government under a federal system.

The second level consists of provincial-level localities, including 23 provinces, five regions of ethnic (aka national) autonomy, four municipalities directly under the central government, and two special administrative regions.

The third level consists of autonomous prefectures, counties, autonomous counties and municipalities set up under the provinces and autonomous regions.

The fourth level consists of townships, ethnic townships (乡) and small towns (镇) set up under counties and autonomous counties.

Also, districts and counties may be set up under the municipalities directly under the central government and relatively large municipalities. In places where districts and municipalities are combined, or municipalities have counties under their leadership, or relatively large municipalities are established, there are five levels of administration, i.e. the central government, provinces (autonomous regions), municipalities (relatively large ones), counties (autonomous counties and municipalities) and townships (ethnic townships and smaller towns). As differs from the local government setup in the early years of the People's Republic, today's provincial-level local government setup is less complex. See the following graph:

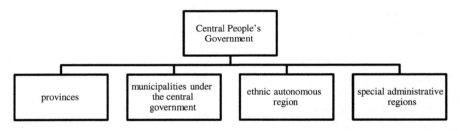

4.4.2 Basic Connotations of "Special Administrative Region"

In China's entire setup of administrative divisions, the special administrative region (SAR) falls in the category of a provincial administrative territory. It is a special provincial territory and a "special locality" different from the general run of provinces and directly administered municipalities as well as from the regions of ethnic [national] autonomy, and has a special legal status. The SAR is, of course, an organic component of China's unified multi-ethnic family as well as a level of government in China unitary government system just like all other localities. It may not exercise national sovereignty or separate itself from China to become an independent country. Its powers, delegated to it by the central government, are derived, not original powers. They are related to the central government as a local government is to a central government, not as a state government is related to a federal government under the federal system.

The main differences between a SAR and an ordinary locality in China (meaning a province, autonomous region or directly administered municipality)—i.e. the characteristics that make it "special"—are as follows:

One, the SAR practices capitalism whereas ordinary localities practice socialism. This is the most "special" characteristic of an SAR and the main reason for setting it up.

Two, the SAR enjoys a high degree of autonomy or self-determination. This self-determination is not only greater than that of ordinary local governments in China but in some respects also greater than that of state governments under a federal system.

Three, the relationship between a SAR and the central authorities must be clearly stipulated in written form.

Four, a SAR's administrative area may not be changed at will. It may not be increased or reduced, and is based on maps of the Hong Kong and Macao special administrative regions issued by the State Council. This is determined by the social systems practiced by the SARs and the ordinary administrative regions, and is a concrete manifestation of the "one country, two systems" principle, a mutual "hands-off" relationship where "neither tries to absorb the other."

Five, the establishment of the SARs and the systems they practice must be determined by the highest organ of state power, i.e. the National People's Congress; these may not determined by the State Council or by the NPC Standing Committee (Article 62 of the Constitution).

Six, there are two kinds of regional autonomy (self-government) in China. One of these is ethnic self-government (aka national autonomy), which is a system of local regional self-government set up mainly to resolve China's ethnic minority issues and ensure that ethnic minority peoples realize their rights of being "masters of their own house." The other kind is the regional administrative self-governance of special localities adopted mainly to bring about national reunification, and the purpose of which is to resolve the problem of getting socialism and capitalism to coexist in one unified country. A difference of substance exists between the two.

Seven, there are strong historical and motivational reasons behind the establishment of the special administrative regions, i.e. they are a sort of special local setup designed uniquely to re-unify Hong Kong, Macao and Taiwan with the Chinese mainland and ensure the prosperity and stability of these regions. Hence, the setting up of such SARs may not be extended at will to China's mainland regions. And differences of substance exist between these special administrative regions (SARs and the special economic zones (SEZs) on the mainland.

In sum, the SARs are local administrative areas unique to China, a new and special type of local setup established on the basis of different social systems.

4.4.3   The Legal Status of Special Administrative Regions

Article 1 and Article 2 of the SAR Basic Laws of both Hong Kong and Macao stipulate that these special administrative regions are inseparable components of the People's Republic of China, that they are highly self-governing local administrative areas within the People's Republic of China and directly under the jurisdiction of the central government. This clearly spells out the legal status of the special administrative regions. The SARs' legal status may be elucidated from three aspects:

First and foremost, the SARs are inseparable components of the unitary system of the unified Chinese state. This means that the SARs may not exercise state sovereignty, nor do they have any independent, self-determined right to break away from the state. This is determined by the structural form of China's unitary state system. Even the component states of a federal nation-state do not have such powers; if they did, the nation-state would cease to exist. Article 1, paragraph ten of the U.S. Constitution, for instance, stipulates that "no state may conclude any treaty or enter into any alliance or coalition... may not sign any agreement or treaty of alliance with another state or foreign country...," clearly indicating that the member states of the United States have no right to become independent. The American people, with gunfire and bloodshed, most emphatically responded to this question during the American Civil War and upheld the integrity of the U.S. Constitution.

Secondly, the special administrative regions are local administrative areas which enjoy a high degree of autonomy. This indicates that a SAR is both a special administrative region and a local government. In a state with a federal system, the term "relationship between the central government and the localities" generally refers to the relations of the central government of member states with the local governments under these states, i.e. city and county governments. They do not refer to the relations between the federal government and their member states, which in a certain sense may be seen as relations between nation-states.[27] In China, the relations of the central authorities with the SARs are certainly not "relations between states"; they are a special form of relationship of the central authorities in a unitary state with localities under those central authorities. No matter how large the powers of the SARs, they are nonetheless local governments, not member states under a federal government, and their legal status is substantially different.

Of all the various local administrative areas in China, the SARs have the largest powers, or in other words "the highest degree of self-determination." That is precisely

---

[27]Take, for example, the federal system of the United States. The relations between the federal government and state governments cannot be seen as what we generally understand as administrative subordination. One could even say there is no subordinate relationship between them, that their relationships are somewhat like those between nations, and that they are merely acting within the bounds set for them by their constitutions. When a federal government conducts itself within the bounds set by its constitution, every member state must defer to it and one might say that the federal government is supreme at this time. However, when the various state governments act within the bounds set for them by their own constitutions, these states are supreme and the federal government must respect the decisions of the state governments. We cannot declare simplistically that the American federal government is the supreme government of the United States.

the unique quality that sets them apart from the general run of localities. A detailed analysis of the power enjoyed by the SARs comes later in this book. However, regardless of the height of the "degree" of power they enjoy and the possibility of these powers being greater those wielded by states under a federal system, these powers are conferred on them by the National People's Congress—the country's highest organ of state power, and are not intrinsic to the SARs. That is a natural requirement of China's unitary state structure. That, however, does not mean China's highest organ of state power may randomly withdraw the powers or convert the SARs into ordinary local administrative areas, since these conferrals of power are fully backed by law and firmly and unshakably installed as basic national policy.

To sum up the above, it is quite evident that the SAR occupies a highly unique position among China's various types of local administrative areas and, where the central government is concerned, is the local administrative area that enjoys the greatest of powers.

Moreover, the SAR is under the direct jurisdiction of Central People's Government. This, too, is an important aspect of the SAR's legal status. We may understand this provision in China's Constitution and the SAR Basic Laws from three aspects. (a) It shows that the SARs are local governments at the provincial level, the highest level among local administrative entities. "Directly under the jurisdiction of the Central People's Government" does not mean that the Central People's Government can interfere at will in the SARs' internal affairs, it means that the SARs have direct access to the China's highest decision-making stratum, communicate with the highest state organs, and request that the central government directly handle relevant matters, thereby giving expression to the principles of national unity and sovereignty. (b) It shows that the SARs are independent of the provinces, autonomous regions, directly administered municipalities and the central ministries and commissions, that no local administrative entity or central ministry or commission may interfere in any matters that the SARs themselves manage according to law, and thereby fully ensure the SARs' right to a high degree of self-governance. It is evident that the SARs' "high-degree-of-autonomy" concept relates not only to the central government but also to the various departments of the central government and the provinces, autonomous regions and directly administered municipalities. (c) This provision also shows that the SARs may directly participate in the management of national affairs in their own name, i.e. that the SARs have the right to form delegations on their own to participate in the work of the NPC and its standing Committee and exercise all rights conferred by the Constitution.

The term "Central People's Government" as used here should be understood as the State Council. Since Article 85 of the Constitution stipulates that "the State Council of the People's Republic of China is the Central People's Government." The SARs should be directly subordinate to the State Council. However, the State Council, as China's highest administrative organ, is also the executive organ of China's highest organ of state power. Hence, while the SARs are directly subordinate to the State Council, they are of course also directly subordinate to the National People's Congress and its Standing Committee.

The relations between the central authorities and the SARs which we will be exploring here refer mainly to the SARs' relations with the following central organs of state power:

The SAR's relation with the National People's Congress and the NPC Standing Committee, or in other words, the SARs' relations with the highest organs of state power;

The SAR's relation with the head of state of the People's Republic of China, or in other words, the SAR's relation with the President of the PRC;

The SAR's relation with the State Council of the People's Republic of China, or in other words, the SAR's relation with highest organ of administrative power;

The SAR's relation with the Central Military Commission, or in other words, the SAR's relation with the highest national organ of military affairs; and

The SAR's relation with the Supreme People's Court and the Supreme People's Procuratorate, or in other words, the SAR's relation with the highest national judiciary and procuratorial organs.

"Relations between the central authorities and the SARs" refers to the SARs' relations with the central organs of state power enumerated above. The SARs have no power relationships with any other state organs.

In Chaps. 5 and 9, I will take the Hong Kong SAR and the Macao SAR as examples to specifically expound the SARs' relations with the central authorities. This will involve the SARs' relation with the various central organs of state power mentioned above. I shall in general use specific matters and incidents—rather than specific departments—as motifs for expounding the bilateral relations between the SARS and the above-mentioned organs of power.

4.5 The Effects of the Establishment of SARs on China's State Structure

It is evident from the nature and status of the special administrative regions that they are provincial-level local administrative regions in China which enjoy a high degree of autonomy. The establishment of these special administrative regions was bound to produce some effects on China's state structure. Chief among them was the further enrichment of the content of China's unitary state system, causing the latter to become more abundant and inclusive. Our previous understanding of the unitary system was overly one-sided in that we equated it with a high degree of centralization of powers. We believed that under a unitary system, the central authorities must concentrate and exercise as many powers as possible, that these not only include powers over foreign diplomacy, national defense, organization of local government, issuance of paper money, Customs, postal administration and so forth which should be under unified central administration by the central government, but also encompass and concentrate under centralized management a series of very specific economic, cultural and social matters. The result was a progressive swelling of the central government departments, of a situation described as "bigger central and smaller local" administration, and of the localities evolving into mere agencies of the central authorities and being left with hardly any self-governing rights. Even in regions of ethnic autonomy we placed excessive and inappropriate emphasis on "coordinating all moves as in a game of chess," and denied them the exercise of any independence or versatility. Already in the 1980s, Deng Xiaoping addressed the matter of excessive concentration of powers and proposed readjustments in the relations between the central and local authorities, devolution of powers, and more self-governance for the localities.[28]

In short, the previous understanding in China of the unitary system was that there could only be a single, homogenous system of local governance nationwide and only one kind of local government, though they might have different appellations. The proposal and implementation of "one country, two systems" and the setting up special administrative regions greatly changed our understanding of the unitary system. We know now that the unitary system does not have to be unvarying, that it may be quite rich in content and include many local systems [of administration]. The precise meaning of the term "unitary system" is that a country has only a single constitution and a single central state power, that the nation's internal and external sovereignty is unitary as are its matters pertaining to national defense, that original powers (原始权力) are retained by the central government, and that the legality of local powers is derived from central-government authorization. However, the relations between the central authorities and the localities may take many different forms, and local powers may vary considerably in extent. In China's case, apart from ordinary provinces in its unitary state system there exist a number of municipalities directly administered by the central government as well as districts of ethnic autonomy in regions where ethnic minorities live in compact communities. And now there are also [two] SARs directly under the jurisdiction of the central authorities and that enjoy a high degree of autonomy. The relations of all of them with the central authorities differ, and may indeed be quite different, but all are top-level locally-administered territories under China's unitary state structure. This disposition could be called a unitary state structure with Chinese characteristics.

The powers of the SARs are quite extensive and may even exceed those of member states of a federal state. But the establishment of the SARs has not changed the nature of China. China has not thereby become a federalist state; it is still a unitary state. Its overall state structure has not changed. It has merely developed and improved the theory and practice of the unitary state system, increased its inclusiveness and enriched its content. China's eventual state structure will quite likely consist of a total of 23 provinces, four directly administered municipalities, five regions of ethnic [national] autonomy and three SARs. The provinces, directly administered municipalities and autonomous regions will be ordinary localities whereas the SARs will be special localities. There will in addition be a number of economic zones and open coastal cities wielding extensive powers and that might be called "quasi-special regions." See following chart:

---

[28]Deng Xiaoping. "Reform of the Party and State Leadership System," carried in *Selected Works of Deng Xiaoping* (1975–1982). Beijing: People's Publishing House, 1983, pp. 280–302.

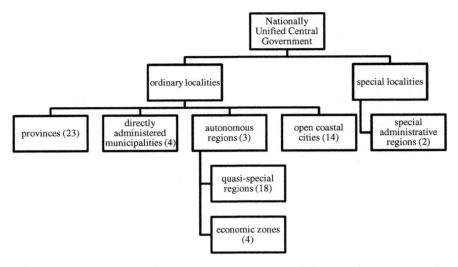

The emergence of the Special Administrative Region setup in China has also impacted the state structure theory in constitutional law, in that it has invalidated the previous method of dividing up the state structure according the extent of the powers wielded by central and local authorities. To wit, special local territories in a unitary state can also wield considerable powers of self-government, and vice versa. The scientific method is to divide up the state structure by such standards as the source of the powers, the nature of the powers, the attribution of "residual powers" and so forth. Discussions on this matter have appeared in other chapters and paragraphs and are not repeated here.

Chapter 5
The Basic Principles for Handling Relations Between the Central Authorities and the Special Administrative Regions

The setting up of the Hong Kong and Macao Special Administrative Regions vastly enriched the contents of China's state structure and its local systems and also raised a new topic for the studies of China's Constitutional Law, to wit, what is the correct way of handling the relations between the central authorities and the localities and especially those between the central authorities and provincial-level authorities?[1] Resolving that new topic called for a completely new way of thinking as well as for serious research using a new concept and a new method. The new concept and new method consisted of the "one country, two systems" put forward by Deng Xiaoping and of the Basic Law of the Special Administrative Region (SAR) formulated on the basis of "one country, two systems." The handling of the relations between the central authorities and the SAR, which included defining the power relationship between the two, had to be done according to the "one country, two systems" formulation and the provisions of the Basic Law; it had to respect history and actualities and proceed in a scientific and rational manner.

---

[1] The term "provincial-level localities" refers to provinces, autonomous regions, municipalities directly administered by the Central Government, and special administrative regions. "The general run of provincial-level localities" as used here refers only to the first three categories and does not include the special administrative regions.

© Foreign Language Teaching and Research Publishing Co., Ltd and Springer Nature Singapore Pte Ltd. 2019
Z. Wang, *Relationship Between the Chinese Central Authorities and Regional Governments of Hong Kong and Macao: A Legal Perspective*, China Academic Library, https://doi.org/10.1007/978-981-13-2322-5_5

5.1 The Nature and Characteristics of the Relation Between the Central Authorities and the Special Administrative Region

The relation between the Central Government and the Special Administrative Region [the Central/SAR relation] possesses both the common characteristics of relations between the central authorities and the localities as well as some special characteristics all of its own.[2]

First of all, the Central/SAR relation possesses the general characteristics of relations between the central authorities and the localities, since it deals with relations between the nation as a whole and its component parts and, in terms of Constitutional Law, has to do with a state's structural form. In China's case, since this country is a unitary state, and since the Central/SAR relation is a relation between the central authorities and the provincial-level localities, it faces first of all the issue of upholding national unity and territorial and sovereign integrity and safeguarding the unified authority of the state, as is also the case with the relations of the central authorities with all of China's provinces, directly administered municipalities and autonomous regions. As to the provinces, directly administered municipalities and autonomous regions, or the special administrative regions—neither may exercise state sovereignty, and all must defer to the Central Government when issues related to state sovereignty are involved. Although an eventual Taiwan Special Administrative Region would be able to retain its own armed forces, it would do so under the premise of not damaging national unity or territorial and sovereign integrity, and "permission to retain armed forces" per se would be authorized and approved by the central authorities. Of course, the issues of local rights of self-determination and of giving play to the localities' zeal and initiative will figure in all kinds of relations between the central authorities and provincial-level localities; they will differ only in magnitude. With the SARs, the issue is that of exercising a high degree of autonomy, whereas with the general run of provincial-level localities the issue is one of the local rights of self-determination. But it is evident that since the SARs are also a kind of provincial-level local administrative region, they share common characteristics with the relations between the central authorities and ordinary provincial-level localities.

However, as compared to the relations between the central authorities and the general run of provincial-level local administrative localities, the Central/SAR relation possesses its own peculiarities and may not indiscriminately copy the methods used for handling the relations between the central authorities and the general run of provincial-level localities; the methods have to comply with the special characteristics of the Central/SAR relation. These special characteristics are manifested in the following aspects:

---

[2]The term "relations between the central authorities and the localities," unless otherwise annotated, refers here only to the relations between the Central Government and provincial-level localities; it does not refer either to the relations between the Central Government and counties, cities or townships, or to the relations between provincial-level governments and counties, cities, or townships.

One, as regards its social character, the Central/SAR relation is one of the forms of relation between socialism and capitalism. As Deng Xiaoping pointed out, "We are pursuing a policy of 'one country, two systems'. More specifically, this means that within the People's Republic of China, the mainland with its one billion people will maintain the socialist system, while Hong Kong and Taiwan continue under the capitalist system."[3] It is clear that the Central/SAR relation also constitutes a relation between socialism and capitalism. For a good many years, China had, under the influence of ultra-Left ideology, consistently believed that socialism could immediately replace capitalism and be practiced worldwide, that socialism and capitalism could not coexist in one country nor could it coexist for any length of time in the world as a whole. Hence, capitalism should be replaced with socialism as soon as possible. After the "Gang of Four" was smashed and with the restitution of Marxism's practical and realistic ways of thinking, China recognized that the ultimate replacement of capitalism by socialism would require a fairly long historical process, and that during this fairly long period of time, socialism would have to coexist peacefully and engage in equal competition with capitalism.[4] This change in China's comprehension of the interrelation between socialism and capitalism emerged precisely at a time when the question of China's reunification was once again raised for discussion. This resulted in a major change in China's ideas about national reunification. China no longer stood for promoting the socialist system nationwide by means of armed force, nor did it insist that the country be united under socialism. And of course, China could not consent to reunifying the country by means of the Three People's Principles or capitalism. Instead, it advocated having the mainland continue implementing socialism and allowing Hong Kong, Macao, and Taiwan to continue exercising capitalism as before—all under the big banner of national reunification. The mainland's socialism would not be applied to swallowing up Hong Kong's, Macao's, or Taiwan's capitalisms, nor could the capitalisms of Hong Kong, Macao, and Taiwan engulf the mainland's socialism. In this regard, Deng Xiaoping explicitly stated China will stick to the Four Basic Principles but will not do so in Hong Kong.[5]

And so, after Hong Kong and Macao returned to China, they should retain the capitalist policies and institutions they had been pursuing. Their economic systems would still pertain to the international capitalist system, and only in terms of political sovereignty would they belong to socialist China. This has already been substantiated in practice after their return to China. It is in this sense that we say the relations between the Central Government and the special administrative regions are relations between capitalism and socialism. The special administrative regions must respect the political sovereignty exercised by the socialist China, while socialist China must also respect the objective realities of the SARs which practice capitalism, and accordingly handle its mutual relations with them in a practical and realistic manner. This situation

---

[3] *Deng Xiaoping on the Hong Kong Issue.* Hong Kong: Joint Publishing (Hong Kong) Company, Ltd., 1993, p. 5.

[4] *Deng Xiaoping on the Reunification of the Motherland.* Beijing: Unity Press, 1995, pp. 19, 24, 36, 41 and 42.

[5] *People's Daily*, April 22, 1986.

does not exist in the relations between the Central Government and the general run of provincial localities in Chinese mainland.

Two, a strong historicism exists in the relations between the central authorities and the special administrative regions, and ample attention should be paid to the SARs' histories and current realities. One might well say that the policy of setting special administrative regions in Hong Kong, Macao, and Taiwan has been generated for historical reasons. Hong Kong had been excised by and "leased" to Britain for almost one and a half centuries, and Macao was occupied by Portugal for more than four hundred years. Taiwan was taken over by Japan from 1895 to 1945, and has then been held by the Kuomintang clique right up to this day.[6] It is against these special historical backgrounds that the three regions merged into the economic system of world capitalism. To bring about the reunification of these special localities with the Chinese mainland, a unique local organizational system had to be set up, since those localities could not be handled in the same manner as the ordinary mainland localities. The objectives of doing so were two: bringing about national reunification and maintaining sustained prosperity and stability in these regions. It is evident that the Central/SAR relations are quite out of the ordinary. The principles and methods used for handling relations between the central authorities and ordinary provincial-level localities cannot be copied indiscriminately, nor can the principles and methods for handling Central/SAR relations be brought to the mainland to handle the relations between the central authorities and ordinary provincial localities. As discussed earlier in Chap. 4, the SARs' setups were established for a very specific purpose; they were special local setups established expressly for the purpose resolving an issue left over from history—the reunification of China—and for bringing Hong Kong, Macao, and Taiwan back to the mainland. The administrative divisions or scopes of application of the SARs cannot be indiscriminately extended, and the histories and realities of these regions have to be given consideration when handling Central/SAR relations.

Three, once the Central/SAR relations were defined, they have had to be legalized, invested with solid content, and institutionalized so that they acquire a high degree of stability, continuity, and feasibility. China had previously neglected the principle of rule of law when handling the relations between the Central Government and the ordinary provincial-level localities. Either there were no laws to act upon, or existing laws were disregarded, or law enforcement was too lax. When handling Central/SAR relations, the "one country, two systems" principle has to be given a legal basis; laws should not be enacted or annulled or changed according to the will of any single individual, that is, a must for maintaining the prosperity and stability of the SARs. Deng Xiaoping had expounded on this matter on many occasions.[7] The formulation of the two SAR Basic Laws was conducted expressly for institutionalizing and legalizing the "one county two systems" program and policies and the relations between the

---

[6]The Kuomintang lost "the Nationalist China presidential elections" held in Taiwan in the year 2000, and the Democratic Progressive Party of Taiwan took over the reins of power. The Kuomintang thereby lost its political power in Taiwan, and substantial changes have taken place in Taiwan's political landscape.

[7]*Deng Xiaoping on the Reunification of the Motherland*, Beijing, Unity Press, 1995.

central authorities and the special administrative regions so that these relations will possess a high degree of stability and continuity, will not undergo changes following changes in leadership personnel, nor be altered as a result of changes in the views of leading persons or in their focuses of attention.

5.2 Basic Principles for Handling Central/SAR Relations

Given the abovementioned characteristics of Central/SAR relations, when handling such relations, the foremost principle both parties should adhere to is the "one country, two systems" principle. This principle is the basic plan and policy China uses to deal with issues related to Hong Kong, Macao, and Taiwan as well as the basic guiding ideology for handling Central/SAR relations. It is therefore necessary to genuinely understand the basic content and spirit of "one country, two systems" and to grasp its scientific connotations if one is to use it correctly to handle Central/SAR relations. In Chap. 3, I have already comprehensively explored the background to the formation of "one country, two systems," its basic contents, and its essence. I will now attempt to go into concrete details and explore some of the basic principles to be observed with handling Central/SAR relations.

5.2.1 The "One Country, Two Systems" Principle

5.2.1.1 The "One Country" Principle

The first thing to be emphasized about "one country, two systems" is the safeguarding of the country's unity and territorial sovereignty and integrity. Put simply, that means there must first of all be "one country." This principle requires that when handling Central/SAR relations, one must first of all assign importance to safeguarding the country's unity and the integrity of the country's territory and sovereignty, that is, the fundamental requirement of "one country." Conversely, if one were to place sole emphasis on the "special nature" of the special administrative regions, merely emphasize "two systems" and neglect or even brush aside "one country," one would surely damage the country's sovereignty and the integrity of its territory when handling Central/SAR relations, the "one country, two systems" exercise would fail, any talk of restoring China's exercise of sovereignty over Hong Kong and Macao would be no more than empty verbiage, and little if any significance would remain in setting up the special administrative regions. One might well say that safeguarding national unity and the integrity of the country's territory and sovereignty is the one and only requirement of the "one country" principle. There will be no "one country" if this requirement cannot be realized. And "two systems" will also fall through without the backing of "one country."

Judging from the provisions of both Basic Laws, all matters related to the central authorities' powers and their regulatory responsibilities are strictly limited within the scope absolutely needed for manifesting state sovereignty and unity,[8] The Basic Laws do not assign to the central authorities unnecessary powers except for those absolutely needed for manifesting state sovereignty and unity. The latter include Article 23 of the Basic Law which requires that the Hong Kong SAR enact laws on its own to prohibit any act of treason, secession, sedition, and subversion against the Central People's Government, as these are necessary for safeguarding the country's unity and sovereignty.

5.2.1.2 The Principle of Respect for the Current Actualities of History and Maintaining the Prosperity and Stability of the Special Administrative Regions

This principle may be summarized as the "two systems" principle. When handling Central/SAR relations, China's unity and sovereignty has to be upheld while close attention must also be given to preventing damage to these regions' sustained prosperity and stability. If, after China's sovereignty over Hong Kong and Macao were restored and the SARs had been set up, Hong Kong and Macao no longer prospered, their societies went into turmoil, their economies slumped, and their people felt insecure, China would have failed to properly implement the basic national policy of "one country, two systems." Safeguarding state unity and sovereignty and safeguarding the SARs' prosperity and stability are two major and indivisible aspects of "one country, two systems," neither of which may be dispensed with.

Hence, when handling Central/SAR relations, full respect must be shown for the histories and actualities of these regions, full respect must be shown for all of the autonomous powers enjoyed by the SARs as stipulated in the Basic Laws, and no department or local authority may intervene in the SARs' internal affairs except as stipulated in the Basic Laws. This has enabled the Hong Kong and Macao regions to achieve greater prosperity and stability after returning to China, and ought to be regarded as a major principle.

5.2.1.3 The Relationship Between "One Country" and "Two Systems."

The relationship between "one country" and "two systems" is one of interdependence. If one went only for "two systems" and not for "one country," we would get is "two countries" instead of "one country, two systems," and this would be very risky. Similarly, if one went only for "one country," did not go for "two systems" and

---

[8]Wang Fengchao. "On the Relations between the Central Government and the Hong Kong Special Administrative Region," carried by the *Hong Kong Wen Wei Po*, 1995-04-05. Also see Ji Pengfei. "Explanations on the Basic Law of the Hong Kong Special Administrative Region of the People's Republic of China (Draft) and Other Related Documents," 3rd Session of the Seventh National People's Congress, 1990-03-28.

handled all matters in the way they are handled in the interior regions, what would ensue is "one country one system," which would also run counter to "one country, two systems" and also be quite hazardous. Hence, neither "one country" nor "two systems" may be overemphasized at the expense of the other. True, the emphasis in both Hong Kong and Macao differed before and after the regions' return to China. And if becoming "one country" had been difficult prior to the regions' return to China, bringing about "two systems" called for special efforts after their return, because the two sides concerned were, after all, existing within "one country" after the respective returns of Hong Kong and Macao to China—that could not be changed!—and the "two systems" in them could willy-nilly draw closer to each other. Both parties concerned had to put extra care and effort into maintaining the "two systems."

According to the "one country, two systems" requirement, both the Central Government and the SARs have to respect and cooperate and refrain from interfering with each other. Each side has to respect the other side's exercise of its statutory powers, and when one side exercises powers assigned to it by a Basic Law, the other side must give it due cooperation and assistance. The Central Government, for example, requires cooperation and assistance from the SARs when it exercises its diplomatic and national defense powers; similarly, the SARs need the Central Government's respect and support when they implement their highly autonomous powers.

As for mutual noninterference, this means that both sides, in the implementation of their powers, shall strictly restrict their implementation to the scope of their statutory powers, shall refrain from interfering in the other side's statutory powers, and refrain from mutual interference in the other side's handling of its own statutory affairs. The Central Government must not interfere in the SARs' handling of local issues as stipulated by the Basic Laws, nor should the SARs interfere in the Central Government's handling of its own affairs. This means—as the Chinese saying goes—that "well water must not encroach upon river waters," nor should river waters intrude upon well waters. The people of Hong Kong have no desire to see the Central Government interfere in their SAR's local affairs, and are fearful lest the interior regions' socialism "erodes" Hong Kong's capitalism and lest the interior regions extend their ways of doing things to Hong Kong. Actually, the interior regions' decision-makers also fear that, subsequent to Hong Kong's return to the mainland, the latter's capitalism will undermine and impact the interior regions' socialism. Hence, they too hope that Hong Kong will not interfere in the interior regions' affairs after it returns to China or that it will intrude its system in the mainland. "The spreading of mainland-type democracy ought to depend on the mainland people's own achievements, and not on externally imposed 'Savior-ism,' as that would only damage the interests of Hong Kong and its people."[9] That is why the "one country, two systems" concept was devised. It is clear that the precise implication of "one country, two systems" is to have "two systems" which are mutually non-interfering; it means that the interior regions will not interfere in the SAR's internal affairs nor will the SARs interfere in mainland affairs; and it means that the mainland's socialism and the

---

[9]Huang Wenfang. "Hong Kong Will Be Better After 1997," carried by the Hong Kong *Ming Pao*, January 1, 1997.

SARs' capitalism will coexist in peace within one country and not interfere with or influence one another.

5.2.2   The Principles of "Hong Kongers Govern Hong Kong," "Macaoans Govern Macao," and a "High Degree of Autonomy"

The implementation of "one country, two systems" also requires the simultaneous implementation in Hong Kong of the principles articulated as "Hong Kongers govern Hong Kong" and "a high degree of autonomy." "One country, two systems" is the foundation; "Hong Kongers govern Hong Kong" and "a high degree of autonomy" are the natural and logical extensions of that foundation.

As long as "one country, two systems" remains unchanged, "high degree of autonomy" and "Hong Kong people govern Hong Kong" will also remain unchanged.

The reason is quite simple. In the early 1980s, the people of Hong Kong very much doubted that the Chinese Communists who embraced communism and socialism could do a proper job of administering a Hong Kong which practices capitalism, and especially since memories of the "ten catastrophic years" [of the Cultural Revolution] have remained fresh in their minds. They feared that the Chinese communists would enforce the ways of the mainland when they would administer Hong Kong and make big mess of things. Their unequivocal opinion was that Hong Kong should not be managed by people from the mainland—an opinion which from the very outset excluded the possibility of the Central Government sending people to manage Hong Kong following the region's return to China. Most wanted "one country," yet also wanted "two systems" and wished to prevent the mainland from administering local SAR affairs. And so, since the British would be gone after Hong Kong's return and would no longer govern Hong Kong's affairs, and since China's Central Government would not be taking charge of Hong Kong's local matters, who should administer those local affairs in Hong Kong?

There was only one solution, i.e., that Hong Kongers themselves take charge of Hong Kong, or in other words, implement "administration of Hong Kong by the people of Hong Kong." Differences of opinion existed on this matter among the populace and within the decision-making stratum, and the Hong Kongers themselves lacked confidence in their ability to properly administer Hong Kong. Under British rule, local Hong Kongers had seldom taken part in decision-making. Moreover, Hong Kong had been rigidly stratified in those days, and local Chinese had no access to the British authorities' highest decision-making level, nor did they know how the British had exercised their rule. Hong Kong had been entirely lacking in democratic transparency. For example, over many years only the governor and chief secretary of Hong Kong as well as the financial secretary and his number two man were informed of the circumstances of Hong Kong's exchange funds. No one else knew. Prior to 1968, Hong Kong's foreign exchange moneys were kept in England, and

Hong Kong lost one-third of its foreign exchange reserves when the British pound sterling suffered a crisis that year. Yet no one in Hong Kong was aware of that.[10] Due, therefore, to the Hong Kongers' lack of political experience, a good many of them in fact opposed "administration of Hong Kong by the people of Hong Kong." If "one country, two systems" and "Hong Kong people govern Hong Kong" were to be implemented, one had first of all to instill confidence in the Hong Kongers that they themselves were able to make decisions and do a good job of administering Hong Kong—and do an even better job than the British had done.

Huang Wenfang, the former deputy secretary-general of the Hong Kong Branch of the Xinhua News Agency who took part in formulating this policy of China's, stated: Getting Hong Kong's people to govern Hong Kong shows that the Central Government fully trusts the Hong Kongers' ability to properly administer Hong Kong. This was a very, very bold concept on the part of the Communist Party. The leaders who put forward this way of thinking could not have done so if they did not possess great daring.[11] It is evident that the Central Government was confident in and fully trusted our Hong Kong compatriots.

Not only would "Hong Kong people govern Hong Kong"; the Central Government would not be allowed to interfere, nor could it gratuitously find fault with or interfere in the Hong Kongers' administration. Whether good or bad, Hong Kong's administration was the Hong Konger's responsibility. Some people maintained that if Hong Kong's administration happened to fail after the region returned to China, such failure was bound to be the outcome of mainland interference. This gave rise to the "high degree of autonomy" proposal. Since it was determined that Hong Kongers should manage Hong Kong, all powers of governance should be wholly relinquished, and full trust should be placed in China's compatriots in Hong Kong and in their intelligence and abilities. And no matter how Hong Kong "messed things up," anything would do so long it did not seek independence, did not flout the Central Government's authority, and complied strictly with the Basic Law. Of course, "high degree of autonomy" did not mean independence or complete dissociation from the Central Government. The Central Government would still be in charge of matters related to foreign diplomacy, national defense, and state sovereignty. The British had wanted to write in "the highest degree of autonomy," but China had not consented, maintaining that doing so would mean a complete breakaway from the Central Government.[12] As long as foreign relation and national defense remained unified under China, powers over any other matters could be boldly ceded to Hong Kong, allowing it to genuinely enjoy a high degree of autonomy. Giving Hong Kong a higher degree of autonomy also means giving the Chinese in Hong Kong a chance to display their abilities. How would one know they were competent or otherwise if they were not given any powers of autonomy or any opportunities to do so? Hong Kong will not have to turn in a

---

[10] Huang Wenfang, "The Historical Course and Implementation of China's Policy Decision to Restore the Exercise of Sovereignty over Hong Kong," Hong Kong: Hong Kong Baptist University, 1997, pp. 38–40.

[11] Ibid., pp. 38–40.

[12] Ibid., p. 61.

single cent to the national treasury, nor will it be required to bear the costs of maintaining garrison forces. So it may well be said the Central Government will derive no direct financial profits or benefits from Hong Kong. How well or poorly Hong Kong is administered will be the Hong Kong people's own business, and they themselves will bear the consequences. That is also in keeping with the legal principle of he who exercises powers should bear the responsibilities and shoulder all consequences.

"High degree of autonomy" is built on the foundation of a high degree of trust. As the saying goes "Do not use people you distrust, and do not distrust the people you use." The Central Government has to fully trust the people of Hong Kong and, as stipulated by the Basic Law, powers that are to be exercised by the special administrative region should be one hundred percent exercised by the special administrative region. The special administrative region per se also has to demonstrate to the central authorities that it is fully trustworthy and capable. Hence, the concepts "Hong Kong people govern Hong Kong" and "high degree of autonomy" are based on a high degree of trust, without which the "high degree of autonomy" will be open to question, that is, a bilateral issue. It is not a unilateral issue, either for the special administrative region or for the Central Government.

In this way, the policy articulated as "Hong Kong people govern Hong Kong and a high degree of autonomy" took shape on the premise of "one country with two systems." There would not have been "Hong Kong people govern Hong Kong" or "a high degree of autonomy" without the "one country, two systems" concept or without full confidence on the part of the Central Government or its trust in the people of Hong Kong. Conversely, there would not have been "Hong Kong people govern Hong Kong" or ultimately "one country, two systems" had there not been that "high degree of autonomy." Hence, "one country, two systems," "Hong Kong people govern Hong Kong," and "high degree of autonomy" are reciprocally linked as an organic whole. The same applies to the three statements regarding Macao—i.e., "one country, two systems," "Macao people govern Macao," and "high degree of autonomy."[13]

Four qualifications or connotations are generally ascribed to that "high degree of autonomy." One, absence of intervention from the Central Government; the Central Government is not to intervene in matters which according to the Basic Laws fall within the scope of SAR self-governance. Two, the decisions made by the SAR governments are final, and the SAR governments are empowered to make final decisions on matters pertaining to powers of autonomy so long as these decisions fall within the scope stipulated by the Basic Laws, and they need not submit such decisions to the Central Government for approval. Three, the SARs possess ample discretionary powers when making major policy decisions, and are empowered, within statutory limits, to freely choose policy decisions which they deem to be logical and reasonable. And, four, the SAR governments have the right, when exercising their statutory functions and duties within the limits stipulated by the Basic Laws, to choose the means and methods they consider appropriate for exercising these functions and duties.

---

[13]In some documents and theses, "high degree of autonomy" is placed before "Hong Kongers govern Hong Kong" and "Macaoans govern Macao." I maintain the connotations are substantially the same and there is no substantial difference due to the order of precedence used in my writings.

5.2.2.1 The Principle of Rule of Law

Since Central/SAR relations are to possess a high degree of stability and continuity, the handling of these relations must adhere strictly to the principle of rule of law so that the regulations may be legalized and institutionalized, so that there may be laws and regulations to go by in all matters, and so that laws and regulations are strictly observed. As discussed earlier, China was previously not much in the habit of legalizing the relations between the central and local governments. Frequent and random changes were made according to the whim or will of those in authority. We must not let such things happen in the handling of Central/SAR relations and must strictly abide by the principle of rule of law.

The chief requirements of the rule-of-law principle are as follows:

First, matters should be handled strictly according to the Basic Laws. The SAR Basic Laws are national basic laws formulated by the National People's Congress on the basis of Article 31 of the Constitution and the "one country, two systems" policy; it is "one country, two systems" presented in the form of law and in the form of the "Basic Law" of the SARs. It stipulates the nature and legal status of the SARs, the relation between the Central Government and the SARs, the basic rights and duties of the SARs' residents, the SARs' political and economic structures, their social systems in terms of education, science and religion, and diplomatic affairs. The Basic Laws are the SAR "mini-constitutions," and as such constitute the basic criterion for handling Central/SAR relations and must be strictly complied with and implemented. When handling Central/SAR relations, matters must be conducted in accordance with the Basic Laws where express provisions exist in those Basic Laws. If such express provisions are not to be found in the Basic Laws, or where matters are eventually found in actual implementation for which the Basic Law provisions are insufficiently explicit, such matters shall also be handled in accordance with the principles and spirit of "one country, two systems" and the Basic Laws, specific laws shall be formulated as soon as possible and, after these are formulated, matters shall be handled strictly according to law. In sum, the foremost requirement of rule of law is that the various Central/SAR relations and the Central/SAR division of powers be legalized and institutionalized and formulated into laws by the nation's highest institutions of power, that these laws be vested with a high degree of authority and not be susceptible to personal intervention, and will thereby acquire stability and continuity. The Basic Laws are the most important of these laws, for which reason first importance must be given to strict adherence to and implementation of the SAR Basic Laws.

The second requirement of the rule-of-law principle is that the Central Government must keep the powers exercised by the SARs strictly within the bounds of legal provisions, or in other words, keep them within the limits needed for upholding national sovereignty and unity. At the same time, the SARs should have no qualms about exercising all powers vested in them by the Basic Laws. The SARs' powers are conferred on them by the Central Government, but that does not mean the central authorities may revoke such conferrals at will. These conferrals come with ample legal safeguards, and both the central authorities and the SARs must handle matters strictly according to law.

The third requirement of the rule-of-law principle has to do with the laws—including the SAR Basic Laws—on Central/SAR relations. The procedures for making amendments to them must be very strict and amendments should not be conducted at will. Making it difficult to add a law to the Constitution—and thereby complicating amendment procedure—is meant expressly to increase the rigor of the said law, to give it stability and greater authority. One might say this is intended to raise the law's "intimidating" effect and to prevent it from being trivialized by would-be amenders. If laws could be amended at will, "the laws" per se would forfeit their intrinsic nature. Precisely for that reason, the SAR Basic Laws have stipulated strict amendment procedures for themselves. For instance, the Article 159 of the Basic Law of the Hong Kong Special Administrative Region stipulates:

> The power to propose bills for amendments to this Law shall be vested in the Standing Committee of the National People's Congress, State Council and the Hong Kong Special Administrative Region. Amendment bills from the Hong Kong Special Administrative Region shall be submitted to the National People's Congress by the delegation of the Region to the National People's Congress after obtaining the consent of two-thirds of the deputies of the Region to the National People's Congress, two-thirds of all the members of the Legislative Council of the Region, and the Chief Executive of the Region. Before a bill for amendment to this Law is put on the agenda of the National People's Congress, the Committee for the Basic Law of the Hong Kong Special Administrative Region shall study it and submit its views.

The same stipulation was made in the Basic Law of Macao.

Not only are the Basic Laws' amendment procedures very strict; also very strict are the procedures for examining and approving amendments to the Basic Laws since these Basic Laws fall in the category of "basic laws" stipulated by the Constitution. In other words, they have to be examined and approved by the National People's Congress; neither the NPC Standing Committee nor any other organ is empowered to amend the Basic Laws. Moreover, an amendment bill must first be studied by the SAR Basic Law Committee under the NPC Standing Committee before it can be placed on the agenda of the National People's Congress. And after the bill is placed on the agenda, it must also undergo ample study by the National People's Congress and approved by more than half of all the deputies before any amendment may be made to a Basic Law.

Even then, it cannot be said that the contents of a Basic Law may be amended at will. The final paragraph of Article 159 of the Basic Law of Hong Kong stipulates: "No amendment to this Law shall contravene the established basic policies of the People's Republic of China." The same provision exists in the Basic Law of Macao. These provisions forbidding amendments are stipulated by the Basic Laws per se, which is to say that no amendment of a Basic Law may contravene the principles or spirit of the Basic Laws. And so, what are the principles and spirit of the Basic Laws? These are "one country, two systems," "Hong Kongers govern Hong Kong," "Macaoans govern Macao," and "a high degree of autonomy." That is to say, no matter how a Basic Law is amended in the future, no changes may be made to these basic principles or this basic spirit, otherwise any amendment shall be null and void.

In order to further boost the authoritativeness of the SAR Basic Laws, the amendment bill modality rather than the "injurious" and "subversive" overall amendment modality is to be adopted when it becomes necessary to amend the Basic Laws, as this may help to permanently preserve the spirit and essence of the Basic Laws. The use of amendment bills could ensure that the basic principles established in the Basic Laws are not violated, and would give the Laws greater stability and continuity.

The fourth requirement of the rule-of-law principle is that, with the exception of laws involving the nation's unity and the integrity of the nation's sovereignty and territory, none of China's nationwide laws shall be implemented in the SARs, that is, a requirement of the "one country, two systems" concept. The mainland's criminal, civil, administrative, and economic laws and regulations, including those on the country political structure, are all socialist in nature and, due to the requirements of "one country, two systems," are not to be implemented in the SARs which exercise capitalism. Moreover, the Hong Kong SAR still pertains to the Anglo-American Common Law system, the legal language of which is mainly English, whereas the Chinese mainland used to belong to the Continental Law legal system, and although it now pertains to the socialist legal system, its legal system still retains the basic characteristics of the Continental Law legal system and therefore cannot be practiced in Hong Kong. As for Macao and Taiwan, although both pertain to the Continental Law legal system, the basic characteristics of their legal systems are also capitalist, and for that reason the mainland's laws cannot be practiced in Macao or Taiwan.

Even though the nationwide laws involving national sovereignty, unity and territorial integrity need to be implemented in the SARs, this must be done in an explicit and unambiguous way, as problems might be caused in actual practice if it is decreed in vague and general terms that laws of this kind are to be exercised in the SARs. Annex III of the Hong Kong Basic Law explicitly lists six nationwide laws which are to be implemented in the SAR[14] As to the way these are to be implemented, Article 18 of the Basic Law stipulates they "shall be applied locally by way of promulgation or legislation by the Region" and not promulgated directly by the Central Government, as a mark of respect for the SAR's high degree of autonomy.

If it should become necessary to add nationwide laws to those listed in Annex III for implementation in the SAR, these should also "be confined to those relating to defense and foreign affairs as well as other matters outside the limits of the autonomy of Region as specified by this Law."[15] And the National People's Congress Standing Committee should first of all solicit the opinions of the SAR Basic Law

---

[14]These six laws are: (1) Resolution on the Capital, Calendar, National Anthem and National Flag of the People's Republic of China; (2) Resolution on the National Day of the People's Republic of China; (3) Order on the National Emblem of the People's Republic of China Proclaimed by the Central People's Government (Attached: Design of the national emblem, notes of explanation and instructions for use); (4) Declaration of the Government of the People's Republic of China on the Territorial Sea; (5) Nationality Law of the People's Republic of China; (6) Regulations of the People's Republic of China Concerning Diplomatic Privileges and Immunities.

[15]Paragraph 3 of Article 18 of the Hong Kong Basic Law.

Committee under it as well as of the SAR government; laws cannot be added at will. Because China's highest legislative organ formulated a number of laws which involved national sovereignty, national defense and foreign diplomacy in the seven years from the ratification of the Basic Law in 1990 to the return of Hong Kong in 1997, the 26th meeting of the Standing Committee of the Eight National People's Congress therefore passed a resolution on July 1, 1997 adding nationwide laws to those listed in Annex III of the Hong Kong Special Administrative Region Basic Law. A total of five new nationwide laws were added, i.e., the Law of the People's Republic of China on the National Flag, the Regulations of the People's Republic of China Concerning Diplomatic Privileges and Immunities, the Law of the People's Republic Of China on the National Emblem, the Law of the People's Republic of China on Territorial Seas and Contiguous Zones, and the Law of the People's Republic of China on Garrisoning the Hong Kong Special Administrative Region. At the same time, implementation of the Order on the National Emblem of the People's Republic of China Proclaimed by the Central People's Government as well as the attachments on the design of the national emblem, the notes of explanation and the instructions for use were discontinued due to the enactment of the National Emblem Law. On June 26, 1998, the NPC Standing Committee passed the Law on the Exclusive Economic Zone and the Continental Shelf of the People's Republic of China, which evidently was also a nationwide law which involved China's territory, national defense, foreign diplomacy and sovereignty, and the NPC Standing Committee therefore determined on November 4, 1998 that this law also applied to the Hong Kong SAR. It is clear that all of these newly added laws of a nationwide character concern China's sovereignty, national defense, and foreign relations, and do not constitute any threat to or in any way affect the Hong Kong SAR's rule of law.

As for the Macao SAR, Annex III of its Basic Law stipulates eight national laws which are to be implemented in that SAR, i.e., the Resolution on the Capital, Calendar, National Anthem and National Flag of the People's Republic of China, the Resolution on the National Day of the People's Republic of China, the Nationality Law of the People's Republic of China, the Regulations of the People's Republic of China Concerning Diplomatic Privileges and Immunities, the Law of the People's Republic of China on the National Flag, The Law of the People's Republic of China on the National Emblem, and the Law of the People's Republic of China on Territorial Seas and Contiguous Zones. When Macao returned to China on December 20, 1999, the 13th Meeting of the Ninth National People's Congress Standing Committee added two laws—the Law on the Exclusive Economic Zone and the Continental Shelf of the People's Republic of China and the Law of the People's Republic of China on Garrisoning the Hong Kong Special Administrative Region—for implementation by the Macao SAR. These ten laws all concern China's sovereignty, national defense, and foreign relations, and the SAR is responsible for implementing them locally by proclaiming them or by exercising legislative means.

Article 18 of both Basic Laws also stipulate that in the event the NPC Standing Committee decides to declare the country is in a state of war, or decides, by reason of turmoil within the Special Administrative Region which endangers national unity or security and is beyond the control of the government of the Region, that the Region is in a state of emergency, the Central People's Government may issue an order applying the relevant national laws in the Region. This is necessary for safeguarding national unity and territorial and sovereign integrity, and is an emergency measure taken in emergency circumstances. Of course, even in those two circumstances, the laws exercised in the SARs may only be those that are "relevant," and not all of them. And when the state of war or the state of emergency comes to an end, the SARs' legal procedures shall revert to their original state.

The last issue that involves the rule-of-law principle is whether the Constitution of the People's Republic of China applies to the SARs. This matter has already been discussed in the Chap. 4 and there is no need to go into further detail here.

The three principles presented above should be complied with when handling Central/SAR relations. They are mutually complementary and indispensable. Safeguarding China's national unity and territorial integrity and safeguarding the SARs' prosperity and stability must be organically integrated with respect for the SARs' high degree of autonomy and refraining from exercising socialism in the SARs; neither of these aspects may be emphasized at the expense of the other. And when handling all matters this type, one must strictly proceed according to law and defer to the requirements of rule of law.

5.2.3 The Main Factors that Affect Central/SAR Relationships

To correctly handle Central/SAR relations, one must gain a clear idea of some of the main factors that affect Central/SAR relations, the better to proactively promote the growth of positive factors and hold the negative and undesirable factors in check and to bring about a healthy and benign development of Central/SAR relations.

5.2.4 The Course of China's Own Reform and Opening up

In Chap. 3, we have already discussed in detail the historical background that gave rise to "one country, two systems" and can see that the "one country, two systems" implemented with regard to the issue of China's reunification is an important aspect of China's Reform and Opening Up, an important component of the grand strategy of Reform and Opening Up, and also one of the contents of Socialism with Chinese characteristics; that it is closely linked with the destiny of Reform and Opening Up in China as a whole.[16] There will be no change in the "one country, two systems" policy decision as long as no changes are made to the entire national strategy of Reform and Opening Up, as long as there is no resurgence of the ultra-"leftist" trend of thought, as long as the practical and realistic line of ideology is held to and carried forward,

---

[16]*Deng Xiaoping on the Unification of the Motherland.* Beijing: Unity Press, 1995, p. 53.

and as long as no change is made to the basic [political] line centered on economic construction. Conversely, the implementation of "one country, two systems" will inevitably be impacted if there are setbacks to the grand strategy of Reform and Opening Up and if the ultra-"leftist" trend of thought rears up again. There is no denying such a possibility. Still, judging from the twenty or more years since "one country, two systems" was put forward, the grand national strategy of Reform and Opening Up has never faltered despite the major changes that have taken place on the mainland, including major changes in state leaders and incidents as big as the one that occurred in 1989. "One country, two systems" has instead been genuinely implemented and put into effect. That has been fully manifested in the formulation of the Basic Laws of two SARs, in the provisions of the Basic Laws on Central/SAR relations as well as in the practical handling of the Central/SAR relations subsequent to the return of Hong Kong and Macao to China.

A typical example of the effects of the Reform and Opening Up process on Central/SAR relations is the Basic Law provision about the original capitalist system and way of life in the SARs remaining unchanged for fifty years. When explaining the reason for these remaining unchanged for fifty years, Deng Xiaoping stated: "We have solemnly promised that our policy toward Hong Kong will remain unchanged for 50 years after 1997. Why 50 years? There is a reason for that. Not only do we need to reassure the people of Hong Kong, but we also have to take into consideration the close relation between the prosperity and stability of Hong Kong and the strategy for the development of China. The time needed for development includes the last 12 years of this century and the first 50 years of the next. So how can we change our policy during those 50 years? Now there is only one Hong Kong, but we plan to build several more Hong Kongs in the interior. In other words, to achieve the strategic objective of development, we need to open wider to the outside world. Such being the case, how can we change our policy toward Hong Kong? As a matter of fact, 50 years is only a vivid way of putting it. Even after 50 years our policy will not change either. That is, for the first 50 years it cannot be changed, and for the second there will be no need to change it. So this is not just idle talk."[17] This clearly indicates that the Central Government's policy design for Hong Kong is very closely tied to the Reform and Opening Up policy strategy of China as a whole, i.e., that by the middle of the twentieth century China intends to become a moderately developed country with a modernization level close to that of Hong Kong. Hence, the Central Government's "one country, two systems" policy toward Hong Kong will also extend to that time and after.

When Lee Kwan Yew, Singapore's Minister Mentor, gave an interview to the Washington Times in May 2001, he said there was nothing which Japan, South Korea, Taiwan, or Hong Kong had already accomplished that China would not be able to do better in future; the United States was incapable of hindering the advance

---

[17]*Deng Xiaoping on the Unification of the Motherland.* Beijing: Unity Press, 1995, p. 59. Actually, the Hong Kong people's per capita GDP in 2000 already attained 187,105 HK yuan, or approximately equivalent to 23,987 U.S. dollars, more than in Canada, Australia, and many other developed countries. See Anson Maria Elizabeth Chan Fang On Sang. "Here and Now, Looking at Tomorrow," carried by the Hong Kong *Ming Pao*, April 19, 2001.

of Chinese mainland.[18] The outside world is unable to hinder China's progress; the only hindrance to China would be China itself, i.e., internal disturbances, corruption, structural problems, and other matters which could prevent ample development in China or even interrupt the process of modernization. Judging from the current situation of China's development, China can achieve political stability and its Reform and Opening Up is irreversible. Hence, one may assert that as long as China's grand strategy of Reform and Opening Up proceeds smoothly, and as long as its modernization drive avoids or undergoes fewer detours, Central/SAR relations will also develop in a benign direction. Advances in reforming China's economic structure will speed up the pace of construction of China's socialist market economy, and the SARs will continue to play an immense role in the construction of China's socialist market economy. Advances in the reform of the political structure and the strengthening and amelioration of the construction of socialist democracy and the legal system, too, will create a benign and relaxed political and legal environment for handling Central/SAR relations.

It is true that Central/SAR relations are highly dependent on the mainland's grand strategy of Reform and Opening Up, yet we must not overlook the fact that an element of independence exists in those relations, and that those relations are not controlled entirely by the mainland's political macroclimate. The relations between the two are affected by factors of even greater complexity. Nonetheless, one may assert that no matter what changes take place on China's mainland, and no matter how many changes take place in China's government leaders and China's government, Central/SAR relations will remain in a relatively stable state. Otherwise, these regions would not be "Special Administrative Regions." Deng Xiaoping has produced some profound expositions in this respect.[19]

5.2.5 The Sustained Stability and Prosperity of the SARs Per Se

This and the first factor are actually two aspects of one and the same contradiction. The first is the Chinese mainland factor, and the second is the SAR factor. Generally speaking, as long as the mainland's advances are sustained and stable, its Reform and Opening Up proceed smoothly, and its socialist market economy advances fairly rapidly, these are bound to vigorously promote the SARs' sustained stability and prosperity. Similarly, if the SARs are able to maintain stability and prosperity and continue to play the role of a window and bridge for China's Reform and Opening Up, they will certainly give impetus to China's Reform and Opening Up and the building up of its socialist market economy. In both these circumstances, Central/SAR rela-

---

[18]U.S.A., *Washington Times*, 2001-05-18.

[19]*Deng Xiaoping on the Unification of the Motherland.* Beijing: Unity Press, 1995, pp. 51–59. *Deng Xiaoping on the Hong Kong Issue.* Hong Kong: Joint Publishing (Hong Kong) Company, Ltd., 1993, pp. 11–12.

tions will proceed as a benign cycle. If the opposite were true, the relations between them would land in a non-benign cycle.

Thanks to the favorable geographical position of the Hong Kong and Macao regions and the acumen and industriousness of their peoples, and also because they are positioned at an interconnecting point between capitalism and socialism and the local governments' policy of proactive noninterference in a free-market economy, their economic development has reached a very high level, and Hong Kong in particular has assumed a pivotal position in the international capitalist economic system. It is, on its tiny stretch of land, exerting enormous economic energy, and the miracle it has wrought is eliciting encomiums from people the world over. Hong Kong has a thriving economy, a stable society, excellent social and public order, and one of the world's lowest crime rates. Its sound legal system and its inhabitants' rigorous law-abiding spirit provide security guarantees for economic transactions and travelers, and figure among the important conditions for the long-term stability and prosperity of its society.

The Macao region is less developed than Hong Kong, but Macao was China's first city to be opened to the outside world. It has had a history of more than 450 years since its doors were thrown open, and for a considerable period of time was all the rage as the largest export trade center in the Far East.

Maintaining the sustained prosperity and stability of the Hong Kong and Macao regions was one of the foremost factors taken in consideration when China resumed its sovereignty over Hong Kong and Macao, and was a major reason for the decision to implement "one country, two systems," set up special administrative regions and confer on them maximum powers of autonomy. These decisions were made not only because China itself was also engaged in construction for modernization, but also out of consideration for the vital interests of the people of Hong Kong and Macao as well as for the international position and prestige of the Chinese nation as a whole. Hence, maintaining the prosperity and stability of these regions after the establishment of the SARs took on special importance for properly handling Central/SARS relations.

We are confident that the economy will see sustained prosperity and stability. The practice of the years after Hong Kong's return to China also proves that its economy is entirely capable of dealing with all difficulties under the management and control of its Chinese inhabitants, of maintaining its customary verve and vitality and continuing its splendid performance. However, whether its society will be able to remain stable requires careful study. According to the provisions of Article 24 of the Basic Law, "The Government of the Hong Kong Special Administrative Region shall be responsible for the maintenance of public order in the Region." The Central People's Government will not interfere in the local affairs of the region, and it will only come forward and intervene only when "something could happen in the region that might jeopardize the fundamental interests of the country" or "something could happen there that would jeopardize the fundamental interests of Hong Kong itself," or when "there might some time arise in Hong Kong a problem that could not be solved without Beijing's intervention." And mainland troops stationed "would be used only if there were disturbances, serious disturbances."[20] Articles 18 and 23 of the Basic Law also set forth provisions corresponding to such matters. Thus the SAR government must conscientiously shoulder the important task of maintaining social order in Hong Kong and upholding its rule of law, so that the Hong Kong region becomes even more prosperous and stable after setting up its SAR and returning to China. Under these circumstances, the Central Government will not intervene in SAR matters and relations between them will be quite harmonious. The same applies to the Macao Special Administrative Region.

5.2.6 International Factors

"International factors" refers to changes in the international political and economic situations which impact China's Central/SAR relations. China's Central/SAR relations are a matter that should fall wholly within the scope of China's sovereign rights. They are China's internal affairs, and no foreign country or international organization should have the right to interfere in them. Yet because of the SARs' unique histories and positions, because Hong Kong and Macao were for long periods of time under the rule of foreigners; because Taiwan, too, was occupied by the Japanese for half a century in past history, and because the United States has meddled in the Taiwan issue after 1949, plus the fact that these three regions all pertain to the world's capitalist system and have very close ties internationally, we have had to take the relevant international factors into consideration when handling Central/SAR relations.

The foremost influence of international factors is the issue of international or regional war and peace. Where China is concerned, its construction of a socialist modernization and the great cause of reunifying the nation both require an international environment of protracted stability and at least several decades of world peace. Only in such a relaxed international climate can we calmly devote our attention to construction and to handling matters of national reunification. The "one country, two systems" proposal and the satisfactory resolution of the Hong Kong and Macao issues were both brought about in a relaxed and peaceful international environment. After China's resumption of sovereignty over Hong Kong and Macao and its setting up of special administrative regions, the issue of international war or peace will continue to have an important bearing on China's handling of Central/SAR relations.

Paragraph 4 of Article 18 of the Basic Law of the Hong Kong Special Administrative Region provides that "In the event that the Standing Committee of the National People's Congress decides to declare a state of war… the Central People's Government may issue an order applying the relevant national laws in the Region." This means that once a change or changes take place in the international situation and the entire country goes into a state of war, the SARs will inevitably be affected, the relevant national laws will have to be implemented in the special administrative regions and Central/SAR relations will enter a state of emergency. We shall, of course, do

---

[20] *Deng Xiaoping on the Unification of the Motherland.* Beijing: Unity Press, 1995, p. 53.

our best to maintain peace, and China has always been a peace-loving nation. After the end of the East-West Cold War, the possibility of a large-scale world war has significantly diminished, the forces for peace in the world have seen constant growth, and maintaining long-term peace in the world is entirely feasible. In a normal and peaceful international situation, Central/SAR relations will be handled in accordance with the policy of "one country, two systems" and the Basic Laws.

The second international factor is the development and the circumstances of capitalism and socialism worldwide. Toward the end of the 1980s, socialism suffered major setbacks in the Soviet Union and Eastern Europe and underwent a "peaceful evolution" at the hands of the Western world. The Soviet Union, as one of the largest socialist states, fell apart, and its socialist cause has come up against enormous difficulties. Meanwhile, rapid changes in the world situation and swift advances in high-end science and technology have furnished new opportunities for the development of international capitalism. Yet, China has stuck to the socialist road despite the vagaries of world events, and at the same time has persevered in taking the path of Reform and Opening Up as well as boldly assimilating advanced production methods and management experience from the West for our own use. It has also unswervingly carried out its "one country, two systems" policy and allowed the Hong Kong and Macao regions to financially remain as members of international capitalism after their return to China and to continue exercising the capitalist system. This is both a mark of China's strength as well as a manifestation of its self-assurance. In these circumstances, the advances of international capitalism have had an important and positive effect on the special administrative regions and on the entire country's Reform and Opening Up, and have indirectly impacted Central/SAR relations.

As concerns each special administrative region and its specific circumstances, the effects of international factors have not been quite the same.

5.2.6.1 The Hong Kong Special Administrative Region

The British factor. The Hong Kong issue has always been a core problem in Sino-British relations. Hong Kong was occupied by the British colonialists ever since the First Opium War, but the Chinese people never gave up on their efforts to restore sovereignty over the region. Whereas the Hong Kong issue was a problem between two sovereign countries before 1997, after China recovered sovereignty over Hong Kong in 1997 the region became a problem within the framework of China's sovereignty. Britain has acquired vast economic and political interests in Hong Kong due to its extended rule over Hong Kong, and British consortiums are extremely influential there. Hence, the "British factor" will be present for a quite long period of time subsequent to China's restoring its exercise of sovereignty over Hong Kong.

In fact, the British side, in the course of negotiations between China and Britain, asked to maintain ties with Hong Kong after 1997. The Chinese side requested clarification on whether that meant "residual sovereignty" and then flatly refused.[21] Britain then switched to other methods in the hope of continuing its influence over Hong Kong. For example, when the Chinese side committed itself to keeping Hong Hong's original system unchanged after resuming its exercise of sovereignty over Hong Kong sovereignty, the British insisted that the term "original" meant the system in existence before June 30, 1997, while the Chinese side insisted that the "original" system referred to the one existing at the time of the signing of the Sino-British Joint Declaration [The Joint Declaration of the Government of the United Kingdom of Great Britain and Northern Ireland and the Government of the People's Republic of China on the question of Hong Kong, signed in 1984], as it feared that Britain would radically alter Hong Kong's system before 1997 and then force the Chinese side to accept it lock, stock, and barrel in 1997 on pain of being accused of reneging on its agreement.[22] Subsequent events showed that China's fears were not uncalled for. As expected, after Christopher Francis Patten, the last governor of Hong Kong, arrived in Hong Kong in 1992, he started to make substantial changes to Hong Kong's original political and legal systems in order to create hindrances to Hong Kong's smooth return to China as well as for the sake of extending Britain's influence over Hong Kong.

As regards the Sino-British Joint Liaison Group, the Chinese side had originally proposed the setting up of this group to convenience liaison between the two sides, but the British side feared that by doing so, a situation might emerge wherein China and Britain would be jointly administering Hong Kong prior to 1997. And so, the Sino-British Joint Liaison Group was established only after China agreed that group's presence could be extended to the year 2000.[23] According to the provisions of Annex II of the Sino-British Joint Declaration, the Sino-British Joint Liaison Group would be established when the Joint Declaration came into force, and it would move to Hong Kong and start working from July 1, 1988 right up to January 1, 2000 when it would conclude its mission. As negotiated between the two sides, the Sino-British Joint Liaison Group would be a liaison agency, not a power institution. Its members and working personnel would conduct their activities within the Group's functions and duties, would take no part in the administration or management of the HK SAR, and would not exercise the function of supervising the SAR government.[24] Hence, the "British factor" and Sino-British relations still exerted a certain influence over

---

[21] Huang Wenfang. "The Historical Course and Implementation of China's Policy Decision to Restore the Exercise of Sovereignty over Hong Kong," Hong Kong Baptist University, 1997, p. 61.

[22] Ibid., p. 61.

[23] Ibid., p. 68.

[24] The Sino-British Joint Liaison Group was a special institution for conducting liaison and consultation on the Hong Kong problem between Chinese and British governments, established in accordance with the provisions of the Sino-British Joint Declaration and its Annex II. The Group's duties consisted in conducting consultations on the carrying out of the Joint Declaration, discussing matters related to the smooth handover of political power over Hong Kong in 1997, and exchanging information and conducting consultations on matters agreed upon by the two sides. The Sino-British Joint Liaison Group also established a number of experts' teams to handle specific matters which required assistance from experts. Each side of the Liaison Group was composed of one ambassadorial-level chief delegate and four other delegates. The Group held at least one meeting

China's handling of Central/SAR relations in this period of time. Britain's influence has of course waned considerably now, though it still expresses "solicitude" over Hong Kong from time to time.

The U.S. factor. The United States has direct economic and political interests in Hong Kong. In 1999, its exports to Hong Kong reached USD 12.5 billion, and in 1998, the United States' direct investments in Hong Kong came to USD 20.8 billion while the amount of loans from U.S. companies came to USD 50 billion. The U.S. has a yearly trade surplus balance of as much as USD 6.9 billion with Hong Kong, and Hong Kong is its 13th biggest trade partner. Around 1200-plus American corporations are doing business in Hong Kong and are hiring some 0.25 million Hong Kongers, or approximately 10 percent of Hong Kong's workforce. Some 50,000 Americans have taken permanent residence in Hong Kong, and this figure does not include those with dual citizenship who are not counted by the Hong Kong government. Approximately, 0.75 million American tourists visit Hong Kong annually.

The United States had little say at first on the Hong Kong problem, but it has consistently shown special "concern" for Hong Kong. Official and nonofficial quarters in the United States one and all display great interest in matters ranging from the initiation of the Sino-British negotiations on the Hong Kong problem to the formulation of the Basic Law, and from the preparations for establishing the special administrative region to appeals for the right of Hong Kongers' children on the mainland to reside in Hong Kong and so forth. Back in 1992, the U.S. Congress drafted a United States-Hong Kong Policy Act which stipulated that the United States would deal with the Hong Kong region differently than with other regions in China, and required that the U.S. State Department submit between 1997 and 2000 an annual report on the year's circumstances in Hong Kong. Subsequently, the U.S. Congress and government on has many occasions expressed "concern" about Hong Kong's democracy after 1997. In March 1997, on the eve of Hong Kong's return to China, the U.S. House of Representatives also passed an act—the Hong Kong Reversion Act—in which it refused to recognize the Provisional Legislative Council. It even called for denying visits to the United State by the members of the Council and for granting special U.S. immigration quotas to persons engaged in Hong Kong's news media. The said Act further expressed the United States' concern regarding Hong Kong's exercise of autonomy after its return to China and suggested measures to be taken by the U.S. government if the Chinese government failed to fulfill its promise of a high degree of autonomy for Hong Kong.[25] According to the United States-Hong Kong Policy Act, the U.S. Department of State should submit annual reports to Congress for three consecutive years about the situation in Hong Kong after the transfer of Hong Kong's political power in 1997. The reports of the first three years gave positive appraisals. Thus

every year in Beijing, London, and Hong Kong, respectively. The Liaison Group was set up on March 27, 1985 when the Joint Declaration went into force. Stationed mainly in Hong Kong as of July 1, 1988, it worked up to the day of its conclusion on January 1, 2000. During its 15 years of existence, the Liaison Group held altogether 47 plenary meetings.

[25]See the U.S. State Department website "relations with Hong Kong": http://usinfo.state.gov/regi onal/ea/uschina/hkact.htm.

in accordance with that Act, the U.S. State Council was not required after 2000 to submit any more annual reports to Congress on Hong Kong's situation. However, the State Department stated in 2001 that it would continue to produce reports on its own initiative. This indicates the extent of the United States' interest in Hong Kong. However, it denied that by doing so it was interfering in Hong Kong's local administration.

Actually, even before Hong Kong's return to China, the United States was thinking of filling in the "international vacuum" created by Britain's withdrawal in 1997 and to "supervise" on behalf of world society the Chinese government's implementation of its special policy on Hong Kong.[26] Its alleged "legal basis" for so doing was that the Sino-British Joint Declaration was an international treaty and therefore internationally binding, hence the way in which China would administer Hong Kong after 1997 should be subject to international supervision. This was in fact a distortion of the Sino-British Joint Declaration. Articles 1 and 2 of the Sino-British Joint Declaration, i.e., that the Chinese government had decided to "restore its exercise of sovereignty over Hong Kong on July 1, 1997" and that the British government would on the same day "return Hong Kong to the People's Republic of China," were indeed internationally binding. As for the sort of policies China implemented on Hong Kong after July 1, 1997, these would be, legally speaking, China's internal affairs. Yet, there still are some people who believe Article 7 of the Sino-British Joint Statement indicated that the Chinese and British government had agreed to "implement the preceding declarations and the Annexes to this Joint Declaration." Article 8 also provides that "this Joint Declaration and its Annexes shall be equally binding." The Chinese side maintains that Article 3 and Annex 1 of the Sino-British Joint Declaration were about policies to be implemented in Hong Kong by China subsequent to 1997, and were merely unilateral policy statements by the Chinese government. And that this had already been declared by the Chinese government at the time of the Sino-British negotiations.[27]

However, the core question is not the legal basis. The main problem is that the United States hopes to turn Hong Kong into another factor for pinning China down. The Hong Kong issue carries much less weight than the Taiwan issue, but the United States, which sees itself as the "world police," will not forgo any opportunity to interfere in China's internal affairs.[28] True, the United States has huge investments in Hong Kong and possesses certain economic interests there. But other countries also have large investments in Hong Kong, yet unlike the United States do not show such "concern" for Hong Kong. The United States' gesticulating and posturing on the Hong Kong issue are wholly for the purpose of interfering in China's sovereign and internal affairs and it stands to reason that China opposes such actions.

---

[26] Huang Wenfang. "Hong Kong Is Bound to Become a Bone of Chinese-American Contention," carried by the Hong Kong *Ming Pao*, April 21, 1997.

[27] Ibid.

[28] Pursuant to the retreat of former colonial nations in the world, many instances have occurred of the United States swiftly filling up vacuums by dint of its national strengths. It began to intervene and insert itself when the French pulled out of Vietnam. It very quickly filled up the "vacuum" after the British withdrew from South Africa. Examples such as these are legion.

5.2.6.2   The Macao Special Administrative Region

Sino-Portuguese relations can very well have influenced the Macao issue. Ever since China and Portugal entered into negotiations on Macao, the Portuguese side took a basically cooperative stand on the issue. This has undoubtedly played a positive role on the benign development of the relations between the Central Government and the Macao Special Administrative Region after China recovered its sovereignty over Macao in 1999. Since Macao returned to China on December 20, 1999, the Macao issue has been entirely a Chinese internal affair and the Portuguese influence there has progressively declined.

Here, too, the U.S. factor cannot be overlooked. U.S. connections with Macao can be traced back several hundred years. In more recent times, American missionaries, merchants, and seafarers have flocked to Macao to proselytize or do business. Here, in 1844, the United States forced the Qing government to sign the Sino-U.S. Mong Ha [Wangxia] Treaty, and China was compelled to open ports to the United States (The Americans call the treaty "the first U.S.-China Friendship Treaty"). Today, approximately fifty percent of Macao's exports are shipped to the United States. After Macao reverted to China in the year 2000, the U.S. Congress immediately passed a United States-Macao Policy Act which "the laws of the United States shall continue to apply with respect to Macao, on and after December 20, 1999, in the same manner as the laws of the United States were applied with respect to Macao before such date," and requesting that the American government "should play an active role…in maintaining Macau's confidence and prosperity, Macau's unique cultural heritage, and the mutually beneficial ties between the people of the United States and the people of Macao."[29] Just as on the Hong Kong issue, the United States has been gesticulating and posturing on the Macao issue in the hope of using that issue to impact Sino-U.S. relations and pin China down. But here, too, the United States' designs will not succeed.

Additionally, China's relations with Japan and with the Southeast Asian countries could also affect the Hong Kong, Macao, and Taiwan regions.

To sum up, irrespective of the vagaries of international relations, and irrespective of how the various "international factors" manifest themselves, Central/SAR relations will all remain as China's internal affairs. Any attempts to "internationalize" the Hong Kong, Macao, and Taiwan issues proved futile in the past, and will be futile going forward. The Chinese people will do a good job of their own affairs, and the Chinese government will appropriately handle all problems that may occur between the Central Government and the SARs, i.e., handle the problems in the spirit of "one country, two systems" and in accordance with the provisions of the Basic Laws.

Among the various factors described above which affect Central/SAR relations, the first two are internal causes , and the third one can only be an external cause.

---

[29] Address by Michael Klosson, U.S. consul-general in Hong Kong and Macao at a reception in Macao on September 22, 1999.

A decisive role will ultimately be played by the advances in China's Reform and Opening Up and by the sustained prosperity and stability of the SARs subsequent to the return of Hong Kong and Macao to China.

5.3 The Division of Functions and Powers Between the Central Government and the Special Administrative Regions

5.3.1 General Theories on the Division of Functions and Powers Between the National and Local Governments (Central and Local Authorities)

We have previously noted that some academics are of the opinion that, in the strict sense, the so-called "division of powers" exists only in federal states. The "division of powers" issue does not exist in unitary states because, theoretically speaking, all powers in a unitary state pertain to the central authorities, and any powers enjoyed by regional governments are authorized (delegated). Hence, there is only "delegation of powers" under the unitary system, and no "division of powers." For convenience's sake in the present discourse the term "division of powers" will be used here when describing the power relations between central and local governments under the unitary system.

Judging from the practice of various countries in the world, the problem of the delimitation of duties and powers exists in all countries—federal and unitary, and it is neither likely nor possible for all state powers to be concentrated and exercised by a Central Government (not to mention federal Central Governments). Even in the most authoritarian countries or historical periods, local governments have enjoyed a certain amount of autonomy. Of course, viewing the matter from a different aspect, the Central Government would be reduced to a mere figurehead and the state would no longer be a state if too many powers are "divided away" by the localities, or if basically all powers are taken over and exercised by the localities. Back in 1851, the British jurist H. A. Smith, in his book local autonomy and centralization advanced the view that neither centralized power nor local autonomy should be emphasized at the expense of the other.

It is apparently a common understanding that there should be an appropriate division of powers between national and local governments (central and local authorities), but different ideas and methods exist in terms of theory and practice on exactly how powers should be divided between the two.

Traditionally, the method of "natural division of powers," or in other words, the "division of powers according to strength" appears to have been adopted in all countries. However, the extent of the powers of the central and local authorities in a country is determined entirely by the way in which the state was formed and by the respective strengths of the central and local authorities. If a state achieved unification and established its nationwide political power by means of armed force, the national government set up in this manner would naturally hold most of the state's powers, would constitute the source of legality for such powers, and would hold the dominant position in central–local relations, whereas the local governments would be of secondary and subsidiary importance and, nationwide, would serve as extensions of the central powers. Conversely, if a country were formed mainly by way of peaceful negotiations, if "local governments" came first and the national government came later, if powers derived their legality from the localities and the people and not from the central authorities, the most frequent outcome of such circumstances was that the localities were stronger than the central authorities, and that in central–local relations the localities held the dominant position and were the principal aspect of contradictions, while the central authorities were of secondary importance and acted in an auxiliary and service capacity. That was, by and large, the way powers were divided into ancient states. Had the First Emperor of Qin unified the six other states not by armed force but through negotiations—in the way the thirteen British colonies of North America had devised a constitution of divided powers and set up the United States of America through negotiations—the history of China's subsequent two thousand years of development would have had to be completely rewritten. But the basic fact was that the First Emperor of Qin had resorted to armed force to unify China, and this set the keynote for China's two thousand years of development, for China's subsequent state structure, and for China's subsequent handling of all relations between central and local authorities. The example of the United States merely proves this theory from the other side of the coin.

With the rise of political rationalism in recent times, people have begun to intentionally design political structures and state modalities which make the exercise of state power more rational and scientific. Where central–local relations are concerned, scholars have advanced a number of theories for politicians to choose from. These have changed the indiscriminate "first-come-first-served principle" and started up the handling of bilateral relations in a scientific and rational way. There are a great many theories about the division of powers between central and local authorities. The French political scientist Andrée Lafoie classified the various central–local relations as political-type division of powers, administrative-type division of powers, and transfers of administrative powers. The American Scholar D. Wright classified the central–local separations of powers as of the separation mode, inclusive mode, and interdependent mode. Whereas the British scholar ROSS divided the power relations between the two according to the degree and nature of their mutual dependence, and came up with four different types, i.e., mutual independence, unilateral local authority dependence on the central authorities, unilateral central authority dependence on the local authorities, and interdependence. Another British scholar found two fundamental types of central–local relations, i.e., the partnership type and the agency type. On this basis, the scientists derived a great many theorems regarding central–local division of powers, such as the agency theory, the partnership theory, the power-dependency relationship theory, the organizational relationship theory, and so forth.[30]

It is true that whether a state exercises the unitary system or the federal system, all must have appropriate divisions of powers and divisions of work. However, the nature of such divisions of powers and divisions of work differ under the different forms of state structure.

Under the federal system, the division of powers between the national government and the member states emerges as a result of "popular" sponsorship and on the basis of equal negotiations. The relation between the two sides is a sort "contractual" relation based on public law, and the division of powers between the federation and its member states is genuine. However, the powers enjoyed by both sides under the "contractual" relation come directly from authorizations by the people, not from mutual authorizations. The powers enjoyed by the national government are derived not from authorizations by the various states, but from direct constitutional authorizations by the people of the country as a whole. On this matter, we once labored under a major misconception. We believed that the powers of the federal government under the federal system were authorized by the member states. That is incorrect, as becomes evident when we look at the Preamble to the U.S. Constitution. Although the Preamble is quite brief, it clears up a very important and basic question—the source of government power. It comes straight to the point with the declaration that "we, the American people" have formulated the constitution of the United States of America. This makes it clear that the powers, whether of the states or the federal government, stem directly from the people; that these powers are divided among the federal government and the state governments by "the people" by means of a constitution, not by means "*sub rosa* deals" between the federation and the states. That is why the U.S. federal constitution has to be passed by a two-thirds majority of the states, and why amendments to the federal constitution, in addition to being passed by Congress, must also be approved by a three-fourths majority of the states. Of course, the powers vested in the states under the federal system are not authorized by the federal government, nor are they directly authorized by the people. Matters are different under the unitary system. All of the powers of countries under the unitary system also pertain to the people, but the people delegate these powers to governments in different ways. The people first delegate the powers *in toto* to the central (national) government, after which the central (national government) "trans-delegates" some of the powers to the local governments in light of the circumstances. The extent of the powers authorized depends entirely on the actual circumstances. The Central Government may delegate very few powers. For example, the powers that the Central Government "delegates" to China's inland provinces are quite limited. Or, they may be quite extensive—in fact, more extensive than the powers vested in diverse states under the federal system, as for instance the high degree of autonomy enjoyed by the Hong Kong Special Administrative Region. Big or small, all of the powers vested

---

[30]For relevant theories, see Michio Muramatsu. *Local Power in the Japanese State (Contemporary Japanese Politics)*, Beijing, The Economic Daily Press, 1989, pp. 2–24. Xing Xiangyang. *Princes in Big State*. Beijing: China Social Press, 1995, pp. 324–338.

in local governments are authorized by the Central Government, not directly by the people. The division of central and local powers is not an outcome of negotiations between the two sides; it is, strictly speaking, the outcome of unilateral acts by the Central Government. Although the people in regions that exercise regional autonomy may elect and produce their own governments, the exercise of local autonomy per se requires authorization by the Central Government, and the magnitude of the powers enjoyed by the local governments is still determined by the Central Government. Thus, the division of central and local powers under the unitary system differs in nature from the division of powers under the federal system, though the actual effects may be similar.

These theories are undoubtedly of a certain reference value for our division of Central/SAR powers. However, any truly scientific and rational divisions of Central/SAR powers in China must be based on actual circumstances and on full consideration of multiple factors, and cannot be resolved entirely by dint of "theorizing."

5.3.2 Regarding the Discussions on the Division of Central/SAR Powers

The above analyses tell us that the Central/SAR power relations are not a matter of negotiation or of equal division of powers between the two sides. They are a matter of a unilateral delegation of powers by the Central authorities, and they differ in substance from power relations under the federal system. Recognizing this fact is most important. Extensive discussions were conducted on this matter during the drafting of the Hong Kong Basic Law. And although people in all quarters agreed there had to be clear division of powers and responsibilities between the Central Government and the special administrative regions, their specific positions on the matter differed.

One position, which was known as the "zero-sum law of distribution doctrine," held that there exists a set amount of government powers in any country, and if the Central Government enjoys excessive powers, the local governments will certainly have fewer powers and vice versa. Hence, if too much emphasis were placed on national sovereign powers when handling Central/SAR power relations, the SARs' autonomous powers were bound to diminish. It would be best if the Central Government retained only two sorts of power—national defense and foreign diplomacy. All other powers should be explicitly delegated to and exercised by the SAR. And only in the aspects of national defense and foreign diplomacy should the Central Government act in its capacity of a Central Authority toward the SAR. In all other respects, the SAR would handle matters on its own, as only that would constitute "a high degree of autonomy" and make it possible to maintain the SAR's prosperity and stability.[31] This position evidently oversimplified state sovereignty. National security was no doubt an important component of state sovereignty, but certainly not its entirety. State sovereignty also includes other content, which I will discuss in detail in subsequent chapters and sections. Even in federalist countries, the powers and duties of the federal government are not restricted to national security and foreign diplomacy. The U.S. federal government, for instance, possesses ample powers over internal affairs under the U.S. constitution.

Other persons held to the "parity status doctrine" which maintained that the Central Government and the SAR region were, in a certain sense, on an equal footing. In other words, the Central Government was the Central Authority over the SAR only on matters of national defense and foreign affairs; on all other matters, the two sides were equal in status. Any disagreements which arose between them on matters of competence should be arbitrated by an independent constitutional court composed of an equal number of judges assigned by both sides, all with the same powers, and it would be best to invite judges from other countries to participate in hearings on Central/SAR authority disagreements. The said court would have supreme authority, and both sides should conscientiously implement its rulings.[32] The basis for presenting the "parity status doctrine" was erroneous. As stated earlier, under the unitary system, the central and local authorities are not equal in status. In any and all circumstances, the Central Government is the Central Government. However, it may refrain from directly exercising all of its powers but instead delegate certain powers to a local government for implementation. As for the resolving of Central/SAR disagreements on competence issues, setting up an independent constitutional court would involve questions regarding China's fundamental political structure and make matters extremely complicated. China's Constitution does in fact provide certain mechanisms for resolving problems, and one could—on this basis and by means of the Basic Law—stipulate a workable and rational plan for resolving such issues. That would ensure SAR participation in the resolution of such disagreements in a certain way, but certainly not on a mutual parity basis.

Some stood for writing in the Basic Law a detailed list of the powers vested in the Central Authorities and the SAR, respectively, and those shared by the two sides. For example, the Central Authorities would be responsible for matters involving state sovereignty, such as national defense and foreign diplomacy, and the SAR would be responsible for its internal affairs and some matters involving foreign relations. Other matters that involve both parties, such as judicial assistance, economic and cultural exchanges, mainlander emigrations to the SAR, and so forth, would be handled through consultation. Matters not explicitly assigned either to the Central Authorities or the SAR or which were designated for resolution by mutual consultation would come under "residual powers." And to show the Central Authorities' determination and sincerity for implementing "one country, two systems," these "residual powers"

---

[31] Advisory Committee for the Hong Kong Special Administrative Region Basic Law: The Basic Law of the Hong Kong Special Administrative Region of the People's Republic of China (Draft), the Consultation Paper: Advisory Report (2), p. 24.

[32] Ibid., p. 29.

would be exercised by the SAR.[33] That position was obviously untenable. If there would be any "residual powers" in the division of Central/SAR powers, possession of these powers was a matter of principle and the powers could not be given over to implementation by any local authority under the unitary system. That is because the Central/SAR relation is one of authorizing unitary powers, and all powers pertain to the central authorities in the first place. If there still are any "residual powers," they should belong to the Central Government. Or at least, they should first belong to the Central Government, and the Central Government shall then decide who should best exercise them.

A few persons maintained that, in addition to the powers enjoyed by the central authorities and the high level of autonomy enjoyed by the SAR, there were some which constituted a "gray area" and it was impossible to determine whether such powers should be exercised by the central authorities or the SAR. There were similar views, which held that new circumstances could eventually emerge which had been unforeseen during the drafting of the Basic Law and jurisdiction over which was not clearly defined in the Basic Law; these powers should best be exercised by the SAR.[34] It should be noted that such things as "gray areas" and "non-defined powers" do not exist under a unitary system, for the simple reason that under the unitary system all matters over which it is uncertain who has jurisdiction should first of all fall under the jurisdiction of the Central Authorities, which will then determine whether the SARs should be authorized to exercise jurisdiction, that is, a principle of the unitary system. It is also why the Basic Laws, after having clearly set forth the various powers enjoyed by the SARs, further specified that the SARs might eventually enjoy other powers granted them by the Central Authorities.

5.3.3   The Divisions of Central/SAR Powers by the Basic Law

For the first time in the history of the development of New China's state structure and the history of its legislature, the Basic Laws of the Hong Kong and Macao SARs specifically and by legislative means have conducted a division of powers between the Central Authorities and a given level of local government. As I have expounded earlier, never in the past had we been accustomed defining the division of central and local powers in the form of laws. Although some such legal regulations did exist, all were too generalized and vague and hardly operable. One might well say that the two Basic Laws have made pioneering forays in this respect. They clearly stipulate the powers to be exercised by the Central Authorities and the SARs as well their limits and conditions, and are eminently operable. As a high-placed official of the State Council's Office for Hong Kong and Macao Affairs has pointed out, the provisions of the Basic Laws are quite clear-cut in terms of the Central Authorities' functions

---

[33]The task force on the Central/SAR Relationship under the Basic Law Advisory Commission of the Hong Kong Special Administrative Region, "Residual Power (Final Power)."
[34]Ibid.

and powers and the affairs they are in charge of administering as well as the Hong Kong SAR's scope of functions and powers.[35]

Viewed from the perspective of legislative techniques, the Basic Laws hew to the method of combining concentrated and dispersed provisions. The Basic Laws each consist of one preamble and nine chapters. The preambles trace the origins of the Hong Kong and Macao problems, China's plans and policies for resolving the Hong Kong and Macao problems, and the constitutional basis and purpose in formulating the Basic Laws. The General Provisions in the first chapters lay out the major political, economic, legal, and social principles for the systems practiced in the SARs and limn the overall outline of "one country, two systems." The second chapters deal with Central/SAR relations and contain concentrated and specific stipulations on the division of functions and powers between the Central Authorities and the SARs. The second chapters as well as the preambles and first chapters are alike in that they may be regarded as the "soul" of the Basic Laws. They outline the main points and the major principles for handling Central/SAR relations are of guiding significance for the stipulations on specific matters in all of the subsequent chapters, and also contain a number of specific and operable provisions on the division of functions and powers. All of the subsequent chapters also involve Central/SAR division of functions and powers regarding various specific matters.

Viewed from the perspective of legislative content, the Basic Laws first of all clearly stipulate that the SARs constitute one of the levels of special local administrative regions under China's unitary state structure (Article 1 and Article 12). Hence, the principles of the unitary system have to be observed when conducting Central/SAR divisions of functions and powers, i.e., that "original powers" pertain to the Central Authorities, and that the legitimacy of the SARs' powers stems from these powers being conferred by the Central Authorities and being neither "inherent" nor "natural," that no matter how great the powers enjoyed the SARs, all are authorized by the Central Authorities, and that the SARs do not have the right to decide on their own to become independent states. Article 2 of the Basic Laws stipulates that the National People's Congress authorizes the Hong Kong (Macao) SAR to exercise, in accordance with the provisions of the Constitution, a high degree of autonomy and enjoy executive, legislative, and judicial power, including that of final adjudication. Actually, an examination of the methods, legislations, and procedures for the drafting of the SAR Basic Laws clearly shows the nature of the division of Central/SAR powers. The Basic Laws, as the fundamental laws that define the functions and powers on both sides, are formulated by China's highest organ of state power; they are not the outcome of bilateral negotiations or consultations, and even less have they been unilaterally formulated by the SARs on their own, despite the presence of numerous Hong Kong and Macao members on the drafting committees

---

[35] Wang Fengchao. "On the Relations between the Central Government and the Hong Kong SAR," *Hong Kong Wen Wei Po*, April 5, 1995.

of the Basic Laws.[36] This means that the division of powers and functions between the two sides was determined by China's highest institution of state power, not by the SARs on their own, nor by negotiations between the Central Authorities and the SARs. This is a matter of fundamental principle and is of decisive significance for both sides on the division of functions and powers regarding specific affairs.

Also, an overview of the Basic Laws' specific regulations on Central/SAR division of functions and powers shows that jurisdiction overpowers is basically determined by the nature of the matter in question, and that the Central Authorities should of course be in charge of matters which manifest state sovereignty and national unity. These include national defense, foreign affairs, state-of-emergency powers, appointments of principal administrative officials, and the powers to formulate, interpret, and revise the Basic Laws. Strictly limiting the Central Authorities' powers are strictly limited to those required for protecting national sovereignty and unity, as this is a requirement of the "one country" principle, provides ample guarantees for the "two systems," and thereby manifests the "one country, two systems" spirit. On the other hand, the provisions of the Basic Laws on the powers exercised by the SARs give full expression to the principle and spirit of "one country, two systems," in that all powers outside and beyond those indispensable for safeguarding national sovereignty and unity and which do not absolutely have to be exercised by the Central Government are exercised by the SARs. According to this principle, some powers which are not closely tied to unity and sovereignty yet are quite important are also authorized for implementation by the SARs, as for example, the power of final adjudication, the power to issue currency, all powers to levy taxes, independent powers for regulating entries and exits, and so forth. Some of these powers are not available to member states of countries under the federal system. And so it is evident that the Basic Laws' provisions on Central/SAR powers are innovations where constitutional studies are concerned, and unprecedented in history. We can also see in them the immense determination and profound sincerity evinced by the Central Government for maintaining the Hong Kong and Macao SARs' prosperity and stability.

In accordance with common legislative practice in other countries, provisions concerning the powers exercised by the central (national) government in the constitutions and constitutional laws of countries under the unitary system are usually generalized provisions, whereas enumerative provisions are adopted for powers exercised by local or regional governments. The reverse is true for states of the federal system; they generally adopt generalized provisions for the laws exercised by national (central) governments but apply enumerative provisions for the powers vested in regional or local governments. However, when studying China's two SAR Basic Laws, we find that a combination of generalized and enumerative provisions is used for the powers of both the Central Authorities and the SARs. While using generalized provisions to define the Central Authorities as the power-authorizing institution (Article 2 and Article 20), the Basic Laws also explicitly enumerate the Central Authori-

---

[36]There were 59 members on the Drafting Committee of the Hong Kong Special Administrative Region Basic Law, 23 of whom were from Hong Kong. And there were 46 members on the Drafting Committee of the Macao Special Administrative Region Basic Law, 22 of whom were from Macao.

ties' powers (Articles 13–15). As concerns the SARs' powers, the Basic Laws use the enumeration method to list the highly autonomous powers to be vested in the SARs (Articles 16–19) while also stipulating in a general manner the SARs' powers which are to be expanded on the basis of continuous authorizations by the Central Authorities (Article 20). This, too, is an innovation.

The powers enjoyed by the Central Authorities and the SARs, respectively, are discussed in detail in the following chapters.

Chapter 6
The Powers of the Central Authorities

In Section Two of Chapter IV, we have been apprised that the term "Central" as used here does not refer to the CPC Central Committee, i.e., the Central Committee of Communist Party of China, nor does it refer only to the Central People's Government, i.e., the State Council, but that it also includes the highest organ of state power, i.e. the National People's Congress and its Standing Committee, as well as the highest institution of state power, i.e., the Chairman of the People's Republic of China, and the highest organ of military power, i.e., the Central Military Commission. As regards the state's highest judiciary organ, i.e., the Supreme People's Court, and the state's highest organ of legal supervision, i.e., the Supreme People's Procuratorate, there is no relationship of administrative subordination between the Central Authorities' judicial organs and legal supervision organs and the SARs' judicial organs and governmental legal organs, since the SARs enjoy judiciary independence in accordance with the SARs' Basic Laws and possess their own powers of final adjudication; the only relations between the two sides are those of judiciary assistance.[1] As for the National Committee of the Chinese People's Political Consultative Conference [CPPCC], its relations with the SARs are not regulated by the Basic Laws since it does not constitute a state organ.

Hence the "Central Authorities" referred to here, as well as including the central judicial and legal supervision organs, also comprises central organs of state power, i.e., the highest organs of state power, the state's leadership institution, the highest

---

[1] The Chinese Constitution defines the People's Procuratorates as state organs for exercising legal supervision and does not regard them as judicial organs. However, for an extended period of time, the People's Procuratorates and the Peoples' Courts on Chinese mainland have both been regarded as judicial organs. Some scholars are now proposing that procuratorates be classified as government administrative departments, as is being done in most other countries and in the Hong Kong and Taiwan regions.

© Foreign Language Teaching and Research Publishing Co., Ltd and Springer Nature Singapore Pte Ltd. 2019
Z. Wang, *Relationship Between the Chinese Central Authorities and Regional Governments of Hong Kong and Macao: A Legal Perspective*, China Academic Library, https://doi.org/10.1007/978-981-13-2322-5_6

organs of administrative power, and the state's highest organ of military leadership. What are called here the "powers enjoyed by the central authorities" refer to the powers enjoyed by these organs and institutions. And in terms of these powers, the Basic Laws contain stipulations of principle as well as specific stipulations.[2]

The provisions in the Basic Laws on the powers enjoyed by the Central Authorities as concerns the SARs may be summed up briefly as the SARs' right to establish/organize, and the organizational powers of the SAR governments, namely the power to appoint and remove principal administrative officials, plus the power to proclaim states of emergency, the power over diplomatic affairs, and powers pertaining to defense matters. Among these powers, the SARs' right to establish/organize is the basis of all other rights and powers and includes the SARs' powers to set up institutions, the rights to formulate, interpret, and revise the SARs' Basic Laws, and the power to retain "residual powers."

6.1 The SAR's Right to Establish/Organize

In constitutional law, "right to establish/organize" is also called "organizational power." This implies the powers to set up government, choose the form of governance, and formulate basic laws of a constitutional nature. These are the "original (primary) rights" of a country's powers. The level of government that exercises these powers is the main indicator that differentiates a unitary government and a parliamentary government. If the national government possesses the original right to establish/organize, and local governments do not have any powers of self-organization, the country pertains to the unitary system. Conversely, if the localities hold the right to establish/organize, and the local and national governments both possess their own rights to establish/organize, the country is a parliamentary state.

Since [China's] central authorities possess the primary (original) right to establish/organize, the localities possess only derived the right of reception, the legality of rights and powers stems from central authorization, the powers enjoyed by the Central Authorities may be unlimited in terms of both theory and principle, and the more the Central Authorities centralize these powers the closer they hew to the principle of the unitary system. In an extremely unitary state, all rights and powers in the country must be centralized under a unified central authority; local governments can only serve as agencies of the Central Authorities and exercise jurisdiction over a given area by passively accepting instructions from the latter. Moreover, they must report all matters big and small to the Central Authorities for adjudication before taking any sort of action; they may not make any decisions on their own. In the feudal societies of ancient times, some ambitious emperors pursued the principle of "all lands under Heaven belong to the ruler, and all persons within their borders are his vassals." For instance, the Qianlong Emperor of the Qing Dynasty was famous

---

[2]The term "Zhong Yang" in the English-language translations of the Basic Law(s) is translated as "Central Authorities." This accurately renders the entire meaning of the Chinese term.

for his autocratically governance and forbade all others from taking a hand in court affairs. In reality, however, he failed to achieve this goal. It is evident that even in a country with the most rigorous unitary system, the central authorities are unable to concentrate all powers in their hands, despite their having ample grounds for doing so in terms of both theory and legal principles.

Although in political practice, the Central Authorities of a country with a unitary system are not able to concentrate on all matters under their unified central control, they must always retain some of the most important and fundamental powers that are directly connected to the country's sovereignty and unity. These include the power to set up institutions in local administrative areas, the powers to formulate, amend, and interpret the organic laws of local governments, and the right to retain "residual powers." These are the basic contents of the right to establish/organize. The right to establish/organize is a power that must be held by the central organs of political power in all countries with a unitary system. It is also the most important of the powers exercised by the central authorities over the localities, the premise and basis of the other powers enjoyed by the central authorities as well as an important manifestation and important guarantee of the country's sovereignty and unity.

Since the SARs constitute one of the levels of the country's local administrative areas, the Central Authorities must necessarily wield the right to establish/organize in the SARs. Both the Constitution and the Basic Laws contain clear-cut stipulations in this respect.

6.1.1 The Power of Institution in the SARs

Both of the Basic Laws state in their preambles: "Upholding national unity and territorial integrity, maintaining the prosperity and stability of Hong Kong (in the interests of the social stability and economic development of Macao), and taking into account its (Macao's) history and realities, the People's Republic of China has decided that upon China's resumption of the exercise of sovereignty over Hong Kong (Macao), a Hong Kong (Macao) Special Administrative Region will be established in accordance with the provisions of Article 31 of the Constitution of the People's Republic of China, and that under the principle of 'one country, two systems,' the socialist system and policies will not be practiced in Hong Kong (Macao)."

It is further stated in the Preamble(s) that: "In accordance with the Constitution of the People's Republic of China, the National People's Congress hereby enacts the Basic Law of the Hong Kong (Macao) Special Administrative Region of the People's Republic of China, prescribing the systems to be practiced in the Hong Kong (Macao) Special Administrative Region, in order to ensure the implementation of the basic policies of the People's Republic of China regarding Hong Kong (Macao)."

This clearly shows that the power of institution in the SARs rests with the Central Authorities, and that the powers to organize the SARs and determine the systems implemented by the SARs also rest with the Central Authorities. The statement that "the People's Republic of China has decided" actually means "the Central Authorities have decided." And the "Central Authorities" and the "People's Republic of China" here both refer to the country's highest organ of state power, i.e., the National People's Congress. In China, only the National People's Congress has the power to determine the establishment of the SARs' administrative systems as well as the powers to stipulate the systems implemented in the SARs and to form and organize the SARs. The decisions to resume the exercise of sovereignty over Hong Kong and Macao and to set up the two Special Administrative Regions were both made by the National People's Congress.

The government of the People's Republic of China and the government of the United Kingdom of Great Britain and Northern Ireland signed the Joint Declaration of the Government of the United Kingdom of Great Britain and Northern Ireland and the Government of the People's Republic of China on the Hong Kong Question (the Sino–British Joint Declaration) on December 19, 1984, after which the Chinese government, in accordance with the provisions of China's Constitution, submitted this important international convention to China's highest organ of state power for deliberation. On April 10, 1985, the Third Session of the Sixth National People's Congress examined and approved the Sino–British Joint Declaration and decided to resume China's exercise of sovereignty over Hong Kong on July 1, 1997. The National People's Congress also decided to set up the Drafting Committee of the Basic Law of the Hong Kong Special Administrative Region of the People's Republic of China, which began to draft a basic law for the HK SAR. The drafting of the Basic Law of the Hong Kong Special Administrative Region of the People's Republic of China was completed after five years of hard work, and this important document was approved by the Third Session of the Seventh National People's Congress on April 4, 1990. The NPC also approved the Decision on Establishing the Hong Kong Special Administrative Region and decided to set up the HK SAR on the same day as China resumed its exercise of sovereignty over Hong Kong. On March 31, 1993, the First Session of the Eighth National People's Congress passed a resolution authorizing the NPC Standing Committee to set up a preparatory work committee for the HK SAR Preparatory Commission. On July 2, 1993, the preparatory work committee for the NPC Standing Committee's HK SAR Preparatory Commission was set up by the decision of the Second Session of the Eighth National People's Congress, and some initial work was begun on preparing for the HK SAR. On January 26, 1996, the National People's Congress HK SAR Preparatory Commission was officially established, and overall preparatory work for the HK SAR officially started up. On July 1, 1997, the governments of China and Britain held a grand ceremony for the transfer of political powers, Hong Kong officially returned to China, the HK SAR's principal officials were sworn in and took office under the auspices of the Central People's Government, and the HK SAR was formally established.

On April 13, 1987, the government of the People's Republic of China and the government the Republic of Portugal signed the Joint Declaration of the Government of the Republic of Portugal and the Government of the People's Republic of China on the Question of Macao (the Sino–Portuguese Joint Declaration). Previously, on April 11 the same year, the Fifth Session of the Sixth National People's Congress had decided to authorize the NPC Standing Committee to deliberate and approve this Declaration. On June 23, 1987, the NPC Standing Committee officially deliberated and approved the Sino–Portuguese Joint Declaration and decided to resume China's exercise of sovereignty over Macao on December 20, 1999. On April 13, 1988, the First Session of the Seventh National People's Congress decided to set up the Drafting Committee of the Basic Law of the Macao Special Administrative Region of the People's Republic of China, which then began to draft a basic law for the Macao SAR. On March 31, 1993, the First Session of the Eighth National People's Congress approved the Basic Law of the Macao Special Administrative Region of the People's Republic of China. The NPC Standing Committee at the same time passed the Decision on the Establishment of the Macao Special Administrative Region of the People's Republic of China and the Decision of the National People's Congress on the Method for the Formation of the First Government, the first Legislative Council and the First Judiciary of the Macao Special Administrative Region, and decided to set up a National People's Congress Preparatory Commission for the Macao Special Administrative Region to be in charge of matters relevant to preparations for setting up the Macao SAR, including preparations to set up the first government of the Macao SAR and formulating the specific methods for setting up its first legislative committee and the first judiciary of the Macao SAR. On May 5, 1998, the setting up of the National People's Congress Macao Special Administrative Region Preparatory Commission was announced in Beijing. The commission was composed of 40 mainland members and 60 members from Macao. The mainland members consisted mainly of persons-in-charge of relevant departments as well as experts and academics closely connected with Macao affairs. The Macao members came mostly from industrial and commercial circles, professional circles and labor, social service, religious and political circles and were of a widely representative nature. Four work teams—political, legal, economic, and sociocultural—were set up under the Preparatory Commission. Within a period of 1 year and 8 months, the Preparatory Commission completed a vast amount of fruitful work on the Basic Law and the relevant regulations of the NPC and its Standing Committee, and completed all preparations for setting up the Macao SAR. On December 20, 1999, the governments of China and Portugal held a ceremony to transfer Macao's political powers, Macao was officially returned to China, administrative officials of the Macao SAR were sworn into office under the auspices of the Central People's Government, and the Macao Special Administrative Region was founded.

It is clear that in all matters—from the decision to resume China's exercise of sovereignty over Hong Kong and Macao to the drafting of the two Basic Laws and to the SARs' preparatory and organizational work—the decisions were made by the National People's Congress, and that the two SARs' Basic Law drafting commissions and the two SAR's preparatory commissions were institutions established under the National People's Congress. No other central institutions of political power, including the NPC Standing Committee and the State Council, had the power to decide on the setting up of those special local administrative institutions, though the NPC relied on them to implement its decisions once the decisions were made.

Since the Central Authorities had the power to set up the SARs, they also had the power to determine the systems implemented in the SARs as well as the power to determine Central/SAR's relations and the division of powers and responsibilities. "One country, two systems" is a special concept implemented in the SARs pursuant to proposals by the Central Authorities. It goes without saying that the National People's Congress did not decide on setting up the SARs or stipulate the systems in them out of thin air, but did so after giving ample consideration to the history and current realities of Hong Kong and Macao and fully hearing the opinions of Hong Kong and Macao personages.

The power of the Central Authorities to set up the SAR institution includes the power of the Central Authorities (i.e., the National People's Congress) to repeal the SAR institution. This is, of course, stated in terms of theory; in reality the National People's Congress will not lightly resort to such an action.

6.1.2   Legislative Authority over the SARs

After the Central Authorities decided to set up the SARs and determined the systems to be implemented in them, they proceeded to give legal form to their decisions and the systems, and formulated constitution-type laws for the SARs. These were the SAR Basic Laws. According to China's Constitution, only the Central Authorities are empowered to formulate SAR Basic Laws; and among the Central Authorities, only the highest organ of state power, namely the National People's Congress, is empowered to formulate such laws. The drafting of the two Basic Laws is a case in point.

An organ that formulates laws must necessarily have the power to amend the laws it formulates, and so the National People's Congress which drew up the SAR Basic Laws must necessarily have the power to amend the SAR Basic Laws. Also, in accordance with China's legal interpretation system, the National People's Congress Standing Committee is responsible for interpreting China's laws, and hence the power to interpret the Basic Laws rests with the NPC Standing Committee. A detailed discussion of this special matter will follow.

6.1.3   The Power to Retain "Residual Powers"

In China, the Central Authorities have the power to clearly define by means of laws the respective powers they and the SARs enjoy. However, in terms of legislative technicalities, there must also be a regulation on who assumes competence when there are matters not regulated by any laws, failing which "power vacuums" and "legal vacuums" will arise and may lead to confusion. Under ordinary circumstances, these "residual powers" pertain to the entity that has the right to establish/organize, and since the SARs' right to establish/organize and the legislative authority over the SARs are both vested in the Central Authorities, any such "residual powers" should pertain to the Central Authorities. This is one of the characteristics of the unitary system. Article 2 of the HK Basic Law stipulates that "the National People's Congress authorizes" the SARs to exercise a high degree of autonomy, and Article 20 stipulates that the SAR "may enjoy other powers granted to it by the National People's Congress, the Standing Committee of the National People's Congress or the Central People's Government." These stipulations imply that if any "residual powers" exist, they should naturally pertain to the Central Authorities even though the Central Authorities may authorize the SAR to exercise these "residual powers."

In sum, the SARs' right to establish/organize, as vested in the Central Authorities, includes the power of institution in the SARs, legislative authority over the SARs and the power to retain "residual powers," the most important of which is the first power—the power of institution in the SARs. The two other powers are derived from the first of those powers.

6.2 The Power to Formulate, Amend, and Interpret the SARs' Basic Laws and to Review Constitutional Violations

In the foregoing text, we have mentioned that legislative authority is an important content of the right to establish/organize, and the formulation of the SARs' Basic Laws is the main form and content of legislative authority. Hence, we will conduct a detailed and separate exposition of the Central Authorities' power to formulate, amend, and interpret the SAR Basic Laws as an important power enjoyed by the Central Authorities. The Central Authorities' power to review constitutional violations by SARs' legislature will be discussed in later chapters and sections.

6.2.1 The Power to Formulate SAR Basic Laws

The SAR Basic Laws are fundamental laws which govern such major matters in the SARs as their political, economic, and cultural systems, the rights and duties of their inhabitants, and Central/SARs relations. They are the basic codes of conduct which the government and inhabitants of the SARs must comply with after the setting up of the SARs as well as the basis of the SARs' legislation. They are also the basic legal instruments which both the Central Authorities and the SARs must abide by, and all legislation that conflicts with the Basic Laws is invalid. In the SARs' legal systems, the Basic Laws are in the foremost position and have the highest legal effect.

As stated earlier, only the Central Authorities in China possess the right to establish/organize in the SARs, the power to stipulate the systems practiced in the SARs and the power to exercise legislative authority over the SARs. Hence, only the Central Authorities have the power to formulate the Basic Laws which stipulate the SARs' basic system. The main formulating entity of the SAR Basic Laws can only be the

Central Authorities, not the SARs per se, and there can only be one main formulating entity; the Central Authorities and the SARs cannot both be the main entities. That is to say, the Basic Laws were not generated through negotiations between the Central Authorities and the SARs. This is also evident from the dates on which the Basic Laws came into existence—the Basic Laws appeared before the SARs did, not after.[3]

The Basic Laws were generated prior to the establishment of the SARs, or in other words while Hong Kong and Macao still remained under the control of Britain and Portugal, respectively, but the drafting of the Basic Laws took place entirely within the bounds of China's sovereignty. They were unilateral legislative acts by the Chinese government and were free from interference by any foreign country or international bloc. Although the formulations of the Basic Laws took international factors into consideration, they were entirely exercises of China's internal law, not international treaties, and differed in substance from the Sino–British Joint Declaration and the Sino–Portuguese Joint Declaration.

Thus, the Central Authorities had ample and full powers to formulate the Basic Laws, as was borne out by the drafting of the two SAR Basic Laws. After the signing of the Sino–British Joint Declaration in 1984, the Central Authorities at once set about drafting the Hong Kong Special Administrative Zone Basic Law. On April 10, 1985, the Third Session of the Sixth National People's Congress passed a decision to set up the Drafting Commission of the Hong Kong Special Administrative Zone Basic Law, on June 18 the Sixth Session of the National People's Congress commissioned the drafting commission, and on July 1 of the same year the drafting commission was officially established. Hence, it can be seen that the Basic Law Drafting Commission was a pro tem special commission of the National People's Congress, and the entire drafting work of the Basic Law was completed by this drafting commission under the auspices of China's highest organ of state power. After nearly five years of work, the Third Session of the Seventh National People's Congress approved the Basic Law of the Hong Kong Special Administrative Region on April 4, 1990.

On April 13, 1988, the First Plenary Session of the Seventh National People's Congress decided to set up the Drafting Commission for the Basic Law of the Macao Special Administrative Region to take charge of the work of drafting the Macao Basic Law. Starting with the convening of the first plenary meeting of the Macao Basic Law drafting commission on October 25, 1988, the commission held a total of 9 plenary sessions plus 72 meetings of professional teams, extensively solicited opinions and suggestions from Macao's residents and social circles, drew up a draft of the Basic Law, and submitted this to the NPC for deliberation. On March 31, 1993, the draft of the Basic Law together with appendices were examined and approved by the First Session of the Eighth National People's Congress. These were signed by the President of China and published with the decision to implement them on December 20, 1999. From drafting to publishing, this Basic Law took four years and

---

[3]The Hong Kong SAR Basic Law was approved by the National People's Congress on April 4, 1990, whereas the Hong Kong SAR was established on July 1, 1997. The Macao SAR Basic Law was approved by the National People's Congress on March 31, 1993, whereas the Macao SAR was established on December 20, 1999.

five months and was formulated on the basis of extensive consultations with residents and various circles in Macao and by absorbing all useful ideas. The drafting of the Macao Basic Law was the crystallization of collective wisdom. It was completed under the direct auspices of the National People's Congress.

Although the Central Authorities possessed the power to formulate the SAR Basic Laws, this is not to say that they could set up laws for the SARs at will, or that they could decline participation by the residents and personages of all circles in Hong Kong and Macao. On the contrary, of a total of 59 members of the Hong Kong SAR Basic Law's drafting commission 23 were Hong Kong personages—a very large proportion. Moreover, the Basic Law's drafting commission entrusted its Hong Kong members with setting up in Hong Kong a widely representative Basic Law consultation committee in order to gather opinions and suggestions from people of all walks of life on the drafting of the Basic Law, so that the Basic Law would be more consistent with public opinion and the actual circumstances of Hong Kong. And the opinions of Hong Kong's people were indeed given the attention they deserved, and were fully reflected in the Basic Laws' articles. It is clear that the Central Authorities, or in other words the NPC, amply recruited the Hong Kong people's participation and fully respected their opinions when exercising its right to formulate the Basic Law.

The drafting of the Basic Law of the Macao Special Administrative Region, too, extensively recruited the participation of personages of all circles in Macao. The Drafting Commission of Basic Law of the Macao Special Administrative Region consisted of 46 persons, 22 of whom were from Macao. The drafting commission also set up a Basic Law consultation committee composed of 90 persons from all sectors, extensively solicited the opinions and suggestions of people of all walks of life in Macao on the drafting of the basic law, and gained the reputation of being "the largest and most extensively representative non-governmental consultation organization in Macao's history."[4] Hence although the power to formulate the Basic Law rested with the Central Authorities, the opinions of all circles in Macao were assimilated.

6.2.2 The Power to Amend the SAR Basic Laws

The power to formulate laws includes the power to amend laws, and the institutions that formulate laws are necessarily at the same time institutions empowered to amend laws. Since the Central Authorities, or in other words the NPC, had and has the power to formulate SAR Basic Laws, they also have the power to amend the SAR Basic Laws it formulated. According to the provisions of Article 62 of the Constitution, the powers to formulate and amend the SAR Basic Laws are vested in the National People's Congress, and no other institution, including the NPC Standing Committee,

---

[4]Ma Wanqi. Briefing on the Work Circumstances of Meetings of the Sponsors of the Consultative Committee of the Macao Special Administrative Region; Quoted from Lan Tian. *Research on Legal Problems of One Country, Two Systems.* Beijing: Law Press, 1997, p. 115.

may exercise those powers. Yet frequent amendments to the Basic Laws are impracticable because the NPC holds only one session per year. The fact that the SAR Basic Laws can only be amended by China's highest organ of state powers indicates the seriousness of Basic Law amendments. Moreover, due to the unique nature of the SARs' Basic Laws, many unique provisions as well as strict limitations have been made to their amendment procedures to ensure the continuity and stability of the Basic Laws and the Central Authorities' policies on the SARs. This is manifested in the following respects:

6.2.2.1   The Power to Propose Amendments

Article 159 of the Basic Law of the Hong Kong Special Administrative Region and Article 144 of the Basic Law of the Macao Special Administrative Region both stipulate that the power to propose amendments to the Basic Law is vested in the Standing Committee of the National People's Congress, the State Council and the Hong Kong (Macao) Special Administrative Region. No other department, institution, or public organization is empowered to propose amendments to the Basic Laws.

From this stipulation, we see that the principal entities empowered to propose amendments to the Basic Laws include both the Central Authorities and the SARs, since these are the main entities involved in the Basic Laws. Why the power to propose amendments should be given to the Central Authorities is easy to understand. It is also logical that both the NPC Standing Committee and State Council have the power to propose amendments to the Basic Laws, since the two are permanent establishments and executive organs, respectively, of the NPC, and both are central political-power institutions directly related to the SARs. And the power to propose amendments to the Basic Laws has been vested in the SARs because the SARs are under the direct jurisdiction of, and specifically implement, the Basic Laws. If the SARs find in their specific operations that certain articles or contents of the Basic Laws are inconsistent with realities, they may propose bills for Basic Law amendments to the National People's Congress in accordance with the procedures stipulated in the Basic Laws.

The Basic Laws stipulate the procedures which the SARs shall comply with for exercising their power to propose amendments, i.e., amendment bills from the SARs shall be submitted to the National People's Congress by the regions' delegations the NPC, after having obtained consent for doing so from two-thirds of the regions' deputies to the NPC, two-thirds of all members of the regions' legislative councils, and the regions' chief executives.

6.2.2.2   Deliberation and Approval

The Basic Laws also stipulate that prior to the inclusion of bills for NPC amendments to the Basic Laws on Congress agendas, the Hong Kong (Macao) Special Administrative Region Basic Law Commission under the NPC Standing Committee (hereinafter referred to as the "Basic Law Commission") shall study the bills and state its opinions about them. As special work institutions under the NPC Standing Committee, the Basic Law Commissions are responsible for studying, and for submitting their views to the NPC Standing Committee, on problems in the relevant articles and contents of the Basic Laws arising in the course of actual implementation. Having these commissions conduct prior examinations of bills for Basic Law amendments is an expression of prudence on the matter of amending the Basic Laws.

After a bill for amending a Basic Law is placed on the agenda of the National People's Congress by its Presidium, it shall be submitted to a general meeting of the Congress for deliberation. When the Congress deliberates such bills, it shall be given ample opportunity to hear the relevant amendment report and the views of residents and people of all circles in the SAR before voting on the matter. In accordance with the NPC's procedures for the formulation of laws, bills for amendments to the Basic Laws acquire legal validity when they obtain a simple majority vote of all deputies to the National People's Congress.

6.2.2.3   Amendment Methods and Principles

Amendments to Basic Laws must take the form of amendment proposals, or in other words, individual amendments shall be made to specific provisions only where amendments are indeed needed. Overall or extensive amendments are inadvisable since amendments of this type are bound to "injure sinews and bones," damage the fundamental legislative intent of the Basic Laws as well as the State's established policies on the SARs, and harm the continuity and stability of the Basic Laws.

6.2.2.4   Contents that May not Be Amended

Both of the Basic Laws stipulate "no amendment to this Law shall contravene the established basic policies of the People's Republic of China regarding Hong Kong (Macao)"; this is a principle which must be complied with when amending the Basic Laws. This is the first time in the New China's legislative history that a law has actually stipulated restrictions or prohibitions against the contents of amendments.[5] The established basic policy of the Central Authorities on Hong Kong and Macao, as based on the Preambles and General Principles of the Basic Laws, is to implement "one country, two systems," refrain from exercising socialist systems and policies in Hong Kong and Macao, authorize the SARs to implement a high degree of autonomy, and maintain their original capitalist systems and ways of life unchanged for fifty years. Any amendments that contravene these established policies by means of making amendments to the Basic Laws are null and void.

There will also be detailed discussions of these issues in later chapters and sections.

---

[5]Xiao Weiyun. *One Country, Two Systems and Hong Kong's Basic Legal System.* Beijing: Peking University Press, 1990, pp. 153–154.

6.2.3   The Power to Interpret the Basic Laws

The power to interpret the Basic Laws is a most complex issue. According to the provisions of Article 67, Item 4 of the Constitution of China, the power to interpret laws rests with the NPC Standing Committee. Due, however, to the fact that Hong Kong is a region that implements the Common Law, its system for interpreting laws is quite different from that in China's mainland regions. Hong Kong's system for interpreting laws is a judicial interpreting system in which courts of law interpret laws. The system implemented in China's mainland is one of the legislative institutions interpreting laws. Hence, many controversies have existed over the power to interpret the Basic Law of the Hong Kong SAR.

The controversies were mainly over the following aspects:

First, whether the power of final interpretation should rest with Hong Kong or Beijing. One point of view maintained that if Hong Kong SAR law courts were no longer vested with full power to interpret constitutional law as previously, "one country, two systems" would change to "one country one system," and nothing would be left of the courts' power of final adjudication. Another point of view held that since the Basic Law included provisions and contents on the powers of the Central Authorities and on Central/SAR relations, if Hong Kong's courts of final adjudication were to unilaterally interpret these provisions and contents and exclude the Central Authorities, "one country, two systems" would be turned into a setup where "two systems exist but not one country," and where the Central Authorities would be dominated by the SAR.[6] Hence, it was absolutely necessary to find a solution satisfactory to both parties and to enable "one country" and "two systems" to become organically conjoined.

To this end, the Basic Law first of all made it clear its power of interpretation was vested in the Central Authorities, since the Basic Law, as a national law formulated by the Central Authorities, first of all, had to comply with China's law interpreting system in terms of the interpretation issue. Hence, the power of final interpretation of the Basic Law had to rest with Beijing, not Hong Kong. There are precedents in other countries for making such systemic arrangements. In Europe, for instance, the laws of the European Union apply to its member states. According to the stipulations of relevant treaties, the power to interpret EU laws is vested in the Court of Justice of the European Union. When the courts of law of member states encounter problems of interpreting EU laws in the process of hearing cases, they may request the Court of Justice of the European Union to produce an interpretation; and if these happen to be cases of final instance, the member states' courts of law must request the Court of Justice of the European Union to produce an interpretation before they make a final ruling.[7] In federalist countries like the United States, the power of final interpretation

---

[6]Huang Yulin. "The Power to Interpret Laws in the Chinese Constitution and the Basic Law of the Hong Kong Special Administrative Region," in Xu Chongde. *The Constitution and Democratic Governance.* Beijing: China Procuratorate Press, 1994, p. 389.

[7]See Huang Yulin. "The Power to Interpret Laws in the Chinese Constitution and the Basic Law of the Hong Kong Special Administrative Region," in Xu Chongde. *The Constitution and Democratic*

of federal laws is also vested in the Federation instead of in the localities. That is even more so in a unitary system state.

Of course, the Central Authorities may, in view of the special circumstances of a SAR, authorize the SAR courts of law to conduct their own interpretations of provisions and contents within the scope of SAR autonomy stipulated by the Basic Laws, so long as their interpretations do not involve the powers of the Central Authorities and Central/SAR relations, and are not rulings of final instance. In such cases, the SAR judicial organs may to all intents and purposes exercise the complete power of interpretation. One should say that such a disposition is logical and reasonable, as it does not run counter to China's present law interpretation system, upholds the "one country" principle while ensuring "two systems," and enables the SARs to exercise all of the interpreting powers stipulated by the Basic Laws.

Second, which central organ should exercise the power of interpreting the Basic Laws—the National People's Congress, the NPC Standing Committee, the State Council, or the Supreme People's Court? Under the current legal system in China, one might say that all of these institutions are vested with a certain amount of legal interpretative power. The National People's Congress as the highest institution of power and the highest legislative organ should be able to interpret laws.[8] The State Council may be able to perform administrative interpretations of laws, but the State Council is an administrative institution and is obviously not suited to interpreting laws of the Basic Law type. The Superior People's Court may produce judicial interpretations on the question of how to make specific use of laws during the judicial process, but its power of judicial interpretation is extremely limited and is unlike that of courts of law under the Common Law system, which can "formulate" laws. Moreover, the SARs are vested with independent judicial powers and powers of final adjudication. Although having the Supreme People's Court interpret the Basic Laws would integrate it with the Common Law system as far as form is concerned, doing so would likely create the misconception that the Supreme People's Court is the SARs' court of final adjudication and that the SARs' judiciaries are not independent. Such being the case, the one and only suitable institution for interpreting the Basic Laws under China's existing constitutional framework is the NPC Standing Committee.

Governance. Beijing: China Procuratorate Press, 1994, p. 389. Also, see Xu Chongde. *A Course on the Basic Laws of Hong Kong and Macao*. Beijing: China Renmin University Press, 1994, p. 69.

[8]There are no clear-cut stipulations in the Constitution on whether the National People's Congress is vested with powers to interpret laws. However, in terms of China's jurisprudence theory and China's legal system, the National People's Congress should, of course, be able to interpret laws since its permanent body, the NPC Standing Committee, can do so. Moreover, the National People's Congress has the power to oversee the implementation of the Constitution, or in other words, the power to investigate violations of the Constitution, and thus, of course, has the power to interpret the Constitution and laws. However, if viewed strictly from legal principles, where a state institution is not clearly and explicitly authorized by the Constitution to exercise certain powers, it may not do so, whatever the institution. A state organ's powers may not be expanded through such means as analogies and implied logical inferences. Since the Constitution only empowers the NPC Standing Committee to interpret the Constitution and laws, that means the Constitution does not empower any other institution, including the National People's Congress, to exercise that power. And that is why the NPC does not have the power to interpret laws. See Chapter X.

As to why laws should be interpreted by legislative organs, the reasoning of China's jurisprudence is that the purpose of interpreting laws is to have an authoritative institution further explain the original intent of the legislation and indicate the true connotations of legal provisions and clauses when their meaning is unclear. In that case, which institutions best understand the original intent of legislation? The institutions that formulate laws, of course. Hence, the best legal explanations are those produced by the legislative institutions per se. There is, in a certain sense, nothing wrong about that argument, and legislative institutions are, of course, the most knowledgeable about the original intent and purpose of the legislation.

However, there have always been scholars who query the system in China where laws are interpreted by legislative institutions; who maintain that this could lead to arbitrariness on the part of legislative institutions and fear that legislation organs could interpret laws as they please without being subject to any restrictions. They maintain that under a good legal interpretation system, laws should be interpreted by a neutral institution such as a court of law, and that once laws have been formulated the legislative organ should stand aside and the fate of the laws should rest in the hands of neutral judges. If legislative organs believe that interpretations of laws by courts of law are incorrect, they may amend the laws or even formulate the laws anew, and legislative organs may use such means to amend or even overturn interpretations by courts of law, but legislative organs should not express any further opinions about the laws once these have been launched.

Regardless of the extent of the criticisms or opinions leveled at China's system of interpreting laws, or whether China's legislative organs frequently exercise this power, such is the current reality in China.[9] If the system is unreasonable, one may propose amendments, but prior to any amendments we must comply with it. Hence, the power of final interpretation of the Basic Laws can be exercised only by the NPC Standing Committee.

For the sake of greater caution and sobriety, the Basic Laws also stipulate that the NPC Standing Committee must solicit the opinions of the SAR Basic Law Committees in the regions to which the Basic Laws pertain before producing any interpretations of the Basic Laws. According to the stipulations of both of the Basic Laws, half of the members of the SAR Basic Law committees are to be from the SAR per se and shall include persons from legal circles. Their task is to study problems that arise in the course of implementing Basic Law provisions and clauses on the functions and powers of the Central Authorities and on Central/SAR relations, and to present their views to the NPC Standing Committee. This is one more guarantee that interpretations of the Basic Laws are consistent with the SARs' actual circumstances.

The third question is how great should the SAR law courts' powers of interpretation be. The dispositions in the Basic Laws in this respect are that the SAR law courts, of course, have full powers of interpreting provisions and clauses when handling cases within the scope of SAR autonomy. Furthermore, the SAR law courts, when handling cases, may also interpret provisions and clauses of the Basic Law that

---

[9]Despite being vested with that important power, for some unknown reason the NPC Standing Committee has in reality seldom exercised it.

fall beyond the scope of [SAR] autonomy, or in other words, provisions and clauses which have to do with matters administered by the Central People's Government or with Central/SAR relations. However, if a SAR court of law needs to interpret these provisions and clauses, and if the interpretation could affect the SAR court's judgment on the case, the SAR's court of final adjudication must request that the NPC Standing Committee produce a final interpretation prior to the SAR law court turning out an unappealable adjudication of final instance. Moreover, the SAR court of law must take the interpretation by the NPC Standing Committee as the criterion when citing the said provision or clause. That, of course, does not affect the force of adjudications produced prior to this stipulation.

This special stipulation, in reality, enables SAR courts of law to interpret all provisions and clauses of the Basic Law; restrictions apply only when the interpretation of provisions and clauses involve the functions and duties of the Central Authorities and Central/SAR relations, and when final adjudications are to be made. In those cases, requests to the NPC Standing Committee shall be made for final interpretations. The purpose of this is mainly to avoid the possibility of discrepancies emerging in the interpretations by the SAR law courts and the NPC Standing Committee—discrepancies which would create confusion in the relations between the Central Authorities and the SARs.

In sum, the drafters of the SAR Basic Law finally resolved difficult constitutional problems by consulting and referencing other countries' experience with regard to the interpretation of laws and basing themselves on China's actual circumstances. The final result finds concentrated expression in Article 158 of the Basic Law of the Hong Kong Special Administrative Region. One may well say that the Basic Law's stipulation on its power to interpret gives full consideration to the actual circumstances of Hong Kong's implementation of the Common Law interpretation system, and is also consistent with the interpretation system under China's law. It is a model of the synthesis of "one country" and "two systems." It is reasonable, logical, and constitutional. Article 143 of the Basic Law of the Macao Special Administrative Region contains similar stipulations. I will further explore issues of the interpretation of the SAR Basic Laws in subsequent chapters and sections in connection with specific cases which have transpired after the establishment of the SARs.

The powers of the Central Authorities with regard to investigating violations of the Constitution will be discussed in the following chapters and sections.

6.3 The Organizational Powers of SAR Governments

Since the Central Authorities vested with the SARs' right to organize/establish and the power to formulate SAR Basic Laws, it follows that they, of course, wield the SARs' organizational powers. This, too, is a most important power among those vested in the Central Authorities since it is a manifestation of the unitary-system principle and of state sovereignty. This power is first and foremost manifested in the fact that both of the Preparatory Commissions were set up by the Central Authorities, that all activities for preparing the SAR governments were sponsored by the Central Authorities[10] and that the Hong Kong and Macao localities did not establish their governments on their own initiative.

However, since the SARs implement the principles of "Hong Kongers govern Hong Kong," "Macanese govern Macao," and "a high degree of autonomy," the Central Authorities have not dispatched officials to the SARs. This makes it clear that the SARs governments are not agencies of the Central Authorities; that they are local government organs composed of the SARs' people per se. The organizational power wielded by the Central Authorities over the SARs is manifested mainly as the power to appoint the Chief Executives and other principal officials. In this respect, Article 15 of the Basic Law of the Hong Kong Special Administrative Region stipulates: "The Central People's Government shall appoint the Chief Executive and the principal officials of the executive authorities of the Hong Kong Special Administrative Region in accordance with the provisions of Chapter IV of this Law." The Basic Law of the Macao Special Administrative Region makes a similar stipulation.

Article 45 of Chapter IV of the Hong Kong Basic Law stipulates that the Chief Executive shall first be selected by election or through consultations and then be appointed by the Central People's Government. Also, according to the provisions of Article 48, the Chief Executive, on being appointed by the Central Government, shall have the power to set up a cabinet for the SAR, to nominate the principal administrative officials and report them to the Central People's Government for appointment, and to recommend to the Central People's Government the removal of these officials, including the secretaries and deputy secretaries of departments, directors of bureaus, the director of immigration affairs and of Customs. And so the Central Authorities effectuate their organizational powers in the SAR government by means of appointing the SAR's Executive Officer and principal officials.

Then, is the Central Authorities' power to appoint the Executive Officer and principal officials a power merely in name and form? Or is it a substantive power? Some people hold that since the policy of the Central Authorities is to have "Hong Kongers govern Hong Kong," the Central Authorities should respect the wishes of the Hong Kongers after an executive officer is generated democratically in the locality, and should simply fulfill the legal procedures and not refuse to grant appointment. This proposition, in fact, replicates the system whereby the British king appoints the prime minister in that the king is bound to appoint as prime minister the leader of the majority party that wins in the general elections. If this system is adopted, however, the organizational power enjoyed by the Central Authorities in the SAR government would be nominal, and "high degree of autonomy" would turn into "complete autonomy." Hence the Central Authorities' appointment of the Executive Officer is in the nature of both a legal procedure and a substantive measure. It represents power in both form and substance. The Central People's Government has the power to refuse to appoint an executive officer designated by the SAR and send [the nomination]

---

[10]Here, Central Authorities refers to the National People's Congress.

back for reconsideration.[11] Yet the Central Government will not directly nominate a candidate of Executive Officer, as that falls within the powers of the SAR. After an executive officer designated by the SAR is appointed by the Central Government, the SAR has to designate another executive officer to be submitted to the Central Authorities for an appointment.

The above Basic Law regulations on the way executive officers are generated make it necessary for executive officers to be responsible to both the SAR and the Central People's Government, and places them under dual supervision by the SARs and the Central People's Government. In the terminology of mainland constitutional studies, this constitutes a system of "dual responsibility and dual leadership," the specific implications of which, of course, differ quite considerably. A SAR executive officer's responsibility toward the Central People's Government does not require him to request instructions and report on all matters, and he may make his own decisions according to the law so long as the Basic Law invests him with powers he may exercise on his own. This amply manifests the principle and spirit of "one country, two systems," and upholds state sovereignty at the same time as it manifests the principle "Hong Kongers govern Hong Kong with a high degree autonomy."

Article 15 of the Basic Law of the Macao Special Administrative Region stipulates that the Central People's Government appoints or dismisses the Macao SAR's executive officer, principal government officials, and attorney-general. Included among the principal government officials are the secretaries of various departments, commissioners, independent commissioners against corruption, directors of audits, and principal persons-in-charge of police departments and customs. Its legislative principles are the same as those of the Hong Kong SAR.

Concerning this matter, the Constitution of China provides that the governors, chairmen and mayors of mainland provinces, autonomous regions, and directly administered municipalities may immediately take office after being elected by local people's congresses and needed not be reported again to the Central People's Government for appointment. Moreover, the leaders of various departments which make up the people's governments of mainland provinces, autonomous regions, and directly administered municipalities are also nominated by the chiefs of local administrations, and only need to be approved by people's congress standing committees at their own levels. They are merely reported to the people's government at the next higher level for the record and need not be approved by higher authorities.[12] Does this mean that the powers of the "highly autonomous" SARs are less extensive than the powers of

---

[11] See Xu Chongde. *A Course on the Basic Laws of Hong Kong and Macao*. Beijing: China Renmin University Press, 1994, p. 65.

[12] Article 101 of the Constitution provides: "Local people's congresses at their respective levels elect and have the power to recall governors and deputy governors, or mayors or deputy mayors, or head and deputy heads of countries, districts, townships and towns." Item 10, Article 39 of the "Organic Law of the Local People's Congresses and Local People's Governments or the People's Republic of China stipulates that the standing committees of local people's congresses at all levels at and above the county level shall, "decide, upon nomination by the governor, chairman of the autonomous region, mayor, prefect of head of the county or district, on the appointment or removal of the secretary-general and the department and bureau directors, commission chairmen and sections

ordinary local mainland governments that do not exercise a high degree of autonomy? Not so. Because the extent of the powers enjoyed by a locality is measured not merely by the way their public servants are generated, but also by the extent of the legally stipulated powers they actually enjoy. Although the administrative chiefs and the principal local administrative officials of the governments of mainland provinces, directly administered municipalities and autonomous regions need not be appointed and approved by higher levels of government, the powers these local governments enjoy are quite limited and cannot be compared with the high degree of autonomous powers enjoyed by the SAR governments. Specific manifestations of this are the provisions in item 4 of Article 89 of the Constitution which state that the functions and powers of the State Council are: "to exercise unified leadership over the work of local organs of state administrations at various levels throughout the country, and to formulate the detailed divisions of functions and powers between the Central Government and the organs of state administration of provinces, autonomous regions, and municipalities directly under the Central Government"; Item 14 provides that the State Council has the function and power "to alter or annul inappropriate orders issued by local organs of state administration at various levels"; and Article 91 provides that "the State Council establishes an auditing body to supervise through auditing the revenue and expenditure of all departments under the State Council and of the local governments at various levels, and the revenue and expenditure of all financial and monetary organizations, enterprises and institutions of the state." Article 110 of the Constitution provides that "local people's governments at various levels throughout the country are state administrative organs under the unified leadership of the State Council and are subordinate to it." This shows that ordinary local governments on the mainland all operate under the direct leadership of the State Council, and that despite the fact that their leaders are generated through elections, their powers are far smaller than the highly autonomous powers of the SARs. Under the unitary system, the powers enjoyed by local governments are not necessarily connected directly with the way in which these powers are generated. Hence, the fact that the chief executives and principal administrative officials are to be appointed once again by the Central Authorities after being elected locally does not affect the SARs' high degree of autonomy, and does not show that the high degree of autonomy enjoyed by the SARs is any smaller than the powers of ordinary local governments on the mainland.

Of course, Article 45 of the HK SAR Basic Law specifies the ultimate method of selecting the Chief Executive, and that is to achieve the ultimate aim of having a broadly representative nominating committee do so by universal suffrage in accordance with the actual circumstances of the HK SAR and the principle of gradual and orderly progression. [sic] Annex I of the HK Basic Law also stipulates if there is a need to amend the method for selecting the Chief Executives for terms subsequent to the year 2007, such amendments must be made with the endorsement of a two-thirds majority of all the members of the Legislative Council and the consent of the Chief Executive, and shall be reported to the Standing Committee of the National

---

chiefs of the people's government at corresponding level and to report such decisions to the people's government at the next higher level for the record."

People's Congress for approval. The Macao Basic Law makes similar stipulations. These provisions point out the direction for the development of democratization in the SARs and express the Central Authorities' commitment to implement thorough-going democracy in the SARs. If the SARs bring about direct selection and elections of Chief Executives by their local inhabitants, this will constitute a milestone in the history of the SARs and mark their entry into a new phase of political development.

As to whether the Central People's Government may or may not remove SAR officials it has appointed, including the Chief Executive: (Translation from the Por-tuguese text—Tr.) "The Central People's Government shall appoint or remove the Chief Executive, the principal officials of the government and the Procurator-General of the Macao Special Administrative Region in accordance with the provisions of this Law." So there is no question that the Central Authorities may appoint or remove the principal officials of the Macao SAR in accordance with the provisions of the Macao Basic Law. However, the Hong Kong Basic Law has no clear-cut provisions in this respect. Article 52 of the Hong Kong Basic Law merely stipulates a number of circumstances under which the HK SAR Chief Executive must resign, to wit, when he or she loses the ability to discharge his or her duties as a result of serious illness or other reasons; or when, after the Legislative Council is dissolved because he or she has twice refused to sign a bill passed by it, the new Legislative Council again passes by a two-thirds majority of all the members the original bill in dispute and he or she still refuses to sign it; or when, after the Legislative Council is dissolved because it refuses to pass a budget or any other important bill, the new Legislative Council still refuses to pass the original bill in dispute. Under these circumstances, the Chief Executive must resign and a new Chief Executive must be elected and appointed in accordance with the provisions of the Hong Kong Basic Law. The issue does not exist of removing the Chief Executive from his or her post.

Item 9 of Article 73 of the Hong Kong Basic Law stipulates procedures for impeaching the Chief Executive, i.e., if one-fourth of all the members of the Leg-islative Council jointly initiate a motion charging the Chief Executive with serious breaches of law or dereliction of duty and he or she refuses to resign, the Council may, after passing a motion for investigation, issue a mandate to the Chief Justice of the Court of Final Appeal to form and chair an independent investigation committee. This committee shall be responsible for carrying out the investigation and reporting its findings to the Council. If the committee considers the evidence sufficient to sub-stantiate such charges, the Council may pass a motion of impeachment by a two-thirds majority of all its members and shall report this to the Central People's Government for decision. Under such circumstances, can the Central Government reject the Hong Kong Legislative Council's motion of impeachment and decide not to remove the Chief Executive from his or her position? The Hong Kong Basic Law per se makes no stipulation in this respect. However, since the result of the impeachment is to be "reported to the Central People's Government for decision," that "decision" presents two possibilities—the impeachment may be approved, or may not be approved. Hence, the Central Government may, logically speaking, make a decision not to consent to the SAR Legislative Council's impeachment of the Chief Executive. Of course, under the circumstances of one-fourth of all of the members of the Legislative

Council jointly initiating a motion charging the Chief Executive of serious breach of law or dereliction of duty, of the Legislative Council mandating the Chief Justice of the Court of Final Appeal to form and chair an independent investigation committee, of the said committee's considering the evidence sufficient to substantiate the charges, and of the Council passing a motion of impeachment by a two-thirds majority of all its members—under such circumstances it is hard to envisage the Central People's Government not consenting to the impeachment of the Chief Executive.

Such being the case, do the Central Authorities have the power to remove the principal officials of Hong Kong SAR of their own volition? The Hong Kong Basic Law contains no provisions on this matter. But does this Law—as well as the stipulation in Article 15 of the Macao Basic Law on the appointment and removal of a principal official of the Macao SAR—include the power to proactively remove principal SAR officials from their positions? One must, first of all, see whether the Central Authorities can, on their own initiative, appoint and remove principal SAR officials, or in other words appoint some person to the post of Chief Executive or some other principal official without going through the procedures of internal elections and negotiations as stipulated by the Basic Laws. That is obviously not possible. When the Central Authorities appoint SAR officials, they must first and foremost fulfill the SARs' relevant democratic and legal procedures, and only then can the candidates be submitted to the Central Authorities for an appointment. Hence, when removing principal officials in the SARs, they must also, first of all, fulfill within the SARs the relevant procedures stipulated by the Basic Laws before submitting them to the Central Authorities for a decision on whether or not to remove the officials.

In the foregoing text, we have already mentioned that the appointment by the Central Authorities of the SARs' Chief Executive and other principal officials is "substantive." And since the appointments are "substantive," so are the removals. However, "substantive" refers to the Central Authorities having or not having the power to reject the lists of appointments or impeachments or removals from office; it does not mean that the Central Authorities may proactively and directly appoint or remove the SARs' principal officials without waiting for the SARs to fulfill the statutory appointment and removal procedures in their respective localities. This should also go for the Chief Executive Election Ordinance passed by the Legislative Council of the Hong Kong SAR on July 10, 2001, which put forward specific stipulations on the election and engendering of the next SAR Chief Executive,[13] including the stipulation that the Central People's Government has the power to remove Chief Executives from office.

6.4   The Power to Declare Emergence State

The term "emergence state" refers to emergency situations brought on in a country by wars with other countries or the emergence of grave and sudden natural disasters, or due to outbreaks of large-scale internal disturbances severe enough to imperil a coun-

---

[13]Hong Kong, *Sing Tao Daily*, July 11, 2001.

try's unity and the stability of its legal state power, leading to grave threats or dangers to normal social order, and to the country's highest organ of state power declaring the termination of the normal order of rule of law either nationwide or in a locality and entering into a state of emergence controls. When emergence state takes place, the state must adopt a number of emergency measures which include declarations of entering into a state of war or a state of emergency, the issuing of emergency orders, the implementation of general or local mobilizations, and the imposition of martial law and curfews or the application of military controls. When the situations that lead to the declaration of the emergence state no longer exist, the country's highest organ of state power announces the termination of the emergence state and the restoration of the normal and peaceful state of rule of law, and social order returns to normalcy.

There are, in general, three kinds of emergence state: (a) states of war in which two or more countries engage in warfare; (b) severe cases of internal chaos; and (c) the occurrence of grave natural calamities. The latter two circumstances are generally referred to as states of emergency. The emergence of such circumstances can severely disrupt the peaceful order of society and gravely impact normal rule of law, and may even result in disintegration of the lawful state regime, drag the country down into a "primitive" and barbarous condition of "a ruler-less state" and inflict grave losses upon the lives and property of its inhabitants. However, since no country can predict the emergence of such emergence state, all countries or regions must "be prepared for danger in times of peace" and "lay up for rainy days." They must consider countermeasures in normal and peaceful times and make corresponding preparations, an important aspect of which is to conduct emergence state legislation and give the state the power to declare emergence state, so that the government may adopt emergency measures based on the law when emergence state do emerge. They must also stipulate the procedures for declaring emergence state so that this power is subject to rigorous restrictions against malpractice or misuse.

As regards legislation for emergence state, the first and foremost thing is to have provisions in the Constitution on the declaration of emergence state. Provisions in this respect are found in the constitutions of all countries in the world. Article 62 of China's Constitution provides that National People's Congress decides on questions of war and peace. Article 67 of China's Constitution provides that the NPC Standing Committee has the power "to decide, when the National People's Congress is not in session, on the proclamation of a state of war in the event of an armed attack on the country or in fulfillment of international treaty obligations concerning common defense against aggression"; the NPC Standing Committee has the power to decide on general mobilization or partial mobilization, to decide on the imposition of martial law throughout the country or in specific provinces, autonomous regions, or municipalities directly under the Central Government; Article 80 provides that the President of the People's Republic of China, pursuant to decisions by the National People's Congress and its Standing Committee, imposes martial law, proclaims a state of war, and issues mobilization orders; Article 89 provides that the State Council has the power to decide on the imposition of martial law in parts of provinces, autonomous regions, and municipalities directly under the Central Government. It is evident that China's Constitution has fairly complete provisions as regards to emergence state.

6.4.1 The Power of the Central Authorities to Implement Emergence State in the SARs

The SAR Basic Laws, as the basic laws of the special administrative regions, should also make stipulations regarding abnormal conditions. That is only rational and normal. However, neither of the two Basic Laws has any stipulations in this respect, and it is not known what the legislators had in mind at the time. The two Basic Laws merely contain indirect provisions when stipulating the circumstances in which national laws apply to the special autonomous regions. Paragraph 4 of Article 18 of the Hong Kong SAR Basic Law stipulates that in the event that the NPC Standing Committee decides to proclaim a state of war or decides that the SAR is in a state of emergency by reason of turmoil within the Hong Kong SAR which endangers national unity or security and is beyond the control of the government of the SAR, the Central People's Government may issue an order applying the relevant national laws in the SAR. The Macao SAR Basic Law makes a similar stipulation. This shows that the Central Authorities may decide that the SARS enter states of emergency under two circumstances: (a) If the entire country enters a state of war, the SAR, as part of the People's Republic of China, shall naturally enter a state of war as well; and (b) if turmoil which endangers national unity or security occurs in a SAR and is beyond the control of the government of the SAR, the Central Authorities are empowered to proclaim that the SAR enters a state of emergency. Under these circumstances, the Central People's Government may issue orders for increasing the application of national laws within the region. These, of course, can only be "relevant national laws," or in other words, national laws relevant to the state of war and the state of emergency. National laws of no relevance may not be implemented in the SARs.[14]

The stipulations of the Basic Laws indicate that only the NPC Standing Committee is empowered to decide that the SAR enters a state of war or a state of emergency. After the NPC Standing Committee has made such a decision, the State Council is specifically in charge of carrying it out. However, in accordance with the provisions of Articles 62 and 67 of the Constitution, the National People's Congress has the first and foremost power to decide on matters of war and peace, whereas the NPC Standing Committee can decide on proclaiming a state of war only when a war breaks out while the National People's Congress is not in session. The provisions of the SARs' Basic Laws should be made consistent with those of the Constitution in this respect, and a provision should be added that the National People's Congress also has the power to proclaim a state of war in the SARs, so as to avoid legislative loopholes.[15]

---

[14] See Xu Chongde. *A Course on the Basic Laws of Hong Kong and Macao.* Beijing: China Renmin University Press, 1994, pp. 64–65.

[15] Although the time span each year in which the NPC is in session is quite brief and lasts only about half a month, it directly exercises the highest state powers in this period, and if a war should break out then, it is obvious that only the NPC and not its Standing Committee will decide on entering a state of war.

The Basic Laws merely stipulate that the Central Authorities have the power to proclaim that the SARs enter an emergence state when wars or serious disturbances break out. As for disturbances or turbulence triggered by serious natural disasters, economic crises or other social issues, so long as they do not imperil state unity and security, and the SARs themselves are capable of keeping them under control, it may be construed that such situations are to be resolved by the SARs themselves. Article 14 of the [Hong Kong] Basic Law stipulates that "The Government of the Hong Kong Special Administrative Region may, when necessary, ask the Central People's Government for assistance from the garrison in the maintenance of public order and in disaster relief." Article 6 and Article 14 of the Law on Garrisoning the Hong Kong Special Administrative Region come up with corresponding stipulations.

6.4.2 The Powers of the SAR Chief Executive for Handling Emergencies

According to Hong Kong's former system, "the Governor in conjunction with the Executive Council" was vested with extensive emergency powers. Hong Kong's emergency regulations stipulated that if the Governor, in conjunction with the Executive Council, believed emergencies or public dangers had arisen, he could formulate regulations he deemed necessary for upholding the public benefit. Under these regulations, the authorities could implement inspections systems, carry out arrests and detentions, conduct emigration and immigration controls, exercise controls over wharfs, ports, and other communications hubs, exercise transport and economic controls, and commandeer or dispose of any properties and enterprises. They could also revise any laws, requisition civilian laborers and so on and so forth. That is to say, the Governor could adopt all measures he deemed necessary when emergencies arose. These contents were stipulated in ten appended legislations. The most important of these was the State of Emergency (Primary) Regulations, which detailed the scope and measures of the emergency measures the Governor could exercise. In the years 1949, 1951, 1952, 1955, 1956, 1958, and 1967, the Governor frequently declared the effectiveness or this or that part of these Regulations. After the return of Hong Kong to China, the Hong Kong SAR's legislation for emergency situations shall have to fit in with the principles and spirit of the Basic Law and the SAR's actual circumstances.[16]

The Basic Laws do not contain clear-cut stipulations on whether the SAR governments have the power to proclaim states of emergency, and only in paragraph two of Article 56 it is specified that the Chief Executive may "adopt measures in emergencies" without first consulting the Executive Council. This shows that the Chief Executive has certain powers for handling emergency situations. Article 58 of the Basic Law of the Macao Special Administrative Region contains a similar stipulation.

---

[16]Lan Tian. *Research on Legal Problems of One Country, Two Systems.* Beijing: Law Press, 1997, pp. 85–86.

6.5   Powers over Diplomatic Affairs

The term "diplomatic affairs" refers to the formal and official economic, political, and economic contacts and exchanges conducted by a country in the capacity of a sovereign nation with other countries, other regions, or international organizations. Diplomatic affairs often directly involve a country's sovereignty and must be conducted in the name of a sovereign nation. Hence, diplomatic powers are state powers that directly concern the sovereignty of countries. Under normal circumstances, the local governments of a country are not vested with diplomatic powers, especially in countries of the unitary system, and diplomatic contacts are under unified administration by the central government.[17]

Under the administrations of Britain and Portugal, the Hong Kong and Macao regions for considerable periods of time had no diplomatic powers. The former Hong Kong government was under the direct jurisdiction of the British Foreign and Commonwealth Office and its diplomatic relations were basically under the unified management of that department. For instance, foreign countries which set up consular institutions in Hong Kong had to obtain permission from England, and the economic agencies set up by the Hong Kong government in other countries or regions were constituents of the British consulates stationed there. To attend relevant international meetings where participants were national entities, Hong Kong had to do so as a member of a British delegation, and if Hong Kong wished to participate in relevant international organizations, it had to do in the capacity and status of "quasi-members." Diplomatic negotiations which directly touched on matters of sovereignty were also managed and controlled by the British. It was only in the 1950s and 1960s when Hong Kong's economic take offs time and again bolstered its international presence that Britain gradually authorized Hong Kong to handle, on its own, a few diplomatic matters which were unrelated to sovereignty.[18]

Macao too basically possessed no power of diplomatic self-determination under Portuguese rule. It was only after the 1976 publication of the Estatuto Orgânico de Macao that a limited amount of diplomatic power was granted to Macao. That Estatuto stipulated that "Macao's relations with foreign countries and the conclusion of international agreements or treaties that represent the power of Macao belong to the President; and that he may entrust the Governor to deal exclusively with the interests of the region" and if "An international agreement or treaty that is implemented in a region should listen to the opinions of local government organizations in advance when it concludes that it has not delegated the above-mentioned mandate."

---

[17]The constitution of the former Soviet Union stipulated that its republics had the right to conduct diplomatic exchanges. However, with the exception of the Ukraine and Byelorussia which for unique historical reasons became members of the United Nations, none of its republics actually joined that international body. Canada's Quebec has the right to conclude international treaties in the cultural aspect with France and other French-speaking countries, but it does not belong in the category of subjects of international law. See Wang Tieya. *International Law.* Beijing: Law Press, 1981, p. 88.

[18]See Xu Chongde. *A Course on the Basic Laws of Hong Kong and Macao.* Beijing: China Renmin University Press, 1994, p. 65.

(Translation from the Portuguese text—Tr.) In this way, Macao too acquired a certain amount of autonomous diplomatic powers of a non-sovereign nature.[19]

Based on the above circumstances, the two Basic Laws both stipulate that the Central People's Government is to be charge of administering SARs-related diplomatic relations. On June 20, 1997, Ambassador Qin Huasun, China's permanent representative to the United Nations, sent a note to the UN Secretary-General regarding the applicability of multinational treaties to the Hong Kong SAR and stated that in accordance with the Sino–British Joint Declaration and the provisions of Article 153 of the Hong Kong Basic Law, international agreements to which the People's Republic of China was not a party but which were already being implemented in Hong Kong after its return to China could continue to be implemented in the Hong Kong SAR. The note contained a detailed explanation of several circumstances related to the implementation of relevant international agreements in the Hong Kong SAR.[20]

With regard to the legal work on international treaties involving Hong Kong, the Foreign Ministry disposed of a number of remnant or follow-up issues concerning the implementation of international treaties before and after the return of Hong Kong to China. This included properly handling, together with treaty signatories, the implementation of treaties which China had already concluded as well as the adaptation to Hong Kong of treaties which China had not yet concluded, in order to secure the signatories' support and understanding. These issues were satisfactorily resolved. Furthermore, with regard to International treaties in which China intended to take part, the Central Government solicited the opinions of the SAR government on the basis of the "one country, two systems" principle and the relevant provisions of the Basic Laws, and made special dispositions for adapting the treaties to Hong Kong in light of Hong Kong's specific needs. The Chinese government, as the party responsible for the SARs fulfilling the rights and duties generated by international conventions, continues to fulfill on behalf of the SARs the labor pacts as well as the agreements on narcotics and the agreements on human rights in which China has or has not participated. It continues to submit reports and transmit data and materials to the institutions that are party to the agreements, and arranges for SAR representatives to join Chinese delegations and attend deliberations and meetings held by the agreements' institutions concerning the reports submitted by the SARs. The Central Government also studies and responds to questions raised by the Hong Kong SAR regarding the adaptation of agreements.

As regards bilateral agreements which involve Hong Kong, the Central Government has, in accordance with the Basic Law, authorized the Hong Kong SAR government to conclude such bilateral agreements, including agreements on civil aviation, protection of investments, transfers of fugitives, transfers of sentenced criminals, and judiciary assistance, and has registered with the United Nations and international civil

---

[19]See Xu Chongde. *A Course on the Basic Laws of Hong Kong and Macao*. Beijing: China Renmin University Press, 1994, pp. 59–60.

[20]Note of Qin Huasun, Permanent Representative of the People's Republic of China to the United Nations and Ambassador Extraordinary and Plenipotentiary, to Secretary-General of the United Nations on Applicability of Multi-Lateral International Treaties to the Hong Kong Special Administrative Region, Gazette of the State Council of the People's Republic of China, 1997 (39).

aviation organizations the bilateral civil aviation agreements signed between Hong Kong and relevant countries.

In addition, the State Council, upon requests from the Hong Kong SAR, has provided the SAR with substantial amounts of other diplomacy-related services, such as producing certificates on whether SAR-designated personnel enjoy diplomatic privileges and immunity, handling matters related to international monetary organizations setting up branch institutions in Hong Kong, and attending to judicial assistance cases between the Hong Kong SAR and other countries.

Among instances of diplomatic work involving the Macao SAR, there was the issue of international treaties which involved Macao. At the end of 1997, China and Macao started bilateral consultations on the adaptation of international agreements to Macao and on issues of the "1999 transition." Prior to the return of Macao to China, the Chinese side consented to the "1999 transition" of 141 agreements and several dozen protocols and amendments (though not including international organization-type agreements and not including agreements of an entirely diplomatic and national defense nature concluded by China), which the Portuguese side had extended and actually applied to Macao. From September 29 to December 17, 1999, the Chinese government successively sent notes to parties concerned with 99 of the 141 agreements (i.e., the 99 that the Portuguese side had extended and actually applied to Macao prior to December 20) about the matter of adapting these agreements to the Macao SAR, and completed the legal procedures. And on December 14, 1999 Ambassador Qin Huasun, China's permanent representative to the United Nations, sent a formal note about these matters to the UN Secretary-General. In the note, the Chinese Government comprehensively set forth China's principled stand and methods regarding the adaptation of international agreements to the Macao SAR, and appended a list of the agreements which China would continue to adapt to the Macao SAR after December 20. Altogether, 158 international agreements have now been adapted to the Macao SAR. The categories they involve cover foreign diplomacy, national defense, civil aviation, Customs, human rights, education, science and technology, culture, prohibition of narcotics, environmental protection, health care, international crime, labor, maritime commerce, private international law, transportation, communications and telecommunications, international organizations, and so forth.[21]

Where bilateral agreements involving Macao are concerned, the Chinese Government has signed (or concluded by means of exchange of notes) agreements on foreign countries setting up consulates in the Macao SAR, or on retaining their consuls general, or regarding consular districts. On December 8, the Chinese Government sent notes to the relevant foreign embassies in China about the effectiveness, after Macao's return to China, of 29 bilateral civil aviation agreements signed with China prior to December 20 with authorization from Portuguese government, confirming China's

---

[21] Note of Qin Huasun, Permanent Representative of the People's Republic of China to the United Nations and Ambassador Extraordinary and Plenipotentiary, to Secretary-General of the United Nations on Applicability of Multi-Lateral International Treaties to the Hong Kong Special Administrative Region, Gazette of the State Council of the People's Republic of China, see Foreign Ministry webpage: http://www.fmprc.gov.cn/chn/2400.html.

consent to the relevant bilateral agreements continuing to be effective in the Macao SAR after December 20.

After the SARs were set up, the Ministry of Foreign Affairs of the People's Republic of China, in accordance with the provisions of the Basic Laws, set up special institutions—offices of commissioners of the Foreign Ministry—to handle diplomatic affairs related to the SARs. Major diplomatic affairs between all countries and international organizations with the SARs would be handled by these institutions. In accordance with the provisions of the Basic Laws, the Central People's Government also authorized the SARs to handle relevant diplomatic affairs on their own according to their Basic Laws. Despite the fact that diplomatic powers are exercised by the Central Government, the SARs, too, enjoy certain powers to handle diplomatic affairs. The powers enjoyed by the SARs in this respect will be specially discussed in the next chapter.

6.6   Powers over National Defense

One of the important basic functions of a country is to provide the territories and people under its jurisdiction with common security defenses in order to repel invasions by other countries, maintain normal and peaceful social order within its territories, and defend the country's sovereignty and territorial integrity. Any country which possesses complete sovereignty also has a unified national defense. In other words, the country's armed forces must be centrally commanded by a unified leadership, and local governments may not engage in military activities. This, on the one hand, is determined by the nature of armed forces per se and national defense and, on the other, is a must for safeguarding national unity. Chinese and foreign history tells us that armed forces, if properly controlled, are powerful weapons for safeguarding national unity and sovereignty; but may disrupt the integrity of a country's unity and sovereignty if poorly controlled. For this reason, the constitution of every country contains extremely rigorous provisions regarding the unity of the country's armed forces. The provision in Article 93 of China's Constitution that "the Central Military Commission of the People's Republic of China directs the armed forces of the country... the Chairman assumes overall responsibility for the work of the Central Military Commission" embodies the principle of a unified Chinese national defense and unified armed forces.

The Central Government is in charge of the SARs' defense. For the Central Government, this is both an exercise of power as well as an exercise of responsibility since the Central Government is responsible for the external security of the SARs. Should an external enemy attempt an incursion, the Central Government has to repel the aggressor and safeguard peace in the SARs. To provide the means for defending the SARs, the Central Authorities must station troops in them. This is required for the SARs' defense and the defense of the nation as a whole as well as being an important reflection of national sovereignty. Some people have opposed the stationing of troops in the SARs, or hold that only a small number of troops should be symbolically stationed there, or maintained that troops should be stationed in remote districts, not in urban regions. All such propositions are wrong, as they are likely to cause loopholes in defense dispositions, and are inadvisable as they place restrictions on state sovereignty.[22] Hong Kongers previously entertained a good many anxieties about garrisoning troops in Hong Kong. When the relevant policies were being drawn up, there were three different views about the way troops were to be stationed: (a) that troops should be stationed in Shenzhen and only symbolically in Hong Kong; (b) that troops be stationed in Hong Kong and have Shenzhen serve as a backup base; and (c) that the troops be stationed in Shenzhen and come to Hong Kong to fulfill their duties when necessary. Not only did the Central Authorities oppose these views, even many in Hong Kong's industrial circles disapproved. They feared that chaos might break out after Hong Kong returned to China, that troops stationed in Shenzhen would be too far off to be effective and that minor incidents could become magnified.[23] The first method, too, was unfeasible for the same reason. Thus, the Central Authorities decided that a certain number of People's Liberation Army troops had to be stationed in Hong Kong.

Situated on the estuary of the Pearl River, Hong Kong has always been a critical area for coastal defense. Troops were stationed there during both the Ming and Qing dynasties. After the British occupied Hong Kong, they had always stationed troops of their three armed services both in the estuary and spread out over the whole of Hong Kong. These were directed by a British commander-in-chief with the rank of major general; the Governor was merely the garrison's nominal commander-in-chief. The chief mission of the British troops stationed in Hong Kong was to "manifest sovereignty and uphold the various conditions conducive to promoting Hong Kong's prosperity, in order to demonstrate the British Parliament's fulfillment of the responsibilities it has undertaken toward Hong Kong." In ordinary times, the main responsibilities of the British troops stationed in Hong Kong were to carry out defense tasks and assist in maintaining Hong Kong's social peace and order. Meanwhile, for quite some time Hong Kong had to defray a considerable portion of the garrison's expenses.[24] For these reasons, China, after resuming its exercise of sovereignty over Hong Kong, had to station troops in the SAR, both for the needs of carrying defense tasks and out of consideration of upholding national sovereignty and unity. Due to the SAR's special circumstances, special provisions were made in its Basic Law in this respect.

In view of the above, the State Council and the Central Military Commission formally started to organize the PLA garrison force in Hong Kong in early 1993. The build-up of this garrison force was completed on January 28, 1996. On December 30 of that year, the 23rd Session of the Eighth National People's Congress Standing

---

[22]Xu Chongde. *A Course on the Basic Laws of Hong Kong and Macao.* Beijing: China Renmin University Press, 1994, p. 62.

[23]Huang Wenfang. *The Decision-making Process and Implementation of China's restoration of sovereignty over Hong Kong.* Hong Kong: Hong Kong Baptist University, 1997, p. 70.

[24]Lan Tian. *Research on Legal Problems of One Country, Two Systems.* Beijing: Law Press, 1997, pp. 68–70.

Committee approved the Garrison Law of the Hong Kong Special Administrative Region of the People's Republic of China, which stipulates the duties of the Hong Kong garrison, the Hong Kong garrison's relation with the Hong Kong SAR government, the duties and disciplines of members of the Hong Kong garrison as well as judicial jurisdiction over members of the HK garrison. This is one of the principal laws specifying the Hong Kong Garrison's activities.

According to the Hong Kong Basic Law, the Troops Garrison Law of the Hong Kong Special Administrative Region, and public announcements by the State Council and the Central Military Commission, the Hong Kong garrison is directly under the command of the Central Military Commission. Its duty is to specifically carry out the defense tasks of the Hong Kong SAR. The Hong Kong garrison does not intervene in the SAR's local affairs. The SAR government and the garrison operate separately according to independent administrative and military systems, do not come under each other's jurisdictions and do not interfere with each other. The Hong Kong garrison, of course, requires full and effective safeguards, which not only need to be furnished by the Central Government, but for which the Hong Kong SAR Government must provide the necessary backing and coordination, and on which the two sides have to maintain contacts and communication.[25]

Chairman Jiang Zemin of the Central Military Commission once pointed out that the stationing of a People's Liberation Army garrison in Hong Kong differs from the PLA'S erstwhile sweeping advances south the Yangtze or the ingress of the "Good Eighth Company" into Nanjing Road, as the historical backgrounds are different. China's resuming its exercise of sovereignty over Hong Kong in 1997 took place according to the principle of "one country, two systems" under which Hong Kongers administer Hong Kong. PLA troops stationed in Hong Kong must take full cognizance of this fact.

According to the provisions of the Hong Kong Basic Law, the PLA garrison in Hong Kong may only go into action under the following situations: (a) when the NPC Standing Committee decides to declare a state of war and the Central People's Government issues an order to implement the relevant national laws in the Hong Kong SAR (Basic Law Article 18), and (b) when turmoil occurs in the Hong Kong SAR which the SAR government is unable to control and which endangers the nation's unity and security, when the NPC Standing Committee decides that the HK SAR has entered a state of emergency, and when the Central People's Government issues an order to implement the relevant national laws in the Hong Kong SAR (Article 18). Once the SAR enters a state of war or a state of emergency, the troops will certainly go into action. The Basic Law also stipulates that the SAR government may request the Central Authorities to dispatch troops to render assistance with maintaining social order and disaster relief when there is indeed the need to do so. In these situations, whether or not troops will be dispatched depends on the SAR government. The garrison troops may go into action only when SAR government requests the Central Authorities that they do so, and the right to make that choice rests with the SAR. It is

---

[25] *People's Daily*, January 30, 1996.

evident that the Basic Law places very stringent restrictions on the use of the Hong Kong garrison forces.

Besides having to abide by national laws, the Hong Kong garrison troops must comply with the laws of the SAR. As regards the resolving of legal issues that involve both the troops and the locality, and especially the handling of issues involving crimes committed by garrison troops and concerning civil disputes, the Troops Garrison Law of the Hong Kong Special Administrative Region makes appropriate stipulations on the relevant issues of judicial jurisdiction. Actual experience since the return of Hong Kong shows that the Hong Kong garrison troops have strictly observed the relevant laws and orders, and have become a powerful force for maintaining the SAR's stability and security.

As regards the matter of military expenditure, Hong Kong bore the major portion of the British forces' expenses in the region prior to Hong Kong's return to China. According to Basic Law stipulations, however, the PLA garrison's expenditures are borne by the Central People's Government, and Hong Kong's residents do not undertake any of the garrison's expenses.

As for Macao, Portugal pulled its garrison troops out of Macao in December 1975. The Estatuto Orgânico de Macao issued for enforcement in February 1976 stipulated that the Portuguese President would pay for Macao's expenses pertaining to external defense. And Article 14 of the Basic Law of the Macao SAR merely stated in general terms that the Central People's Government would be responsible for the SAR's defense affairs. Since Macao's territory is quite small and the region is surrounded by China's territorial lands and seas, the Central Government at first made no decision to station a garrison in the Macao SAR. However, as the date of Macao's return to China approached, the Central Authorities decided that a garrison should be stationed in Macao. In this connection, the 10th Session of the Ninth National People's Standing Committee passed the Garrison Law of the Macao Special Administrative Region on June 28, 1999, which stipulates matters relevant to the stationing of a garrison in Macao. The biggest difference between the Macao garrison and the Hong Kong garrison is that Article 3 of the Macao Garrison Law stipulates that the Macao SAR government may, when necessary, ask the Central People's Government to have the Macao garrison render assistance in maintaining social order and disaster relief. There is no such stipulation with regard to the Hong Kong garrison, and the Hong Kong SAR government is wholly responsible for the SAR's social peace and order.

According to the provisions of the Basic Law(s), the Central Authorities, in addition to the six powers enumerated above, are vested with other powers related to national sovereignty and unity. An example is the powers of the chief of state. The SARs require that the Chairman of the People's Republic of China shall represent the chief of state when they accept relevant orders promulgated by the Chinese Central Authorities. There is also the power of the NPC Standing Committee to conduct filings for the record of the laws formulated by the SARs' legislative organs, the power to return motions for reconsideration, and the Central Government's responsibility for handling Hong Kong and Macao SARs' affairs which involve Taiwan. These will be discussed later.

6.7 The Handling of "Residual Powers"

"Residual powers" refers to powers which the drafters of constitutions have not delegated to any party for implementation when dividing up powers among state organs and especially between the national government (federal or central) and local regional governments. To prevent the emergence of legislative "blanks" leading to "power vacuums," those who formulate constitutions and laws sweepingly stipulate that the power to administer unassigned matters should be retained by the central (federal) authorities or the local (member state) authorities. These residual powers are not necessarily minor powers, and may sometimes be quite considerable.

There are two aspects to assigning jurisdiction over "residual powers." One is when matters emerge over which laws have failed to assign clear jurisdictions, some department or other may first take over jurisdiction to prevent a "legislative vacuum" which could result in matters, especially sudden emergencies, being no one's concern. From the perspective of political science, all situations which should be covered by state powers must be covered, and "power blanks" must be avoided when drafting constitutions. The other aspect is that jurisdiction over "residual powers" is an important criterion for evaluating state structures. If residual powers are given over to local or regional governments, the country is a federal state; otherwise, it is unitary. That is because residual powers are frequently closely tied to the sources of a country's "primary powers" and state sovereignty, and the entity that possesses residual powers is often the possessor of the country's "primary powers." That is why in the constitutions of many countries, residual powers are often vested in the country's comprehensive and highest organs of state power. In countries of the unitary system, the issue of jurisdiction over residual powers does not exist since all powers of the localities are conferred to them by the central authorities. If any power over which jurisdiction is unclear does exist, it should pertain to the central authorities. That is an important principle of the unitary system.

The first country to define jurisdiction over residual powers in its constitution was the United States. The 10th Amendment of the U.S. Constitution stipulates: "The powers not delegated to the United States by the Constitution, are reserved to the states respectively, or to the people." The constitution of many other countries followed this example. In general, the constitutions of countries which implement the federal system adopt enumerationism for the powers of the federal government. All powers which the constitutions do not clearly say should be exercised by the federal government are reserved for the member states or the people.

Article 2 of China's Constitution clearly provides that "All power in the People's Republic of China belongs to the people." The final item of Article 62 provides that the National People's Congress is "to exercise such other functions and powers as the highest organ of state power should exercise." And the final item of Article 67 provides that the Standing Committee of the National People's Congress is "to exercise such other functions and powers as the National People's Congress may assign to it." This amply demonstrates that in China, the people are the owners of all state powers, including, of course, "residual powers" if these do exist; and that the

National People's Congress which represents the people as a whole may exercise all of the highest state powers, and may also authorize its permanent institution, namely its Standing Committee, and its executive organ, namely the State Council to exercise the corresponding powers. As for the powers of the localities, including those of the SARs, all of these are delegated by the state's highest organs of state power, and for that reason the Constitution does not explicitly delegate powers to the localities but keeps them at the highest organs of state power.

Articles 2 of both of the SAR Basic Laws provide that the National People's Congress authorizes the SARs to exercise a high degree of autonomy and enjoy executive, legislative, and independent judicial power, including that of final adjudication. This shows very clearly that regardless of the magnitude of the powers, all are delegated by the Central Authorities, and moreover, that the "residual powers" which the Central Authorities do not explicitly authorize the SARs to exercise are retained and exercised by the National People's Congress and its permanent institutions.

However, the SAR Basic Laws have made some unusual dispositions in this aspect in terms of legislative techniques. First of all, they make some generalized provisions as regards the Central Authorities' powers, and then adopt the enumeration method for individual provisions. As regards generalized stipulations, Article 12 of the Basic Laws provides that the SAR is a local administrative region that enjoys a high degree of autonomy in the People's Republic of China, that it is directly administered by the Central People's Government, and that it also has the right to reserve the "residual powers" described above. The enumerative-type individual provision refers to Articles 13–15 and Articles 158 and 159 of the Basic Law regarding the various powers exercised by the Central Authorities. These have been discussed in detail heretofore. Although enumerative-type stipulations are used to "restrict" the powers exercised by the Central Authorities, or in other words, to strictly limit the powers exercised by the Central Authorities regarding the SARs to the aspects enumerated, and ensure they are "kept within the bounds absolutely necessary for manifesting state sovereignty and unity," they also serve to affirm and ensure that the Central Authorities do exercise those powers.[26]

Second, the Basic Laws, as well as making use of enumerative provisions about the powers exercised by the SARs, i.e., detailed stipulations of the various powers authorized by the Central Authorities for implementation by the SARs (to be discussed in detail in the next chapter), they also use the method of generalized provisions to stipulate that the SARs are empowered to accept further authorizations from the Central Authorities, as indicated in Article 20 of the Basic Law: "The Hong Kong Special Administrative Region may enjoy other powers granted to it by the National People's Congress, the Standing Committee of the National People's Congress or the Central People's Government." I call this power "the power to accept 'other powers' granted by the Central Authorities." This stipulation shows on the one hand that the Central Authorities possess sovereignty over the SARs, retain "residual powers" and

---

[26]Wang Fengchao. "On the Relations between the Central Authorities and Hong Kong Special Administrative Region," carried in *Hong Kong Wen Wei Po*, April 4, 1995.

have the "power to authorize" and, on the other, that the SARs have the "power" or "right" to continue accepting "other powers" authorized by the Central Authorities.

As stated earlier, a provision like this one has appeared in the Constitution only when providing for the functions and powers exercised by the NPC Standing Committee and the State Council. It would seem to be of little actual significance, but that is not true since it constitutes the legal ground for the Central Authorities to continue granting the SARs certain other powers in the future. The absence of such a provision would mean that the Central Authorities would not be able to grant other powers to the SARs, nor would the SARs be able to accept any more of such powers and that their powers would be strictly limited to those specifically listed in the Basic Laws. Hence, this provision bears substantial significance. The State Council has previously obtained powers granted by the NPC Standing Committee beyond the scope stipulated by the Constitution on the strength of provisions similar to those of Article 89 of the Constitution.[27]

It is evident that when handling this issue, the drafters of the Basic Law also broke with customary legislative conventions and devised a versatile solution to the "residual powers" question without sacrificing principles. In other words, the Central Authorities retained all "residual powers" while the SAR had the power to again accept "other residual powers" granted by the Central Authorities.

6.8   The Origins, Nature, and Exercising of the Central Authorities' Powers

6.8.1   The Origins of the Central Authorities' Powers

It may be asked: Why are the Central Authorities "empowered" to exercise these powers over the SARs, and why do the Central Authorities have the "power to authorize powers"? What are the grounds and basis for their exercising these powers? This involves the issue of the source of the legitimacy of political authority in terms of political science and jurisprudence. If explained by means of Hans Kelsen's Pure Theory of Law, it means that the source of legitimacy of all of a country's laws and norms derives from the country's Basic Norm, or Grundnorm. If the Grundnorm changes, the basis for the source of legitimacy and the power of the laws as a whole

---

[27]On April 10, 1985, the 3rd Session of the Sixth National People's Congress decided to authorize the State Council to formulate, when necessary, provisional stipulations or ordinances regarding issues related to economic systems and opening up to the outside on the basis of the Constitution and on the premise that these did not conflict with the basic principles of relevant laws and the relevant decisions by the NPC and its Standing Committee. These would be published and implemented and reported to the NPC Standing Committee for the record. Wu Jialin. *Constitutional Jurisprudence.* Beijing: Qunzhong Press, 1992, p. 294.

will change accordingly, as will the entire structure of laws and powers.[28] The Basic Grundnorm he refers to is, in reality, the orthodoxy of state power, which may also be called Sovereignty. New state powers generated by revolutions or coups d'état or by general elections inevitably set up a new Grundnorm, whereupon state powers are repartitioned.

The Sino–British Joint Declaration and the Hong Kong Basic Law both stipulated at the very outset that China would restore its exercise of sovereignty over Hong Kong on July 1, 1997 and that Britain would return Hong Kong to China at the same time. This would become a political reality, and at midnight on June 30, 1997, at the moment when Hong Kong's handover ceremony took place, the entire Grundnorm in Hong Kong changed. The transfer of sovereignty signaled a change in the source of legitimacy of powers. The directives that came from London used to be highest and the most authoritative. Now, however, powers which needed to obtain grounds for their legitimate existence had to first of all secure the consent of and authorization from China's central state power.[29]

The matter is quite simple. The Central Authorities have the right to exercise those powers over the Hong Kong SAR because Hong Kong has since ancient times been China's territory, and China has now retrieved its exercise of sovereignty from British hands. This has given China the power to establish a new Grundnorm in Hong Kong and implement new governance and, in a certain sense, constitutes a "sovereignty revolution." For the same reason, this also goes for Macao.

6.8.2   State Sovereignty

State sovereignty is the highest power of a country's government to independently handle internal and external matters, namely a country's power to rule its own territory and people. It is the most fundamental and most important of a country's powers.

---

[28] See Wacks R. "One Country, Two Grundnormen? The Basic Law and the Basic Norm." In Wacks R. ed. *China, Hong Kong and 1997 Essays in Legal Theory.* Hong Kong University Press, 1993, pp. 155–162.

[29] Britain once proposed during Sino–British negotiations on the future of Hong Kong that it wanted to exchange sovereign powers for administrative powers. In other words, Britain would return sovereignty over Hong Kong to China after July 1, 1997 yet retain administrative powers over the region in a bid to extend its rule over Hong Kong, but this was categorically rebuffed by the Chinese government. Sovereignty and administrative powers cannot be separated. Sovereignty is incomplete when it does not include administrative powers. It is impossible to envisage a situation where Hong Kong's sovereignty would have been exercised by China while its administrative powers would be wielded by the British. The principles of public law sometimes differ from those of private law. Under `private law`, a corporation's business rights and ownership rights may be separated, and the operator is not necessarily the owner. Under `public law`, however, the ownership rights and "operating rights" are always conjoined and one cannot imagine a situation where a country "hires" a foreigner to act as president or prime minister and administer the state. Hence, exchanging sovereign powers for administrative powers is not at all workable.

Sovereignty is a state's most important attribute—an attribute which in the complete sense is intrinsic to, and not acquired by, states, and for which reason is inalienable.

Sovereignty, as a country's innate right, is expressed in three respects: It is internally the highest right of rule, namely it is a country's right to administer all people and matters within its territory and all of its nationals outside of its territory; the right to determine the political and economic systems it practices; the right to determine the division of its administration regions, and so forth. For example, China has decided to implement the socialist political, economic, and cultural systems on the mainland while it sets up special administrative regions, implements the capitalist system, and adopts management methods different from those on the mainland in Hong Kong and Macao. These are matters which fall within the scope of China sovereignty. Externally, sovereignty is manifested as the right to independence and the right to resist and defend oneself against encroachments by other countries, or in other words, a country's rights and powers to be free from any outside interference, to handle its external matters independently, and to defend its security and territorial integrity.

It is precisely the principle of state sovereignty that gives political authority to a country's government, that confers legitimacy to its rule over its lands and people, and that enables it to establish the country's Grundnorm and install its ruling institutions and legal systems. As for the ways in which sovereignty is acquired, this matter goes too far beyond the present subject and will not be explored here.[30]

In sum, all the powers the Central Authorities enjoy in the special administrative regions stem from state sovereignty, and the sovereignty of the People's Republic of China over Hong Kong and Macao constitutes the source of legitimacy of the powers of the Central Authorities.

6.8.3 Standards for the Central/SAR Division of Functions and Powers

The above analyses show that the Central/SAR division of functions and powers, as guided by the "one country, two systems" policy, follows two principles. The first principle is that, in accordance with the nature of the matters—i.e., in accordance with the nature and characteristics of the matters per se and the spirit of the "one country, two systems" concept—functions and powers which ought to be exercised

---

[30]For writings on state sovereignty and political authority, read Frederick Engels. "On Authority," *Selected Works of Marx and Engels*, vol. 2. Jean-Jacques Rousseau. *On the Origin and Basis of Human Inequality*. Kelsen H. *The Pure Theory of Law*, trans Max Knight. Berkeley and Los Angeles: University of California Press, 1967. Kelsen H. General. *Theory of Norms*, trans M. Hartney, Oxford, Oxford University Press, 1991. Also see *General Theory of Law and State*, trans Wedkerg A, Cambridge: Harvard University Press, 1945. Harris J. W. *When and Why Does the Grundnorm Change?* carried in Cambridge Law Journal, 1971 (29), p. 103. Hart H. L. A. *The Concept of Law*, Oxford, Clarendon Press, 1961. (USA) J. Harold Berman. *Law and Revolution*, trans He Weifang and Gao Hongjun, Beijing, Encyclopedia of China Publishing House, 1993.

by the Central Authorities shall be exercised by the Central Authorities, as, for example, matters pertaining to defense; and powers which ought to be exercised by the SARs shall be legislated and exercised by the SARs themselves, such as economic and cultural affairs. The second principle concerns the division of functions and powers in accordance with the powers and functions of the country's national government (the Central Government) and its local governments. Matters which fall within the scope of national government functions and powers, such as safeguarding state sovereignty and defending the integrity of the nation's territories, are mainly the functions and powers of the Central Government and for that reason are, of course, taken charge of by the Central Government, whereas matters which fall within the scope of local government functions and powers, such as the maintaining of public peace and order, come under the jurisdiction of the SAR governments. Thus, when the Basic Laws' drafting committees were "assigning" the functions and powers of the Central Authorities and the SARs, they were by no means intentionally siding with either the Central Government or the SAR governments, nor were they deliberately or artificially "assigning" certain powers that should be exercised by one party over to another party; they were partitioning powers scientifically and rationally in line with the needs of upholding national unity and maintaining SAR prosperity. Powers which needed to be exercised by the Central Authorities went to the Central Authorities; those which needed to be exercised by the SARs went to the SARs. The overriding principles were "one country, two systems," "a high degree of autonomy" plus scientific and rational dispositions under which sovereign powers stayed with the Central Authorities while administrative powers went to the SARs.

Specifically, the division of functions and duties in the Basic Laws falls under these circumstances: (a) Certain powers are exercised wholly by the Central Authorities, such as that of national defense. (b) Certain powers are exercised by the Central Authorities, but when doing so the Central Authorities embrace SAR participation, as, for instance, the Central Authorities' power to interpret SAR Basic Law. (c) Certain powers pertain to the Central Authorities which, however, do not exercise the powers but authorize the SARs to do so while the Central Authorities supervise the exercising of these powers. For example, the Central Authorities possess full powers over foreign affairs but authorize the SARs to handle foreign economic and trade affairs on their own, according to statutory titles and procedures and under supervision from the Central Authorities. (d) Certain powers are exercised by the SARs while the Central Authorities merely play a supervisory role. For instance, legislative powers pertain to the SARs whereas the Central Authorities exercise supervision simply by placing the legislation on file. (e) Some powers are wholly exercised by the SARs, such as judiciary powers, the power of final appeal, and the power to manage finance and trade.

It is clear that the Central Authorities are proactively pursuing a policy of non-interference in the SARs and that Central Authorities step forward only when it is indeed necessary for them to do so. Other than sovereignty plus "the power to authorize powers" and "retain powers," all of the powers enjoyed by the Central Authorities are of a sovereign and servicing nature. In the matters of defense and foreign relations, for instance, the Central Authorities' rights and powers are oriented in the main toward services and responsibilities. Rights imply duties, and powers also imply responsibilities. The fact that the Central Authorities enjoy the above-mentioned powers means that they must assume responsibilities toward the SARs in those aspects and may not let the SARs sustain the slightest losses or make any mistakes in those respects. Similarly, the SAR governments fully enjoy by law all powers needed to maintain prosperity and stability, and this also entails responsibilities. In other words, the SAR governments must, within the scope of their own functions and duties, be responsible toward the Central Government above them, be sure to prevent anything that could harm the country's unity and sovereignty, and at the same time be responsible to the population under them and do their utmost to safeguard the SARs' continued prosperity and stability. Holding a position calls for fulfilling certain duties, and holding powers requires conscientious efforts toward fulfilling all the responsibilities entailed. This goes for both the Central Government and the Special Administrative Regions.

Chapter 7
The Powers Enjoyed by the Special Administrative Regions

From the detailed analyses in Chapter V of such matters as the division of duties and powers between the Central Authorities and the Special Administrative Regions, the principles for such divisions, and the handling of "residual powers," one sees that the powers vested in the Central Authorities are those necessary for safeguarding national unity and sovereignty. All other powers have been granted by the Central Authorities to the SARs for implementation. Besides enjoying a high degree of autonomy, the residents of the SARs also enjoy the power to participate in the administration of affairs of a national nature, and the SARs also have the power to accept other powers and authorizations granted to them by the Central Authorities and to handle affairs that were originally to be administered by the Central Authorities.

This chapter focuses on discussing the diverse powers enjoyed by the SARs, which include in the main: (a) the high degree of autonomy enjoyed by the SARs; (b) the SARs' power to participate in the administration of affairs of a national nature; and (c) the SARs' power to accept "other powers" granted by the Central Authorities. Of course, the SARs also bear corresponding responsibilities for safeguarding national unity and sovereignty. A general principle is that under the "one country, two systems" setup, the SARs must undertake responsibility both for their own prosperity and stability and for safeguarding national unity and sovereignty.

It is evident that the "special administrative regions" referred to in this chapter include not only the SARs' Chief Executives and the SARs' government organizations of all levels but also the SARs' residents. The powers enjoyed and the responsibilities borne by a SAR are to be seen as the various powers and the various responsibilities exercised by the residents and governments of the SAR as a whole.

© Foreign Language Teaching and Research Publishing Co., Ltd and Springer Nature   181
Singapore Pte Ltd. 2019
Z. Wang, *Relationship Between the Chinese Central Authorities and Regional
Governments of Hong Kong and Macao: A Legal Perspective*, China Academic
Library, https://doi.org/10.1007/978-981-13-2322-5_7

7.1 The High Degree of Autonomy Enjoyed by the SARs

In constitutional science, "power of local autonomy" refers to the powers and functions of a locality to handle affairs of a local nature on its own. Under the structure of a unitary system, the autonomous powers enjoyed by the locality are not "innate" but are granted "subsequently (ex post facto)" by the central government. In other words, the Central Authorities, on condition of not affecting the unified exercise of state sovereignty, grants powers of administering local affairs which it should be administering itself, to local governments for the latter's self-determined administration, and Central Authorities merely play a supervisory role. The exercise of autonomous powers is limited, in that it may not obstruct national sovereignty or national unity. If local autonomous powers obstruct national sovereignty or national unity, the Central Authorities will revoke these autonomous powers. Hence, the autonomy of any locality is limited, and is certainly not "autonomy" without any limits whatsoever, and "complete autonomy" does not exist. As stated above, under a unitary system there is, strictly speaking, no such thing as local autonomy with divisions of powers between the central authorities and the localities. There is only the granting of powers; no division of powers. In other words, the central authorities grant the local authorities certain limited powers to manage local affairs. As to the amount or degree or type of the powers granted, these are determined by the central government. This differs in substance from the equal division of powers between federal government and the various member states under the federal system.[1]

Articles 2 of both the Basic Laws of the Hong Kong and Macao SARs stipulate: "The National People's Congress authorizes the [Hong Kong] Special Administrative Region to exercise a high degree of autonomy and enjoy executive, legislative and independent judicial power, including that of final adjudication, in accordance with the provisions of this Law." Paragraph 3 of Article 13 of the Basic Law also stipulates: "The Central People's Government authorizes the [Hong Kong] Special Administrative Region to conduct relevant external affairs on its own in accordance with this Law." These are the basic contents of the high degree of the autonomy exercised by the SARs.[2]

7.1.1 Powers of Administrative Management

Broadly speaking, "powers of administrative management" refers to such social affairs as economics, culture, municipal governance, public security, social welfare, etc., and to the conduct of everyday self-management in these sectors. These are the basic duties and functions of government. Under the traditional unitary system, the central government normally maintains control over numerous powers of adminis-

---

[1] Wang Shuwen. *A Guide to the Basic Law of the Hong Kong Administrative Region.* Beijing: CPC Central Committee Party School Press, 1990, pp. 107–108.
[2] See Footnote 1.

trative management, while local governments often merely passively exercise the central authorities' relevant policies and decrees. The Hong Kong and Macao SARs are granted and enjoy administrative powers by the Central Authorities in accordance with the "one country, two systems" and "a high degree of autonomy" principles. Article 16 of the Hong Kong Basic Law stipulates: "The Hong Kong Special Administrative Regions shall be vested with executive power. It shall, on its own, conduct the administrative affairs of the Region in accordance with the relevant provisions of this Law." The Macao Basic Law makes a similar stipulation.

The Macao Basic Law has not adopted the enumerative method or listed in detail the powers of management over administrative affairs enjoyed by the SAR, because the scope of its administrative affairs are so extensive and cover so many aspects of social life that it would be virtually impossible to produce a clear and complete listing. However, since there may not be any loopholes in the governments' management of administrative affairs, Article 16 of the Basic Law first of all carries a generalized stipulation regarding the powers of managing administrative affairs enjoyed by the SAR, so that when new matters emerge in local society the SAR it will not be left helpless because no powers are authorized in the Basic Law and thereby result in "power vacuums" and social chaos.

Chapters V and VI in the Basic Laws fairly explicitly and specifically stipulate the main powers of administrative management enjoyed by the SAR(s). These include, in the economic aspect, finances, banking, trade and industrial and commercial sectors, land, maritime transport, and civil aviation. They also cover education, science, culture, sports, religion, labor, and social services. All these are specific administrative actions. The SAR governments are also vested with extensive powers in terms of abstract administrative actions.

7.1.1.1 Functions and Powers in Terms of Abstract Administrative Actions

(1) The power of administrative decision-making. SARs' chief executives have the power to formulate various policies for the SARs' governments and are the SARs' highest decision-making institutions.

(2) The issuance of administrative orders and the formulation of administrative-type laws and regulations. The SARs' chief executives are empowered to issue administrative orders and formulate administrative-type laws and regulations in order to specifically execute the national-type laws implemented in the SARs and the laws passed by the SARs' legislative councils.

(3) The power to present legislative bills. The SARs' governments are empowered to present drafts of laws to the legislative councils, and the chief executives empowered to sign law proposals approved by the legislative councils and issue these as laws.

7.1.1.2 The Power to Appoint and Remove Personnel

The SARs' chief executives have the power to propose candidates for persons in charge of all the SARs' principal government departments and to report them to the Central People's Government for an appointment. The SARs have the power to appoint and remove judges in SAR courts of all levels, including judges at the SARs' courts of final adjudication. The SARs are empowered to appoint and remove other civil servants.

7.1.1.3 Functions and Powers in Terms of Specific Administrative Actions

(1) Public security powers. In accordance with the Basic Laws, the SAR governments are responsible for maintaining social public security in the SARs on their own. In this respect, the SAR governments are empowered to set up diverse disciplinary forces in the SARs, maintain normal social order and public security in the SARs, and punish various criminal activities.

(2) Economic management powers. The Hong Kong and Macao SARs are continuing to implement capitalist market economies. Under a market economy, the government adheres to a policy of "positive non-intervention" toward residents' economic behavior. Hence, the SAR governments' economic management powers differ from the economic management powers of mainland governments. The SAR governments do not manage their economy by means of directly administering the businesses of each and every specific enterprise; they merely provide various services from a macroscopic perspective for developing the market economy. The role of the governments in the market economy can only be one of arbiter; certainly not one of arbiter-cum-player. The SAR governments will continue to adhere to this "do-nothing," or in other words "positive non-interventionist," economic policy. The macroeconomic management powers in this respect include in the main:

One, the right of independent finances. The SARs implement a policy of financial independence. All financial revenues are used for the SARs' own purposes and are not handed over to the Central People's Government. Nor does the Central People's Government levy taxes in the SARs.

Two, the right of independent taxation. The SARs practice a system of independent taxation. They legislate their own laws on tax categories, rates of taxation, tax relief and exemptions, and other matters related to taxation.

Three, the right of an independent fiscal system. The SAR governments have the power to formulate their own financial and monetary policies, uphold the freedom of operations of financial enterprises and the monetary market, and conduct management and supervision by law. The SAR governments have the power to issue currencies, and shall have the power designate banks to issue or continue to issue currencies under statutory authority. SARs do not apply foreign exchange control policies and implement and ensure the free flow of capital within, into and out of the regions. The SAR governments possess the power to manage and control foreign exchange funds. The right to independently issue currencies, in particular, is a power that no member state under a federal system can enjoy, and "one country one currency" is the normal state of affairs. Yet under the circumstances of China's implementing "one country, two systems," the special administrative regions may continue to use their own currencies. It is evident that they are "special" in more than the ordinary sense.

Four, the SAR governments formulate their own industry policies, protect investments according to law, promote technical advances, promote and coordinate the development of various trades such as manufacturing, commerce, tourism, real estate, transport, public utilities, services, agriculture and fisheries, and formulated their policies for environmental protection. The SARs develop their new industries on their own.

Five, the SARs maintain their status as free ports and do not impose any tariffs unless otherwise prescribed by law. They continue to pursue the policy of free trade and safeguard the free movement of goods, intangible assets, and capital. The SARs maintain their status as separate customs territories. The SARs also have the right to issue their own certificates of origin for products in accordance with prevailing rules of origin.

Six, the power to manage land. The land and natural resources within the SARs belong to the state, and are managed, used, developed, leased, or assigned by the SAR governments to individuals and legal persons for their use and development. The revenue thereof pertains to the SAR governments.

Seven, maritime shipping management rights. The SARs maintain and perfect their previous systems of shipping management, define on their own their specific functions and responsibilities in respect of maritime shipping, continue as authorized by the Central People's Government to maintain shipping registers and continue to issue related certificates under their own laws, using the title "Hong Kong, China" or "Macao, China." With the exception of foreign warships, access for which requires special permission from the Central People's government, all ships enjoy access to the ports in accordance with the laws of the two regions. Private shipping businesses and shipping-related businesses and wharfs continue to operate freely.

Eight, civil aviation management rights. The Hong Kong SAR continues to implement the previous system of civil aviation management, takes its own responsibilities for routine business and technical management of civil aviation, and signs air service agreements with authorization from the Central People's Government. Article 134 of the Hong Kong Basic Law stipulates that the government of the Hong Kong SAR is granted powers to manage other matters related to civil aviation. The Macao Basic Law, too, stipulates that the Macao SAR may formulate various civil aviation management systems with specific authorization from the Central People's Government. (3) Education management powers. The SAR governments are authorized to formulate their own policies on the development and improvement of education, including policies on the educational system and its administration, and including policies on the language of instruction, the allocation of funds, the examination system, the system of academic awards, and the recognition of educational qualifications.

(4) Medical management powers. The SAR governments formulate their own policies for developing Western and traditional Chinese medicine and for promoting medical and health services.

(5) Science and technology management powers. The SARs governments are empowered to formulate their own policies on science and technology and for protecting by law achievements, patents, discoveries, and inventions in scientific and technological research, and decide their own scientific and technological standards and specifications applicable to their own region.

(6) Cultural sector management powers. The SARs formulate their own policies on culture, and manage on their own the cultural sector in their regions, including literature and the arts, journalism, publishing, radio, film and television, and so forth.

(7) Sports sector management powers. The SARs formulate, on their own, the policies on sports in their own region for the sake of developing the SARs' sports sectors.

(8) Autonomous social welfare policy. The SAR governments have the right to develop, on their own, policies for the advancement and improvement of social welfare on the basis on basis of their previous social welfare systems.

(9) Professional qualification assessment powers. On the basis of retaining its previous system of assessing professional qualifications, the Hong Kong SAR government is empowered to formulate, on its own, measures for assessing the vocational qualifications for various professions.

(10) Labor management powers. The SAR governments formulate, on their own, their laws and policies on labor.

7.1.2 Legislative Powers

"Legislative powers" refers to the powers to formulate, amend and abrogate laws. Conducting legislative controls over society is an important basic function for a government. In China, the legislative system comprises two levels—central legislation and local legislation. Central legislative power, aka national legislative power, is exercised by the National People's Congress and its Standing Committee. Local legislative powers are exercised by the people's congresses and their standing committees of relatively large cities authorized to do so by provinces, autonomous regions, directly administered municipalities and the state as well as by the people's congresses of special administrative regions authorized to do so by the state. The local-type laws and regulations formulated by local state-power organs may not conflict with the Constitution, laws, or the State Council's administrative laws and regulations. The state-power organs of ethnic autonomous localities (i.e., autonomous regions, autonomous prefectures, and autonomous counties) may produce certain alternative provisions to state laws and may formulate Autonomy Regulations and Separate Regulations in light of the political, economic, and cultural characteristics of the local ethnic peoples, which take effect after being reported to and approved by the National People's Congress Standing Committee or the standing committee of a people's congress at the next higher level. Autonomous Regulations and Separate Regulations are also local-type regulations.

The legislative powers enjoyed by the SARs by their nature also belong in the category of China's local legislation. However, they are quite different from the ordinary kind of local legislation on the Chinese mainland as described above. According to the "one country, two systems" principle, the Hong Kong SAR retains its previous legal system in basically unchanged form, and nationwide-type laws are not implemented in the SAR unless otherwise prescribed in writing. Hence the SAR's legislative powers are down to earth, innovative, and not merely "implementational" in nature. The SARs legislative organs must effectively assume responsibility for exercising legislative control over the SARs. The great majority of ordinary local legislatures in Chinese mainland, including those in ethnic autonomous localities, are in the nature of "implementers" of state laws. Also, ordinary local legislatures perform on the basis of the Chinese Constitution, mainland laws, and administrative laws and regulations, whereas SARs legislatures perform on the basis of the SAR Basic Laws and may not violate the Basic Laws. Moreover, the scopes of SAR legislative powers are far greater than those of ordinary local legislatures. So long as any of the matters within the scope of SAR autonomy do not involve national defense and foreign relations or relations with the Central Authorities, the SAR legislative organs have the power to exercise legislative controls.

For the same reason, since the legislative powers enjoyed by the SARs were also granted to them by the Central Authorities, the organ that did the granting has the right to supervise the exercise of the legislative powers. The Basic Laws carry specific stipulations in this respect.

First of all, paragraph two of Article 17 of the HK Basic Law stipulates that laws formulated by the SAR legislative organs must be reported to the NPC Standing Committee for the record. "Reporting for the record" implies that the formulated laws and their relevant legislative materials are sent to the NPC Standing Committee so that it may be informed about these matters and have them on record, but, of course, does not include the implication that the NPC Standing Committee does the approving. In this respect, the Basic Law stipulates immediately afterward that "the reporting for the record shall not affect the entry into force of such laws." This shows that the laws formulated by the SAR legislative organs may immediately go into force, so long as all of the local legislative procedures have been completed, and that placing on the record has no effect in this matter. "Placing on the record" and "going into force" have different implications.

Second, paragraph three of Article 17 of the Basic Laws also stipulates that if the NPC Standing Committee, after consulting the Basic Law committees under it, considers that any law enacted by a Region's legislature is not in conformity with the provisions of the Basic Laws regarding affairs within the responsibility of the Central Authorities or regarding the relationship between the Central Authorities and the Region in question, the Standing Committee may return the law in question but shall not amend it. Any law returned by the NPC Standing Committee is immediately invalidated. These invalidations do not have retroactive effect, unless otherwise provided for in the SARs' laws.

Thus, it is evident that the NPC Standing Committee enjoys certain powers of supervision over legislation by the SARs. The exercise of such supervision involves certain requirements and procedures. First, the NPC Standing Committee's supervision over the SARs' legislatures is restricted to whether the legislation relevant to the supervision complies with the provisions in the Basic Laws on matters administered by the Central Authorities and the relations between the Central Authorities and the SARs. Laws legislated by the SARs within the scope of their autonomous administration are merely subjected to routine filings for the record. Second, if the NPC Standing Committee maintains that the SARs' legislature violate the Basic Laws' relevant stipulations and reconsiderations are in order, the opinions of the relevant Basic Law committees must be solicited before the laws are returned to the SARs. This is an obligatory procedure, as it enables the NPC Standing Committee to exercise supervision with greater precision. Third, if the NPC Standing Committee finds that relevant SAR legislature fails to comply with the relevant stipulations in the Basic Law, it merely returns the relevant laws to the SAR and does not amend them. The laws returned by the NPC Standing Committee are either invalidated or amended by the SAR; the power to decide rests with the SAR. As for the laws that are amended, these must still be reported to the NPC Standing Committee for the record. The fact that the NPC Standing Committee does not make amendments to the laws it sends back shows that the Central Authorities respect the SARs' legislative powers. Also, the laws sent back by the NPC Standing Committee will lose their legal validity. However, the invalidation of the said laws has no retroactive effect, unless otherwise provided for by the SARs' laws. This way of handling such matters avoids the possibility of retroactivity causing a series of legal problems on the one hand, and enables consideration of special circumstances.[3]

There are no specific regulations in the Basic Laws regarding the time within which laws are to be reported to the NPC Standing Committee for the record after being formulated by the SARs. Nor are there any regulations regarding either the specific NPC Standing Committee department which accepts the reports for the record, or the time and specific procedures for examining the said reports. In actual practice, it is the NPC Standing Committee's legislative affairs commission that takes specific charge of matters related to filing for the record. Such regulations have yet to be supplemented or perfected by means of legislation.

According to Hong Kong's original constitutional disposition, the British government enjoyed very extensive legislative powers over Hong Kong. First of all, Article 9 of the Letters Patent stipulates "We do also reserve to Ourselves, Our heirs and successors, Our and their undoubted right, with the advice of Our of their Privy Council, to make all such laws as may appear to be necessary for the peace, order and good government of the Colony." This shows that the British government had the power to directly formulate laws for Hong Kong in the form of the British queen doing so

---

[3]This oversight of the SARs' legislatures by NPC Standing Committee is, in reality, a special sort of examination for unconstitutionality. This matter will be discussed in detail in subsequent chapters and sections.

together with the Privy Council. Second, paragraph two of Article 7 of the Letters Patent authorized the Governor-General to exercise legislative powers together with the Legislative Council. However, Article 8 stipulated that "We do reserve to Ourselves, Our heirs and successors, full power and authority to disallow, through one of Our Principal Secretaries of State, any such law as aforesaid." That is to say, the British government had absolute veto power over the Hong Kong's local legislature. Moreover, the Royal Instructions also stipulated ten kinds of laws for which Britain's authorization had to be obtained before they could be formulated.[4]

As noted by Professor Yash Ghai of Hong Kong University: "British authority in Hong Kong (broadly defined) rested on a mixture of prerogative and statute ... Briefly the legal situation, as clarified in the Colonial Laws Validity Act 1865, provided for the plenary powers of the British Parliament to make laws for Hong Kong. The British Government had extensive powers of law making as well, derived from prerogative as well as legislation and exercised principally through Orders in Council. It could authorize institutions in Hong Kong to make laws and establish courts, but no law locally enacted could contravene a provision of an act of parliament which applied of its own force in Hong Kong."[5] It is evident that the legislative powers enjoyed by Hong Kong were highly restricted under British rule. And by comparison with the Basic Laws, we find that the legislative powers enjoyed by the Hong Kong SAR are quite extensive.

The Macao SAR also has the power to establish its local legal system and to formulate various laws applicable to local circumstances, including criminal codes, civil codes, commercial codes, and procedure codes. Some such laws are formulated by the central federal authorities in countries with federal systems. Hence, there has been a substantial increase in the legislative powers of the Macao SAR as compared to previous times.

Another matter related to the legislative powers enjoyed by the SARs is the fact that when national-type laws are to be exercised in the SARs, these must be announced locally by the SARs on their own or implemented through their own legislation instead of being directly announced and implemented by the Central Authorities. This, too, is a mark of respect for the SARs' legislature. As for the national-type laws implemented by the SARs, the Basic Laws list specific examples in Annex III. Although the NPC Standing Committee may increase or reduce the laws listed in Annex III after soliciting the opinions of the Basic Law Commissions under it, all of the national-type laws listed in the Annex and implemented in the SARs must be strictly limited to laws on national defense and foreign relations and other laws which do not fall within the scope of SAR autonomy. Thus, the implementation of these laws will not affect the exercise of the Regions' legislative powers.

---

[4] Miners N. *The Government and Politics of Hong Kong*. Hong Kong: Oxford University Press Hong Kong Ltd., 1994, p. 259.

[5] Ghai Y. *Hong Kong's New Constitutional Order* (Second Edition). Hong Kong; Hong Kong University Press, 1999, p. 14.

7.1.3 Independent Judicial Powers and the Power of Final Adjudication

"Judicial Powers" refers to the jurisdiction exercised by the state's judicial departments over the legal disputes which arise between citizens, between citizens and the
government and legal persons, between legal persons, between the government and
legal persons, or between government institutions, and the power of final adjudication is the power of final jurisdiction. Since the object of administration of justice is
to produce fair judgments when disputes arise between two parties (including when
the government is a party), and to determine who is right and who is wrong and
soften contradictions and solve disputes, judicial rights must be independent—independent not only in terms of society, but also in terms of administrative departments.
Hence, the constitutions of all countries stipulate provisions with regard to judicial
independence. China's constitution also has similar provisions, namely Article 126
of the Constitution which provides that "The people's courts exercise judicial power
independently, in accordance with the provisions of the law, and are not subject to
interference by any administrative organ, public organization or individual."

In accordance with the "one country, two systems" policy, judicial power is one
of the important contents of the SARs' autonomous powers. Article 19 of the Hong
Kong Basic Law stipulates: "The Hong Kong Special Administrative Region shall be
vested with independent judicial power, including that of final adjudication." Here,
the implication of "independent" is not only independence in terms of other organs,
public organizations, and individuals, but also and more importantly in terms of the
Central Authorities and the mainland. In other words, after the SARs have been set
up, the Central Authorities do not interfere with their judiciaries, and all of the SAR
courts, besides continuing to retain their own localities' original legal system and the
original limitations placed on court adjudicative powers, exercise jurisdiction over
all cases in the SARs.

An important content and characteristic of independent judicial powers is the
power of final adjudication vested in the SARs. In fact, the constitutions of all countries in the world grant the power of final adjudication to their countries highest
courts. This is an important manifestation of a country's having a unified judiciary.
Even in Hong Kong under British rule, its courts were never vested with the power of
final adjudication. In former times, if any parties to civil or criminal lawsuits refused
to accept judgments by Hong Kong's highest court, they could, upon fulfilling certain
procedures, lodge appeals with the Judicial Council of Britain's Privy Council, and
only the judgments by that Judicial Council were final rulings. The former judiciary
in Macao was even more dependent on Portugal. However, China, after resuming its
sovereignty over Hong Kong and setting up a SAR, did not take back the power of
final adjudication to have it exercised by the Central Authorities, but instead granted
that power to and let it be exercised by the SARs. This tells us that the SARs' judicial
powers are quite complete and independent, and that the Central Authorities have no
intention of intervening in the SARs' judicial affairs. Accordingly, the SARs have set
up their own courts of final adjudication in order to exercise the power of final adju-

dication, while other, ordinary courts in the SARs exercise ordinary judicial powers. The Hong Kong SAR court of final adjudication may also, when necessary, invite judges from other areas where the Common Law is applicable to participate in trials.

After Hong Kong was occupied by Britain in the mid-nineteenth century, it gradually introduced and imported England's Common Law system.[6] It built up a complete set of rule-of-law institutions in light of local characteristics and formed a fairly mature and independent body of legal professionals. Hong Kong's well-developed rule-of-law system has had direct links with the international community, provided strong guarantees for Hong Kong's economic take-off and did an excellent job of protecting the security of market deals and the investments placed in Hong Kong by all countries. Hence, it was only natural that its legal system, geared as it was to the developed capitalist market, should be retained. Accordingly, Article 8 of the Basic Law stipulates: "The laws previously in force in Hong Kong, that is, the Common Law, rules of equity, ordinances, subordinate legislation and customary law shall be maintained, except for any that contravene this Law, and subject to any amendment by the legislature of the Hong Kong Special Administrative Region."

However, since the HK SAR government has no jurisdiction over such state actions as national defense and foreign relations, and since in accordance with the normal practice of countries in general, local governments should not exercise jurisdiction over state acts, the SARs' courts of law, too, should not exercise jurisdiction over legal matters which involve such state acts as national defense and foreign relations.[7] The state's declarations of war, peace negotiations, conclusions of treaties, cessions or annexations of territories, recognitions of foreign governments, and so forth are all exercises and direct manifestations of state sovereignty which courts are not able to adjudicate. According to the customary practice of the Common Law, if an ordinary lawsuit adjudicated by a court of law happens to involve state acts, the court must ask administrative organs to provide relevant evidence concerning the facts and issues. And the documents concerned provided by the administrative organs possess binding power over the courts, which must use these documents as grounds for producing judgments.

Therefore, paragraph three of Article 19 of the Hong Kong Basic Law stipulates that the courts of the HK SAR have no jurisdiction over the acts of state such as defense and foreign affairs. The courts of the SAR shall obtain a certification from the Chief Executive on matters concerning acts of state such as defense and foreign affairs whenever such questions arise in the adjudication of cases. These certifications

---

[6]Strictly speaking, "U.K. Law" or "British Law" is a concept different from that of "English Law." U.K. Law, or British Law, is the general term for the legal system practiced in all regions of Great Britain, whereas "English Law" consists of the laws applied only in the region of England.

[7]After Britain signed the Treaty of Rome and became a member of the European Economic Community, some persons lodged a complaint with courts of law claiming that doing so would restrict the supreme authority of the British Parliament and place it under the control of the EU Treaty. England's Court of Appeal refused to accept the case, citing as its reason that it was not empowered to examine treaties concluded by the state. See Wang Shuwen: *Introduction to the Basic Law of the Hong Kong Special Administrative Region.* p. 113, Beijing: CPC Central Committee Party School Press, 1990.

shall be binding on the courts. Before issuing such certifications, the Chief Executive must obtain certifying documents from the Central People's government. This is a requirement for upholding state sovereignty, and it conforms to the customary usage of all other countries.

The Macao Basic Law has similar regulations on this matter. Only, the circumstances of Macao's legal system are quite different from Hong Kong's. First of all, Macao' laws also fall in the rubric of the Continental Law system and differ from Hong Kong's Common Law. Second, Macao's legal system used to be very skimpy, basically made use of Portuguese laws, and was barely "localized" prior to Macao's return to China. Hong Kong's legal system on the other hand was highly developed; most of it had already been "internalized" as local law, and constituted a complete system on its own. Also, Macao's legal institutions were basically all under the control of Portuguese persons in 1999 prior to Macao's return to China, and there was a severe dearth of local legal talent. Not so in Hong Kong, where there was an abundance of local talent who had already gradually assumed control over vital legal institutions before Hong Kong's return to China in 1977. Hence, the key to any intention by the Macao SAR of making good use of its own independent judicial powers and powers of final adjudication lay in the progress made in building up Macao's legal system and the growth of Macao's local legal talent.

Although the SARs exercised independent judicial powers and had no relations of jurisdiction or vocational guidance with China's Supreme People's Court and Supreme People's Procuratorate, conflicts between the SARs' laws and mainland laws were bound to increase, and mutual judicial assistance was necessary between the two regions. Before the SARs' were returned to China, conflicts between mainland laws and the laws of Hong Kong and Macao were resolved mainly by means of China and Britain or China and Portugal adhering to international private law channels. Judicial assistance was also conducted in accordance with the methods of international judicial assistance. However, after China had resumed its exercise of sovereignty over Hong Kong and Macao and established the two SARs, respectively, further adherence to channels of international private law to resolve the two regions' legal conflicts and to judicial assistance became quite inappropriate. After Hong Kong and Macao returned to China, a situation had arisen of the concurrent existence of multiple legal jurisdictions in China. Hence, I agree with the proposal of some scholars to formulate a law on interregional conflicts in China and a law on interregional judicial assistance in order to resolve legal conflicts among legal jurisdictions and the issues of judicial assistance under the circumstances of the concurrent existence in China of several different legal jurisdictions after the SARs' establishment. We may use some of the principles of international private law as reference, but should certainly not copy them lock, stock, and barrel.[8] This matter will be discussed in detail in the later chapters and sections.

The power of SAR courts of law to conduct constitutionality reviews (examinations) will be discussed in Chapter XI.

7.1.4   The Power of the SARs to Handle Foreign Affairs Matters on Their Own

Hong Kong is a large international-type metropolis. It is also one of the most thriving modernized industrial and commercial port cities in the Asia-Pacific region and an important center of finance, trade, shipping, and communications in the world. Although Macao is smaller than Hong Kong, it is also an international-type city, a member of many international organizations and treaties, and also has a special status in world society. In recent history, due to the closed-door policy pursued by the Qing government, the Hong Kong and Macao regions became China's main channels to the outside world, and world society's understanding of China—this huge ancient civilization in the Orient—was derived mainly through those two windows. In this way, the Hong Kong and Macao regions also became a place where Eastern and Western cultures gathered and communed. Hong Kong's society has become an internationalized and modernized Chinese society; it has established close ties with the whole world's capitalist system, and has a thousand and one links with international society. If these ties are severed, Hong Kong and Macao would lose their verve and vitality. An important reason for Hong Kong's and Macao's success is that they are societies open to the whole world. Meanwhile, the whole of China's mainland is in the process of implementing a policy of opening up to the outside. To maintain the prosperity and international status of the Hong Kong and Macao regions, it is absolutely necessary for the Hong Kong and Macao SARs to be vested with certain powers of handling foreign affairs on their own. True, the two SAR Basic Laws

---

[8]See Huang Jin. *Research of Interregional Conflict Law*. Xuelin Press, 1991, pp. 219–255. Han Depei and Huang Jin. "Formulating the Law of Interregional Conflicts to Solve the Interregional Conflicts of Laws Between Our Chinese Mainland and Taiwan, Hong Kong and Macao," carried in Journal of Wuhan University Social Science Edition, 1993 (4), p. 54. Huang Jin. "Interregional Conflict of Laws and Its Solution—Also on 'One Country, Two Systems': Interregional Legal Conflicts with China," carried in Huang Bingkun. *The Legal Issues of "One Country, Two Systems"*, Hong Kong: Sanlian Bookstore, 1989, p. 104. Judicial Assistance Bureau, Ministry of Justice, People's Republic of China and Association of China 's Private International Law: *Proceedings of International Judicial Assistance and Interregional Conflict Law*. Wuhan: Wuhan University Press, 1989. Chang Zheng and Wang Guangyi. *Legal Discussion on the Relationship Across the Taiwan Strait*. Chengdu: Sichuan University Press, 1992. Taiwan Law Research Center of Fujian Province et al. Xiamen: Lujiang Press, 1992. Zeng Xianyi and Guo Pingtan ed. *Legal Issues in the Exchanges Across the Taiwan Strait*. Zhengzhou: Henan Peoples Press, 1992. Wang Zhiwen. "The Development and Comparison of Legal Conflicts between the Two Sides of the Taiwan Straits," carried in Hua Gang faction, 1992 (21), p. 171.

both stipulate that the Central People's Government is in charge of matters related to foreign affairs in the SARs. However, the SARs have the power, in accordance with provisions in the Basic Laws or as authorized the Central People's Government, to handle, on their own, foreign matters related to economics and culture. This is an important aspect of their autonomous powers. Chapter VII of the Basic Laws makes special stipulations in this connection.

The powers enjoyed by the SARs to handle foreign affairs comprise in the main the following aspects:

(1) Taking part in relevant foreign affairs negotiations. The two Basic Laws both stipulate that representatives of the SAR governments may, as members of delegations of the People's Republic of China, participate in negotiations at the diplomatic level conducted by the Central People's Government in matters that directly affect the regions.[9] Here, "negotiations at the diplomatic level directly affecting [the regions]" includes diplomatic negotiations conducted specially by the Central Peoples' Government with foreign governments or international organizations for the benefit of one or the other SAR, and also includes other diplomatic negotiations conducted by the Central People's Government with foreign countries or international organizations which may involve SARs' interests. Under both of these circumstances, the SARs' government may dispatch representatives to take part in the negotiations as members of delegations of China's Central Government.

(2) Conducting foreign economic and cultural exchanges on their own initiative. The two Basic Laws both stipulate that the SARs may, on their own and using the name "Hong Kong, China" or "Macao, China," maintain and develop relations and conclude and implement agreements with foreign state and regions and relevant international organizations in the appropriate fields, including the economic field and the trade, financial and monetary, shipping, communications, tourist, cultural, and sports fields. That is to say, the economic and cultural contacts by the Hong Kong and Macao regions with the international society are not severed because of China's resumption of sovereignty over the regions and its setting up of the SARs. On the contrary, the Hong Kong and Macao regions should play even better roles on the international economic and cultural stage, and their international positions should be further enhanced. The SARs may, as necessary, set up official or semi-official institutions in other countries simply by reporting these actions to the Central People's Government for the record. Similarly, foreign governments and international organizations may establish consular missions or other official and semi-official institutions in the SARs with approval from the Central People's Government of the People's Republic of China. All such acts are conducive to maintaining and developing the Hong Kong and Macao regions' economic and cultural contacts with the world.

(3) The power to participate in international organizations and international conferences. This includes a number of aspects.

---

[9]Xiao Weiyun. *One Country, Two Systems and the Basic Law of the Macao Special Administrative Region.* Beijing: Peking University Press, 1993, p. 117.

(1) Participating in international organizations and international conferences between states. In accordance with the stipulations of the Basic Laws, the SARS may send representatives as members of delegations of the People's Republic of China or in a capacity permitted by the Central People's Government or by the international organization or international conference concerned, to participate in international organizations or international conferences that are held in terms of state entities and that concern appropriate fields related to the SAR in question, and to express their views under the title "Hong Kong, China" or "Macao, China." Once a SAR takes part in international organizations and international conferences between and among states, it not only may express its opinions under the title "Hong Kong, China" or "Macao, China," but may also take a stand different from that of the Central People's Government.[10]

(2) Participating in international organizations and international conferences not limited to those held by states.
The Basic Laws also stipulate that the SARs may, using the name "Hong Kong, China" or "Macao, China," participate in international organizations and international conferences not limited to those held by states. This refers mainly to people-to-people and nongovernmental international organizations and international conferences, as for instance the International Disabled Persons Rehabilitation Association.

(3) Continued participation in relevant international organizations.
The Basic Laws also stipulate that the Central People's Government shall take steps for the SARs to continue to retain their status in international organizations they had already joined before their return to China. In these cases, the Central People's Government takes the necessary steps to enable the SARs to continue to retain, in an appropriate form, their status in international organizations in which the People's Republic of China has participated and Hong Kong or Macao have also participated in one form or another. As regards international organizations in which the People's Republic of China has yet to participate but in which Hong Kong or Macao have already joined in one form or another, the Central People's Government, where necessary, enables the SARs to continue their participation in an appropriate form. These stipulations have been made after giving ample consideration to Hong Kong's and Macao's actual circumstances and to the charters of the relevant international organizations.

(4) Application of international agreements.
There are three situations. One, the application to the SARs of all international agreements which China has formally concluded with other countries is determined by the Central People's Government in accordance with the circumstances and needs of the SARs and after soliciting the views of the SAR governments. Two, international agreements to which the People's

---

[10] Xiao Weiyun. *One Country, Two Systems and the Basic Law of the Macao Special Administrative Region.* Beijing: Peking University Press, 1993, p. 117.

Republic of China is yet to become a party but which are already implemented in Hong Kong and Macao may continue to be applied in the said SARs. For example, both Hong Kong and Macao have separately joined the World Trade Organizations (WTO, i.e., the former General Agreement on Tariffs on Trade), and although China eventually joined the WTO only at the end of 2001, it nevertheless allowed Hong Kong and Macao to retain their original status in that organization, using the name "Hong Kong, China" or "Macao, China," between the time it resumed its exercise of sovereignty over the two regions and the end of 2001. Three, the Central People's Government, where necessary, authorizes the SARs or assists them in the making of appropriate arrangements for the application other relevant international agreements in the SARs.

(5) The power to separately issue passports and travel documents.

Article 154 and Article 139, respectively, of the two Basic Laws stipulate that, with authorization from the Central People's Government, the SARs' governments have the power to issue, in accordance with law, passports of the PRC Hong Kong SAR and passports of the PRC Macao SAR to all Chinese citizens who hold permanent identity cards of the two regions and also travel documents of the PRC Hong Kong or Macao SARs to all other persons lawfully residing in the Regions. These passports and documents are valid for trips and visits to all countries and regions in the world, and clearly, state the holders' right to return to the SARs.

The SAR governments have the power to apply immigration controls on entries into, sojourns in, and departures from the Regions by persons from foreign states and regions.

The Central People's Government assists or authorizes the governments of Hong Kong and Macao to conclude visa exemption agreements with foreign countries or regions.

(6) Mutual establishment of missions by foreign countries and the SARs.

First, the SARs may, as needed, establish official or semi-official economic and trade missions in foreign countries simply by reporting such acts to the Central People's Government for the record.

Second, as regards foreign countries setting up institutions in the SARs, foreign countries may set up consular and other official or semi-official missions in the SARS with approval from the Central Government of the People's Republic of China. The consular missions or other official missions set up in Hong Kong or Macao by countries which already have formal diplomatic relations with China may be maintained. Consular missions or other official missions set up in Hong Kong or Macao by countries which have yet to establish formal diplomatic formal relations with China may, according to the circumstances of each case, be permitted to remain or be changed to semi-official missions. Countries not recognized by the People's Republic of China may only establish nongovernmental missions in the SARs.

The above-described circumstances show that the SARs enjoy quite substantial autonomous powers in terms of foreign affairs. After the return of Hong Kong and Macao to China, the SARs' international latitude for foreign exchanges has not contracted as some people had reckoned, but has instead undergone constant expansion.

7.2   The SARs' Right to Participate in National Affairs

Not only do the SARs enjoy a high degree of autonomy, they also have the right to participate in the administration of [China's] national affairs. After China resumed its sovereignty over the Hong Kong and Macao regions, Chinese citizens among the residents of Hong Kong and Macao regions, including Chinese citizens among the regions' permanent and non-permanent residents, all became citizens of the People's Republic of China. As Chinese citizens, they naturally have the right to take part in the administration of nationwide affairs, in discussions and decisions on the state's fundamental policies, and especially in the discussions and decisions on matters concerning the SARs. Since the people's congress system is China's fundamental political system, residents of the SARs should also participate in state governance by way of the people's congresses. However, their mode of participation differs from that of the mainland regions because the SARs do not implement the people's congress system.

7.2.1   The SARs' Delegates and Delegations Who Attend the National People's Congresses

Article 21 of the Basic Laws stipulates that Chinese citizens who are SAR residents are entitled to participate in the management of state affairs according to law. In accordance with the quota for deputies and the method of electing deputies determined by the National People's Congress, the SAR's National People's Congress deputies elected locally from among Chinese citizens in each SAR take part in the work of the highest institutions of state power. That is to say, the SARs, as provincial-level local political regimes, have the power to organize their own independent delegations who are to directly participate in the work of the State's highest organs of state power and exercise all rights granted to people's deputies by the Constitution. These deputies may advance proposals in the name of their own delegation, participate in the voting on relevant bills and resolutions and so forth, and through such actions may uphold the interests of their own special administrative region on the one hand and, on the other, exercise the right the Constitution confers on Chinese citizens to be masters of their own house.

As for the method by which SARs elect deputies to the National People's Congress, the Basic Laws do not contain any specific stipulations in this respect. On March 14, 1997, the 5th Session of the Eighth National People's Congress approved the Measures for the Election of Deputies of the Hong Kong Special Administrative Region of the People's Republic of China to the Ninth National People's Congress, which stipulates that election of deputies from the Hong Kong Special Administrative Region deputies to the Ninth National People's Congress is to be sponsored by the NPC Standing Committee. A quota of 36 deputies is to be elected by the Hong Kong SAR to the Ninth National People's Congress. The deputies elected by the Hong Kong SAR to the NPC have to be Chinese citizens from among the residents of the Hong Kong SAR. The specific method of election consists of setting up an Election Council for Deputies to the Ninth National People's Congress sponsored by the NPC Standing Committee, and this Election Council elects the 36 Hong Kong SAR deputies to the National People's Congress. As provided by the Resolution of National People's Congress on the Measures for Generating the First Government and Legislative Council of the Hong Kong Special Administrative Region, the first government of the Hong Kong SAR is to be composed of Chinese Citizens from among the Selection Committee of the First Government of Hong Kong SAR and of members of the Eight National Committee of the Chinese People's Political People's Conference and of the HKSAR Provisional Legislative Council of the Hong Kong Special Administrative Region" as well as of Chinese citizens among inhabitants of the Hong Kong SAR and Chinese citizens who are members of the Eighth National Committee of the Chinese Political Consultative Conference (CPPCC) and of the Hong Kong SAR's Provisional Legislative Council but not members of the Election Council. The persons concerned may declare unwillingness to participate in the Election Council. The list of Election Council members is published by the NPC Standing Committee.

The first session of the Election Council was convoked by the NPC Standing Committee. It selected eleven members of the Election Council to make up a presidium, which has chosen one of its members to serve as its executive president. The Presidium presides over the Election Council, which may formulate specific election measures upon proposals by the Presidium. A group of ten or more members of the Election Council may nominate candidates for delegates. Candidates for delegates jointly nominated by each member of the Election Council may not exceed the quota for elections. The Election Council conducts elections by the competitive multi-candidate method, and the number of candidates for National People's Congress delegates is to exceed the election quota by 20–50%. Elections are to be directly held if the quota of nominated candidates does not exceed the competitive ratio of 20–50% of the election quota. Where the number of candidates nominated exceeds the election quota by 50% or more, all members of the Election Council are to cast their votes and the formal list of candidates is established according to the sequential order of the number of votes received by each candidate and when the differential ratios are not exceeded by one half, whereupon voting for the election proceeds.

The voting is conducted by secret ballot. An election conducted by the Election Council is null and void if the number of votes cast exceeds the number of voters, but is valid if the votes equal or are fewer than the number of voters. A ballot is invalid if the number of persons nominated on it exceeds the requisite number of candidates, but is valid if the number of candidates nominated on it is equal to or less than that required. The candidates with the most votes are elected. Where the number of votes is the same and an election cannot be determined, voting is repeated for the candidates with the same number of ballots and those with the most ballots are elected. The results of the elections are announced by the Presidium and then reported to the Deputies Credentials Committee of the National People's Congress Standing Committee. Based on reports issued by the above-mentioned Credentials Committee, the NPC Standing Committee confirms the deputies' credentials and issues a list of deputies.[11]

In accordance with this method, the Hong Kong SAR has elected its own 36-member NPC delegation, formed an independent delegation and begun to participate in meetings of the National People's Congress and its Standing Committee, and has thereby begun to represent the SAR's Chinese citizens in the exercise of their solemn constitutional powers.

Similarly, on March 15, 1999 the Second Session of the Ninth National People's Congress approved the "Measures for the Election of Representatives of the Macao Special Administrative Region to the Ninth National People's Congress," which stipulates that the Macao Special Administrative Region's election of deputies to the Ninth National People's Congress is sponsored by the NPC Standing Committee, and that the Macao SAR's quota of representatives to the Ninth National People's Congress is 12 persons. The deputies elected by the Macao SAR to the National People's Congress must be Chinese citizens at least 18 years old from among the residents of the Macao SAR. The Macao SAR has set up a National People's Congress Deputies Election Council to elect deputies from the Macao SAR. In accordance with those Measures, the Macao SAR has, after its establishment, already elected its 12 deputies, formed its own delegation, and begun to represent Macao's Chinese citizens in the exercise of their constitutional powers.

From the long-term perspective, the SARs' National People's Congress deputies should be gradually elected by the SARs' Chinese citizens through local elections. This is the direction for future development. However, on this matter, the SARs must take the pace of democratization on the mainland into consideration.

As regards mainland personnel sent to various institutions established in the SARs by the Central Authorities and by various mainland regions, these personnel are also Chinese citizens but they are not SAR residents and consequently may not participate in the elections of SAR deputies to the National People's Congress, nor may they be elected to or work as SARs' representatives at the National People's Congress or its

---

[11] *People's Daily*, Beijing, March 15, 1997.

Standing Committee. They must return the regions from which they were originally dispatched to exercise their democratic rights.[12]

In addition to the SARs being empowered to elect and dispatch representatives to work at the National People's Congress and its Standing Committee, personages from Hong Kong and Macao have also been invited by National Committee of the CPPCC to take part in the work of the CPPCC as representatives by special invitation. As stated in the Preamble of China's Constitution, the CPPCC is a broadly based representative organization of the united front which has played a significant role in the country's political and social life, in promoting friendship with other countries and in the struggle for socialist modernization and for the reunification and unity of the country. In March 1993, Article 4 of the Constitutional amendment passed by the Eighth National People's Congress further stipulated that "the system of multi-party cooperation and political consultation led by the Chinese Communist Party will exist and develop for a long time to come." Hence, despite the CPPCC not being a state organ, it nevertheless plays an important role in the country's political life. Some academics regard it as the "upper house" of China's "parliament," but this comparison is inaccurate, since China's CPPCC is by its nature fundamentally different from the Upper House of the British Parliament or the U.S. Senate.

Nevertheless, in a certain sense, it shows us the importance of the CPCPC. According to the provisions of the CPCPC Constitution, the main functions and duties of the CPCPC consist of political consultation and democratic oversight and organizing the administration and discussion of state affairs by the various parties, organizations, and personages participating in the CPCPC. The 9th National Committee of the CPCPC specially invited 119 Hong Kong personages and 26 Macao personages to join in the work of the CPPCC, and set up special committees for Hong Kong, Macao, and Taiwan compatriots to take charge of Hong Kong, Macao and Taiwan affairs and overseas Chinese affairs. As the 9th Central Committee of the CPCPC counts a total of 2272 members, the proportion of Hong Kong and Macao members in it is fairly high.

The SARs deputies to the National People's Congress enjoy the same rights at NPC meetings as the deputies elected to the NPC by all provinces, municipalities and autonomous regions, and the SARs members of the Chinese People's Political Consultative Conference enjoy the same rights and treatment as members from all provinces, municipalities and autonomous regions. They also enjoy some other special conveniences. For example, in accordance with a Circular issued by the General Office of the State Council on December 9, 1982, the relevant departments contact Customs authorities in advance when NPC deputies and CPPCC members from the SARs enter or exit China's border controls on official business, and they are then exempted from customs checks. All of their traveling expenses to and from Beijing when they come to take part in NPC and CPPCC meetings are defrayed by the two institutions. When NPC deputies and CPPCC members from Macao travel in mainland areas, the relevant departments issued certifications to the airlines, railways,

---

[12]See Wang Shuwen. *Introduction to the Basic Law of the Hong Kong Special Administrative Region*. Beijing, CPC Central Committee Party School Press, 1990, p. 115.

ships, and other means of transportation they take, and all fares were paid in *renminbi* at the same rates as for domestic travelers.[13] Today, of course, all outside residents and foreigners who travel in China enjoy the same treatment as Chinese nationals and pay fares at the same prices, and the issue of "special consideration" for NPC deputies and CPPCC members no longer exists. Another example: the General Customs Administration, after consultations with the General Office of the State Council and the General Office of the CPPCC, on May 9, 1986 issued a another Circular which requires that Customs authorities favor Hong Kong and Macao NPC deputies and CPPCC member entering and exiting China's border controls with exemptions from Customs checks on the strength of their Home Return Permits [i.e., Mainland Travel Permits for Hong Kong and Macao Residents—Tr.].[14] These dispositions are meant as personal expressions of courtesy from the Central Government to NPC deputies from the Hong Kong and Macao regions as well as conveniences for them in their work so that they may better serve the people of the Hong Kong and Macao regions.

7.2.2   The Relations Between the SARs' NPC Deputies and the SAR Governments

According to the provisions in the Constitution, NPC deputies elected by the provinces, municipalities, and autonomous regions on the mainland must "in public activities, production and other work, assist in enforcement of the Constitution and the law… Deputies to the National People's Congress should maintain close contact with the units which elected them and with the people, heed and convey the opinions and demands of the people and work hard to serve them."[15] The Organic Law of the National People's Congress states: "Deputies to the National People's Congress should maintain close contact with the units that elected them and with the people. They may attend, without voting rights, meetings of the people's congresses of the units that elected them, so as to heed and convey the opinions and demands of the people and work hard to serve them."[16] The Localities' Organic Law also stipulate that deputies to local people's congresses of all levels "should maintain close contact with the units or voters that elected them, publicize laws and policies, assist the governments at their levels in carrying forward their work, and conveying the opinions and demands of the masses to the National People's Congress and its Standing Com-

---

[13]Circular of the General Office of the State Council Concerning the Entry-exit Procedures for Deputies to the National People's Congress and Members to the National People's Political Consultative Conference Who Reside in the Regions of Hong Kong and Macao and Other Related Matters When They Return to the Inland.

[14]"Circular on Granting Courtesy Exemptions from Customs Inspections to National People' Congress Deputies and National People's Political Consultative Conference Members of the Hong Kong and Macao Regions on the Strength of Their Credentials," issued by the General Administration of Customs on May 9, 1986.

[15]Article 76 of the Constitution.

[16]Article 41 of the Organic Law of the National People's Congress.

mittee and to the People's Government. The deputies of the people's congresses of provinces, autonomous regions, directly administered municipalities, autonomous prefectures, and cities with districts may attend meetings of the people's congresses of the units that elected them."[17] That is to say, mainland National People's Congress deputies have certain powers in terms of decision-making in local affairs, and may attend local people's congress meetings. For example, National People's Congress deputies elected in Guangdong Province are empowered to attend meetings of the people's congress of Guangdong Province, and have the statutory duty to supervise the circumstances of the implementation of work and laws by the local governments.

However, the relations of the SARs' National People's Congress deputies with the SARs cannot be handled as simply as they are on the mainland. The deputies may not attend the meetings of SAR legislative organs, and may not interfere in governance implemented by the SAR governments. That is because the work these deputies do is with the Central Authorities, and the decision-making they take part in concerns fundamental nationwide policy, and they are to direct their attention on national affairs. Of course, situated as they are in the country's highest organ of state power, they should also represent the SAR peoples and governments.

According to relevant NPC Standing Committee regulations, the National People's Congress deputies from the Hong Kong SAR are required to adhere to the following work principles: They may not interfere in the work of the SARs; they may not interfere in affairs within the scope of SAR autonomy; they may not conduct inspections in the SARs; they may not accept appeals or complaints from Hong Kongers regarding the SAR government or organs; they may discuss state affairs and raise opinions about mainland draft legislations; they may refer to the NPC Standing Committee opinions, criticisms, and suggestions regarding all aspects of mainland affairs; they may transmit to the NPC Standing Committee opinions, appeals, and complaints from Hong Kongers concerning all aspects of mainland affairs; they may inspect mainland organs and units; and they may, upon invitation, attend meetings held by the NPC Standing Committee and special commissions.[18] It is evident that the SAR's NPC deputies are strictly limited to mainland affairs.

The problem is that the SAR Basic Laws contain no clear stipulations regarding the duties and responsibilities of these deputies. Article 21 of the Hong Kong Basic Law merely stipulates: "Chinese citizens who are residents of the Hong Kong Special Administrative Region shall be entitled to participate in the management of state affairs according to law. In accordance with the assigned number of seats and the selection method specified by the National People's Congress, the Chinese citizens among the residents of the Hong Kong Special Administrative Region shall locally elect deputies of the Region to the National People's Congress to participate in the work of the highest organ of state powers." Nor do any other laws or documents, including the "Measures Whereby the Hong Kong Special Administrative Region Shall Elect Deputies to the Ninth National People's Congress," and the "Mea-

---

[17] Article 32 of the Organic Law of the People's Republic of China on the Local People's Congresses and Local People's Governments.

[18] *Mingpao Daily News*, U.S.A., January 10, 2001.

sures Whereby the Macao Special Administrative Region Shall Elect Deputies to the Ninth National People's Congress," contain any stipulations regarding the duties and responsibilities of the SARs' deputies to the NPC. One can see that the intent of such legislation was to avoid as far as possible any intervention by the SARs' National People's Congress deputies in the work of the SAR governments, and in particular by voiding the powers of these National People's Congress deputies in their own "electoral districts," namely the SARs. The purpose in so doing is to ensure the implementation of "one country, two systems," and to "keep well water and river water from encroaching upon each other." As State Chairman Jiang Zemin pointed out to Hong Kong's NPC deputies when he took part in a meeting of the National People's Congress in 1998: "Hong Kong deputies may represent their Hong Kong compatriots only by participating in the management of national affairs. They should not intervene in any matters of the SAR government."[19]

Precisely for that reason, when Hong Kong's NPC deputies asked to set up an independent office in Hong Kong, they were tactfully turned down by the NPC Standing Committee, which feared that such an office might affect the exercise of governance by the Hong Kong SAR government and interfere with the SAR's high degree of autonomy. The Basic Law makes it quite clear that supervision over the SAR government is the duty and responsibility of the Hong Kong SAR's Legislative Council; not the duty or responsibility of the Hong Kong' National People's Congress deputies. They may keep in touch with the SAR government through the Central People's Government Liaison Office in Hong Kong.[20]

Nonetheless, Article 159 of the Hong Kong Basic Law also stipulates that if the Hong Kong SAR proposes to make amendments to the Basic Law, "Amendment bills from the Hong Kong Special Administrative Regions shall be submitted to the National People's Congress by the delegation of the Region to the National People's Congress after obtaining the consent of two-thirds of the deputies of the Region to the National People's Congress, two-thirds of all the members of the Legislative Council of the Region, and the Chief Executive of the Region." Article 144 of the Macao Basic Law contains a similar stipulation. That is to say, the Regions' NPC deputies do have certain duties and responsibilities in the Regions, and moreover very important responsibilities, i.e., participating in bills for amending the Basic Laws and representing the SARS in presenting to the NPC bills for amending the Basic Laws. Such powers are by no means "void"; they are very substantial. Does that mean the SARs' NPC deputies may only participate in major SAR affairs, i.e., crucial bills for amending the Basic Laws, and may only "observe" rather than participate in minor everyday matters? If they may not participate in or have some say about the management of certain local affairs in the Regions, how will they determine at crucial moments whether the Basic Laws need to be amended? And how will they go about such important decision-making? And how will they represent the SARs' interests in the highest organs of state power? Thus, the matter of the duties and responsibilities of the SARs' NPC delegates should be conscientiously studied and

---

[19] *South China Morning Post*, Hong Kong, March 10, 1998.

[20] *South China Morning Post*, Hong Kong, March 4, 1998.

reasonably resolved. Reference should be taken from the relevant regulations and experience in other countries, and the deputies were given a certain participatory though the not meddlesome role in the SARs' local exercise of governance.

7.2.3   The Matter of SAR Chinese Citizens Holding Office in the Central Government

As regards the right of the SARs to participate in the management of nation wide affairs, and specifically as regards the holding of official positions by SARs' Chinese citizens, the latter should enjoy the same rights as mainland Chinese citizens do. Hong Kong and Macao are currently importing professional talent from the mainland, and in fact, Hong Kong and Macao talent can also be used on the mainland. After China joined the World Trade Organizations, China as a whole has become more and more open, and the world is establishing an increasing presence in China. These are tendencies which will only grow in momentum. But China is at present coming up against a problem of grave shortages of persons trained in foreign affairs and, in particular, monetary affairs, law, and foreign trade. As China opens up in all aspects, every department may face the problem of external contacts and exchanges, which are no longer limited exclusively to foreign affairs institutions. China is short of talent in this respect, and this often results in serious damage to the interests of our country and people. China is an ancient land with a history of five thousand-plus years of civilization, but, regrettably, the current international order has been built up by Westerners, and so when handling various external affairs we have been constrained to abide by rules of the game devised by Westerners and to use their languages and methods. This is a reality.

It is because China lacked persons well versed in contacts with foreign countries, because its functionaries were incapable of conveying their views by means of the language and methods familiar to Westerners, and because they continued to use documents and methods couched in antiquated officialese, that they frequently put in double the efforts to gain half the anticipated results, held up important national affairs and inflicted huge losses on the economy. Yet it was precisely in these respects that Hong Kongers developed their fortes. Hong Kong has a great many persons skilled in international trade, monetary affairs, and law. They are very fluent in standard English and loyal to their country, and the Central Government may quite confidently make use of their valuable talents—which is also a Constitutional right for Hong Kongers. Previously, the positions held by Hong Kong and Macao compatriots in Central Government institutions were limited to those in the NPC Standing Committee and the CPPCC. In recent years, the Central Government has begun to place Hong Kongers in some important administrative posts, although far from enough has been done so far.

In fact, a retrospect of China's recent history shows that in spite of Hong Kong being still under British rule, not a few outstanding Hong Kongers gave up their comfortable lives and went to Beijing to serve their country. The most outstanding example is that of the noted lawyer Wu Tingfan (Wu Tung Fang 1842–1922), who was engaged by the Qing Government to be Minister for the Amelioration of Laws. Under his sponsorship, the modernization of China's feudal laws began, laying the foundations for current Chinese law (including the laws of the Taiwan region). The China of past times can hardly be mentioned in the same breath as today's China, and China's mainland has also turned not a few talented people. But Hong Kong's outstanding professionals are just as employable.

7.3   The Power to Accept "Other Powers" Granted by the Central Government

The various powers enjoyed by the SARs have been discussed in Sections A and B, and it is "quite hard to visualize that any other power required for bringing about a high degree of autonomy has not yet been granted to the Hong Kong Special Administrative Region."[21] That, however, is not to say the SARs may enjoy only those powers. Right after presenting a detailed list of the various highly autonomous powers enjoyed by the SAR, the HK Basic Law posits in Article 20 that "the Hong Kong Special Administrative Region may enjoy other powers granted to it by the National People's Congress, the Standing Committee of the National People's Congress or the Central People's Government." That is to say the powers enjoyed by the SARs are not limited to those specifically listed in the SAR has the power to accept other powers granted by the Central Authorities, even though the Central Authorities have, in the Basic Law, already specifically granted the SAR all of the major powers necessary for the exercise of a high degree of autonomy.

Earlier, I have already discussed the Basic Laws' handling of "residual laws," i.e., that on the general premise of affirming the Central Authorities' full authority for maintaining unity, the Basic Laws make versatile dispositions in terms of legislative techniques and use methods that include both enumerative and generalized provisions on the functions and powers vested in the Central Authorities, and thereby clearly establish the Central Authorities as the granters and possessors of all powers including "residual powers" and enumeratively defines the major powers that must be exercised by the Central Authorities. At the same time, the Basic Laws include both enumerative and generalized stipulations with regard to the functions and powers enjoyed by the SARs. They first list the various powers enjoyed by the SARs, and then makes a generalized stipulation in Article 20 that the SARs have the power to continue accepting "other powers" granted by the Central Authorities. This provides a legal basis for the Central Authorities to eventually, and as needed, grant the SARs various powers other than those stipulated in the Basic Laws, and for the SARs to accept other powers granted by the Central Authorities. These arrangements, as

---

[21]See Wang Shuwen. *Introduction to the Basic Law of the Hong Kong Special Administrative Region*. Beijing, CPC Central Committee Party School Press, 1990, p. 117.

well as upholding the Central Authorities' authority in maintaining unity and the unitary system exercised in China, also grant, to a maximum extent, a high degree of autonomous power to the SARs and furnish a versatile disposition for the putative adoption of special handling methods if and when special problems do arise. They also provided a fairly good solution to a constitutional dilemma which at one time gave rise to considerable debate.

During the drafting the Hong Kong Basic Law, some persons proposed that other than clearly defining the powers enjoyed, respectively, by the Central Authorities and the SARs, "residual powers" should be explicitly given over to the SARs. They, however, knew little about the difference between federal and unitary systems, nor were they clear as regards jurisdiction over state powers under the unitary system. Other persons argued that even though "residual powers" pertained to the Central Authorities, why shouldn't the Central Authorities nominally assign "residual powers" to the SARs and thereby show some good faith and bolster the Hong Kongers' confidence? However, these persons did not understand that "residual powers" was by no means a "nominal" issue but was tied very closely to a country's sovereignty and political structure. Thus the Basic Law drafting committee rejected the above-described opinions, and adopted dispositions that stood on principle while showing resilience. This is manifested in Article 20 of the Basic Laws of Hong Kong and Macao.[22]

As for the departments which can grant "other powers," including the National People's Congress, the NPC Standing Committee and the State Council, are all empowered to grant "other powers" to the SARs in light of existing circumstances and within the scopes of their duties and responsibilities.

Detailed discussions on this matter have already been conducted in Chapter VI.

7.4   The SARs' Responsibility for Upholding State Unity and Sovereignty

In constitutional studies, "rights" and "duties" are homologous concepts, and the entity that enjoys rights must also undertake corresponding duties. "Powers" and "responsibilities," too, are homologous concepts, and entities which possess certain powers must at the same time undertake corresponding responsibilities.

Also discussed previously is the circumstance that the Central Authorities and the SARs both bear dual responsibilities for safeguarding national unity and sovereignty and safeguarding the SARs prosperity and stability. The Central Authorities, as those who exercise national sovereignty, have the right to exercise all powers necessary for safeguarding national unity and sovereignty, and as well as taking complete responsibility for national unity and sovereignty, they must also take responsibility for the SARs' continued prosperity and stability. On the other hand, since the SAR

---

[22]See Wang Shuwen. *Introduction to the Basic Law of the Hong Kong Special Administrative Region.* Beijing, CPC Central Committee Party School Press, 1990, pp. 116–117.

governments enjoy all powers needed for exercising a high degree of autonomy, they must conscientiously undertake the corresponding responsibilities; in other words they must take responsibility both for safeguarding the SARs' prosperity and stability and for upholding the country's sovereignty and unity within their own Region. An important principle of constitutional studies is that exercise of power is always accompanied by corresponding responsibilities whereas irresponsible power may not be allowed to exist.

Constitutions in all countries—whether of the federal system or the unitary system—stipulate the responsibilities local governments should bear for safeguarding national sovereignty and unity. Article 1, Section 10 of the U.S. Constitutions stipulates that no State shall enter into any treaty, alliance or confederation... keep troops of ships of war in times of peace, enter into any agreement or compact with another State, or a foreign power, or engage in war, unless actually invaded, or in some imminent danger as will not admit of delay.[23] Paragraph three, Article 72 of the French Constitution stipulates: "In the departments and the territories, the delegate of the Government shall be responsible for national interests, administrative supervision and the observance of the law."[24] The Basic Law (Constitution) of the Federal Republic of Germany stipulates that if a *Land* fails to comply with its obligations under this Basic Law or other federal laws, the federal government, with the consent of the Bundesrat, may take the necessary steps to compel the *Land* to comply with its duties. For the purpose of implementing such coercive measures, the federal government or its representative shall have the right to issue instructions to all *Länder* and their authorities.[25] The constitutions of other counties carry similar stipulations. It is evident that safeguarding the country's unity and sovereignty is a basic function and duty of local governments in any country. Even the Crimes Ordinance of Hong Kong before its return to China contained stipulations forbidding actions that endangered the British royalty and betrayed Britain.[26] China's Constitution provides that people's congresses and their standing committees in all localities and people's governments of all localities must ensure compliance with and implementation of the Constitution, laws and administrative rules and regulations (Articles 99, 104, and 107) and consciously uphold the country's unity and sovereign integrity.[27] China's criminal law also has corresponding regulations in this respect.

The SARs, as special local administrative regions in China, and the SAR governments, as unique forms of local government, are like all other local administrative regions and local government in terms of safeguarding national unity and sovereignty and bear the same responsibilities. Article 23 of the Hong Kong Basic Law stipulates:

---

[23]Li Daokui. *The American Government and American Politics.* Beijing: China Social Sciences Press, 1990, p. 756.

[24]Peking University Department of Law. *Selections of Constitutional Materials,* 5th collection. Beijing: Peking University Press, p. 21.

[25]Peking University Department of Law. *Selections of Constitutional Materials,* 5th collection. Beijing: Peking University Press, p. 110.

[26]See Wang Shuwen. *Introduction to the Basic Law of the Hong Kong Special Administrative Region.* Beijing, CPC Central Committee Party School Press, 1990, pp. 116–117.

[27]*Constitution,* Articles 99, 104 and 107.

"The Hong Kong Special Administrative Region shall enact laws on its own to prohibit any act of treason, secession, sedition, subversion against the Central People's Government, or theft of state secrets, to prohibit foreign political organizations or bodies from conducting political activities in the Region, and to prohibit political organizations or bodies of the Region from establishing ties with foreign political organizations or bodies."

Article 42 of the Hong Kong Basic Law stipulates that Hong Kong residents and other persons in Hong Kong shall have the obligation to abide by the laws in force in the Hong Kong Special Administrative Region.

The Macao Basic Law makes similar stipulations.

The above provisions in the Basic Laws very specifically place responsibility on the SARs for safeguarding national unity and sovereignty within the SARs. This is not only the responsibility of the Central Authorities or the garrisons stationed in the SARs by the Central Authorities. The stipulations require that the SARs enact laws on their own and prohibit the activities listed in Article 23 on their own. These are also guarantees the SARs should make with regard to their "one system" [in other words, to uphold their capitalist system]. This stipulation in the Basic Laws is both an empowerment of the SARs and a demand upon the SARs, and the SARs should enact laws in this respect when appropriate. The fact that the Central Authorities have not directly implemented the legislations concerned in the SARs is a mark of respect for the SARs autonomy. Since the Criminal Law of the People's Republic of China is, in accordance with the "one country, two systems" principle and the relevant provisions in the Basic Laws, not applicable in the SARs, the SARs should legislate laws on their own to prohibit the occurrence of the actions listed above. This will be a mark of taking responsibility toward the Central People's Government and Chinese people as a whole as well as taking responsibility toward the SARs' own social stability and prosperity and toward all of their residents.

The stipulation in Article 23 of the Basic Law covers in the main the following aspects: One, acts of treason and splitting the nation; two, acts of sedition and subversion against the Central People's Government; three, theft of state secrets; and four, foreign political organizations conducting political activities in the Regions and establishing ties with the Regions' political organizations and bodies. Such actions are bound to pose threats to country's unity and the integrity of its territorial sovereignty, and the SARs should legislate laws to prohibit them. Should there be turmoil in the Regions which the SAR governments are unable to control and that endanger national unity or security, the NPC Standing Committee has the power, in accordance with Article 18 of the Basic Laws, to decide that the Regions are in a state of emergency, in which case the Central People's Government may issue orders applying the relevant national laws in the Regions. And when necessary, the SAR governments may, in accordance with paragraph 3 of Article 14 of the Basic Laws, ask the Central People's Government for help from the garrison forces in fulfilling the SARs' responsibility for maintaining national unity and sovereignty.

The residents of the SARs, as citizens of the People's Republic of China, also bear responsibility for consciously safeguarding the country's unity and sovereignty and for helping the SAR governments fulfill their statutory duties and responsibilities.

To sum up the above, we can see that the Basic Laws' division of duties and responsibilities between the Central Authorities and the SARs is indeed scientific, perfectly logical and reasonable. Powers which should fall within scope of the SARs' high degree of autonomy and which ought to be exercised by the SARs are not deliberately or "artificially" assigned for exercising by the Central Authorities. Nor are powers which are needed for safeguarding the nation's unity and sovereignty and which ought to be exercised by the Central Authorities deliberately or "artificially" assigned for exercising by the SARs. The division of duties and powers is conducted entirely in line with the "one country, two systems" principle and policy, in accordance with the different functions of central governance and local governance, and on the basis of the nature of the matters concerned. Powers which ought to be exercised by the Central Authorities go to the Central Authorities, and those which are best exercised by the SARs are exercised by the SARS. Although a division of functions and powers between the Central Authorities and the SARs has been expressly stipulated in writing in the two Basic Laws and both sides should each attend to their own duties and responsibilities, that by no means implies that the two sides are completely isolated or inflexible or even opposed to each other. On the contrary, they should coordinate and cooperate. They share a common responsibility for safeguarding the nation's unity and sovereignty within the SARs and in promoting the SARs' continued prosperity and stability. They constitute an indivisible whole.

Chapter 8
The Handling of the Relevant Relationships

In previous chapters we have made a detailed analyses of the relations of the Central Authorities with the Special Administrative Regions (i.e. Central/SAR relations) and especially of the respective functions and powers of the SARs, in the course of which I have touched on the relations of the organs of state power—including the National People's Congress and its Standing Committee, the State Council, the State President and the Central Military Commission—with the SARs. In this chapter we will explore the relations of SARs with the various Central People's Government departments, the various provinces and autonomous regions and the directly administered municipalities, and the relations between the SARs as well as the eventual relations between the Central Authorities and a Taiwan Special Administrative Region. Among these relations, those of the various departments of the Central People's Government, the various provinces and autonomous regions and the directly administered municipalities with the SARs are, in themselves, important aspects of the Central/SAR relations and have a certain bearing on the above relations. Doing a good job of handling these relations and is most important for handling Central/SAR relations.

8.1 The Relations of the Central People's Government Departments with the SARs

8.1.1 State Council Organization

The term "Central People's Government departments" as used here refers to the various ministries, various commissions, various directly administered institutions and administrative institutions under the Central People's Government, or in other

© Foreign Language Teaching and Research Publishing Co., Ltd and Springer Nature Singapore Pte Ltd. 2019
Z. Wang, *Relationship Between the Chinese Central Authorities and Regional Governments of Hong Kong and Macao: A Legal Perspective*, China Academic Library, https://doi.org/10.1007/978-981-13-2322-5_8

words, under the State Council. All of these ministries and commissions are central state administrative organs, each of which exercises control over a certain aspect of national administrative work under the unified leadership of the State Council. The legal status of the various ministries and commissions is the same; the only difference is that the matters over which the commissions assume responsibility are generally of a comprehensive and wide-ranging nature, whereas the ministries for the most part only involve certain aspects of specific matters. The National Family Planning Commission, for instance, is a comprehensive department because the implementation of family planning involves many departments and sectors, for which reason the State has set up a commission to make overall arrangements for all matters in the relevant sectors. The operations of the Ministry of Justice and other ministries are, on the other hand, highly specialized and they are responsible for only one certain aspect of some specific work. According to the provisions of China's Constitution, the heads of all ministries and directors of all commissions are nominated by the State Council and are approved for appointment by the National People's Congress or its Standing Committee. The various ministries and commissions implement a responsibility system for their heads and directors who exercise unified leadership over the nationwide work of the various ministries and commissions and answer to the State Council.

After various structural reforms over the years, the State Council presently consists of 25 ministries and commissions. These are the Ministry of Foreign Affairs, National Development and Reform Commission, Ministry of Science and Technology, National Ethnic Affairs Commission, Ministry of National Security, Ministry of Civil Affairs, Ministry of Finance, Ministry of Land and Resources, Housing and Urban-Rural Development, Ministry of Water Conservancy, Ministry of Commerce, National Health and Family Planning, Audit Office, Ministry of Defence, Ministry of Education, Ministry of Industry and Information Technology, Ministry of Public Security, Ministry of Supervision, Ministry of Justice, Human Resources and Social Security, Ministry of Environmental Protection, Ministry of Transportation, Ministry of Agriculture, Ministry of Culture, People's Bank of China.[1]

There is one special entity directly under the State Council, that is the State-owned Assets Supervision and Administration Commission of the State Council (SASAC) and 15 institutions directly under the State Council, including the Customs General Administration, the State Administration for Industry and Commerce, the State Administration of Press and Publication SARFT, the State Administration of Work Safety, the National Bureau of Statistics, the State Intellectual Property Office, the State Administration for Religious Affairs, the State Administration of Machine, the State Administration of Taxation, the General Administration of Quality Supervision, inspection and Quarantine, the General Administration of Sport, the State Food and Drug Administration, the State Forestry Administration, the National Tourism Administration, the Counselor's Office of the State Council.[2]

---

[1] *People's Daily* Online Edition, April 17, 2000.
[2] *People's Daily* Online Edition, December 28, 2000.

The State Council has four administrative bodies: the State Council's Overseas Chinese Affairs Office, the State Council's Legislative Affairs Office, the State Council's Hong Kong and Macao Affairs Office, the Research Office of the State Council. The State Council's Hong Kong and Macao Affairs Office is a special institution which directly administers SAR affairs. The State Council's Taiwan Affairs Office and the CPC Central Committee's Taiwan Affairs Office used to be one institution with two different signboards. It is now listed as an institution directly under the CPC Central Committee.

The State Council also has under it thirteen government-affiliated ministerial-level institutions, such as the Xinhua News Agency, the Chinese Academy of Social Sciences, the Development Research Center of the State Council, the China Earthquake Administration, the China Banking Regulatory Commission, the China Insurance Regulatory Commission, the National Natural Science Foundation of China, the Chinese Academy of Engineering Chinese Academy of Engineering, the National School of Administration, the China Meteorological Administration, the China Securities Regulatory Commission and the National Social Security Fund Council. Furthermore, there are 16 state bureaus administered by the State Council's ministries and commissions, as for example the National Bureau of letters and visits, the National Energy Board, the State Tobacco Monopoly Bureau, the National Civil Service, the National Mapping Geographic Information Bureau, the China Civil Aviation Administration, the National Heritage Board, the State Administration of Foreign Exchange, the National Food Administration, the National Defense Science and Industry Bureau, the State Administration of Foreign Experts Affairs, the State Oceanic Administration, the National Railway Administration, the State Post Office, the State Administration of Traditional Chinese Medicine, and the National Coal Mine Safety Supervision Bureau. In addition, there are 3 council coordinating agencies under the State Council, as for example the Leading Group Office of Poverty Alleviation and Development of the State Council, the State Council South Water Diversion Construction Committee Office, and the State Council Three Gorges Project Construction Committee Office.

After various structural reforms over the years, the State Council Ministries presently consists of 25 ministries and commissions: Ministry of Foreign Affairs, Ministry of National Defense, National Development and Reform Commission, Ministry of Education, Ministry of Science and Technology, Ministry of Industry and Information Technology, State Ethnic Affairs Commission, Ministry of Public Security, Ministry of State Security, Ministry of Supervision, Ministry of Civil Affairs, Ministry of Justice, Ministry of Finance, Ministry of Human Resources and Social Security, Ministry of Land and Resources, Ministry of Environmental Protection, Ministry of Housing and Urban-Rural Development, Ministry of Transport, Ministry of Water Resources, Ministry of Agriculture, Ministry of Commerce, Ministry of Culture, National Health and Family Planning Commission, People's Bank of China and National Audit Office.

There is one special organization directly under the State Council, State-owned Assets Supervision and Administration Commission of the State Council. There are also 15 organizations directly under the State Council, they include General Administration of Customs, State Administration of Taxation, State Administration for Industry and Commerce, General Administration of Quality Supervision, Inspection and Quarantine, State Administration of Press, Publication, Radio, Film and Television, General Administration of Sport, State Administration of Work Safety, China Food and Drug Administration, National Bureau of Statistics, State Forestry Administration, State Intellectual Property Office, National Tourism Administration, State Administration for Religious Affairs, Counselors' Office of the State Council, Government Offices Administration of the State Council.

The State Council has four administrative offices which assist the Premier in handling specific matters in given aspects. These include Overseas Chinese Affairs Office of the State Council, Hong Kong and Macao Affairs Office of the State Council, Legislative Affairs Office of the State Council and Research Office of the State Council. The State Council's Hong Kong and Macao Affairs Office is a special institution which directly administers SAR affairs. The State Council's Taiwan Affairs Office and the CPC Central Committee's Taiwan Affairs Office used to be one institution with two different signboards. It is now listed as an institution directly under the CPC Central Committee.

The State Council also has under it 13 government-affiliated ministerial-level institutions including Xinhua News Agency, Chinese Academy of Sciences, Chinese Academy of Social Sciences, Chinese Academy of Engineering, Development Research Center of the State Council, Chinese Academy of Governance, China Earthquake Administration, China Meteorological Administration, China Banking Regulatory Commission, China Securities Regulatory Commission, China Insurance Regulatory Commission National Council for Social Security Fund and National Natural Science Foundation. There are 16 administrations and bureaus under the Ministries & Commissions: State Bureau for Letters and Calls, State Administration of Grain, National Energy Administration State Administration of Science, Technology and Industry for National Defense, State Tobacco Monopoly Administration, State Administration of Foreign Experts Affairs, State Bureau of Civil Servants State Oceanic Administration, National Administration of Surveying, Mapping and Geoformation, National Railway Administration, Civil Aviation Administration of China State Post Bureau, State Administration of Cultural Heritage, State Administration of Traditional Chinese Medicine, State Administration of Foreign Exchange and State Administration of Coal Mine Safety. There are three deliberation and coordination agencies under the State Council: Leading Group Office of Poverty Alleviation and Development of the State Council, Office of the Construction Committee of the South-to-north Water Diversion Project of the State Council and Executive Office of Three Gorges Project Construction Committee of the State Council.

It is evident the Central People's Government of China is structurally quite ponderous. This is attributable in the main to the earlier implementation of a planned economy. The United States is a country with a highly developed market economy and the U.S federal government today has 14 official ministerial-level institutions.[3] The departments of China's State Council will be further adjusted and their numbers reduced along with the development of China's market economy and the deepening reform of China's administrative system.

8.1.2   The Relations of the Central People's Government Departments with the Governments of the Provinces, Autonomous Regions and Directly Administered Municipalities

Article 89 of the Constitutions provides that the functions and powers exercised by the State Council includes: stipulating the tasks, functions and responsibilities of the various ministries and commissions; exercising unified leadership over the work of the various ministries and commissions and exercising leadership over national-type administrative work which does not fall in the domain of the various ministries and commissions; and, exercising unified leadership over the work of state administrative organs of all levels in localities nationwide, and stipulating the specific divisions of functions and powers of state administrative organs of the Central Authorities and the provinces, autonomous regions and directly administered municipalities.

The Constitution also provides that local people's governments of all levels answer to the next higher level of state administrative organs and report their work to them. The local people's governments of all levels nationwide are state administrative organs under the unified leadership of the State Council and all are subordinated to the State Council. The "Organic Law of the Local People's Congresses and Local People's Governments of the People's Republic of China" also carries similar provisions, among which Article 57 also stipulates that the various work departments of people's governments of provinces, autonomous regions and directly administered municipalities are under the unified leadership of the people's governments at the same levels, and are led by, or subject to vocational guidance from, the competent departments of the State Council.

We can see from these provisions and stipulations that, (1) in terms of their administrative level, the people's governments of provinces, autonomous regions and directly administered municipalities are the same as the State Council's various ministries and commissions in that all are administrative organs one level lower than, and under the unified leadership of, the State Council. The difference is that the

---

[3] The U.S. Federal Government has 14 departments: the Department of State (which in fact should be translated into Chinese as the "Ministry of Foreign Affairs"), the Department of Defense, the Department of Justice, the Interior Ministry, the Department of Education, the Department of Finance, the Departments of Trade, the Department of Agriculture, the Department of Energy, the Department of Transportation, the Department of Housing and Urban Development, the Department of Labor, the Department of Health and Human Resources, and the Department of Veterans' Affairs. There is also an Executive Office of the President.

former are Level One local governments in charge of an area or region and known as "块块" (i.e. "blocs"), whereas the latter are Level One government departments in charge of a vocation or industry and known as "条条" (i.e. "vertical sectors"). In terms of law, there are no relations of administrative subordination between the two, only relations of cooperation. (2) In the provinces, a dual leadership system is implemented for the various vocational or industrial departments of the people's governments of autonomous regions and directly administered municipalities, i.e. they are subject to the unified leadership of people's governments at their respective levels as well as to vocational guidance by the competent State Council departments.[4]

8.1.3   Relations of the Central People's Government Departments with the Special Administrative Regions

Despite the vast structure of China's Central People's Government, few of its institutions are in direct contact with the SARs or have anything to do with SAR affairs. In that case, how are the SARs, as special administrative regional governments in the nature of provincial-level local administrations, related to the various ministries and commissions of the State Council? According to the provisions of the Basic Laws, the relations between the Central Authorities and the SARs are those between "the leader and the led, the supervisor and the supervised, and the authorizer and the authorized." The Central People's Government is empowered to manage the SAR-related matters that fall outside the SARs' scope of autonomy. However, the relations of the State Council's diverse ministries and commissions with the SARs differ from the relations of the State Council per se with the SARs, and although all are administrative organs one level below the State Council, the scope of their functions and responsibilities are different. The State Council's ministries and commissions are functional departments which administer a given specialization or vocation nationwide, whereas the SAR governments are special local governments under the State Council which administer a given region of the People's Republic of China. According to the "one country, two systems" principle and the provisions of the Basic Laws, the relations between the SARs and the administrative organs under the State Council are relations of "mutual non-subordination, mutual non-interference and mutual respect"[5] rather than relations between leaders and the led. The SAR governments are only responsible directly to the State Council in terms of the domains or territories under their jurisdiction.

The State Council's various ministries and commissions may not interfere in the internal affairs of the SARs. As a rule they do not set up institutions in the SARs, and if it becomes necessary to set up a formal agency in a SAR, the consent of the SAR government must be obtained and the matter must be reported to the Central

---

[4]Wu Jialin. *Constitutional Jurisprudence*. Beijing: Qunzhong Press, 1992, p. 318.

[5]Xiao Weiyun. *One Country, Two Systems and the Basic Law of Macao Special Administrative Region*. Beijing: Peking University Press, 1993, p. 120.

People's Government, i.e. the State Council, for approval. After such agencies have been established, they too are not empowered to interfere in SAR affairs. If it becomes necessary in engage in business contacts with a SAR government, this may take place only upon mutual consultation between the two parties. The agencies and their staffs must comply with the laws of the SAR and respect the SAR's high degree of autonomy, and any unlawful or criminal acts on their part are to be handled by the SAR's judiciary.

As for the relations of other departments (ministries, commissions, offices, etc.) of the Central People's Government with the departments (bureaus, etc.) of the SAR governments, these do not entail either superior-subordinate leadership relations or business guidance relations; both sides constitute completely independent systems. The various vocational departments of the SAR governments are not subject to the dual leadership system, are accountable only to the SAR governments and need not report their work to the corresponding business departments of the Central Government. They are free of any administrative subordinate relationship, or in other words, SAR staff members at all levels are accountable only to the SAR government; whereupon the SARs' Chief Executives are then responsible and accountable for all matters to the Central People's Government and the SARs. For example, no relation of administrative subordination exists between the National Ministry of Finance and the SARs' finance departments, and the Ministry of Finance is not empowered to issue orders to the latter. Both are accountable directly to the State Council or to the SAR governments respectively in terms of the areas under their respective jurisdictions. The various policies formulated and enforced by the various departments of the Central People's Government have no binding force on the SAR governments, and the SAR governments' various departments formulate their own policies entirely according to local circumstances.

8.1.4   Institutions Stationed in the SARs by the Central Authorities

In line with the provisions of the Basic Laws, the Central People's Government is charge of the SARs' foreign relations and defense affairs, and for this reason the Ministry of Foreign Affairs and Ministry of National Defense, which represent the diplomatic and defense functions and duties of the Central People's Government, exercise these two powers in the SARS on behalf of the State Council.

The Hong Kong, Macao and Taiwan Department of the Ministry of Foreign Affairs specifically implements the Central Government's policies regarding the Hong Kong, Macao and Taiwan issues, and coordinates and handles Hong Kong, Macao and Taiwan matters which involve foreign countries. On the very same dates respectively that Hong Kong and Macao returned to China, the Ministry of Foreign Affairs set up and stationed special commissioner's offices in the Hong Kong and Macao SARs to take specific charge of handling foreign affairs matters related to the two SARs.

According to the Hong Kong Basic Law, the main functions of duties of the special commissioners' office in Hong Kong include: (1) handling foreign relations matters which Central People's Government is responsible for administering and which are related to the SAR. (2) Coordinating and handling matters related to the participation of the Hong Kong SAR in relevant international organizations and international conferences; coordinating and handling matters related to the establishment of offices in Hong Kong by international organizations and institutions; and coordinating and handling matters related to the holding of inter-governmental international meetings in the Hong Kong SAR. (3) Handling the applicability of international agreements to the Hong Kong SAR; assisting in the handling of matters relevant to bilateral agreements discussed and concluded by the Hong Kong SAR with foreign countries and which require authorization by the Central People's Government. (4) Coordinating and handling matters related to the consular missions or other official and semi-official missions set up by other countries in the Hong Kong SAR. (5) Handling matters related to visits to the Hong Kong SAR by foreign state aircraft and foreign warships. (6) Handling other matters devolved upon them by the Central People's Government and the Ministry of Foreign Affairs. According to the requirements of these functions and responsibilities, the office set up by the Ministry of Foreign Affairs in the SAR has established a number of functional departments.[6]

Similarly, Office of the Commissioner of the Ministry of Foreign Affairs in the Macao SAR is both an institution for dealing with SAR-related foreign relations matters for which the Central People's Government is responsible for handling and a channel that the Macao SAR government can use to communicate with the Central People's Government on foreign affairs matters. Its functions and responsibilities are basically the same as those of the Office of the Commissioner of the Ministry of Foreign Affairs in the Hong Kong SAR and include handling and assisting the Macao SAR Government with the handling of Macao-related foreign affairs; coordinating and dealing with matters related to the consular missions or other official and semi-official missions established by other countries in the Macao SAR and the handling relevant consular business; and coordinating and dealing with the Macao SAR's issues concerning international organizations, international meetings, international agreements and laws and other issues involving Macao's foreign affairs. Established under Office of the Commissioner of the Ministry of Foreign Affairs in the Macao SAR are four functional departments, namely a policy research department, a comprehensive business department, a consular affairs department and a general affairs department. In addition to one commissioner and one assistant commissioner, each of the above functional departments is equipped with an appropriate number of officials.

According to the provisions of the Basic Laws, the Central People's Government is responsible for the SARs' defense. Hence, on the dates when the respective SARs

---

[6]The Ministry of Foreign Affairs. "What Work has the Central People's Government Performed in Terms of Foreign Relations after Hong Kong's Return to China?" See the home page of the Foreign Ministry of the People's Republic of China, http://www.fmprc.gov.cn/chn/2651.html.

were established, the State Council's Ministry of Defense and the Central Military Commission stationed troops in the SARs for fulfilling the task of SAR defense.

Also, the original branch offices of the Xinhua News Agency in Hong Kong and Macao have been rightfully re-designated as liaison offices of the Central People's Government stationed in the Hong Kong and Macao SARs. They handle matters other than those concerning foreign affairs and national defense and other than those that fall within the scope of SAR autonomy.

The Office of the Commissioner of the Ministry of Foreign Affairs, the troops stationed in the SARs, and the Central People's Government's liaison offices stationed in the SARs are three principal Central Authority institutions in the SARs. They are there to develop relations with the SAR governments, but relations of cooperation only; their activities will be kept strictly within the limits stipulated by the Basic Laws and will not intervene in matters that fall within the domain of SAR autonomy. The operations of these three institutions stationed in the SARs will be discussed in detail later.

8.2   Relations Between Ordinary Local Governments and the SAR Governments

The term "ordinary local governments" refers to the general run of provinces, ethnic autonomous regions and directly administered municipalities on the mainland. All constitute the highest levels of local administrative regions under the unified leadership of the State Council. In terms of the leadership system, dual leadership is implemented over these ordinary localities in accordance with the provisions of the Constitution; in other words, the people's governments of these provinces, autonomous regions and directly administered municipalities are under the unified leadership of the State Council and accountable to the State Council, and also under the leadership of the people's congresses and people's congress standing committees at their respective levels and accountable to the state power organs at their own levels. The relations among them are relations of complete equality without reciprocal subordination or intervention; relations of equal cooperation and mutual assistance.

The relations of these local administrative regions with the SARs are a particular kind of relation among localities in a sovereign state. To wit, they are the relations between ordinary localities and special administrative regions in the People's Republic of China. There is no administrative subordination among them, even with Guangdong Province. Historically speaking, the Hong Kong and Macao regions once formed parts of Guangdong Province and, prior to the regions' return to China, their representatives participated in the work of the Guangdong provincial people's congress and its standing committee and, as members of the Guangdong delegation, attended meetings of the National People's Congress. However, that does not mean any relations of subordination or guidance exists today between Guangdong Province and the Hong Kong and Macao SARs. Their status in China's administrative framework is one of complete equality. There is no reciprocal subordination or reciprocal intervention. They both implement their own respective policies in their respective areas of jurisdiction, and are directly accountable respectively to the State Council. No mainland province, autonomous region or directly administered municipality may intervene in SAR affairs.

Due to historical and geopolitical reasons, Hong Kong and Macao's contacts with Guangdong Province had been more frequent than with other regions in China. Guangdong Province's relevant departments had long ago concluded bilateral agreements with the relevant Hong Kong British authorities and Macaoan Portuguese authorities. On this basis, Guangdong Province established a liaison officials system with Hong Kong and Macao and wrote up a set of "Working Rules for Liaison Officials" According its provisions, Guangdong liaison officials represented Guangdong Province's relevant departments in liaising with the relevant Hong Kong British and Macao Portuguese authorities concerning border matters and other counterpart affairs. The methods of liaison consisted mainly of meetings or talks at ports of entry, or correspondence when necessary. The liaison officials were appointed upon approval by Guangdong Province's competent authorities and, after the appointments, the lists of liaison officials had to be officially communicated by Guangdong Provincial Government via the Hong Kong Office of the Xinhua News Agency or Nam Kwong Company in Macao to the Hong Kong British authorities or the Macao Portuguese authorities and also transmitted by the Guangdong Province Public Security Department, the Guangdong Province Armed Police Forces and the Guangdong Customs Branch Office to the border inspection and customs stations. Only then could the liaison officials go about their tasks. The term "meetings" meant reciprocal requests for meetings of both parties' liaison officials at border entry ports. At such meetings, Guangdong liaison officials merely transmitted the opinions and suggestions of the relevant Guangdong departments or listened to the opinions and suggestions of the other party's relevant authorities, or explained circumstances and issues which the Guangdong side required clarification. They did not engage in discussions. "Talks" referred to meetings between liaison officials from both sides—or with the direct participation of relevant representatives from both sides as arranged by the liaison officials—at which opinions were exchanged or consultations or negotiations or work summaries were conducted on designated issues. For the holding of, or participation in, all such consultations, a consultation plan had to be devised in advance and reported to the competent authorities for approval. Important consultations had to be reported to the Guangdong Provincial Government or to the competent State Council departments for approval, and then implemented by the entity that sent out the liaison officials or by competent provincial authorities. After the event, an account of the proceedings had to be sent to the leading organ which approved the talks. The establishment of the liaison official system resolved a good many issues between Guangdong and Hong Kong or Macao and had a highly salutary effect.[7]

---

[7]"Working Rules for Liaison Officials," issued by the People's Government of Guangdong Province on December 28, 1984.

After the establishment of the SARs, the various mainland provinces, autonomous regions and directly administered municipalities normally did not set up offices or agencies in the SARs. If they indeed needed to set up agencies in the SARs, they had to obtain approval from the SAR governments and approval from the Central People's Government. These consisted mainly of formal and official work institutions set up in the SARs by the people's governments of provinces, autonomous regions and directly administered municipalities. These approved institutions and their staffs were obliged to comply with the various SAR laws, and any illegal or unlawful acts on their part were to be handled according to law by the SARs' judiciary departments.

As stated above, the present relations of the various provinces, autonomous regions and directly administered municipalities with the SARs are entirely equal interregional relations devoid of reciprocal subordination or intervention. That is not to say they cannot set up any relations of interregional cooperation. On the contrary, such relations of interregional economic and cultural cooperation are bound to increase in the wake of the progressive opening up of China's mainland areas. The Hong Kong and Macao regions, too, need to continue relying on the mainland's advantages as regards material resources and manpower for developing their economies and thus remain invincible in international competition. Guangdong, Fujian and Hainan provinces, in particular, had very close economic and trade relations and cultural contacts with the Hong Kong and Macao in the past, and most of Hong Kong's and Macao's current inhabitants have their origins in these provinces. All of the above factors make for closer relations between these provinces and the SARs and, in terms of economic development, the various parties can draw on their respective strong points and advance together toward prosperity for all.

The civil organizations of China's mainland regions and those of SARs are also mutually independent in yet another aspect. For instance, the relations of the SARs' civil organizations with those in China as a whole in such respects as education, science, technology, culture, sports and religion should also be dealt with "according to the principle of reciprocal non-subordination, mutual non-intervention and mutual respect."[8] The business contacts and cooperation among these civil organizations are based on complete equality.

Another issue related to mainland and SAR relations after China resumed its exercise of sovereignty over Hong Kong and Macao and set up the SARs is that of the entry and exit of immigrants from either side, and border controls. Concerning the entry-exit system, SAR residents entering the mainland regions still come and go freely, and do so more conveniently than before. However, mainland residents still have to go through approval procedures for entering the Hong Kong SAR even though they no longer need to apply for visas at a British embassy, and still cannot go in and out of the SAR as they please. Moreover, the number of mainlanders who can settle down in the SAR will be determined only after the Central People's Government's competent authorities solicit the opinions of the SAR government.

---

[8] Wang Fengchao. "On the Relations between the Central Authorities and the Hong Kong Special Administrative Region," carried in the *Hong Kong Wen Wei Po*, April 5, 1995.

This issue appears to have become quite serious and is perturbing both the SAR and central governments.

The SAR governments may set up offices in Beijing to conduct unified coordination and handling of diverse SAR affairs and look after SAR residents doing business in and touring the mainland. The Hong Kong SAR set up such an office in Beijing in March 1999. Its duties and functions are: to provide the Central People's Government, the various departments of provinces and municipalities and non-governmental organizations with information about the Hong Kong SAR; brief the Hong Kong SAR government about new developments on the mainland; conduct negotiations with relevant mainland departments about specific matters as directed by the Hong Kong SAR government; maintain contacts with the various departments of the Central People's Government and with the representative offices in Beijing of various provinces and municipalities; handle Hong Kong SAR-related entry formalities; maintain contact with Hong Kong SAR civil organizations set up on the mainland; provide logistical support to Hong Kong SAR government delegations visiting the mainland on official business; provide substantive assistance to Hong Kong residents located in Chinese mainland; and obtain Hong Kong entry visas for foreign citizens located on the mainland.[9]

The Macao SAR will also be setting up an office in Beijing with the consent of the State Council. According to the draft regulations on "Establishing a Beijing Office for the Macao Special Administrative Office" approved on June 28, 2001, the Beijing Office will be directly under the Macao Chief Executive and its main functions and duties shall include: assisting the Chief Executive in comprehensively planning the Macao SAR's relations with the Central People's Government and the mainland, taking charge of liaison with the various Central departments and the offices in Beijing of the various provinces, autonomous regions, and directly administered municipalities, making publicity on the mainland about the current state of the Macao SAR's social and cultural affairs and developing tourist and cultural exchanges between the two sides. It will, in particular, promote tourism with Macao as the destination. develop liaison, consultation and negotiations with relevant mainland departments in such fields as economics and trade, tourism, culture, training and promoting exchanges and cooperation, as directed by the Chief Executive, and provide the Macao SAR with logistical and information assistance.[10]

As for legal conflicts and issues between the mainland and the SARs, these, as stated earlier, may not be handled by applying the principles of international private law or the principles of ordinary jurisprudence in Chinese mainland. They will have to be resolved in accordance with laws on interregional conflicts formulated separately by the Chinese mainland in light of actual circumstances.

Another relevant question is that of the SARs' areas of jurisdiction. There were already many different arguments prior to Hong Kong's return to China about the areas under the Hong Kong SAR's jurisdiction. Some said Hong Kong's domain after

[9]See the Hong Kong Special Administrative Region Beijing Office website: http://www.info.gov.hk/b.jo/.
[10]Macao government network news: http://www.macau.gov.mo/index_cn.html, June 28, 2001.

1997 would extend to Shenzhen, that the border between Hong Kong and Shenzhen would cease to exist and the two regions would merge into a single entity.[11] Facts have proved this understanding to be wrong because the SAR's domain was determined by the Basic Law as clearly defined by the State Council, and is not to be changed at will. Secondly, the SARs were established for specific historical reasons, and one may definitely state that no special administrative region can be formed just anywhere in Chinese mainland, and that the territory of a SAR is not to be enlarged or reduced without good reason. Finally, and most importantly, according to the "one country, two systems" policy, the special administrative regions' capitalist system and mainland's socialist system co-exist simultaneously within a unified People's Republic of China and People's Republic of China, and "one party should swallow up the other."[12] Enlarging or shrinking the domain of a SAR would violate that principle, would it not? Shenzhen and Zhuhai are special economic zones, but they are still socialist in nature, whereas Hong Kong and Macao are special administrative regions which engage in capitalism. The two are different in nature and cannot be intermingled. And so, after the forming of the SARs, strict administrative boundaries still exist between Shenzhen and Hong Kong and between Zhuhai and Macao, as defined by official maps of the territories of the two SARs issued by the State Council on July 1, 1997 and December 20, 1999 respectively.

It is quite clear that when handling the SARs' relations with the various Central People's Government departments and with the various provinces, autonomous regions and directly administered municipalities, all sides must rigorously implement the "one country, two systems," "a high degree of autonomy," "Hong Kongers administer Hong Kong," and "Macaoans administer Macao" principles. They must handle matters strictly according to the SARs' Basic Laws, and no department or local government may intervene in SAR affairs if it is not specifically authorized to do so by the Basic Laws. What is called "a high degree autonomy" applies not only to the Central Government (since its administrative authority is strictly limited to aspects defined by the Basic Laws and all other matters are subject to Basic Law's own legislative authority); it applies even more to the provinces, autonomous regions and directly administered municipalities in China since they have no say in SAR affairs nor may they intervene in any SAR government matters.

The two SAR Basic Laws are laws implemented not only within the SARs; they are also basic laws of a national nature in that the Central Government departments and all mainland provinces, autonomous regions and directly administered municipality are required to implement and rigorously abide by them when handling matters concerning the SARs.

---

[11] Wang Fengchao. "On the Relations between the Central Authorities and the Hong Kong Special Administrative Region," carried in the *Hong Kong Wen Wei Po*, April 5, 1995.

[12] *Deng Xiaoping on the Reunification of the Motherland*. Beijing: Unity Press, 1995, p. 18.

8.3 Relations Between and Among the Special Administrative Regions

The Hong Kong Special Administrative Region was established on July 1, 1997, and the Macao Special Administrative Region was established on December 20, 1999. And if Taiwan is in future peacefully unified with the mainland, China will have a third Special Administrative Region. How the relations between and among these Special Administrative Regions are handled will affect the handling of the relations between the Central Authorities as well as the prosperity and stability of the Special Administrative Regions.

Because Hong Kong and Macao were under British and Portuguese jurisdiction respectively before their return to China, the relations between them in those days were handled by the Hong Kong British government and the Macao Portuguese government according to the principles of International relations, as between two different countries. Due to geographical and historical factors, the Hong Kong British and Macao Portuguese governments shared common interests and views about the future of Hong Kong and Macao, and their common concern was to maintain stability under the rule of the British and Portuguese authorities in those regions. Macao was smaller in terms of its territory and population, and its politico-economic future was basically tied to Hong Kong's. Macao benefitted from Hong Kong's prosperity and stability, and it certainly could not thrive on its own if Hong Kong fell into chaos or recession. Hence, Macau's Portuguese government paid great attention to drawing on Britain's experience in ruling Hong Kong by engaging in frequent political and economic exchanges. There were, of course, conflicts between the two on many issues, but never to the extent of affecting their long-term relations.

The relations between the two regions underwent a fundamental change after both returned to China, set up their respective SARs, and came respectively under the direct jurisdiction of the Central People's Government. First of all, the international factor no longer existed in their relations, which are now relations between two neighboring local administrative territories within one sovereign nation. The principles concerning international law no longer apply, and have been replaced by China's relevant domestic legislation and by agreements on cooperation between two SARs. Secondly, although there are considerable differences between the two in terms of land area, population, economics, political clout and culture, their positions within the framework of China's constitutional system are those of equals, and both have become local provincial-level administrative regions directly subordinate to the Central Authorities. They are not reciprocally subordinate, nor do they intervene in each other's affairs. Their relations are those of mutual respect and mutual cooperation between two local administrative regions.

However, the relations between them differ from those among the mainland provinces and those between the SARs and the mainland. They are relations between two special administrative regions of the People's Republic of China that practice capitalism. Hence, both political and economic factors must be taken into consideration when relations between the SARs are handled; and both present-day and historical factors must be considered.

Although the Macao SAR is equal in status with the Hong Kong SAR in terms of politics and law, it is still in the main reliant on Hong Kong economically, and since Hong Kong also needs to make use of Macao, economic contacts between the two are very close. As regards disputes that arise between them, these are to be resolved by the Central Authorities if they are major disputes of a principled or political nature. If they are ordinary legal disputes of a civil nature, it is evident that the principles of international private law can no longer be cited where the application of laws is concerned. Such disputes have to be resolved through negotiations between the two regions, or resolved when a mainland Chinese law on inter-regional conflicts is eventually formulated.

As regards the relations of Taiwan with the Hong Kong and Macao SARs, the Kuomintang refused to acknowledge the Sino-British Joint Declaration when it was concluded between China and Britain and when Hong Kong's return to China was already an established fact, and it only acknowledged later that "Hong Kong has returned to the Chinese nation."[13] After the setting up of the Hong Kong and Macao SARs, issues involving Taiwan are no longer matters of foreign diplomacy, nor are they local SAR matters. They should pertain to matters other than foreign affairs and national defense and which do not fall within the scope of SARs autonomy, and therefore belong under the jurisdiction of the Central Government. On June 22, 1995, Qian Qishen, Vice-Premier of the State Council and Director of the Preliminary Working Committee of the Hong Kong Special Administrative Region Preparatory Committee announced on behalf of the State Council seven basic principles and policies for handling HK SAR matters involving Taiwan after 1997. And on January 16, 1999, as chairman of the Preliminary Working Committee of the Macao Special Administrative Region, Qian Qishen again announced seven basic principles and policies for dealing with Macao issues involving Taiwan. These basic principles and policies are fundamentally the same. All were formulated in accordance with the basic national policy of "one country, two systems" and in line with the "one China" policy—after a great deal of investigation and research was conducted in the actual circumstances of Hong Kong and Macao—in order to furnish the Hong Kong and Macao SARs with basic parameters for handling Taiwan related issues.

The Hong Kong SAR's relations with Taiwan after "97" (the 1997 events) and the Macao SAR's relations with Taiwan after "99" (the 1999 events) are a special component of the cross-Strait relations as well as a special factor affecting Central/SAR relations. Of the Taiwan-related issues arising after the establishment of the Hong Kong and Macao SARs, all those that involve state sovereignty and cross-Strait relations are to be dealt with in line with Central People's Government dispositions, or handled by the Hong Kong and Macao SAR governments under Central People's Government guidance. As concerns non-governmental contacts and exchanges between Hong Kong and Taiwan or between Macao and Taiwan, the legitimate rights

---

[13] Huang Wenfang. *The Decision-making Process and Implementation of China's restoration of sovereignty over Hong Kong.* Hong Kong: Hong Kong Baptist University, 1997.

and interests of our compatriots in Hong Kong, Macao and Taiwan are to be protected. Accordingly, the basic principles and policies defined by the Central People's Government for handling the HK SAR's Taiwan-related issues after "97" and the Macao SAR's Taiwan-related issues after "99" include the following: (1) currently existing Hong Kong/Taiwan and Macao/Taiwan non-governmental contacts and relations, including economic and cultural exchanges and human traffic, are to remain basically unchanged; this is in keeping with the Basic Laws' provision that Hong Kong's and Macao's previous systems shall remain unchanged for 50 years; (2)Taiwan residents and various types of capital in Taiwan are encouraged and welcome to come to Hong Kong and Macao to engage in capital investment, trade and other industrial and commercial activities, and the legitimate rights and interests of Taiwan residents and various type of capital in Hong Kong and Macao are to be protected by law; (3) according to the "one China" principle, airlines and shipping lines between the Hong Kong and Macao SARs are to managed as "special regional routes," and maritime and airline communications between the SARs and the Taiwan regions are to be conducted in accordance with the principle of reciprocity; (4) Taiwan residents may enter and exit the special regions in accordance with the laws of the Hong Kong and Macao SARs, or they may go to school, seek employment or settled down locally; for Taiwan residents' convenience in entering and exiting the SARs, the Central People's Government has made special arrangements as regards their ID documents; (5) Hong Kong and Macao SARs' non-governmental organizations in such aspects as education, science, technology, culture, the arts, sports, professions, medicine/well-being, labor, social welfare, social work and so forth and their religious bodies may maintain and develop relations with the relevant non-governmental institutions and organizations in the Taiwan region on the principles and basis of reciprocal non-subordination, mutual non-intervention and mutual respect; (6) contacts and intercourse between the Hong Kong and Macao SARs and the Taiwan region under diverse titles, such as commercial negotiations, signing agreements and setting up agencies, are to be reported to the Central People's Government for approval or specifically authorized by the Central People's Government, and approved by the SARs' Chief Executives; and (7) already-existing Taiwan agencies and their staff members in Hong Kong and Macao may continue to stay there, but in terms of their actions they must strictly abide by the Basic Law of the Hong Kong Special Administrative Region of the People's Republic of China and the Basic Law of the Macao Special Administrative Region, may not violate the "one China" principle, and may not engage in activities that harm the security, prosperity and development of Hong Kong and Macao or that do not tally with their registered descriptions.[14]

It is evident that the foundation for the Central People's Government's basic principles and policies for defining and handling Hong Kong's Taiwan-related post-"97" issues and Macao's Taiwan-related post-"99" issues are the "one China" principle

[14]Qian Qishen. "Basic Principles and Policies of the Central People's Government for Hong Kong's Handling of Taiwan Related Issues after '97'," at the Fifth Plenary Meeting of the Preparatory Work Committee of the Hong Kong Special Administrative Region Preparatory Commission, June 22, 1995. And "Seven Basic Principles and Policies for Handling Macao's Taiwan Related Issues after '99'," Beijing, *People's Daily*, January 16, 1999.

and the "one country, two systems" policy. As long as the Taiwan side's activities in Hong Kong and Macao adhere to the "one China" principle and Taiwan does not engage in "two Chinas" or "one China, one Taiwan" activities that harm national unity, everything may proceed as usual. Due to their unique status, Hong Kong and Macao may play a special role in developing cross-Strait relations and ultimately realizing national unification.

If Taiwan is eventually unified with the mainland in accordance with the "one country, two systems" principle and sets up a special administrative region, the principles and methods for resolving relations between Hong Kong and Macao SARs should also apply to the relations between the "Taiwan special administrative region" and the Hong Kong and Macao SARs, with, of course, extra consideration given to Taiwan's characteristics. These matters remain to be defined and specified by China's relevant legislation at some future time.

In sum, the methods used for handling either the relations of various mainland entities with the SARs or the relations between and among the SARs must be in the form of laws and systems that imbue them with the qualities of operability and long-term stability. This is most important for upholding national unity and sovereignty and for maintaining the SARs' prosperity and social stability.

8.4 Taiwan's Relations with Other Regions

As stated earlier, the "one country, two systems" policy was from the very outset put forward to deal with the issue of Taiwan's unification with the mainland, and it is only by chance that the concept was first used for solving the Hong Kong and Macao issues. So it is only logical that the "one country, two systems" policy is being used to resolve the Taiwan issue. This proves that "one country, two systems" is feasible and widely applicable on the one hand and, on the other, has accumulated valuable experience for the future use of 'one country, two systems' concept in Taiwan and for setting up a Taiwan special administrative region.[15]

Due to Taiwan's unique historical and political factors, an eventual Taiwan special administrative region will not only enjoy the high degree of autonomy enjoyed by the Hong Kong and Macao SARs; its relations with the Central Authorities and the mainland will also be somewhat different from those of the Hong Kong and Macao SARs with the Central Authorities and the mainland. This will be manifested as follows:

First, in terms of the relations between the Central Authorities and a Taiwan special administrative region, the Center Authorities commits itself to permitting Taiwan to retain its original system. After reunification, Taiwan' socio-economic system

---

[15]I maintain that consideration ought to be given to the name of the eventual Taiwan special administrative region. To highlight Taiwan's difference from Hong Kong and Macao, Taiwan, instead of being named the "Taiwan Special Administrative Region," might be called the "Taiwan Region" or some other appropriate name.

and life style would remain unchanged. An eventual Taiwan special administrative region would enjoy a high degree of autonomy; it would have administrative powers, legislative powers and judicial powers including the power of final adjudication, it would retain its own armed forces, and it would administer its own party, political and military systems. The Central Government would undertake not to dispatch troops to, or station administrative personnel in, Taiwan and to set aside a number of seats for Taiwan in the Central Government.[16] The Central Authorities' plans and policies for Taiwan would be formulated as a "Basic Law of the Taiwan Special Administrative Region" which would then be legalized. Meanwhile, patriotic persons of all walks of life in Taiwan would participate extensively in the formulation of the "Basic Law of the Taiwan Special Administrative Region" and give full expression to their views on relevant issues, and ample importance would be attached to their opinions.

On such major issues as how to bring about national unification, the Central Authorities will listen attentively to opinions from all sectors in Taiwan. "Under the premise of one China, any issue can be discussed, including ways which both sides find appropriate for conducting discussions on formal negotiations between both banks of the [Taiwan] Strait." Here, the statement "'Under the premise of one China, any issue can be discussed' of course includes all kinds of issues of concern to the Taiwan authorities."[17] That will include ways of achieving national unification, the relations between the Central Authorities and a Taiwan special administrative region, the high degree of autonomy to be enjoyed by a Taiwan special administrative region, the powers of the people of Taiwan to participate in administering affairs of a nationwide nature and so forth. The Central Authorities will not simplistically apply the model for resolving Hong Kong and Macao issues to the handling of Taiwan issues or to the eventual handling of relations between the Central Authorities and a Taiwan special administrative region; the methods will be more versatile and more indulgent. As long as the fundamental principle of one China is upheld and no attempts are made to bring about "two Chinas" or "one China and one Taiwan" or any covert form of "Taiwan independence" such as "division and separate governance," "an interim two Chinas" and so forth, all issues of concern to the Taiwan authorities could be resolved by means of cross-Strait negotiations.

Thus after Taiwan is eventually unified with the mainland, two situations would exist among the three special administrative regions. First, the Hong Kong and Macao SARs would each handle their relations with the Central Authorities according to their own Basic Law. Secondly, the eventual Taiwan special administrative region would have autonomous powers far greater than those of the Hong Kong and Macao SARs, and would possess its own armed forces. As a result, there would be four tiers in China's eventual state structure in terms of the Central Authorities' relations with provincial-level localities and the magnitude of the powers vested in the localities: Tier 1 would consist of the relations of the Central Authorities with a Taiwan special administrative region. Tier 2 would consist of the relations of the Central Authorities

---

[16]Jiang Zemin. "Continue to Strive to Speed Up the Completion of the Great Cause of Reunifying the Motherland," (January 30, 1995), carried in the *People's Daily*, February 1, 1995.

[17]See footnote 16.

with the Hong Kong and Macao SARs. Tier 3 would consist of the relations of the Central Authorities with the national minority autonomous regions. And Tier 4 would consist of the relations of the Central Authorities with the ordinary provinces and directly administered municipalities. It is clear that the eventual establishment of a Taiwan special administrative region will further enrich the relations of the Central Authorities with China's provincial-level localities and add variety and diversity to China's state structure.

Secondly, the relations of the Central Government's various departments and the mainland's provinces, autonomous regions and directly administered municipalities with a Taiwan special administrative region and with the various departments of a Taiwan special administrative region government would be reciprocally non-subordinate and mutually non-interventionist, and mutual cooperation would be of an entirely voluntary and negotiated nature.

Thirdly, the relations of a Taiwan a special administrative region with the Hong Kong and Macao SARs should also be cooperative relations of reciprocal non-subordination, mutual non-intervention and mutual respect, and these three regions should each be directly accountable to the national central government. It is to be expected that their interrelations in various sectors would be more easy and convenient since in terms of social systems all pertain to capitalist societies and they would share similarities as regards economic, cultural and social institutions.

And so, when a Chinese law on interregional conflicts is formulated at a future date, it should also include solutions for legal conflicts between a Taiwan SAR and the mainland and between a Taiwan SAR and the Hong Kong and Macao SARs, as these would, by their nature, be legal conflicts between different territorial legal units within a unified China.

Chapter 9
The Institutions for Handling Central/SAR Relations and Their Operations

In the foregoing chapters we have specifically explored the origins of "one country, two systems" and the establishment of SARs, the principles for handling Central/SAR relations, the division of duties and responsibilities between the Central Authorities and the SARs, and the handling of several combinations of relations relevant to Central/SAR relations. In this chapter we shall explore the institutions which handle Central/SAR relations and their work principles.

According to the provisions of both SAR Basic Laws, the SARs are directly subordinate to the Central Authorities, and the organs of the Central Authorities which take part in handling SAR matters include the National People's Congress and its Standing Committee i.e. the highest organ of state power, the State Council i.e. the highest state administration, and the Central Military Commission i.e. the supreme national military command. Here, we will explore the roles and the operational procedures and systems of the National People's Congress Standing Committee and the State Council in their handling of Central/SAR relations.

9.1 The Highest Organs of State Power

9.1.1 The Nature of the Highest Organs of State Power

According to the provisions of China's Constitution, all powers in China pertain to the people, and the organs through which the people exercise state power are the National People's Congress and the local people's congresses at all levels (Article 2 of the Constitution). All state administrative organs, judicial organs, procuratorial organs and military organs are generated by and accountable to the people's congresses,

© Foreign Language Teaching and Research Publishing Co., Ltd and Springer Nature   231
Singapore Pte Ltd. 2019
Z. Wang, *Relationship Between the Chinese Central Authorities and Regional*
Governments of Hong Kong and Macao: A Legal Perspective, China Academic
Library, https://doi.org/10.1007/978-981-13-2322-5_9

and are supervised by them (Article 3, Article 62, Article 63 and Article 94). The National People's Congress is the highest organ of state power, and its permanent body is the Standing Committee of the National People's Congress which exercises the highest state power when the National People's Congress is not in session (Article 57 and Article 67). This clearly indicates the nature of the China's highest organ of state power.

State power, which is the embodiment and main content of state sovereignty, includes in the main the power of legislation, the power of administration, the power to command armed forces, and state judiciary power. The highest state powers, as the highest and ultimate embodiment of state sovereignty, include the state's highest power of legislation, the state's highest power of administration, the state's highest power over military affairs, and the state's highest power of jurisprudence, all of which powers constitute a complete entity. In China's feudal society, the highest state powers rested in the hands of one ruler whereas in a today's democratic society they are held by the people. Of course, in capitalist countries they are in reality held by the bourgeoisie whereas in a socialist country they are held by the people as a whole led by the working class. Yet since not everyone among the people in a socialist country can directly exercise their highest powers, only the highest organs of state power generated by means of equal suffrage exercise the highest state powers. In China, this is the National People's Congress and its Standing Committee. Hence the National People's Congress and its standing establishment constitute China's highest organ of state power.

It is evident that the highest organ of state power not only exercises legislative functions (this is of course its most important function), but also administrative functions, military affairs functions and judicial functions. This can also be seen from the provisions in China's Constitution regarding the functions of the NPC and the NPC Standing Committee, i.e. that the NPC organizes and generates the state's highest administrative organs, the state's highest military organs and the state's highest judicial organs and confers upon them respectively the state's highest administrative powers, the state's highest military powers and the state's highest judicial powers. And when any problems arise that these organs themselves are unable to resolve or disputes arise among them over extents of authority, they are to submit these issues for resolution to their common highest authorizing organ and highest organ of state power—the National People's Congress.

Hence, in China, the highest organ of state power not only confers the powers vested in all local governments, it also confers all powers upon the highest state administrative organ, the highest state judicial organ and the highest military organ. This is the full constitutional meaning of "highest state power" and "highest organ of state power." In China, the National People's Congress may discuss all matters— political, economic, cultural, military, foreign diplomatic and jurisprudential, and may discuss and determine all major state affairs.

Yet the fact that the highest organ of state power exercises administrative, military and judicial functions and possesses all of the highest state powers does not mean that it directly or by itself exercises all of these state powers. On the contrary, it has to devise various executive organs or agencies of its own, i.e. administrative, military and judicial organs, which exercise their respective administrative, military and judicial functions and, together, implement the duties and responsibilities of the highest organ of state power, while the highest organ of state power itself it retains and directly exercises a number of important powers of a representative and fundamental nature. These powers include: One, the highest state legislative power. Two, the power to devise and set up the state's highest administrative, military and judicial organs and to confer the corresponding state powers on these organs respectively. Three, the power to exercise supervision over the work of the state organs it has generated, which includes conducting inspections, listening to their work reports and raising queries. Four, when, in their work, these organs come up against a major issue of especial importance or a new issue emerges for which no clear jurisdiction exists and they are unable to make determinations so that they have to submit these issues to the highest organ of state power for decision—i.e. for exercising the power of ultimate decision on major state matters including major administrative, judiciary and military matters—it is frequently in such situations that highest organ of state power's administrative, military and judicial functions find direct expression. Five, the power of adjudication when competence disputes arise between the supreme state organs it has itself generated.

The powers and functions of the National People's Congress of China are of a comprehensive nature, cover all of the aspects mentioned above, and are entirely different from the "separation of the executive, legislative and judicial powers" in the West. It is evident that in China, the State Council is not the only organ which executes the highest state powers. The highest state judiciary and the highest military command are, strictly speaking, also executive organs, but the functions they exercise are different. They form a pyramid-like structure, as shown below:

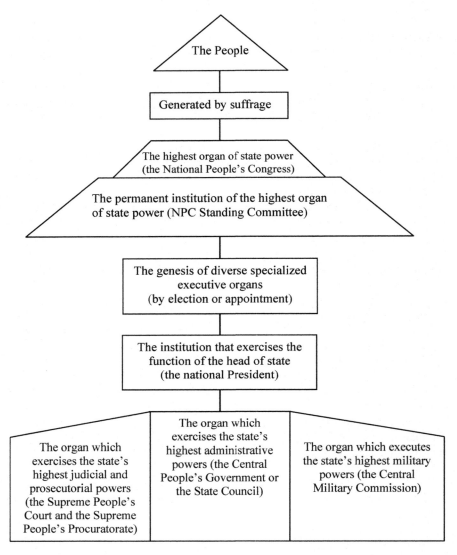

Once one understands the highest state powers as defined by the Constitution and the nature and functions of the highest organs of state power, it is easier to explain the various powers vested by the National People's Congress and the NPC Standing Committee in the SARs, as defined in the SARs' Basic Laws.

From the above analyses we can see that the first and foremost organ in China which has handled Central/SAR relations and determined the destiny of the SARs is the National People's Congress and its Standing Committee. This has been and is manifested chiefly as:

(1) Determining that sovereignty was to be resumed over Hong Kong and Macao, and approving the international agreements with Britain and Portugal respectively on the Hong Kong and Macao issues, i.e. the Sino-British and Sino-Portuguese joint declarations.

(2) Deciding to implement "one country, two systems" and devising the SAR set-up.

(3) Formulating, revising and interpreting the SAR Basic Laws, stipulating the various systems implemented in the SARs, handling Central/SARs relations, determining the division of powers between the Central authorities and the SARs, and empowering the SARs to implement a high degree of autonomy and enjoy extensive autonomous powers.

The highest organ of state power also exercises certain powers to conduct constitutionality reviews (examinations) in the SARs

(4) Making the preparations for setting up the SARs.

(5) Putting the SAR Basic Laws into effect after the establishment of the SARs, conducting supervision over the high degree of autonomy exercised by the SARs, and exercising the power to decide such major SAR-related matters as declarations of war and peace and announcing emergency situations.

Since all of these powers are important manifestations of national sovereignty as well as major matters of a fundamental and long-term nature for the SARs, they must therefore be decided and exercised by plenary sessions of the National People's Congress or of the NPC Standing Committee.

9.1.2 The SAR Basic Law Committees of the NPC Standing Committee

According to the provisions of Article 28 of the Organic Law of the National People's Congress passed by the First Plenum of the Fifth National People's Congress on December 10, 1982, the NPC Standing Committee could, as needed, set up work committees. The directors and deputy directors of these work committees were to be appointed or removed by the NPC Standing Committee. After the SARs' establishment, the highest organ of state power, for the sake of exercising the relevant powers in items (2) and (4) listed above, decided to set up respectively the Hong Kong and Macao Special Administrative Region Basic Law committees under its permanent institution, the NPC Standing Committee. According to National People's Congress decisions on April 4, 1990 and March 31, 1993 respectively, these two committees are work committees under the jurisdiction of the NPC Standing Committee and subordinate to it.

These Basic Law committees are in the nature of work institutions of the NPC Standing Committee. They are not power institutions, and as such cannot exercise powers on behalf of the NPC Standing Committee; they can only provide the NPC Standing Committee with opinions and suggestions on relevant issues which the latter may or may not accept. They may be regarded as special consultation and work institutions set up by the NPC Standing Committee uniquely for the purpose of handling SAR affairs. This shows how seriously the highest organ of state power takes its handling of SAR affairs.

According to National People's Congress resolutions, the duties and functions the Basic Law committees are to study issues in the implementation of Articles 17, 18, 158 and 159 of the Hong Kong Special Administrative Region Basic Law and Articles 17, 18, 143 and 144 of the Macao Special Administrative Region Basic Law respectively, and to offer opinions and suggestions thereon to the NPC Standing Committee.

Accordingly, the specific tasks of the Basic Law Committees include the following:

(1) When the NPC Standing Committee exercises its power to supervise laws legislated by the SARs per se, and if it believes that a law formulated by a SAR legislative institution fails to comply with Basic Law provisions regarding Central Authority-administered matters or Central/SAR relations and intends to return the law to the SAR legislative institutions, the NPC Standing Committee shall, before sending the law back, first send it to the Basic Law committee concerned for studies and listen to the committee's opinions before making it own decision.

(2) When the NPC Standing Committee decides whether or not to implement in the SARs national-type laws concerning national defense, foreign relations and other affairs which according to their Basic Laws do not fall with the scope of SAR autonomy, or to make additions to, or deletions from, the National-type Laws listed in Annex III of the Basic Laws, it first solicits the opinions of the Basic Law Committees.

(3) If SAR courts, in the process of trying cases, need to make interpretations of Basic Law provisions concerning Central People's Government-administered affairs or Central/SAR relations, and if the interpretations of such provisions affect the adjudications on the cases, the SARs' Courts of Final Instance (Appeal) must, before making their final non-appealable judgments, seek an interpretation of the provisions concerned from the NPC Standing Committee, and the SAR courts must use the interpretation by the NPC Standing Committee as the criterion when they cite the provisions. Before the NPC Standing Committee makes an interpretation of a Basic Law, it must solicit the opinions of the Basic Law Committees under its jurisdiction. As I have said earlier, the highest state powers as provided for in China's Constitution include judicial powers, and the highest organ of state power strictly speaking also possesses judicial functions. Under normal circumstances it does not exercise judicial powers, but it may, when necessary, directly exercise certain judicial functions. From the viewpoint of Common Law, the NPC Standing Committee's interpretation of the Basic Laws constitutes the exercise of judicial functions. And China's highest organ of state law does indeed possess such a function.

(4) When the National People' s Congress is about to accept bills for amending SAR Basic Laws and prior to placing such bills on the agenda of the NPC Standing Committee, it must first address these bills to the SAR Basic Law committees for them to study and offer their opinions.

As regards the composition of the Basic Law committees, the Hong Kong committee is made up of twelve persons while the Macao committee is made up ten persons, half of whom are SAR persons and the other half mainland persons. Since the committees' work is primarily legal in nature, the persons who make up the committees must include persons from the legal profession. All members are appointed by the NPC Standing Committee for terms of five years. The committee members from Hong Kong and Macao must be Chinese citizens who reside permanently in the SAR concerned and have no right-of-abode in any other country. They are to be nominated jointly by the Chief Executive, the Chairman of the Legislative Council and the Chief Justice of the Court of Final Appeal of the SAR concerned, and appointed by the NPC Standing Committee.

These two Basic Law Committees were set up on July 1, 1997 and December 20, 1999 respectively, and have drafted their respective detailed work regulations and work systems. The Hong Kong Basic Law Committee has already conducted special research on interpretations of the Basic Law and has offered its opinions and suggestion to the NPC Standing Committee. Since the said committees are set up within the framework of legislative institutions, their work procedures, too, basically consist of legislative procedures. Some scholars have suggested that these committees' work procedures undergo judicial conversion, and that the committees should be converted from political institutions into independent judicial institutions, or into an independent agency capable of adjudicating conflicts and disputes in the two regions.[1] Such a conversion, if it does take place, would give rise to a "revolutionary" change in China's Constitution and the SAR Basic Laws.

9.2 The Highest Organ of State Administration

9.2.1 The State Council

According to China's Constitution, the state's highest administrative organ is the executive organ of the highest organ of state power, i.e. the Central People's Government, and that is precisely the nature of the State Council.[2] The State Council is a comprehensive institution which exercises the highest administrative powers nationwide under the highest organ of state power. The Constitution defines the functions of the State Council, which include exercising unified leadership over administrative work nationwide, exercising unified leadership over the work of state administrative organs

---

[1]Legal quarters in Hong Kong did put forward such a suggestion.

[2]Article 85 of the Constitution.

at all levels nationwide, managing foreign affairs and concluding treaties and agreements with foreign countries, exercising leadership and management over national defense construction projects nationwide, and exercising other functions vested in it by the National People's Congress and the NPC Standing Committee.[3] The State Council has thus played and currently plays a most important role in handling Central/SAR relations. Chief among these are: (1) representing the Central Government in discussing and resolving the Hong Kong and Macao issues with Britain and Portugal, signing the relevant agreements, and reporting these to the National People's Congress and its Standing Committee for approval; (2) implementing relevant decisions by the National People's Congress and its Standing Committee, assisting in the formulation of the SAR Basic Laws, advancing proposals for revising the Basic Laws and making preparations for setting up the SARs; (3) implementing the "one country, two systems" and the SAR Basic Laws, exercising control over the SAR governments, and administering affairs which according to the Basic Laws are to be administered by the Central People's Government; (4) taking charge of SARs-related foreign affairs as well as authorizing the SARs to handle foreign affairs on their own in accordance with the provisions of the Basic Laws; (5) taking charge of SAR defense matters and assuming the costs of stationing troops there; and (6) appointing the SARs' Chief Executives and principal officials in accordance with the relevant provisions of the Basic Laws.

It is evident that the functions of the State Council in handling SAR affairs have been and are currently quite important and quite specific. These are also responsibilities toward the SARs taken by the State Council in its status as the National Central Government.

When exercising those functions, the State Council usually must do so in its own name and not in the name of some institution or department within the State Council. For example, the final signing of the Sino-British and Sino-Portuguese joint declarations, the proposals for amendments to the Basic Laws, the appointments of SAR chief executives and principal officials—all of these powers had to be exercised in the name of the Central People's Government of the People's Republic of China. Foreign affairs could and may be handled by the Ministry of Foreign Affairs under the direct leadership of the State Council. National defense matters when the Hong Kong garrison was being organized and set up have been conducted and fulfilled in the form of notices jointly issued by the State Council and Central Military Commission. In future, everyday defense affairs shall be the responsibility of the Ministry of Defense representing the State Council.[4]

---

[3] Article 89 of the Constitution.

[4] Communiqué of the State Council of the People's Republic of China, 1996(2), February 12, 1996.

9.2.2 The Hong Kong and Macao Affairs Office of the State Council

Although the State Council's above-mentioned powers of jurisdiction over the SARs must usually be exercised in the name of the State Council, this does not mean all specific work related to the matters described above must be personally attended to by the Premier and Vice-Premiers or approved by plenary sessions or by executive meetings of the State Council. The Premier of the State Council may set up special administrative bodies to assist him in handling affairs in this connection. The Hong Kong and Macao Affairs Office of the State Council is such an administrative body.

Article 11 of the Organic Law of the State Council provides that the State Council may, according the needs of its work and the principle of streamlining and efficiency, set up a number of administrative bodies to help the Premier handle special matters. The establishment of these administrative bodies is to be discussed and determined by plenary sessions or by executive meetings of the State Council. The persons in charge of them are to be appointed or dismissed by the Premier and are not to be categorized as members of the State Council. Their function is to handle matters of a special nature that do not fall within the jurisdiction of any ministry, commission or directly affiliated agency. For example, Taiwan affairs do not pertain to the jurisdiction of any commission or directly affiliated institutions, and the State Council has therefore specially set up the Taiwan Affairs Office to take charge of Taiwan work. The State Council has also set up such special institutions as the Hong Kong and Macao Affairs Office, the Overseas Chinese Affairs Office, the Special Economic Zones Office, the Office of Foreign Affairs, the State Council Research Office.

On August 12, 1978 the CPC Central Committee endorsed and issued a Report on the Preparatory Meeting for the Work Related to Hong Kong and Macao Affairs. It pointed out in the report that to start up work on the Hong Kong and Macao issues it was necessary to do in-depth investigations and studies and seek truth from facts, that all work should proceed from actual local circumstances and not by copying or transposing methods used in the mainland, that one should emancipate one's minds, take bold action, be innovative, speed up the pace and make more contributions toward the realization of China's four modernizations. It was also decided to set up the Central Hong Kong and Macao Working Group to assist the central authorities in administering Hong Kong and Macao work.[5] The State Council's Macao and Hong Kong Affairs Office was set up at the same time.

According to the provisions of the State Council Reform Plan approved on March 16, 1993 by the first session of the Eighth National People's Congress and the "Notice on the Institutional Set-ups of the State Council" (document Guo Fa [1993] No. 25), the State Council's Hong Kong and Macao Affairs Office is the State Council's

---

[5]Li Mo. *The Great Exhibition of New China.* Guangzhou: Guangdong Tourist Press, 1993, p. 863. Actually, during the Cultural Revolution the CPC Central Committee already had a leading group for Hong Kong and Macao work, which was under the direct charge of Zhou Enlai. See Huang Wenfang. *The Decision-Making Process and Implementation of China's Resumption of Sovereignty over Hong Kong and Macao.* Hong Kong Baptist University, 1997, p. 6.

administrative agency in charge of exercising centralize management over Hong
Kong and Macao affairs, and its main functions and duties are: (1) to conduct investigations and studies of the political, economic, cultural and social circumstances of
the Hong Kong and Macao regions and grasp major trends and tendencies in good
time order to provide information and suggestions for formulating plans, policies
and strategies for Hong Kong and Macao work; (2) to formulate specific policies and
measures for implementing the "one country, two systems" concept and promote the
peaceful unification of the motherland; (3) to study and formulate plans and policies
for the Chinese government to reinstate its exercise of sovereignty over Hong Kong
and Macao and bring about a smooth takeover of political power, and take charge
of organizing specific matters in the Hong Kong and Macao SARs; (4) to plan and
make dispositions for various items of work during the transition periods in Hong
Kong and Macao; (5) to do a good job of various items of work for implementing the
Basic Laws in the Hong Kong and Macao SARs; (6) to assist the Foreign Ministry
in taking charge of foreign affairs work related to Hong Kong and Macao and direct
the work of the Sino-British and Sino-Portuguese joint liaison teams and the land
committees (teams); (7) to formulate, examine and approve policies and measures
that involve Hong Kong and Macao rules and regulations and coordinate the relations between the mainland and the Hong Kong and Macao regions; (8) to formulate
specific policies for the interactions between the Hong Kong and Macao regions in
the political, economic, cultural and social domains, and to organize joint implementation with departments concerned; (9) to do a good job, jointly with various
localities and departments, of reception work for Hong Kong and Macao personages
of all sectors who come to the mainland on visits or for work; (10) to, jointly with the
relevant departments, examine and approve institutions set up in the Hong Kong and
Macao regions by various regions and departments, examine and approve personnel
permanently stationed in the Hong Kong and Macao regions, and offer suggestions
to the State Council regarding the examination and approval of persons concerned
who visit the Hong Kong and Macao regions; and (11) to undertake other matters
assigned to it by the State Council.

In line with the above-described functions and duties, the Hong Kong And Macao
Affairs Office of The State Council set up seven (functional) departments, namely
the Secretarial and Administrative Department, the Comprehensive Department, the
Political Affairs Department, the Liaison Department, the Department of Exchanges,
the Law Department and the Party Committee (the Personnel Department).[6]

It is clear that the Hong Kong and Macao Affairs Office of the State Council
has been a highly important and comprehensive department of the Central People's
Government for specifically handling Hong Kong and Macao affairs. After the return
of Hong Kong and Macao and especially after the establishment of the SARs, it is
continuing to play a most important role in handling Central/SAR relations. Through
its work, the Hong Kong and Macao Office is able to avoid inadvertent interference

---

[6]The Secretarial Bureau of the General Office of the State Council and the Department of General
Affairs of the State Commission Office of Public Sectors Reform. *Organizations and Institutions
of the Central People's Government*. Beijing: China Development Press, 1995, pp. 396–399.

in SAR affairs by various central government departments and by local governments in the mainland due lack of understanding of the Basic Laws. The SAR governments on their part also need to gain more understanding of the mainland regions through the Hong Kong and Macao Affairs Office. It is as Director Liao Hui of the State Council's Hong Kong and Macao Affairs Office has said: the function and duty of the Office is to help with communications between the SAR governments and the departments of the Central People's government and local institutions, do a good job as a "gatekeeper," a "liaison man" and an "attendant," and render services to the governments and general public of the SARs.[7]

9.2.3 The Liaison Office of the Central People's Government in the SARs

Other than the Hong Kong and Macao Affairs Office of the State Council, representative institutions have also been set up in Hong Kong and Macao regions by the Central People's Government. These are the Hong Kong Branch of the Xinhua News Agency and the Macao Branch of the Xinhua News Agency.

The Xinhua News Agency Hong Kong Branch was set up in 1947, and its main function at the time was to take charge of the CPC Central Committee publicity and liaison work. After the People's Republic of China was founded in 1949 and China and Britain established diplomatic relations, it became an agency in Hong Kong of China's central news institution—the Xinhua News Agency as well as a representative institution in Hong Kong of the State Council of Chinese People's Republic. However, the British government in Hong Kong never gave it due recognition. It was only after the publication of the Sino-British Joint Declaration in 1972 that the British government in Hong Kong gradually accorded it treatment commensurate with that for an official representative institution. After the Hong Kong issue was raised between China and Britain, the resolution of that issue was placed on the Chinese government's agenda, and in 1983, the Xinhua News Agency HK Branch, which had at first been affiliated to the Hong Kong and Macao Affairs Office of the State Council, became directly affiliated to and led by the State Council. It administrative ranking was raised by one level to that of a ministerial institution.[8]

The Macao Branch of the Xinhua News Agency, set up in September 1988, was both the agency in Macao of the China's state news institution, the Xinhua News Agency, and the representative institution of the State Council in Macao. It keeps the State Council informed about circumstances in Macao and undertakes tasks assigned

---

[7]Director of the Constitutional Affairs Bureau of Hong Kong SAR. "An Exploration of Central/SAR Relations," address at the seminar on "Hong Kong Is My Home, Implement the Basic Law," April 3, 1998.

[8]Li Jun. *Encyclopedia of Taiwan, Hong Kong and Macao.* Beijing: Hualing Press, 1992, pp. 612–613.

by the State Council. Its functions, before it was set up, were exercised by the Macao Nam Kwong Trading Company.[9]

These two Xinhua branch offices have, in the process of solving the Hong Kong and Macao issues and formulating the two SAR Basic Laws, played the role of liaising with Hong Kong and Macao and providing timely reports about the opinions and suggestions of people of all sectors in the two regions. They also played a substantial role in organizing and coordinating the preparations for the two SARs. After China resumed its sovereignty over Hong Kong and Macao and the two SARs came under the State Council' s direct jurisdiction, the nature of the work of these two institutions underwent major changes. The better to implement "one country, two systems," "governance of Hong Kong by Hong Kongers," "governance of Macao by Macaoans," the high-degree-of-autonomy policy and the two SAR Basic Laws as well as to support the SAR governments in exercising governance according to the Basic Laws and ensure that the Central People's Government's work institutions in Hong Kong and Macao fulfill their functions and duties according to the powers vested in them, it became necessary to make some adjustments to the titles and functions of these two Xinhua News Agency branch offices.

After discussions and approval at the twenty-fourth executive meeting of the State Council on December 28, 1999, starting on January 18, 2000 the Xinhua News Agency HK Branch and the Xinhua News Agency Macao Branch were renamed the Liaison Office of the Central People's Government in the Hong Kong Special Administrative Region and the Liaison Office of the Central People's Government in the Macao Special Administrative Region respectively." On January 15, 2000 the State Council sent letters to the governments of the Hong Kong and Macao SARs and officially issued the "Notification Concerning the Renaming of the Hong Kong Branch and Macao Branch of the Xinhua News Agency."

According to the requirements of the notifications, the duties of the liaison offices of the Central People's Government stationed in the SARs include: (1) Liaising with the Office of the Commissioner of the Ministry of Foreign Affairs in the Hong Kong SAR, the Office of the Commissioner of the Ministry of Foreign Affairs in the Macao SAR and with the People's Liberation Army garrisons in Hong Kong and Macao; (2) contacting and assisting relevant departments in Chinese mainland in administering Chinese-funded institutions in Hong Kong and Macao; (3) promoting exchanges and cooperation in economic, education, science, culture, sports and other fields between Hong Kong and Macao and Chinese mainland; (4) liaising with people of all circles in the Hong Kong and Macao societies, enhancing exchanges between the mainland and Hong Kong and Macao, and reflecting the opinions of Hong Kong and Macao residents about the mainland; (5) handling Taiwan-related affairs; and (6) undertaking other tasks assigned by the Central People's Government.[10]

---

[9]Li Jun. *Encyclopedia of Taiwan, Hong Kong and Macao*. Beijing: Hualing Press, 1992, pp. 612–613.

[10]"Notification Concerning the Renaming of the Hong Kong Branch and Macao Branch of the Xinhua News Agency," State Council, 15 January 2000.

The liaison offices in the Hong Kong and Macao SARs of the Central People's Government and their personnel are to rigorously abide by the Basic Laws and local laws and carry out their functions and duties according to law. The SARs should also provide them with the work conveniences and immunities necessary for fulfilling their duties and responsibilities.

After the renaming of the Hong Kong and Macao branch offices of the Xinhua News Agency, the Central People's Government's institutions in the SARs are as follows: The liaison offices of the Central People's Government in the SARs, the commissioners of the Foreign Ministry in the SARs, and the People's Liberation Army garrisons in the SARs. The news business once shared by the HK and Macao branches of the Xinhua News Agency have, upon application by the Xinhua News Agency, been taken up by the Xinhua News Agency's Hong Kong and Macao branches which have been registered with the SAR governments respectively, and the SAR governments have provided conveniences for their registrations and the work they do.

In the two preceding sections we have seen that on the matter of solving the issue of Hong Kong and Macao's return to China and handling Central/SAR relations, the highest organs of state power, i.e. the National People's Congress and its standing committee, were the decision-making organs, that the highest administrative organ, i.e. the State Council, was the specific executing organs, and that the two were very closely connected. The two SAR Basic Law committees under the NPC Standing Committee and the Hong Kong and Macao Affairs Office of the State Council, while carrying out the "one country, two systems" plan and policy, are to handle Central/SAR relations strictly according to the provisions of the Basic Laws, work together with due division of labor, maintain close connections, and strive together to uphold the country's sovereignty and unity and maintain the SARs' prosperity and stability.

9.3 Work Principles that Must Be Followed

The National People's Congress and its Standing Committee, the State Council, the NPC Standing Committee SAR Basic Law committees, and the State Council's Hong Kong and Macao Affairs Office are the Central Authorities' institutions for handling the interrelations between the Central Authorities and the SARs (Central/SAR relations). Their specific work systems for the handling of Central/SAR relations may differ due to differences in the nature of these institutions. For instance, the National People's Congress and the NPC Standing Committee and their affiliated Basic Law committees for the most part use the methods of meetings and panel discussions whereas the State Council and the Hong Kong and Macao Affairs Office under it generally employ administrative methods and administrative head responsibility system. However they must all abide by a number of common work principles. These principles have been touched upon in all previous chapters and will only be briefly summarized here.

9.3.1   Abiding by the "One Country, Two Systems" and "A High Degree of Autonomy" Guidelines

"One country, two systems" and "a high degree of autonomy" are China's basic state policy for solving the Hong Kong, Macao and Taiwan issues as well as the fundamental guiding ideology for handling Central/SAR relations. Hence, when solving every specific issue that involves Central/SAR relations, we must unswervingly and implement to the letter the "one country, two systems" and "a high degree of autonomy" guidelines. "One country" and "two systems" are not opposed to one another; they are mutually complementary. Isolated and one-sided emphasis on either of the two is a biased approach, fails to grasp the essence of "one country, two systems" and may cause mistakes and confusion in actual practice. The two must be organically integrated and the "one country, two systems" spirit must be comprehensively and correctly understood and applied.

9.3.2   Dealing with Matters Strictly According to Law

"Law" here refers to the SAR Basic Laws. The two Basic Laws are basic laws of a national character formulated in accordance with the Constitution by China's highest organ of state power—the National People's Congress—and directly related to the special administrative regions. They are "one country, two systems" expressed in the form of law, institutions, regulations and specific practice, and as such are the fundamental charter for handling Central/SAR relations. Whether it is the National People's Congress and its Standing Committee or the State Council, or whether it is the Basic Law committees of the State Council's Hong Kong and Macao Affairs Office, or whether it is the SAR governments—all must earnestly implement the Basic Laws and handle matters strictly according to the Basic Laws. On no account are they to cast aside the Basic Laws. Without the guarantees of the Basic Laws there can be no mention of "one country, two systems," and upholding national unity and sovereignty and upholding the SARs' prosperity and stability becomes empty verbiage. The Hong Kong and Macao regions and especially Hong Kong have formed a good tradition of rule of law amidst international capitalist competition, for which reason the Central Authorities should, as befits a great country, carry forward the Chinese nation's tradition of keeping its promises, eliminate all sorts of interference, deal with matters strictly according to the Basic Laws, and carry out each and every article of the Basic Laws.

9.3.3 The Principle of Incorporating SAR Participation

Although the initiative in Central/SAR relations rests with the Central Authorities, all relevant Central authorities must fully incorporate participation by Hong Kong and Macao personages when handling mutual relations, extensively listen to opinions in all quarters and respect the opinions of the SAR governments and people, as only thus can decisions be made that conform to realities. Actually, when the National People's Congress was formulating the SAR Basic Laws, it very extensively integrated the participation by people of all quarters in Hong Kong and Macao, and in addition set up Basic Law advisory committees the functions and duties of which were to assemble and report to the drafting committees the opinions and suggestions of people of all walks of life in Hong Kong and Macao regarding the Basic Laws and accept requests for consultations from the drafting committees. This is unprecedented in China's legislative history. The Basic Laws themselves, when stipulating that the Central Authorities' exercise powers, also stipulated ways in which the SARs should incorporate SAR participation. Subsequently, the State Council's Hong Kong and Macao Affairs Office invited consultants on Hong Kong affairs from among people of all walks of life in Hong Kong, and the Xinhua News Agency Hong Kong Branch too invited consultants on regional affairs—in both cases doing so for the sake of extensively absorbing the opinions of people in Hong Kong and Macao. Fifty percent of the members of the SAR Basic Law committees were from Hong Kong and Macao. This too was done to integrate ample participation from the SARs in their decision making. The Hong Kong and Macaoan deputies in the National People's Congress and the Hong Kong and Macauan members of the CPPCC have already played a significant role in this respect and will continue to do so in the future.

9.3.4 Mutual Respect, Mutual Support and Common Development

Other important work principles which must be adhered to when handling Central/SAR relations are mutual respect, mutual support, and common development. The Central Authorities must respect the SARs' high degree of autonomy, firmly implement the principle of Hong Kongers governing Hong Kong and Macauans governing Macao and on no account intervene in SARs' matters that according to the Basic Laws fall within the scope of their autonomy. Conversely, the SARs must also respect the Central Authorities' unified authority, consciously safeguard the country's unity and the integrity of its sovereignty, respect the Central Authority's right of jurisdiction over matters which according to the Basic Laws pertain to Central Authority administration, and provide active coordination and support in this respect. Because they have done so, the two sides have established benign interrelations within the framework of the Basic Laws. The capitalist SARs and the socialist mainland have been coexisting peacefully, making advances in common,

and together contributing to lasting peace, order, prosperity and stability of the whole
of China including the SARs and to the great rejuvenation of the Chinese nation in
the twenty-first century.

9.4   How Central/SAR Relations Have Been Handled After 1997

Four years have elapsed since the Chinese government resumed its exercise of
sovereignty over Hong Kong on July 1, 1997, and more than a year has passed
since the Chinese government resumed its exercise of sovereignty over Macao on
December 20, 1999. Realities have shown that the "one country, two systems"
national policy is correct and that the two SAR Basic Laws are feasible. The Central
Authorities and the SARs have swiftly adapted to their new roles, are appropriately
exercising their respective statutory powers, and have been basically successful in
handling their mutual relations.

9.4.1   The Central Authorities' Exercise of Their Statutory Powers After the Two Regions' Return to China

Admittedly, devising ways to handle the SARs' affairs under "one country, two
systems" has been an entirely new challenge where China's Central Government
is concerned. After China set up a highly centralized administrative management
system in the 1950s, the Central Government became accustomed to dictating orders
to the localities and using administrative means to directly manage society and the
localities. There have been some changes in this situation since Reform and Opening
Up, but because the Constitution stipulates too many functions and duties for the
Central Government, it is very hard to keep Central Authorities' fingers out of a
great many pies.[11] After the establishment of the Hong Kong and Macao SARs,

---

[11]Most of the provisions in Chapter One on "General Principles" of China's Constitution stipulate
the state's functions and responsibilities, and virtually every article contains the term "state," yet in
many cases the term "state" refers to the Central Government. Moreover, Sections 1–4 of Chapter
Three of the Constitution specifically stipulate various powers, functions and responsibilities for the
Central Authorities. If merely some simple institutional reforms are made to the Constitution but no
amendments that would reduce the government's and mainly the Central Government's functions
and duties (which in reality are often burdensome), such reforms could hardly be thoroughgoing. The
reason is quite simple. It is because, legally speaking, the Central Authorities are obliged to exercise
the functions and duties assigned to them by the Constitutions. For example, paragraphs 4, 5, 6 and
7 of Article 89 of the Constitution stipulate that State Council is to exercise unified leadership over
the work of local organs of state administration at various levels throughout the country, formulate
the detailed division of functions and powers between the Central Government and the organs of
state administration of provinces, autonomous regions, and municipalities directly under the Central
Government, draw up and implement the plan for national economic and social development and

however, the Central Authorities have, in terms of handling its relations with the SARs, proceeded strictly in accordance with the Basic Laws, and one can say it has done so quite successfully. It has not infringed on the SARs' high degree of autonomy or interfered in local affairs within the scope of the SARs' autonomy. Around the time of Hong Kong's return to the motherland, in particular, the Central Authorities sent out notices nationwide requesting a correct understanding of the special relationship between the Central Authorities and the SARs so as to clear up any misunderstandings in the mainland regions. In 1996, the CPC Central Committee and the State Council jointly issued a notice on correctly handling a number of issues in the relations between the mainland and Hong Kong.[12] And after Hong Kong's return to China, the General Office of the CPC Central Committee and the General Office of the State Council jointly issued a "Notice on the Publishing of the 'Circular on the Circumstances of Hong Kong's return'"[13] and the General Office of the State Council issued a "circular on issues concerning the investments of Chinese Citizens of the Hong Kong Special Administrative Region in the mainland of China."[14] All of these were important documents on the specific standards for handling Central/SAR relations.

9.4.1.1   SAR Defense Matters

The Central Authorities had taken charge of the SARs' defense matters In accordance with the provisions in the SAR Basic Laws and the two Garrison Laws. The People's Liberation Army garrisons in Hong Kong and Macao are duly and according to law fulfilling their duties of defending the SARs and have established excellent work relations with the SAR governments. Basically gone are the SAR residents' previous feelings of apprehension about the People's Liberation Army. Moreover, the SARs no longer pay defense costs as they did under the British and they may devote all their energies and resources toward developing economic and cultural endeavors. And although Chinese residents in the SARs are also Chinese citizens, they need not do military service like their compatriots on the mainland. Hence one can say that in

---

the state budget, direct and administer economic affairs and urban and rural development, and direct and administer matters concerning education, science, culture, public health, physical culture and family planning. All of these are mandatory stipulations that the Central Authorities are obliged to comply with, failing which they could be accused of dereliction of duty. Hence, if these stipulations are not amended in terms of the Constitution, any streamlining of administration, devolution of powers or institutional reforms would have little or no effect.

[12]Notice of the CPC Central Committee and the State Council on Correctly Handling a Number of Issues in the Relations between the Mainland and Hong Kong. Zhong fa (1996) No. 8.

[13]"Notice of the CPC Central Committee and the State Council on the Publishing of the 'Circular on the Circumstances of Hong Kong's return'" Zhongbanfa (1997) No. 8.

[14]"Circular of the General Office of the State Council on Issues Concerning the Investments by Chinese Citizens in the Hong Kong Special Administrative Region in the Mainland of China," December 22, 1997.

these respects the Hong Kong and Macao SARs and their inhabitants are enjoying greater benefits after the regions' return to China.

The main duty of the SARs' garrison forces is to take charge of the SARs' defense. Starting on July 1, 1997, the HK garrison units have conducted numerous surveys each year of Hong Kong's topography, terrain configuration and infrastructure, and familiarized themselves with Hong Kong's natural environment. They formulate plans for the defense of major targets in the SAR, make dispositions for the entry of foreign ships and planes into Hong Kong's harbors, conduct sea and air patrols and alerts, and in addition help the SAR government with maintaining social order and conducting disaster relief. The Hong Kong garrison has also focused on conducting enhanced drills and maneuvers for possible outbreaks of crises. The headquarters of the U.S. Pacific naval forces has, after conducting surveys of the Hong Kong garrison forces, stated its belief that the Hong Kong garrison has formed a competent fighting set-up with advanced facilities. This shows that the Hong Kong garrison has developed its fighting capabilities and is ready to undertake the mission of defending the SAR.

However, the main apprehensions of people of all walks of life in Hong Kong are not about the garrison's ability to undertake the defense of the SAR. On this point there are in reality no apprehensions because there are no doubts concerning the PLA's combat effectiveness. The Hong Kong residents' greatest apprehension lie in whether the garrison forces could affect the lives of SAR residents, and the whole world is waiting to see whether this Communist armed force which has previously been completely at odds with capitalism can get along with capitalist Hong Kong and especially whether it will interfere in SAR governance, or whether it will help to implement the "one country, two systems" concept. Despite the assurances contained in the Basic Law and the Garrison Law, the residents cannot set their minds at ease. As stated once in a Hong Kong newspaper: "Where Hong Kong's residents are concerned, the PLA forces stationed in Hong Kong exist as though shrouded in a veil of mystery, and even a light traffic collision is major news that can set the whole city agog."[15] A year later, however, the attitude of Hong Kong's residents toward the armed forces stationed in Hong Kong has changed considerably, and newspapers have begun to carry such headlines as "Hong Kongers: PLA Not Scary Any More" and "Hong Kongers' Jitters about PLA Greatly Decline" when reporting on the PLA.

The HK Basic Law stipulates that garrison personnel must abide both by national laws and the laws of the HK SAR, in addition to observing military discipline. That is without precedent in PLA history. In a rule-of-law society like Hong Kong, all aspects of the garrison forces' life and training involve legal issues, and they very strictly abide by these laws and disciplines, ranging from major matters such as military training, conducting air or maritime missions from Hong Kong, entering or exiting its borders, maintaining communications, etc. down to such things as target practice in their barrack areas. Advance notice of all of these must be sent to the SAR government's relevant departments and published in the Government Gazette. The garrison forces in Hong Kong have all along exercised strict closed-type manage-

---

[15] *Hong Kong Economic Journal*, July 23, 1997.

ment, and their officers and men carry on their activities within their barrack areas. Shifts from one barrack area to another required by their work are subject to strict reviews and approvals. The garrison forces' strict adherence to laws and discipline are confirmed not only by the SAR government and people but have been highly commended internationally. In its "United States-Hong Kong Policy Act Report" issued on April 25, 2000, the Asian Affairs Bureau of the U.S. State Department said that the PLA forces stationed in Hong Kong to a large extent continued to maintain a "low-key" and "symbolic" presence, and that after smoothly taking over the military facilities of the British garrison in Hong Kong, they have "vanished" from public sight. As regard how they along with SAR residents, owing to substantial differences in the Hong Kong residents' political beliefs, value concepts, ways of life and daily habits from those of mainland people, their way of handling relations with the residents of Hong Kong cannot be modeled on the traditional methods used in Chinese mainland; a new type of civilian-military relationship that fits in with Hong Kong's society and the customs and habits of its residents have had to be established. Hence some of the PLA's traditional ways of doing things developed over many years have been discontinued here. For instance, to abide by Hong Kong's laws and regulations on noise-control and in consideration of the habits of Hong Kong's residents, the garrison forces do not blow bugles or vociferously shout orders during military drills. Some systems previously non-existent among PLA units in Chinese mainland have been set up, such as the press spokesman office system and the once-a-year "Open Barracks Day." These inform the general public in good time about some of the garrison forces' activities and reduce the aura of "mystery" surrounding them. According to a social poll conducted by a Hong Kong university, the Hong Kong residents' satisfaction rate with the garrison has reached 71.9%, and one social organizations' survey of the Central Authorities' Hong Kong agencies' implementation of the "one country, two systems" concept show that as many as 93 percent of Hong Kong residents express satisfaction with the HK garrison.[16]

The Macao garrison, after entering the Macao SAR on December 20, 1999, has rapidly built up a fighting capability and, besides undertaking the SAR's defense matters, has also, in accordance with the Macao Basic Law and the Macao Garrison Law, helped the SAR government with maintaining social peace and order and conducting disaster relief, established good interactions with the SAR government people and plays a significant role in maintaining social stability in the Macao SAR, and is thereby acclaimed by the SAR's government and people.

9.4.1.2 Foreign Affairs

Since the establishment of the SARs, the Commissioners stationed by the Foreign Ministry in the Hong Kong and Macao SARs have conducted affairs strictly according to the Basic Laws, respected the SARs' high degree of autonomy and, on the basis of the principle of "mutual respect, mutual trust, mutual support and close cooperation,"

---

[16]The above-mentioned materials were furnished by the Southern Weekly of June 28, 2001.

have refrained from intervening in the SAR governments' handling of local affairs, set up good cooperative relations and effective work mechanisms with the SAR governments, and worked out and accumulated successful experiences in respect of diplomatic work involving Hong Kong and Macao.

Hong Kong is an international-type city and the foreign affairs it involves are quite complex and many-sided. Since Hong Kong's return to China, the foreign ministry's Commissioner in Hong Kong has, in accordance with the relevant provisions of the Hong Kong Basic Law, conscientiously handled a great deal of foreign affairs which involve Hong Kong and for which the Central Government is responsible, and assisted the SAR government in dealing with a vast amount of foreign affairs. In terms of handling affairs with relevant international organizations and international agreements, the Commissioner in Hong Kong has by law examined and consented to the HK SAR joining relevant international organizations and to the relevant international organizations setting up offices in Hong Kong; assisted the SAR government in drawing up the UN sanction law and legislated laws for the execution of relevant decisions on sanctions passed by the UN Security Council; many times assisted SAR government officials, including foreign nationals, in attending relevant international meetings in the capacity of members of Chinese government delegations; authorized the SAR government to issue on its own credentials for participating separately in international meetings; applied in the name of the Central Government and on behalf of the SAR government for operating international exhibitions and international meetings; assisted the SAR government in sponsoring the holding of numerous inter-governmental international meetings; and promoted and guided the SAR government in cancelling the "port of first asylum" policy for refugees.

In terms of treaty & law and the bilateral domain, the Commissioner in Hong Kong has issued to the SAR government a good many documents of authorization, authorizing the SAR to negotiate and sign with relevant counties bilateral agreements concerning civil aviation, flights across borders, protection of investments, handing over of escaped criminals, transfer of sentenced persons, assistance in criminal judicature and other domains; issued one-time authorizations for the SAR government to negotiate with other countries (including those with which no diplomatic relations have been established) agreements or administrative dispositions for mutual abolition of visas; and has examined and approved many initialed texts of bilateral agreements which the SAR government needs to submit to the Central Government for approval. In the bilateral domain, the commissioner has solicited the opinions of the SAR government on the applicability to Hong Kong of numerous treaties and conventions involving national defense and foreign relations; has on numerous occasions assisted the SAR government in the submission of reports and materials to relevant convention mechanisms; and the Commissioner has accepted and examined a great many criminal, civil and commercial judicial assistance cases concluded between Hong Kong and other countries.

Take, for example, the International Covenant on Civil and Political Rights. According to the provisions of the Basic Law of the Hong Kong Special Administrative Region, the relevant provisions in the Covenant which apply to Hong Kong continued to be effective after Hong Kong's return to China. China at that time was not a party to the Covenant, but the Chinese government, in order to manifest the "one country, two systems" principle, taking the provisions of the Covenant in reference, the Chinese government nonetheless transmitted reports concerning Hong Kong's implementation of the relevant Covenant provisions to the United Nations Human Rights Council, and the reports were written by the HK SAR government on its own. The HK SAR's government delegation also accepted the UN Human Right Council's deliberations on these reports. This is ample proof that Chinese government places a high degree of importance on the state of human rights in the Hong Kong SAR and the SAR's fulfillment of international covenants.

From 1997 to 2001, the Hong Kong SAR has concluded approximately sixty binding bilateral agreements with numerous countries and regions. Moreover the seventy bilateral agreements concluded prior to Hong Kong's return to China are still effective. The range of applicability of many of those agreements are limited to Hong Kong and do not include other localities in Chinese mainland. In addition to concluding binding agreements, the Hong Kong SAR has signed non-binding arrangements with other countries, regions or international organizations.[17]

In terms of consular work, the Commissioner in Hong Kong has handled Chinese government agreements with many countries on establishing a consular presence in Hong Kong, and has affirmed the appointments of consuls-general and honorary consuls and issued various types of visas, passports and other certificates. In terms of protocol work, the Commissioner has transmitted to the SAR government requests by important foreign guests to visit or pass through Hong Kong, requests to accord them VIP treatment, or requests to meet SAR leaders. China's institutions abroad have also rendered active assistance in informing Chinese embassies and consulates abroad about the Chief Executive's and high-ranking SAR officials' intentions to conduct visits abroad. The Commissioner has also approved requests by foreign military vessels or aircraft to land in Hong Kong. Depending on the circumstances, the Commissioner has of course also denied requests by foreign warships to visit Hong Kong.

As regard the provision of consular protections to Hong Kong persons residing in other countries, due to the fact that not a few of the latter hold British national (overseas) passports (namely BN(O) passports) issued before Hong Kong's return to China, some countries still regard them as British nationals. However, if holders of BN(O)s get into trouble in other countries, Britain's consular institutions abroad are reluctant to extend protections to them. In such cases, the Foreign Ministry's Commissioner in Hong Kong quite clearly points out that in accordance with a statement in *the Sino-British Joint Declaration on the Hong Kong Question* to the effect that all Chinese compatriots in Hong Kong are Chinese citizens, whether or not they hold British Dependent Territories Citizens Passports, Chinese embassies and consulates abroad will, to the best of their abilities, extend consular protections and services to Hong Kong Chinese residents who hold BN(O)passports, if so requested by the person or persons in question. Consequently, China's embassies and consulates abroad

---

[17]The Government of the Hong Kong Special Administrative Region. *2000–2001 Master Calendar*, June 30, 2001.

have provided consular protections and services to Hong Kongers who have landed in trouble in other countries, and have worked closely with relevant Chinese embassies and consulates and with the SAR government to jointly handle numerous consular cases which involve Hong Kong. In terms of the news media, the Commissioner in Hong Kong has examined and approved applications by foreign reporters visit places on China's mainland and has frequently approved Hong Kong reporter's interviews with visiting delegations of Chinese leaders.[18]

The statement points out that the HK SAR takes part in international organizations and international meeting in different capacities. To international organizations and meetings where the participants are countries and states, the Hong Kong government also sends representatives as members of delegations of the People's Republic of China. The HK SAR may also in the capacity of an official member and using the name "Hong Kong, China" participate alone in international organizations and meetings in which the participants are not countries and states.

In addition, quite a number of international organizations have set up offices and agencies in Hong Kong.

The Commissioner in Macao too, has since the time China resumed its exercise of sovereignty over Macao in December 20, 1999, handled numerous foreign affairs involving Macao in line with the provisions of the Macao Basic Law, and has vigorously protected the interests of the Macao SAR and its residents.

9.4.1.3   The Handling of Other Matters Which Do not Fall in the Category of a High Degree of Autonomy

According to the provisions of the Basic Laws, the Central Authorities, in addition to being responsible for the SARs defense and diplomatic matters, are also responsible for interpreting and making amendments to the Basic Laws, for exercising the powers of placing laws formulated by the SAR legislatures on the record and returning these laws for reconsideration, for appointing the SARs' chief executive and high-ranking officials, and for the Central Authorities announcing emergency situations in the SARs. After the establishment of the Hong Kong SAR, the NPC Standing Committee on one occasion interpreted two articles of the HK SAR Basic Law, and although there were differences of opinion, the NPC Standing Committee did not overstep the boundaries authorized by the HK Basic Law and its interpretations of the Basic Law were supported by the majority of Hong Kong residents. The NPC Standing Committee's conduct of routine examinations for putting legislation by SAR organs on the record have, up to now, not resulted in any SAR legislations being returned. This shows that it fully respects the SARs' exercise of legislative powers.

---

[18]The foregoing materials come from the Ministry of Foreign Affairs. "What Kind of Work Has the Central Government Done in Terms of Hong Kong-Related Diplomacy after Hong Kong's Return to China." See the Chinese People's Republic Ministry of Foreign Affairs homepage http://www.fmprc.gov.cn/chn/2651.html.

The State Council has, after the local nominations and elections of chief executives of the two SARs, appointed the chief executives according to law. The State Council has also duly fulfilled its function in appointing principal administrative officials submitted by the SAR governments, and thereby fully respected the wishes of the SARs' people and governments. In the handling of SAR matters involving Taiwan, the Central Government has also solved the relevant issues in light of the circumstances and in accordance with the "one country, two systems" and "one China" principles.

9.4.1.4 Protections for Investments in Chinese Mainland by SAR Residents

Around the time the Chinese government resumed its sovereignty over Hong Kong, many localities and persons on the mainland believed that since Hong Kong would be brought back under China's jurisdiction, policies similar to those for mainland residents could be adopted for dealing with issues that involved Hong Kong, including issues of Hong Kong residents' investments in Chinese mainland. Hence, some mainland localities began to launch policies designed to attract medium-sized and small investors from Hong Kong and stipulating that:

(a) Hong Kong residents could, on the basis of voluntary compliance, apply for and operate individually-owned industrial and commercial businesses or set up private enterprises, and that their businesses and methods would receive the same treatment as those operated by mainland residents. These stipulations run counter to China's current laws, regulations and policies for the use of foreign capital and are also inconsistent with the fundamental spirit of "Notice of the CPC Central Committee and the State Council on Correctly Handling a Number of Issues in the Relations between the Mainland and Hong Kong" and "Notice of the CPC Central Committee and the State Council on the Publishing of the 'Circular on the Circumstances of Hong Kong's return'" Zhongbanfa (1997) No. 8. Hence, with approval from the State Council, the General Office of the State Council on December 22, 1997 issued "Circular of the General Office of the State Council on Issues Concerning the Investments by Chinese Citizens in the Hong Kong Special Administrative Region in the Mainland of China," indicating that after China had resumed sovereignty over Hong Kong, corporations, the current laws, regulations and the corresponding procedural regulations for enterprises with foreign investment should continue to apply to enterprises and other economic organizations or individuals coming to the mainland to place investments. If the administrative regulations which various mainland localities were studying and preparing to launch or had already launched and implemented for absorbing investment from medium-sized and small investors were inconsistent with the current laws, regulations and corresponding procedural regulations, the launching or implementation of such administrative regulations should be terminated at once. The Notice also requested that in future, when all mainland provinces, municipalities, autonomous regions and localities were formulating laws and regulations of a local nature related to the Hong Kong SAR, they should solicit the opinions of the State Council's relevant competent departments, and on major matters should report the circumstances to the CPC Central Committee and State Council for approval. It is evident the Central Government is doing its best to dispel misunderstandings and strictly implement the "one country, two systems" requirements in terms of handling investments by Hong Kong residents in Chinese mainland.

9.4.1.5   Assistance to the Offices of the SAR Governments in Beijing

With approval from the State Council, the General Office of the State Council issued the "Notice on Providing Conveniences to and Other Matters Concerning the Beijing Office of the Hong Kong Special Administrative Region" on August 25, 2000, requesting that all provinces, autonomous regions, people governments of municipalities directly under the central government and all ministries, commissions and institution directly under the State Council provide various conveniences to SAR government office in Beijing. For instance, law enforcement personnel were not to enter the premises of the Hong Kong Office in Beijing without the consent of the person responsible at the Hong Kong Office in Beijing or a representative authorized by that person. Law enforcement personnel are not to inspect or examine archives, documents and materials stored at the venue of the Hong Kong Office in Beijing as well as archives, documents and materials placed, or in the process of being transported, in envelopes with designated markings. Customs at all entry ports are to pass such envelopes without examination on the strength of designated marking or labels filed on record with Customs by the Hong Kong Office in Beijing. In case of special circumstances where law enforcement organs need to examine envelopes with the above-mention designated markings or labels, the examination may proceed only in the presence, or with the consent, of the person in charge at the Hong Kong Office in Beijing or his authorized representative. People's governments at all levels and their departments are not to commandeer vehicles or other equipment and property pertaining to the Hong Kong Office in Beijing. Office equipment and motorized means of transport shipped into the mainland by the Hong Kong Office in Beijing and household articles for personal use shipped into the mainland by the director or deputy director of the Office should be exempted from customs duties upon Customs determination that their quantity falls within reasonable limits; other permanent staff may also be accorded the above duty-free treatment for personal-use household articles imported to the mainland within six months of their assuming office. When entering or exiting mainland entry ports, the director and deputy directors of the Hong Kong Office in Beijing may be accorded the courtesy of exemption from customs checks and examinations. The Office is of course required to observe mainland laws and refrain from engaging in commercial and other profit-making activities in Chinese mainland. Articles of public and private use shipped into Chinese mainland by the Hong Kong Office in Beijing are not to be transferred without approval from the customs authorities. Transfer formalities are to be completed at Customs according to regulations for articles transferred with Customs approval. It is obvious that the treatment given to the SAR Office in Beijing by the Central Authorities is equivalent to that given to foreign embassies and quite different from that accorded to any other province, municipality or autonomous region, and gives full expression to the "one country, two systems" principle. The Macao SAR government's office in Beijing has enjoyed the same treatment after it was established. One sees from the way the Central Authorities handed these specific SARs-related matters that the Central Government's commitments to "one country, two systems" and "a high degree of autonomy" were turning into realities.

A telephone public opinion poll conducted by the Asia-Pacific Institute of the Chinese University of Hong Kong in November 2000 has found that Hong Kong's residents are quite positive about the practice of "one country, two systems" after Hong Kong's return to China; 45.9% of those polled expressed satisfaction or considerable satisfaction with the circumstances of Hong Kong's implementation of "one country, two systems" while only 26.6% expressed dissatisfaction or great dissatisfaction. Obviously, satisfied persons considerably outnumber the dissatisfied. Analysis by that institute shows that the reasons for Hong Kong residents feeling satisfied with the practice of "one country, two systems" are mainly as follows. One, the absence of any interference by the Central Government in Hong Kong's exercise of its internal affairs after it returned to China has substantially dispelled the intense anxiety they felt about Beijing interference prior to Hong Kong's return. Two, the Central Government's open expressions of strong support and assistance for the HK SAR's efforts to stabilize Hong Kong's economy after the outbreak of the Asian Financial Crisis have gained trust in the Central Government from not a few Hong Kong residents. Three, the increasingly pivotal position of mainland China's economy for Hong Kong has, on the one hand, enhanced the residents' sense of national pride and, on the other, reduced their resistance to the mainland. Hence, despite the existence of various kinds of problems, Hong Kong's residents do accept the practice of "one country, two systems."[19]

9.4.2 The SARs' Practice of Exercising a High Degree of Autonomy

After Hong Kong and Macao SARs were established, the SAR governments have taken specific actions based on the provisions of the Basic Laws to implement "one country, two systems" and "a high degree of autonomy." The SAR governments are administering local affairs according to law within the range of their autonomy, boldly exercising autonomous rights, upholding democracy, rule-of-law and economic development in the SARs and keeping up a good momentum.

In terms political democracy and freedom, Hong Kong and Macao, after their return to China, cast off more than a century of foreign rule and set up autonomous governments administered by local persons, with local Chinese citizens assuming the positions of chief executives and other principal administrative, judicial and legislative officials. This is a milestone in the history of democratic development in

---

[19] *Hong Kong Daily News*, November 23, 2000.

Hong Kong and Macao; the Chinese residents of Hong Kong and Macao have finally become masters of their own house politically and have taken a key step forward in terms of political democracy. This is also a new venture in the development of China's local government institutions and provided a brand new experience for the reform of the mainland's system of local government. Take for example freedom of the press—a most significant indicator. In early 2001, the Hong Kong radio station asked the Public Opinion Programme of Hong Kong University to conduct a survey on "Asian media in the eyes of Hong Kongers." The results showed that nearly half of those interviewed expressed satisfaction with the overall performance of Hong Kong's media, but felt that the Hong Kong news media's performance was only so-so in terms of sense of responsibility and credibility. It ranked first among Asian media in terms of freedom of expression.[20]

In terms of economic freedom, not a few of the world's authoritative research and evaluation institutions, as for instance the U.S. Heritage Foundation, the Harvard Institute for International Development, the World Economic Forum, the International Institute for Management Development, the Economist Intelligence Unit and others, for many years in a row acclaimed Hong Kong as a place with the world's greatest economic freedom. Also, taking Canada's Fraser Institute as an example, with the support of more than fifty research institutes worldwide it put out, in early 2001, a report on world economic freedom in the year 2000 and continued to assess Hong Kong as a location with the world's greatest economic freedom. This annual report graded 123 countries and regions worldwide according to 21 indices, including scale of government, economic and judicial systems, currency policy and stability of prices. The writers of the report opined that personal right of choice, guarantees for private property and freedom of transaction constitute the core of economic freedom, and that Hong Kong and Singapore continued to rank first and second in these respects. Several new items were added in the year 2001 survey, among them an index for more extensive economic freedom and another for openness of trade. The main factors for economic freedom were "personal choice, protections for private property, and freedom of exchange." The writers assembled materials on indexes of economic freedom and, juxtaposing these with various indexes for social progressiveness, found that countries with the greatest economic freedom had the least poverty, the swiftest economic growth and the highest marks for United Nations HDI (Human Development Index). Taking all factors into consideration, the report maintained that Hong Kong currently had the world's most free economic setup.[21]

In terms of economic achievement, the per capita GDP for Hong Kongers reached 187,105 HKD in 2000.[22] The Hong Kong Monetary Authority announced on April

---

[20]See *People's Daily* Online, http://www.sina.com.cn, April 10, 2001.

[21]The economic freedom indexes of Hong Kong, Singapore, New Zealand, Britain, the United States, Australia, Switzerland and the Netherlands rank as the ten foremost in the world. Chinese mainland ranks 75th and Taiwan, 38th among the 123 countries and regions surveyed. Hong Kong *Ming Pao*, April 19, 2001. HK government webpage: http://www.info.gov.hk/gia/general/200104/20/0420296.htm.

[22]Anson Maria Elizabeth Chan Fang On Sang. "Reviewing the Past, Waiting for the Future," carried in *Ming Pao*, April 19, 2001.

9 that by the end of March, 2001 Hong Kong's official foreign currency reserves would reach USD 114,600,000,000, equivalent to about eight times Hong Kong's currency in circulation. The Hong Kong SAR's foreign exchange reserves rank third in the world, after Japan and Chinese mainland.[23] Some people used to believe that Hong Kong's economic achievements were the result of British control and that Hong Kong would have fallen into chaos without the British.[24] This "myth" has collapsed, and under China's control Hong Kong has become economically more vibrant than before it returned to China.

Internationally, appraisals of "one country, two systems" and of China's handling of Central/SAR relations are very positive. On February 9, 2000, Doug Bereuter, chairman of the Asia and the Pacific Sub-Committee of the Foreign Affairs Committee of the U.S. House of Representatives, clearly indicated that the situation in Hong Kong two and a half years after its return to China was to a large extent positive, that free capitalism had been upheld and Hong Kong continued to formulate and implement its independent economic policies.[25] Even the annual reports on the circumstances of Hong Kong and Macao which the U.S. State Department submitted to the U.S. Congress fully affirmed the "one country, two systems," "high degree of autonomy," "Hong Kongers managing Hong Kong," "Macaoans managing Macao" and the two Basic Laws implemented by the Chinese government. The Human Rights Report (No. 25) issued by the U.S. State Department on February 26, 2001, too, had to concede that: "Hong Kong reverted from British to Chinese sovereignty on July 1, 1997 (the handover). As a Special Administrative Region (SAR) of the People's Republic of China (PRC), Hong Kong enjoys a high degree of autonomy except in defense and foreign affairs and remains a free society with legally protected rights." "The 4000 Chinese troops sent to Hong Kong in 1997 to replace the British military garrison have maintained a low profile and have not performed police functions." "Hong Kong is a major international trade and finance center. It is the principal gateway for trade and investment with China. A thriving free market economy operates with limited government interference. The economy, which provides residents a high standard of living, is in the midst of a strong recovery from the 1997–1998 international financial crisis. Per capita gross domestic product (GDP) is $23,523 (HK$183,483)." "The Government generally respected the human rights of residents, and the law and judiciary generally provide effective means of dealing with individual instances of abuse.—Despite the ban on the Falun Gong in Chinese mainland, the Falun Gong remained legally registered and generally free to continue its activities in Hong Kong."[26] [Back translation by the translator.] Despite the fact that the U.S. State Department issued these comments for sake of interfering in

---

[23] See Xinhua Net http://news.xinhuanet.com/china/20010410/489556.htm, April 10, 2001.

[24] Huang Wenfang. *The Decision-Making Process and Implementation of China's Resumption of Sovereignty over Hong Kong and Macao.* Hong Kong Baptist University, 1997, p. 9.

[25] See Hong Kong Government web page: Free Economy System, http://www.freeconomy.org/fre economy/eng/main.htm.

[26] U.S. State Department. 2000 Annual Human Rights Report, February 26, 2000. http://usinfo.sta te.gov/regional/ea/mgck/hrhonkong.htm

China's internal affairs, it had to—if only from this one aspect—affirm the success of the "one-country-two-systems" exercise. As regards the Macao SAR, the U.S. State Department also issued a so-called "Macao Policy Act Report" on May 16, 2001 in which it was constrained to acknowledge that the one year of actual practice after Macao became a special administrative region of the People's Republic of China in December 20, 1999, that China had honored its commitments on Macao autonomy and that Macao was being administered by Macaoan officials and formulating policies in accordance with its own characteristics and interests. Macao, it said, continued to be a free society and its residents enjoyed basic civic freedoms on a daily basis. Macao residents enjoyed the freedoms of assembly, speech and association, and the freedom to petition the government. The operations of Macao's news media were free from government interference, and moreover, ever since the transfer of autonomy, the news media had greater freedom to express themselves, were demanding that government officials take assume more responsibilities and increase transparency, and news commentaries were directing more criticism of the SAR government than against the former Portuguese colonial government. Macao's judiciary was independent and free from political interference, appointment procedures were impartial, appointments were life-long, and remunerations ample. In many respects, the United States saw Macao a partner "with which it was increasingly willing to cooperate." As concerns such matters as the protection of intellectual property rights, anti-money laundering legislation, gambling business management, controls over strategic trade and crackdowns on money-laundering activities. Macao's high degree of autonomy was an important sign that the Chinese Government held to its international commitments, that the Macao was developing in a positive direction under China's sovereignty, and that the Macao government was striving to improve Macao's economy, resolve long-lasting problems of criminality and uphold the free and unique life-style of the Special Administrative Region.

As Senior Minister of Singapore Lee Kuan Yew pointed out in an address to the Chinese University of Hong Kong in December 2000, in the three years since Hong Kong's return to Chinese mainland one had not seen any heavy-handed interference by Beijing in Hong Kong's affairs. ... Hong Kong's constitutional could be inspected in 2007, and if the Hong Kongers are able to convince Beijing's leading stratum that the Hong Kongers are willing to conduct matters according to the Chinese Constitution and the Basic Law, it is possible that Hong Kong will be allowed to have a more representative and participatory government. ... If Hong Kong is to advance, it should strive to formulate a set of objectives that are effective and practicable and that fall within the restrictions of the power structure of the People's Republic of China and the Hong Kong special administrative region.[27] This tells us that international public opinion was quite positive with regard to the successful implementation of "one country, two systems" in Macao and Hong Kong.

Another important indicator of international society's widespread confirmation of the SAR's high degree of autonomy is the acknowledgement the SAR's passport

---

[27]Lee Kuan Yew's Address at the Ceremony for Accepting an Honorary Doctorate of Law Conferred by the Hong Kong Chinese University. See Hong Kong *Ming Pao*, December 17, 2000.

has gained in various countries. On April 5, 2001 Iceland and Norway officially announced that they were according visa-free treatment to HK SAR passports of the People's Republic of China. This has resulted in the number of countries according visa-free access to HK SAR passports finally exceeding the number of countries giving visa-free treatment to British BN(O) passports for HK residents prior to Hong Kong's return to China—a total 89 countries are now according visa-free access to SAR passports; three more that to the BN(O)s. At the same time Japan has announced that the term of validity for SAR passport visas has been extended to three years. By now, more than 1.4 million persons in Hong Kong have applied for and obtained SAR passports.[28] The European Union has previously already accorded visa-free entry to its borders to HK SAR passport holders without setting any preconditions, and has giver Macao SAR passport holders the same treatment. By the end of June, 2001, ninety-one countries had accorded visa-free treatment to HK SAR passport holders of the People's Republic of China. This was the international society's best expression of confidence in "one country, two systems."

Prior to Hong Kong's return to China, not a few Hong Kongers were apprehensive lest the PRC'S SAR passports newly issued by the SAR government would not be acknowledged by other countries, in particular countries in Europe and the Americas. Hence many Hong Kongers, for the sake of convenience in business and travelling, applied for the British National (Overseas) passport (BN[O]) issued in previous times to Hong Kongers by the then Hong Kong British authorities. It is evident people in those days lacked confidence in whether "one country, two systems" could be realized, and were greatly concerned over whether Hong Kong could continue to maintain its prosperity and stability after its return to China. Many Hong Kongers even moved abroad. Hong Kong's return to China, however, did not plunge Hong Kong into chaos or trigger a "flood of refugees." Although Hong Kong was heavily impacted by the Asian Financial Crisis, it very quickly recovered and continued to maintain prosperity and stability. This proved to International society the enormous success and vitality of the "one country, two systems" concept. In less than four years after Hong Kong's return to China, the acknowledgement the HK SAR has won from international society has already surpassed that garnered by Hong Kong as a British "dependency" prior to 1997. This, as well as demonstrating the successful implementation of the "one country, two systems," also shows that the "Hong Kongers administer Hong Kong" and "high degree of autonomy" setup is superior to Hong Kong's administration under the British authorities.[29]

In 2001, the Hong Kong SAR government engaged a survey company to conduct an extensive investigation of Hong Kong's situation. The upshot was that 49% of American businesses felt that there had been no change in Hong Kong. Leaders in all walks of life in Hong Kong universally opined that Hong Kong was "Asia's international metropolis" and "an important city for the mainland." However not a few persons had warned that Hong Kong should not let itself be seen as "merely one of mainland China's cities." They were also concerned that assets would be lost as

---

[28]*Hong Kong Wen Wei Po*, April 6, 2001.

[29]*Hong Kong Wen Wei Po*, March 16, 2001.

the Chinese government conducted reforms, and that Hong Kong would gradually be distanced from Western society. The Hong Kong authorities, however, are striving to promote Hong Kong's status as an international metropolis and are confident the results of the above investigations will help the SAR government adopt measures to further raise Hong Kong's international status.[30]

Since the Hong Kong SAR's establishment, the Central Government has not intervened in matters that fall within the scope of Hong Kong's high degree of autonomy. Hong Kong continues to pursue capitalist operations, and there has been a considerable increase in the number of large multinational corporations setting up headquarters in Hong Kong. HK SAR government statistics show that some 3001 companies with foreign capital set up regional headquarters in Hong Kong prior to June 1, 2000. Hong Kong assimilated foreign capital to the tune of USD 64,400,000,000 in the year 2000. An investigation by the British magazine *The Economist* shows that Hong Kong is still the first choice of multinational corporations for setting up headquarters in the Asia-Pacific region. A survey of 8000 North American, European and Japanese multinational enterprises conducted by *The Economist*'s "intelligence service" over the last two years indicates that 35% of these enterprises indicated they would list Hong Kong as their first choice if they were to set up headquarters in the Asia-Pacific region; 30% chose Singapore and only 9% opted for Tokyo. Meanwhile, a sustained drop in Hong Kong's crime rate has placed it among the safest of the world's biggest cities. Large numbers of Hong Kong émigrés are returning to Hong Kong, while the number of Hong Kongers moving abroad has declined for six straight years, reaching a record low for the previous 20 years. The number of those going abroad in 2000 has fallen by 7% over the previous year. These figures indicate that Hong Kongers are fully confident in Hong Kong's prospects and confirmed the successful implementation of "one country, two systems."[31]

---

[30] *Yahoo News*, May 11, 2001.

[31] For the above data, see the *People's Daily* Overseas Edition, January 10, 2001, as well as the Xinhua News Agency, June 29 and June 30, 2001.

Chapter 10
Case Study: The Central/SAR Relations Since 1997

Although not much time has elapsed since China resumed the exercise of sovereignty over Hong Kong, a number of issues and cases have occurred involving Central/SAR relations. Examples are those regarding the legality of the establishment of a provisional legislative council, the issue of revising a number of laws dating back to "bygone dynastic eras," the adaptation of laws (by replacing such terms and concepts as "British imperial" and "official" with "national"), the issue of the legal status of the Xinhua News Agency HK Branch Office, the issue of whether the director of the Xinhua News Agency HK Branch Office has been constrained by the "Personal Data (Privacy) Ordinance," the Hu Xian [Aw Sian] Incident, and so forth. Among these cases, those which have caused fairly big repercussions are the issue of the legality of the SAR Provisional Legislative Council, the issue of the right of abode in Hong Kong, cases of the desecration of the national flag, the Zhang Ziqiang (Cheung Tze-Keung) Case and the Li Yuhui Case. One of the chief reasons for the emergence of these unique legal issues is that in accordance with the Basic Law, both regions retain their own legal and judicial systems and, in terms of law, "one country, two systems" became "one country two laws [legal systems]." This plus the increasingly close economic, financial, and civil exchanges between the regions have made many legal issues quite complicated. The problems would not exist if "one country one system" or "one country one law" was being implemented. However, as compared to these legal issues, "one country, two systems" is more fundamental and should not be negated because it has given rise to legal problems of one sort or another. On the contrary, such cases and issues ought to be handled in accordance with the "one country, two systems" principle and the Basic Laws. The handling of such cases and problems is also a direct test of the "one country, two systems" principle and the Basic Laws, and the handling of each case has deepened people's understanding of "one country, two systems" and the Basic Laws.

© Foreign Language Teaching and Research Publishing Co., Ltd and Springer Nature Singapore Pte Ltd. 2019
Z. Wang, *Relationship Between the Chinese Central Authorities and Regional Governments of Hong Kong and Macao: A Legal Perspective*, China Academic Library, https://doi.org/10.1007/978-981-13-2322-5_10

10.1   The Hong Kong Special Administrative Region v. Ma Wei

10.1.1   Facts of the Case

On July 1, 1997, right after the establishment of the Hong Kong SAR, a unique, landmark-type case emerged to test the viability of the Basic Law and the "one country, two systems" principle, i.e., the Hong Kong SAR v. Ma Wei [Ma Wai-Kwan] case.[1] Three defendants in the case had been charged on August 11, 1995 with the Common Law offense of conspiring to interfere with the course of justice, the former British government in Hong Kong had submitted to the court a bill of indictment, and the court had begun to hear the case on January 3, 1997. This was originally a simple Common Law criminal offense. Then, on July 1, 1997, the Chinese government resumed its sovereignty over Hong Kong, the British administration was terminated, Hong Kong became a special administrative region of the People's Republic of China, Hong Kong's former legally constituted authorities ceased to exist, and the HK SAR entered into force. On July 3, a new SAR court of law resumed hearings on this case. However, the defendants' senior counsel suddenly demanded that the government should withdraw the charges. The reason he gave was that the government's bill of indictment submitted to the High Court of Hong Kong had automatically become invalid, or in other words, offenses committed prior to the establishment of the SAR no longer counted. Since the matters involved in the case were of major import, however, the presiding judge straightaway transferred the case to the Appeals Tribunal of the High Court for examination and adjudication.

The debate, in this case, was focused mainly on the following two aspects: One was the new HK SAR's "maintaining" and "adoption" of Hong Kong's original laws an Actus legitimus. Two was the SAR's establishment of a provisional legislative council legitimate?

10.1.2   Was the "Maintaining" and "Adoption" of Hong Kong's "Former" Laws an Actus Legitimus?

The Hong Kong Basic Law indeed stipulates that "laws previously in force in Hong Kong, that is, the common law, rules of equity, ordinances, subordinate legislation and customary law shall be maintained, except for any that contravene this Law, and subject to any amendment by the legislature of the Hong Kong Special Administrative Region." However, did this "maintaining" have to be effected by means of a "volitional" act of adoption on the part of the National People's Congress via its Standing Committee or by the HK SAR legislature—an act which specifically

---

[1] Hong Kong SAR v. Ma Wai-Kwan, David, Chan Kok-Wai, Donny and Tam Kim-Yuen, (1997) HKLRD 761.

adopts these "previously-in-force" laws of the Hong Kong SAR? Or are these previous laws automatically converted into laws of the new special region when Hong Kong is returned to China? The defense's senior counsel held that in accordance with Basic Law provisions all previous laws, in order to be adopted as laws of the new special region, had to be specifically adopted as laws of the HK SAR by means of a "volitional" act of adoption by the National People's Congress through its Standing Committee or the Hong Kong SAR legislature. Yet, the NPC Standing Committee not only had not done so, but had conversely annulled the "Application of English Law Ordinance" (Chapter 88 of the Hong Kong Ordinances) because it conflicted with Hong Kong's Basic Law. The legality of the SAR's Provisional Legislative Council also came in question, and for these reasons, the chief defense counsel maintained that the Common Law no longer existed in Hong Kong after the transfer of Hong Kong's political power on July 1 and no longer formed part of the HK SAR's laws. Since the relevant charges in the case were offenses under the Common Law prior to Hong Kong's return to China, said the chief counsel, they should have been annulled after China resumed its sovereignty over Hong Kong.

However, the Hong Kong government's chief prosecutor maintained that in accordance with the HK Basic Law, the Common Law was a component part of the law of the HK SAR and did not require any special act of adoption. All that was needed were annulments by means of specific announcements of laws which were no longer applicable. Whatever the case, the NPC Standing Committee had indeed already adopted laws previously in force in Hong Kong as laws of the Hong Kong SAR.

Whether the Common Law still exists in Hong Kong after the transfer of Hong Kong's political power has to do with the interpretation of the relevant provisions of the Basic Law. And to interpret the Basic Law, one may analyze the formulation of the Basic Law, starting with the Sino-British Joint Declaration—the basic norm for the "legitimacy" of the transfer. The essence of the Sino-British Joint Declaration and the Basic Law consists of maintaining the social, economic, and legal systems of Hong Kong prior to its return to China unchanged for the next fifty years. That was a key factor in the transfer of political power. As senior government barristers have stated: Articles 8, 18, 19, 81, 87, and 160 of Hong Kong's Basic Law clearly indicate the basic spirit that the Hong Kong SAR should automatically keep Hong Kong's original laws and judiciary systems unchanged. To wit,

Article 8 stipulates: The laws previously in force in Hong Kong, i.e., the Common Law, rules of equity, ordinances, subordinate legislation and customary laws shall be maintained, except for any that contravene the Basic Law and subject to amendment by the legislature of the Hong Kong Special Autonomous Region.

Article 18 (1) stipulates: The laws in force in the Hong Kong Special Administrative Region shall be the Basic Law, the laws previously in force in Hong Kong as provided for in Article 8 of this Law, and the laws enacted by the legislature of the Region.

Article 19 (1) (2) stipulates: The Hong Kong Special Administrative Region shall be vested with independent judicial power, including that of final adjudication. The courts of the Hong Kong Special Administrative Region shall have jurisdiction over all cases in the Region, except where restrictions are placed on the power of adjudication of the counts as regards their continued retention of Hong Kong's previous legal system and principles.

Article 81 (2) stipulates: The judicial system previously practiced in Hong Kong shall be maintained except for those changes consequent upon the establishment of the Court of Final Appeal of the Hong Kong Special Administrative Region.

Article 87 stipulates: In criminal or civil proceedings in the Hong Kong Special Administrative Region, the principles previously applied in Hong Kong and the rights previously enjoyed by parties to proceedings shall be maintained.

Article 160: Upon the establishment of the Hong Kong Special Administrative Region, the laws previously in force in Hong Kong shall be adopted as laws of the Region except for those which the Standing Committee of the National People's Congress declares to be in contravention of this Law. If any laws are later discovered to be in contravention of this Law, they shall be amended or cease to have force in accordance with the procedure as prescribed by the Law. Documents, certificates, contracts, and rights and obligations valid under the laws previously in force in Hong Kong shall continue to be valid and be recognized and protected by the Hong Kong Special Administrative Region, provided that they do not contravene this Law.

The term "shall continue to be" as used in these articles clearly and unmistakably indicates that Hong Kong's "previously-in-force" laws did not need any special procedures and could directly become SAR laws on July 1, 1997 unless some of those "previous" laws were explicitly annulled by the NPC Standing Committee. As for whether the term "adopt" in Article 160 meant there should be special procedures for "adopting," the chief prosecutor in the case maintained that this article should not be viewed in isolation that the entirety of the Basic Law as well as other relevant articles should be taken into consideration, and that no conflicts existed in the Basic Law's context on this matter. As for the Article per se, it contains the implication that the previous laws should naturally continue to be effective and need no special procedures. The matter is even clearer upon closer perusal of the Sino-British Joint Declaration.

On February 23, 1997, the 24th session of the Eighth National People's Congress Standing Committee, after examining proposals by the Hong Kong Special Administrative Region Special Committee on the issue of handling Hong Kong's previous laws, passed the "Decision on Article 160 of the Basic Law of the Hong Kong Special Administrative Region of the People' Republic of China on Handling Laws Previously in Force in Hong Kong," and not only further specified that Hong Kong's previous laws, including the Common Law, rules of equity, ordinances, subordinate legislation, and customary law should be automatically adopted as laws of the Hong Kong SAR, except for any that contravened the Basic Law, but also drew up a detailed list of Hong Kong's previous laws which entirely or partially contravened the Basic Law and which the NPC Standing Committee decided not to adopt as laws of the Hong Kong SAR. This Decision by the NPC Standing Committee in itself constituted an act of "adopting" Hong Kong's original laws as well as an "inquiry into the constitutionality" of Hong Kong's previous laws. The fact that the NPC Standing Committee annulled the "Ordinance on the Application of English Law" because the Ordinance contravened the Hong Kong Basic Law did not affect the effectiveness of the Common Law in the Hong Kong SAR.

10.1.3   The Issue of the Legality of the Provisional Legislative Committee

As regard the legality of the Hong Kong SAR's Provisional Legislative Committee, the senior defense counsel maintained that the actions of the SAR's Provisional Legislative Committee on July 1, 1997 of approving the Hong Kong Reunification Ordinance, adopting previous laws as laws of the Hong Kong SAR, and its retention of pending legal proceedings had no legal standing because the Provisional Legislative Council was not an entity generated by the Basic Law and therefore not a legislative institution of the Hong Kong SAR, and the laws it established were naturally ineffective.

The chief prosecutor maintained that when the National People's Congress approved the Basic Law in 1996, it simultaneously approved the Decision on the Method for the Formation of the First Government and the First Legislative Council of the Hong Kong Special Administrative Region, in which it decided to set up a National Congress preparatory committee for the Hong Kong SAR within the year 1996 and that this committee would be "in charge of planning matters relevant to the formation of the Hong Kong Special Administrative Region." Owing to unilateral violations of mutual agreements by the British side, the Chinese side decided that the members of the former British legislative council would not be allowed to automatically "cross over" during the 1997 transition, and as a result, the new HK SAR faced the reality of not having a legislative institution. Hence, on March 24, 1996, the HK SAR preparatory committee decided to set up the Provisional Legislative Council as a provisional legislative institution for the SAR.

On March 14, 1997, the Eighth National Congress examined the "Work Report of the National People's Congress Hong Kong Special Administrative Region Preparatory Committee" by Qian Qichen, Chairman of the SAR Preparatory Committee, and passed a resolution which "approved the report."

In other resolutions, the National People's Congress maintained that: "In the year since the National People's Congress Hong Kong Special Administrative Region preparatory committee has been set up, it has performed highly productive work." It is held that, based on the Chinese People's Republic Hong Kong SAR Basic Law and the NPC and its Standing Committee's policies with regard to "one country, two systems," "a high degree of autonomy," and "Hong Kongers manage Hong Kong," the preparatory committee had passed a series of resolutions, decisions, and proposals, including the *Decisions on the Election Procedure of Selection Committee, Decisions on Setting Up Provisional Legislative Council in Hong Kong Special Administrative*

Region, Suggestions on Explanations Concerning the Implementation of Nationality Law of the People's Republic of China in Hong Kong Special Administrative Region, Suggestions of SCNPC on Handing the Existing Law of Hong Kong, Decisions on the Operation of the First Chief Executive of Hong Kong Special Administrative Region and Provisional Legislative Council Before June 30, 1997. It had organized and set up the Selection Committee for the first government of the HK SAR, chaired the selection committee in selecting and producing the HK SAR's first Chief Executive and members of the Provisional Legislative Council, and put forward suggestions and opinions for major economic and legal issues related to the Hong Kong's political power handover and peaceful transition and to arrangements for activities to celebrate the Hong Kong's return. It had laid the foundations for the formation of the HK SAR and Hong Kong's peaceful transition, and done other work conducive to Hong Kong's long-term stability and prosperity. The National People's Congress expressed the hope that the HK SAR Preparatory Committee would keep up its good work, continue to support the first Chief Executive of the HK SAR in his work, and make efforts toward successfully completing the tasks given to it by the National People's Congress.

This clearly shows that the establishment of the Provisional Legislative Council was not only a matter within the scope of functions of the SAR Preparatory Committee, but that it had also obtained the confirmation and recognition of the National People's Congress. From any perspective, the legality of the Provisional Legislative Council allows of no doubt.

10.1.4   The Verdict of the Court and Commentary

After careful consideration, the Appeals Tribunal of the SAR High Court on July 29, 1997 passed its verdict, which was to be the first constitutional ruling in the history of the Hong Kong SAR. The appeals tribunal maintained that in accordance with the provisions of Articles 8, 18 and 160 of the Hong Kong Basic Law, the Common Law "previously in force" prior to Hong Kong's return to China was obviously still in effect. Hence, the government's bill of indictment prior to Hong Kong's return to China had not automatically become invalid after China restored its exercise of sovereignty over Hong Kong on July 1, 1997. Article 8 of the Hong Kong Basic Law quite explicitly pointed out: "The laws previously in force in Hong Kong, that is, the common law, rules of equity, ordinances, subordinate legislations and customary law shall be maintained, except for any that contravene this Law, and subject to any amendment by the legislature of the Hong Kong Special Administrative Region." The judge maintained that the use of the term "shall be" in Article 8 of the Basic Law indicated that it was unnecessary for the HK SAR government to institute any procedures, and that Hong Kong's previous laws, except for any that contravened Hong Kong Basic Law, would be automatically adopted as laws of the Hong Kong SAR. That was indisputable.

The verdict of the High Court maintained that the Basic Law is a unique document consisting of at least three tiers (significances), namely international, national, and constitutional. It stated that the Basic Law is not merely the result of an international agreement, i.e., the Sino-British Joint Declaration. It is also a Chinese law of a nationwide character as well as the constitution of the Hong Kong Special Administrative Region. The Basic Law puts into effect the general and specific policies covered by the Joint Declaration, which focuses on maintaining Hong Kong's current social, economic, and legal systems unchanged for fifty years. The aim of the Basic Law is to ensure the implementation of these basic general and specific polities so as to maintain the Hong Kong SAR's stability and prosperity. Hence, continuity after the handover of sovereignty is of the utmost importance. The Basic Law is a unique document which reflects the treaty concluded between two countries as well as involves the relationship between a suzerain state and an autonomous region, which practices a different system, and it also stipulates the framework and functions of a government's various branches and lists the rights, interests, and responsibilities of its citizens. Thus, it can be seen that the Basic Law possesses significance at the least at three levels—international, national, and constitutional. In addition, attention should be paid to the fact that Basic Law was drafted by lawyers without training in the Common Law. The Basic Law was drawn up in Chinese and also has a legal English version. However, if any discrepancies emerge between the two, the Chinese version shall serve as the criterion. From the background and characteristics of Basic Law as described above, interpreting the articles of the Basic Law is no easy matter. It is evident that the abovementioned court of law believed that other that the changes required by China's restoration of its exercise of sovereignty over Hong Kong, the overall intention in the Basic Law's abiding strictly to the Sino-British Joint Declaration was to strive for stability during Hong Kong's transition, and the previous systems should be continued. Hence, the argument that the previous laws could be "retained" and "adopted" only by going through official procedures was not the original intent of the Basic Law and was rejected by the court.

As regards the juridical status of the SAR's Provisional Legislative Council, the court of appeals maintained that the Provisional Legislative Council was a provisional organization of the SAR set up by the SAR preparatory committee under the National People's Congress that this was an act performed by China as the sovereign state over Hong Kong, and that the Hong Kong SAR's courts as local courts did not have the right to query the laws approved by the sovereign state or the acts it performed. Even before Hong Kong's return to China, Hong Kong courts could not subject to examination any legislations or acts performed with regard to Hong Kong by the British Parliament or by the British queen in conjunction with the Privy Council. According to China's Constitution, the National People's Congress is China's highest organ of state power and together with the NPC Standing Committee, exercises the country's legislative powers. Accordingly, the Appeals Tribunal was of the unanimous opinion that the Provisional Legislative Council was an institution set up according to law by the Special Administrative Region's Preparatory Committee exercising powers invested in it by the National People's Congress in accordance with Chinese law, and that the

Hong Kong court as a local court in one of China's special administrative regions did not have the right to query either this national action by the sovereign state or the reason or reasons behind the setting up of this organization. The jurisdictions which the Hong Kong SAR court had the right to exercise in this case include the following: Whether the National People's Congress had produced any resolutions or decisions to set up the SAR Preparatory Committee; whether the SAR Preparatory Committee had produced any decision or resolution to set up the Provisional Legislative Council, and whether the establishment of the Provisional Legislative Council had indeed been in line with decisions or resolutions by the National People's Congress and SAR Preparatory Committee. If there were no problems in these respects, then no problems existed. Moreover, after the National People's Congress had deliberated the SAR Preparatory Committee's work report on March 14, 1997, it in fact "decided to approve the report" and acknowledged the legal status of the Provisional Legislative Council, despite the absence of any reference to the setting up of the Provisional Legislative Council in the Basic Law.

Thus, based on the above facts, the court maintained that the SAR's Provisional Legislative Council was a legislative institution legally set up in accordance with relevant National People's Congress decisions and resolutions, and the legislations passed by the Provisional Legislative Council, including the Hong Kong Reunification Ordinance approved on July 1, 1997, of course possessed legal validity. Hence, the government's indictment previously submitted to the Hong Kong High Court prior to Hong Kong's return to China was still in force after China resumed its sovereignty over the Hong Kong, and the acts that infringed on laws "previously in force" still should be prosecuted.

This "landmark" verdict not only further confirmed the applicability of the Basic Law in Hong Kong and the legality of the Provisional Legislative Council; it also confirmed that the acts-of-state of the Chinese government as the sovereign state were not to be challenged by the local judiciary. Seen from the perspective of political system and rule of law, the significance of this verdict lay in the fact that it firmly established the rule of law of the new Hong Kong SAR, confirmed the Hong Kong SARs' new legal authority established by China's highest organ of state power, and also, indirectly via the judiciary, and further confirmed the legitimacy of the acts-of-state taken to restore China's sovereignty over Hong Kong. It also demonstrated to the world that after coming back under China's sovereignty, the Hong Kong SAR remained as a civilized society with a sound rule of law and independent judiciary in which any disputes could be peacefully and satisfactorily resolved by means of judicial procedures, including such "sensitive" and highly political cases such as the one currently under review. In China's mainland regions, issues regarding constitutional litigation are still in the discussion phase. However, the new Hong Kong SAR is not prevented from conducting "abstract" judicial examinations of legislative acts because such a system does not yet exist in China's mainland regions. This, too, fully meets the "one country, two systems" requirement.

In the entire litigation process, although the acts-of-state of China's highest organs of state power were confronted with judicial challenges, neither the National People's Congress, the NPC Standing Committee or the State Council, nor any institution or individual on China's mainland have intervened in HK SAR court's examinations of the case, nor have they exerted any pressure on any party to the litigation. Nor has the new SAR government exerted any pressure on the court. The only things that have taken place are argumentations on the basis of reason and strictly in accordance with the law, the fighting of "legal battles," and peaceful judicial solutions of problems. This fully reflects the Central Authorities' sincerity with regard to implementing the SAR's "high degree of autonomy" and "Hong Kongers administering Hong Kong"; it showed that the Hong Kong SAR enjoyed a high degree of judicial independence, and that the SAR judiciary is independent not only of the local government but also of the Central Authorities.

This case has also involved complex issues of the SAR courts' power to inquire into the constitutionality of laws. These will be explored later.

10.2   Litigation on the Right of Abode of Children Born to Hong Kongers in Chinese Mainland and the Relevant Constitutional Laws

10.2.1   Background to the Litigation

For a long period of time, there were no border controls between Chinese Mainland and Hong Kong. Hong Kong residents were free to come to the mainland, and mainland residents were also free to work and settle down in Hong Kong. Since Hong Kong's economic and social conditions were not much better than those of the mainland prior to the 1950s, not many mainlanders insisted on going to work and settle down in Hong Kong. In the late 1950s, however, due to the effects of "Left" ideology and policies on the mainland, the number of people migrating to Hong Kong constantly increased, giving rise to the problem of border controls between the two regions. Still later, more and more mainlanders hoped to move to Hong Kong when Hong Kong's economy took off and the economic gap between the regions kept widening. When China began to open up to the outside and economic and trade exchanges between the two regions livened up, the number of Hong Kongers coming to the mainland to do business also proliferated, and some of them had children either through legal marriages or illicit cohabitation. These children born to Hong Kongers residing on the mainland as well as other individuals who for various reasons wished to move to Hong Kong gave rise to a vast tide of migrants and exerted immense migratory pressures on Hong Kong society. This became a permanent thorn in mainland–Hong Kong relations and ultimately led to a major constitutional and legal problem (to avoid using the term "crisis") confronting the two regions after Hong Kong's return to China.

Attachment 1 of the Sino-British Joint Declaration touched on this issue, and Hong Kong SAR Basic Law carries provisions in this respect. Paragraph 4 of Article 22 stipulates:

"For entry into the Hong Kong Special Administrative Region, people from other parts of China must apply for approval. Among them, the number of persons who enter the Region for the purpose of settlement shall be determined by the competent authorities of the Central People's Government after consulting the government of the Region."

Article 24 of the Hong Kong Basic Law stipulates:

"Residents of the Hong Kong Special Administrative Region ("Hong Kong residents") shall include permanent residents and nonpermanent residents.

The permanent residents of the Hong Kong Special Administrative Region shall be:

(1) Chinese citizens born in Hong Kong before or after the establishment of the Hong Kong Special Administrative Region;
(2) Chinese citizens who have ordinarily resided in Hong Kong for a continuous period of not less than seven years before or after the establishment of the Hong Kong Special Administrative Region;
(3) Persons of Chinese nationality born outside Hong Kong of those residents listed in categories (1) and (2);
(4) Persons not of Chinese nationality who have entered Hong Kong with valid travel documents, have ordinarily resided in Hong Kong for a continuous period of not less than seven years and have taken Hong Kong as their place of permanent residence before and after the establishment of the Hong Kong Special Administrative Region;
(5) Persons under 21 years of age born in Hong Kong of those residents listed in category (4) before or after the establishment of the Hong Kong Special Administrative Region; and
(6) Persons other than those residents listed in categories (1) to (5), who, before the establishment of the Hong Kong Special Administrative Region, had the right of abode in Hong Kong only.

The abovementioned residents shall have the right of abode in the Hong Kong Special Administrative Region and shall be qualified to obtain, in accordance with the laws of the Region, permanent identity cards which confirm the right of abode."

The provisions of Paragraph 4 of Article 22 of the Basic Law are quite clear. For entry into the Hong Kong SAR, no matter for what purpose or reason, people from other parts of China must apply for approval in Chinese mainland and be in possession of legal documents. This, of course, includes both short-term visits and permanent residence. This Basic Law provision fundamentally negates the concept that mainland residents may freely enter and exit Hong Kong after the region's return to China. Indeed, due to the vast number of people hoping to take up permanent residence in Hong Kong, the only possible solution was for the Central Government to determine a reasonable arrangement for the number of people and time of entry into Hong Kong after consulting the government of HK SAR. In other words, it was not possible to satisfy the wish of all people to settle permanently in Hong Kong or to let all persons qualified for permanent residency to arrive on the same day. The intention of the Basic Law legislation was undoubtedly well meant and quite apparent.

The problem lay in the definition for "permanent residents" in Article 24 of the Basic Law, in which item (1) of paragraph 2 stipulated in accordance with *jus soli* that "Chinese citizens born in Hong Kong before or after the establishment of the Hong Kong Special Administrative Region" were permanent residents of the Hong Kong SAR, and item (2) stipulated that "Chinese citizens who have ordinarily resided in Hong Kong for a continuous period of not less than seven years before or after the establishment of the Hong Kong Special Administrative Region" were also permanent Hong Kong SAR residents. However, item (3) stipulated that "persons of Chinese nationality born outside Hong Kong" of these two above categories of persons were also HK SAR permanent residents. This gave rise to an actual problem, i.e., did persons born in Chinese mainland when both their parents or one parent were not yet permanent HK residents but both or one parent later obtained permanent residency because of working in Hong Kong or other reasons—have the right of abode in Hong Kong? The Basic Law provisions were not clear about that.

The problem drew attention again during the preparations for the Hong Kong SAR, and for that reason the fourth plenary session of the National People's Congress Hong Kong Special Administrative Region Preparatory Committee (hereinafter Preparatory Committee) issued in August 1996 an "Opinion on the Implementation of Paragraph Two of Article 24 of the 'Basic Law of the Hong Kong Special Administrative Region of the People's Republic of China'." This Opinion clearly pointed out: "Item (3) of Paragraph two of Article 24 of the Basic Law on Chinese nationals born outside of Hong Kong provides that when the Chinese national per se is born, either both or one his or her parents must be persons who have already obtained permanent residency in Hong Kong in accordance with Item (1) or Item (2) of paragraph two of the Basic Law." This specifically excludes the right of abode in Hong Kong for mainland residents born when neither of their parents had yet become a permanent Hong Kong resident. This was confirmed again by means of the "Resolution on the Work of the National People's Congress Hong Kong Special Administrative Region Preparatory Committee" passed by the Fifth Meeting of the National People's Congress on March 14, 1997.

Accordingly, the Hong Kong SAR Provisional Legislative Council formulated the 1997 Immigration (Amendment) (No. 2) Bill and the 1997 Immigration (Amendment) (No. 3) Bill after Hong Kong's return to the China, which stipulated that to obtain permanent residency rights in Hong Kong, the children born to Hong Kong residents in Chinese mainland should be born to parents, one or both of whom were already permanent residents of Hong Kong. Children who claimed to possess right of abode in the Hong Kong SAR should produce certificates of right of abode or other acknowledged ID certifications to prove possession of right of abode and obtain one-way permits to settle down in Hong Kong issued by mainland public security organs. The bills' effective dates were retroactive to July 1.

These two legislations by the Hong Kong SAR Provisional Legislative Council were in accordance with Article 17 of the Basic Law promptly reported to the NPC Standing Committee for the record, and since the NPC Standing Committee did not hold that these bills violated the Basic Law's articles on matters administered by the Central Authorities or on Central/SAR relations and had not returned the bills to the SAR, the two legislations were entirely valid.

10.2.2 Relevant Lawsuits and Their Effects

Once the 1997 Immigration (Amendment) (No. 2) Bill and the 1997 Immigration (Amendment) (No. 3) Bill were made public, the parents of more than a thousand children affected thereby maintained that the bills violated the Basic Law and immediately took the HK SAR government to court and demanded that the two legislations be subjected to judicial examination. This gave rise to the Wu Jialing & Wu Dandan v. Immigration Department Director case, the Chen Jinya case, and other relevant cases.[2]

On January 26, 1998, a court of first instance of the Hong Kong Special Administrative Region exercised the power of judicial examination and ruled that the Provisional Legislative Council's revision of the provisions of abovementioned Immigration Bills—which deprived Chinese mainland-born children born to persons who were not yet Hong Kong permanent residents of their right of abode in Hong Kong—contravened the provisions of the Basic Law, and the court therefore negated the legal validity of the revision of the immigration bills. After losing out on this lawsuit, the Hong Kong SAR government, concerned lest the ruling would lead to vast numbers of mainland persons flooding into Hong Kong, immediately submitted an appeal to the Tribunal of Appeals of the Hong Kong's High Court.

On April 2 of that year, the Tribunal of Appeals made a ruling that the plan implemented by the HK SAR on the certification of right of abode was legal, and that if children, including out-of-wedlock children, born in Chinese mainland to Hong Kong permanent residents, arrived in Hong Kong prior to July 1, 1997, they would have the right of abode in Hong Kong. The Tribunal of Appeals overturned the verdict by the court of first instance and ruled that when the children were born, either one or both of their parents should already be a permanent Hong Kong resident for the children to be qualified for obtaining the right of abode in Hong Kong. This case was immediately referred to the Hong Kong SAR's highest court, namely its Court of Final Appeal, for a final ruling.

Having heard the case, the Hong Kong SAR Court of Final Appeal on January 29, 1999 produced a final verdict on the right of abode cases of children born to Hong Kong residents in Chinese mainland. The verdict stated that the stipulations

---

[2]CACC 216/1999, the High Court of the Hong Kong Special Administrative Region; FACC14/1998, the Final Court of Hong Kong Special Administrative Region; (1999) 1 Hong Kong Law Reports and Digest 315 (English Version), 731 (Chinese Version).

on the abovementioned emigration bills did not comply with Basic Law regulations: That the children born to Hong Kong residents, as referred to in Item (3), paragraph two of Basic Law Article 24, covered children born to parents both prior and after the latter became permanent Hong Kong residents, and that the term "children" included those born both in and out of wedlock; and that the restriction, as iterated in paragraph 4 of Basic Law Article 22 on "people from other parts of China" entering Hong Kong, did not apply to these persons. As regards the Hong Kong court's "constitutional jurisdiction," namely judicial examination power, the verdict pointed out that Hong Kong courts could examine not only the laws passed by Hong Kong's local legislative councils or the acts of Hong Kong's administrative organs to see whether they complied with Hong Kong's new "constitution," namely the Basic Law, and declare these null and void if they failed to comply, they could also examine the relevant legislations by the National People's Congress or the NPC Standing Committee to see whether these complied with the Basic Law, and could also similarly declare them null and void if these were found to contravene the Basic Law.

This verdict at once triggered widespread discussion among people of all walks of life on the mainland and in Hong Kong because it touched upon many fundamental issues in terms of constitutionality, judicial theory, ethics, and even social science. Legal quarters on the mainland were concerned about verdict's narrative regarding the possibility of Hong Kong's courts to examine legislation by the National People's Congress or the NPC Standing Committee, and held that Hong Kong's courts were not empowered to carry out constitutionality reviews of the country's highest organs of state power, and that legislation by the country's highest organs of state power was not to be challenged by any judicial organ.[3] To dispel misgivings in mainland China, the HK SAR Government on February 24 wrote a letter to the SAR Court of Final Appeal requesting clarification of the verdict's narrative and maintaining this was an issue of a constitutional nature. After a brief hearing, the HK SAR Court of Final Appeal on February 26 produced a supplementary explanation to the verdict,

---

[3]Mainland legal experts, who at that time were in Zhuhai attending a political and legal affairs group meeting of the Macao SAR Preparatory Committee, held a seminar regarding this matter on February 6, 1999. All of them had taken part in the drafting of the "Macao Special Administrative Region Basic Law" and the preparatory work for the Hong Kong SAR. Regarding the issue of the "court's constitutional jurisdiction" in the verdict, they pointed out: "According to the provisions of the Constitution, the National People's Congress is the country's highest organ of state power, and the NPC's legislative acts and decisions are not to be challenged or negated by any institution," and "Examining Hong Kong's laws for whether they comply with the Basic Law is the right of the NPC Standing Committee, not the right of the Court of Final Appeal." (Carried in "Mainland Legal Profession Personages Voice Opinions Concerning Verdict By HK SAR Court of Final Appeal," see *People's Daily*, February 8, 1999.) Here, the mainland experts explicitly pointed out that the SARs' courts were not empowered to implement judicial examinations of whether legislation by the National People's Congress and its Standing Committee were consistent with the Basic Law. But they did not clarify whether the SAR courts had the right to exercise judicial examination of legislation by the SAR's own legislative institutions or, in particular, whether local legislation conducted on matters within the scope of autonomy complied with judicial examinations implemented under the Basic Laws—a right that the SAR courts had in reality always exercised with regard to local legislation.

and explicitly pointed out: "The judicial jurisdiction of the SAR courts is derived from the Basic Law. Article 158 (1) of the Basic Law explains that the right of interpretation of the Basic Law pertains to the NPC Standing Committee. The power to interpret the Basic Law exercised by this Court when examining cases is derived from authorization from the NPC Standing Committee based on Articles 158 (2) and 158 (3)." It stated that the Hong Kong Court of Final Appeal, "in the verdict of January 29, 1999, did not query the power of the NPC Standing Committee to interpret the Basic Law vested in it by Article 158, and should the NPC Standing Committee conduct an interpretation of the Basic Law, the Special Region's court must ensure that the interpretation prevails." Any powers exercised by the National People's Congress and the NPC Standing Committee contingent on the provisions of the Basic Law and on procedures stipulated by the Basic Law are not to be queried.

In China's history, there have indeed never been any courts of law, including the Supreme Court or local institutions, that have dared to examine laws formulated by the highest organ state power, and so the intense reaction from mainland China's legal quarters was not at all surprising. The supplementary explanation by the Hong Kong regional Court of Final Appeal did clear up the doubts expressed in mainland legal circles and dispel a possible politico-legal conflict. However, it was unable to suppress the controversy over the verdict in Hong Kong itself. The HK SAR government, as the losing party in the lawsuit, obviously held to an understanding of the relevant article different from that of the SAR's Court of Final Appeal. The HK SAR government's main concern was that the verdict would all at once result in a sudden and substantial uptick in the number of qualified mainland residents coming to settle down in Hong Kong. Statistics based on investigations by the HK SAR Government indicated that in line with the Court of Final Appeal's verdict, the number of persons in Chinese mainland newly qualified for right of abode in Hong Kong would increase by 1.76 million (about 0.69 million among the first generation of persons; and after this first generation had resided continuously in HK for seven years or more, some 0.98 million persons among their progeny would qualify for abode in Hong Kong). Estimates by the HK SAR Government indicated: "Assimilation of these new immigrants will bring huge pressures to bear on Hong Kong. There is no way that Hong Kong's territorial and social resources will be able to cope with the educational, housing, medical and health, social welfare and other needs of this massive number of new immigrants. The social problems and consequences thus triggered will gravely affect Hong Kong's stability and prosperity and cannot be borne by Hong Kong."[4]

---

[4]Dong Jianhua. "Report on the Problems Encountered in the Implementation of the Relevant Provisions of the Basic Law of the Hong Kong Special Administrative Region to the Central People's Government of China," 1999-05-20.

10.2.3 The "NPC Interpretation"

The HK SAR government maintained that the relevant verdict by the Court of Final Appeal involved a matter of principle—how the Basic Law should be understood, and the management of mainland residents entering Hong Kong also involved Central/SAR relations. Hence, the HK SAR government decided to formally request the State Council for assistance, in the hope that the State Council would ask the NPC Standing Committee to produce interpretations of the Basic Law articles concerned in accordance with the relevant provisions of the Constitution and the Basic Law. The State Council accepted the HK SAR Government's request and officially, in the form of a proposal, put forward to the NPC Standing Committee a "Bill Requesting Interpretation of Article 22, Paragraph 4 and of Article 24, Paragraph 2, Item (3) of the Basic Law of the Hong Kong Special Administrative Region of the People's Republic of China." In accordance with the provisions of the Basic Law, the NPC Standing Committee, first of all, solicited the opinions of the NPC Standing Committee Hong Kong Special Administrative Region Basic Law Committee under it. The twelve mainland and Hong Kong members of that committee thereupon held discussions on the ways and means and contents of an "NPC Interpretation," and then submitted their opinions to the NPC Standing Committee. On June 26, 1999, the NPC Standing Committee formally discussed the State Council's Bill and decided to produce a legislative interpretation of the relevant articles of the Hong Kong Basic Law in accordance with the provisions of Article 67 Item (4) of the Constitution and Article 158, paragraph one of the Basic Law.

In the text of the Interpretation, the NPC Standing Committee stated that the questions involved in the bill presented by the Hong SAR Government and the State Council involved interpretation of the articles concerned of the Hong Kong Basic Law in the Hong Kong SAR Court of Final Appeal's verdict of January 29, 1999, and that the said relevant articles concerned matters administered by the Central Authorities as well as Central/SAR relations. However, the Court of Final Appeal, prior to producing its verdict, had not requested an interpretation from the NPC Standing Committee in accordance with the provisions of Article 158, paragraph three of the Hong Kong Basic Law, nor did the interpretation by the Court of Final Appeal comply with the original intent of the legislation. Hence, the NPC Standing Committee was now producing an interpretation of the provisions of Article 22, paragraph 4 and Article 24, paragraph two, Item (3) of the Basic Law.

The said Interpretation pointed out that the provisions in Article 22, paragraph four of the Hong Kong Basic Law referred to the circumstance that persons in all provinces, autonomous regions, and municipalities under the central government, including the children of Chinese nationality born in Chinese mainland to permanent residents of Hong Kong, who for whatever reason requested to enter the Hong Kong SAR were required, in accordance with the provisions of laws and administrative regulations, to apply to the relevant authorities in the locality where they were situated for fulfilling procedures of approval and were required to hold effective certifications issued by the relevant authorities to be able to enter the Hong Kong SAR. Otherwise, all mainland persons, including the children of Chinese nationality born in mainland China to permanent Hong Kong residents, who entered the Hong Kong SAR, would be doing so illegally if they did not fulfill the corresponding procedures of approval in accordance with the provisions of the relevant laws or administrative regulations of the state.

As regards the provisions of Article 24, paragraph two of the Hong Kong Basic Law: "The permanent residents of the Hong Kong Special Administrative Region consist of: (1) Chinese citizens born in Hong Kong before or after the establishment of the Hong Kong Special Administrative Region: (2) Chinese citizens who have ordinarily resided in Hong Kong for a continuous period of not less than seven years before or after the establishment of the Hong Kong Special Administrative Region; (3) Persons of Chinese nationality born outside Hong Kong to those residents listed in categories (1) and (2)." Here, the provision in Item (3) on "persons of Chinese nationality born outside Hong Kong to those residents listed in categories (1) and (2)" referred to persons who were born either before or after the establishment of the Hong Kong SAR, and who, when born, had either two parents or one parent who complied with the conditions stipulated in either Item (1) or Item (2) of Article 24 of the Basic Law of the Hong Kong Special Administrative Region of the People's Republic of China. In other words, both or one of the person's parents must already have legal permanent residency in the Hong Kong Region when the person concerned was born, and could not qualify as such at some later date.

The NPC Standing Committee further pointed out that the original legislative intent expounded in this interpretation and the legislative intent of other items in paragraph two of the Hong Kong Basic Law had, in reality, already been expressed in the "Opinion on the Implementation of paragraph two of Article 24 of the 'Basic Law of the Hong Kong Special Administrative Region of the People's Republic of China'" approved by the fourth plenary session of the National People's Congress Hong Kong Special Administrative Region Preparatory Committee and issued on August 10,1996, but that it had not drawn attention at the time. This further interpretation by the NPA Standing Committee of the stipulations of the two Basic Law articles was finally solving questions about the right of abode in Hong Kong of children in Chinese mainland born to Hong Kongers. If Hong Kong SAR courts needed to cite the relevant provisions of the Hong Kong Basic Law when reviewing relevant cases, they were to use this interpretation as the criterion.[5]

---

[5]"The NPC's Interpretation of Article 22, Paragraph 4 and Article 24, Paragraph 2 Item 3 of the Basic Law of on the Hong Kong Special Administrative Region of the People's Republic of China." Beijing: *Legal Daily*, 1999-06-27.

10.2.4   Follow-up Controversies and Problems of the "NPC Interpretation"

Although the NPC Standing Committee's interpretation of the Hong Kong Basic Law finally solved the legal issues concerning the right of abode in Hong Kong, related litigations kept cropping up and controversies were extremely acute. These were reflected in the following issues.

10.2.4.1   The Constitutional and Legal Interpretation System

China's Constitution vests the NPC Standing Committee with right of constitutional and legal interpretation, and the system exercised in Chinese mainland is one whereby the constitution and laws are interpreted by legislative organs, or in other words by a "legislative interpretation" system. Interpretations by legislative organs are final and authoritative. Not only must all administrative organs and social organizations abide by and implement them; judicial organs, too, when handling specific cases must also decide cases on the basis of the relevant interpretations. According to the "Resolution about Reinforcing the Legal Interpretation" passed on June 10, 1981 by the Fifth NPC Standing Committee, all the provisions of laws and decrees, the texts of which need to be further defined or supplemented, are to be interpreted or further defined by means of decrees issued by the NPC Standing Committee. All problems in laws and decrees specifically used in court adjudication work are to be interpreted by the Supreme People's Court. All problems in laws and decrees specifically employed in procuratorial work by the procuratorates are to be interpreted by the Supreme People's Procuratorate. If there are conflicts of principle between interpretations by the Supreme People's Court and the Supreme People's Procuratorate, these are to be submitted to the NPC Standing Committee for interpretation or decision. This means that if the Supreme People's Court has queries about the texts of laws per se, or if its interpretation differs from that of the Supreme People's Procuratorate, it is to apply to the NPC Standing Committee for final legal interpretation.

Article 43 of the Legislation Law of the People's Republic of China further confirms that all of the special committees of the State Council, Central Military Commission, Supreme People's Court, Supreme People's Procuratorate, and National People's Congress as well as the standing committees of the people's congresses of provinces, autonomous provinces, and municipalities directly under the central government may submit requests to the NPC Standing Committee for the conduct of legal interpretations.

It is obvious that in Chinese mainland, if judicial organs come across situations where legal provisions are unclear when they hear a case, they should temporarily halt the hearing and first seek a legal interpretation of the law or laws from the Supreme People's Court. If the Supreme People's Court is unable to clearly interpret the relevant laws, it may seek final legislative legislative interpretations from the NPC Standing Committee. This is China's "legislative interpretation" system. However, the NPC Standing Committee's interpretation of laws does not mean it hears cases on behalf of judiciary organs; it merely exercises the right of final interpretation of laws, not the right of final adjudication of cases. In Chinese mainland, people do not consider that the National People's Congress Standing Committee, by conducting final interpretations of laws, infringes upon the Supreme People's Court's right of final adjudication, because the NPC Standing Committee does not hear cases on behalf of the Supreme People's Court; it merely conducts final interpretations of laws, whereas judicial final adjudications are still conducted by the Supreme Court.

Moreover, if people's courts have queries about how to make specific use of laws and decrees when hearing cases, they may request that the Supreme People's Court produce an interpretation. These interpretations possess legal force. The scope of the legal judicial interpretation made by the Supreme People's Court is limited to issues of the specific use of laws and decrees during hearings, and these interpretations may not run counter to the original intent of the laws and decrees. Relative to legislative interpretations, judiciary interpretations are of an auxiliary and less important nature while the former are of first importance.[6] In fact, legislative interpretations are not often used and constitutional interpretations even less so. There have never been cases of the Supreme People's Court applying to the NPC Standing Committee for interpretation of an article of law based on the needs of hearing a specific case. Conversely, the NPC Standing Committee does not base its interpretations of laws on hearings of specific cases, and that gives it greater latitude for interpretations.[7] that is, where the difference lies between legislative and judiciary organs. Legislative organs, like administrative organs, exercise their powers actively and on their own initiative, whereas judiciary organs adhere to the principle of "leaving things alone if there are no complaints," and exercise their judiciary powers passively. If final interpretations of laws were to be exercised by judicial organs, they would similarly morph into "passive interpretations." That, actually, describes the law interpretation system under the Common Law.

Under the Common Law system, the power of final judicial adjudication and the powers of constitutional and legal interpretation are all vested in courts of law. Under that system, after legislative organs have formulated laws they no longer have any say in them and the fate of the laws rests in the hands of courts of law. Due to the strict exercise of judicial independence, judicial organs do not solicit the opinions of legislative or administrative organs if they require interpretations of laws when handling cases. If legislative organs disagree with the interpretations by courts of law, they may amend or even repeal or reformulate the relevant laws, but they do not interpret them. That is, the system for legal interpretations under the Common Law. Under British rule, too, the Hong Kong courts of law enjoyed very limited powers of legal interpretation, and the system's basic spirit was the same as that practiced in other Common Law regions. Based on Hong Kong's special circumstances, this

---

[6]Zhang Zhiming. "China's Law Interpretation System." carried in Liang Zhiping. *Problems of Interpreting Laws*. Beijing: Law Press China, 1998, p. 165.

[7]Xu Chongde. *The Constitution of China (Revised)*. Beijing: China Renmin University Press, 1996, p. 210.

system of legal interpretation was retained after Hong Kong returned to mainland China.

The problem faced today is that the HK SAR's Basic Law has been formulated by the National People's Congress of Chinese mainland, which traditionally practices the Continental Law, whereas the Basic Law serves the HK SAR, which hews to the Common Law. When handling interpretations of Basic Law issues, legislators are confronted with a dilemma. They must take mainland China's legal interpretation system into consideration and at the same time keep in mind the legal interpretation system under Hong Kong's Common Law. The ultimate compromise is the provision in Article 158 of the Basic Law, which stipulates that in accordance with the provisions of China's Constitution, the power of interpretation of the Basic Law, like that of all other laws in China, is vested in the NPC Standing Committee. This brings the Basic Law in conformity with the mainland's law interpretation system and manifests the "one country" requirement. Yet, at the same time, the legal interpretation system under Hong Kong's Basic Law is also retained, since the NPC Standing Committee authorizes Hong Kong SAR's courts of law to interpret provisions of the Basic Law when they hear cases. But if a provision to be interpreted has to do with matters administered by the Central People's Government or with Central/SAR relations, the HK SAR Court of Final Appeal must ask the NPC Standing Committee to come up with an interpretation of the relevant provision before the HK SAR court produces a non-appealable final judgment. And, when citing the said provision, the Hong Kong SAR court of law must use the NPC Standing Committee's interpretation as the criterion. Previously made verdicts, however, are not affected by this compromise. It is evident that this legal interpretation system was carefully designed to merge the mainland's system of legislative institutions interpreting laws with Hong Kong's system of courts of law interpreting laws, and thereby simultaneously satisfying both the "one country" and "two systems" requirements. This is a new and unique disposition for a constitutional system.

10.2.4.2 Did the NPC Standing Committee Overturn a Judgment by the Hong Kong SAR Court of Final Appeal?

A widely circulated but erroneous view maintains that an interpretation of the Basic Law produced by the NPC Standing Committee overturned a judgment by the Hong Kong SAR Court of Final Adjudication. The fact is that, first of all, the NPC Standing Committee's interpretation of the Basic Law during the case concerned on January 29, 1999 did not affect the right of abode in the Hong Kong SAR obtained by the litigant as adjudged by the Hong Kong Court of Final Appeal. In other words, the interpretation did not affect the rights and duties conferred on the parties concerned in accordance with the judgment, nor was the interpretation retroactive. It was effective only for matters which would take place in the future, i.e., it was effective only for mainlanders other than the parties concerned in the case. The NPC interpretation would serve as the criterion for whether mainlanders eventually coming to settle down in Hong Kong complied with the conditions set by the provisions in Article 24, paragraph two, Item (3). Hence, it could not be said that the NPC Standing Committee overturned the Hong Kong Court of Final Appeal's original judgment. That the handling by the NPC Standing Committee did not simplistically impose a uniform solution on the matter showed, from one aspect, that the Standing Committee honored the Hong Kong SARs' power of final adjudication.

Some persons maintain the NPC Standing Committee's act of interpreting the Basic Law infringed on the power of final adjudication enjoyed by the Hong Kong SAR. This view is incorrect. As stated earlier, under the Common Law system the power of final interpretation and the power of final adjudication are combined, and both are exercised by the highest court (of final instance). However, in China's system of law, the power of final interpretation and the power of final adjudication are not combined; they are not exercised in a unified manner by one single institution but are exercised by two institutions, respectively. According to the provisions of China's Constitution, the power of final interpretation of laws is exercised by the NPC Standing Committee, while China's power of final adjudication is exercised by the Supreme People's Court.[8]

Similarly, as regards the matter of interpreting the HK SAR Basic Law, the mechanism laid down in the Basic Law is, as said earlier, that the "power of final interpretation" of the Basic Law is vested in the NPC Standing Committee, but the "power of final adjudication" rests with the Hong Kong Court of Final Appeal. Separating the "power of final interpretation" and the "power of final adjudication" is, on the one hand, consistent with China's legal system and also a combination of "one country" and "two systems." It is precisely in this sense that the NPC Standing Committee did not interfere in the SAR court's power of final appeal, since it is not a "court of final instance" for the SAR's Court of Final Appeal. The NPC Standing Committee merely exercised the Basic Law's power of final interpretation; it does not replace the SAR court of law in the hearing of cases. The power of final appeal (power of final adjudication) is still exercised by the SAR court; hence, the NPC Standing Committee does not interfere in the Hong Kong SAR court's judicial power of final appeal. The NPC Standing Committee is fully cognizant of the importance of maintaining Hong Kong's judicial independence and certainly will not interfere in the Hong Kong SAR's judicial power of final appeal as stipulated in the Hong Kong SAR's Basic Law.

Of course, under the Common Law system, the verdicts of courts of law may serve as precedents, and in the eventual handling of similar cases, courts of law should honor previous judgments. This is the *stare decisis* principle. However, if a legislative organ formulates or amends a law that involves issues in a case and changes the rules for relevant issues previously set by courts of law pursuant to the courts' own judgments, then the courts of law must honor the law formulated or amended by the legislative organ when dealing with future cases of the same category. This is also a principle of the common law, namely the principle that "statutory laws supersede case laws," and situations in which a statutory law replaces a case law may occur in any region

---

[8]*Constitution of the People's Republic of China*, Articles 67 and 127.

or country that practices the Common Law.[9] Hence, the NPC Standing Committee's conducting an interpretation of the Basic Law upon a request from the State Council should be seen as a normal occurrence, either under the mainland's system of law or under the Common Law. The fact that the NPC Standing Committee handled the matter the way it did instead of simplistically imposing a uniform solution shows that it respected the HK SAR's power of final adjudication.

Under the systems of "one country, two systems" and "one country multiple laws," China still has only one institution that exercises the power of final interpretation of laws, namely the NPC Standing Committee. However, it now already has three institutions which exercise the power final adjudication, i.e., the mainland's court of last instance, which is the Supreme People's Court situated in Beijing, and two courts of final appeal situated in the Hong Kong and Macao SARs, respectively. There are no relations of administrative subordination among these three courts of last instance (final appeal), and each exercises its own power of final adjudication in its respective jurisdiction.

Actually, setups in which the final power of interpretation and the final power of adjudication are exercised by different institutions are not rare in the world. Countries on the European continent do not subscribe to the British- and American-type "judicial superiority theorem"; they usually separate the final power of interpretation and the final power of adjudication, and have these powers exercised by different institutions. In countries on the European continent, the power of final interpretation of laws is usually exercised by constitutional courts (or constitutional committees) while the power of final adjudication is exercised by ordinary supreme (high) courts. In Germany, for example, in accordance with the provisions of the German Federal Constitution and in response to requests from the federal government, various states and one-third of the members of the Bundestag are empowered to examine the laws of the Federation and various states to determine whether these violate the federal constitution or laws; and if courts of law at various levels find that federal laws or the laws of certain states violate the federal constitution when they are examining specific cases, they must submit the law or laws concerned to a federal constitutional court for examination and judgment before they go on with hearing the cases.[10] The only difference is in the names of the institutions in various countries, which exercise the power of final interpretation of the laws. Some are called constitutional courts; others are called constitutional commissions or committees. In China, it is the NPC Standing Committee which exercises that power. In China's Taiwan, it is the Council of Grand Justices of the Judicial Yuan that interprets laws and the constitution. According to the current "Constitution of the Republic of China" [Taiwan] and its judicial system, when courts of law at all levels in the Taiwan region including the supreme court and the supreme administrative court hear cases, they may interpret ordinary laws, but if they find that a law is in violation of the constitution or that the interpretations of the relevant law by the supreme court and the supreme adminis-

---

[9]Wesley-Smith P. *The Sources of Hong Kong Law*. Hong Kong: Hong Kong University Press, 1994, p. 33.

[10]Li Hongxi. *The Theory of Judicial Review*. Taipei: National Taiwan University, 1990, p. 265.

trative court do not coincide, they must temporarily suspend the hearing and apply to the Council of Grand Justices of the Judicial Yuan for an interpretation of the relevant provisions of the constitution, or for a judgment on whether the relevant law or laws violate the constitution, or produce a unified interpretation of the law(s) in dispute, and only then can they hear the case on the basis of the above acts. Although the names of the institutions which exercise the power of final interpretation of laws differ, their *raisons d'être* are the same.

There will be an in-depth discussion of the matter of constitutional reviews in the next chapter.

10.2.4.3   Analysis of the Nature of the NPC Standing Committee's Interpretation of the Basic Law

Some people may think that what the NPC Standing Committee is doing here is not legislating laws anew or amending laws but that it interprets laws. However, because the way legislatures interpret law is unfamiliar to Common Law regions, people living under the Common Law do not understand it and reject this way of interpreting laws. In 1902, the British House of Lords (in reality Britain's Supreme Court) examined a case, and the Chief Justice Lord Halsbury voluntarily recused himself because he had drafted the law involved in the case. He said he noted that the worst person to choose for interpreting a case law is the one who wrote it in the first place, because that person is quite likely to "confuse his intent" in drafting the law with the connotations of the words he actually uses.[11] This remark indicates the exclusionary nature of the Common Law system as regards legislative interpretation.

Prior to the "NPC Interpretation," there were indeed Hong Kongers who suggested that the NPC had best amend the Basic Law and further define its legal terminology rather than use the method of interpreting laws to solve problems. However, the premise to amending a law is that an error exists in the law per se, whereas the relevant provisions of the Basic Law contained no errors. And so, amending the Basic Law was not feasible and the only recourse was to interpret the law. Actually, the NPC Standing Committee's interpretation in 1996 and 1998 on the matter of implementing the Nationality Law [of the People's Republic of China] in the Hong Kong and Macao SARs was a very good example of mainland legislative interpretation, yet no one at the time raised any objections to the content and method of this legislative interpretation.[12]

---

[11]Guan Shuxin. "Legislators Are the Worst Choice for Interpreters of the Law," carried in *A Frank Discussion on the Law*, Hong Kong Bar Association, 2001.

[12]On May 15, 1996, the 19th Session of the Eighth National People's Congress Standing Committee passed the "Explanation Concerning Some Problems in the Implementation of the Nationality Law of the People's Republic of China in the Hong Kong Special Administrative Region." Taking into consideration Hong Kong's historical background and current realities, this explanation adopted flexible methods, which satisfactorily resolved difficult problems engendered by the implementation of China's Nationality Law in the Hong Kong SAR. On September 29, 1998, the 6th Session of the Ninth National People's Congress Standing Committee produced the "Explanation Concerning

The legislative interpretation issue involves China's constitutional system. Under China's Constitution, the NPC Standing Committee is the permanent body of the nation's highest organ of state power as well as the body that exercises the country's legislative power. In China's constitutional theory, the power to interpret laws is a power subsidiary to the power of legislation, and the interpretation of the laws is one of the major functions of the NPC Standing Committee as a legislative organ. Hence, its acts of interpreting laws are legislative in nature, and should be regarded as a kind of special legislative action. This is the same as some institutions in Chinese mainland which work out detailed rules for implementation after laws have been formulated, the difference being that the Basic Laws' "detailed rules of implementation" are formulated by the NPC Standing Committee and that these formulations are not completed once and for all but take place many times over diverse issues. Due to the political nature of the Constitution and constitutional laws, interpretations of the Constitution or constitutional laws differ from the interpretations of ordinary laws, and in no country in the world are they regarded as purely judiciary activities. As H. Kelsen said, it is more correct to see interpretations of the Constitution as legislative acts rather than as purely judiciary acts.[13]

In terms of their methods and procedures, current interpretations have also adhered to the general legislative procedures of the NPC Standing Committee. The State Council put forward a bill to the NPC Standing Committee requesting interpretation of the (Hong Kong?) Basic Law, whereupon the NPC Standing Committee's Council of Chairmen held a meeting to decide whether to accept the State Council's bill. The Council of Chairmen examined the bill and deemed it both necessary and appropriate for the NPC Standing Committee to conduct an interpretation of the relevant provisions of the Basic Law in order to ensure its implementation. Hence, the Council of Chairmen decided to submit the State Council's bill to the General Assembly of the NPC Standing Committee for discussion. On June 22, 1999, the Council of Chairmen submitted the bill, together with an explanation, to the 10th meeting of the Ninth National People's Congress Standing Committee for examination. The 10th meeting of the Ninth National People's Congress Standing Committee conducted a careful examination, solicited the opinion of the NPC Standing Committee's Hong Kong Special Administrative Region Basic Law Committee and, on June 22, 1999 approved the interpretation of the relevant provisions of the Basic Law.[14] Hence, as regards the process as a whole, the NPC Standing Committee's act of interpreting the Basic Law should be seen as a special act of legislation.

The Legislation Law of the People's Republic of China passed by the third meeting of the Ninth National People's Congress on March 15, 2000 has also specifically stipulated the procedures and effects of interpretations of the law, and has confirmed

---

Some Problems in the Implementation of the Nationality Law in the Macao Special Administrative Region" and made similar special dispositions regarding the nationality issue of Macao residents after Macao's return to China.

[13]Li Hongxi. *The Theory of Judicial Review.* Taipei: National Taiwan University, 1990, p. 265.

[14]Beijing, *People's Daily*, June 23, 1999 and June 27, 1999.

that interpretations of laws by the National People's Congress Standing Committee possess equal force as the laws themselves.[15]

10.2.4.4 May a Chief Executive Ask the State Council to Request Interpretations of Law by the NPC Standing Committee?

Article 158 of the Hong Kong Basic Law authorizes only the SAR Court of Final Appeal to seek interpretations of relevant provisions of the Basic Law by the NPC Standing Committee when reasons for doing so emerge as stipulated by law; it does not authorize the Chief Executive of the Hong Kong SAR to do so. However, if he conducts a comprehensive survey of the entire process of the interpretation of the Basic Law in question, the Chief Executive of the SAR does not violate the Basic Law's provisions. According to Article 43 of the Basic Law, the Chief Executive of the Hong Kong Special Administrative Regions is the head of the Hong Kong Special Administrative Region and represents the Region. That is to say, the Chief Executive is not only the head of the Region's administrative departments but also the head of the entire Special Administrative Region and may represent any department in the Region. This is different from the structure of local government in mainland China where a provincial governor is only the head of the province's administrative departments and may not represent all of the province's institutions.

Article 43 of the Basic Law also stipulates that the Chief Executive of the Hong Kong Special Administrative Region is legally accountable to the Central People's Government and to the Hong Kong Special Administrative Region. And, Article 48 stipulates that among the powers and functions exercised by the SAR Chief Executive, the responsibility for implementing the Basic Law as well as other laws which in accordance with the Basic Law apply in the Hong Kong Special Administrative Region. Hence, the Chief Executive is to report on his work to the Central People's Government, brief the Central People's Government on the SAR's implementation of the Basic Law, and be responsible to the Central People's Government. The matter in question was a work report by the SAR Chief Executive to the State Council regarding a major affair, which took place in the course of the implementation of the Basic Law. As is indicated by the title "Report on Seeking Assistance from the Central People's Government in Solving Problems Encountered in the Implementation of the Provisions Concerned of the Basic Law of the Hong Kong Special Administrative Region of the People's Republic of China," this was a normal act of reporting on work performed and of seeking Central Government help in solving problems which he himself could not solve.[16] As for the SAR Government's suggestion in the report about an interpretation of the Basic Law that was merely a suggestion, and it was entirely up to the State Council to decide whether it would accept the suggestion and whether it would submit a bill to the NPC Standing Committee requesting interpretation of the Basic Law. Hence, the Chief Executive was merely making a normal

---

[15] *Legislative Law of the People's Republic of China*, Article 47.

[16] Beijing, *People's Daily*, June 23, 1999.

report on his work to the Central Government to whom he was directly responsible. And only after the State Council had studied the "report" sent up by the SAR Chief Executive and felt that the matter was indeed of major import did it, on its own initiative, propose and submit the bill on interpreting the provisions concerned in the Basic Law. Thus, in a certain sense, that National Congress interpretation of the Basic Law was a voluntary act by the NPC Standing Committee made upon the request of the State Council.

Strictly speaking, from the perspective of law, whether or not the SAR Chief Executive proposed an interpretation of the Basic Law played no decisive role on whether or not the People's Congress ultimately interpreted the Basic Law. The reason is that even if the SAR Chief Executive's Report or proposal had not existed and no person or institution had made any proposal, the NPC Standing Committee still had the power, based on the provisions of Article 158, Chapter One of the Basic Law, to interpret the Basic Law on its own initiative, without its interpretation being premised on a proposal by any institution or individual, because the Basic Law does not place any limitations on the NPC Standing Committee's power to make interpretations. Nor were the NPC Standing Committee's interpretations of the Basic Law based on the presence of lawsuits in courts of law. Professor Yash Ghai of Hong Kong University has conducted in-depth expositions and studies on this matter.[17]

10.2.4.5 Remedial Measures for Judgments of Final Instance: Other Countries' Experiences

In reality, situations where judgments by supreme courts are amended or even changed by means of legislation due to legislative or administrative organs disagreeing with a certain supreme court judgment are quite common in other countries. Envisage a final verdict made by a supreme court in some country or region for which there is no possibility of appeal because that court is already the highest and most final. Assuming that the verdict is problematic and the emergence of the problem or problems is due not to corruption or abuse of law or other factors outside of the law, and that the problem is a normal and permissible "judiciary error," or that the chief justice indeed entertains a different opinion, or that the administrative and legislative institutions hold different views about the same matter—which situations are also quite normal and may occur in any country or region. What should be done when such circumstances emerge?

One should of course uphold judicial independence and must not overturn supreme court judgments. There is no question about that. However, are there any remedial measures for future cases, and how should one go about such remedial measures? I once probed this matter with William Van Alstyne, the well-known American constitutionalist and professor at the Duke University School of Law. He said two

---

[17] Profound discussions on this matter have been published by Professor Yash Ghai of Hong Kong University. See Ghai Y. *Hong Kong's New Constitutional Order*. Hong Kong University Press, 1997, p. 193.

remedial measures are possible when such things occur. One is for the Supreme Court to select and try another identical or similar case and make a new judgment, and thereby amend the previous "problematic" judgment. The other way is to change the norms established by the Supreme Court's judgment by means of congressional legislation or even by amendments to the constitution. Of course, such legislation could be effective only for future matters and would not affect the legal force of the original judgment. Both of these methods have been applied in the United States.[18]

There have also been frequent cases of the United States Supreme Court voluntarily rectifying problems or errors in previous judgments by means of making fresh judgments. People do not allege that other institutions are intervening in the judiciary, since this happens because the Supreme Court itself becomes aware of the existence of problems, or changes its mind. The best-known example is the one in 2000 during the U.S. presidential elections, when spearheaded by five "conservative" judges, the U.S. Supreme Court changed its consistent stand, intervened in state electoral affairs, repealed a judgment by the Florida Supreme Court, ordered the termination of Florida's manual recounting of votes, and thereby put George W. Bush in the White House. Al Gore, nursing his grievance, had to concede defeat and his political career suffered a major setback. That fact is that the Supreme Court, headed by those five conservative judges, had never previously intervened in state or local electoral affairs, and had maintained that such elections, including state elections for federal presidents, came under the jurisdiction of states and localities that the federal institutions including the federal Supreme Court ought not to intervene, and that the states' supreme courts should be the highest institutions—i.e., the courts of final appeal or instance—in terms of handling any controversies in such elections. The other four liberal judges had previously always maintained that the Supreme Court could and should intervene in such elections. Most interestingly, in this unprecedented "Bush v. Gore" case, each and every judge reversed his or her consistently held stand. The five conservative judges suddenly became quite "liberal" and announced that the federal court was empowered to intervene in state elections, while the four liberal judges all at once grew quite "conservative" and insisted that state elections fell outside the jurisdiction of the Supreme Court. It is obvious that despite the U.S. judiciary and judges being independent in terms of their structure and systems and being free of what we usually refer to as "structural problems" or "institutional problems," the judges themselves are subject to various influences and have their own political inclinations which affect the courts' verdicts. This case is a typical example of a supreme court changing its previous judgments by means of a new judgment.

As for "altercations" among the U.S. federal administrative institutions, the federal Congress and the Supreme Court, these defy enumeration. If federal administrative institutions or the federal Congress disagrees with judgments by the Supreme Court, they will unceremoniously root for the amendment of existing laws or the formulation of new laws. And, if the Supreme Court is dissatisfied with amendments of laws by Congress or with a new legislation, it will conduct a tit for tat review of some

---

[18]Conversation between the author and Prof. William Van Alstyne of Duke University (U.S.) on March 28, 2001.

new case and, with a new judgment, announce that Congress's latest legislation violates the constitution and is therefore null and void. After several such clashes, the ultimate solution is to resort to a constitutional amendment and resolve the issue by getting the general public to speak up and express its opinions on amending the constitution. During such constitutional amendments, the public may support the Supreme Court, or may support Congress and the administrative institutions. And the outcome may be the "correction" of a "problematic" Supreme Court judgment, whereas the administrative and legislative organs must also run the risk of being criticized by public consensus for having affected judicial independence.

Take, for example, a well-known case of burning the national flag. In the 1989 Texas v. Johnson case, by a 5 to 4 count, the nine justices of the Supreme Court passed a verdict asserting that the act of a protestor burning an American flag outside a Republican national convention in 1984 was protected by the First Amendment, and it thereby repealed legislation by the state of Texas. The Supreme Court maintained that burning the flag was an overt and open act of a political nature, and the government should not prohibit the expression, whether verbal or otherwise, of some point of view simply because the general public found that view offensive and was outraged by it, even though the act had to do with the national flag. In terms of its wording, the First Amendment would seem to protect freedom of speech in the narrow sense. However, we have felt for a long time that it protects not only verbal and written language but also other forms of manifesting freedom of thought. Texas maintained that prohibiting the burning of the national flag was intended to uphold peace and order and to protect the national flag, which symbolizes the nation and national unity. But the Supreme Court rejected this claim. The court's judgment sorely displeased the American government. It immediately initiated and passed the "Flag Protection Act of 1989," which defined deliberately setting fire to and desecrating the national flag as a crime. However, in the 1990 United States v. Eichman case, the Supreme Court once again confirmed that any act of burning the national flag was protected by the First Amendment that the Flag Protection Act of 1989 was unconstitutional, and therefore null and void.[19]

This Supreme Court judgment prompted a decision by the US Congress to propose a bill for amending the Constitution and defining acts of burning and desecrating the national flag as a crime under the Constitution. If this constitutional amendment was passed, it would authorize Congress to approve a law that would prohibit burning or in any other way desecrating the national flag. Starting in 1989, the U.S. Congress made consistent efforts to pass a constitutional amendment that would prohibit the burning and desecration of the U.S. national flag. In 2000, the amendment was successfully approved in Congress by a 305 to 124 vote, but ended up again in failure with four votes short in the Senate. During a more recent instance on July 17, 2001, Congress passed the amendment by 298 to 125 votes and sent the case to the Senate for approval. Previous experience has always shown that Senate has refused to pass such constitutional amendments and scotched all such attempts on the

---

[19]Van Alstyne W.W. *First Amendment: Cases and Materials (Second Edition)*. Westbury, New York: The Foundation Press, Inc., 1995, p. 315.

invariable contention that they violated the First Amendment's provisions regarding the protection of citizens' freedom of speech. If a constitutional amendment is to, finally, go into effect in the United States, it must obtain the support of two-thirds of the representatives in the Congress and Senate, respectively, and then must be approved by 38 of the 50 states. No doubt, the U.S. Congress will continue striving for constitutional amendments to protect the national flag.[20]

Thus, if we look at the "NPC Interpretations" from this perspective, we do not feel they are such a serious problem. Although they are "interpretations of the law" rather than legislations or amendments of the law, all are essentially the same, as discussed above. It always takes much wrangling and argumentation, and time before truths are genuinely identified and recognized.

10.2.4.6   Other Relevant Cases

On July 20, 2001, the Hong Kong SAR Court of Final Appeal again produced two judgments on the right of Chinese mainland residents to reside in Hong Kong. The first concerned the right of abode in Hong Kong of children born to mainlanders located in the Hong Kong SAR. The subject, in this case, was a three-year-old boy named Zhuan Fengyuan, born in Hong Kong in September 1997. At the time, his parents both held two-way permits as nonresidents. After giving birth to Zhuang Fengyuan in Hong Kong, they had no choice but to return to Chinese mainland since they were not permanent Hong Kong residents, but they left Zhuang Fengyuan in the care of his grandfather in Hong Kong. From then on the child stayed in Hong Kong. Before a year was up, however, the Hong Kong government decided to extradite him to the mainland, whereupon his parents filed a lawsuit. During the hearings at the preliminary trial and appellate court, the judges ruled in favor of the appellants, but the Hong Kong government disagreed and eventually filed an appeal with the Hong Kong SAR Court of Final Appeal. After examining the case, the five justices at this court rejected the appeal, upheld the original judgment of the Hong Kong High Court's Court of Appeals, and unanimously ruled that Zhuang Fengyang had the right to live in Hong Kong and to obtain permanent residency there.[21]

The basis for the judgment of the SAR Court of Final Appeal was Article 24 of the Basic Law. Article 24 clearly stipulates: "… permanent residents of the Hong Kong Special Administrative Region shall be: (1) Chinese citizens born in Hong Kong before or after the establishment of the Hong Kong Special Administrative Region; …" The justices maintained that, despite Zhuang Fengyuan's parents not being permanent Hong Kong residents when he was born, both were Chinese citizens and this, according to Article 24, did not affect Zhuang Fengyuan's right of abode in Hong Kong since the wording of the provisions of Article 24 merely mentioned place of birth and did not say whether the child's father or mother had to have right

---

[20]*Los Angeles Times*, 18 July 2001.

[21]The case Director of Hong Kong Immigration Department v. Zhuang Fengyuan (Chong Feng-yuen), Court of Final Appeal Civil Lawsuit No. 26 of the Year 2000.

of residency. The Court of Final Appeal also maintained that the Article concerned a matter within the Region's scope of autonomy, and there was no need to seek an interpretation of law from the NPC Standing Committee.

After this judgment was made, the Hong Kong government said it honored the tribunal's judgment. The government's spokesman held that the Court of Final Appeal, in its judgment on the Zhuang Fengyuan case, had clearly stated that it accepted the constraints in the NPC Standing Committee's interpretation of the Basic Law. As adjudication on the case had already concluded, the SAR government would accept and implement the judgment concerned. As for the opinions of the NPC Standing Committee's Legislative Affairs Commission, the SAR government stated it would study the latter's opinions and would carefully consider these opinions when handling future cases. Thereupon, in accordance with this judgment, Zhuang Fengyuan at once obtained the right of abode and permanent residency in Hong Kong.

On the Central Authorities' part, due to the fact that said judgment touched upon the application of the "Interpretation Regarding Chapter Four of Article 22 and Item (3) of Chapter Two of Article 24 of the Basic Law of the Hong Kong Special Administrative Region of the People's Republic of China," the spokesman of the Commission of Legislative Affairs of the NPC Standing Committee (NPC Standing Committee CLA) voiced the following opinion: We have remarked that since the NPC Standing Committee produced an interpretation of the relevant provisions of the Hong Kong Basic Law on June 26, 1999, the Hong Kong SAR courts have, in judgments that involve cases of the right of abode in Hong Kong, on numerous occasions stressed that the interpretations made by the NPC Standing Committee regarding the Basic Law are binding upon the courts of law of the Hong Kong SAR and have served as grounds for judgments on some cases. However, the judgment on July 20 by the Hong Kong SAR Court of Final Appeal on the Zhuang Fengyuan (Chong Feng-yuen) case is not quite the same as the relevant interpretation by the NPC Standing Committee, and we express concern about this.[22]

Hong Kong has long had a serious problem with mainland women coming to Hong Kong to give birth to children. The situation was extremely grave before Hong Kong's return to China, and although it improved somewhat after Hong Kong's return, the Hong Kong government is still worried that the above judgment might trigger illegal immigration of more pregnant women from the mainland to bear children in Hong Kong, increasing the pressure on Hong Kong's local medical services, welfare, and education. According to statistics from the Immigration Department, in the 43 months from July 1, 1997 to January 31, 2001, as many as 1991 Chinese citizens were born in Hong Kong, some of whom were born to mainland Chinese citizens legally in Hong Kong and others to Chinese citizens illegally in Hong Kong. The Hong Kong SAR stated its intention to strengthen cooperation with mainland public security organs in preventing the emergence of large-scale illegal entries into Hong Kong to bear children.

---

[22]Beijing, *The People's Daily*, 22 July 2001, p. 2.

At the legal level, the NPC Standing Committee's CLA stated that the said judgment was not quite the same as the NPC Standing Committee's nterpretation of Article 22, paragraph 4 and of Article 24, paragraph two, Item (3) of the Basic Law of the Hong Kong Special Administrative Region of the People's Republic of China. The said Interpretation had pointed out that the first three items of Article 24, paragraph two of the Hong Kong SAR Basic Law stipulated that permanent residents of the Hong Kong SAR consisted of (1) Chinese citizens born in Hong Kong before or after the establishment of the Hong Kong Special Administrative Region; (2) Chinese citizens who had ordinarily resided in Hong Kong for a continuous period of not less than seven years before or after the establishment of the Hong Kong Special Administrative region; and (3) Persons of Chinese nationality born outside Hong Kong of those residents listed in categories (1) and (2). Here, the stipulation in Item (3) on "persons of Chinese nationality born outside Hong Kong of those residents listed in categories (1) and (2)" meant that whether the child concerned was born before or after the establishment of the Hong Kong SAR, one or both of that child's parents had to conform with the provisions of items (1) or (2) of paragraph two of Article 24 of the Basic Law of the People's Republic of China. It was evident that the NPC Standing Committee was emphasizing that both or at least one of the parents must already be permanent Hong Kong residents if the child was to obtain the right of abode in Hong Kong. Apparently, the SAR Court of Final Appeal had a different understanding of this matter. As to whether the Hong Kong SAR would seek to amend the Basic Law so as to fundamentally solve the problem—that would be determined by the attitudes of the SAR Government and the NPC Standing Committee.

On the same day, in the case of Tan Yaran, Chen Weihua, and Xie Xiaoyi v. Director of Immigration, four out of five chief justices adjudged that Tan Yaran, Chen Weihua, and Xie Xiaoyi did not have the right of abode in Hong Kong. All of the latter were children adopted through legal means in Chinese mainland by permanent Hong Kong residents. The parents disagreed with the High Court's verdict against giving their children the right of abode, and appealed to the Court of Final Appeal for the right abode for the children in accordance with Article 24 of the Basic Law. After deliberation, the Court of Final Appeal held that Item (3) of Article 24 of the Basic Law specified that the term "born ... to" in the sentence "children of Chinese nationality born outside of Hong Kong to Chinese citizens" indicated that these children had to be biological offspring and could by no means be interpreted as including adopted children. This stipulation focused on the time of birth and indicated that the relationship was to be biological that it did not include parent–child relations resulting from adoption because at the time of birth no relationship existed yet between the persons and the adoptive parents.[23]

On January 10, 2002, the Hong Kong SAR Court of Final Appeal put a close to a series of cases on right of abode in Hong Kong, which had consumed four years and caused a considerable uproar. In that series of lawsuits which involved some 5000

---

[23]Case of Tan Yaran, Chen Weihua and Xie Xiaoyi v. Director of Immigration, FACC20/2000, FACC21/2000. The HK SAR government, based on humanitarian considerations, later exercised its powers of discretion and accorded Tan Yaran the right of abode in Hong Kong.

persons, the Court of Final Appeal decided that around one thousand could stay in Hong Kong and obtain right of abode, or had "reasonable expectations" of staying on in Hong Kong. As regards these "reasonable expectations" cases, the Hong Kong Government's Immigration Department once again reviewed the cases and handled them by exercising its powers of discretion. The other four thousand or so persons would have to return to Chinese mainland and reapply for resettlement in Hong Kong through legal channels.[24]

We can see from these judgments that the Court of Final Appeal was functioning independently when reviewing these cases. The government won some of the cases, and lost others. The Court of Final Appeal was not deliberately ingratiating itself with either the SAR government or the Central Government. The Court of Final Appeal's understanding of the Basic Law could have differed from that of the SAR government or the Central Authorities, but that was quite natural. Meanwhile, if the SAR government or the Central Authorities disagreed with judgments by the Court of Final Appeal, they could seek interpretations of the Basic Law or amendments of the relevant provisions.

10.3 Desecrating the National and Regional Flags

10.3.1 Basic Facts of the Case

The Hong Kong Special Administrative Region v. Wu Gongshao and Li Jianrun case concerning the desecration of the national flag took place at a public demonstration activity organized by the Hong Kong Alliance in Support of Patriotic Democratic Movements of China on January 1, 1998.[25] This previously approved demonstration included a march from the Victoria Park to the Hong Kong Government Central Government Offices on Lower Albert Road. During the march, someone saw the two respondents (defendants) waving a besmirched flag of the People's Republic of China and a besmirched flag of the Hong Kong SAR. At the end of the march, they tied the two flags to the balustrade of the Hong Kong Government Central Government Offices. Both flags were subsequently removed by the police, who found that they had been severely defiled. A circular section had been cut from the national flag, the largest of the five stars on it had been daubed with black ink, the star-shaped design had been perforated, and the obverse side of the flag was similarly damaged. The four smaller stars of the star-shaped design had also had the word "shame" scrawled on them in black ink, and on the obverse side, a black cross had been smeared on the lowest of the four smaller stars in the central section. Meanwhile, the flag of the SAR had a piece torn out, depriving it of part of its bauhinia design. The remaining

---

[24]Chen Shaobo. "'Right-of-Hong Kong-Abode Fracas' Lawsuit Costing 27 Million Concludes," *People's Daily*, January 11, 2002.

[25]CACC563/1998, the High Court of Hong Kong Special Administrative Region; FACC4/1999, the Final Court of Hong Kong Special Administrative Region.

portion had a black cross smeared on it, and three of the remaining four red stars in the design also bore black crosses. The word "shame" had also been smeared on the flag in black ink. Another Chinese character above it was indecipherable due to part of the flag being torn away. The flag's obverse side had also suffered similar damage. During the march, two of the defendants had shouted the slogan. "Set up a democratic China." It was reported that one of the defendants had said to the media: "Tearing and smearing the national and regional flags are acts meant to express dissatisfaction with and opposition to non-popularly elected rulers."

The SAR government brought lawsuits against the two defendants for desecrating the national and regional flags as well as for violating Article 7 of the National Flag Ordinance and Article 7 of the Regional Flag Ordinance, respectively. The magistrate court convicted the defendants, who thereupon filed appeals with the High Court's Court of First Instance. With both parties together filing appeals, the case was transferred to the High Court's Court of Appeals on December 8, 1998. The Court of Appeals allowed the appeals and annulled the guilty verdicts against the two defendants on March 23, 1999.[26] The Hong Kong Government then went on with an appeal to the Court of Final Appeal. The Appeals Commission of the SAR Court of Final Appeal ruled acceptance of the appeal on March 20, 1999, maintaining that the case involved a major legal issue, namely, whether Article 7 of the National Flag Ordinance and Article 7 of the Regional Flag Ordinance violated the Basic Law. The Hong Kong SAR Court of Final Appeal reviewed the case in October 1999 and produced a verdict on December 15.

10.3.2   The Court's Verdict

The court deemed that this case not only involved numerous complex human rights, constitutional, and legal issues, but it also touched upon Central/SAR relations. The first issue was that of freedom of speech and freedom of expression. As the SAR Court of Final Appeal stated: The disputed point in this appeal case is whether the acts of desecrating the national flag and regional flag ought to be classified as mandatory articles of criminal offenses and whether they conflict with the guarantees of freedom of expression. Article 27 of the Basic Law explicitly guarantees the freedom of speech of Hong Kong residents and stipulates: "Hong Kong residents shall have freedom of speech, of the press and of publication; freedom of procession and of demonstration, and the right and freedom to form and join trade unions, and to strike." Article 39 of the Basic Law further stipulates: "The provisions of the International Covenant on Civil and Political Rights, the International Covenant on Economic, Social and Cultural Rights, and international labor conventions as applied to Hong Kong shall remain in force and shall be implemented through the laws of the Hong Kong Special Administrative Region. The rights and freedom enjoyed by Hong Kong residents shall not be restricted unless as prescribed by law. Such restrictions shall

---

[26](1999) 1 HKLRD 783. Also see (1999) 2 HKC 10.

not contravene the provisions of the preceding paragraph of this Article." Hence, the International Covenant on Civil and Political Rights applies to Hong Kong, and the Hong Kong Bill of Rights Ordinance has included the said Covenant in Hong Kong's local legislation.[27] Article 19 of the said Covenant stipulates the freedom of expression: "(1) Everyone shall have the right to hold opinions without interference. (2) Everyone shall have the right to freedom of expression; this right shall include freedom to seek, receive and impart information and ideas of all kinds, regardless of frontiers, either orally, in writing or in print, in the form of art, or through any other media of his choice. (3) The exercise of the rights provided for in paragraph two of this article carries with it special duties and responsibilities. It may therefore be subject to certain restrictions, but these shall only be such as are provided by law and are necessary: (a) For respect of the rights or reputations of others; (b) for the protection of national security or of public order (ordre publique); or of public health or morals."

Since the freedom of expression stipulated in Article 19 of the International Covenant on Civil and Political Rights (ICCPR) applied to Hong Kong, the question is whether the acts of the two defendants fell in the category of the normal exercise of freedom of speech and expression, whether their opinions could only be expressed by means of desecrating the national and regional flags, and whether they violated Article 7 of the National Flag Ordinance and Article 7 of the Regional Flag Ordinance passed by the Hong Kong Legislature, and whether these two Ordinances infringed on the provisions protecting freedom of speech in the Basic Laws and the International Covenant on Civil and Political Rights.

According to Article 18 of the Hong Kong Basic Law and the July 1, 1997 decision of the National People's Congress Standing Committee, the National Flag Law passed by the NPC Standing Committee on June 28, 1990 falls in the category of national laws, which are to be implemented in the Hong Kong SAR. Article 19 of the said National Flag Law stipulates: "Whoever desecrates the National Flag of the People's Republic of China by publicly and willfully burning, mutilating, scrawling on, defiling or trampling on it shall be investigated for criminal responsibilities according to law; where the offense is relatively minor, he shall be detained for not more than 15 days by the public security organ in reference to the provisions of the Regulations on Administrative Penalties for Public Security." On the same day as the National Flag Law was passed, the NPC Standing Committee passed the Decision on Punishment for the Crime of Insulting the National Flag and National Emblem of the People's Republic of China, stipulating that "public and willful desecration of the national flag and national emblem of the People' Republic of China by burning, mutilating, scrawling on, defiling or trampling upon them shall be punished by three years of imprisonment, criminal detention, public surveillance or deprivation of political rights." Article 299 of the new Criminal Law formally defines this crime.

Article 18 of the Basic Law also stipulates that the national laws practiced in the Hong Kong SAR are not exercised in the locality directly but are "publicized and legislated locally by the Hong Kong Special Administrative Region." Accord-

---

[27] *Ordinances of Hong Kong*, Chapter 383.

ingly, the Hong Kong provisional legislative council formulated a "National Flag Ordinance" to implement the National Flag Law in the Hong Kong SAR. Article 7 of the National Flag Ordinance was related to the case in question and stipulated: "Whoever desecrates the National Flag of the People's Republic of China by publicly and willfully burning, mutilating, scrawling on, defiling or trampling on it commits a crime and, once convicted, may be administered a Level 5 fine (i.e., 50,000 HK dollars) and incarcerated for three years. "

To protect the SAR's flag, the SAR legislature also passed a "Regional Flag Ordinance," which stipulated that the Region's flag and its emblem are the symbol and hallmark of the Hong Kong SAR and that every Hong Kong resident should respect and cherish the Region's flag and its emblem. Article 7 therein stipulates: "Whoever publicly and willfully desecrates the Region's Flag and Region's Emblem by burning, mutilating, scrawling on, defiling or trampling on them commits a crime and, (a) once convicted by public prosecution procedures, may be administered a Level 5 fine (i.e. 50,000 HK dollars) and incarcerated for three years. And (b) if convicted by simplified procedures, may be administered a Level 3 fine (i.e. 30,000 HK dollars and imprisoned for one year."

The Court of Final Appeal ruled that the National Flag is the symbol of a state and represents the state's dignity, unity, and territorial integrity, and that the SAR's Regional flag is a symbol of the Region as an indivisible and special part of the People's Republic of China under the "one country, two systems" policy. The intrinsic importance of the National Flag and the Region's Flag is to be seen in the fact of the raising of the National Flag and the Region's Flag with the advent of midnight on July 1, 1997, heralding the historic occasion of the handover ceremony marking the resumption of the exercise of sovereignty by the People's Republic of China over Hong Kong. Moreover, the Chairman of the People's Republic of China followed this up with a pronouncement, which started with the words: "The Flag of the People's Republic of China and the Flag of the Hong Kong Special Administrative Region of the People's Republic of China have been solemnly raised over Hong Kong." Given the circumstances of the case, the Court of Final Appeal maintained that the acts of the two defendants in the case constituted the crime of desecrating the National Flag and the Regional Flag by means of defilement.

The Court of Final Appeal maintained that freedom of expression is a basic freedom in a democratic society as well as the core of the way-of-life system of Hong Kong and other civilized societies. Hence, courts of law must adopt broad and relaxed interpretations of the guarantees of constitutionality, and such freedoms should include the freedom of expression of ideas repugnant or disagreeable to most people and the freedom to criticize the actions of government organs or officials. However, the court maintained that legislative prohibitions of the desecration of the National Flag and the Regional Flag are a limited and not an extensive restriction of the freedom of expression, because whatever the message expressed by the relevant person or persons, the legislation concerned merely prohibits one form of expression, namely the form of expression that desecrates the National Flag and the Regional Flag; it does not prohibit the freedom to express a similar message through the use of some other form. Even the scrawling of laudatory statements on the National Flag or Regional Flag instead of the scrawling of messages that usually express opposition may constitute what is defined as crime in Article 7 of the two regulations, i.e., the crime of desecrating the National Flag and Regional Flag by means of scrawling upon them. The reason for this is that a legal provision intended to protect the dignity of flags of symbolic significance must provide the flags with overall and across-the-board protections from desecration.

Furthermore, the right of freedom of expression is not absolute, as is clearly indicated by the International Covenant on Civil and Political Rights. It confirms that the exercise of the right of expression must have special responsibilities and duties attached to it and must therefore be subject to certain restrictions. These restrictions must be spelled out by laws, and take into account what is necessary: "(a) For respecting of the rights or reputations of others; (b) for the protection of national security or of public order (ordre publique); or of public health or morals."

Firstly, the restriction on freedom of expression must be spelled out by law, and the two legal provisions involved in this case are as provided by law and comply with these requirements. Secondly, it must be seen whether these restrictions are intended to uphold public order. The court maintained that as concerns the time, place, and circumstances in which Hong Kong is currently situated, Hong Kong already pertains to a new constitutional order after its return to China. Hong Kong became an indivisible part of the People's Republic of China since July 1, 1997, when the People's Republic of China restored its exercise of sovereignty over Hong Kong and set up the Hong Kong Special Administrative Region in accordance with the "one country, two systems" principle. Under these circumstances, protecting the National Flag and the Regional Flag is a manifestation of our legal social interests and falls within the scope of the concept of public order. The legal interests described above form part of the public welfare and the overall interest. Hence, the legislative restrictions are intended to uphold the public order and the overall interest.

Of course, even though the abovementioned legal rights fall within the scope of public order as stipulated by law and the Legal and Civil Rights Covenant, the court had to conduct a thorough inquiry into whether the limitations exercised on the freedom of expression were necessary for protecting these legal interests which fall within the scope of public order. The court maintained that the two legal provisions involved in the present case of defining the desecration of the National Flag and Regional Flag as criminal offenses were a form of limited restriction of the freedom of expression, the purpose of which was to protect the National Flag as symbol of the state and the Regional Flag as symbol of region, and thereby protect the indisputable legal benefits, which these flags have brought to the nation and the region. Since the restrictions exercised by such legislation were limited, they survived the test of "whether or not they are necessary." The compatibility of these limited restrictions with the purpose quested by the application of these limited restrictions did not overstep the bounds of their mutual compatibility. And, since the National Flag and Regional Flag possessed special symbolic significance, shielding them from desecration played a major role in attaining the abovementioned purpose. Hence, the court maintained that there was an ample justification for ruling that the acts of desecrating the national and regional flag were criminal offenses, and that there were ample grounds for applying restrictions to the protected right of freedom of expression. Moreover, other countries also formulate laws to protect their national flag as well as classify desecrations of their national flags or similar actions as criminal offenses punishable by incarceration. The court cited a number of typical cases abroad of desecrating national flags to further prove its point. This showed that ranking the desecration of national flags as a criminal offense is also seen as a necessary measure to protect public order in other democratic societies. Hence, Article 7 in the National Flag Law and Article 7 in the Regional Flag Ordinance were necessary for upholding public order; the application of restrictions on freedom of expression in the articles of both of these laws were supported by ample grounds and complied with the Hong Kong's "constitution."

In the final section of its ruling, the Court of Final Appeal commended the determination showed by the three judges in the abovementioned court for protecting the freedom of expression, but it ruled that the government's appeal should be allowed because the Court of Final Appeal believed there was no basis for claiming that the two queried legislations were incompatible with the freedom in question. The two matters, it stated, might overlap peripherally but were fundamentally different at their cores. And so, there were intrinsic and basic differences in terms of both content and form between flags and emblems and totems and other symbols that licitly represented a community and narratives which transmitted some specific message, whether the said community consisted of a small group of persons or a vast nation, and whether the said specific message was trite and insignificant or highly controversial. It was only natural that a society should wish to protect its symbolic objects, and it was possible for a society to uphold freedom of speech while protecting its flag and emblems, even though doing so was certainly no easy matter. Such a situation could be achieved if the legislation protecting the flag and the emblem was clear and concise, did not involve the essential contents of what was being expressed, was limited simply to maintaining the flag's and the emblem's neutrality in terms of forms and methods of expression, and kept away from politics or dissensions. Thus, the court confirmed that the two legislations in the case concerning the protection of the national flag and the regional flag against public and deliberate desecration both complied with these criteria, and that the court was not applying any restrictions whatsoever to the contents that might be expressed. As regards the forms of expression people might use, the only restriction the law applied was to prohibit the desecration of objects that people would not dream of desecrating even if no such legislation existed. Such restrictions did not suppress the expression of any thoughts, and no overt expressions of any opinions would be inhibited whether these were the overt expression of political opinions or of any other opinions.

In reply to a question posed in a plausible statement by the chief counsel representing the second defendant—i.e., what would be the limits placed on the permitted application of restrictions—the court opined that the restrictions would go no further since these had already reached the limits permitted by the (Hong Kong) constitution; that under the protections for the National Flag and emblem and the Regional Flag and emblem, all persons in Hong Kong would, in accordance with Hong Kong laws, enjoy equal opportunities to speak out freely, say whatever they wished and in whatever manner they wished to say it, and feel confident that this situation would be sustained.

10.3.3 The Central/SAR Relations Involved

At issue in this case was the matter of freedom of speech, freedom of expression, and their legal restrictions. Cases like this one have occurred in many countries, most countries have produced similar legislations, and one might say that the basic stand of all countries and localities is also basically the same.[28] As stated in the judgment by the Court of Final Appeal, the court had indeed had to do its best to protect the freedoms of speech and expression—the cornerstones of democracy, and the Basic Laws and the International Covenant on Civil Rights confirmed this stance. There was no question about that. And, in reality, Hong Kong society has consistently enjoyed the rights to these freedoms. However, the court was similarly—and in accordance with laws which included the International Covenant on Civil Rights—constrained to show concern for public order and the overall interests of society. It could not attend to one thing and neglect the other, to the detriment of society. The court was fully justified in making such a judgment. The case was unique in that it involved not only the relationship between freedom of expression and upholding public order but that, just as importantly, it also involved Central/SAR relations. The "public order and the overall social interest" which the court had to uphold in this case referred not only to the public order and overall social interest of the Hong Kong SAR but also encompassed the interests of the nation as a whole. The judges had to establish a balance not only between the local populace's statutory freedom of expression and the Hong Kong region's public order and overall social interest, but also strike a balance between the local populace's statutory freedom and the entire nation's public order and overall social interest—an aspect Hong Kong's judges had no need to consider before the region's return to the mainland in 1997.

As noted by Hong Kong's Chief Justice on the judgment, Hong Kong found itself under a new constitutional order in terms of the time, location, and environment in which it was located after its return to China. On July 1, 1997, the People's Republic of China restored its exercise of sovereignty over Hong Kong and set up the Hong Kong Special Administrative Region in accordance with the "one China two systems" policy, turning Hong Kong into an inseparable part of the People's Republic. Under this circumstance, not only did the Hong Kong SAR's overall interest lie in protecting the Region's flag from desecration; the Hong Kong SAR's overall interest also lay in protecting the flag of the nation from desecration in the exercise of Hong

---

[28] As related previously, the United States is an exception. However, the U.S. Congress has since 1989 consistently tried to pass a constitutional amendment which would prohibit the burning and desecration of the American national flag and overthrow the Supreme Court's position in the cases Texas v. Johnson and United States v. Eichman that the act of burning the American flag is protected by the U.S. Constitution's First Amendment.

Kong's local laws, and the well-being and overall interest of the Hong Kong SAR's populace also lay within the scope of the concept of public order that the Court had to protect. In order to uphold this public order and overall interest, it was permissible to institute reasonable and necessary restrictions on the ways of exercising the freedom of expression. This judgment by the Hong Kong SAR Court possessed a profound and far-reaching effect, since it indicated that after Hong Kong's return to China, the HK SAR Court no longer limited its purview of Hong Kong's overall interest and public order to the Hong Kong region; that it recognized that safeguarding the image and the overall interest of the nation as a whole in the exercise of Hong Kong's local laws was consistent with the Hong Kong SAR's overall interest and necessary for the SAR's public order. It was quite praiseworthy of the Court that it had recognized, so soon after the HK SAR returned to China, that the interests of the country as a whole were at one with the HK SAR's local interests and should be given the same protections. That was something the judges who reviewed previous appeals had obviously failed to comprehend.

Of course, judges anywhere who make such rulings are usually subject to a great deal of pressure. The handling of such sensitive cases has always been a difficult matter, and cases concerning the freedoms of speech and expression and their legal restrictions are a perennial source of headaches for judges in any country or region. People are likely to be critical of any judges who place any restrictions on freedom of speech according to law, even though these judges are specifically permitted to do so by either their local laws or international covenants on civil rights. Specifically, in the present case, it is possible that people might not have been very reproachful of the judges if they had placed restrictions on freedom of expression for reasons of protecting the Hong Kong SAR's regional flag and public interests, as that would have been less difficult for the general public to understand. The problem lay in the other important reason for the judges applying restrictions on the freedom of expression was to protect the national flag of China and the interests of China as a whole, in the recognition that doing so was necessary for protecting the overall interests of and upholding public order in the Hong Kong SAR. That was not comprehensible or acceptable to all persons. Although the times had already advanced beyond 1997, people's state of mind had yet to completely cross that temporal hurdle.

We must, however, state that the judges' ruling was entirely correct and natural. There are times when it is not easy to protect citizens' rights and freedoms from governmental encroachments and to rule that the government has lost its case. That calls for withstanding considerable pressure, especially when rule of law is incomplete and no ample guarantees exist for judicial independence. There are also times when the overall interests of society and public order are rigorously upheld by law, and when lawsuits are ruled in favor of the government and against the ordinary people. Such times, too, are quite trying and place heavy pressures on the judges. But these situations cannot be helped and fall within the judges' functions and duties. Where the HK SAR's judges are concerned, the chief justices not only have to strike a reasonable balance between these two situations, they must, according to law, place the overall interests of the nation in the same important position as the interests of the Hong Kong SAR and effectively protect them due to the reality that Hong Kong has been restored to China and is implementing "one country, two systems." Understanding the consistency of the nation's interests and the interest of the HK SAR and doing a proper job of handling SAR/Central relations is not only the job of the SAR's Chief Executive and legislative and administrative organs; it is also the job of the SAR's judiciary even though there are no direct relations between it and the Central organs. In a society that exercises rule of law as rigorously as Hong Kong, further defining social norms and establishing codes of conduct in many matters calls for the filing of lawsuits. The importance of the case in question lay in the fact that it opened up a new "world outlook" for the Hong Kong SAR's judiciary.

10.4 The Zhang Ziqiang Case (Cheung Tze-Keung) and the Li Yuhui Case and Issues of Criminal Jurisdiction

10.4.1 The Facts of the Cases

In the Zhang Ziqiang case, Zhang and his gang of 36 persons engaged in acts of illegally buying and selling and transporting explosives, illegally buying and selling guns and ammunition, smuggling guns and ammunition and committing acts of abduction and robbery, and harboring felons in Hong Kong and Guangdong. On December 5, 1998, the Guangdong Province Superior People's Court passed a final judgment under which five principal criminals were sentenced to death and their associates were sentenced to life or long terms of imprisonment as well as additional punishments. The severity of these legal sanctions drew strong reactions in Hong Kong and Macao, China as a whole and even overseas.

The circumstances of this so-called "fat cat" case were so grave as to break numerous records in the histories of crime in both China and Hong Kong. Back in June 1991 and March 1992, Zhang Ziqiang had colluded with his cohorts on the mainland to seal off streets in Hong Kong with AK-47s, spray constables with gunfire, and loot seven gold shops on Kwun Tong Muh Wah Street and Tai Po Road of gold ornaments worth more than seven million HK dollars, causing great consternation throughout Hong Kong. On July 12, 1991, he connived with others in his gang to stage an armed hold up of a bank's money van in a cargo depot at Hong Kong's Kai Tak Airport and seized 170 million HK dollars. Two months later, he was apprehended and sentenced to 18 years of imprisonment, but was released in June 1995 due to insufficient evidence. He nursed a bitter hatred for Hong Kong's disciplinary departments and government for what he perceived as mistreatment during his stint in prison.

From 1995 to March 1998, this gang committed numerous murders and robberies in Guangzhou and Shenzhen; repeatedly attacked Hong Kong prisons; kidnapped the eldest son of a tycoon named Lee and ransomed the boy for 1.07 billion HK dollars; abducted Guo, chairman of a real estate group, and obtained 700 million HK dollars as ransom; planned to throw an incendiary device at the residence of a rich Macaoan named Ho but called it off only after a constable discovered their intentions; transported 800 kg of explosives, 2000 detonators, and 500 m of blasting fuse from Chinese mainland to Hong Kong, plotted to take revenge on the government and continue to engage in acts of terror, abduction, and other crimes; made phone calls threatening Hong Kong's Secretary for Security; planned to carry out a series of bombings in Hong Kong including on its Stanley Prison and to abduct Anson Chan, the second highest official in Hong Kong at that time, and thereby threw everyone in a panic. The sheer amount of money involved in their crimes and brazenness of the kidnappings were quite astounding. After Zhang Ziqiang had abducted Lee's eldest son, he neither made anonymous phone calls nor wrote menacing letters but swaggered in person to the Lee mansion to pick up the ransom money. And, when saw the luxurious accoutrements there he came straight out with his name and an extortionist ransom figure. The boasts of this criminal gang that it would carry out kidnappings from all of Hong Kong's ten wealthiest families by turns plunged all wealthy households in the region into a state of terror and trepidation.

Of the 36 principal defendants in this case, 18, including Zhang Ziqiang, were permanent residents of Hong Kong and 18 were mainlanders. Their crimes straddled both sides of the border and involved both Hong Kong and mainland areas. Some were carried out in Hong Kong and others in Guangdong Province, others took place partly in Hong Kong and partly on the mainland, and still others were hatched on the mainland and executed in Hong Kong, but the outcomes and effects involved both regions. Thus, the case entailed complicated issues of criminal and judicial jurisdiction and fell under dual jurisdictions. Both regions possessed judicial jurisdiction and handling rights over this case under mainland and Hong Kong law.

As the Zhang Ziqiang case was being tried by a mainland court, Li Yuhui, a resident of Shantou in Guangdong Province, under the pretext of spreading the Gospel at Telford Gardens in Hong Kong, induced five Hong Kong residents to imbibe a poisonous potion which killed all five on the spot, and then absconded to the mainland with a large sum of money. The police in Shantou subsequently arrested him and confiscated illicit moneys amounting to more than a million yuan. Prior to that, he had been constantly scheming and preparing to engage in murder and robbery in Hong Kong, and had purchased mainland poisons, which he took to Hong Kong. After the Shantou police had completed its investigations, the Shantou People's Procuratorate prosecuted the case at the Shantou Intermediate People's Court, and Li Yuhui was sentenced to death. This case, too, was a complex one over which courts in both regions had jurisdiction. Like the Zhang Ziqiang case, it was a landmark case involving relations between the two regions after Hong Kong's return to China, and the way in which the conflict of jurisdictions was to be handled would be a test of the correct handling of Central/SAR relations.

10.4.2 The Conflict Between the Two Regions' Criminal Jurisdictions

10.4.2.1 Criminal Jurisdiction in Chinese Mainland

Whether these two cases should be accepted and dealt with by mainland courts depended on the mainland's relevant legal provisions as well as the facts of the cases. According to China's Code of Criminal Procedure amended in March 1996 and China's Criminal Law amended and approved in March 1997, China's main principle for handling criminal jurisdiction is that of territorial jurisdiction, after which come the principles of personal jurisdiction, protective jurisdiction, and universal jurisdiction. Due to the complexity of jurisdiction issues, no country or region adopts a single principle of jurisdiction.

Article 24 of the Code of Criminal Procedure established the principle of territorial jurisdiction as: "A criminal case shall be under the jurisdiction of the People's Court where the crime was committed." This basic principle of criminal jurisdiction is implemented in many countries and regions worldwide. As for the definition of "place where the committed," Article 6 of China's Criminal Law states: "This law shall be applicable to anyone who commits a crime within the territory and territorial waters and space of the People's Republic of China, except as otherwise specifically provided by law... If a criminal act or its consequence takes place within the territory of territorial waters or space of the People's Republic of China, the crime shall be deemed to have been committed within the territory of and territorial waters and space of the People's Republic of China." According to a "Judicial Explanation" issued by the Supreme People's Court in June, 1998, the principle is established of taking the place of the commission of the crime as the main criterion and the result of the commission of the crime as the secondary criterion for defining the location of a crime, to wit: "Crime scene" refers to the location where the crime has taken place. In terms of property crimes for the sake of taking illegal possession, "crime scene" includes the location where the crime has taken place and the result-of-the crime location where the criminal actually takes possession of the property.[29] As for the definition of "crime," in accordance with the relevant provision of China's Criminal Law, a "crime" includes the specific act of carrying out the crime and the act(s) of preparing to carry out the crime, as stipulated in Article 22: "Preparation for a crime refers to the preparation of the instruments or the creation of the conditions for a crime." Preparation for a crime may be attached to the principal act of the crime to establish the crime, or may be used independently to secure a conviction.

In the Zhang Ziqiang case, many of the crimes committed by Zhang and his cohorts were prepared in Chinese mainland. For example, their acts in Guangdong of unlawful purchasing and selling and transporting explosive devices, unlawfully purchasing and smuggling guns and ammunition and the multiple instances in Guangzhou, Shen-

---

[29]"Explanation of a Number of Questions Regarding the People's Republic of China Criminal Procedure Law," Supreme People's Court Judicial Committee, June 29, 1998.

zhen, and Dongguan of plotting and planning abductions of rich businesspeople in Hong Kong were obviously conducted in preparation for carrying out abductions, bombings, and other crimes in Hong Kong. However, according to mainland law these acts per se constituted independent crimes, jurisdiction over which pertained to mainland law enforcement and judicial organs. Despite the fact that these acts were only preparations made for carrying out crimes in Hong Kong, jurisdiction could still be exercised over them as "preparations for crimes" in accordance with the above-mentioned provisions of China's Criminal Law. Most countries and regions in the world have confirmed this principle, i.e., that courts of law may exercise jurisdiction over acts of preparing for crimes carried out in their respective areas of judicial juris-diction, even though the results of the crimes occurred outside their respective areas of judicial jurisdiction. Thus, as concerns jurisdiction over this crime, the mainland's public security organ was empowered to investigate the crime, the mainland procu-ratorial organ was empowered to prosecute the crime, and the mainland's court of law was empowered to try the case.

As for the Li Youhui Case, although the crime and its results both took place in Hong Kong, its planning and preparations were made on the mainland, the perpetrator himself was a mainland resident, and he was first caught by mainland public security authorities, hence jurisdiction pertained to mainland law enforcement and judicial organs.

10.4.2.2   The Hong Kong SAR's Judicial Jurisdiction

There is no question that the Hong Kong SAR law enforcement and judicial organs had jurisdiction over the two cases as well. As regards the Zhang Ziqiang case, that was not only because the principal culprits Zhang Ziqiang et al. were permanent residents of Hong Kong but also because the principal criminal acts in the case—the gold store robberies and the rich family abduction—had also taken place in Hong Kong. And, in the Li Yuhui Case, the criminal act and its results both took place in Hong Kong. Whether in accordance with the principle of personal jurisdiction or the principal of territorial jurisdiction, the Hong Kong SAR law enforcement and judicial organs had, pursuant to Hong Kong SAR law, indisputable jurisdiction over both cases. However, does the fact that both cases were ultimately handled by main-land judicial authorities mean that the mainland infringed on the Hong Kong SAR's judicial independence and its high degree of autonomy? Due to differences between the criminal laws and penalties in the two localities—the death penalty was prac-ticed on the mainland but had been abolished in Hong Kong—the results of different courts of law in the two localities handling the case according to different systems of laws were quite different. Although both crimes were indeed most heinous, their cir-cumstances extremely odious and the results extremely grave, the maximum penalty meted to these persons if Hong Kong had exercised jurisdiction would have been life imprisonment, not the death penalty. Was the handling a deliberate circumvention of law in order to put those persons to death? Due to the presence of a great many factors, the jurisdiction issue for the two cases was quite complicated.

10.4.2.3   The Principle of First Acceptance

When conflicts of jurisdiction occur and two or more judicial territories possess jurisdiction over the same case, the customary practice in other countries is to adopt the principle of first acceptance, which means that the court which was actually the first to accept the case to exercise de facto jurisdiction; and that other judicial organs which also have jurisdiction either to forfeit that right, or to exercise it symbolically. One of the benefits of this principle is that suspected criminals may be apprehended and the crimes may be punished promptly and effectively, minimizing the effects of crimes as much as possible and preventing them from expanding. Hence, this is a basic principle internationally acknowledged for handling conflicts of judicial jurisdiction.

The Zhang Ziqiang case was first cracked by the Guangdong police, the 36 suspects were also apprehended by the Guangdong police, a mainland procuratorial organ was subsequently the first to prosecute the case and a mainland court was the first to accept it. Hence, the trying of the case by the mainland judiciary complied with the acknowledged jurisdictional principles of first acceptance and actual control. Meanwhile, the Hong Kong SAR government did not sit idly by. It had initiated an investigation into the activities of Zhang Ziqiang et al. However, in accordance with Hong Kong law it lacked sufficient evidence to justify taking coercive action or to file charges with a Hong Kong SAR court, so that no Hong Kong court had actually accepted the case, and one might also say that no conflict of jurisdiction had occurred.[30]

As for the Li Yuhui Case, since the suspect had absconded to the mainland after committing the crime, the Hong Kong SAR police had not been able to arrest him and it was again the mainland police authorities who first broke the case and arrested the culprit. The mainland prosecutorial authorities had been the first to press charges and a mainland court had been the first to accept the case, so that it conformed to the criminal jurisdiction principle of first acceptance.

The chance coincidence of these two cases led to a misunderstanding among some in the legal profession, causing them to believe that the mainland authorities had intentionally circumvented the law and deliberately applied principles and theories of jurisdiction favorable to themselves. In other words, when a Hong Konger broke mainland laws on the mainland or broke laws of both regions simultaneously in both regions, the mainland authorities applied the principle of territorial jurisdiction (i.e., the location where the crime took place) and the principle of first acceptance to determine judicial jurisdiction, as for instance in the Zhang Ziqiang Case; but when a mainland resident broke Hong Kong's criminal laws in Hong Kong, the mainland authorities conversely used the nationality principle plus the principle of first acceptance to determine judicial jurisdiction. This gave one the impression that whether a Hong Konger broke laws on the mainland or a mainlander broke laws in Hong Kong, the mainland authorities could always find a theory or principle favorable

---

[30]Wang Zhongxing. "Why the Mainland Has Criminal Jurisdiction over the Case of Hong Kong Resident Zhang Ziqiang," carried in Hong Kong, *Chinese Law*, 1999(3), p. 4.

to themselves and assume criminal jurisdiction. This way of looking at it only took account of the superficial and incidental and overlooked the essence of the matter.

10.4.2.4   The Conflict Between the Criminal Judicial Jurisdictions of the Two Regions and the Transfer of Suspects

The conflict between the criminal judicial jurisdictions of the two regions is manifested in two situations: (a) Hong Kong residents committing crimes in mainland China, and (b) mainland residents committing crimes in Hong Kong. How criminal judicial jurisdictions and the transfer of the suspects concerned ought to be determined in such cases are acute legal issues that have beset the two regions for quite some time.

Regarding the first situation, if a permanent Hong Kong resident commits a crime wholly on the mainland, breaks mainland laws, and is detained by mainland police, the case does not involve Hong Kong factors other than the perpetrator's identity as a permanent Hong Kong resident and that he has not committed any crime according to Hong Kong Law. As Prof. Chen Hongyi of Hong Kong University's Law School has said, under such circumstances the mainland courts of law possess complete jurisdiction. All that the Hong Kong SAR can do, in accordance with conventional international practice, is ask the mainland court of law to handle the relevant case strictly according to mainland laws and international human rights standards.[31] As to whether the Hong Kong SAR judicial institutions ought to handle such cases or how they handle the cases after the mainland courts have dealt with them according to law—that is the SAR's own business.

But what if a permanent Hong Kong resident commits a crime entirely on the mainland, breaks mainland criminal laws and then flees back to Hong Kong, and is detained by Hong Kong police? In such circumstances, if the crime he has committed on the mainland has, according to Hong Kong laws, also violated Hong Kong's criminal laws, the Hong Kong SAR courts possess jurisdiction in line with the principle of first acceptance. The mainland may also request that the suspect be transferred to the mainland for handling in line with relevant agreements on judicial assistance between the two regions (if there are such agreements). If, in accordance with Hong Kong SAR laws, crimes committed on the mainland do not violate Hong Kong's criminal law and do not constitute crimes in Hong Kong, the handling of such cases depends on the criminal judicial assistance dispositions between the two regions. Under normal circumstances, both sides have the obligation to mutually extradite criminals in accordance with the reciprocity principle.

In some cases, China's mainland judicial organs do not possess judicial jurisdiction. For example, in situations where a Hong Kong permanent resident commits a crime wholly in Hong Kong, where the preparation, commission, and consequences

---

[31] Chen Hongyi. "Interaction between Hong Kong and Mainland Legal Institutions after Returning to China," carried in, *Hong Kong twentyfirst Century Blueprint* (Liu Zhaojia ed.). Hong Kong: Hong Kong Chinese University Press, 2000.

of the crime all take place in Hong Kong and bear no relation to the mainland, and where the perpetrator has fled to the mainland after committing the crime and has been apprehended by mainland public security authorities—in such circumstances, the mainland has no basis for judicial jurisdiction and the only thing the mainland can do is hand the suspect over to Hong Kong's police and judicial organs for disposal. And in reality the mainland and Hong Kong police authorities have always cooperated in such matters; in other words, the mainland authorities have transferred to Hong Kong those of its residents who have committed crimes in Hong Kong and fled to the mainland, provided the suspects' crimes are unrelated to the mainland. These are normal transfers of suspects. If Zhang Ziqiang had prepared and carried his criminal acts solely in Hong Kong, and the consequences of those acts had been limited to Hong Kong and contained no elements involving the mainland, the mainland police authorities would have had to transfer him to Hong Kong's police authorities even though they had been the first to apprehend him, since the mainland had no judicial jurisdiction over the matter.

The problem today is that in accordance with Hong Kong's current laws, the Hong Kong police authorities have no obligation to transfer mainland residents who have committed crimes on the mainland, and then fled to the Hong Kong and whose crimes are unrelated to Hong Kong. The reason is that transfers of suspects between the two regions are unidirectional. Prior to Hong Kong's return to the mainland, repatriations and the transfers of suspects between the two regions were conducted according to relevant agreements between the governments of China and Britain. After Hong Kong's return to China, the two regions have not concluded any agreements in this respect and interaction has been limited to cooperation between the police authorities of Guangdong and Hong Kong on some individual cases.

As regards the second aspect, i.e., the handling of a case where a mainland resident commits a crime in Hong Kong, one may first consult the provisions concerned in China's Criminal Law. On the handling of Chinese citizens who commit crimes outside China's borders, Article 7 of the Criminal Law stipulates: "This Law shall be applicable to any citizen of the People's Republic of China who commits a crime prescribed in this Law outside the territory and territorial waters and space of the People's Republic of China; however, if the maximum punishment to be imposed is fixed-term imprisonment of not more than three years as stipulated in this Law, he may be exempted from the investigation for his criminal responsibility." This shows two different situations in the way China handles its own citizens who commit crimes abroad. First, if the said citizens' criminal acts outside China are not crimes according to China's Criminal Law and the suspect is apprehended in the country where the crime was committed, the courts in the country where the crime was committed possess complete jurisdiction, and all China can do is to request the courts in the said countries to handle the relevant cases strictly according to those countries' laws and international human rights criteria. If the said suspect's crime in another country breaks that country's laws but do not break China's laws and the suspect flees back to China, under such circumstances the outcome may depend on whether agreements on judicial assistance or repatriation exist between the two sides. Jurisdiction over criminal cases is in keeping with the law that is practiced; there is no possibility that China's courts will handle the said suspect according to the law of the country where the crime took place. China's courts can only handle penalties for crimes in accordance with China's Criminal Law. Acts that are not crimes in terms of China's Criminal Law cannot be handled by China's courts; they can be handled only by courts in the country where the crime took place. However, whether the court in the said country is able to exercise jurisdiction depends on whether the said country succeeds in extraditing the suspect.

The second situation is that, where the said citizen's criminal act abroad also violates China's Criminal Law and is also a crime under China's Criminal Law, China's courts have jurisdiction over it according to the nationality principle, but whether they can exercise jurisdiction again depends on the circumstances. If the said suspect is arrested in the country where he committed the crime, and the court in the country where the crime was committed has already convicted and punished him, Chinese courts still may exercise jurisdiction and still may convict and punish him, but since the defendant has already been subjected to criminal punishment in another country, he need not be punished again. However, if the said suspect has not been apprehended in the country where he committed the crime and has fled back to China, how he is handled in such circumstances also depends on whether any agreement on judicial assistance of extradition exists between the two sides.

However, the complexity of criminal judicial jurisdiction involving Hong Kong and Macao lies in the fact that neither of these regions is a foreign country, yet according to the provisions of the SAR Basic Laws, China's Criminal Law is not implemented in the Special Administrative Region. Hence, the above provisions of China's Criminal Law cannot be directly applied to the Hong Kong and Macao SARs. So, how is the problem to be resolved? Prof. Chen Hongyi of Hong Kong University Law School has proposed that the Supreme People's Court and the Supreme People's Procuratorate must issue a judicial interpretation, which supplements the relevant provisions of Article 6 and Article 7 of China's Criminal Law so that they apply to the situation of mainland citizens who commit crimes in Hong Kong.

As regards the handling of the Li Yuhui Case jurisdiction issue, the main reason for the mainland court's exercise of jurisdiction over the Li Yuhui Case was that his criminal act was partially completed in Chinese mainland, to wit, the planning and the preparation of objects used in the crime were completed in Chinese mainland, and mainland institutions were the first to arrest the suspect and handle the case. If Li's criminal act had been entirely conducted in Hong Kong, including the planning and preparations, and if he had not fled back to the mainland after committing the crime and had been arrested in Hong Kong by the Hong Kong police, no mainland factor would have figured in the case apart from the suspect being a mainland resident. Under such circumstances, despite the mainland court having jurisdiction according to the personality principle, the Hong Kong court had priority jurisdiction according to the territorial and first acceptance principle and had the right to try and punish the offender. As stated earlier, after the Hong Kong court had tried and punished the criminal, the mainland court would also have the right to exercise jurisdiction again in accordance with the mainland's Criminal Law if the criminal had returned to the mainland and had also broken the law in accordance with the mainland's Criminal

Law, but it might not necessarily impose an another criminal penalty. If the suspect's act that broke Hong Kong's criminal laws had not constituted a crime under the mainland's Criminal Law, and if he had fled back to the mainland after committing the act and had then been arrested by mainland police—would the mainland have had any judicial jurisdiction under such circumstances? It is clear that since his act would not have constituted a crime under the mainland's Criminal Law, the mainland court would not be able to try the case. Under such circumstances, whether or not the suspect would be transferred to the Hong Kong SAR would depend on the principle of reciprocity and the specific provisions of agreements on mutual legal assistance between the two sides.

Hence, what is urgently needed at this time that both sides should hold consultations as soon as possible to draft agreements on extraditions of suspects and exercising criminal judicial assistance between the two sides on the basis of the "one country, two systems" policy and the provisions of Hong Kong's Basic Law, and to produce regulations on the issues concerned. It should be pointed out that the mainland courts' exercise of judicial jurisdiction over the Zhang Ziqiang and Li Yuhui cases did not violate the Hong Kong SAR's judicial independence or its high degree of autonomy. That is because these were issues of the rules of judicial procedures, and once such rules are established, it's the same for either party. Moreover, the mainland authorities possessed ample legal and theoretical grounds for exercising judicial jurisdiction. Conflicts of criminal judicial jurisdiction are highly complex problems, and problems of this or that sort exist not only between Hong Kong/Macao and the mainland; a great many similar problems are also to be seen in and among other countries. These need to be resolved between the parties concerned according to the principle of equality and mutual benefit.

10.5 Judicial Assistance in Civil and Commercial Matters Between the SARs and Chinese Mainland

If criminal judicial assistance between the SARs and the mainland is a complex issue, judicial assistance in civil and commercial matters between the two regions and the mainland is an even more complicated matter. Yet, just like criminal judicial assistance between the two regions, judicial assistance between the two regions in civil and commercial matters consists of cooperation between two independent judicial sectors in within one sovereign state in which both sides adhere to the basic policy of "one country, two systems" and strictly comply with relevant provisions of the Basic Law, abide by the principle of effective negotiation and mutual benefit, respect each other's judicial system and judicial independence and at the same time make allowances for historical and present-day realities, refer to the relevant provisions of international treaties and adhere to already-existing and mature approaches in order to make rational dispositions for matters of civil and commercial assistance. Generally speaking, there are no major differences of principle between the two sides in these respects; the main issues are those of legal techniques and details.

As regards the Hong Kong–Macao judiciary, the mainland authorities have always strictly differentiated between cases involving Hong Kong and Macao and those involving foreign countries. They have never regarded Hong Kong and Macao cases as cases involving foreign relations, for which reason the ways and means they used to handle these cases have been somewhat different. In an "annotated document" on December 6, 1984, the Supreme People's Court noted that in accordance with the provisions in Article 9 of the Nationality Law of the People's Republic of China and Item 7 of the Ministry of Public Security's Internal Regulations on Implementing the Nationality Law as well as the spirit of the Chinese side's Memorandum attached to the Sino-British Joint Declaration on the Question of Hong Kong, citizens of Hong Kong and Macao who held British Dependent Territories citizen passports or ID certificates issued by the Macao Portuguese authorities could not be treated as possessing British or Portuguese nationality, and the civil lawsuits they filed or responded to in mainland law courts could not be handled as foreign cases.[32] Hence, neither conventions on international judicial assistance nor China's laws on handling foreign cases applied to cases, which involved Hong Kong and Macao. Civil and commercial judicial assistance matters between Hong Kong–Macao and the mainland consisted in the main of the serving of judicial documents, mutual acknowledgement and implementation of arbitration decisions, mutual acknowledgement and implementation of court rulings, and mutual coordination on the enforcement and obtaining of evidence.

10.5.1 Entrustment and Service of Civil and Commercial Judicial Documents

Internationally, the mutual service of judicial documents is very common among transnational and cross-jurisdictional judicial institutions. The Convention on the Service Abroad of Judicial and Extrajudicial Documents in Civil or Commercial Matters, aka the Hague Service Convention, ratified in 1965 is the main treaty for standardizing the serving of judicial documents among various countries. The British government joined this convention in November 1967, and in July 1970 extended the application of this convention to Hong Kong. As to the situation between Hong Kong and Chinese mainland, due to the scarcity of civil and commercial cases reciprocally involving Hong Kong and Macao and in order to facilitate cooperation between the judicial institutions of these two regions in this respect, the Guangdong Supreme People's Court and the Hong Kong High Court signed a "Macao-Hong Kong Agreement" on July 1, 1988 on the serving of civil and serving of civil commercial judicial

---

[32]"Annotated Reply on the Question of Whether Cases of Hong Kong and Macao Compatriots Holding Passports Issued by the Hong Kong British or Macao Portuguese Authorities Filing Or Responding to Civil Lawsuits in Mainland People's Courts May be Regarded as Foreign Cases," issued by the Supreme People's Court on December 6, 1984.

documents between Macao and Hong Kong, which contained seven provisions on specific matters. This was a normative document, which standardized the service of judicial documents by and between the two regions.

On March 2, 1991, the 18th Session of the Seventh National People's Congress Standing Committee decided to approve China's joining the Convention, which came into force in China on January 1, 1992. On March 4, 1992, the Supreme People's Court, the Ministry of Foreign Affairs, and the Justice Department jointly issued "Notice on the Enforcing the Relevant Procedures of the 'Convention on the Service Abroad of Judicial and Extrajudicial Documents in Civil or Commercial Matters'" (*Waifa* [1992] No. 8). After soliciting the opinions of the State Council's Hong Kong and Macao Office, the aforementioned Supreme People's Court, Foreign Ministry, and Justice Department decided that when serving judicial documents and extrajudicial documents, the Hong Kong High Court and mainland people's courts could take into reference Document *Waifa* [1992] No. 8 issued by the Supreme People's Court, the Foreign Ministry, and the Justice Department. Consequently, prior to Hong Kong's return to China, the serving of judicial documents by Hong Kong and Chinese mainland proceeded in the main in accordance with the Hague Convention.

After the establishment of the Hong Kong SAR, the Hague Service Convention which applied to the serving of judicial documents between different countries obviously could no longer apply to the circumstances of Hong Kong and Chinese mainland. The agreement between Macao and Hong Kong too did not fit in with the new requirements as it was limited to Macao and Hong Kong, and the complex procedures, low efficiency, and lengthy time cycle for serving judicial documents between the two regions created a great many inconveniences for the judicial institutions and parties concerned in the two regions. Hence, the two regions urgently needed a new mechanism and instrument for solving the serving of documents. Moreover, the Hong Kong Basic Law already provided a basis for doing so. Article 95 stipulated: "The Hong Kong Special Administrative Region may, through consultations and in accordance with law, maintain juridical relations with judicial organs of other parts of the country, and they may render assistance to each other." After numerous consultations between the relevant judicial organs of the two regions and extensive solicitations of opinions from legal quarters and relevant sectors in the two regions, the parties concerned finally reached a unanimous agreement on the mutual entrustment and service of civil and commercial judicial documents between Chinese mainland and the Hong Kong SAR. On December 30, 1998 the 1038th session of the Judicial Committee of the Supreme People Court approved the "Arrangements by the Supreme People's Court on the Mutual Entrustment and Service of Civil and Commercial Judicial Documents between Courts of the Mainland and the Hong Kong Special Administrative Region," and published the contents of the agreement in the form of a judicial interpretation (*Fashi* [1999] No. 9). Meanwhile, on the basis of a unanimous opinion reached by the Supreme People's Court and representatives of the Hong Kong SAR, the Hong Kong SAR on the same day published the agreement in the form of an amendment to the SAR's High Court Rules.

From the perspective of the consultation process and the form of publication, one can see that Hong Kong, after its return to China, indeed enjoys independent judicial powers that Hong Kong and Chinese mainland still pertain to two different and mutually independent judicial jurisdictions.

The judicial documents referred to in the aforementioned the "Arrangements" include in Chinese mainland: Copies of complaints, copies of appeals, powers of attorney, summons, verdicts, mediations, rulings, written decisions, notices, certificates, and acknowledgements of receipt; whereas in the Hong Kong SAR they include: Copies of complaints, copies of appeals, summons, pleadings, affidavits, judgments, verdicts, awards, court notice, court orders, and proofs of service. According to the "Arrangements," mutual entrusting and serving of civil and commercial judicial documents between mainland people's courts and Hong Kong SAR courts must all be conducted via mainland higher people's courts in various localities and the Hong Kong SAR High Court. The mainland's Supreme People's Court may directly entrust the Hong Kong SAR High Court with the service of judicial documents. The "Arrangements" requires that when the entrusting party request the serving of judicial documents, it must issue a letter of entrustment with its stamp affixed on the letter, and must specify on the letter, the title of the entrusting organ, the family and given name or the title of the recipient of the served document, the detailed address of the recipient, and the nature of the case. The letter of entrustment must also be prepared in the Chinese language. If the attached judicial document is not in the Chinese language, a Chinese translation must be furnished. As concerns the time limit for the serving, in accordance with the "Arrangements," the entrusted party must serve the documents whether or not the date or time limit for the court appearance has expired. The entrusted party is to fulfill the serving after receipt of the letter of commission in a timely manner and shall not do so more than two months after receipt of the letter of entrustment at the latest. After the serving of a judicial document, mainland people's courts shall issue an acknowledgement of receipt and the Hong Kong SAR High Court shall issue certificate of service. If the entrusted party is unable to serve [a document], it shall note the cause that hindered service or the reason and date of rejection on the acknowledgement of receipt or the proof of service, and shall promptly send back the letter of entrustment and all appended documents. The "Arrangements" stipulate that the service of judicial documents should proceed in accordance with the procedures stipulated by laws where the entrusted party is located. The entrusted party does not bear legal responsibility for the contents or consequences of the legislative documents entrusted for service by the entrusting party. The costs for the entrusted service of judicial documents are reciprocally waived by both parties. However, the entrusting party shall bear the costs incurred by the service if it requests a specific form of service in its letter of entrustment, as for instance service by a specifically designated person. This is also consistent with the provisions of Article 265 of the Law of Civil Procedure. The aforementioned "Arrangements" also stipulates that in the event that new problems emerge in the relevant provisions, which are in the course of being carried out and which need to be amended, the matter should be resolved through consultations between the Superior People's Court and the Hong Kong SAR's High Court. It is evident that the Dispositions contains fairly specific stipulations with regard to the serving of civil and commercial judicial documents between the two regions. The Hong Kong SAR, too, has amended its Rules of the

High Court by including similar contents and adapting them to local circumstances. Hence, both the mainland and the Hong Kong SAR already have laws to follow in terms of serving judicial documents.

10.5.2 Reciprocal Implementation of Arbitral Decisions

As regards China's recognition and implementation of arbitral decisions by other countries, Article 269 of China's Law of Civil Procedure lays out the following principle: "If an award made by a foreign arbitral organ requires the recognition and enforcement by people's court of the People's Republic of China, the party concerned shall directly apply to the intermediate people's court where the party subjected to enforcement has his domicile or where his property is located. The people's court shall deal with the matter in accordance with the international treaties concluded or acceded to by the People's Republic of China or with the principle of reciprocity." The handling of this matter among different countries has proceeded mainly in accordance with the 1958 New York Convention (the Recognition and Enforcement of Foreign Arbitral Awards Convention). Britain was a member state of that convention and extended the force of the convention to Hong Kong. China acceded to the convention in December 1986. Thus, mainland China's recognition and enforcement of arbitral awards involving Hong Kong prior to Hong Kong's return to China were conducted basically in accordance with this convention. Moreover, the "Explanation Regarding a Number of Questions Concerning the Hearing of Cases of Economic Disputes Involving Hong Kong and Macao" passed by the Supreme People's Court on October 19, 1989 also touched upon some arbitral matters, albeit in a very incomplete manner. The Hong Kong side, could, in accordance with the provisions of the New York Convention, request that Hong Kong courts recognize and enforce arbitral awards produced by New York Convention signatory states or participating regions, and the Hong Kong courts could, after examining the requests and deeming that these conform to the relevant legal provisions, confirm their efficacy and enforce them according to law, or conversely could turn down the requests. As regards arbitral awards by non-signatory countries or regions of the New York Convention, the parties concerned could of course also resort to the method of renewed appeals to request enforcement of the original arbitrations.[33]

However, after Hong Kong's return to China, the New York Convention obviously no longer applied to handling enforcements of arbitral awards between the two regions. Hence, after lengthy consultations, the two regions worked out a new agreement, and on June 18, 1999, the 1069th meeting of the Judicial Committee of the Supreme People's Court approved the Arrangements on the Mutual Enforcement of Arbitral Awards between the Mainland and the Hong Kong Special Administrative Region and published the contents in the form of a judicial interpretation (*fashi* [2000] No. 3) on January 24, 2000. The Hong Kong SAR simultaneously

---

[33] *Ordinances of Hong Kong*, Chapter 341.

published the "Arrangements" in the form of an amendment to its relevant laws and implemented the agreement in the SAR.

In accordance with the provisions of the agreement, the Hong Kong SAR courts agreed to enforce the awards made by mainland arbitral institutions in line with the Procedural Law of the People's Republic of China. Since there were a great many arbitral institutions on the mainland, a list of such institutions drawn up in accordance with Procedural Law was provided to the Hong Kong SAR by the Legislative Affairs Office of State Council through the State Council's Hong Kong and Macao Affairs Office, and mainland people's courts agreed to enforce awards produced by Hong Kong in accordance with the HK SAR's Arbitration Ordinance. The specific arrangements were: if one party to an arbitration award produced in the mainland or in Hong Kong failed to honor the award, the other party could apply for enforcement by a court of law concerned where the subject of the application had his domicile or where his property was located. The term "court of law concerned" refers, in the mainland, to an intermediate people's court where the subject of the application has his domicile of where his property is located and, in Hong Kong, to the High Court of the Hong Kong SAR. If the subject of the application has places of domicile or locations of property in both the mainland and the Hong Kong SAR, the applicant may not simultaneously submit applications to the courts concerned in both places. Only if enforcement by the court of law in one region does not suffice to reimburse the subject's debts may the applicant apply to the court in the other region for enforcement of the inadequate portion. The total amount of the arbitration award enforced consecutively by the courts in both regions may not exceed the amount awarded.

The applicant who requests that a court concerned enforces an arbitral award produced on the mainland or by the Hong Kong SAR is required to submit an application for enforcement and a copy of the arbitral award plus an arbitration agreement. The agreement shall specifically state the matter(s) stipulated in the enforcement application, the time frame and procedures for the enforcement, the enforcement fee, and define matters that may be arbitrated as not to be enforced. For instance, enforcement of the said ruling may be annulled where mainland courts maintain that enforcement of the said arbitration award would violate the public interest of mainland society, or where Hong Kong SAR courts affirm that enforcement of the said arbitration award in the Hong Kong SAR violates the public policies of Hong Kong. The agreement shall also stipulate that when problems are encountered in the course of enforcing the agreement and amendments are needed, these shall be resolved through consultations between the mainland's Supreme People's Court and the Hong Kong SAR Government.

There are now laws to be followed on the matter of reciprocal enforcement of arbitral awards by the two regions. It should be noted, however, that what has been resolved is merely the mutual enforcement of the two regions' arbitration rulings, and that different opinions exist as to whether "enforcement" includes "recognition" of the intent of the other party's ruling.

10.5.3 Mutual Recognition and Enforcement of Court Rulings

Prior to Hong Kong's return to China, reciprocal recognition and enforcement in the handling of rulings by Hong Kong and mainland courts of law may be viewed in light of the relevant arrangements established at the time between China and Britain. However, mainland courts basically did not recognize rulings produced by Hong Kong courts of law. For example, the Supreme People's Court, in its annotated reply in May 1974 to the Shanghai Higher People's Court regarding the enforcement of Hong Kong–Macao divorce cases, explicitly pointed out that although the Hong Kong court of law had already produced a verdict in accordance with Hong Kong law on the Qian Xingyi and Wu Zhangming divorce case, a separate hearing and verdict should be conducted by the Shanghai court in accordance with mainland Chinese law, and the Hong Kong court's verdict would not be recognized.[34] After that time, limited recognition was gradually accorded in individual cases to verdicts by Hong Kong courts. On September 20, 1991, the Supreme People's Court, in an annotated reply to the Heilongjiang Higher People's Court, indicated that regarding the application submitted by Chinese citizen Zhou Fangzhou requesting recognition of the effectiveness of a local Hong Kong court's judgment on the dissolution of her marriage to British subject Zhuo Jian, intermediate people's courts with jurisdiction should accept such cases. If reviews after acceptance of such cases showed that the said judgments did not violate the basic principles of China's laws or social public interests, rulings could be made to recognize their legal effectiveness.[35]

Along with the sharp increases in cases related to Hong Kong and Macao after the establishment of the Hong Kong SAR, it became necessary to further institutionalize the mutual recognition of court judgments on both sides, which would otherwise have led to a considerable waste of human, material, and financial resources. In 1998 alone, courts of law nationwide accepted 4162 HK—and Macao-related cases, 3630 of which involved Hong Kong and 532 involved Macao, an increase of 39.24% over 1997. Yet, neither Hong Kong nor Macao have reached any agreements or made any reciprocal arrangements with Chinese mainland on reciprocally recognizing and enforcing the other side's judgments.

As regards mainland China, the Civil Procedure Law has come up with provisions on recognizing and enforcing judgments and rulings by courts in other countries, but these provisions obviously do not apply to the Hong Kong and Macao SARs, and can only serve as reference. Article 266 of the Civil Procedure Law stipulates: "If a party applies for enforcement of a legally effective judgment or written order made by a people's court, and the opposite party or his property is not within the territory of

---

[34]"Annotated Reply on the Matter of the Enforcement of Hong Kong and Macao Divorce Cases," Supreme People's Court, May 17, 1974.

[35]"Annotated Reply on the Matter of Whether Chinese Courts Should Accept the Application by Chinese Citizen Zhou Fangzhou to a Chinese Court Requesting Recognition of the Effectiveness of the Judgment by a Local Hong Kong Court on a Divorce," the Supreme People's Court, September 20, 1991.

the People's Republic of China, the applicant may directly apply for recognition and enforcement to the foreign court which has jurisdiction. The people's court may also, in accordance with the relevant provisions of the international treaties concluded or acceded to by China, or with the principle of reciprocity, request recognition and enforcement by the foreign court." This shows that when a situation emerges where a judgment by a people's court requires recognition and enforcement in a foreign country, the party concerned may, first of all, go directly to the country concerned and apply to the foreign country's courts with jurisdiction for recognition and enforcement of the judgment or ruling by the Chinese court. In these situations, reliance on actions by the party concerned offers very little if any hope of success if no treaties or reciprocal arrangements exist between the two countries. Hence, the parties concerned may also apply to China's courts for requesting that the relevant foreign courts recognize and enforce the judgments or rulings of the Chinese courts. Under such circumstances, the matter is fairly simple if both countries have joined international treaties regarding mutual recognition of court judgments or both sides have concluded the relevant bilateral agreements, and the other side will be obligated by international law to enforce the judgments by Chinese courts. In the absence of such treaties or agreements, the two sides may mutually recognize and enforce judgments by the other side's courts based on the principle of reciprocity and by means of handling individual cases.

As regards the matter of China recognizing and enforcing judgments by foreign courts, Article 267 of the Civil Procedure Law stipulates: "If a legally effective judgment or written order of a foreign country requires recognition and enforcement by a people's court of the People's Republic of China, the party concerned may directly apply for recognition and enforcement to the intermediate people's court of the People's Republic China which has jurisdiction. The foreign court may also, in accordance with the provisions of the international treaties concluded or acceded to by that foreign country and the People's Republic of China or with the principle of reciprocity, request recognition and enforcement by a people's court." And Article 268 stipulates: "In the case of an application or request for recognition or enforcement of a legally effective judgment or written order of a foreign court, the people's court shall, after examining it in accordance with the international treaties concluded or acceded to by the People's Republic of China or with the principle of reciprocity and arriving at the conclusion that it does not contradict the basic principles of law of the People's Republic of China nor violates State sovereignty, security and social and public interest of the country, recognize the validity of the judgment or written order, and, if required, issue a writ of execution to enforce it in accordance with the relevant provisions of this Law; if the application or request contradicts the basic principles of the law of the People's Republic of China or violates State sovereignty, security and social and public interest of the country, the court shall not recognize and enforce it." Here, the reciprocity principle is basically adopted for the relevant foreign countries that recognize and enforce the judgments and rulings by Chinese courts.

Where Hong Kong is concerned, it has always exercised two systems toward judgments by foreign courts, i.e., the Statutory Law system and the Common Law system. The term "Statutory Law system" refers to the exercise of a registration procedure based on Hong Kong's "Foreign Judgments (Restriction on Recognition and Enforcement) Ordinance,"[36] "Foreign Judgments (Reciprocal Enforcement) Ordinance,"[37] and "Judgments (Facilities for Enforcement) Ordinance,"[38] and whereby Hong Kong courts directly enforce the relevant judgments. However, this system applies only to countries and regions with bilateral agreements or reciprocal arrangements with Hong Kong. For those countries and regions, which do not have mutual agreements or bilateral arrangements with Hong Kong, only the Common Law system may be applied. This is a procedure that calls for the rehearing of cases in Hong Kong courts. In other words, a party concerned which has won a lawsuit in a court in some other judicial district may regard the judgment of his successful lawsuit as a sort of debt established between the parties concerned and may file a renewed lawsuit in a Hong Kong court of law, whereupon that court determines whether it has judicial jurisdiction over the matter in the original lawsuit. If the court determines that it does have jurisdiction, it may use the foreign court's judgment as an attachment to its own judgment and then enforce it. In this way, the foreign court's judgment is recognized and enforced in the form of a renewed judgment made by a Hong Kong court of law. According to Hong Kong's Foreign Judgments (Reciprocal Enforcement) Ordinance, the registration procedure is preferable to the Common Law procedure. In other words, if a bilateral agreement or a reciprocal arrangement exists with Hong Kong, the matter may be directly registered and enforced, while the procedure of filing a renewed lawsuit is used only when no such arrangement is present.[39] It is obvious that the Statutory Law system of direct registration is more convenient and economical than the Common Law system.

It is only logical that the stipulation and method of Hong Kong recognizing and enforcing the judgments of foreign courts could be applied to handling the judgments of mainland courts. The key to the matter is that both sides should enter into negotiations as soon as possible. Since Chinese mainland is able to reach agreements with so many foreign countries, and Hong Kong too is able to conclude agreements and engage in good cooperative relations with so many foreign countries, there is decidedly no reason why Chinese mainland and the Hong Kong SAR should be unable to reach agreement on the mutual recognition and enforcement of court judgments.

It should also be noted that, as differs from criminal justice, the judicial jurisdiction exercised by a local court in the domain of civil and commercial affairs does not require the application of the laws of the same locality; the court which exercises jurisdiction may apply the laws of another locality as the lex causae. The Economic Division of the Guangzhou Intermediate People's Court, when examining a dispute

---

[36] Ordinances of Hong Kong, Chapter 46.

[37] Ordinances of Hong Kong, Chapter 319.

[38] Ordinances of Hong Kong, Chapter 9.

[39] Huang Ji'er. "Judicial Assistance on Civil and Commercial Affairs between the Hong Kong Special Administrative Region and the Mainland," carried in *Chinese Laws*, 1998 (9), p. 16.

involving a Hong Kong loan borrowing contract on June 17, 2000, for the first time made a judgment by applying a relevant Hong Kong ordinance in order to uphold by law the legal rights and interests of the party concerned. In 1996 and 1997, respectively, the Hong Kong Meidaduo Finance Co., Ltd. extended a loan of HK $126 million to the Ruichang Company, which then provided a 46-story building in Hong Kong as collateral for the loan, while the Hong Kong Julong and its legal representatives Li Jungang and Wen Meijuan signed "irrevocable guarantees." Ruichang was subsequently unable to repay the principal and interest as contracted. Ruichang thereupon filed a suit with the Hong Kong SAR High Court, requesting that the above parties reimburse it for the loan principal and interest, and the court ruled in its favor. However, the defendants were still unable to repay the monies, whereupon Meidaduo publicly auctioned off Ruichang's collateral real estate, but obtained from it a price of only HK $65.1 million. By December 1998, the four defendants still owed the plaintiff principal and interest totaling some HK $87.29 million. Since the four defendants were in possession of numerous properties in Guangzhou, Meidaduo filed a lawsuit with the Guangzhou Intermediate People's Court on the premise that Guangzhou could serve as a locale for enforcing its property demands. After reviewing the case, the Guangzhou Intermediate People's Court stated that the case had already been tried by a Hong Kong court, but that no judicial agreements existed as yet between Chinese mainland and Hong Kong, which stipulated that applications could be made for the recognition and enforcement of Hong Kong court judgments in Chinese mainland and, moreover, the parties concerned had not, in the relevant agreements, selected a court capable of exercising jurisdiction over the case. Therefore, the plaintiff, under the circumstance of its rights and interest not having obtained effective guarantees, filed a lawsuit with a mainland court, which could serve as a locale for enforcing its property demands. In accordance with the Civil Procedure Law of the People's Republic of China, the Guangzhou Intermediate People's Court could exercise jurisdiction over this case; and since the various parties concerned had agreed to choose Hong Kong laws as the laws applicable to their contract dispute, those laws could, in light of the provisions of the PRC's General Principles of Civil Law, be applied to the case. Accordingly, the Guangzhou Intermediate People's Court adjudged that in accordance with the provisions of the Hong Kong SAR's "Money Lenders Ordinance" and Hong Kong's current laws regarding loan collaterals, the plaintiff had won the lawsuit and that the four defendants should, within ten days of the judgment going into effect, repay principal and interest to the tune of HK $ 87.29 million.[40] This matter shows that numerous ways and means are available for cooperation on civil and commercial lawsuits between the two regions.

---

[40] *China News Agency*, May 18, 2000.

10.5.4 Cooperation in Conducting Investigations and Obtaining Evidence

Conducting investigations and obtaining evidence in transnational and cross-border civil and commercial lawsuits are an important content of international judicial assistance. But any agreement in this respect has long been absent between Hong Kong and Chinese mainland, and each has adhered to its own customary practices. Hong Kong's cooperation with other countries in civil and commercial lawsuits has proceeded mainly in accordance with the 1970 Hague Convention on the Taking of Evidence Abroad in Civil and Commercial Matters and based on the corresponding provisions drawn up in line with this Convention in such laws as the SAR's Rules of the High Court[41] and its Evidence Ordinance.[42] Chinese mainland has participated in this Convention only since July, 1997.

Article 262 of China's Civil Procedure Law stipulates: "In accordance with the international treaties concluded or acceded to by the People's Republic of China or with the principle of reciprocity, the people's courts of China and foreign courts may make mutual requests for assistance in the service of legal documents, in investigation or collection of evidence or in other litigation actions." And Article 263 stipulates: "The request for the providing of judicial assistance shall be effected through channels provided in the international treaties concluded or acceded to by the People's Republic of China; in the absence of such treaties, they shall be effected through diplomatic channels. A foreign embassy or consulate accredited to the People's Republic of China may serve documents on its citizens and make investigations and collect evidence among them, provided that the laws of the People's Republic of China are not violated and no compulsory measures are taken. Except for the conditions provided in the preceding paragraph, no foreign organization or individual may, without the consent of the competent authorities of the People's Republic of China, serve documents or make investigation and collect evidence within the territory of the People's Republic of China." This shows that there are two ways through which China and foreign countries may engage in cooperation in judicial investigations and collection of evidence. One is by conducting these according to international treaties concluded or acceded to by China and the other is by conducting these through diplomatic channels according to the principle of reciprocity if either of the two sides has not acceded to the relevant international treaties. Foreign embassies and consulates stationed in China may conduct investigations and collect evidence among the country's citizens so long as they do not violate the laws of the People's Republic of China and do not resort to compulsory measures.

However, neither the above provisions of the 1970 Hague Convention on the Taking of Evidence Abroad in Civil and Commercial Matters, nor the abovementioned provisions of the Civil Procedure Law are applicable to cooperation between mainland China and the Hong Kong SAR on the handling of investigations and evidence

---

[41]Ordinances of Hong Kong, Chapter 4.

[42]Ordinances of Hong Kong, Chapter 8.

collection, even though they may be taken as reference. The former provisions are those of an international convention and do not apply to Hong Kong and mainland China since the relations between the two are not those between different countries. Nor are the latter applicable, because in accordance with the Basic Law they do not fall in the rubric of national laws implemented in Hong Kong. This is a very ticklish problem frequently encountered in the handling of laws involving the two regions. The only solutions to it are like the one in 1998 when the two regions reached agreement on the entrustment and service of civil and commercial judicial documents, and like the one in 1999 when they reached agreement on mutual enforcement of arbitral awards; i.e., when both sides consulted on an equal footing to reach agreements based on the principles of reciprocity, mutual respect, and referencing the practices of international conventions, and then each working out legal procedures according to their own legal systems to implement the agreements. That is how it should be for cooperation on examinations and evidence collection as well.

Chapter 11
Reviews of Constitutionality, Rule of Law, and National Unity

Matters of national unity and of handling relations between the whole and the component parts of a nation are generally seen as political issues apparently unrelated to rule of law. Indeed, these matters are highly political in nature and are very frequently determined by the decision-makers' political acumen and farsightedness. However, the role of rule of law in resolving matters of national unity should by no means be underestimated. Rule of law alone is insufficient to solve such problems, but these problems cannot be resolved by politics without rule of law, and even though temporarily solved, they are not resolved for any length of time. Where rule of law is well exercised, it plays an immense role in upholding national unity and stability and in dealing with the relations between the whole and the component parts of a nation. In a certain sense, all resolutions of a political nature are final and thorough and hold good for all time only if they are put into full effect by means of laws.

Previous chapters and sections in this book have carried frequent references to the role of rule of law in the resumption of China's sovereignty over the Hong Kong and Macao regions and in the handling of Central/SAR relations, especially in Chapter V where I conducted specific explorations in the matter of rule of law. In the present chapter, I shall no longer discuss rule of law in general terms; its importance obviously does not require any further elaboration. I wish to emphasize one matter in the discussion on rule of law, namely, reviews of constitutionality. Why does this need discussion? That is because reviews or examinations of constitutionality or non-constitutionality are the cornerstones of rule of law, a most fundamental component of rule of law. When people in China mention rule of law, the first thing that comes to mind is legislation. In developed countries and regions, however, rule of law certainly does not consist solely of legislation even though legislators invariably strive to devise the most detailed and concrete laws. Yet once these are applied in real life, one suddenly finds that human behavior is much more diverse and "unruly" and that the laws painstakingly worked out by so many experts all seem very unsophisticated and feeble. That is something that cannot be helped. The same

© Foreign Language Teaching and Research Publishing Co., Ltd and Springer Nature Singapore Pte Ltd. 2019
Z. Wang, *Relationship Between the Chinese Central Authorities and Regional Governments of Hong Kong and Macao: A Legal Perspective*, China Academic Library, https://doi.org/10.1007/978-981-13-2322-5_11

of course goes for the Constitution—the "law of laws." That is why in the rule-of-law and judicial systems of all countries, there must be an authoritative institution for interpreting laws which serves as a living "legal spokesman" in charge of clarifying muddled and unclear issues in laws, and why there must be a system for reviewing constitutionality, or lack thereof.

One of the chief contents of reviews of constitutionality is to resolve dissensions over administrative competence between national governments (central governments or federal governments) and district governments (local governments) in light of constitutions or constitution-type laws (as for instance the SAR Basic Laws). Where these issues are well resolved, national unity can be effectively promoted and consolidated. Where they are poorly resolved, tensions arise between national and district governments (central governments and localities), and in serious cases may give rise to national schisms. Hence, a good, fair and effective institution for solving dissensions of a constitutional nature is of prime importance for a country. That is why I have entitled this chapter "Reviews of Constitutionality, Rule of Law and National Unity."

The Central–SAR relations in China are no exception. The SAR Basic Laws have been formulated, the "one country, two systems" concept, a "high degree of autonomy," "Hong Kongers administer Hong Kong," and "Macaoans administer Macao" have entered into law, and basic legal frameworks, legal institutions, and rule-of-law hardware are in existence, and all that remains to be done is to put these to specific use. These are issues of enforcement of law and administration of justice; primarily of the administration of justice. And the highest forms of administration of justice and rule of law are reviews of constitutionality. Hence the core issue today of the handling of Central/SAR relations is actually that of reviewing constitutionality, or in other words, of determining who interprets the SAR Basic Laws, and who has the right to make the final decisions, who is the final arbiter and what are the criteria and procedures for arbitration when situations of lack of distinctness and clarity emerge in the powers and relations between the central authorities and the SARs.

Why don't the relevant institutions formulate some document in the nature of "detailed rules for the implementation of the SAR Basic Laws" and give more concrete expression to the Basic Laws? That would save people the trouble of conducting reviews of constitutionality and make things more convenient, would it not? Every time an important law is formulated in Chinese mainland, the State Council or some other institution issues detailed rules for its implementation, or the Supreme People's Court published a highly detailed and specific judicial interpretation to further clarify the connotations of the law's articles and to enhance its operability for the judges. The reason why the Basic Laws cannot be handled in this way is that their main areas of implementation are in an entirely different jurisdictional domain. Such things are not done Under Hong Kong's Common Law system. The highest courts (i.e., a court of final appeal) in Common Law locales do not conduct detailed interpretations of laws for the use of the courts of all levels before the laws go into effect; they only interpret laws when lawsuits are in progress. The Common Law system sets forth the precise meanings of articles of law during hearings of specific lawsuits to determine whether a certain article violates the highest law (the constitution or a basic law). These court ordinances in reality serve as the laws' "detailed rules of implementation." Hence under the Common Law system, laws are not merely written legislations but also include a great many relevant cases which in a certain sense carry greater import. That is why the "case reports" in the Common Law domain actually serve as "law reports" for schools of law and lawyers!

In that case, who formulates the "detailed rules of implementation" or the "judicial interpretations" for the Basic Laws of the Special Administrative Regions? Certainly not the State Council or the Supreme People's Court. The Supreme People's Court does not have the power to conduct reviews of constitutionality, nor are there any special institutions for reviewing constitutionality (constitutional courts) in mainland China. China's Constitution and the SAR Basic Laws have vested this power in two institutions—the NPC Standing Committee and the SARs' Court of Final Appeal. Only these two institutions or systems have the power to formulate "detailed rules of implementation" or "judicial interpretations" for SAR Basic Laws. The NPC Standing Committee and the SARs' Court of Final Appeal each operate within their own judicial systems; the former fulfills its obligations primarily through such means as constitutionality reviews and Basic Law interpretations, while the SARs' Courts of Final Appeal fulfill their duty of interpreting the Basic Laws and conducting constitutionality reviews by means of hearing cases and producing judgments. The NPC Standing Committee exercises the power of final interpretation for the Basic Laws, while the SARs' Courts of Final Appeal wield the power of final judgment over all cases in the SARs. Hence the SARs' Basic Laws differ from other laws in China in that they do not consist merely of their own articles plus a basket of judicial interpretations devised for these articles by the Superior People's Court, but made up of Basic Law case interpretations, which are constantly being clarified and enriched by a numerous Basic Law cases. Under the Common Law system, rules of law are in fact being "fought out" by means of fighting lawsuits. The specific connotations of many articles of law are clarified in the course of engaging in lawsuits only, and judges or constitutionality review institutions spell out the original intent of legislations in their respective judgments or writs of explanation. Hence when studying the Basic Laws one must study not only the texts of the Basic Laws; more importantly, we must see how the NPC Standing Committee and the SARs' Court of Final Appeal have exercised their respective powers of examining constitutionality and read up on the abundant interpretations and cases concerned.

This Chapter is devoted mainly to exploring issues of the reviews of constitutionality in Chinese mainland and the SARs. One may now say that rule of law in the SARs and the destiny and future of the SARs are closely tied to the entire process of rule of law and the improvement and perfection of the entire constitutionality review system in China. The practice of the SARs in the years after their founding proves that the establishment and perfection of the constitutionality review system is not merely a core issue in the mainland's rule-of-law construct but has also become a key to handling Central/SAR relations. In the final section, I shall, from a still broader perspective, expound on the general relations between rule of law and national unity as well as on the methods of bringing about and maintaining national unity.

11.1   China's System for Reviewing Constitutionality

11.1.1   "Limited Government" and Judicial Reviews

Contemporary rule of law has established two basic systems and principles. One of these is the legal person system established in terms of private law, i.e., the restricting of the rights and duties of the individual within given limits and allowing the individual to undertake limited risks and responsibilities only, and in this way prevents loss of all property by all persons in a company if the company goes bankrupt. This is the "Co., Ltd." system. This system in fact socializes—also called "democratizes"—economic rights, commercial risks, and responsibilities, lets more people share rights at the same time as they share responsibilities. And because the risks and responsibilities borne by individuals are smaller than those in previously unlimited companies, the behavior of company operators and administrators must be subjected to strict supervision and constraints, and this has given rise to a whole system of corporate laws and laws for market dealings. Such is the mission of civil and commercial law.

Relative to the limited company system is the second and perhaps the most important system established by contemporary rule of law—the "limited government" system.[1] As the economic pattern of human society transitioned from a natural economy (or planned economy) to a market economy, governments also had to correspondingly evolve from "unlimited government" over to "limited government," in the way that "unlimited companies" evolved into "limited companies." There are three levels of significance to "limited government." The first is that the power of any government must be limited; it must not be unlimited. The government must not be enabled to do everything. Governments are not omnipotent. Although the powers of modern governments are considerably smaller that they used to be, they also bear far fewer risks and political hazards, and they need not live in constant fear and angst as the feudal emperors once did; this is beneficial for government stability and for government personages. Secondly, government powers are not only subject to restrictions, they must also be supervised and constrained, and uncontrolled government powers are not to be permitted. Three, when governments misuse their powers, there must be legal mechanism for promptly revealing and correcting these abuses. Accordingly, many countries have devised entire sets of constitutional (public law) systems, most important among them being the judicial review system, or referred to more broadly as the "system for reviews of constitutionality." The principal mission of constitutions is to standardize acts of government and governance.

However, during studies of the history of constitutions, I have come across a very interesting phenomenon. All persons who devise constitutions and all politicians hold

[1] As the English term for "有限公司" is "company limited," I am translating "有限政府" correspondingly as "government limited." If all governments could append "Ltd." at the end of their formal appellation, just as "Ltd." is added at the end of the commercial name of a company with limited shares, this might serve as a reminder to governments that their powers are limited and subject to constraints.

that reviews of constitutionality are most important, but whether due to deliberate evasion or to unintended oversight, few are the countries with constitutions that contain provisions about powers to conduct constitutionality reviews, and many even do not contain the term "review of constitutionality," the earlier constitutions in particular. However, systems for constitutionality reviews are indeed in operation in all countries. What grounds are there for such a claim? Customary constitutional practice. People have actually had the nerve to leave the establishment such an important system as constitutionality reviews to so-called "constitutional practice!" It is in truth a most ironic fact in the history of mankind's governance and rule of law that the existence of such an important mechanism for ensuring and upholding rule of law lacks any constitutional or even legal basis; that, strictly speaking, constitutionality still remains in the "primitive" and "lawless" state of being determined according to the "first-come-first-served principle" prevalent in the rudimentary handling of property ownerships. Was this a deliberate act by the drafters of constitutions of leaving a "rule-of-law vacuum" to test the political wisdom and rule-of-law awareness of later generations? I have no idea. Take for example the American founders and "inventors" of the system of constitutionality reviews. If the U.S. Supreme Court had not—in that famous judgment in 1803—been the first to claim that the power of judicial examination (i.e., the right of conducting reviews of constitutionality) pertained to itself and beat others to filling this curious and rare vacuum left by the constitution's drafters, one can hardly imagine that today's U.S. Supreme Court would have such a great authority and that the United States would be exercising its present "separation of powers." The behavior of the young U.S. Supreme Court in 1803 is reminiscent of the way the early colonists seized stretches of land and announced possession of these the moment they arrived on the New Continent, and declared that "outsiders" should keep out! However, one cannot but acknowledge the astuteness and courage of the then US Supreme Court headed by Chief Justice John Marshall.

That state of affairs clarifies at least one thing, i.e., building up rule of law does not mean simply going about legislation; legislation, no matter how rigorous, always has loopholes. The establishment of rule of law also depends on awareness, and especially on the political wisdom, foresight and insight of the country's "founders," their devotion to rule of law, and their sense of responsibility toward history. Respect for previously established conventions and customs is also an important component of rule of law and a manifestation of the fine qualities of the citizens in a country ruled by laws. The rule-of-law loopholes left to us by the drafters of constitutions are of course very daunting and are predicated on the assumption that all people are sages. With a view to avoiding chaos, subsequent drafters of constitutions in various countries have usually assigned the exercise of the powers of judicial examination or constitutionality reviews to this or that institution, since history has time and again demonstrated that people's awareness is fickle and unreliable—indeed a deplorable aspect of human nature. When setting up a "government limited," constitutionality reviews must be established, and the best way to set up constitutionality reviews is by means of written, documentary legislation, even though legislation is not omnipotent.

Throughout the long years of Chinese feudal society, the powers of the feudal emperors and feudal governments were unrestricted and were never subject to any supervision or constraints, nor were there any legal mechanisms capable of preventing government misuse of powers or examining government actions. From first to last the emperors were plenipotentiary; emperors were "the whole caboodle."[2] Over a long period of time, people were helpless before government behavior. Legal methods which might have enabled them to query or challenge government acts were nonexistent, no legal succor was available to them when their rights were trampled upon, and any ideas about "people suing officials" were mere wishful thinking. With the founding of the New China in 1949, numerous efforts were made with regard to restraining and supervising government and setting up a system for examining constitutionality. Provisions in this respect were, in particular, inserted in the new Constitution formulated in 1982. Article 41, for instance, clearly stipulated:

> Citizens of the People's Republic of China have the right to criticize and make suggestions regarding any state organ or functionary. Citizens have the right to make to relevant state organs complaints or charges against, or exposures of, any state organ or functionary for violation of the law of dereliction of duty; but fabrication or distortion of facts for purposes of libel or false incrimination is prohibited. The state organ concerned must deal with complaints, charges or exposures made by citizens in a responsible manner after ascertaining the facts. No one may suppress such complaints, charges, and exposures or retaliate against the citizens making them. Citizens who have suffered losses as a result of infringements of their civic rights by any state organ or functionary have the right to compensation in accordance with the law.

Yet for an extended period of time, China did not devise a practical set of constitutional and legal mechanisms which would genuinely ensure the rights of its citizens to supervise or even challenge government actions. It was not until the Standing Committee of the Seventh National People's Congress (hereinafter referred to as the "NPC Standing Committee") passed the Administrative Procedure Law of the People's Republic of China on April 4, 1989 that a genuine breakthrough took place.[3] Article 2 of this Law specifically provided that "if a citizen, a legal person or an organizations considers that his or its lawful rights and interests have been infringed upon by a specific administrative act of an administrative organ or its personnel, he

---

[2]From the time China started to bring in Western law at the end of the Qing Dynasty and up to the time before 1949, new-type companies with limited shares were set up. This system was terminated after the new government was established in 1949. After the "cultural revolution" ended in 1977, China embarked on its Reform and Opening Up endeavors and only then were modern corporations of limited liability set up. These are still being improved and perfected today. However, China has not yet made much progress in terms of establishing "limited government."

[3]Implementation of the Administrative Procedure Law began on October 1, 1990. Previously, in accordance with Article 3, paragraph two of the Civil Procedure Law (Trial) formulated by the NPC Standing Committee on March 8, 1982, i.e., that "This law is applicable to administrative cases which are handled by the people's court," citizens and organizations which disagreed with handling by administrative organs could file lawsuits with courts. Accordingly, more than 130 laws and administrative regulations as well as a large number of local regulations gave citizens the power to bring suits against specific government administrative acts. However, before the Administrative Procedure Law came into effect, no complete system for administrative procedures was formed, nor did courts of law accept or hear many administrative cases.

or it shall have the right to bring a suit before a people's court in accordance with this Law." Thereafter, Chinese citizens and legal persons could, when their rights and interests were infringed upon or violated by the government, demand an explanation through a people's court in accordance with the law, and ordinary people could go to courts to sue officials and the government. This was considerable progress. At the outset the ordinary people, the government and the courts "were not used to" doing this, and it was big news whenever the mayor of a city was taken to court as a defendant. Today, twelve years later, "people suing officials" is no longer newsworthy in China, and not only are township, country, and municipal governments repeatedly placed in the defendant's seat in people's courts, even provincial governments and ministries and commissions of the State Council are being requested to appear in court. Today, China's ordinary citizens are increasingly awakening to their rights and interests, and are more and more willing to "take on" government authorities in courts of law. Meanwhile, China's judges may still depend on the government for their "rice bowl," yet more and more dare say "no" to the government, and passing judgments against the latter is no longer a novelty. The implementation of the Administrative Procedure Law is an important landmark in the progress of China's rule of law.[4]

On May 12, 1994, the Eighth NPC Standing Committee passed the Law of the People's Republic of China on State Compensation, which provided in Article 2 that "If a state organ or a member of its personnel, when exercising functions and powers in violation of the law, infringes upon the lawful rights and interests of a citizen, legal person or other organization and causes damages, the aggrieved party shall have the right to recover damages from the state in accordance with this law." This was another supervision and constraint of a substantive nature on state organs and their personnel.

However, whether the State Compensation Law or the Administrative Procedure Law or any other relevant law which exists today—all place considerable restrictions on citizens or legal persons who challenge government acts through judicial channels. The main restriction is that citizens, legal persons, and other organizations may only seek judicial supervision or judicial redress for "specific administrative acts" by the government. Article 11 of the Administrative Procedure Law lists the specific administrative acts against which lawsuits may be filed in courts of law, and Article 12 specially lists the government acts against which lawsuits may not be filed. Paragraph two of this Article identifies "administrative rules and regulations, regulations, or decisions and orders with general binding force formulated or announced by administrative organs." That is to say, citizens may go to courts to protest against a certain specific administrative measure taken by the government,

---

[4]In 1990, when implementation of the Administrative Procedure Law had just begun, courts of law nationwide accepted and heard 13,006 administrative cases in the whole of that year, 30.92% more than in 1989; hearings on 12,040 cases were concluded, an increase of 23.59% over the previous year. From October to December 1990, courts of law heard 5258 administrative cases, 96.56% more than in the same period of the previous year. Ren Jianxin. "Work Report of the Supreme People's Court." Beijing: *People's Daily* (April 13, 1991), p. 3. In 2000, local courts nationwide heard and passed judgments on a total of 86,000 administrative lawsuits. Xiao Yang. "Work Report of the Supreme People's Court," Xinhua News Agency, Beijing, March 21, 2001.

but may not seek judicial examinations of normative documents formulated by the government and legislative acts performed by the government—usually referred to as "abstract administrative acts" in China's law circles. You may go to court and sue the police for incorrectly imposing a fine on you, but you may not go to court and say that the law, regulation or rule on which the policeman based his fine is wrong, and you may not request a judicial examination of the problematic law, regulation or rule. Even if you do file a lawsuit in this respect, no court of law will accept it.[5]

Hence in China, there are at present only limited judicial examinations. One can only seek judicial examinations for specific administrative acts, and courts of law cannot examine the state's legislative acts to determine whether they violate the Constitution, whether they are reasonable, or whether they should be repealed or retained. Does that mean the state's "abstract acts," i.e., legislative acts, are not subject to any restrictions or supervision? No, it does not. China's Constitution stipulates a special system for examining constitutionality. In other words, there are two kinds of supervision for state acts under Chinese law. One is supervision over specific acts, and the other is supervision over "abstract acts." Responsibility for the two is taken, respectively, by two different institutions. The former is under the charge of ordinary courts of law, and responsibility for the latter falls to institutions which examine constitutionality.

11.1.2 China's Institutions Responsible for Examining Constitutionality and Their Competence

China exercises a national congress system, which is similar to the British parliamentary system. Under this system, China, in terms of its Constitution, exercises "sovereignty of the National People's Congress," akin to Britain's "sovereignty of the Parliament." China's Constitution defines the National People's Congress as "the highest organ of state power." China's highest administrative organ (i.e., the State Council), highest judicial organ (i.e., the Supreme People's Court) and highest state organ for legal supervision (i.e., the Supreme Procuratorate) are generated by the National People's Congress, answer to it, and are under its supervision. The head of the state (i.e., the Chairman of the State) is elected by it, and the national institution for commanding the armed forces, i.e., the Central Military Commission is also generated by the National People's Congress by means of elections, and it answers to the latter. It is evident that China's entire state apparatus is set up by, revolves around, and centers on the National People's Congress.[6] The Constitution also carries detailed provisions regarding the other powers pertaining to the National People's Congress

---

[5]Luo Haocai. *China's Judicial Review System.* Peking University Press, 1993, p. 23. "*Si fa fu he* (Judicial Review)" is usually translated into Chinese as "Judicial Examination (*si fa shen cha*)" in Chinese mainland, but mostly as "Judicial Review" in Hong Kong and Taiwan.

[6]China's Constitution in reality implements "sovereignty of the people." Article 2 of the Constitution expressly stipulates "All power in the People's Republic of China belongs to the people." However, among the provisions in Article 62 of Constitution on the functions and powers exercised by the

and its permanent institution the NPC Standing Committee, including the state's legislative power, the power to determine major affairs of state, the power to supervise the state's other institutions and so forth. Among these powers is the power to conduct constitutionality reviews.[7] However, that is not to say that the power to conduct constitutionality reviews is to be exercised solely by the National People's Congress. On the contrary, in accordance with the relevant provisions of China's Constitution, there are other institutions that have the power to implement constitutionality reviews. The Legislation Law passed by the Ninth National People' Congress on March 15, 2000 went a step further in terms of building up the constitutionality review system by further defining China constitutionality review institutions. Article 88 stipulated: "The limits of power for annulling or altering laws, administrative regulations, local regulations, autonomous regulations, separate regulations or rules are as follows:

a. The National People's Congress has the power to annul or alter any inappropriate laws enacted by its Standing Committee, and to annul any autonomous regulations or separate regulations which have been approved by its Standing Committee but which contravene the Constitutions or the provision of the second paragraph in Article 66 of this Law;

b. the Standing Committee of the National People's Congress has the power to alter or annul any administrative regulations which contradict the Constitution and laws, to annul any local regulations which contradict the Constitution, laws or administrative regulations, and to annul any autonomous regulations or separate regulations which have been approved by the standing committees of the people's congresses of relevant province, autonomous regions, or municipalities directly under the Central Government but which contravene the Constitution or the provision of the second paragraph of Article 66 of this Law;

c. the State Council has the power to alter or annul any inappropriate rules of the departments of local governments;

d. the people's congress of a province, autonomous region or municipality directly under the Central Government has the power to alter or annul any inappropriate local regulations formulated or approved by its standing committee;

e. the standing committee of a local people's congress has the power to annul any inappropriate rules formulated by the people's government at the same level;

National People's Congress, the final paragraph states "… to exercise such other functions and powers as the highest organ of state power should exercise." The Constitution does not stipulate who should determine, and which powers and functions are to be "such other functions and powers as the highest organ of state power should exercise." Moreover, this paragraph in the two earlier constitutions had stipulated that the National People's Congress should exercise all other functions and powers it believed it should exercise. That is to say, those two constitutions conferred unlimited powers to the National People's Congress and in effect equated and lumped together the people's representative organs under it with the people per se. Actually, it is the people who should truly possess all powers, as stipulated in Article 2 of the Constitution, and under any circumstances, there should be limits to the powers of the people's representative organs.

[7]Cai Dingjian. *The National People's Congress System*. Beijing: Law Press, 1998, p. 267.

f. the people's government of a province or autonomous region has the power to alter or annul any inappropriate rules formulated by people's governments at the next lower level; and

g. the authorizing organ has the power to annul any of the regulations formulated by an authorized organ that transcends the authorized limits of power or contravenes the authorized purpose, and when necessary, may revoke the authorization."

One can see that China's system for constitutionality examinations is both multi-tiered and multi-elemental, and that the power to exercise constitutionality examinations has both centralized and dispersed aspects. In accordance with the provisions of the Constitution and the Legislation Law, the National People's Congress, the NPC Standing Committee, local people's congress at all levels and their standing committees, and even the State Council and provincial-level local government have certain powers to conduct constitutionality examinations, but that the subjects of the exercise of constitutionality examinations differ, as do the extents of the powers.

11.1.2.1 The Constitutionality Examination Powers of the National People's Congress

Article 62 of the Constitution stipulates the powers vested in the National People's Congress, item two of which is "to supervise the enforcement of the Constitution," and the 11th of which is "to alter or annul inappropriate decisions of the Standing Committee of the National People's Congress." These are regarded as the constitutional grounds for the constitutionality examination powers vested in the National People's Congress. Accordingly, the NPC's constitutionality examination powers may be divided into two aspects, the first of which is "to supervise the enforcement of the Constitution," and the other of which is the power to examine review the decisions of the NPC Standing Committee.

As regards the first aspect, Chinese scholars generally maintain that the stipulation "to supervise the enforcement of the Constitution" means conferring constitutionality examination powers on the National People's Congress. And so, on which institutions can the National People's Congress exercise these powers? First of all, the Constitution clearly provides that the National People's Congress is empowered to alter or annul inappropriate decisions made by the NPC Standing Committee. Thus, there is no question but that the National People's Congress's right of constitutionality examinations first of all extends to the NPC Standing Committee. However, can the National People's Congress exercise its power of constitutionality examinations to other institutions, such as the State Council? Or must it exercise its power of constitutionality examinations to other institutions through the medium of the NPC Standing Committee? That is because the Constitution does not provide that the National People's Congress may alter or annul decisions made by the State Council or other institutions; it only stipulates that other institutions must answer to it and submit to its supervision, as in the corresponding stipulations of Articles 3, 62, 63, 67, 94, 128 and 133 of the Constitution. I feel that constitutionality examinations are meant to be included here. Especially when these are perused in conjunction other articles of the Constitution one can assert that the subjects of the constitutionality examinations by the National People's Congress is not limited solely to the legislative actions of the NPC Standing Committee but also includes supervision over the enforcement of the Constitution (including both "abstract acts" and "specific acts") by the *Yi Fu Liang Yuan* (acronymic jargon used in political circles to denote the Central People's Government, Superior People's Court and Superior People's Procuratorate—Trans.) and by the Central Military Commission. Here "supervision" also implies constitutionality examinations. That is why the *Yi Fu Liang Yuan* must report their work at the annual meetings of the National People's Congress. As to how the National People's Congress is to supervise the enforcement of the Constitution and how it is to correct and handle acts that violate the Constitution, the Constitution makes no provisions. In terms of actual operations, the National People's Congress, because of its own limitations and various other reasons, can hardly conduct actual constitutionality examinations of these institutions despite its being empowered to do so.

Regarding the second aspect of the constitutionality examination of the NPC Standing Committee by the National People's Congress, it is generally considered that the basis for such examinations is Article 62, item 11 of the Constitution, i.e., that the National People's Congress is empowered "to alter or annul inappropriate decisions of the Standing Committee of the National People's Congress." As to the term "inappropriate," its connotations here are flexible and its reach can be quite extensive. In other words, it includes decisions that are unconstitutional and illegal as well as those that are irrational. Here, the term "decisions" includes laws approved by the NPC Standing Committee as well as its everyday decisions. So it is safe to say that the constitutionality examination powers of the NPC Standing Committee are quite broad.

Where a modern rule-of-law country is concerned, the most important power after its constitution has been formulated is that of constitutional interpretation. Surprisingly, China's Constitution does not vest this important power in its highest organ of state power—the National People's Congress; it confers the power on its permanent institution, the NPC Standing Committee (Article 67, items 1 and 4 of the Constitution). And so the Constitution permits the National People's Congress to exercise the power of constitutionality examination but does not allow it to exercise the right to constitutional interpretation. This stipulation is quite puzzling and hard to understand. May the National People's Congress, as the parent body of the NPC Standing Committee, interpret the Constitution and the laws? If the National People's Congress may not do so, what should it do when it comes across situations where the Constitution or laws need to be interpreted with regard to laws formulated by the NPC Standing Committee and during the exercise of constitutionality examinations of the *Yi Fu Liang Yuan?* Should it "request" its subordinate institution—the NPC Standing Committee—to conduct an "authoritative interpretation" of the Constitution or the law, and then, on the basis of this "authoritative interpretation," pass a constitutionality judgment on the legislation by the NPC Standing Committee or the acts of the *Yi Fu Liang Yuan* which are suspected of violating the Constitution? This obviously fails to make sense in terms of either logic or realities.

Some persons may explain it this way: Since the National People's Congress is the highest organ of state power and the parent institution of the NPC Standing Committee, and since its subordinate institution, the NPC Standing Committee, has the power to interpret the Constitution, the logical inference is that the National People's Congress naturally also possesses the power to interpret the Constitution. I maintain that this inference is wrong, because in accordance with the basic principles and requirements of rule of law, where any state institutions are concerned, the powers they may exercise must be expressly set forth and stipulated in writing in the Constitution; they may not exercise powers which are not explicitly granted to them by the Constitution. And State power may not be "inferred" by ordinary logic. Where the actions of citizens are concerned, absence of explicit prohibitions implies consent, but where state institutions are concerned, the requirements of rule of law are exactly the opposite in that the absence of explicit authorization constitutes forbiddance. And so I do not believe that because the NPC Standing Committee possesses the power to interpret the Constitution, its parent institution the National People's Congress automatically also has the power to interpret the Constitution.

True, the National People's Congress may alter or annul inappropriate decisions by the NPC Standing Committee, including decisions by the NPC Standing Committee to conduct examinations of the constitutionality of given laws, regulations or actions. However, this does not imply that the National People's Congress has the power to interpret the Constitution. This disposition in the Constitution is not due to the drafters of the Constitution neglecting or overlooking the matter, because it is obvious that when the drafters of the Constitution defined the functions and duties for "supervising the enforcement of the Constitution" they explicitly conferred these on two separate institutions—the National People's Congress and the NPC Standing Committee, whereas they conferred the power to "interpret the Constitution" solely to the NPC Standing Committee. It is evident that under the construct of China's present Constitution and legal system, the power to interpret the Constitution and laws is an independent power which is not necessarily linked with the exercise of the power to examine constitutionality.

Historically, the National People's Congress has never exercised the power of constitutionality examinations on other institutions, yet has conducted self-examinations of the constitutionality of its own legislation. If one looks for examples of the conduct of constitutionality examinations by the National People's Congress, there are the constitutionality examinations it has done on the two Special Administrative Region Basic Laws of Hong Kong and Macao. China's Constitution is a socialist-type constitution which defines the political, economic, cultural, and social systems of China's socialism. However, the Basic Law of the Hong Kong Special Administrative Region approved by the Seventh National People's Congress on April 4, 1990 stipulates that "the socialist system and policies shall not be practiced in the Hong Kong Special Region, and the previous capitalist system and way of life shall remain unchanged for 50 years." This clearly violates China's Constitution. Hence some Hong Kong personages feared that the Hong Kong SAR Basic Law would in future be subjected to constitutional litigation and possibly declared unconstitutional and annulled. For this reason, at the same time as the Seventh National People's Congress approved the

Hong Kong SAR Basic Law, it also adopted a Resolution which resolved the issue of whether the Hong Kong SAR Basic Law violated the Constitution. The full text of the Resolution is as follows:

The Third Session of the Seventh National People's Congress adopted the Basic Law of the Hong Kong Special Administrative Region of the People's Republic of China, including Annex I: Method for the Selection of the Chief Executive of the Hong Kong Special Administrative Region; Annex II: Method for the Formation of the Legislative Council of the Hong Kong Special Administrative Region and Its Voting Procedures; and Annex III: National Laws to be Applied in the Hong Kong Special Administrative Region as well as the designs of the regional flag and regional emblem of the Hong Kong Special Administrative Region. Article 31 of the Constitution of the People's Republic of China stipulates: "The state may establish special administrative regions when necessary. The systems to be instituted in special administrative regions shall be legally prescribed by the National People's Congress in the light of specific conditions." The basic law of the Hong Kong special administrative region is formulated on the basis of the Constitution of the People's Republic of China in accordance with the specific conditions of Hong Kong and complies with the Constitution. The system, policies, and law implemented after the establishment of the Hong Kong Special Administrative Region are based on the Basic Law of the Hong Kong Special Administrative Region. The Basic Law of the Hong Kong Special Administrative Region of the People's Republic of China goes into effect as of July 1, 1997.

That Resolution was very succinct. Most importantly, it confirmed that the Hong Kong SAR Basic Law was "formulated on the basis of the Constitution of the People's Republic of China in accordance with the specific conditions of Hong Kong" and therefore "complies with the Constitution." As to how it is formulated in accordance with the Constitution, it cites the provisions of Article 31 of the Constitution on the establishment of special administrative regions and on authorizing the National People's Congress to formulate the systems to be implemented in the special administrative region. That was in effect an examination of constitutionality, or in other words, the conduct of an examination of unconstitutionality (also called an examination of constitutionality) at the same time as the National People's Congress approved the Basic Law of the Hong Kong Special Administrative Region. After the examination, the National People's Congress deemed it constitutional; that it did not violate the Constitution, thereby thoroughly ruling out the possibility of someone eventually maintaining that the Hong Kong SAR Basic Law violated the Constitution and filing a constitutional lawsuit. That was the first time in the New China's legislative history that the National People's Congress publicly conducted an examination of the unconstitutionality (constitutionality) of a law as well as the first time that it formally published a conclusion of such an examination. The organs, procedures, times, methods, and the making of such conclusions may all require further discussion, but their contributions toward initiating a historical precedent must be fully recognized.[8]

---

[8]The powers vested in the National People's Congress by Article 31 of China's Constitution are extremely broad and may be described as unlimited because they authorize the National People's

Similarly, when the Eighth National People Congress approved the Macao Special Administrative Region Basic Law on March 31, 1993, it also conducted a constitutionality examination of the Basic Law and passed a similar Resolution, and thereby resolved its constitutionality issue. In China, the Hong Kong and Macao issues are of course special cases. Apart from these, China's highest organs of state power have not exercised the right of constitutionality examinations vested in them by the Constitution.

These two examples of constitutionality reviews have also resolved, in the form of a conventional practice, the question of which institution should conduct constitutionality reviews of the National People's Congress's own legislation. The Constitution has only stipulated that the National People's Congress may conduct constitutionality reviews of legislations by the NPC Standing Committee, but Constitution has not made any stipulation concerning constitutionality reviews of the National People's Congress's own legislations. In accordance with that convention, the National People's Congress is to be responsible for the conduct of reviews of whether its own legislation is constitutional or otherwise. In other words, the subject of National People's Congress constitutionality reviews is not only the NPC Standing Committee, but itself as well. And whether doing so is reasonable or not, that has already become an unwritten constitutional convention.

11.1.2.2   The Constitutionality Review Powers of the NPC Standing Committee

Since the National People's Congress holds only one meeting a year, and since each meeting lasts only half a month and counts 3000 delegates, it is so overloaded with work that is unable to undertake the functions and duties of conducting constitutional examinations. Hence the Constitution has conferred the power of conducting constitutional examinations primarily on the NPC Standing Committee, which now possesses a whole range of constitutionality examination powers, namely, the power to interpret the Constitution, the power to supervise the enforcement of the Con-

---

Congress to formulate—and to implement in a given territory—a system which comes in conflict with the country's fundamental system as stipulated by China's Constitution. Actually, Article 31 is unnecessary, since Article 62, item 15 of the Constitution stipulates that the National People's Congress has the power to exercise "such other functions and powers as the highest organ of state power should exercise." Hence the National People's Congress is, in line with this item, fully entitled to formulate systems and laws that are inconsistent with the Constitution's basic principles. This shows similarities with Britain's parliamentary sovereignty. In Britain, the parliament may formulate or not formulate any laws, which includes formulating or not formulating laws that limit parliamentary sovereignty. For example, the European Communities Act 1972, approved by the British Parliament in 1972, acknowledging that the legal force of the Treaty of Rome and the EU laws was greater than the force of the domestic laws it had formulated, and eliminated their supremacy in terms of their relations with the European Union. Hence, a Lord Chancellor asserted that no Parliament could restrain the acts of future parliaments. O. Hood Phillips. *Constitutional and Administrative Law (Seventh Edition)*. London: Sweet & Maxwell Ltd., 1987, p. 61. Gong Xiangrui. *Comparing the Constitution and Administrative Law*. Beijing: Law Press, 1985, p. 60.

stitution, and the power to interpret laws. Article 67 of the Constitution provides that the first function and duty of the NPC Standing Committee is to "interpret the Constitution and supervise its enforcement"; its fourth function and duty is "to interpret laws," its seventh function and duty is "to annul those administrative rules and regulations, decisions or orders of the State Council that contravene the Constitution or the law," and its eighth function and duty is "to annul those local regulations or decision of the organs of state power of provinces, autonomous regions, and municipalities directly under the Central Government that contravene the Constitution, the law or the administrative rules and regulations." It is clear that the NPC Standing Committee has ample powers of conducting constitutionality reviews.

First, the NPC Standing Committee has the power to interpret the Constitution and constitutional laws. As stated above, this is a power exclusive to the NPC Standing Committee. Although interpretation of the Constitution is highly important, the NPC Standing Committee has infrequently exercised this power, and few instances of its doing so can be found. An example of interpreting the Constitution often cited by scholars is the "Decision on Having the State Security Organs Exercise the Public Security Organs' Functions and Powers of Investigation, Detention, Preliminary Examination and Arrests" approved by the Second Session of the Sixth NPC Standing Committee on September 2, 1983. This Decision which contained a reinterpretation and explanation of the contents of Article 37 and Article 40 of the Constitution, vested the State Security organs with the same powers as exercised by the Public Security organs. Apart from this, I have not been able to find examples of the NPC Standing Committee directly interpreting provisions in the Constitution.

Since references to China's Constitution may not be used in lawsuits, the NPC Standing Committee's interpretations are not connected with specific case hearings, and for that reason, scholars call them "abstract interpretations."[9] Current interpretations of the Constitution by the NPC Standing Committee are not linked with case hearings in courts of law, and rarely have there been judges who have come across Constitutional matters or even legal matters they do not understand when they hear cases and have therefore had to ask the NPC Standing Committee for interpretations thereof. Such a system has not yet taken shape in China.[10] And situations have never arisen where interpretations of the Constitution or national laws have been requested

---

[9]Xu Chongde. *The Chinese Constitution (Revised Edition)*. Beijing: Law Press, 1985, p. 210.

[10]One of the exceptions is when, because of differences of opinions between the Superior People's Court and the Superior People's Procuratorate on the meaning of the provision in Article 93, paragraph 2 of the Criminal Law "other persons who perform public service according to law," the NPC Standing Committee was asked to conduct a legislative interpretation, and the 15th Session of the Ninth NPC Standing Committee passed a decision on April 29, 2000 to conduct an interpretation of the meaning of the provision "other persons who perform public service according to law" in paragraph two of Article 93 of the Criminal Law. However, even though that rare request for an interpretation was put forward on the initiative of the Superior People's Court and the Superior People's Procuratorate, its "extrinsic" manifestation finally took the form of an initiative by the NPC Standing Committee, i.e., the interpretation took place as a motion for a legal interpretation put forward by the NPC Standing Committee's Council of Chairmen to the NPC Standing Committee's Legislative Affairs Commission, and not as a direct proposal for the interpretation of a law by the Superior People's Court to the NPC Standing Committee, although I myself am quite sure that

in the course of legislation or administration because questions about such matters have been encountered.

Probably the only exceptions are Hong Kong and Macao. Article 158 of the Basic Law of the Hong Kong Special Administrative Region stipulates: "… if the courts of the Region, in adjudicating cases, need to interpret the provisions of this Law concerning affairs which are the responsibility of the Central People' Government, or concerning the relationship between the Central Authorities and the Region, and if such interpretation will affect the judgments on the cases, the courts of the Region shall, before making their final judgments which are not appealable, seek an interpretation of the relevant provisions from the Standing Committee of the National People's Congress through the Court of Final Appeal of the Region. When the Standing Committee makes an interpretation of the provisions concerned, the courts of the Region, in applying those provisions, shall follow the interpretation of the Standing Committee. However, judgments previously rendered shall not be affected." In these circumstances, the interpretation of the Basic Law by the NPC Standing Committee becomes directly concerned with the judgment of specific cases. Article 143 of the Basic Law of the Macao Special Administrative Region carries a similar provision. Since the two SAR Basic Laws are laws of a constitutional nature, the NPC Standing Committee's interpretations of them are also interpretations of a constitutional nature. Hence, they have initiated a new precedent in the history of China's rule-of-law construct, namely, constitutional interpretation acts by the NPC Standing Committee (including interpretations of laws of a constitutional nature) have begun to produce judicial results. They are no longer purely "abstract," but have started to relate to judgments on specific cases.

The NPC Standing Committee has made very few interpretations of provisions of the Constitution, but it has rendered interpretations of laws of a constitutional nature. For example, prior to the return of Hong Kong to China, the British government issued British National (Overseas) passports (BNOs) to many Chinese residents in Hong Kong, and the Hong Kong SAR Basic Law stipulated that these Chinese residents would automatically become Chinese residents, yet China's Nationality Law which would go into force in Hong Kong does not recognize dual citizenship. How the Nationality Law would be implemented after Hong Kong's return was a big problem. Hence, the Eighth National People's Congress Standing Committee approved the "Interpretation of a Number of Questions Regarding the Implementation in the Hong Kong Special Administrative Region of the Nationality Law of the People's Republic of China" on May 15, 1996. In consideration of Hong Kong's historical background and current situation, the said Interpretation stipulated that all Chinese compatriots in Hong Kong would be citizens of China, whether they held British Dependent Territories Citizens passports or BNOs. On the other hand, they could, starting on July 1, 1997, continue to use effective travel documents issued by the British government (including BNOs) to travel in other countries or regions, but possession of these British travel documents would not entitled them to British

---

internal documentary exchanges took place on the matter between the Superior People's Court and the NPC Standing Committee.

consular protection rights in the Hong Kong SAR or in other regions of the People's Republic of China. The nationality issue of Chinese citizens of the Hong Kong SAR who possessed residency rights in other countries would be handled in the same way. Thus, difficulties occasioned by the implementation of China's Nationality Law in the Hong Kong SAR were resolved by means of interpretation of law. The NPC Standing Committee made similar arrangements for solving the nationality issue of Macao residents after Macao's return to China. The Nationality Law is a law of a constitutional nature, hence its interpretations may also be regarded as interpretations of a constitutional nature.

Another typical example is the first time—on June 26, 1999—that the NPC Standing Committee rendered an interpretation of two provisions of the Hong Kong SAR Basic Law in response to a request from the State Council. The reason for that interpretation was the content of a judgment made on January 29 by the Hong Kong SAR's Court of Final Appeal on a case involving the right of abode of children born in Chinese mainland to Hong Kong residents, which differed from the Hong Kong SAR government's understanding of the relevant Basic Law provisions. The SAR government maintained that the judgment concerned by the Court of Final Appeal involved a matter of principle of how the Basic Law should be understood, and that the way of managing the entry of mainland residents into Hong Kong also involved Central/SAR relations. Hence the SAR government had asked the State Council to request that the NPC Standing Committee render interpretations of the two Basic Law articles in accordance with the relevant provisions of the Constitution and the Basic Law. The NPC Standing Committee had accordingly solicited the opinions of its affiliated Hong Kong Special Administrative Region Basic Law Committee and thereupon rendered interpretations regarding the two relevant articles of the Basic Law, thereby resolving the issue of the right of abode in Hong Kong of children born in Chinese mainland to Hong Kong inhabitants. However, the NPC Standing Committee's interpretations did not affect the right of abode in Hong Kong obtained by the parties to the lawsuit concerned adjudicated by the Hong Kong SAR's Court of Final Appeal on January 29, 1999, because such interpretations were not retroactive and only affected future matters. The Hong Kong SAR's courts should follow the NPC Standing Committee's interpretations when passing judgments on future relevant cases.[11] This case and the relevant interpretations have already been discussed in detail in the previous Chapter.

On the whole, the NPC Standing Committee has not yet rendered many interpretations of the Constitution and laws of a constitutional nature, and those it has rendered basically involve Hong Kong and Macao.

Two, the power to supervise enforcement of the Constitution. Because the NPC Standing Committee is a permanent institution of the National People's Congress, it can basically exercise all of the powers exercised by the latter. It can in particular fully exercise the highest state powers during the lengthy periods when the National People's Congress is not in session, including the power of constitutionality reviews. However, if one pays closer attention one will easily discover that the Constitution's

---

[11] Beijing, *Legal Daily*, June 27, 1999.

written provisions regarding the power of constitutionality reviews for the National People's Congress differ from those for the NPC Standing Committee. For the former, Article 62 of the Constitution, in addition to the general provision "to supervise the enforcement of the Constitution," also states "to alter or annul inappropriate decisions of the Standing Committee of the National People's Congress." However, Article 67 of the Constitution, when stipulating the NPC Standing Committee's power of constitutionality reviews, in addition to the provision "to supervise its enforcement" merely indicates "to annul those administrative rules and regulations, decision or orders of the State Council that contravene the Constitution or the law" and "to annul those local regulations or decisions of the organs of state power of province, autonomous regions, and municipalities directly under the Central Government that contravene the Constitution, the law, or the administrative rules and regulations." The connotations of "inappropriate decisions" and "contravene the Constitution and the law" obviously differ. As stated earlier, "inappropriate" not only includes "contravene the Constitution and law" but may also include "irrational." Hence the NPC Standing Committee's exercise of constitutionality review powers in terms of the State Council, provinces, autonomous regions, and municipalities directly under the Central Government is limited to the aspect of "contravening the Constitution and the law." In other words, only reviews of a legal character are conducted, with attention only given to whether there are any violations of the Constitution and laws; the Constitution makes no provisions as to whether the NPC Standing Committee may review factual matters. Whereas for the National People's Congress, the Constitution stipulates that it may conduct legal reviews and may also review the rationality of factual matters.

Yet as concerns the subjects of constitutionality reviews conducted by the National People's Congress and the NPC Standing Committee, the range covered by the latter is obviously much wider. Article 67, Item 8 of the Constitution stipulates that the NPC Standing Committee is empowered "to annul those local regulations or decisions of the organs of state power of provinces, autonomous regions, and municipalities directly under the Central Government that contravene the Constitution, the law or the administrative rules and regulations," which is to say that the power of conducting constitutionality reviews is not only laterally directed toward the *Yi Fu Liang Yuan*, but is also vertically oriented; it may examine the local laws and regulations formulated by the organs of state power of provinces, autonomous regions, and municipalities directly under the Central Government to determine whether these are constitutional. In this sense, the NPC Standing Committee's power to conduct constitutionality examinations is greater than that of the National People's Congress. It is evident that China's Constitution has vested the power and responsibility to conduct constitutionality examinations mainly in the NPC Standing Committee instead of the National People's Congress.

Where constitutionality examinations directed at the State Council are concerned, the Constitution has vested that duty and responsibility in both the National People's Congress and the NPC Standing Committee. However the Constitution stipulates a division of work in this respect between the National People's Congress and the NPC Standing Committee. Specifically, the National People's Congress is responsible for general supervision. For example, during the yearly reviews of government work reports, the NPC Standing Committee is responsible for "annulling the administrative laws and regulations formulated by the State Council that contravene the Constitution and law," which is to say that the NPC Standing Committee is responsible for reviewing the State Council's "abstract administrative acts" to determine whether they are constitutional. As for whether the National People's Congress may review the State Council's "abstract administrative acts," I believe it cannot, because the Constitution does authorize it to do so, and it cannot exceed its functions. Similarly, the National People's Congress also may not examine the local laws and regulations formulated by the organs of state power of provinces, autonomous regions, and municipalities directly under the Central Government to determine whether these are constitutional, since this is the NPC Standing Committee's duty and function. But of course the National People's Congress may use its powers to conduct constitutionality examinations of the constitutionality of the NPC Standing Committee's acts of constitutionality examinations, and the Constitution vests it with full powers to do so.

Just like the National People's Congress, the NPC Standing Committee has immense powers of conducting constitutionality reviews, but it has virtually never exercised them. With regard to the *Yi Fu Liang Yuan*, it usually only exercises general, nonspecific supervision and has not conducted constitutionality examinations of any specific matters, and the same goes for constitutionality examinations of local legislation. Does this mean that the *Yi Fu Liang Yuan* and all provinces, municipalities under the Central Government and autonomous regions stick so closely to rules that instances of unconstitutionality never occur? That is obviously impossible. So what happens when unconstitutionalities are discovered? Usually, the matter is solved internally. The NPC Standing Committee usually asks the institutions concerned to correct the unconstitutionalities on their own, and thus allows them to "save face." That is why one does not see the National People's Congress or the NPC Standing Committee making a big fanfare of publicly examining the laws formulated by the State Council of local power institution for unconstitutionalities, of listening to arguments from all quarters, and then solemnly passing a judgment (or verdict) on whether unconstitutionality has taken place. Such situations are not likely to occur in China with its present political and legal culture.

Three, the NPC Standing Committee also has the power to interpret laws. The power to interpret laws and the power to conduct constitutionality examinations are closely connected. Interpretation of laws is bound to be involved when constitutionality examinations of laws are conducted. China's Constitution, in addition vesting the power of interpreting the Constitution and laws in the NPC Standing Committee, also empowers it with the power to interpret ordinary laws. Chinese mainland implements a system whereby legislative organs interpret the law, or in other words, the "legislative interpretation" system. Interpretations by legislative organs are final and authoritative. Not only are all administrative institutions and social organizations to follow these interpretations, judicial organs must also base themselves on the relevant interpretations when handling specific cases and rendering judgments. Moreover, as stated earlier, if people's courts have questions about how to specifically apply laws and regulations when hearing cases, they may request interpretations by the Supreme People's Court. Such interpretations also carry legal force, but the judicial interpretations made by the Supreme People's Court are limited in scope to the specific application of laws and regulations during court trials and may not contravene the original intent of the laws and regulations. Relative to legislative interpretations, judicial interpretations are merely of an auxiliary nature.

China's Legislation Law further confirms that the NPC Standing Committee has the power to interpret laws. Article 42 of that Law stipulates that when the specific meaning of the provisions of a law requires further elucidation, or when new situations arise after the law has been formulated and the basis for applying the law requires clarification, the NPC Standing Committee may make an interpretation. The State Council, the Central Military Commission, the Supreme People's Court, the Supreme People's Procuratorate, and the various special commissions of the National People's Congress as well as the standing committees of the people's congresses of provinces, autonomous regions, and municipalities directly under the Central Government may request interpretations of laws by the NPC Standing Committee. There are no provisions regarding requests for interpretations of law by citizens or by parties to lawsuits in particular. The procedures for law interpretations are basically the same as for legislation. China's Legislation Law also stipulates that law interpretations by the NPC Standing Committee carry the same force as laws. Up to the present, the NPC Standing Committee has made a few interpretations of ordinary laws, but as yet has not conducted any examinations involving the constitutionality of any laws. Those interpretations, of course, usually do not involve the hearing of specific cases.

11.1.2.3   The Powers of Constitutionality Examination by Local People's Congress of Various Levels and Their Standing Committees

Strictly speaking, only the National People's Congress and the NPC Standing Committee are vested with the powers of constitutionality examinations. However, in accordance with the provisions of the Constitution and laws, local people's congresses at all levels and their standing committees also have certain powers of constitutionality examinations and may make legally binding judgments on matters involving the Constitution. Article 99 of the Constitution stipulates that local people's congresses at various levels have the power to alter or annul inappropriate decisions by their own standing committees. For instance, the people's congress of a province has the power to examine a certain local law or regulation formulated by the permanent institution—the standing committee—of its people's congress in order to determine whether it conforms to the national law or the Constitution, and may alter or annul the law or regulation if it finds it "inappropriate." The term "inappropriate" here include "inappropriate" in terms of constitutionality, or in other words, violations of provisions in the Constitution by local rules or regulations formulated by the standing committees of provincial people's congresses. Article 104 of the Constitution also stipulates that the standing committee of a local people's congress at and above the county level (hereinafter "local people's congress standing committee") has the power to supervise the work of the people's government, people' court and people's procuratorate at the corresponding level, and has the power to examine and annul inappropriate decisions and orders of the people's governments at the corresponding level. For instance, a provincial people's congress standing committee has the power to examine local government regulations formulated by that provincial government. Local people's congress standing committees also have the power to examine inappropriate decisions by people's congresses at the next lower level. For example, the provincial people's congress has the power to examine local regulations which the people's congress of a municipality directly under the province has formulated for that municipality. The term "inappropriate" here also includes "inappropriateness" in terms of constitutionality, and local people's congress standing committees may also conduct constitutionality examinations of subjects (institutions) under their supervision. Items 4 and 5 of Article 88 of the Legislation Law make the same stipulations. These powers, vested in local people's congresses and their standing committees are similar in nature to the NPC Standing Committee's power to conduct constitutionality reviews. All are powers to conduct constitutionality reviews and differ only in that they are exercised at local levels. In recent years, local people's congress standing committees, in stark contrast with the NPC Standing Committee, have been most active in terms of exercising their powers of conducting constitutionality examinations, and their supervision over local people's government has gradually become institutionalized.

11.1.2.4 Problems in the Powers of Other Institutions to Conduct Constitutionality Examinations

a. Problems in the State Council's Constitutionality Examination Powers

In terms of jurisprudence, the State Council, as the state's highest administrative institution, should not have the power to conduct constitutionality examinations because of a constitutionality examination, in essence, a special and independent judicial act as well as a kind of judicial power. Administrative institutions should not have judicial powers and even less should they have the power of constitutionality examination which is the most important of judicial powers. Yet Article 89 of China's Constitution stipulates that the powers exercised by the State Council include "to alter or annul inappropriate orders, directive and regulations issued by the ministries or commissions" and "to alter or annul inappropriate decisions and orders issued by local organs of state administration at various levels." I believe that, strictly speaking, these powers of the State Council do not fall within the scope of constitutionality examinations. They can only be regarded as "abstract administrative acts" conducted within an administrative institution for the purpose of self-supervision and self-examination; they are still administrative acts by nature, not acts of constitutionality reviews or judicial acts. They are the same, by nature, as the stipulation in Item 6 of Article 88 of the Judicial Law, i.e.: "The people's government of a province or autonomous region has the power to alter or annul any inappropriate rules formulated by people's governments at the next lower level." Administrative institutions may also, on their own initiative, correct some unconstitutional matters by means of self-examination and self-supervision. However, the ultimate constitutionality of the regulations formulated by administrative institutions and of the self-examinations of these regulations still has to be determined by the NPC Standing Committee or even the National People's Congress.

b.   Problems in the Powers of Courts of Law to Conduct Constitutionality Examinations

China's Constitution per se neither affirms nor negates the power of courts of law to conduct constitutionality reviews, just as there is nothing in the text of the U.S. Constitution which affirms or denies that the U.S. Supreme Court has the power to conduct constitutionality reviews. However, a judicial interpretation issued by China's Supreme People's Court in 1955 excluded that possibility and from then on China's courts of law, including the Supreme People's Court, have drawn a clear line against enforcement of the Constitution.[12] Although people are constantly seeking judicial aid from courts of law because their constitutional rights are being violated, the courts usually reject such cases and judges always do their best to avoid constitutional issues when hearing cases. Some audacious judges, when forced by circumstances, will cite the Constitution when judging cases but such cases have never involved constitutionality examinations.[13]

---

[12]On July 30, 1955, Supreme People's Court document *Yanzi* No. 11298 carried an annotation addressed to the then High People's Court of Xinjiang Province. It maintained in the annotation that the Constitution does not carry provisions on how indictments and sentencing should be conducted in criminal affairs. Hence, "in criminal judgments, it is not advisable to cite the Constitution as grounds for indictments and sentencing." The Superior People's Court did not give a reason for this; it merely said that the Constitution is a country's basic law and the "mother" of all laws, and quoted a statement by Chairman Liu Shaoqi expounding the importance of the Constitution. Yet no mention was made in the annotation that the Constitution may not be cited in judgments on civil, economic, and administrative matters or that the Constitution should not be applied in criminal lawsuits. It merely said that it was inadvisable to quote the Constitution as grounds for indictments and sentencing in criminal judgments. Moreover, saying it was "inadvisable" to quote the Constitution did not entirely exclude the possibility of doing so. Information Center of the State Council Legislative Affairs Bureau. *The Full Collection of Chinese Laws and Regulations: Judicial Interpretation*. Beijing: China Procuratorate Press, 1998.

[13]Actually, there are now more and more ordinary lawsuits which involve the Constitution, and there are situations where the people's courts also cite the Constitution in their judgments. See Libel Case Du Rong v. Shen Yafu and Mao Chunlin; Damages Reimbursement Dispute Case Zhang Lianqi and Zhang Guoli v. Zhang Xuezhen; Right of Reputation Infringement Dispute Case Wang Faying v. Women's Literature and Three Other Magazines; and Character and Reputation Defamation Case Qian X v. Qu Chen Shi Daily Necessities Co., Ltd. See Information Center of the State Council Legislative Affairs Bureau. "Legislative Interpretations" of the Complete Library of Chinese Laws and Regulations, China Procuratorial Press, 1998. I have analyzed the five above cases in my article "May China's Constitution Be Used in Lawsuits?" See Wuhan. *Zuel Law Journal*, 1999, Volume 5. See Beijing, China Renmin University Center for Book and Newspaper Information. *Constitutional Law and Administrative Law* (the Duplicate Newspaper and Periodical Materials), vol. 1, 2000. Zhou

There was a small breakthrough in this respect in the Administrative Review Law approved by the Ninth NPC Standing Committee on April 29, 1999. Article 7 therein stipulates that when citizens, legal persons or other organizations apply for an administrative review of a specific administrative act, they may, if they maintain that a certain "rule" on which the said specific administrative act is based is unlawful, at the same time apply to the reviewing institution for a review of the said "rule." Such "rules" include those set by State Council departments, those set by local people's governments at and above the county level and their work departments, and those set by town and township people's governments. Article 5 therein also stipulates that if the applicant disagrees with the decision of the administrative examination, he may file an administrative lawsuit with a people's court in accordance with the Administrative Review Law. This signifies that courts of law may review not only specific administrative acts but may also review the "rules" on which these acts are based to determine whether they are tenable, thus breaking out of the restriction against courts of law reviewing abstract administrative acts. This should be affirmed as an improvement.[14] Of course, none of the rules and regulations [*guizhang*] set by the various departments and commissions of the State Council and by local people's governments are subject to applications for reviews or judicial examinations, to say nothing about legislations [*fagui*] and laws [*falü*].

A case that took place in 1998 appears to have disclaimed the contention that courts of law may not exercise the power to conduct constitutionality reviews. On December 15, 1998, a judge at an intermediate people's court in the Jiuquan region of Gansu Province, when adjudicating an administrative lawsuit on the protection of consumer rights, determined that the "Ordinance on the Supervision and Management of the Quality of Gansu Province Products"—a local regulation formulated by the Gansu People's Congress Standing Committee—did not comply with two national laws, namely, the Law on Product Quality and the Law on Administrative Punishments, and therefore refused to judge the case in accordance with the local ordinance formulated by the Gansu People's Congress Standing Committee, and in effect terminated the force of that local ordinance. That was the first time a judge of a local court independently exercised a judicial examination of a state legislative act and determined whether or not the judicial act complied with the law (i.e., a higher level law) and whether or not it should be applied.

After this judgment was made, the Gansu Province People's Congress Standing Committee held a special meeting of directors to hear the circumstances the case. They determined that the written judgment rendered by the Jiuquan region's intermediate people's court had "gravely violated the legislative rights vested in the local people's congress and its standing committee by the Constitution and the local organic law, that it exceeded the limits of judicial power and failed to correctly comprehend laws and regulations, and that the unlawful judgment had directly damaged the solemnity of local laws and regulations and adversely affected the uniformity of

Wei. "The Trial Study on the Provisions of the Basic Rights of the Constitution of China," Hong Kong, *Journal of Chinese Law and Comparative Law*, 1997–1998, Volume 3, Number 2.

[14]Wang Liming. *A Study on Legislative Reform*. Beijing: The Law Press, 2000, p. 294.

the socialist legal system." They maintained that "this is a serious instance, seldom seen throughout the country, of a judicial organ violating the law in the process of adjudication." The Gansu People's Congress stated that in accordance with the relevant laws, if a judicial organ maintains, in the process of adjudicating a case, that a certain local regulation conflicts with or contradicts laws, administrative regulations or local laws and regulations, it should report this to the provincial people's congress standing committee, or it may submit reports level-by-level to, and seek instructions from, the higher authorities all the way up the National People's Congress Standing Committee. But it is absolutely forbidden to make arbitrary rulings beyond its authority or produce self-willed interpretations of the said laws or regulations. Hence the Gansu People's Congress held that in this case, the Jiuquan intermediate court should only have conducted an examination and adjudged the legality of the specific administrative act of the administrative institution concerned; it should never conduct any criticism or interpretation of a law or regulation or determine that these are ineffective. Hence the Gansu People's Congress requested that the Gansu Provincial High People's Court bring up the case for trial and annul the judgment by the Jiuquan Intermediate People's Court. The Gansu High People's Court subsequently retried the case, and annulled the Jiuquan Intermediate People's Court's original administrative adjudication.[15]

The courage of the judge in this case was indeed commendable, yet I still agree with the opinion of the Gansu People's Congress Standing Committee, because in accordance with the provisions of the present Constitution and laws, when parties concerned or a judge has queries about the constitutionality, legality or rationality of a law, an administrative regulation or a local regulation or ruling, they should seek a resolution by the National People's Congress and not try to have the court itself resolve the matter. Whether such a system is rational or not, it is a provision in the Constitution, it is law, and before any changes are made, everyone should abide by it. This is a basic principle of rule of law. The question is: how should the judge ask the NPC for an interpretation of the law or even an interpretation of the Constitution, and what procedures ought to be followed. There are no explicit provisions or precedents for doing so as yet. I maintain that when the judge had encountered that situation, he could have first suspended the hearing and asked the people's congress to "interpret the law," as the people's congress had suggested, and then reviewed the case according to the people's Congress's interpretation and see whether this worked. If it did, it would set a precedent; it would link up people's congress "interpretations of law" and its exercise of constitutionality examinations with the hearings of specific court cases.

Courts of law are not only unable to review NPC legislation, they are also not authorized to examine rules and regulations formulated by the government, including those formulated by local governments, and may only exercise this power indirectly by using other means. A judgment made by a Beijing court in December 2001 is an example of a court implementing October 24, a different sort of judicial examination.

[15]"Did a Court Scrap a People's Congress Ruling?," Beijing, *China Economic Times*, September 5, 2000, October 24, 2000.

In the case of Chauffeur Zhou X versus the Chaoyang Traffic Police Detachment of the Beijing Public Security Traffic Administration Bureau, the Chaoyang Beijing Public Security Traffic Administration Bureau's Chaoyang Traffic Detachment on March 12, 2001 made a public security penalty decision to impose a fine of RMB 200 *yuan* on the defendant for driving through a red light. Its basis was the Beijing Municipal Regulations on Road Traffic Management approved by the Beijing People's Government on December 9, 1997, and Article 38 of the local government regulations stipulated that a fine of no less than 200 yuan and no more than 500 yuan could be imposed for a traffic violation of driving through a red light. However, Article 28 of the Regulations of the People's Republic of China on Administrative Penalties for Public Security adopted by the Eighth NPC Standing Committee on May 12, 1994 stipulated that violations of traffic signs and signals while driving motor vehicles were punishable by a fine of no more than five yuan or a warning.

The Court of First Instance maintained that the defendant was being rightfully punished according to law for a violation of traffic regulations, but that this had to be done within the scope of legal regulations. Article 28 of the Regulations of the People's Republic of China on Administrative Penalties for Public Security had already stipulated that violations of traffic signs and signals while driving motor vehicles were to be punished by a fine of no more than five yuan or a warning, and the Law on Administrative Punishments of the People's Republic of China also stipulated that the people's governments of municipalities directly under the Central Government could make specific stipulations within the scope of laws and regulations. The basis for the punishment meted to the defendant was Article 38 of the Beijing Municipal Regulations on Road Traffic Management, but the Court stated that "the Beijing Municipal Regulations on Road Traffic Management are rules formulated by the Beijing Municipal Government, and the punishment stipulated by these rules for violations of traffic signs and signals while driving motor vehicles obviously exceed the range of punishment stipulated by the Regulations of the People's Republic of China on Administrative Penalties for Public Security; hence, the punishment meted by the defendant on the plaintiff in accordance with the said government regulations is an erroneous application of the law." The court ultimately determined that the traffic administration department's penalty decision violated the law, and it produced a verdict against the traffic department. The Court of Second Instance upheld the original verdict.[16] In this case, since the court had no jurisdiction over constitutional cases and could not conduct abstract judicial examinations of any legislation including administrative legislation, and since it could not declare the local rules null and void even though these local rules obviously violated national law and even violated the Constitution, it could only tactfully sidestep the issue of the legality and the constitutionality of the local rules and merely declare that the specific administrative acts conducted in accordance the said local rules were invalid. Although the court had in reality exercised an abstract judicial examination of the local legislation, the

---

[16] Administrative Judgment (2001) *Chao xing chu zi* No. 35 of the Beijing Municipal Chaoyang District People's Court, in the case Zhou X v. the Mobile Unit of the Chaoyang Traffic Police Detachment of the Beijing Municipal Traffic Administration Bureau.

court could not say that or let that be manifested in its written judgment, for that might lead to a similarly embarrassing situation encountered by the Gansu Jiuquan court as related earlier.[17]

According to China's constitutional setup and the constitutionality examination system, courts may not examine any legislative acts by people's congresses and governments, and they have no power to conduct constitutionality examinations. People's congresses may, conversely, supervise the courts' judicial activities and even subject the courts to individual case supervision. The NPC Standing Committee has formulated provisions for national supervision of individual cases, but these have been temporarily shelved due to opposition from academics. However, many local people's congresses have made efforts in this direction and some have already formulated corresponding local rules and regulations. An example is the "Regulations on the Supervision of the Work of Judicial Institutions by People's Congresses and Their Standing Committees at all Levels in Zhejiang Province," passed by the Ninth People's Congress Standing Committee of Zhejiang Province on December 28, 2000. Courts of law, too, have frequently stated on their own initiative that they would accept supervision by the people's congresses. The first to do so was the Superior People's Court which on December 24, 1998 published "A Number of Opinions on the People's Courts Accepting Supervision from the People's Congresses and Their Standing Committees," in which Article 7 stipulated that "if people's congresses and their standing committees request, through statutory procedures for supervision, that people's courts examine major cases which the people's courts have already adjudicated or which exert a major influence on the locality, the people's courts should conscientiously conduct examinations thereon; and where cases have indeed been erroneously adjudged they shall rectify the judgments in accordance with statutory procedures for examinations and supervision; and if there is nothing inappropriate about the judgments, they shall submit a written report on the results and reasons therefor." And on December 29, 2000, the Superior People's Court again issued a "Decision on Strengthening Communication with People's Congress Delegates" so as to better coordinate supervision by the people's congresses over the courts.

It is evident that under the present setup, although the courts possess certain powers of judicial review, they play no part at all in constitutionality examinations but conversely have become the subjects of constitutionality examinations. I maintain that in accordance with the Constitution, people's congresses may indeed supervise courts of law and even implement constitutionality examinations of the latter, especially today when judicial corruption has become extremely grave. If people's congresses are to conduct individual case supervision over people's courts, there is nothing reprehensible about that, but the Constitution will have to be amended to make it clear that the people's congresses possess that judicial function. If people's congresses were authorized to carry out individual case supervision by a simple act of legislation, it would be unconstitutional because the Constitution has not authorized

---

[17]Li Feng, Yang Wenxue and Zhou Huagong. "City Trots Out 'Indigenous Rule.' Should We Pay ¥5.00 or ¥200.00 for Crashing Red Lights?" Carried in the *Da Zhong Daily*, December 22, 2001. Also see *Jing Hua Daily*, December 15, 2001.

people's congresses to intervene in the hearing of specific cases; it merely authorizes them to exercise general supervision over the people's courts.

Worth noting is that a judicial interpretation approved by the Judicial Committee of the Superior People's Court on June 28, 2001 for the first time made use of the Constitution to handle a lawsuit regarding a violation of the right to education, pointing out that "according to the facts in this case, Chen Xiaoqi et al., by infringing on Qi Yuling's right of personal name, infringed on the basic right of acquiring an education enjoyed by Qi Yuling in accordance with the provisions of the Constitution, caused specific damages and consequences, and should bear the corresponding civil liabilities."[18] Huang Songyou, chief of the First Civil Tribunal of the Supreme People's Court, stated that a considerable number of the basic rights enjoyed by China's citizens under the provisions of the Constitution have long been in a state of "torpidity" or "semi-torpidity" in judicial practice, and that citizens' right to education is precisely such a right—one which is specifically provided for in the Constitution, yet has not been accorded concrete form in terms of the norms of the common law. That "annotated response" for the first time broke the "silence" and clearly pointed out that the basic rights enjoyed by citizens through the Constitution should be protected when infringed upon, even if they have not been converted into rights in terms of the norms of the common law. That judicial interpretation upheld the basic right to an education enjoyed by citizens under the Constitution and may well have initiated the first instance of the judicialization of the Constitution. In China's judicial practice, China's Constitution had never been cited as a direct legal basis in China's legal documentation. Huang Songyou averred that the awkward position of the Constitution when applied in Chinese law is due on the one hand to its status as a fundamental law in the China's legal system and its preeminent legal authority and, on the other, to the fact that much of its content has long been relegated to a "purely nominal standing" in judicial practice and has never produced any real legal effect. If the contents of Constitutional provisions cannot be implemented in the field of jurisprudence, they fail to ensure the basic rights that citizens should enjoy under the Constitution and are unable to find their due place in a rule-of-law society.[19]

This was indeed a highly commendable judicial interpretation and is likely to develop into a judicial activity of landmark significance. It shows that citizens' constitutional rights can be ensured through ordinary judicial proceedings, and it has created a precedent of a court of law directly using the Constitution to protect the rights of citizens. If things continue in this way, there is much hope for the development of China's rule of law. Although China's courts of law do not yet conduct constitutionality examinations, that does not mean courts should turn a blind eye and do nothing in cases of infringements of citizens' constitutional rights. It is entirely

---

[18]"Annotated Response by the Supreme People's Court on Whether Civil Liability Should Be Borne When Infringements of the Right of Personal Name Are Used to Infringe on the Constitutionally Protected Basic Right of Citizens to Obtain an Education," document *Fa shi* (2001) No. 25, approved on June 28, 2001 by the 1183rd meeting of the Judicial Council of the Supreme People's Court and implemented as of August 13, 2001.

[19]Cui Li. "Protecting the Right to an Education in the Name of the Constitution; A Judicial Interpretation Occasioned by a Spurious-Name Lawsuit," Beijing, *China Youth Daily*, August 15, 2001.

possible for courts to handle these cases in the way the Supreme People's Court handled such cases, to start by doing things that can be done, and gradually establish areas of jurisdiction for courts of law on constitutional issues.

From this case, we may draw the conclusion that in China, the power to conduct constitutionality reviews is at present exercised from the top downward by people's congresses and their standing committees. The National People's is the highest constitutionality review institution, and the NPC Standing Committee is the principal institution of constitutionality examinations and local people's congresses at all levels and their standing committees exercise the power of conducting constitutionality examinations of the actions of the subjects of supervision in their respective jurisdictions. However, the ultimate power of constitutionality examinations is exercised by the National People's Congress and its Standing Committee. Under the Common Law system, courts at all levels may exercise the power of constitutionality reviews, but the ultimate power of constitutionality review is exercised by the highest court. China's system of constitutionality examinations have merely replaced "courts of law" with "people's congresses," and replaced judicial procedures with "quasi-legislative procedures." China's legislative organs not only legislate but also are in charge of constitutionality examinations. This may be the reason why China's National People's Congress is not merely a legislative organ but the state's "highest organ of power."

c. The Procedures and Principles of China's Institutional Examinations

China's Constitution per se contains no provisions at all regarding the procedures for constitutionality examinations. It was the Legislation Law that first contained some such provisions. First of all, as regards provisions concerning the principals (i.e., plaintiffs) in constitutionality examinations, Article 90 of the Legislation Law contains stipulations on which organs or institutions may put forward requests for constitutionality examinations. It includes this stipulation: "When the State Council, the Central Military Commission, the Supreme People's Court, the Supreme People's Procuratorate and the standing committees of the people's congresses of the provinces, autonomous regions and municipalities directly under the central government consider that administrative regulations, local regulations, autonomous regulations or special regulations contradict the Constitution or laws, they may submit to the Standing Committee of the National People's Congress written requests for examination...," and since these are "requests," they are comparatively forceful and may not be offhandedly rejected.

What is fairly outstanding is that Article 99 stipulates at the same time: "When state organs other than those mentioned in the preceding paragraph, public organizations, enterprises and institutions or non-enterprise institution or citizens consider that administrative regulations, local regulations, autonomous regulations or special regulations contradict the Constitution or laws, they may submit to the Standing Committee of the National People's Congress written requests or make a written proposal to the Standing Committee of the National People's Congress for examination, and the working offices of the Standing Committee shall study the suggestions and shall, when necessary, refer them to the relevant special committees for examination and suggestions." In this way, the power to "propose" a constitutionality review is given to ordinary social groups and individual citizens, despite the fact that it is merely a proposal, but it actually enters the examination process only "when necessary." Moreover, the Article restricts the subjects for examination to administrative regulations and rules and makes no provisions as to whether citizens may file "complaints" about national laws and government regulations. Its limitations are quite obvious. Yet, this is, after all, the first time in China's Constitutional history that ordinary citizens are connected with constitutional examinations. In terms of the principals of constitutionality examinations, the Legislation Law took a small, albeit crucial, step forward.

After the NPC Standing Committee accepts such "requests" or "proposals" for constitutionality examinations, its work institutions first of all distribute these to the relevant special committees for examination. If these special committees determine that an administrative regulation, local regulation or special regulation runs counter to the Constitution or laws, they may submit a written examination opinion to the formulating institution; or the Law Committee and the relevant special committees may convene a joint examination meeting, ask the formulating institution to attend the meeting to explain the circumstances, and then send a written examination opinion to the formulating institution. The formulating institution must, within two months, submit its opinion on whether changes should be made and provide feedback to the National People's Congress Judicial Committee and the relevant special committees. If, after conducting examinations, the National People's Congress Judicial Committee and the relevant special committees maintain that the administrative regulations, local regulations or special regulations indeed conflict with the Constitution or national laws but the formulating institutions do not make changes, they may submit written examination opinions to the Council of Chairmen and put forward motions for annulment, and the Council of Chairmen shall decide whether to request that examinations and decisions be made at meetings of the Council of Chairmen. These provisions would appear to be simple, but in fact also constitute no small progress because they, after all, provide basic clues to and procedures for solving the constitutionality examination issue. We have learned that citizens have already submitted requests and proposals to the NPC Standing Committee for conducting examinations of rules and regulations and that some have been trying out this new power in the hope of becoming a "Chinese Marbury."[20] Crucially, though, this procedure must be started up as soon as possible.

Chapter V of the Legislation Law entitled "Scope of Application and Filing" fairly specifically stipulates the principles for examining laws, regulations, and rules and stipulates the levels of effect of the Constitution, laws, regulations, and rules. First, as regards legal effect, that of the Constitution is the highest, and no laws, administrative regulations, local regulations, autonomous regulations and separate regulations or rules may conflict with it. Two, the legal effect of national laws is higher than that of administrative regulations and local regulations and rules, and

---

[20]William Marbury was the plaintiff in the Marbury v. Madison case which was instrumental in establishing the United States' judicial review system in 1803.

that of administrative regulations is higher than that of local regulations and rules. And then there is the legal effect of local laws which is higher than the legal effect of the rules and regulations of governments at or below the corresponding levels. And the legal effect of the rules and regulations formulated by the governments of provinces and autonomous regions is higher than that of the rules and regulations formulated by people's governments of comparatively large cities in the province's administrative areas. However, if certain adaptive provisions are legally made to certain laws, administrative regulations or local regulations of the autonomous regulations or to separate regulations of regions that practice ethnic regional autonomy, the provisions of the autonomous regulations or separate regulations shall prevail in the autonomous areas concerned. Where authorized adaptations are made to certain laws, administrative regulations or local regulations of the SARs, the provisions of the SAR regulations shall prevail in the SARs concerned. The departmental rules formulated by the various ministries and commissions of the State Council and the departmental rules and local rules formulated by local governments are of equal effect amongst the departments and local governments, and application of these rules shall be confined within their respective limits of authority.

Also, as regards the solving of inconsistencies which exist between laws, regulations, and rules, if there are conflicts between laws and different stipulations that have been made on the same matter, rulings thereon are to be produced by the NPC Standing Committee. If there are inconsistencies between administrative regulations formulated by the State Council on the same matter, rulings thereon are to be produced by the State Council. If there are inconsistencies between local regulations and rules, and if there are inconsistencies between new and old separate regulations formulated by one and the same organ, the formulating organ is to produce rulings thereon. If there are inconsistencies between the provisions of local regulations and departmental regulations on one and the same matter and the State Council maintains that the local regulations should prevail, the provisions of the local regulations shall prevail, but if it is maintained that the departmental regulations should prevail, then the NPC Standing Committee shall be requested to make a ruling. Where there are inconsistencies between departmental regulations and between departmental regulations and local government regulations on one and the same matter, rulings thereon are to be produced by the State Council. Where there are inconsistencies between the provisions of regulations and laws formulated upon authorization by people's congresses, rulings thereon are to be made by the NPC Standing Committee. Where laws, regulations, decrees, rules, and separate regulations have been formulated by one and the same organ and there are inconsistencies between the special provisions and general provisions, the special provisions shall prevail. Where there are inconsistencies between new and old provisions, the new provisions shall prevail. No laws, administrative regulations, local regulations, autonomous regulations, separate regulations, and rules may be retroactive, except where special regulations are formulated in order to better protect the rights and interests of citizens, legal persons, and other organizations.

The Legislation Law also stipulates that legislation by any organ may not transcend the organ's limits of power, may not contravene legal procedures, and lower level legislation may not violate the provisions of higher level legislation. To relieve the general public as much as possible from problems of complying with laws and regulations due these being too vague or ambiguous, the Legislation Law stipulates that any inconsistencies between the provisions of regulations on one and the same matter should be eliminated through rulings thereon and one aspect of a law or regulation may be changed. If the provisions of some regulations are deemed inappropriate, they should be amended or revoked. All of these stipulations mark considerable progress. Their performance will be tested in practice.

d.   The Characteristics and Problems of China's Constitutionality Reviews

Under the Common Law system in Britain and the United States, constitutionality reviews are conducted by courts in general, whereas in Europe's Continental Law system they are placed under the charge of special constitutional courts. It is evident from the analyses conducted above that China's Constitution and legal system have devised a special system of constitutionality reviews, the powers of which are exercised neither by courts in general, as under the Common Law system, nor by constitutional courts (committees) as in Europe under the Continental Law system. They fall under the unified top-down responsibility of the National People's Congress and its Standing Committee as well as the local people's congresses and their standing committees, and are exercised chiefly by the National People's Congress and the NPC Standing Committee. Objectively, therefore, China already has an initial and operable constitutionality review system, and it is unfair to say that China is entirely devoid of such a system. China's constitutionality review system has been built on the theoretical basis of the "sovereignty of the National People's Congress." In other words, the power of the people is unified and indivisible, and the National People's Congress represents the will and interests of the people of the entire nation and is the state's highest institution of state power, and it would be inappropriate if another independent institution were to review its legislation for constitutionality or otherwise. This would appear to be logical, but numerous problems exist in actual practice in this system of constitutionality reviews.

First, due to the complexity and multiplicity of the institutions that conduct constitutionality reviews, it is often the case that one matter falls under the jurisdiction of two or even more institutions, which in reality results in no one taking charge of the matter and constitutionality reviews having no effect. For example, the NPC Standing Committee and the standing committees of people's congresses of provinces, autonomous regions, and municipalities directly under the central government are all empowered to conduct constitutionality reviews of local legislation formulated by provinces, autonomous regions, and municipalities directly under the central government. And the State Council and the provincial-level people's congress standing committees, too, have the power to conduct constitutionality reviews of the local regulations and rules formulated by provincial-level people's governments. But among all of these institutions, there is in reality not a single institution with special powers to truly assume responsibility. Hence the necessity of setting up a special institution for constitutionality reviews.

Two, the power to interpret the Constitution and [national] laws is at times detached from the power of constitutionality reviews. The best example of this is the National People's Congress which has the power to conduct constitutionality reviews but not the power to interpret the Constitution and laws. This, in practice, is likely to produce awkward situations, as discussed earlier.

Three, the most crucial issue is that constitutionality reviews were originally meant in the main to examine laws and regulations for constitutionality or lack thereof. In other words, the subjects of constitutionality reviews were not limited to administrative institutions and even less to judicial organs. On the contrary, they were to be directed at legislative organs to see if the state's formal legislation conformed to the Constitution. Yet the system of constitutionality reviews established by the present Chinese Constitution is led precisely by the legislative organs and simply adds a function to these organs. However, doing so causes a direct conflict of interests. The National People's Congress and its Standing Committee, as legislation organs, conduct interpretations and examinations of the laws they themselves formulate, and they themselves judge whether these are constitutional or otherwise; local people's congresses, too, produce legislations and then interpret and examine them, and in this way serve as their own judge and jury. It cannot be denied that the people's congresses are capable of producing impartial judgments as well as impartially interpreting the Constitution and exercising the power of constitutionality reviews, but the system must absolutely be designed on the premise of what to do in the eventuality of the people's congresses failing to be just and impartial! We should, in institutional terms, absolutely avoid the emergence of conflicts of interest and should not allow contradictions to exist in terms of the institutional design.

Four, the procedures for constitutionality reviews are imperfect. Although the Legislation Law has devoted efforts to setting up procedures for constitutionality reviews, these efforts still fall short of requirements. Because China's constitutionality reviews are conducted by legislative organs, the procedures for constitutionality reviews are in reality mechanically applied legislative procedures, and "requests" or "proposals" for constitutionality reviews are handled and regarded as special motions addressed to the people's congresses. However, procedures for constitutionality reviews are in essence special judicial procedures and should not be legislative procedures. Under the Common Law system, constitutionality reviews are none other than judicial reviews by courts of law, and their procedures are none other than judicial procedures. In countries of the Continental Law system, although there are independent constitutional courts [tribunals], judicial procedures are also employed to conduct constitutionality reviews.[21]

Five, today when local courts of law need interpretations of laws in the course of hearing cases, the usual way is to seek "judicial interpretations" from the Supreme People's Court rather than seek "legislative interpretations" by local people's congress standing committees or by people's congresses at a higher level. If, under such circumstances and in accordance with the present system of constitution-

---

[21]Liu Qingrui. *Comparative Constitutional Law*. Taipei: San Min Book, 1993, ed. 6, pp. 276 and 320.

ality reviews, the Superior People's Court is unable to produce an interpretation and resolve the problem, or "the problem does not fall in the category of laws or decrees specifically applied by the court to adjudge the case," or where "further definition is required of the specific meaning of the provisions of the law," or "new situations have arisen after the formulation of the law and clarification is required or the grounds for applying the law" (Article 42 of the Legislation Law), or where an interpretation by the Superior People's Court differs from an interpretation by the Supreme People's Procuratorate, the Supreme People's Court should seek a final "legislative interpretation" of the law concerned by NPC Standing Committee. Similarly, since courts of law, in accordance with the current constitutionality review mechanism, do not have the power to conduct constitutionality reviews, in situations where a judge adjudging a case finds that a law or decree violates the Constitution, he should suspend the hearing, request the initiation of a constitutionality review by the NPC Standing Committee, and then resume the hearing in accordance with the findings of the constitutionality review. However, as stated earlier, there has almost never been an instance, known to the outside, in which the Superior People's Court has applied to the NPC Standing Committee for an interpretation of the provisions a law based on the needs of a court hearing. As for a court of law applying to the NPC Standing Committee for an "interpretation of the Constitution" because of its inability to understand a Constitutional issue during a court hearing, no such case has ever occurred. That does not mean courts have never come across unconstitutional laws and regulations or obscure constitutional and legal issues. It only means they have not yet formed the habit of getting the NPC Standing Committee to solve issues of interpreting laws and interpreting the Constitution and conducting constitutionality reviews, despite explicit provisions on such matters in the Constitution. People have long been under the impression that courts do not handle constitutional issues and that the NPC Standing Committee does not deal with specific issues.

Related to the above is the conceptual misunderstanding still prevalent among many people that constitutional reviews are a function of legislative organs, that constitutional reviews are legislative acts. The fact is that constitutional reviews ought to be a special kind of judicial activity, a country's most important judicial activity, since it concerns a country's most important and most fundamental "law"—the Constitution. Unless that concept is rectified, no changes of any kind are possible.

e.   Thoughts about Perfecting China's Constitutionality Review System

It is evident from the foregoing analyses that the key to the matter is setting up a specialized and independent institution for constitutionality reviews. China's constitutional scholars have for many years discussed this issue, and official quarters have expressed willingness to consider it.

Chen Peixian, Vice-Chairman of the NPC Standing Committee, when delivering a work report to the National People's Congress on behalf of the NPC Standing Committee on March 31, 1988, formally proposed: "It is necessary to earnestly sum up experience gained in the last few years in carrying out supervision work, establishing special institutions for supervision work, formulating supervision work provisions on the contents and scope of supervision and the procedures and methods of supervision, so that supervision work is gradually systematized and standardized. Meanwhile, the fundamental solution of the supervision issue is contingent on the deepening of the reform of the political system."[22] However, this matter remains unresolved to this day. In the wake of constant deepening of China's Reform and Opening Up and the constant diversification of social interests, the lack of clarity of the functions and duties of various institutions and in the divisions of powers between the central and local authorities has led to increasingly serious legal conflicts, and the current mechanisms for resolving such conflicts can hardly cope with the needs of social development.

Meanwhile, the return of Hong Kong and Macao to China has given rise to new situations in Central/SAR relations, and mainland mechanisms for the handling of Central and local relations are inappropriate for solving conflicts arising between the Central Authorities and the SARs. The two SAR Basic Law Committees set up by the National People's Congress serve, in a certain sense and in reality, as special constitutionality review institutions, or in other words, as institutions which judge whether there have been violations of the SAR "mini-constitutions"—the SAR Basic Laws. However, these two committees are merely work institutions of the NPC Standing Committee. They are not institutions of power and can only provide counseling and opinions; they cannot make decisions. And since they are situated within the National People's Congress, in terms of their nature, they still form part of a legislative institution, and there is nothing judicial about them. Nor is there anything judicial about their work procedures. Furthermore, these two committees are only in charge of supervising the implementation of the Basic Laws, not the Constitution of the country as a whole.

As for how to set up an constitutionality review institution, scholars have put forward many suggestions, all confined to the following: One, set up, as in European countries, a constitutional court independent of all other institutions including the National People's Congress; two, vest the power of constitutionality reviews in the existing supreme courts, as is done in the British and U.S. legal systems; three, set up under the NPC Standing Committee a constitutional council (also called "court"); and four, set up under the National People's Congress a constitutional council (also called "court").[23]

The first two of the above concepts would involve changes in China's current political system, be quite costly, come up against considerable resistance, and take considerable time. The third concept would not solve any problems as the current NPC Standing Committee in reality already has an institution of this sort. I personally believe the fourth plan to be fairly feasible. First of all, it conforms to China's fundamental political system today and China's current constitutional system. And the National People's Congress would still be China's highest organ of state power.

---

[22] Beijing, *People's Daily*, April 19, 1988, p. 2.

[23] cf. Hu Jinguang. "An Exploration into the Judicial Applicability of China's Constitution," Beijing, Academic Journal of China Renmin University, 1997 (5). Miao Lianying. "Tentative Ideas on Setting up an Institution Dedicated to Constitutional Reviews," Wuhan, *Zuel Law Journal*, 1998 (4). Bao Wanzhong. "Set up a Composite Examinations System Combining a Constitutional Committee and a Superior Court," Shanghai, *Law Science*, 1998 (4).

This would avert social unrest due to extensive amendments to the Constitution and reduce the likelihood of resistance.

First and foremost, China's Constitution has actually established the fundamental principle of "National People's Congress sovereignty," and the people's congress system constitutes the state's basic political system. Hence the powers vested in the National People's Congress as the country's highest organ of state power consist not only of legislation but should also include administrative and judicial powers. In terms of scientific principles, they should include all state powers. However, the National People's Congress does not exercise all of those powers on its own. Administrative powers, for example, are exercised by the country's highest organ of administrative power—the State Council which it has established for that purpose, and judicial powers are exercised by the courts which it has set up. For itself, it has retained the most important powers—those of legislation, constitutionality reviews and so forth. If, under the National People's Congress, a constitutional court or a constitutional council is set up, that in reality would be the National People's Congress setting up another institution to take care of the implementation of constitutional matters, just like setting up the State Council in order to take charge of the state's administrative matters. Thus in terms of politics and the Constitution, that would be consistent with the current system, and the people's congress system would be kept.

Although this constitutional court or constitutional council would be generated by the National People's Congress, its judges should hold office permanently or for extended periods of time. It should also have ample material guarantees, and be independent in its work from any other institution, including the National People's Congress because it would also be reviewing legislation by the National People's Congress to determine whether it complies with the Constitution. Some people say that since it would be set up under the National People's Congress, it could hardly, if at all, produce independent judgments. Actually, I believe that the crux lies in the provision of effective guarantees in terms of legal and material conditions and tenures of office. If these conditions are met, it would make no difference under which institution they are established. For example, the British Parliament is in fact Britain's highest organ of state power, and may, in theory, exercise all state powers. To this day, Britain's judicial power of final adjudication is still exercised by the British Parliament. In fact, the main duty and function of British Parliament's upper house is to exercise the judicial power of final adjudication. The only difference is that what is known as a supreme (highest) court or constitutional court in other countries is called the House of Lords in Britain, and that other countries give it independent status whereas Britain keeps the institution within the Parliament. However, keeping it within the Parliament does not affect its independent judgments. So the crux of the matter is not its name or where it is located, but rests primarily in whether real guarantees are provided and in the development of a suitable constitutional and legal culture.

If there were such an independent constitutional court (council), the National People's Congress and the NPC Standing Committee could devote themselves solely to legislative functions and duties. So long as no other institutions or persons questioned their legislations or requested constitutionality reviews, one could assume that the legislations were constitutional. Moreover, the two SAR Basic Law committees currently established by the NPC Standing Committee could also be dissolved, and responsibility for the constitutionality reviews of all laws could be delegated to that institution. Should any situations of unclear division of authority emerge between the Central Authorities (including the National People's Congress and its Standing Committee) and the Special Administrative Regions, these could be solved by an independent constitutional court. This would be fair and reasonable, would internationally conform entirely to the principle of rule of law, and would be beneficial to the implementation of the "one country, two systems" concept. It would also be more convincing for Taiwan, as it would demonstrate to Taiwan that any eventual disputes over authority between Taiwan and the mainland after the complete unification of China would be adjudicated by an independent constitutionality review institution instead of in a one-sided manner by a mainland entity. That would allay the anxieties of a good many personages in Taiwan. The judges of the state's constitutional court after reunification should, of course, be from the mainland, Taiwan, and the Hong Kong and Macao SARs, and consist of outstanding jurists and judges from all of the above regions. This matter is of extreme importance for realizing the final unification of the nation.

Currently, as a transitional measure, we should first of all publicly and formally make it clear that the National People's Congress and the NPC Standing Committee are also China's constitutionality review institutions, that they are China's "constitutional courts" or "constitutional councils," and that they accept and hear "requests" and "proposals" put forward by various institutions, social organizations and individual citizens as stipulated by the Legislation Law. And since people's courts would not be permitted to exercise the power of constitutionality reviews, it should be specified that when people's courts encounter situations where "interpretations of the law" and "interpretations of the Constitution" are necessary when adjudging a case they must first suspend the hearings and, through specified procedures, immediately submit the case to the National People's Congress or the NPC Standing Committee for them to fulfill the "constitutional courts'" duty of conducting constitutionality reviews and interpretations of the law. Since the SAR "supreme courts" are required by the two SAR Basic Laws to take the National People's Congress and the NPC Standing Committee as their constitutionality review institutions, there would be no reason not to require that mainland courts at all levels, including the Superior People's Court, follow suit. Thus, having made it clear that China also has constitutionality review institutions, it will be possible to further straighten out the relations among China's state organs, and a major deficiency will have been made good in terms of China's rule of law. In future, when conditions become ripe, we could separate out and give independent status to the constitutionality review functions of the National People's Congress and the NPC Standing Committee and then set up a special institution for constitutionality reviews.

Establishing and improving China's constitutionality review system is today a matter of especial significance and urgency. First of all, after joining the WTO, China at once faced real problems of how to handle constitutional cases. If some foreigner maintained during a lawsuit that a certain law, or administrative regulation or decree was unconstitutional or violated WTO rules and requested that the court conduct a review thereof, what should our court say in reply? If the court could not review such cases, and the attorneys submitted the case to the NPC Standing Committee as per the provisions of Article 99 of the Legislation Law and engaged in litigation at the NPC Standing Committee, how should we respond?

And another thing: One of the main aspects of the inadequacy of China's rule of law is illegal legislation, or even lawless legislation. Why do some departments and localities dare, by means of legislation, to "legitimately" raise the signboards of departmental protectionism and local protectionism? And why is it that efforts to crack down on departmentalism and local protectionism have never been successful? The main reason is that both of these "protectionisms" have their own protective umbrellas and conform to laws. And where do such "laws" come from? They are created by departmental and local legislation. Violations of the law by legislative means may be said to "derange our very foundations." They are more malignant than ordinary transgressions, and even more serious and pernicious than crimes committed by taking advantage of one's functions and duties. That is why placing legislation under effective reviews and supervision by independent courts or constitutionality review institutions is one of the most pressing tasks we now face.

11.2 The Constitutionality Review System of Special Administrative Regions Under "One Country, Two Systems"

In the above section, I have dwelt on the system of constitutionality reviews in mainland China, and we can see that in accordance with China's present constitutional structure, the institution in China which is truly vested with complete power to conduct constitutionality reviews is the NPC Standing Committee, despite the absence of sufficiently clear-cut constitutional or legal definitions. As pointed out at the beginning of this chapter, in accordance with the provisions of China's Constitution and the actual circumstances of the special administrative regions, the Basic Laws of the Special Administrative Regions confer the power to "formulate" the "implementing regulations" or "judicial interpretation" of the SAR Basic Laws "judicial interpretation" to the National People's Congress and the SAR's Court of Final Appeal. That is to say that two entities enjoy the power of constitutionality reviews in the SARs, i.e., the National People's Congress and the SAR's Court of Final Appeal. Both of these institutions bear responsibility for supervising the implementation of the SAR Basic Laws in the Special Administrative Regions. This is also one example of the combination of "one country" and "two systems." The present section explores matters related to the implementation of the relevant Basic Law constitutionality review powers of the NPC Standing Committee and the SAR courts, respectively.[24]

11.2.1 Constitutionality Reviews of SAR Legislation by the NPC Standing Committee Under "One Country, Two Systems"

From the analyses in the foregoing section, we see that the NPC Standing Committee has the power not only to implement constitutionality reviews of the actions of the *Yi Fu Liang Yuan* but also of legislation by provincial-level people's congresses. Similarly, the NPC Standing Committee is vested with the power to conduct constitutionality reviews of legislation by the SARs. That includes the powers to conduct reviews of the originally-existing laws of Hong Kong and Macao, and certain powers to conduct constitutionality reviews of new laws formulated by SAR legislation organs. The power which the NPC Standing Committee enjoys to conduct constitutionality reviews of SAR laws and the SARs' new legislation is not only based on the Constitution; the NPC Standing Committee has always been China's institution for conducting constitutionality reviews, and is amply authorized to do so by the SARs' Basic Laws. This is demonstrated in the following aspects:

11.2.1.1 The Power of the NPC Standing Committee to Place on Record and Review SAR Legislation

The two SAR Basic Laws both stipulate that the SARs enjoy the power of legislation. However, the laws formulated by the SAR legislative institutions are to be placed on record with the NPC Standing Committee. Although this placing on the record does not prevent the laws from going into force, if the NPC Standing Committee feels that any of the laws formulated by the SAR legislations fail to conform with the provisions in the Basic Law on matters under Central Government administration and Central/SAR relations, it may return the relevant law to the SAR, without, however, making any amendments. Prior to sending the law back, the NPC Standing Committee is to solicit the opinions of its affiliated SAR Basic Law Committees. Laws sent back by the NPC Standing Committee immediately become ineffective. Once a law becomes ineffective, it has no retroactive effect unless otherwise stipulated by SAR laws.[25] This stipulation in the Basic Laws in reality confers limited power to exercise constitutionality reviews on the NPC Standing Committee by means the placing-

---

[24] Although the term "constitution" in "constitutionality reviews" refers to the SAR Basic Laws, and in reality refers to reviews of actions that violate the SAR Basic Laws. I have borrowed the universally accepted concept "constitutionality review" for convenience in presenting this narrative.

[25] Article 17 of the "Basic Law of the Hong Kong Special Administrative Region" and the "Basic Law of the Macao Special Administrative Region."

on-record method. To this day, however, the NPC Standing Committee has never exercised this power.

Regarding this matter, the Basic Laws have in reality established a special system of placing on the record. The usual "placing on the record" does not contain any implication of "approval." However, since the NPC Standing Committee may send back—which means refuse to place on record—SAR legislation which it considers to be inconsistent with the relevant provisions of the Basic Laws, it must, prior to sending back the law, make an judgment on whether the law intended for placing on the record conforms to the provisions of the Basic Laws; this "judgment" may be seen as a special "constitutionality" review. Hence, the NPC Standing Committee does enjoy a certain power of "constitutionality" review with regard to SAR legislation. Of course, this "constitutionality" refers to provisions in the Basic Laws on matters administered by the Central Authorities and Central–SAR relations. As long as the legislation made by the SARs on the basis of the Basic Laws and on matters within their scope of autonomy does not involve provisions relevant to matters administered by the Central Authorities or Central–SAR relations, the NPC Standing Committee only exercises the usual placing on the record. A great deal of cerebration went into this special system of placing on the record.

In Chinese mainland and autonomous regions is also reported for the record to NPC Standing Committee. If the NPC Standing Committee maintains that a certain local legislation by a certain province is unconstitutional, it may, in accordance with the provisions of Article 67 of the Constitution directly annul the legislation by the province concerned, instead of sending it back. In Chinese mainland, the NPC Standing Committee enjoys complete powers of conducting constitutionality reviews over ordinary legislation by the localities and administrative legislation by the State Council.

11.2.1.2 The Power to Interpret the SAR Basic Laws Enjoyed by the NPC Standing Committee

Although the power to interpret the Constitution and laws differs from the power to conduct constitutionality reviews, there is no question but that the power to interpret the Constitution and Laws constitutes an important content of the power to conduct constitutionality reviews, and that its exercise immensely affects the conduct and results of constitutionality reviews. Article 158 of the Hong Kong Basic Law and Article 143 of the Macao Basic Law stipulate that "the power to interpret this law pertains to the National People's Congress Standing Committee," which in reality further affirms that the NPC Standing Committee enjoys the power to conduct constitutionality reviews over the SARs. Issues relating to this matter have been amply discussed earlier. Please see Sect. 10.2 of Chap. 10.

11.2.1.3   The Power of the NPC to Conduct Constitutionality Reviews of Originally-Existing SAR Laws

Article 60 of the [HK] Basic Law stipulates: "Upon the establishment of the Hong Kong Special Administrative Region, the law previously in force in Hong Kong shall be adopted as laws of the Region except for those which the Standing Committee of the National People's Congress declares to be in contravention of this Law. If any laws are later discovered to be in contravention of this Law, they shall be amended or cease to have force in accordance with the procedure as prescribed by this Law."

This provision further empowers the NPC Standing Committee, when the SAR is established, to conduct reviews, first of all, of original laws which existed prior to the forming of the SAR; the only standard for such reviews is the SAR Basic Law. When any such laws are found to conflict with the Basic Law, they have been declared null and void. All others have been accepted as SAR laws. These are very typical constitutionality reviews. The NPC Standing Committee has accordingly conducted a hitherto unprecedented constitutionality examination, which has quite possibly been the most extensive in constitutional history and reviewed laws of unequaled number and complexity.

The system of laws in Hong Kong prior to its return to China was most complicated. Its constitutional laws were the Letters Patent and Royal Instructions, and these comprised at least five major categories of laws: One, an countless number of British common laws and equity laws suited to Hong Kong; two, written laws suited to Hong Kong formulated by the British Parliament, the number of which had already been reduced to 29 from 70 prior to Hong Kong's return; three, Hong Kong local case laws which starting in 1905 were compiled into the *Hong Kong Case Law Reports* of which there were some 200 volumes; four, ordinances and subordinate legislation formulated locally in Hong Kong, of which there were 36 volumes of *Ordinances of Hong Kong*, totaling nearly 30,000 pages and more than 640 chapters; and five, some customary laws left over from the Qing Dynasty. In addition, the British authorities of Hong Kong before its return to China had hurriedly amended numerous laws based on the Hong Kong Bill of Rights Ordinance in the hope that China would keep these unchanged after Hong Kong's return. One can well imagine the sheer magnitude of conducting constitutionality examinations, in comparison with the Basic Laws, of each and every one of these numerous and complex laws, most of which were, moreover, in English!

Hence, the relevant departments had already begun, in early 1992, to organize examinations of Hong Kong's originally-existing laws. The National People's Congress Standing Committee Hong Kong Special Administrative Region Planning Committee's Preparatory Work Committee (hereinafter "Preparatory Committee") was established in July 1993. Under it was a legal team responsible for comprehensively studying and examining Hong Kong's existing laws and putting forward suggestions for handling them. In the course of two and half years of arduous work, the special legal team(s) had already studied and examined all of Hong Kong's existing written laws by the end of 1995. In January 1996, after the National People's Congress Hong Kong Special Administrative Region Planning Commission

("Planning Commission" for short) was established, the newly established Planning Commission's legal team again conducted repeated, in-depth and careful studies of the proposals made by the Preparatory Committee's special team(s) "Finally, the committee members reached a common understanding, i.e., that all situations that conflicted with the Basic Law had to be appropriately dealt with. However, when doing so, a basic principle should assure, namely, that Hong Kong's existing laws should remain basically unchanged. In terms of specific ways of handling, one could focus on the different characteristics of situations that conflicted with the Basic Law and adopt different means (of handling them)."

Based on the opinions of the legal team(s), the SAR Planning Commission formally submitted to the NPC Standing Committee a "Proposal on the Matter of Handling Hong Kong's Original Laws" in which it put forward specific proposals for dealing with various situations in Hong Kong's original laws which conflicted with the Basic Law. On February 23, 1997, after having examined the Hong Kong SAR Planning Commission's Proposal, the 24th Session of the Eighth National People's Congress Standing Committee approved the "Decision on Handling the Originally-Existing Laws of Hong Kong on the Basis of Article 160 of the 'Basic Law of the Hong Kong Special Administrate Region'" (hereinafter referred to as the "Decision"). The Decision made detailed stipulations on the ways to deal with various types of laws originally existing in Hong Kong, including common laws, equity laws, ordinances, and customary laws. This was an overall "constitutionality review" of Hong Kong's original laws.

Hence, the relevant departments had already begun, in early 1992, to organize examinations of Hong Kong's originally-existing laws. The National People's Congress Standing Committee Hong Kong Special Administrative Region Planning Committee's Preparatory Work Committee (hereinafter "Preparatory Committee") was established in July 1993. Under it was a legal team responsible for comprehensively studying and examining Hong Kong's existing laws and putting forward suggestions for handling them. In the course of two and half years of arduous work, the special legal team(s) had already studied and examined all of Hong Kong's existing written laws by the end of 1995. In January 1996, after the National People's Congress Hong Kong Special Administrative Region Planning Commission ("Planning Commission" for short) was established, the newly established Planning Commission's legal team again conducted repeated, in-depth and careful studies of the proposals made by the Preparatory Committee's special team(s) "Finally, the committee members reached a common understanding, i.e., that all situations that conflicted with the Basic Law had to be appropriately dealt with. However, when doing so, a basic principle should assure, namely, that Hong Kong's existing laws should remain basically unchanged. In terms of the specific ways of handling the laws, one could focus on the different characteristics of situations that conflicted with the Basic Law and adopt different means (of handling them)."

Based on the opinions of the legal team(s), the SAR Planning Commission formally submitted to the NPC Standing Committee a "Proposal on the Matter of Handling Hong Kong's Original Laws" in which it put forward specific proposals for dealing with various situations in Hong Kong's original laws which conflicted with the Basic Law. On February 23, 1997, after having examined the Hong Kong SAR Planning Commission's Proposal, the 24th Session of the Eighth National People's Congress Standing Committee approved the "Decision on Handling the Originally-Existing Laws of Hong Kong on the Basis of Article 160 of the 'Basic Law of the Hong Kong Special Administrate Region'" (hereinafter referred to as the "Decision"). The Decision made detailed stipulations on the ways to deal with various types of laws originally existing in Hong Kong, including Common Laws, equity laws, ordinances, and customary laws. This was an overall "constitutionality examination" of Hong Kong's original laws.

The Decision first of all affirmed that "the originally existing laws of Hong Kong, including common laws, equity laws, ordinances, subsidiary legislation and customary laws, except for those which come in conflict with the Basic Law, shall be adopted as laws of the Hong Kong Special Administrative Region." Hong Kong's originally-existing laws were then divided into categories, differentiated in various ways, and handled with different methods. The first type consisted of some of Hong Kong's originally-existing laws and subsidiary legislations in Annex 1 of the Decision which were determined to be in conflict with the Basic Law; it was therefore decided not to adopt them as laws of the Hong Kong SAR. There were altogether 14 of these laws and subsidiary legislations, as for example The Application of English Law Ordinance (Chapter 88), The Royal Hong Kong Regiment Ordinance (Chapter 199), and The Legislative Council (Electoral Provisions) Ordinance (Chapter 381). These were mainly laws and their subsidiary legislations which manifested Britain's colonialist rule over Hong Kong plus those concerning the dispositions for Hong Kong's three-level structural elections for implementing the "three violations" political reform plan.[26]

The second type consisted of Hong Kong's originally-existing laws and subsidiary legislations, some of the provisions of which were determined to be in conflict with the Basic Law; these conflicting provisions were not adopted as laws of the Hong Kong SAR whereas other portions were retained. Many of Hong Kong's laws and subsidiary legislations were of this type. Hence, in order not to affect the integrity of Hong Kong's laws, Article 4 of the Decisions stipulated: "To Hong Kong's originally-existing laws which will be adopted as laws of the Hong Kong Special Administrative Region starting on July 1, 1997, necessary amendments, adaptations, limitations and exceptions shall be made during their application in order to comply with the status of Hong Kong after the People's Republic of China restores its exercise of sovereignty over Hong Kong and with the relevant stipulations of the Basic Law." These would include Article two of the Immigration Ordinance (Chapter 115), the Bill of Rights Ordinance (Chapter 383), the Personal Data (Privacy) Ordinance (Chapter 486), major amendments to the Societies Ordinance (Chapter 151) after July 17, 1992, and major amendments to the Public Order Ordinance (Chapter 245) after July 27, 1995.

---

[26]The "three violations" political reform plan refers to the "three violations" political reform plan unilaterally touted by the British government after 1992 in violation of the Sino-British Joint Statement, and in violation of the Basic Law and the understandings reached between the foreign ministers of China and Britain in 1990 through the exchange of correspondence.

Additionally, the Decision stipulated specific principles for the handling of a number of common problems. If the originally-existing laws and auxiliary legislations had to with the Hong Kong SAR's diplomatic affairs, and if they came in conflict with the national laws implemented in the Hong Kong SAR, they should take the national laws as their criterion and should comply with the international rights and interests enjoyed by the Central People's Government and with the international duties undertaken by the Central People's Government. Any provisions which accorded privileged treatment to Britain or other countries of the British Commonwealth would not be retained, but reciprocity provisions between Hong Kong and Britain o other countries and regions of the British Commonwealth would not be subject to these restrictions. Provisions regarding the rights, exemptions and duties of British troops stationed in Hong Kong, if they did not conflict with the Basic Law and (China's) Garrison Law, would be retained and applied to the armed forces stationed in Hong Kong by the Central People's Government of the People's Republic of China. Provisions concerning the effectiveness of laws in the English language superseding those in the Chinese language would be interpreted as the Chinese and English languages both being formal languages. Laws in the English language quoted in legal provisions, if they did not harm the sovereignty of the People's Republic of China and did not come into conflict with the Basic Law, could, as a transitional disposition, continue to referenced and applied prior to amendments being made to them by the Hong Special Administrative Region.

The third type consisted of originally-existing laws and auxiliary legislations in Hong Kong, virtually all of which used some names and terminology—such as the term "Her Majesty"—that conflicted with the Basic Law. The Decision adopted the substitution principle to resolve this widely existing situation. The specific regulations for the substitutions were are follows:

a. In all provisions which contained "Her Majesty," "Royal," "The British Government," "Lord High Commissioner" and other such terms and phrases, the said terms and phrases should be correspondingly constructed as the Central Authority or other competent organs of China; in other circumstances, they should be constructed as the Government of the Hong Kong Special Administrative Region.

b. In all provisions which referred to "Her Majesty's Most Honorable Privy Council" or "the Privy Council," these terms and phrases should be constructed as the Court of Final Appeal of the Hong Kong Special Administrative Region or other relevant central organs of China.

c. From all names of government institutions or semiofficial institutions labeled with the title "imperial," the term "imperial" should be deleted and constructed as the corresponding institution of the Hong Kong Special Administrative Region.

d. All titles which referred to "this Colony" should be constructed as the Hong Kong Administrative Region.

e. All titles or terminology which referred to "the Supreme/Highest Court" and "the High Court" should be correspondingly constructed as the High Court and the Court of Final Appeal of the High Court.

f. All such titles and terminology as "governor," "governor-in-council," "chief secretary," "secretary for justice," "chief judge," "chief secretary for administration," "secretary for constitutional affairs," "commissioner of customs and excise," and "puisne judge," shall be correspondingly constructed as Hong Kong Special Administrative Region Chief Executive Officer, Chief Executive in Council, Chief Secretary for Administration, Secretary for Justice, Judge of the Court of Final Appeal or Chief Judge of the High Court, Secretary for Home Affairs, Secretary for Constitutional Affairs, Commissioner of Customs and Excise, and High Court Judge.

g. All titles and terminology regarding the legislative bureau, judicial organs or the administrative organs and their staff should be correspondingly constructed and applied in light of the relevant provisions of the Basic Law.

h. All provisions which refer to "The People's Republic of China" and "China" and similar titles and terminology shall be constructed as the People's Republic of China including Taiwan, Hong Kong, and Macao. All provisions which individually or simultaneously refer to Chinese mainland, Taiwan, Hong Kong, and Macao and such titles and terminology shall correspondingly construct these as components of the People's Republic of China.

i. All provisions which refer to "foreign countries" and similar titles and terminology should be constructed as all countries or regions other than the People's Republic of China; all provisions which refer to "foreign nationals" and similar titles and terminology shall be constructed as all persons other than citizens of the People's Republic of China.

j. All provisions which state that "the provisions of this ordinance do not affect, and shall not be regarded as affecting the rights and interests of Her Majesty, her heirs or her successors" should be constructed as "the provisions of this ordinance do not affect and shall not be regarded as affecting the rights and interests enjoyed by the Central Authorities or the Government of the Hong Kong Special Administrative Region in accordance with the provisions of the Basic Law and other laws."

To prevent instances of missed examinations, the Decision finally stipulated that if an originally-existing Hong Kong law was found to conflict with the Basic Law after being adopted as a law of the Hong Kong Special Administrative Region, it could be amended or its effect terminated in accordance with the procedures in the provisions of the Basic Law.

This was an all-embracing constitutionality examination of the originally-existing laws of Hong Kong, conducted in accordance with the Basic Law—an examination of immense scale and far-reaching influence. In that process, there were no controversies regarding the examination of and amendments to the great majority of the laws since the examinations and amendments were of a technical nature. No amendments were made to the substantive contents of the originally-existing laws, and therefore no substantive changes took place in the rights and duties relationships of social laws.

A fairly acute controversy occurred over the issue of how to deal with the Human Rights Law and the Personal Data (Privacy) Ordinance which were formulated and deliberately raised to high positions by the Hong Kong British government in the post-transitional period (time just before the transitional period?). In June, 1991, the Hong Kong British government, in disregard of opposition by the Chinese side, formulated the Human Rights Law, in which the provisions of Article 2 Item (3) on the interpretation of the said Law and purpose of its application, the provisions of Article 3 regarding its "influence on previous laws" and the provisions of Article 4 on the "definition of future laws" caused the Human Rights Law to override other laws in Hong Kong. Article 3 Item (2) of the Personal Data (Privacy) Ordinance also contained provisions that gave that ordinance an overriding status. The Hong Kong British government intended to have these two laws override the SAR's Basic Law and turn them into constitutional legal documents which in future would be above the Basic Law and become grounds for the future conduct of judicial reviews by SAR courts of law. Subsequently, the Hong Kong British government attempted to gain the upper hand by "striking first" prior to Hong Kong's return to China: Based on these new "constitutional" legal documents, it conducted, through the legislative bureau, an extensive and wide-ranging "urgent" revision of more than forty of Hong Kong's "original" laws, including the Societies Ordinance and Public Order Ordinance. This in fact was a preemptive "constitutionality examination" by the Hong Kong British authorities of Hong Kong's originally-existing laws. Here, however, the Human Rights Law and the Personal Data (Privacy) Ordinance played the role of "constitution."

In that case, could the Hong Kong British government formulate a basic laws norm of an overriding nature for China's special administrative region? There is no question that it could do so, prior to Hong Kong's return to China (although it frequently violated relevant agreements and understandings reached between China and Britain), and it had the power to formulate for Hong Kong constitutional norms which served Hong Kong courts of law as grounds for conducting judicial reviews (constitutionality examinations). However, the power to formulate Hong Kong's constitutional norms became China's after July 1, 1997. The basis for constitutionality examinations was now being stipulated by China, The constitutional laws of an overriding status formulated unilaterally by the Hong Kong British government naturally became ineffective, and the constitutionality examinations conducted by the National People's Congress Standing Committee and the SAR courts could only be based on the SAR's Basic Law. The reason was quite simple. Hong Kong's return to China had brought about a fundamental change in Hong Kong's basic norms.[27] Hence the National People's Congress was justified in suspending the provisions concerned in the two ordinances, since doing so was a matter of basic respect for China's sovereignty.

Another problem is: Exactly how long a period of time is meant by the term "originally-existing" in the Basic Law provision "the originally-existing laws remain basically unchanged"? The Hong Kong British government granted Hong Kong residents little freedom during the more than a hundred years they ruled Hong Kong,

---

[27]Chen Hongyi. "Hong Kong's Return: Legal Reflections," carried in Beijing, *Jurists*, 1997(5), pp. 51–55.

but began to unilaterally make extensive changes, based on the Human Rights Law, to originally-existing laws just a few years before Hong Kong' return to China, and then tried to coerce China into accepting these new "originally-existing laws." China of course refused to do so. And so the NPC Standing Committee maintained during its examinations that the newly amended provisions would not be adopted as laws for the special administrative region. China maintained that the starting date for "originally-existing" referred to 1984 when China and Britain signed their Joint Declaration and at the latest should not exceed 1990 when the Basic Law was approved, whereas Britain obviously maintained that "originally-existing" meant anything prior to July 1, 1997.

As Qian Qichen, chairman of the Hong Kong Special Administrative Region Preparatory Committee said in his Work Report of the National People's Congress Hong Kong Special Region Preparatory Committee on March 10, 1997 at the Fifth Session of the Eighth National People's Congress: "Based on the decisions by the Basic Law and the National People's Congress on the Basic Law, only the Basic Law possesses the status of overriding the other laws of Hong Kong. Meanwhile, the Hong Kong Bill of Rights Ordinance contains provisions of the said law which possess an overriding status and which come in conflict with the Basic Law. Moreover, the Hong Kong British authorities have made use of the overriding status of the said law to unilaterally conduct extensive and wide-ranging amendments to Hong Kong's originally-existing laws. These acts by the British side have violated the Sino-British Joint Declaration and the provision of the Basic Law that 'the current laws shall remain basically unchanged'."[28]

Yet the Chinese side has handled this problem with great circumspection. It has not imposed an arbitrary solution nor completely annulled these provisions which conflict with the Basic Law. It has instead stipulated that these two laws may on the whole be adopted as laws for the Hong Kong SAR, and that only the provisions in them that involved their overriding status be deleted. The major revisions made by the Hong Kong British authorities to the Societies Ordinance after July 17, 1992, and to the Public Order Ordinance after July 27, 1995, due to the overriding status of the Bill of Rights Ordinance, of course had to be annulled. However, to prevent the emergence of legal vacuums when the SAR would be established, it was decided that the SAR government would formulate new ordinances of its own to replace those annulled. As to what kind of ordinances should be formulated to replace them, that was the SAR government's own concern. And so, "annulling" did not necessarily mean restoring the original laws and provisions. It is clear that the Chinese government stuck to principles in handling such problems and displayed a good deal of versatility.

Yet another problem is how, in accordance with the Basic Law, one should examine and handle the unwritten laws—common laws, equity laws, and customary laws—originally in existence in Hong Kong.[29] Although the "substitution" principle in the

---

[28]Beijing, *People's Daily*, March 11, 1997.

[29]Xi Wen. "A Landmark in the History of Hong Kong's Legal Development: A Brief Discussion on the Decision of the NPC Standing Committee on the Handling of Hong Kong's Originally Existing Laws," carried in Hong Kong, *China Law*, 1997(2), p. 14.

Basic Law for the handling of the Hong Kong's originally-existing laws similarly applies to these unwritten laws, it merely consists of changes of titles and terminology but not changes in the laws' substantive contents. As regards substantive examinations, the legal team(s) of the Preparatory Committee maintained: "In accordance with Common Law principle for interpreting laws, the principles and conventions in these laws which come in conflict with the Basic Law shall, after the implementation of the Basic Law on July 1, 1997, of course become ineffective. And if these laws are to be applied in future when Special Administrative Region courts of law hear cases, explanations, and judgments that comply with the Basic Law should be made in accordance with the provisions of the Basic Law. Hence, the common laws, equity laws, and customary laws among Hong Kong's originally-existing laws may be brought in compliance with the Basic Law by means of new precedents in judicial practice and there is no need to examine each and every one of them."[30] This handling method in reality confers upon SAR courts the power to conduct examinations of these laws on whether they violate the Basic Law. It complies with the basic principles of common law and equity law, and enables courts of law to amend earlier case precedents by means of later case precedents and thereby develop the laws. After 1997, the Hong Kong SAR courts may continue to reference the judgments by courts in Britain and other Common Law countries. On the whole, however, the Hong Kong SAR courts should gradually form their own set of judicial precedents in light of the SAR's own circumstances.

During this unprecedented and special constitutional examination, the NPC Standing Committee has shown itself to be practical and realistic. It has adopted a highly tolerant attitude and appropriately handled the transition of Hong Kong originally-existing laws. It has altered Hong Kong's legal system and set up a new "basic norm" and legal order, yet has refrained from fracturing or rupturing Hong Kong's original legal system or causing upheavals in Hong Kong society, and has brought about a stable transition in Hong Kong's political power and legal system. In the handling of controversial issues, the NPC Standing Committee, as well as adhering to principle, has displayed considerable versatility and breadth of mind and manifested the Central Authorities' determination and sincerity to scrupulously abide by the Joint Declaration and the Basic Law and implement "one country, two systems," "Hong Kongers administer Hong Kong," and a high degree of autonomy.[31]

As stated by Prof. Cheng Hongyi, head of the Faculty of Law of Hong Kong University: "To sum up, one might say that the '97 transition has had a very light impact on Hong Kong's original laws. Whether in terms civil or commercial matters, criminal matters, public law and even human rights, Hong Kong's original laws may—as stated in the Joint Declaration—be said to remain 'basically unchanged,' and the Hong Kong Special Administrative Region's laws are, as always, protecting

---

[30] Xi Wen. "A Landmark in the History of Hong Kong's Legal Development: A Brief Discussion on the Decision of the NPC Standing Committee on the Handling of Hong Kong's Originally Existing Laws," carried in Hong Kong: *China Law*, 1997(2), p. 13.

[31] Zeng Yuwen. "Treat Hong Kong's Original Laws with Tolerance," Hong Kong, *Ta Kung Pao*, Feb. 5, 1977.

the rights and interests of individuals and corporate persons."[32] This may be described as a successful constitutionality examination.

Similarly, the Twelfth Session of the Ninth National People's Congress Standing Committee on October 31, 1999, with assistance from the National People's Congress Macao Special Administrative Region Preparatory Committee, conducted an all-round and systematic constitutionality examination of the originally-existing laws of Macao in light of the Macao Basic Law, approved the Decision on Handling the Originally-Existing Laws of Macao in Accordance with Article 45 of the Basic Law of the Macao Special Administrative Region of the People's Republic of China, and conducted an examination and handling of Macao's originally-existing laws by categories. Altogether twelve of Macao's originally-existing laws, decrees, administrative laws and regulations and normative documents were determined to be in conflict with the Basic Law and were therefore not adopted as laws of the Macao SAR. Three other laws and decrees were also determined to be in conflict with the Basic Law and not adopted as laws of the Macao SAR, but before the Macao SAR formulated new laws, relevant matters could be handled in accordance with the principles of Basic Law provisions and with reference to the originally used methods. Eighteen of Macao's originally-existing laws and decrees contained some provisions which were deemed to be in conflict with the Basic Law and were not adopted as laws of the Macao SAR, but the continued application was made of their other provisions. Most other laws and decrees did not conflict with the Basic Law, but the titles and terminology used for some of them used had to be changed, and the Decision stipulated the principles for the substitution of these titles and terminology. The Decision also stipulated that starting on the day the SAR was established, necessary changes be made to Macao's originally-existing laws which were adopted as laws of the Macao SAR, and that necessary alterations, adaptations, restrictions, or exceptions be made so these laws would comply with Macao's status and its relevant Basic Law provisions after China's resumed its exercise of sovereignty over Macao, and would be consistent with the principles of other provisions. Should Macao's originally-existing laws which were adopted as laws of the Macao SAR be later found to come in conflict with the Basic Law, they could be amended or cease to have effect, in accordance with the provisions and statutory procedures of the Basic Law. The examination of Macao's originally-existing laws likewise did not have a fundamental impact on Macao's originally-existing legal system and complied with Basic Law's principle that Macao's originally-existing laws should remain basically unchanged. It was also a successful constitutionality examination.

The originally-existing laws of Hong Kong and Macao were not formulated by the SARs' legislative organs. However, since these were to be adopted as the SARs' laws, the NPC Standing Committee, as the organ for conducting SAR constitutionality examinations, of course had the power to conduct overall constitutionality examinations of those laws, decrees, and documents. These overall and systematic examinations of Hong Kong's and Macao's originally-existing laws, completed

---

[32]Chen Hongyi. "Hong Kong's Return: Legal Reflections," carried in Beijing, *Jurists*, 1997 (5), pp. 51–55.

within a concentrated time frame and with concentrated manpower and material resources by the NPC Standing Committee, changed over to everyday for-the-record examinations of legislation by the SARs' legislative organs after the SARs were established.

Also, may the NPC Standing Committee implement constitutionality examinations of administrative acts by the SARs' administrative organs? The Basic Law merely stipulates that, for the administrative acts by SAR administrative organs, the SAR Chief Executive is to be accountable to the Central People's Government and the HK Special Administrative Region in line with the provisions of the Basic Law.[33] In terms of actual practice, the fact that the SAR Chief Executive reports on his work to the Premier of the State Council at regular intervals may be regarded as a specific manifestation of "accountability to the Central People's Government." Yet the Basic Law does not stipulate that the SAR Chief Executive and administrative organs must be accountable to the NPC Standing Committee, hence it might be said that the NPC Standing Committee does not have direct powers to conduct constitutionality examinations over the administrative acts of the SAR administrative institutions.

Another question: Since the NPC Standing Committee has the power of constitutionality examinations over the SARs, is the National People's Congress, as the higher authority over the NPC Standing Committee, also an organ for conducting constitutionality examinations of the SARs?[34] In the first section, I have already expounded the circumstance that in China Constitution and political system, the National People's Congress undoubtedly enjoys the power of constitutionality examinations—which is also of the highest level—despite the fact that the objects of National People's Congress constitutionality examinations being chiefly the NPC Standing Committee and its own legislations.[35] As stated earlier, up to the present, examples of the National People's Congress conducting constitutionality examinations are those, in 1990 and 1993, respectively, of determining whether the SAR Basic Laws of Hong Kong and Macao violated their own regions' "mini-constitutions" (their Basic Laws). Other than these, the China's highest organ of state power has not as yet exercised the power of constitutional examinations. Since the two SAR Basic Laws have both vested the power to exercise their Regions' constitutionality examinations in the NPC Standing Committee, I believe that under normal circumstances the National People's Congress will not directly exercise the power of constitutional examinations in the SARs, but will indirectly exercise supervision over the SARs through the acts of the NPC Standing Committee, including the NPC Committee's legislative and legal interpretations as well as its for-the-record examinations of SAR legislation.

---

[33] Article 43 of the Basic Law of the Hong Kong Special Administrative Region.

[34] Here, "constitution" of course means the Basic Law of the Special Administrative Region.

[35] Article 62 of the Constitution of the People's Republic of China.

11.2.2 Constitutionality Examination Powers of SAR Courts Under "One Country, Two Systems"

11.2.2.1 The Grounds for SAR Courts Exercising Constitutionality Examinations

There is still a good deal of debate on the SAR courts' power to conduct constitutionality examinations. This matter did not draw sufficient attention when the Basic Laws were formulated, and this reason the Basic Laws do not contain clear stipulations on the SARs' constitutionality examinations system, and even less do they stipulate whether the SAR court may or may not exercise the power of the constitutionality examinations (the power of legislative examinations). However, since Article 11 of the Basic Law provides that "no law enacted by the legislature of the Hong Kong Special Administrative Region shall contravene this Law," and this shows that the Basic Law is the SARs' highest legal norm, that the SARs possess a genuinely overriding status and the highest legal force, and that no other legislation by the SARs may contravene the Basic Laws. This provides a constitutional foundation for setting up the SARs' mechanism for constitutionality examinations, because there has to be a mechanism for judging whether the SARs' legislations contravene the Basic Laws, and that is the constitutionality examinations.

In that case, which organ is to judge whether the SAR legislations contravenes the Basic Law? As said earlier, the NPC Standing Committee is one of them, but not the only one, nor does it frequently exercise that power. Some scholars maintain that the NPC Standing Committee may be a SAR institution which conducts constitutionality examinations. However, "the laws which the NPC Standing Committee are able to examine in accordance with Article 17 of the Basic Law are limited to a certain portion of the laws formulated by the legislative organs of the Hong Kong SAR, or in other words, the Hong Kong laws which come in conflict with matters administered by the Central Authorities and with the provisions on Central/SAR relations. As regards other laws formulated by the Hong Kong SAR legislative organs, if they come in conflict with the provisions of the Basic Law other than those mentioned above, the NPC Standing Committee should not have the power to conduct examinations. In that case, by which constitutional organ or organs should these laws be examined? … If the organs of the Central Government do not have the power for constitutionality examinations of laws of this type, it ought to pertain to the organs of the Hong Kong SAR." That this power ought to belong to the legislative organs of the Hong Kong SAR clearly was not the intention of the Basic Law's formulators, otherwise Article 11 of the Basic Law would not have stipulated that the laws formulated by the SAR's legislative organs were not to contravene the Basic Law, and if the legislative organs found that their previous legislations were unconstitutional they could very well have used such methods as amending or reformulating the laws to correct them instead of adopting the method of constitutionality examinations.[36]

---

[36]Dai Yaoting. "Constitutional Law," carried in Chen Hongyi et al. *Outline of Hong Kong Law.* Hong Kong: Joint Publishing (H.K.), 1999, pp. 117–118.

Article 8 of the Basic Law stipulates: "The laws previously in force in Hong Kong, that is, the common law, rules of equity, ordinances, subordinate legislation and customary law shall be maintained, except for any that contravene this Law, and subject to any amendment by the legislature of the Hong Kong Special Administrative Region." Article 81 stipulates: "The judicial system previously practiced in Hong Kong shall be maintained except for those changes consequent upon the establishment of the Court of Final Appeal of the Hong Kong Special Administrative Region." Under the Common Law system prior to Hong Kong's return to China, Hong Kong had already formed a constitutionality examination system for which the ordinary judicial organs, that is courts of law, were responsible, namely, the Judicial Review system. Under this system, Hong Kong courts of law enjoyed the power to conduct constitutionality examinations. Based on those provisions in the Common Law, this judicial review system was naturally retained after the Hong Kong's return to China. Article 80 of the Basic Law also stipulated: "The courts of the Hong Kong Special Administrative Region at all levels shall be the judiciary of the Region, exercising the judicial power of the Region." The "law" comprising the "judiciary" naturally first of all included the Region's fundamental law, i.e., the Basic Law, and the courts at all levels of the Region were responsible for supervising the implementation of the Basic Law. In addition, Article 158 of the Basic Law vested the courts of the Region with the power to interpret the provisions of the Region's Basic Law in the adjudication of cases. Hence, it is only logical that the SAR courts should at the same time conduct constitutionality examinations. From various perspectives, it was clear that the SAR courts should continue to enjoy the power to conduct constitutionality examinations after Hong Kong's return to China and that the SAR courts could find grounds in the Basic Law for exercising the power to conducted constitutionality examinations.

Moreover, some scholars maintain that as compared to past practice, there was somewhat more latitude for judicial reviews (constitutionality examinations) by SAR courts of law. That was first and foremost because Hong Kong had for the first time in its history obtained the power of final adjudication which is usually linked with constitutionality examinations. All courts of law which enjoy the power of final adjudication usually also have the power of constitutionality examinations.[37] The power of final adjudication is meaningless if one does not have the power of judicial reviews (constitutionality examinations).[38] Hong Kong's previous court of final appeal used to be Britain's Privy Council Judicial Committee, and that committee had the power to conduct constitutional reviews of whether Hong Kong's local laws formulated by Hong Kong's governor together with the Legislative Council contravened the Letters Patent and Royal Instructions and to repeal unconstitutional local legislation. After Hong Kong's return to China, the Privy Council Judicial Committee was replaced

[37]Chen Hongyi. "On the Hong Kong SAR Courts' Power of Constitutional Examinations." carried in Beijing: *Peking University Law Journal*, 1998(5), p. 12.
[38]Just as discussed earlier, China's mainland is an exception in that the Superior People's Court is mainland China's Court of Final Instance, yet it is not vested with the power of constitutionality examinations, which power is exercised by another institution, i.e., the National People's Congress and its Standing Committee.

by the Hong Kong SAR Court of Final Appeal. This, for Hong Kong, was a fundamental change, and with its acquisition of the Hong Kong SAR power of Final Judicial Adjudication, it also obtained the corresponding power of constitutionality examinations.

Also, many of the Basic Law provisions regarding the protection of human rights "were likely to be cited during lawsuits as grounds for requesting the court to adjudge certain legal norms as being in contravention to the Basic Law and invalid." This did not exist in Hong Kong's previous constitutional system. "Seen from this perspective, the implementation of the Basic Law may possible lead to a broadening and elevation of the Hong Kong courts' power of judicial examination of legislation."[39]

Thirdly, as compared with Hong Kong's original political system in which powers were highly concentrated in the governor of Hong Kong, the political system of the Hong Kong SAR has tended more toward the principle of separation-of-powers principle, which is most apparent among the SAR's legislation, administration, and judiciary. This has given the SAR's judiciary more opportunities to intervene in and solve disputed between the legislation and administrative institutions and other political controversies.[40]

Prof. Chen Hongyi also maintains: "The Basic Law is a constitutional document of greater comprehensiveness and specificity than the Letters Patent and it has become a grand blueprint and overall plan for the future development for Hong Kong society. When the courts of the Hong Kong Special Administrative Region exercise constitutionality examinations in accordance with the Basic Law, the role they play is of an authoritative guardian of the implementation of the Basic Law, a solemn and sacred task that carries heavy and long-term responsibilities."[41] It is of course more advantageous to have a complete constitutional law implemented by a court of law, and the Basic Law, on which nearly five years of careful formulation were expended, of course possesses more advantages in terms of constitutionality examinations than the Letters Patent.

Hence, the courts of the HK SAR "conduct (judicial) examinations of greater extent under the Basic Law than the originally-existing system. It is a system of a greater scope, and the Basic Law provides many guarantees for rights and freedoms. It is a more standardized system, especially as regards issues of the economic and social policies. Matters concerning fiscal politics, education, professional organizations, religious freedoms, civil aviation, guarantees for the pensions of civil servants—to cite just a few examples—may all be constitutional matters," and all may be subjected to constitutional examinations. "The tendency today is to broaden the scope of judicial jurisdiction, and courts of law may have jurisdiction over any issues which include constitutional interpretations, even though they may not be able to handle them

---

[39]Wacks R. "The Judicial Function," carried in *The Future of the Law in Hong Kong* (Wacks ed.). Hong Kong: Oxford University Press, 1989, p. 133.

[40]Chen Hongyi. "Legal Reflections on Hong Kong's Return to China," carried in *The Jurist*, 1997(5), p. 61.

[41]Chen Hongyi. "Legal Reflections on Hong Kong's Return to China," carried in *The Jurist*, 1997(5), p. 61.

very specifically."[42] Prof. Chen Hongyi maintains: "Post-'97 Hong Kong courts had broad latitude for developing Hong Kong's laws, to the extent of setting up a legal system based on the Basic Law and 'one country, two systems' and Hong Kongers' 'high degree of autonomy.' What Hong Kong courts need is not simply abundant professional legal knowledge and the ability to clearly discern the details of cases; they must also have a high degree of political acuity."[43] That is the best description of the challenges facing the new SAR courts.

11.2.2.2 The Practice of the SAR Courts in Conducting Constitutionality Examinations

The practice of Hong Kong in the four or more years since returning to China demonstrates that the Hong Kong's courts have indeed exercised that power on many occasions. In relevant lawsuits, they have implemented constitutionality examinations of whether Hong Kong SAR local legislative and administrative acts have violated the Basic Law, and some judgments have also involved issues of China's Constitution. Though examinations of lawsuits related to the Basic Law, the SAR courts have begun to "gradually set up interpretations of Basic Law provisions, and make their meanings and scope of application more distinct." These cases have included the HKSAR v. Ma Wei Case (regarding the retention of Hong Kong's originally-existing laws stipulated by the Basic Law and the legality of the Provisional Legislative Council),[44] the Association of Expatriate Civil Servants of Hong Kong v. the Chief Executive of HKSAR (concerning the definition of "legal procedures" in Article 48, item (7) of the Basic Law),[45] Chim Pui Chung v. the President of the Legislative Council (concerning Article 79, item (6) of the Basic Law as to whether the relieving a member of the Legislative Council of his position requires waiting for the completion of an appeal),[46] the Association of Expatriate Civil Servants of Hong Kong v. the Secretary of the Civil Service (concerning the issue of contract officers transferring to permanent officers having to comply with Chinese spoken and written language requirement and not violating Article 100 of the Basic Law),[47] the case of Weng Kunli and other persons (concerning Article 10, paragraph one of the Provisions on the Transfer of Sentenced Person complying with Article 153 of the Basic Law),[48] the Chan Wah v. Hang Hau Rural Committee and Another and Tse Kwan Sang v. Pat Heung Rural Committee, Secretary for Justice (concerning the interpretations regarding the lawful traditional rights and interest of the indigenous inhabitants of

---

[42]Yash G. *Hong Kong's New Constitutional Order.* Hong Kong University Press, 1999, p. 306.

[43]Chen Hongyi. "Legal Reflections on Hong Kong's Return to China," carried in *The Jurist*, 1997(5), p. 61.

[44](1997) Hong Kong Law Reports and Digest 761: (1997) Hong Kong Cases 315.

[45](1998) 1 HKLRD 615.

[46](1998) 2 HKLRD 552.

[47]HCAL No. 9 of 1998.

[48](1999)3 HKLRD 316.

the "New Territories" in Basic Law Article 40 and interpretations regarding the right of permanent residents of the Hong Kong SAR to vote and the sand for election in Basic Law Article 26),[49] the Cheung Man Wai Florence v. The Director of Social Welfare (the stipulation in the Social Workers Regulations that social workers must register in compliance with Basic Law Article 144 and 145),[50] Commissioner for Ratings and Valuation v. Agrila Limited (concerning the matter of the meaning of "ratable value" in Basic Law Article 121 not being limited to its sense in the Rating Ordinance),[51] Chan Shu Ying v. The Chief Executive of the HKSAR (concerning the matter that the Provision of Municipal Services (Reorganization) Ordinance is consistent with Basic Law Article 68, item (3), Articles 97, 98 and 160, and Annex II),[52] and Ng Kung-siu and Anor v. HKSAR (on the relationship between protecting the national and regional flags and freedom of expression).[53]

The HKSAR courts also exercise constitutionality reviews when adjudicating a series of lawsuits on the right of abode in Hong Kong of children born in the mainland to Hong Kong persons. These cases involved the definition of permanent Hong Kong inhabitants in Article 24 of the Basic Law, the procedures for mainland inhabitants to settled down in Hong Kong in Article 22, and provisions of the International Covenant on Civil and Political Rights and the effectiveness of the interpretations of the Basic Law by the NPC Standing Committee in Article 39 of the Basic Law. During their hearings on these cases, the SAR court of various levels on numerous occasions carried out judicial reviews of the SAR's legislative and administrative acts. As mentioned earlier, there is acute controversy over some issues, and as newly set up SAR courts after Hong Kong's return to China these face the problem of how to integrate into the new system of constitutional governance. That takes time and patience, as "one country, two systems" is after all something new, and no one dares assert they already know how to go about it. In any case, the HKSAR courts' exercise of the power to conduct constitutionality examinations is a reality which must be faced, and crux at this time is how to do a good job of handling the relations between the SAR courts and the NPC Standing Committee in terms of exercising that power. On the other hand, clarification of the meanings of many provisions of the Basic Law through interpretations of the Basic Law by the SAR courts epitomizes the characteristics and advantages of having judicial organs interpret the constitution and the law.

The more important of these cases include the Kam Nga and others v. Director of Immigration,[54] Ng Ka Ling and Others v. Director of Immigration,[55] Lui Sheung Kwan and another v. Director of Immigration,[56] Lau Kong Yung and 16 Others v. the

---

[49]137 and 139/1999, CACV 278 and 279/1999.

[50]HCAL 25/1999.

[51]CACV 107/1999.

[52]HCAL 151/1999.

[53](1999) 1 HKLRD 783.

[54](1999) 1 HKLRD 304.

[55](1999) 1 HKLRD 315, 3391–3401.

[56](1998) 1 HKLRD 265.

Director of Immigration,[57] etc. On July 20, 2001 the HKSAR Court of Final Appeal again made three important judgments, namely, the Tam Nga Yin and others v. the Director of Immigration (whether or not children adopted from China's mainland by permanent Hong Kong inhabitants through legal channels comply with the definition in Basic Law Article 24 for permanent SAR inhabitants),[58] the Director of Immigration v. Chong Fung Yuen (whether or not Chinese citizens who themselves were born in Hong Kong of parents who were not permanent inhabitants of Hong Kong comply with the conditions in Basic Law Article 24 for being permanent SAR Inhabitants),[59] Fateh Muhammad v. Commissioner of Registration (the seven years of ordinary and continuous residence as stipulated in Article 24, Item (2) of the Basic Law does not include the time served under criminal detention in Hong Kong),[60] etc.

Some of the cases listed above had already been studied and analyzed in Chapter XI. It is evident that the HK SAR courts had already taken charge of the interpretation and supervision of the Basic Law in the SAR. Through the SAR courts' judicial acts, the meanings of many of the Basic Law's provisions were further clarified and the Basic Law was enhanced and developed. The SAR courts, and mainly the judgments passed by the Court of Final Appeal, are in the process of formulating the detailed rules for the implementation of the Basic Law, and these judgments, plus the NPC Standing Committee's interpretations of the Basic Law and the text of the Basic Law, together constitute the entirety of the Basic Law. Studying the Basic Law not only requires studying the text of the Basic Law, it also calls for studying the interpretations of the Basic Law by the NPC Standing Committee and the judgments made by the SAR courts as they exercise the power of constitutional reviews. This presents an entirely new challenge to Chinese mainland law workers who are accustomed to placing reliance on written legislations.

As regards Macao, it only had court of first instance (Tribunal Judicial de Base) when it was under Portuguese administration, and appellate cases were accepted directly by Portuguese courts. Meanwhile, constitutionality reviews of relevant laws could only be submitted to Portugal's constitutional courts,[61] since Macao itself had no power to conduct constitutionality reviews. The circumstances in Macao had been quite different from those Hong Kong. Previously, Hong Kong had already had a history of, and experience in, judicial reviews as well as a complete judicial system, whereas Macao strictly speaking had no judicial reviews (namely, constitutional reviews of abstract government acts), and a complete judicial system had been set up there only a short while before Macao' return to China.[62] Hence the Macao SAR's

---

[57]FACV 10/1999; FACV 11/1999.

[58]FACV 20/2000; FACV 21/2000.

[59]CFAV 26/2000.

[60]CFAV 24/2000.

[61]Zhao Bingzhi and Gao Dezhi. *Macao Legal Issues.* Chinese People's Public Security University Press, 1997, pp. 16–17.

[62]Xiao Weiyun. *One Country, Two Systems and the Macao SAR Basic Law.* Peking University Press, 1993, p. 232.

judicial organs had never exercised the power of constitutionality reviews over the SAR's legislation.

11.2.3   Interaction Between the NPS Standing Committee and the SAR Courts on the Matter of Constitutionality Examinations

If the SAR courts exercised the power of constitutional reviews, how did they handle its relations with the NPC Standing Committee's power of constitutionality examinations? Chinese mainland and the SARs practiced two different systems of constitutionality examinations and, frankly speaking, neither side sufficiently understood the other side. In the view of mainland personages, it was invalid and indeed inconceivable for a court to announce that a law approved by a legislative organ violated the constitution. For how could a judge appointed under a democratic system overthrow a decision by a body elected by the people? That was incomprehensible for people living under the Continental Law system, yet quite normal under the Common Law system. Similarly, in the view of Hong Kong personages, it was also unthinkable that the highest organ of state power (organ of legislation) would examine laws and actions to see whether these were constitutional, because how could one and the same institution examine its own decisions for constitutionality? There is an adage under the Common Law that a person cannot act as his own judge. Yet in under the people's congress system in Chinese mainland, doing so complies with the system and is quite normal. Such a problem would not emerge if the two localities exercised their power of constitutionality examination or power of judicial examination each within their own respective domains. But how should the problem be handled when constitutionality cases occur that involve both places?

Question 1: Under the Common Law, courts of law may examine the laws passed by legislation organs. But are the National People's Congress and its Standing Committee the highest organs of state power for the SARs? There should be no question about this, and the China's highest organs of state power are also the SARs' legislative organs and have the power to legislate for the SARs. In that case, may the SAR courts examine the laws passed by the National People's Congress and its Standing Committee to see whether they contravene the Basic Law?

The answer is no. First of all, Hong Kong courts before Hong Kong's return to China did not have the power to implement constitutional reviews of British parliamentary legislation, and doing so was impossible even under the original Common Law system.[63] There was some broadening of the extent of the constitutional reviews by the courts after Hong Kong's return, but laws and resolutions by the National People's Congress and its Standing Committee were excluded from the scope of their

---

[63]Chen A. H. Y. "The Court of Final Appeal's Ruling in the 'Illegal Migrant' Children Case: Congressional Supremacy and Judicial Review" carried in "Law Working Paper Series" Paper No. 24, *Faculty of Law*, Hong Kong, the University of Hong Kong, March 1999.

constitutional reviews, and this should be seen as the "restriction" on the courts' judicial power "imposed by the legal system and principles previously in force in Hong Kong," as stipulated in Article 19 of the Basic Law. Also, the legislative acts for the SAR by China's highest organs of power are acts of state that represent the exercise of state sovereignty. In accordance with the provisions of Article 19 of the Basic Law, the Hong Kong SAR courts of law have no jurisdiction over acts of state such defense and foreign affairs. And since no such jurisdiction exists, neither do constitutional reviews. Hence in fundamental terms, the HK SAR courts may not conduct constitutionality examinations of the legislation, including interpretations, by the National People's Congress and its Standing Committee. If, in the course of adjudicating lawsuits, SAR courts encounter questions of fact concerning acts of state, including state legislation, they should, in accordance with the provisions of Basic Law Article 19, obtain a certificate from the Chief Executive with regard to such questions, and the certificate shall be binding on the courts. And before issuing such a certificate, the Chief Executive shall obtain a certifying document from the Central People's Government.

In that case, what should be done if legislation, including interpretations of laws, directed at the SARs by the National People's Congress and its Standing Committee conflict with the Constitution or a Basic Law? This is a cause of concern for many people. If such a circumstance does emerge, it should be solved by constitutionality examination organs in China's mainland, or in other words, it should be handled by a constitutionality examination institution on the mainland. As discussed in Sect. 11.1, in accordance with the provisions of China's Constitution the institution currently empowered to conduct constitutionality examinations of acts by the NPC Standing Committee is the National People's Congress. Hence, if problems occur in the constitutionality examinations of the SARs by the NPC Standing Committee, and if interpretations of the Basic Laws by the NPC Standing Committee contravene the legislative principles of "one country, two systems," "a high degree of autonomy" and "Hong Kongers administer Hong Kong," the way to remedy these is to ask the National People's Congress to repeal the decisions concerned by the NPC Standing Committee. If the decisions concerned by the National People's Congress are wrong, there is, according to the Constitution's current provisions, no way to remedy such situations and, as said earlier, one can only depend on the National People's Congress to remedy things itself. Whether this is reasonable or feasible is another matter. If the mainland's system of constitutionality examinations is insufficiently sound at this time, one should improve and perfect the mainland's constitutionality examinations system as soon as possible, but one should not take this as an excuse to strip the Central Authorities of the power of constitutionality examinations they should exercise. And for that reason the process of building up rule of law and the perfection of the constitutionality examinations system in the country as a whole directly affects rule of law and social development in the SARs.

In reality, as discussed in the foregoing section, according to the current constitutional system the constitutionality examinations institutions of the various provinces, autonomous regions and municipalities directly under the central government—and their people's congresses and people's congress standing committees—also may not conduct constitutionality examinations of legislations by their higher legislative organs, namely, the legislations by the National People's Congress and its Standing Committee, not to mention constitutionality examinations by the Supreme People's Court of legislations by the National People's Congress. On this matter, there is nothing special about the SAR Special Laws. They do not accord any special treatment to the SARs; the treatment is the same as for ordinary localities on the mainland, i.e., the Central Authorities retain the power the conduct final constitutionality examinations, even though they may not make much use of that power.

Of course, saying so does not negate the fact that the SAR courts of law have the power to conduct interpretation of relevant laws legislated by the National People's Congress and its Standing Committee. And since the SAR counts have the power to interpret the Basic Law, they of course have the power to interpret other legislations by the National People's Congress and its Standing Committee. If they find situations where such legislation contravenes the Basic Law, they must, in line with the current mechanism for solving such situations, temporarily suspend adjudication, ask the NPC Standing Committee to conduct interpretations or constitutionality examinations of the National People's Congress laws suspected of contravening the Constitution, and then conduct further adjudication in line with the NPC's interpretations or examination results. If some legislation has to be repealed because it contravenes the Basic Law, that can only be done by the NPC itself. Any future developments and changes in this respect will hinge on the progress of rule of law in Chinese mainland.

Question 2: The National People's Congress and its Standing Committee have the power to conduct examinations of legislation by SAR legislative organs. In that case, can they implement constitutionality examinations of the judgments by SAR courts? According to the provisions of the Basic Laws, the SARs enjoy independent judicial powers and powers of final adjudication. As stated earlier, the National People's Congress and its Standing Committee are not the SARs' "courts of final instance" or "supreme courts" and do not conduct constitutionality examinations of the judgments made by the SAR courts within their scopes of jurisdiction. The NPC Standing Committee has the power to interpret the Basic Laws in accordance with the provisions of the Basic Laws, but that is not a judicial power of the power of final adjudication; it is a power subsidiary to the power of legislation and bears legislative characteristics. Hence in my view, acts of interpreting the Basic Laws by the NPC Standing Committee fall in the category of legislative acts and not judicial acts. In terms of jurisprudence, "interpreting" is a concept different from that of "making a judgment" or "trying a case." The NPC Standing Committee does try specific cases; it merely explains the specific connotations of legal provisions. According to the provisions of the Basic Laws, the power to try cases pertains to the SAR courts. If an instance of unconstitutionality occurs in a judgment by a SAR court, it should be corrected and resolved by means of the SAR's own judicial mechanism and constitutionality examinations mechanism. Should the mainland [authorities] disagree with the SAR court's judgment concerned, they may seek an interpretation of the Basic Law by National People's Congress or even amend the Basic Law through statutory procedures, but they may not try the case in place of the SAR court.

In Chinese mainland, there is still some controversy about whether the National People's Congress and it Standing Committee may exercise "individual case supervision" over judgments by mainland courts. The NPC Standing Committee is preparing to draft a set of detailed rules on the supervision of court trials. However, we have learned that the NPC Standing Committee will not directly handle or examine and approve specific cases. It will only urge courts to rectify and resolve the cases concerned on their own in accordance with the law.[64] I maintain that people's congresses should not replace courts of law in court trials simply because the quality of court trials on the mainland is fairly low and even corrupt practices exist, since doing so would damage another important constitutional principle, namely, the principle of independent adjudication by courts of law, and be disadvantageous for the courts' establishing authority and credibility. Low quality of court-of-law adjudication should be resolve by means of improving the quality of the judges and reforming the judicial system. One must not "throw out the child with the bath water," attend to one aspect and lose sight of the other, and as a result lose more than we gain.

Some people maintain that since the British House of Lords is also vested with judiciary functions, China's NPC Standing Committee can also exercise certain judiciary activities. Moreover, the Constitution provides that the National People's Congress and its Standing Committee are our country's highest organs of state power,[65] and "highest power" should include judiciary powers. I maintain that neither of these two contentions is tenable under China's present constitutional structure. First of all, the British House of Lords is qualified in the British constitution as possessing judiciary functions and is in fact an important constituent of Britain's courts—a circumstance formed in the course of history and not something "learned" at random.[66] However, China is not a bicameral state, and the NPC Standing Committee is not qualified by the Constitution as possessing judicial functions and therefore cannot exercise judicial activities. As for "highest power," I maintain that this refers to the various powers listed in Articles 62 and 67 of the Constitution and does not include judicial powers. "Highest power" means "the highest powers" and only "the highest powers," not "all powers," and cannot take the place of all of the constitutional powers exercised, respectively, by other state organs. As I have said above, if one insists on having the National People's Congress and its Standing Committee exercise judicial powers, like the British House of Lords, that can be done, but one must first amend the Constitution, expand the duties and powers of National People's Congress and its Standing Committee and incorporate judicial powers in Articles 62 and 67. In this way, the National People's Congress and its Standing Committee will become China's actual constitutional court or highest court, and their mode of operations and procedures will all undergo corresponding changes.

---

[64]On August 24, 1999, the NPC House Judicial Committee asked the 11th Session of the Ninth National People's Congress for an examination of the draft of the regulations on exercising supervision over major cases of lawbreaking in the work of conducting trials and inspections. See the Beijing *Guangming Daily* of August 25, 1999.

[65]Constitution of the People's Republic of China, Article 57.

[66]Ward R. *English Legal System*, London, Butterworths, 1998, p. 166.

If, in Chinese mainland, the NPC Standing Committee does not directly implement constitutional examinations of mainland court-of-law adjudications, there will be even less reason for the NPC Standing Committee to directly exercise constitutionality examinations of adjudications by the courts of the "highly autonomous" Special Autonomous Regions.

Let us assume that in future, the NPC Standing Committee adopts judicial procedures when exercising the power of constitutionality examinations and even makes it clear that is China's constitutional court, or that eventually another constitutional court or council is set up under the National People's Congress which shall be independently in charge of constitutionality examinations and rule of law is brought about in China, does that mean the SARs' powers of final adjudication will be "handed up" to NPC Standing Committee or a constitutional court? I do not believe that is possible, because the SARs' powers of final adjudication are not only protected by the Basic Laws; they are also protected by the two Joint Declarations. Even if rule of law realized in China and the system of constitutionality examinations is perfect, the powers vested in national constitutionality examinations institutions will still be those stipulated in the Basic Laws (i.e., interpretation of the Basic Law and the record review of SAR legislation). The power of final adjudication will still pertain to the SARs.

Question 3: The blending (bonding) of two different systems of constitutionality examination. During the adjudication of Lau Kong Yung and 16 others v. the Director of Immigration, Non-Permanent Judge Sir Anthony Mason of the SAR Court of Final Appeal pointed out that in accordance with the Basic Law, the SAR continued to apply the Common Law and the Common Law judicial system. One of the basic contents of the "one country, two systems" principle was to incorporate the Common Law system under the grand framework of the Chinese Constitution through the medium of laws of a national nature. And there had to be a point of connection between the SAR courts and the relevant Chinese institutions. In a country where the Common Law is universally implemented, local courts are generally connected with nationwide constitutional courts or nationwide supreme courts. However, we are involved not only with two different systems but also with two different legal regimes. Under the principle of "one country, two systems," Article 158 of the Basic Law provides a quite different method of connection because Article 158 (which is consistent with Article 67, paragraph four of the Chinese Constitution) vest the power to interpret the Basic Law in the NPC Standing Committee instead of in the Supreme People's Court, and then the NPC Standing Committee authorizes the SAR courts to interpret on their own the provisions of the Basic Law which fall within the scope of SAR autonomy when they adjudicate cases. In the Common Law system, interpretation of laws includes interpretation of the constitution and is handled by the courts when they adjudicate cases. In China, however, according to Article 67, Item (2)4 of the Chinese Constitution, the NPC Standing Committee has the power to interpret laws, because China's Constitution has not adopted the concept of division of powers under the Common Law, and according to Article 57 of China's Constitution the National People's Congress is the highest organ of state power and the NPC Standing Committee is its permanent body. The NPC Standing Committee's power to, and function of, interpreting the laws is obviously not exercised when cases are being adjudicated. And for that reason the term "adjudicating cases" as mentioned in Article 158 of the Basic Law clearly indicates that the power of interpretation enjoyed by SAR courts is limited to the adjudication of cases, and that it is different from the ordinary and self-initiated power of interpretation enjoyed by the NPC Standing Committee in accordance with Article 67, Item (4) of the Constitution and in accordance with Article 158, paragraph one of the Basic Law.[67] It is evident that the system of interpreting laws and the system of constitutionality examinations in mainland China may seem quite strange to the judges and lawyers under the Common Law.

Take for example the 1999 "People's Congress Interpretation of the Law." The SAR Basic Laws have not conferred the power of final interpretation of the Basic Laws to the SAR courts of final appeal (instance), nor do the SAR courts of final appeal (instance) enjoy the Basic Laws' power of final "constitutionality" examinations. These powers are indeed powers pertaining to the NPC Standing Committee according to the Constitution and the Basic Laws. When the HK SAR Court of Final Appeal was adjudicated the right of abode cases, it should have asked the NPC Standing Committee to interpret the Basic Law, but it did not do so. That shows the new SAR courts will need some time to understand and familiarize themselves with the mainland's Constitution and legal system, and need time to gradually adapt to the new political and legal environment under "one country, two systems."

The SAR courts of final appeal (instance)—as the SARs' "highest courts"—need to take independent responsibility for the SARs' rule of law and jurisprudence, and should minimize as much as possible their requests to the NPC Standing Committee for "interpretations of the law." The NPC Standing Committee of course does not want to make too many interpretations of the Basic Laws, and in particular must not interfere with the independent judicial powers of the SAR courts of final appeal (instance) so as to avoid giving the impression that the SAR courts ask Beijing for instructions on each and every matter and thus adversely affect the international prestige of SAR jurisprudence. Also, it is indeed no small matter and a very difficult step for a judicial institution under the Common Law to request that a SAR court of final appeal ask a legislative institution (even though China's Constitution qualifies the National People's Congress as the highest organ of state power) for an interpretation of a law (even though it is a law of a constitutional nature). The difficulty rests in the fact that NPC Standing Committee is a legislative institution and has not been explicitly defined as a constitutionality review institution or a judicial Institution, and the difficulty of asking a newly established SAR Court of Final Appeal to take such a step can well be imagined when Chinese mainland has not made it clear that the NPC Standing Committee is China's institution for conducting constitutionality examinations and when the mainland's Supreme People's Court has yet to formally apply to the NPC Standing Committee for any interpretation of the Constitution or a

---

[67]FAVC 10/1999; FAVC 11/1999.

law.[68] I entertain no doubts about the punctiliousness and steadfastness of the SAR Court of Final Appeal's five chief justices with regard to rule of law. All of them are honest and upright persons who have practiced their vocations for many years, accumulated profound professional knowledge and enjoy high prestige in society. I have not the least doubt about their loyalty to China (although some are not citizens of China) and their deep love for the Hong Kong SAR. I know they sincerely uphold China's unity, and that they wish to create a salutary business environment for Hong Kong and maintain Hong Kong's fine international reputation through their impartial administration of justice. If requesting assistance from the NPC Standing Committee should become absolutely necessary and unavoidable, they would not avoid doing so, out of their deep sense of responsibility for their profession and the SAR's prosperity. The key to the problem is that rule of law in Chinese mainland is still far from being sufficiently sound and that basic and important rule-of-law institutions are yet to be fully established. Relying on the current mainland legal institutions and mechanisms to handle SAR affairs would certainly be far from satisfactory. As some scholars have noted, were the Basic Laws to stipulate that [China's] Supreme People's Court exercise the power of final interpretation of the Basic Laws, SAR legal quarters and international society would be more likely to accept such an arrangement, and it would be more convenient for SAR courts of final appeal to apply to the Supreme People's Court for interpretations of the Basic Law.

Assuming also that mainland China's Supreme People's Court were vested with the power to conduct constitutionality examinations or that there was an independent constitutional court (council) that exercised the power of constitutionality examinations, and that it was highly independent, the SAR would not have had to be vested with the power of final adjudication during the Sino-British and Sino-Portuguese negotiations, and it would have been entirely possible to have the Supreme People's Court or a constitutional court (council) handle constitutional cases concerned in a unified manner (of course, under such circumstances the SARs should dispatch a given number personages from legal circles to the Supreme People's Court or the constitutional court to serve as chief justices). That is because even in a country like the United States which implements a federal system, the power of final adjudication is exercised by the supreme court of the federation, not by the supreme courts of the states.[69] One could say that doing so would be a sign of the Central Government's sincerity and determination for "one country, two systems." I, of course, have no doubts at all about China's sincerity and determination to implement "one country two system" in the Hong Kong and Macao regions. No Chinese leader hopes that things will deteriorate in Hong Kong and Macao after they return to China. In fact, I feel that an objective reason for vesting the SARs with the power of final adjudication

---

[68]There have already been discussions on this issue in previous sections. Although the Supremed People's Court has many times "communicated" internally with the NPC Standing Committee, there have never been any reports in the media about its openly requesting the latter for interpretations of the Constitution and laws.

[69]It is said that during the Sino-British negotiations, the British side had not expected that China would give Hong Kong SAR the power of final adjudication. China offered to give that power to the Hong Kong SAR.

is that rule of law is not sound yet in Chinese mainland and judicial independence has yet to be fully established. Hence the only alternative was to voluntarily forgo the power of final adjudication and for the very first time implement the coexistence of multiple legal systems in a single country, and devise a one-and-only setup in the world with at least three courts of final instance in one country.[70]

And so, assuming that it has been made clear that the National People's Congress and the NPC Standing Committee are China's institutions for constitutionality examinations, that there are entirely feasible procedures for constitutionality examinations and for interpreting the Constitution and laws, and that many citable mainland precedents and cases exist—requests by SAR courts of final appeal to the NPC Standing Committee for interpretations of the basic laws would be more easy to justify before the outside world and more likely be accepted by SAR legal circles and people in all walks of life, since that would be the system currently employed in China. The problem is that the mainland has not clearly defined the National People's Congress and the NPC Standing Committee as China's institutions for constitutionality examinations, and although the Constitution has clearly stated that the NPC Standing Committee may interpret laws, we must acknowledge the fact that prior to the emergence of matter related to Hong Kong and Macao's return, the NPC Standing Committee may be said to have almost never had interpreted any laws. As related earlier, examples of the NPC Standing Committee interpreting law virtually have to do with the Hong Kong and Macao affairs. And only in the year 2000 when the Legislation Law was formulated were some provisions made in terms of procedures for interpreting laws, and one might say that no such rules existed in the past. Under these circumstances, how could one expect the SARs' courts of final appeal to gladly and naturally address constant requests for "interpretations of law" from a legislative institution even though it was the state's highest organ of power?

Thus, the two different legal concepts and two different constitutionality examination systems would need a considerable period of time to bond with each other. Where the SAR courts were concerned, their exercise of the power of constitutionality reviews was far more frequent than that of courts before their return to China, the matters decided were far more important, and their scope was much broader. However, "we cannot simply say that the broader the scope of the courts' power of constitutionality examination the better, or say that the more the courts negate legislative or administrative measures during the exercise the power of constitutionality examination the better. The power of constitutionality examination frequently leads to the courts getting involved in the handling of some social and public policy issues of a controversial nature, or in seeking coordination between various conflicting rights and interests or value concepts. The courts must learn to how to appropriately make use of the sharp weapon of the power of constitutionality examination, and to find the appropriate position of courts as judicial organs and the guardians of constitutional

---

[70]China is currently the only country in the world to have three courts of final appeal, namely, the mainland's Supreme People's Court in Beijing, the Hong Kong SAR's Court of Final Appeal and the Macao SAR's Court of Final Appeal. Also, the Council of Grand Justices of Taiwan's Judicial Yuan is Taiwan's current "constitutional court," or in other words, Taiwan's "court of final instance." Hence, China in fact has four courts of final instance now.

laws in the entire political and legal system including legislation, administration and jurisprudence."[71] One might well say that the SAR courts are at present seeking an appropriate position for themselves under the SARs' new constitutional system and in the complex mainland and SAR politico-legal systems. Such positioning is usually not something that legislation can solve; it must be gradually found through trial and error in the practice of constitutionality examination.

Similarly, as concerns the SARs' "higher-up" constitutionality examination institution, namely, the NPC Standing Committee, the Basic Laws do not place many direct limitations on the exercise of the power of constitutionality examination by the NPC Standing Committee or by the National People's Congress. Under the system where ordinary judicial organs or special constitutional courts are in charge of constitutionality examinations, these constitutionality examinations are legislative acts in terms of their nature; they are normally passive, follow the principle of "disregard if no complaints," and conducted in connection with specific cases. However, these principles do not apply under the China's system where legislative organs are responsible for constitutionality examinations. Theoretically, the people's congress [NPC] may, in view of the circumstances and on their [its] own initiative, exercise constitutionality examinations of their [its] own legislation, the acts of the Central Government, and whether the SARs' legislation and administration contravene the Basic Laws. However, I feel that in the exercise of constitutionality examinations, the RD should adhere to some basic principles.

These principles would include: One, the criteria for the RD's exercise of constitutionality examinations of the SARs are the SAR Basic Laws, and in particular the provisions of the Basic Laws on matters under Central Government jurisdiction and Central/SAR relations; not the Constitution of China.

Two, since the Basic Laws stipulate that the RD amendments of the Basic Laws may not contravene the Central Authorities' "established basic policies" for the SARs,[72] which in fact are provisions of the Basic Laws which may not be amended, the RD's constitutionality examinations of the SARs' must also comply with the RD's "established basic policies" for the SARs. These "established basic policies" are "one country, two systems," "Hong Kongers administer Hong Kong," "Macauans administer Macao" and a high degree of autonomy. These constitute the bottom line the RD must abide by when conducting constitutionality examinations.

Three, even though the RD may on its own initiative exercise the power of constitutionality examinations of the SARs, it [the RD] must do so very cautiously, use that power as little as possible, and do so relatively passively and only when there are complaints.

Four, the power of constitutionality examinations exercised by RD may not replace the work of the SARs' legislative organs. If the SARs' legislation is declared "un-

---

[71] Chen Hongyi. "On the Hong Kong SAR Courts' Power of Constitutional Examinations," carried in Beijing, *Peking University Law Journal*, 1998(5), p. 18.

[72] Article 159 of the Basic Law of the Hong Kong Special Administrative Region and Article 144 of the Macao Special Administrative Region.

constitutional," the SARs' legislative organs should redo the legislation on their own; the Central Authorities should not conduct legislation in place of the SARs.

Five, even though an RD constitutionality examination of a SAR is a kind of act conducted by legislative organs and applied chiefly to procedures for legislation, one should in future consider the adoption of some sort of "quasi-judiciary" procedure, given that constitutionality examinations are by nature a sort of judiciary act. Moreover, one should in future strengthen the work of the NPC Standing Committee's Basic Law Committee, and the RD should conscientiously listen to the committee's opinions before making any decisions. The operations of the committee should be more standardized as regards, for instance, conducting hearings on relevant issues.

Six, the scope of the constitutionality examinations of the SARs by the NPC Standing Committee is focused mainly on the contents of Basic Law provisions vis a vis matters under the Central Authorities' jurisdiction and Central/SAR relations, but is not necessarily limited to these, which is to say that it has comprehensive powers of constitutionality examinations. However, the NPC Standing Committee normally does not exercise the power of constitutionality examinations of SAR legislation within the SARs' scope of autonomy. Doing that is mainly the duty and function of the SAR courts.

It is evident that the NPC Standing Committee has had a reorientation problem on this issue; after all, SARs are different from the ordinary provinces, municipalities, and autonomous regions in Chinese mainland. How, in the circumstances of implementing "one country, two systems," should the NPC Standing Committee do a good job of serving as guardian of the Basic Laws, of neither neglecting its duties or overstepping its powers, of protecting the country's overall interests and at the same time fully respecting and guaranteeing the SARs' judicial independence and power of final adjudication, and exercising its own powers to just the right extent. That is an entirely new problem. The mainland authorities should prefect their own legal interpretation system and constitutionality examination system as quickly as possible. This is needed both for developing the mainland's own rule of law and for handling Central/SAR relations and realizing and upholding national unity.

11.3 Rule of Law and the Country's Unity

An indispensable factor of a state is its national territory. It is the simplest piece of political common sense that a country must its own land. How such land is obtained and how to bring about and maintain the country's long-term unity are common and eternal problems that have confronted all countries and their leaders both here and abroad and modern and ancient times. No leader is willing to become the ruler of a subjugated state and be spurned by his progeny and descendants. To this day, most of the wars in human history have been brought about by struggles over land, unification, and independence. Leaders in both China and abroad and in times both ancient and contemporary may well be said to have endured all sorts of hardships, racked their brains to the limit and devised all kinds of methods to realize and maintain their country's unity. Their ideals were same, but the effects have been quite different. Some have achieved unity quite easily and kept it very long. Others have battled it many years without achieving unification. During studies of history both Chinese and foreign I have found there are in the main two ways of achieving and maintaining a country's unity. One is the "Chinese world order principles" employed by China's kings and emperors in ancient times, and the other is the experience of the contemporary West of using rule-of-law theory to safeguard national unity. These are diametrically different world outlooks and methodologies, but their actual effects are very much the same.

I have previously discussed constitutionality examinations, and it is quite evident that one cannot overemphasize the need to perfect a country's rule of law, firmly establish a constitutionality examination system and raise these to the height of realizing and maintaining national unity. The process of transforming China's legal system and setting up rule of law is not merely mainland China's business; it also directly affects the SARs' prosperity and stability and Central/SAR relations. Hong Kong's and Macao's reunification with China has been realized, and Taiwan's reunification with the mainland is merely a matter of time. While striving for national unification, the Chinese mainland needs to make ample preparations not only in terms of politics but also in the aspect of rule of law. It must constantly improve and perfect the rule-of-law infrastructure so that China's rule of law suits the needs of reunification and constantly expand its inclusiveness and independence. Otherwise, many similar circumstances with occur in future, such as having once more to forgo the power of constitutionality examinations because of our lack of a constitutionality examination system and an independent constitutionality examination institution. Moreover, the lack of an independent constitutionality examination institution may make persons in Taiwan feel that the absence of an independent arbitration institution for adjudicating disputes arising between the banks of the Taiwan Strait, if and when these are eventually unified, will increase man-made hindrances to unity. Even though the SARs implement "one country, two systems" and "acting on one's free will," there are bound to be numerous cross-Strait disputes which will need interpretation of both regions' constitutional laws. Hence, Chinese mainland must as soon as possible set up and perfect its own constitutionality examination system, set up an independent constitutionality examination institution, truly begin to practice serious constitutionality examinations, and truly set up rule of law. Only thus will mainland China exert greater attraction and cohesiveness, and only then will it have greater confidence, possess more bargaining chips and be unlikely to forfeit more powers when it will conduct unification talks with the Taiwan authorities. And in this way, the Hong Kong and Macao SARs will have greater confidence in their high degree of autonomy and feel more self-possessed and justified in their handling of "interpretations of law." Most importantly, people will truly feel that China has already established rule of law and that China is a rule-of-law state. Due to the absence of an independent constitutionality examination institution, people have always felt that rule of law has not been firmly established in China despite considerable progress in this respect in the past few years.

Here, I would like to compare the two philosophies and methods for upholding unity in ancient China and the contemporary West. From this, we may discern the unique effect of rule of law in bringing about and maintaining national unity where modern countries are concerned.

11.3.1 The "Chinese World Order Principles"

Generally speaking, ancient China's feudal dynasties implemented policies of conciliation and appeasement to bring about the dynasties' unity. The feudal emperors took an extremely relaxed and open attitude toward all ethnicities, and basically adopted an attitude of national equality and no discrimination against ethnic minorities as well as accorded them petty favors so that they would constantly feel the warmth and benefits of belonging to the "big family." For example, Tai Zong, the well-known emperor of China's Tang Dynasty, with a view to pacifying Tibet, married off his daughter Princess Wencheng to the Tibetan King Songtsan Gampo in exchange for peace and Tibet's recognition of the suzerain status of the Central Plains. Thus it is not hard to explain why ancient China was able to establish a vast empire and maintain it for so long, despite the lack of advanced means of communication. The ancient kings and emperors needed highly developed powers of affinity and cohesiveness and even personal charisma in order to attract ethnic minorities from distant border regions to come and pay sincere homage. This was a prime example of "governance through inaction." One might also call it "rule of man," since unity was indeed realized through loyalty or allegiance to an individual or a household or surname, and when that individual or surname no longer ruled, the country too no longer existed.

After the outbreak of the Revolution of 1911, the various provinces one after another declared independence, and on November 30 the Mongolian Royal Lama, with support from Russia, pretended they wished to take an armed contingent to Beijing to pledge allegiance,[73] only to declare independence soon after. Their main excuse: "Mongolians previously were allied only with the Manchu Qing Imperial Household and therefore never became allied one-on-one with the Chinese Empire. Now that the Manchu Imperial Household has fallen, Mongolia's relations of allegiance have accordingly come to an end." The Mongolians "have a blood relationship with the Manchus, and have therefore been ranked as close and affectionate depen-

---

[73] The Lama stated perfidiously: "We Mongol people of the Khalkha Fourth *Bu* have benefitted from the favor of the Great Qing for more than two hundred years and will not sit idly by. Jebtsundamba Khutuktu has already spread a summons to arms and called up four thousand cavalrymen from the Fourth League to enter the Capital City and Protect the Qing Emperor. Please issue provisions and weapons immediately according to the numbers of men so that we may set forth, and give explicit orders within three hours today whether approval is accorded." Cheng Chongzu. *Recent History of Outer Mongolia*, ed. 1, Taipei, Wen Hai Press, 1965, p. 10. However, very soon after that, on December 28, 1911, Jebtsundamba Khutuktu held a ceremony for his ascension to the throne, proclaimed his own dynastic title and set up a Mongolian central government.

dencies for more than two hundred years. The termination of the Qing Dynasty has severed the relations between Mongolia and China."[74]

The real reason for Outer Mongolia becoming independent was Russia's support, but the high-sounding excuse given was that the Manchu Qing Dynasty had already been overthrown and the Mongolians were loyal only to the Manchu dynasty, not the Hans. It is evident that in a feudal society, the upholding a country's the unity depends to a great extent on kinship, or "orthodoxy."

Scholars in Taiwan sum up the principles whereby ancient China upheld its unity as the "Chinese World Order Principle" of "China's World Empire," which included the "status order principle," the "pursuit of new principles" and the "Theoretical Issues Tributary System." By the "status order principle" is meant that the Chinese traditional world order concept is based on the doctrine of propriety whereas the modern Western world order concept is based on the doctrine of rule of law. The difference is that the "propriety establishes rules prior to existence of the fact, while rule-of-law establishes rules after the existence of the fact." For "rule of propriety" one must first establish "status" and "order." "Status" consists of "title" and "position." By establishing status one fixes the order of importance, by establishing order one implements the order of importance. Hence to establish status one must first rectify the name. Once the name is rectified, one may, in proper order, establish status, and then, according to the status, seek the proper sequence. When one knows the proper sequence, all matters may be administered in apple pie order. In accordance with this theory, the Chinese World Empire set up a system of suzerain–vassal feudal stratum levels. This system determined the principal–subordinate relations between suzerain and vassal states, the recruitment sequence, the amount of armed forces, the sequence of nobility titles, the formats of official documents, the relations among vassal states, and so forth.

In 1808, after Japan's Meiji Restoration, the Japanese government, in a letter to the King of Korea, used such terms as "imperial" and "imperial edict" which could only be used by the emperor of the "Chinese World Empire" and which the Korean government denounced as "a violation of status" and "unsightly" and angrily

---

[74] After the Yuan Shikai government was established, it never acknowledged Outer Mongolian independence. When the Chinese-Russian-Mongolian Agreement was signed on June 7, 1915, China was compelled to accept the name over the reality while Russia did just the opposite. Outer Mongolia acknowledged China's suzerainty, while China and Russia acknowledged that Outer Mongolia had autonomy and that it formed part of China's territory. Outer Mongolia was not empowered the sign international agreements with other countries, and the title "Jebtsundamba Khutuktu" of Outer Mongolia was conferred by the President of the Republic of China. China and Russia were to station the same number of troops and officials in Outer Mongolia. On June 1, 1916, [China's] Central Government, in accordance with the Chinese-Russian-Mongolian Agreement, held a solemn investiture for Jebtsundamba Khutuktu of Outer Mongolia, and Outer Mongolia relinquished its independence. However, the fact is that Outer Mongolia was already independent, or one should say, had already become a dependency. Zhang Qixiong. *Negotiations on Jurisdiction over Outer Mongolian Sovereignty 1911–1916*, Institute of Modern History, Academia Sinica, 1995, pp. 39 and 262.

returned to Japan and thereby aroused grave animosity between Japan and Korea.[75] In 1882, when a military mutiny took place in Korea, Japan sent out its troops. The Qing government also dispatched troops at once in the name of "rectifying chaos in a subordinate state." It also arrested Prince Daewon and brought to Beijing to be put on trial for the crime of disregarding the title conferred by China's emperor on the Korean King, or supposedly having "denigrated the king but in reality belittled the Emperor." This was a typical case of a violation of the existing status system, leading to turmoil in the old order. Scholars have pointed out that, seen from the perspective of modern international law, the terms used in the Japanese document did not pose any particular problem and states ought to be on an equal footing. However, according to the "status order principle" this was an absolute no-no. The Chinese emperor had conferred a title on the Korean King, who then ruled his stated in accordance with the principle that "the power of the King is conferred by the Emperor," and it was only right and proper that the Chinese Emperor should concern himself with the internal affairs of a subordinate state. This theory had always held sway in ancient China, but obviously differed from the theory of modern international law.[76]

The so-called "Theoretical Issues Tributary System" means implementing the almanac on which is recorded the title of reign set by the dynastic emperor in order to signify allegiance to the Chinese emperor. At the outset of each Chinese dynasty, the new calendar promulgated by the emperor must be emplaced to show that the new emperor takes the throne, replaces the old with the new, and establishes the new system of law upon the mandate of heaven, and that subordinate states must also change their almanacs under the supervision of the Ministry of Rites or the Ministry of Colonial Affairs Where the West is concerned, a calendar or almanac is an ordinary instrument of calculating dates and in no way can be related to the unification or the splitting of a state. However, these constituted an important method for maintaining a unified Empire.[77] An example is the letter sent in September 1878 by China's special envoy to the vassal state of Ryuku to the consuls of the United States, France, and the Netherlands, condemning Japan and declaring the United States, France, and the Netherlands had "signed agreements using the terminology of the Qing Dynasty reign title, and if the Qing Dynasty's tributary affairs are not conducted as usual, the afore-mentioned agreements are equal to scraps of waste paper."[78]

The so-called "tributary system principle" means that since China its peripheral states constitute a unified "Chinese world empire," and have concluded agreements with these states respective on sovereign–subordinate relations, a tiered tributary system must be implemented to highlight the sovereign–subordinate relationship and the vertical monarch–subject relationship between them, in order to standardize the

---

[75]*Foreign Affairs Book of Korea (Japan) I*, Document No. 8, Soul, Chengjin Cultural Press, 1980. *Logs of Iwakura Tomomi Vol 2*, Tokyo, Hara Shobo, 1968, pp. 20–22.

[76]Zhang Qixiong. *Negotiations on Jurisdiction over Outer Mongolian Sovereignty 1911–1916.* Beijing: Institute of Modern History, Academia Sinica, 1995, pp. 12–14.

[77]Zhang Qixiong. *Negotiations on Jurisdiction over Outer Mongolian Sovereignty 1911–1916.* Beijing: Institute of Modern History, Academia Sinica, 1995, pp. 14–16.

[78]Compiled by Matsuda Michiyuki: A personal letter from RyuKyu Kingdom's officials in Tokyo to foreign minister in Japan, Ryukyu independence movement Volume 2, Tokyo, 1981, p. 424.

affiliate relationship between rulers and ruled. That is to say, the chief of a neighboring "barbarian" vassal state which the Chinese emperor deemed to deserve the "status" of a state was conferred the title of "king," the state became a "kingdom," and was thereby elevated as member of the "Chinese World Empire," could participate in the activities of the "big family," its existence would acquire legality and orthodoxy, and the state itself would acquire an assurance of security. In addition to issuing an imperial edict during the conferring of titles, the emperor would also confer a "gold-plated silver seal" which symbolized the legality and authority of power. Status was genuinely established after the conferring of titles. The emperor possessed the power to punish and dethrone those conferred the title of "king." Tributes were to be paid after the conferring of titles. The Collected Statutes of the Qing Dynasty contained detailed stipulations on the various requirements for offering tributes, including the rankings of the tribute envoys and size of their entourage, the time, the etiquette for audiences with the emperor and so forth. Based on the Confucian spirit of "giving more and taking less," the emperor was required to respond to the tributes brought by vassal states with generous "rewards" and bestow tax exemptions on tribute trading by vassal states, or in other words, reward tributes with trade and thereby cultivate a sense of association and cohesion and an awareness of community among peripheral vassal states.[79] Bringing tributes was not merely a sort of etiquette to show loyalty to the emperor, it was also a commercial activity, a unique activity of "diplomacy," and an important domestic affairs activity of the Chinese empire.

Ancient China depended on these "Chinese world order principles" and on a kind of "quasi-kinship" relation to maintain long-term unity in this vast empire. If there was any element of "law" here, it was a sort of *ius naturale* rather than any legal "hardware" of recent and modern times.

11.3.2 State Unity Perspective Based on Constitutions and Rule of Law in the Modern West

The "Chinese World Order Principle" was merely a theory for maintaining state unity in ancient China; it is hardly applicable either in other countries in the West, or in today's China. States with extensive territories have also been founded in the contemporary West. These states are usually set up on the basis of "contracts" which have been acknowledged by two or more parties and depend on perfected systems and rule of law to bring about and maintain state unity. This is a modern method of realizing and upholding unity.

Take, for example, the United States. The territory of the United States covers approximately 9.63 million km^2 (9.16 km^2 of land and 470 thousand km^2 territorial water). As a nation of immigrants, it is, with its highly pluralist composition, probably the most complex of countries. Caucasian white peoples make up 75.1% of its

---

[79]Zhang Qixiong. Negotiations on Jurisdiction over Outer Mongolian Sovereignty 1911–1916, Academia Sinica Institute of Modern History, pp. 16–19.

population; African black people, 12.3%; Asians, 3.6%; native Indians and Alaskans, 0.9%; other races, 5.5%; and biracial or multiracial, 2.4%. In the United States as a whole, Hispanics or Latinos already make up 12.5% of the entire population, more than number of African blacks and constituting the largest ethnic minority. Eleven percent of the 280 million inhabitants of the United States are born in other counties. Between 1990 and 2000, more than 13.3 million new arrived in the U.S., so that the number of people there born abroad surpassed 30.5 million and constituting 3.5 immigrants for every 1000 of the population.[80] The complex population makeup of the United States, given its multinational background, does not have a unified culture or any unified faith or political conviction. Statistics show that 56% of the U.S. population adheres to Protestantism; 28% to Roman Catholicism, two percent to Judaism, and 10% are atheists. The Americans do not even have a common language. In many settings and especially in the family, many do not use the English language, each speaks his "own tongue," and the English language proficiency of adults is limited.[81]

This may be the most complex country in human history. The multiplicity and complexity of its population composition is quite rare, and it would be impossible to hold together a country with such a non-homogenous ethnic background if not for the existence of good mechanisms. Although the United States is a very young country, it has in the last two hundred or more years developed an immense attraction and has constantly drawn other regions to join this new commonwealth which now counts 50 members and shows a tendency toward continual expansion. For instance, Puerto Rico of the Caribbean Islands may very well become the 51st U.S. state. According to the results of numerous nonbinding votes in the past, the great majority of its people approve of maintaining its current situation or completely becoming a U.S. state, very few have approved of independence. In the voting in December 1998, 50.3% approved of maintaining the status quo, 46.5% voted for becoming a U.S. state, and only 2.5% voted for independence (4.4% in 1993).[82] In the 225 years

---

[80] U.S. Census Bureau, Census 2000 Redistricting (Public Law 94–171) Summary File, Tables PL 1 and PL2. http://www.census.gov/prod/2001pubs/c2kbr01-1.pdf.

[81] U.S. *Qiao Bao* (China Press), 2001-08-07.

[82] Puerto Rico, a U.S. dependency in the Caribbean Islands, formulated a constitution in 1952 which took effect after being approved by the U.S. Congress. This constitution stipulated that Puerto Rico would implement local autonomy while maintaining close relations with United States, that it would obtain a status in the commonwealth associated with the United States, and that the United States would provide it with security and defense. The Puerto Ricans are U.S. citizens, enlist in the U.S. armed forces and take part in U.S. primary elections but not the presidential elections; Puerto Rica has a representative in the U.S. House of Representative but no voting rights. Internally, there has always been controversy in the Puerto Rico over whether to maintain the status quo, or to completely join the United States and become its 51st state, or to become completely independent. Puerto Rico has a territory of 8897 km^2 and a population of about 3.9 million; in 1999 its GDP was more than USD 38 billion, and its GDP per capita about USD 9800. If it joined the United States, it would territorially be its third smallest state and slightly bigger than Delaware and Rhode Island. Its population would rank 23rd in the United States. Whether Puerto Rico is able the hold a binding referendum to determine its own destiny will hinge on a decision by the U.S. Federal Government on whether to confer on it the right of self-determination. The U.S. House of Representative passed a bill ("Resolution 856") giving the Puerto Ricans the right to self-determination, but the bill still needs to be approved by the U.S. Senate and signed by the U.S. President to become effective. Puerto

since the founding of the United States, its state structure has been extremely solid and stable and has exhibited no possibility of dividing or partitioning. Not only does the U.S. possess extensive territories and a powerful cohesiveness, it is also a unique hegemon in today's world. What has made it possible for such a country to emerge, flourish, and keep on upholding its national unity? I believe this ought to be attributed to its constitution, its rule of law, and its unique federalism.

The United States constitution and the federal system it has established have met the people's natural need for a national identity yet have not required excessive sacrifices of freedoms and rights. It citizens possess dual state and federal status. There are, via the constitution, clear divisions of power between the states and the federal government, and in the case that controversies arise, these are impartially solved through intervention by an independent judicial institution, and in many cases, the judiciary tends toward protecting the rights of the states. Hence, the states are quite at ease about being a member of the federation, and do not feel upset or that they are asked to make big sacrifices. The U.S. constitution also explicitly refuses to let federation member states secede from the federation. The U.S. constitution has made indelible contributions to the long-term security, prosperity, and stability of the United States. Of course, the U.S. federal system and its legal system have also undergone a tortuous course of development and survived a good many severe tests. The U.S. North-South War in the 1860s was a severe blood-and-fire test for American-type federalism. The American people defended the country's unity with their blood and lives and unequivocally rejected any attempt to split their country. No issues of asserting independence ever occurred after that war and U.S.-type federalism began to advance toward maturity.

At 10 o'clock, deep in the night of December 12, 2000, and in the midst of a cold winter, all people in the United States waited beside their TV sets and with mixed emotions listened to the judgment by the nine justices of the U.S. Supreme Court on their country's destiny, and impressing people with the power of rule of law. In the process of a "pitched battle" and after having consciously studied the Supreme Court's massive and complicated written judgment together with his lawyers, Democratic Party Candidate Al Gore made a genuine and sincere speech, admitting defeat and declaring that despite his extreme disagreement with the Supreme Court's judgment, he accepted it. For the sake of the people's unity and the strengthening of democracy, he voluntarily accepted defeat and wished to work together with the new president to heal the divisions and the harm done to the nation by the intense election. He also called on his supporters to let their love for their country supersede their disappointment and to rally closely under the leadership of the new president, because "this is America." They should reunite after the fierce contention, for now was the time to admit that the American people's strength was greater by uniting them than by dividing them, and the country's interests supersede all else. During the U.S. presidential elections in 2000, the Federal Supreme Court, as the United

---

Rico's sole representative in the Federal House of Representatives still does not have the right to vote in the referendum that would decide the destiny of his own people and country. According to the U.S. constitution, no state is free to secede from the federation.

States' most authoritative institution for adjudicating federal and state disputes, categorically intervened in the presidential election and causing the reputation of the world's most powerful court to suffer a heavy blow. It thereby became the "biggest loser" in the entire elections and the United States' tradition of the supremacy of the judiciary was placed in doubt. However, from another side, we can see that rule of law and judicial independence have the advantage of being able to peacefully resolve all disputes, including political ones, through judicial channels, and that power successions issues can be solved without resorting to force. If such circumstances took place in certain third world nations, the flames of war would rage and the countries would break up.

To sum the United States' means whereby state unity is upheld and relations among the whole and the component parts are handled, the first is democracy; in other words, the orthodoxy and legality of all power come from the electorate; legally elected governments are not to be illegally overthrown. When the U.S. Senate attempted to impeach President Clinton in 1997 and 1998, one of his main defenses was that he had become president through two fair elections by the American people and that the Senate had no right to negate the wishes of the American public.

The second is federalism. That is, equivalency, or in other words, based on the different nature of a country's powers, dispensing them out among various levels of government for implementation. This division of powers is fixed by an inflexible constitution and any amendments to the constitution must be approved by both the federation and its member states. Discussions on the federal system have been presented in previous sections.

The third is supremacy of the judiciary. The essence of constitutional government and rule of law rests in the fact that all disputes between the federation and its constituent parts can be fairly and reasonable resolved through an independent judiciary system, and that the federal judiciary system has become the guardian angel of the constitution and the state. It is quite obvious that the United States would not exist if it were not for its constitution and rule of law. That society and that country are built entirely on their constitution and rule of law. So much so that some Americans complain about the United States having nothing else but laws. Although the United States conducts citizens' education and education in patriotism and makes some efforts to build a common culture and common ideals and aspirations, the existence of that country is not maintained by such "software." There can be no unification of thinking in a country as heterogeneous as the United States, and it seems that no U.S. government has ever thought of unifying the thinking of its populace. The existence of United States is held together by such "hardware" as the U.S. constitution, rule of law and an independent judiciary, which form a sharp contrast with ancient China's "birthright order theory," "pursuit of new principles" and "tributary system theory." China in ancient times depended mainly on "software" to maintain the country's unity. "Hardware" was also in existence, such as the appointments of local officials and the conferring of nobility titles, but reliance was placed first of all "software."

Both theories and both systems described above are able to maintain the long-term unity of countries. The first method strives to create kinship ties or "quasi-kinship" ties, to create a large family, and hold the whole country together under one roof, so to speak. The second method relies on the rule of law generated through equal negotiations to hold all the component parts together. The shortcoming of the first method is that it possesses virtually no renewal mechanisms of its own, and with the passage of time it is prone to accumulating dross and collapsing on its own. Hence feudal dynasties usually come to end with the aging of the feudal state apparatus. This system does not fall on account of any policy of conciliation per se; if properly exercised there would be nothing wrong with this policy and it would feasible. The problem lies in the fatal flaws that riddle the political systems of China's feudal dynasties. As regards the second method, there is indeed no apparent way of "sabotaging" it, even if someone wished to do so. It appears to be quite impossible for a country like the United States to get bogged down in internal and external troubles or demands for independence from its localities. Although there may sometimes be sharp contradictions and conflicts between the federal government and the states, the issues can always be peacefully resolved due to the presence of a sound judicial mechanism, and there is little likelihood of matters ending up in armed conflicts and open warfare.

Problems are very likely to arise when strong men maintain unity through sheer power. In terms of physics, such unipolar structures are unstable and likely to break down at any time. A one-legged stool cannot stand erect. Stability is possible only when strength (state power) is equally distributed. If state power is overly concentrated at one end—for instance at and by the Central Authorities—the state becomes top-heavy and could keel over. If state power is overly concentrated in the localities, the state finds itself in a precarious position. Hence, when state power is overly concentrated, whether at the central government or at the local governments, that is not good news for the country. The same applies when there is only one superpower in world society; one can hardly hope for much peace in the world, and a country in which power is too concentrated can hardly achieve stability. These countries must adjust their state structures, adjust the distribution of their power, legalize and institutionalize it, genuinely establish constitutional government and rule of law, and institute a set of good judicial mechanisms for solving disputes. Only then will there be logical administration, harmony among the people, and long-term stability. There is virtually no other choice for modern countries. They can only depend on such "hardware" as firm rule of law to bring about and uphold national unity, and depend on rule by law to solve the conflicts and controversies that emerge in the country as a whole and its localities.

Postscript: New Problems and a Few Reflections

This concludes the writing of this book, but a good many new problems remain to be studied. And, as I carry on in-depth explorations into these subjects, I have had new ideas about some deep-seated theories on the Common Law and Continental Law systems, which I now present in this Postscript so as to share them with the reader.

A. A Profusion of New Problems

Even as I wrote this book, a variety of new and thorny issues cropped up between the Chinese mainland and the Special Administrative Regions. Social developments have constantly tested the "one country, two systems" setup as well as the political acumen of the Chinese in the two different regions. One of the focal issues is the Falun Gong. The Central People's government explicitly defined the Falun Gong as an evil cult and banned it in 1999. Should Hong Kong, as a Special Administrative Region, keep in step with the Central authorities and also ban the Falun Gong? That has indeed tossed a "hot potato" to the HK SAR. Although the SAR's Chief Executive has expressed agreement with the Central Government's definition of the Falun Gong and described it as an evil cult, the SAR government has not banned it. Falun Gong activities in Hong Kong have not been prohibited by the government. Its practitioners still openly ply their crafts in the SAR and continue to mount parades and demonstrations without interference from the SAR government. Articles and ads regarding the Falun Gong appear regularly in the press, and the SAR government has frequently stated that it has no intention of banning the Falun Gong by legislative means.

Judging from the means and methods the SAR government uses for handling the Falun Gong, the SAR is proceeding strictly according to the "one country, two systems" setup, and the SAR government is indeed adhering strictly to the principle of rule of law. They are acting strictly according to SAR laws. The SAR government will not interfere in any activity as long as it does not come in conflict with SAR laws. But once they do violate SAR laws, the SAR government will not stand by with folded arms. That is the usual international practice; all issues are resolved

© Foreign Language Teaching and Research Publishing Co., Ltd and Springer Nature Singapore Pte Ltd. 2019
Z. Wang, *Relationship Between the Chinese Central Authorities and Regional Governments of Hong Kong and Macao: A Legal Perspective*, China Academic Library, https://doi.org/10.1007/978-981-13-2322-5

through rule of law. The SAR, as a government, must pay close attention to the activities of the Falun Gong since the latter has, after all, been identified by the Central Authorities as an evil cult and has had a huge effect in China and abroad. "The government would be irresponsible if it acts deaf and dumb on this matter."[1]

Although the SAR government has neither officially declared the Falun Gong an evil cult nor proscribed it, the SAR government is indeed responsible for warning or advising Hong Kong's residents about its concerns. That is something governments anywhere would and should do. And it is only natural and positive for Hong Kong's Chief Executive to state his views on the Falun Gong. If Hong Kong's residents do not heed his advice and continue to engage in its crafts, they shall be responsible for their behavior. And if any criminal offenses are involved, the SAR government should investigate and prosecute matters as they stand. That would be typical of the handling of issues by means of rule of law. Doing so would reflect the "one country, two systems" principle, comply with rule of law and show respect for basic human rights. And in fact, throughout the SAR's handling of this matter, the Central Government has not intervened in the SAR government's exercise of governance. It has scrupulously adhered to the spirit of the "one country, two systems" and "Hong Kongers administer Hong Kong" principles. It understands the SAR's circumstances, is fully confident that Hong Kongers are able to do a good job of administering Hong Kong and that the SAR government can do a good job of dealing with this matter, and it has set a fine precedent for correctly handling Central/SAR relations.

Another event that has had an international effect is that of Li Shaomin returning to Hong Kong to take a teaching post. Li Shaomin is an American of Chinese descent and now teaches at the City University of Hong Kong. In July, 2001, he was convicted by a people's court in Beijing of espionage and was expelled from the country. Based on "one country, two systems" considerations, the SAR government allowed Li Shaomin to return to Hong Kong. However, the SAR immigration official announced a caveat to him at the airport: They were permitting Li to cross the border on the basis of the terms of a work visa. They reminded him that during his stay in Hong Kong, he may not engage in anything that does not comply with his work visa or that violates the terms of his work visa, failing which his work visa will be canceled at any time. And, they again warned him, they did not want him or any person to do anything that violates Hong Kong's interests. If he does, they would cancel his document at any time. Li Shaomin also signed a consent form.[2] These were the terms for allowing him to enter the country. On August 3, 2001, the City University of Hong Kong decided to allow Li Shaomin to continue teaching at the university. The authority concerned at the university stated that this decision was entirely the university's own decision, that no political factors had been taken in consideration and only academics were contemplated. The SAR

---

[1]Elsie Leung Oi-Sie. "The Rule of Law and Human Right" (the speech at the luncheon party of the Japan Society of Hong Kong), July 5, 2001.
[2]People.cn, Hong Kong, June 13, 2001.

government stated that it respected academic freedom, but it would not allow anyone to conduct spying activities in Hong Kong, since that would harm the interests of Hong Kong and the country.

Could a person who had been convicted of espionage by a mainland judicial organ and expelled from the country continue to work in a Chinese Special Administrative Region, and even teach in a university? That was a question the drafters of the Basic Law had no way of foreseeing. There were two questions here: First, according to the Basic Law, China's criminal law does not apply in the SAR and the mainland's criminal charges differ from the SAR's. However, the crux of the question is: where the party concerned has committed the crime of espionage and the Basic Law stipulates that the SAR is also responsible for safeguarding the unity and security of the state (Article 23 of the Basic Law), is it appropriate to permit a person convicted by China of the crime of espionage to continue teaching in a Chinese university (even though it is located in a Chinese Special Administrative Region)? And second, in the term "expel from the country" (i.e., *quzhu chu jing* in Chinese, which translates literally as "drive out of the borders"— Translator's note), does "borders" mean "national boundaries" or "border lines"? And should the SARs be included within those "borders"?

Under "one country, two systems," the mainland and the Hong Kong SAR pertain to two different judicial jurisdictions, the mainland's criminal law has no effect in the SAR, and there is a difference between "legal jurisdiction" and "administrative region." There is a certain basis in the Basic Law for the way the SAR government handles the Li Shaomin event. The SAR government's course of action has, of course, been criticized by some people who maintain that even under "one country, two systems" such a person should not be permitted to enter the region, or even teach at a university.

The United States has expressed approbation for the SAR government's handling of the matter. It so happened that the U.S. government submitted its yearly report on Hong Kong soon after the event, and stated therein that the Chinese government was continuing to honor its "one country, two systems" commitment and respect the Hong Kong SAR's high degree of autonomy. The Hong Kong government, (it said,) was continuing to uphold its residents' basic civil rights and interests and to safeguard the freedoms of speech and assembly, rule of law was still being upheld, and its civil servants were continuing to maintain neutrality. Hong Kong was still one of the most free cities in Asia.

We can see from the handling of this event that the SAR's entry and exit controls fall within the range of SAR autonomy, and the SAR institutions' employment system is also determined by the SAR institutions themselves. The Central Government does not interfere in the SAR's autonomy, nor does it interfere in any SAR institution's staff employment policy, even though doing so may concern the handling of highly sensitive political cases like this one. However, the SAR should also consciously uphold the nation's unity and security, since this is the SAR's responsibility toward the nation. We may rest assured that sensitive matters involving interregional relations will constantly occur in the future. The Central Authorities and the SARs have already gained some experience in dealing with such thorny issues. So long as one rigorously adheres to "one country, two systems" and acts according to the Basic Laws, solutions will always be found, whatever the problems one encounters going forward.

B. **The Governance Philosophy of Common Law**

Recently, as I have been reading up on some works about the Common Law, I have acquired some new understandings about that law, and I am writing them up so that all may peruse them. The Common Law is definitely not a mere legal system; it is a philosophy about governing a state.

Rule of law is a modern way of governing a country. When we mention this new "way" of governing a country, the first thing that comes to mind is legislation, i.e., getting legislative organs to formulate a vast amount of laws and "net" all aspects of social life in a "network of laws." This would apparently constitute "rule of law" and allow one to rest at ease. However, the three of life is forever putting forth new foliage, and all perfect laws and all real-time legislation may seem to become out of date or retrogressive, and therefore someone must be there to interpret the laws. This is especially true for constitutional laws which are required to be highly stable and unchangeable and may not be frequently amended. Hence, there must inevitably be a special institution that constantly expounds and elaborates written legislation. And so, which organ or institution should be interpreting the constitution and laws. Different legal systems have different stipulations on this matter, yet under any legal system, courts of law are at least one of the organs which interpret the law. Under the Common Law, however, the courts' role is not limited merely to interpreting already formulated written legislation. Courts of law have a more important use, i.e., judges may, by means of adjudicating cases, passively create new legal norms. In this rests the quintessence of the Common Law.

The basic attitude taken by the Common Law toward any new things emerging in the course of social development is: when anything first puts on its appearance, it first remains in an apparently "lawless" state, and society is allowed to regulate the thing on its own, and if society is able to "manage" the matter on its own, the state will not intervene with legislation. That is because if all things are at once put under legislative restraints the moment they emerge, social development is bound to be held up. Any legislation, no matter how liberal, will exert certain restrictions on the full expression of people's creativity and on ample social development, and cause certain "injuries" to society. Hence, according to the Common Law viewpoint, instead of "the more laws the better," too many laws are seen as a hindrance to social advance; best not start out by erecting legislative controls, but let society move forward by dint of conducting daring experiments and breaking new paths.

The governance logic of the Common Law consists in first assuming that everything is feasible and legal. Nothing is illegal or unlawful if laws contain no specific regulations thereon. If no one objects to your actions, that means doing what you do is acceptable and is therefore legal. However, if something "goes wrong," problems arise and someone raises objections to your actions and goes to court to challenge your behavior, then his honor the judge examines you have done and decides whether it is O.K. and whether it accords with "the law." And at this time, the judge comes forward to tell you what "the law" is on this matter. And only at this time does the question of "the law" and the state coming forward arise; if not, the state will simply stay out of the picture. Under the Common Law system, there are no cases which a court of law may not take on, and no cases which the judge may not adjudicate. Common Law courts will, in general, not shut their doors on a case because written legal grounds are absent, as that would be deemed irresponsible. Situations—such as in China—where a court's scope of case acceptance is determined by law and where a court may decide at its discretion which cases it can decline and thereby reject "troublesome" ones would be unthinkable for the Common Law.

Hence in a Common Law environment, rule of law is not equivalent to legislation. On the contrary, rule of law refers mainly to judicature, and a main characteristic of the judicature as compared to legislation and administration is passivity, or in other "if no charges are pressed, leave the matter alone." When discussing rule of law In the Common Law context, the first things that come to mind are the judge's independence and the high standard of the judicature; not large amounts of legislation by the legislature (this, conversely, may be precisely the focus of "regulation" by rule of law). Social government must take into account the social costs, minimize these costs as much as possible, and reduce the price paid when society sets norms for people. It is best to let society form its own norms and mechanisms for development. Legislative actions frequently deal blows at large swaths of people whereas the judiciary merely focuses on individual cases. Using the method of handling individual cases is a relatively economical way for governing society. Letting the judiciary rather than the legislature or the administration "take charge of" society is the least costly way of governing society.

However, this sort of "rule-of-lawism" under the Common Law is not anarchism. What it wants is "proactive" nonintervention, governance with the least action (*wuwei*), avoid causing "disturbances," and refraining from forcible suspensions of the normal course of social development. There, however, must be reasonable government regulation. The government may of course exercise controls by means of legislation if it deems that necessary. But no government legislation should not be retroactive or go after past practices and should have effect on people's behavior before a law comes into force. Moreover, when something new begins to emerge in society and the government wants to exercise preemptive actions and controls, it may legislate and formulate "legal" norms. But the final decision on whether the government's legislation is reasonable and the law is justifiable is produced by independent courts of law. Neither the formal laws formulated by legislative organs nor the administrative rules and regulations produced by administrative organs are the ultimate or most authoritative standards. These legal standards "made by people" must also undergo examination by court judges, and the people have the right to address a judge and tell him they find the legislation comical, useless or even "illegal" and request that the legislation be repealed. The government can of course dispute such claims, say that the legislation is for society as a whole and that is quite scientific and rational. The ultimate verdict will depend on the judge's assessment.

How does the judge make his assessment? What serves as his criterion? Is the criterion the national Constitution or is it some constitutional law, as for example the Basic Law of a Special Administrative Region? Such are the origins of judicial reviews or constitutionality reviews. It is clear that the judge is the arbiter between the government and the people, and that the highest criterion of arbitration is the fundamental law formulated by the people, namely the Constitution. Under the Common Law, the judge's highest duty is to uphold the Constitution, not the law. What is rule of law? We often say that the object of rule of law is to regulate "officials," and "officials" consist of legislative officials, administrative officials, and judicial officials. In a certain sense, the object of rule of law is to "regulate" legislation and regulate "administration." In other words, independent judicial judges "regulate" legislative officials and administrative officials according to the Constitution and common sense. Hence, the Common Law concept of ruling is that "rule of law" consists of "rule by the judge." This is a passive sort of rule, a rule by individual cases. It is not rule by legislation, not an active or overall type of rule. The objective of the law is to protect the people, not to strike down criminals. Rather let slip ten thousand lawless elements than wrong a single innocent person.[3] The government is a supervisor and monitor. It is not the dominator or leader of social development. It is the people who are the masters and dominators of society. Judges are the wellspring of law, the ultimate arbiters, and formulators of everything that is nonstandard.

The benefits of governing a country and society in this manner are: First, it will enable society to undergo ample growth and development, people's potentials will be fully tapped, society will undergo ample "dilation," and this will bring about a big-society-small-government setup with an exceptionally strong self-governing capability. The putative premise for this is that society will no longer need "mom-and-dad officials," that the people are more intelligent than the government, and that the people, by dint of their intuitive knowledge and education, know how to manage themselves. By that time, the government will not be more intelligent than the ordinary people, and the ordinary people will not seem to never grow up and to need government controls and "education" in all matters.

Second, under this governance model, given that the state does not take readily to legislative intervention, society develops and grows in a natural and normal manner with few traces of "manmade" elements. One of anarchism's arguments is that irrespective of the kind of government control or intervention, any prior state legislation constitutes crude interference in the normal development of society, and

---

[3]Liu Dajun, currently a judge at the International Court for Former Yugoslav War Criminals, once conducted a splendid comparison of the concepts of the Common Law and Chinese law. Taking criminal law as an example, he said that any criminal law has two functions—cracking down on crime and protecting the people. However he maintained the criminal law of the Common Law puts first importance on protecting the people, while China's criminal law places first emphasis on cracking down on enemies, and these two concepts have in reality given rise to two different judicial practices. From a speech by Judge Liu Dajun at Tsinghua University on December 20, 2001.

excessive government interference makes it difficult if not impossible for society to grow into a towering, fully developed tree. It is like farmers using large amounts of farm chemicals to grow vegetables; owing to their abundant use of such chemicals, vegetables may indeed be free of plant diseases and insect pests and may appear to be verdantly "healthy" but will have forfeited much of their nutritional value. A great loss indeed! Moreover, the health of those who consume them will be imperiled and thereby defeat the original purpose. The same goes for social development. The logic of the Common Law is that one should, as far as possible, allow society to grow naturally in accordance with its intrinsic laws of development. "Subduing the enemy without going into battle and governing with a minimum display of force"—such is the best form of governance.

Third, under this form of governance, society's development is relatively balanced and stable. "Balanced" here means the balance between society and government. Too much government interference in society is bound to end up in inflated government institutions, in the formation of a top-heavy "big government and small society" as well as a lack of balance. The true essence of the Common Law and Equity Law consists in putting society and government in an equal and balanced condition by means of an independent judicial system. This will enable society to develop in even and stable manner. Social development will be ample, normal and balanced, and therefore stable and relatively free of conflicts, making it possible to attain long-term stability and a prosperous country with its people living at peace.

Furthermore, this form of proactively non-interfering rule-of-law governance may to the maximum extent eliminate social inequality and promote socialism. Since the government will not join in the competition when new things emerge, new opportunities will be equally available for all members of society. Also, the government will in general not intervene with advance legislation, so that there will be no possibility of man-made privileges arising. Even if conflicts and problems do emerge, these can be mediated and resolved by independent judges without bias or partiality. This will eliminate as far as possible the emergence of grave social injustices because a great many social injustices are in reality caused by excessive government intervention and not generated spontaneously in society. The problem often rests in the government per se. Let me put it this way: When everyone is swimming in the vast sea of society, all people are equal and compete freely. However, if the government also gets into the water, or when it interferes excessively in the swimming activities, a great many injustices may arise. Hence the Common Law idea is that under such circumstances, the government only needs to stay ashore and supervise, and if someone is physically exhausted and needs help, the government can come forward at this time to provide succor. Or if someone relies on his or her superior strength and techniques and tries to lord it over a region and set up a monopoly, giving rise to injustices, the government which is ashore and responsible for supervision should intervene and oppose the monopolies or unequal dealings. Such is the role the government should play under the circumstances of a market economy.

This would seem to be quite loose and relaxed way of governance. However once one violates a law and a judge also confirms that the country's legislation is "lawful," the penalty is very stern. For instance, under the common law, a violation of the law is a crime, and any violation of the law, big or small, must be tried in court, and all must be dealt with by the judge. China regards violations of the law and the commission of crimes as two different concepts. For instance, theft, embezzlement, and taking bribes are not seen as committing crimes if the amounts involved are minor. These need not go through a judge and may be given administrative penalties, or not penalized. Under the Common Law, however, the pilfering, embezzlement, or theft of even a cent or penny is a crime and must be prosecuted and handled by a judge. In terms of their nature, the embezzlement of one cent or penny and the embezzlement of a hundred million are the same. That is why there have been cases in Hong Kong where thefts of five HK dollars were punished as crimes. Is lawbreaking regarded as a crime only when it reaches a certain extent? That, in the Common Law view, is being excessively loose and relaxed.

As so it would appear that in countries or regions where the Common Law is practiced, the most "powerful" are not the popularly elected government officials or members of parliament but the court judges. And that is indeed the case. This mode of social governance is centered on the judiciary, and hews to the "judiciary supremacy theorem." Judges are the core of the system. Judges may repeal what is called the government's legislation, and judges may "formulate" truly authoritative "laws" by means of adjudication.[4] This way of social governance might seem strange; letting a group of judges who have no basis in public opinion govern society would seem undemocratic. This in fact is a form of elitist governance similar to Aristotle's "Master of Philosophy" mode of governance. In other words, selecting some elders, wise men, and persons in society who truly understand "law" (not "the laws")—instead of popularly elected officials and parliament members who are dominated by public opinion and often impulsive—to adjudge right and wrong and make final decisions on important matters and major constitutional issues.

Under these circumstances, what sort of judges one chooses takes on considerable importance since judges are embodiments of law and the highest and the ultimately authoritative arbiters of all disputes in society. Judges should be the elite of mankind; they should be deities who are incapable of ever committing any errors, and the people truly cannot accept that a judge can make any mistakes. I have remarked two very amusing instances of "deification." Under rule by man, people regard the highest administrative official as a "deity" and are filled with curiosity about everything that has to do with him (or her). Yet under rule of law, people idolize judges as "deities." The judges also think of themselves as deities

---

[4]Although Britain practices the Common Law, due to the fact that Britain pursues "parliamentary sovereignty," the Parliament is the highest authority and judge can only faithfully execute the Parliament's position. However, changes have already occurred in this situation following Britain's entry into the European Union, and Parliamentary supremacy has been shaken.

and keep themselves shut apart as though they belong to a different world. I have personally experienced such a situation. Arriving at a luncheon, a Hong Kong judge noticed that journalists were present and asked me to "clear the premises." Veteran journalists were requested to leave, and only then did he seat february himself. I asked why, and he said it would unbecoming to let "commoners" watch how a grand justice eats his food. That would be too detrimental to his image. So it was not surprising that the judge was unwilling to grant interviews. Once, a reporter happened to come across Chief Justice Andrew Li spending a weekend holiday at an open-air training camp playing basketball with some middle school students, and the Chief Justice was grinning broadly. Greatly intrigued, the reporter at once spread the news, as it was a rarity to catch a grand justice with "an expression of youthful exuberance." (*The Hong Kong Ming Pao*, January 19, 2001) That a judge playing with a ball could actually be newsworthy showed the veneration felt for judges by the general public.

Such stringent demands are put to judges because the matters society entrusts to the judges are too manifold and too weighty. The people's lives, homes, and possessions—everything rests in the hands of the judges, who could even determine the destinies of the state and society. Hence, the conditions for choosing judges not only include expertise in law but also comprehension of fundamental rights. As well as being fair and impartial, they are required to be moral elites, wise men, and seniors; they are probably the modern-day versions of the elders who took charge of all important clan affairs in the early days of humanity! Judges should be seniors, whereas administrative officials and parliament members may be a bit younger.[5] In fact, by organically combining popularly elected government officials and popularly elected parliaments with judicial organs independently operated by social elites, one can achieve a setup that is ruled by law, that is scientific and rational, and that is probably a relatively ideal mode of governance.

Implementation of the Common Law (Case Law) not only requires that judges be of high quality, the quality of the populace must also universally reach a certain elevation. That is because many social rules and regulations must be formed spontaneously among the people and the judges must respect the people's customs and practices. If the people are of a generally low level of education and of poor quality, turmoil could reign in society, making it impossible to exercise any sort legal self-governance.

I am not suggesting that China should adopt the Common Law system lock, stock, and barrel. That is not possible. However, in-depth exploration into the Common Law's governance philosophy will be of benefit to our understanding of how to correctly handle Central/SAR relations and how to correctly handle relations between the government and society under the conditions of developing a market economy, and provide inspiration for China's current rule-of-law reform and even

---

[5]U.S. President Jeb Bush's nomination of Clarence Thomas, an Afro-American lawyer only 43 years of age, as U.S. Supreme Court Justice in 1991 was met with sharp criticism in American society. In addition to other objections, the critics stated that he was too young and inexperienced to assume such an important position.

the reform of its political system. I feel if it were possible to develop a set to Case Laws with Chinese characteristics, this would definitely not be a bad thing for improving and perfecting China's rule of law. A clear-cut advantage of the Common Law system characterized chiefly by Case Laws is that due to its principle of going by precedents, it will obviate the repetitive incidence of similar cases and prevent different courts of law from passing different judgments on the same kind of cases. Here in China, we often see cases occurring time and again. For instance, a court will adjudge that a certain fine levied by the government is illegal and Citizen A should be reimbursed, whereupon the government department concerned implements the verdict and gives Citizen A back his money. However, because the court's verdict lacks the force of a precedent and the "regulation" whereby the government levied the fine is still effective, the government will fine Citizen B when he finds himself in the same situation. Ergo, similar lawsuits may occur over and over again in court and different judges may pass entirely different judgments on the same cases. This is certainly not a rule-of-law situation. Hence, I suggest that when conditions are ripe we ought to develop China's own Case Laws.

C. **More on China's State Structure**

If asked what kind of a state structure China has, you might unhesitatingly reply "unitary." If you are asked why this is so, you would certainly say China's Constitution provides it. However, if you leaf through the pages the Constitution, you will be surprised to find that there are no provisions in the Chinese Constitution saying that "China implements the unitary system," and even the term "unitary" cannot be found. The "Report on the Revised Draft of Constitution of the People's Republic of China" delivered by Constitution Revision Committee Vice-Chairman Peng Zhen on November 26, 1982, too, does not clearly stipulate what sort of state structure China has. Hence, one could say that the text of China's Constitution per se does not explicitly state what kind of state structure China implements. People have long said that China is a state with a unitary system. Constitution textbooks in China argue repeatedly and at great length on why China implements the unitary system and the system's various advantages, and arbitrarily insist that Marxism had always been inclined toward implementing the unitary system as soon as possible where conditions permit. These statements are in fact inaccurate. Not to mention that many socialist countries implement federalism, and even the Soviet Union practices a complex system of super-federalism, the most important fact is that the Chinese Constitution itself does not explicitly stipulate what kind of state structure China is to implement.

China's constitutional scholars have long been quoting the sentence in the Constitution "The People's Republic of China is a united multi-ethnic state founded in common by all ethnicities in the country" to serve as the constitutional basis for China's implementation of the unitary system. Actually, this sentence does not suffice to denote China's state structure; it merely explains China's ethnic circumstances. The important thing is that any state in the sense of being an integrated whole (including federalist states) is a united state, and many states are multiethnic. The United States and Russia are also united countries and are extremely multiethnic. They have far more ethnic groups than China and their circumstances are far more complex than China's, yet can we say that that they are "united countries" because they implement a federal system? It is obvious that they are not merely united countries; they are very united countries, and they by no means go soft on acts which may split the country. Proof of this is that the United States did not scruple at fighting a civil war to uphold the country's unity and that Russia deployed vast numbers of troops to crack down on Chechen separatism. We, on the other hand, have consistently equated "national unity" with the unitary system—which is like saying that a country must go for the unitary system if it wishes to be united, and that it is not united if it implements federalism. This is obviously untenable. This may perhaps be a correct proposition where China is concerned, i.e., that federalism, if implemented in China, may result in splits. However, we cannot universalize this proposition and maintain that the same applied to all countries; that for all countries, the unitary system is better than the federalist system. That is not true.

Thus, the provision in the Chinese Constitution that China is a "united multi-ethnic state" does not suffice to explain the state structure which China implements. And, strictly speaking, the Constitution does not specify China's state structure. That is not an oversight on the part of those who wrote the Constitution. Of those who participated in the drafting of China's Constitution in 1982, many were well-known constitutionalists who knew heft and importance of state structures. I surmise that the Constitution does not make clear-cut provisions about such an important issue primarily because the constitutionalists intended to leave sufficient leeway for future development and give China's state structure a certain amount of flexibility. For example, the establishment of Special Administrative Regions as specified in Article 31 of the Constitution in reality gives the National People's Congress unlimited power to create new systems. The Constitution merely specifies that the state may set up Special Administrative Regions when doing so is necessary. As for what kind of systems is to be implemented in the SARs, free rein is given to the National People's Congress and no restrictions are specified. Article 62 of the Constitution stipulates the various powers vested in the National People's Congress, the last one of which specifies that the NPC exercises "other duties and functions that should be exercised by the highest organ of state power." That is a very broad and sweeping authorization. The NPC can use this provision of the Constitution to make extensive innovations in terms of the state structure.

In the main body of this book, I have also mentioned that I do not doubt that China is effectuating a genuine unitary state structure. However, its constitutional basis is not the provision in the Constitution's preface regarding "a united multi-national state." Instead, one should find an indirect basis via the specific divisions in the Constitution between the functions and duties of the central state organs and local state organs, as I have already recounted earlier to some extent. I will bring up the matter again here. My intention is to say that despite China's implementing the unitary system, the Constitution per se has in fact reserved space for ample development of reforms of the state structure. For the sake of developing a socialist market economy, for the sake of adapting to the new situations in central/local relations China will face after joining the World Trade Organization, and especially for the sake of bringing about the country's ultimate reunification and of correctly handling Central/SAR relations, we must not stand still, refuse to make progress, and hold fast to established practices but should seek guidance from the "one country, two systems" policy, seek truth from facts, and boldly innovate. If we courageously expound and give thought to all means and methods beneficial to resolving the issues of unification China currently faces, we are bound to ultimately find or "invent" ways and means of solving such issues suited to China's national conditions.

Finally, I would like to address a fashionable topic—the relations between the WTO and "one country" and "two systems." Prior to China's joining the WTO, investors in Hong Kong, Macao, and Taiwan received, in Chinese mainland, certain facets of preferential treatment unavailable to foreigners. This was quite normal because Hong Kong, Macao, Taiwan, and Chinese mainland are "one country," and foreigners fully understood this. And so, Hong Kong, Macao, and Taiwan compatriots were recipients of "one country" benefits, which in turn increased the country's cohesiveness and were helpful internationally to forming a sense of "one China." Now that China has joined the WTO, Hong Kong, Macao, and Taiwan investors have to accept treatment as foreigners and we are regarding our own flesh-and-blood compatriots as aliens. This only increases centrifugal forces and, internationally, may strengthen the impression of China's non-unity. That runs counter to China's Constitution and law. For instance, Chinese mainland insists that Chinese residents in Hong Kong, Macao, and Taiwan are legally Chinese citizens. Then why is it that they—also Chinese citizens—may not take part in China's judicial examinations or practice the trade on the mainland? In terms of the qualifications for judicial examinations, we certainly do not place any restrictions on Chinese citizens, do we?[6] I am confident that opening the legal services market to Hong Kong, Macao, and Taiwan lawyers will gain understanding internationally. China is one country but counts four separate customs territories and qualifies as four independent WTO members, whereas the 15 independent EU states qualify as a single WTO member! Ironic, is it not? And so I say here and now that we must open up internally before opening up to the outside. If we must indeed first open up to the "outside," then we should first find appropriate ways and means of opening up to Hong Kong, Macao, and Taiwan so they may sense that their true interests rest in "one China," that "one China" is the real McCoy and not just an empty political slogan. As Premier Zhu Rongji once said, this is would be "a deal among one's own people." I sincerely hope we Chinese will make use of our wisdom to handle the issues of reunifying the country and the WTO matter, and in doing so achieve a win-win or multi-win situation.

---

[6]According to the provisions in Article 13 of the Measures for the Implementation of State Judicial Examinations (Trial) jointly issued by the Supreme People's Court and the Supreme People's Procuratorate on October 31, 2001, enrollees for the state judicial examinations should possess the following qualifications: 1) Is a citizen of the People's Republic of China, 2) Upholds the Constitution of the People's Republic of China and has the right to vote and be elected, 3) has full civil capacity, 4) complies with the academic and professional qualifications stipulated by the Law on Judges, Law on Prosecutors, and Law on Lawyers, and 5) is of good character.

Bibliography

Revista Jurídica de Macau《澳门法律学刊》, 第1–4期.

An Zuozhang: *Compendium of Chinese History*, Jinan: Shangdong Education Press, 1986.

Andrew Byrnes, Johannes Chan: *Public Law and Human Rights, a Hong Kong Sourcebook*. Hong Kong: Butterworths Asia, 1993.

Cai Dingjian: *The National People's Congress System*, Beijing: Law Press, 1998.

Cao Peilin: *Foreign Political System*, Beijing: Higher Education Press, 1992.

Chen Hongyi: *Hong Kong's Legal System and Basic Law*, Hong Kong: Wide Angle Press, 1986.

Chen Hongyi: *A Preliminary Study of Hong Kong's Transition Period*, Seminar of the Open College of Further Education of Hong Kong, Dec. 1995.

Chen Huifen: *The Record Event of China-UK Hong Kong*, 1994.

Chen Jialing: *Handbook of Local Government*, Wuhan: Wuhan University of Technology Press, 1989.

Chen Liankai: *China, Chinese Ancient Tribes in the East, Foreigners, Birthplace of China, Chinese People*. "The Multi-unity of Chinese Nation" edited by Fei Xiaotong, Beijing: Minzu University of China Press, 1989.

Chen Yunsheng: *Brief Theory of Regional Ethnic Autonomy*, Shenyang: Liaoning University Publishing House, 1985.

Chen Guangzhong: *Collection of Cross-strait Legal Studies*, Beijing: Preparation Office of Cross-strait Legal Academic Seminar, 1993.

Chen Hongyi, Chen Wenmin: *Human Rights and the Rule of Law—the Challenge of Hong Kong's Transition*, Hong Kong: Guangjiao Mirror Press Co. LTD, 1987.

Chen Hongyi: *The Concept of "One Country, Two Systems" and Its Application in Hong Kong, Macao and Taiwan*, Seminar of the Faculty of Law of the University of Hong Kong and Macao Society of Public and Comparative Law, Dec. 1994.

Chen Hongyi: *View the 1997 Transition on Hong Kong-Taiwan from the Legal Point*, Hwa Kang Law Review, Issue 23 (Offprint), Oct. 1995.

Chen Hongyi: *Law and Politics of Hong Kong*, Hong Kong: Wide Angle Press, 1990.

Cheng Chaoze: *Out of the Valley of China*, Shenzhen: Haitian Press, 1995.

Cheng Handa: *History of the British political system*, Beijing: China Social Sciences Press, 1995.

Cheng Linsheng: *Deng Xiaoping's Thought of One Country*, Two Systems, Shenyang: Liaoning People's Publishing House, 1992.

Clement Shum: *General Principles of Hong Kong Law*. Hong Kong: Longman Hong Kong, 1994.

David Clark, Gerard Mcloy: *Hong Kong Administrative Law (Second Edition)* Butterworths Asia, 1993.

© Foreign Language Teaching and Research Publishing Co., Ltd and Springer Nature
Singapore Pte Ltd. 2019
Z. Wang, *Relationship Between the Chinese Central Authorities and Regional
Governments of Hong Kong and Macao: A Legal Perspective*, China Academic
Library, https://doi.org/10.1007/978-981-13-2322-5

Deng Kaisong, Huang Qichen: *Collection of Macao History (1553-1986)*, Guangzhou: Guangdong People's Publishing House, 1991.

Deng Kaisong: *Macao History: 1840-1949*, Macao: Macao Historical Society, 1983.

Deng Xiaoping: *Deng Xiaoping on the Construction of Democracy and Legal System*, Beijing: Law Press, 1994.

Deng Xiaoping: *Deng Xiaoping on Hong Kong*: Joint Publishing (H.K.), 1993.

Deng Xiaoping: *Deng Xiaoping on the Reunification of the Motherland*, Beijing: Unity Press, 1995.

Deng Xiaoping: *Selections from Deng Xiaoping*, Beijing: People's Publishing House, 1993.

Deutsch, K. The Nerves of Government: *Models of Political Communication and Control*. New York: Free Press, 1966.

Diao Tianding: *Outline of Local National Institutions in China*, Beijing: Law Press, 1989.

Diao Tianding: *Research of Local National Institutions in China*, Beijing: Qunzhong Press, 1985.

Ding Zhongzhu: *On the Scientization of National Administration*, Beijing: Qunzhong Press, 1987.

District Court Law Reports. Hong Kong Government.

Dong Chengmei, Wang Zhenmin: *The Truth and Falsehood of Democracy*, Chengdu: Southwestern University of Finance and Economics Press, 1994.

Dong Likun: *The Theory and Practice of Hong Kong Law*, Beijing: Law Press, 1990.

Elazer, Daniel: "The Shaping of Intergovernmental Relations in the Twentieth Century," *The ANNALS of the American Academy of Political and Social Science, Vol 359 (May)*.

Evans, Dafydd Meurig Emrys: *Common Law in a Chinese Setting: the Kernel of the Nut? An Inaugural Lecture delivered on Oct. 1970*. Hong Kong: Publication Centre of Asian Studies, Hong Kong University, 1971.

Fang Liwen: *Introduction to the Law on Regional Ethnic Autonomy*, Urumqi: Xinjing People's Press, 1986.

Feng Tejun: *Political Economy and International Relations in the Contemporary World (Second Edition)*, Beijing: China Renmin University Press, 1993.

G. R. Sayer: *Hong Kong 1862–1919, Years of Discretion (Second Impression)*. Hong Kong: Hong Kong University Press, 1985.

G.B. Endacott: *Government and People in Hong Kong 1841–1962, a Constitutional History*. Hong Kong: Hong Kong University Press, 1964.

Ge Jianxiong: *Unity and Division*, Beijing: Joint Publishing, 1992.

Geoffrey Parker, Li Yiming (Translate): *Western Geopolitical Thoughts of the Twentieth Century*, Beijing: Chinese People's Liberation Army Publishing House, 1992.

George Leonard Staunton, Ye Duyi (Translate): *An Authentic Account of an Embassy from the King of Great Britain to the Emperor of China*, Hong Kong: Joint Publishing (H.K.), 1994.

Guan Ou: *Summary of Local Autonomy*, Taiwan: San Min Book Press, 1983.

H. L. A. Hart, Zhang Wenxian etc. (Translate): *The Concept of Law*, Beijing: Encyclopedia of China Publishing House, 1996.

Hanf, K. and Scharpf, F.: *Inter-organizational Policy Making: Limits to Co-ordination and Central Control*. Thousand Oaks: Sage Publications, 1980.

Hans Kelsen, Shen Zonglin (Translate): *The General Theory of Law and State*, Beijing: Encyclopedia of China Publishing House, 1996.

Harold Traver, Jon Vagg: *Crime and Justice in Hong Kong*. Hong Kong: Oxford University Press, 1991.

Hong Chenghua, etc.: *Chronicle of the Evolution of the Political System of the People's Republic of China (1949–1978)*, Beijing: Spring and Autumn Publishing House, 1987.

Hong Kong Affairs Society: *Hong Kong's Political and Legal System During the Transition Period*, Hong Kong: People Semimonthly Published, 1984.

Hong Kong Government: *Legal System in Hong Kong*. Hong Kong: The Government Printer, 1991.

Hong Kong Government Gazette. Hong Kong Government.

Hong Kong Hansard (Official Report of LegCo. Proceedings). Hong Kong Government.

Hong Kong Journal (1980–1994). Hong Kong Journal Ltd.

Hong Kong Law Reports. Hong kong Government.

Hong Kong People's Association: *Introduction of Hong Kong Law*, Hong Kong: The Commercial Press, 1987.

Hsu, Berry Fong-chung: *The Common Law in Chinese Context*. Hong Kong: Hong Kong University Press, 1992.

Hu Guoheng: *The Road to Prosperity*, Hong Kong: Hong Kong Economic Society, 1993.

Huang Jin, Huang Feng: *Interregional Judicial Assistance Study*, Beijing: China University of Political Science and Law Press, 1993.

Huang Jin: *Research of Interregional Conflict Law*, Shanghai: Xuelin Press, 1991.

Huang Jin: *Theory and Practice of Interregional Judicial Assistance*, Wuhan: Wuhan University Press, 1994.

Huang Renyu: *A Way for Modern China*, Hong Kong: China Hwa Book Co., 1995.

Huang Tao: *One Country, Two System (No. 5)*, Beijing: China Literature and History Publishing House, 1988.

Huang Wenfang: *The Course and Practice of China's Decision to Restore Its Sovereignty over Hong Kong*. Hong Kong: Hong Kong Baptist University, 1997.

Huang Yi: *Hong Kong Issue and One Country, Two Systems*, Beijing: Vastplain Publishing House, 1990.

Ian Scott: *Political Change and the Crisis of Legitimacy in Hong Kong*. Hong Kong: Oxford University Press, 1989.

IAOC Law: *Federalism and decentralization: constitutional problems of territorial decentralization in federal and centralized states*. Boulder: Westview Press, 1987.

Jiang Bikun: *History of China's Modern Constitutional Constitution*, Beijing: Law Press, 1988.

Jiang Jiwu: *Local Autonomy and Elections*, Taiwan: Big China Books, 1984.

Johannes Chan, H L Fu and Yash Ghai ed: *Hong Kong's Constitutional Debate-Conflict over Interpretation*. Hong Kong: Hong Kong University, 2000.

K.C. Wheare: *Federal Government*, Hong Kong: The Commercial Press (Hong Kong) Limited, 1991.

Lan Tian: *Research on Legal Issues of "One country, Two systems" (General Volume)*, Beijing: Law Press, 1997.

Lau Siu-kai, Kuan Hsin-chi: T*he Ethos of the Hong Kong Chinese*. Hong Kong: The Chinese University Press, 1988.

Laws of Hong Kong. Hong Kong Government.

Li Changdao, Gong Xiaohang: *Basic Law Perspective*, Hong Kong: China Hwa Book (Hong Kong) Co., 1990.

Li Da: *US-Taiwan Relations and China's Unity*, Hong Kong: Wide Angle Press, 1987.

Li Da: *"One Country, Two Systems""and Taiwan*, Hong Kong: Wide Angle Press, 1987.

Li Daokui: *The American Government and American Politics*. Beijing: China Social Sciences Press, 1990.

Li Jiaquan, Guo Xiangzhi: *Review and Prospect on Cross-strait Relations*, Beijing: Current Affairs Press, 1989.

Li Ming: *Hong Kong's Politics and Society in Flux*, Hong Kong: China Hwa Book Co., 1987.

Li Yongchun, Luo Jian: *The Theory and Practice of Political System Reform Since the Third Plenary Session of the Eleventh Central Committee*, Beijing: Spring and Autumn Publishing House, 1987.

Li Zepei: *The Law of Hong Kong*. Beijing: Law Press, 1992.

Li Zong'e: *Hong Kong Daily Law (Six Copies)*, Hong Kong: The Commercial Press (Hong Kong), 1995.

Liang Fulin: *The New Look of China-Hong Kong Relationships after 1997*, Hong Kong: Wide Angle Press, 1995.

Liang Fulin: *Detect Hong Kong before and after Transition*, Hong Kong: Wide Angle Press, 1994.

Linda Pomerantz-Zhang: *Wu Tingfang (1842–1922), Reform and Modernization in Modern Chinese History*. Hong Kong: Hong Kong University Press, 1992.

Liu Zhaode: *Hong Kong Politics in Transition*, Hong Kong: Wide Angle Press, 1993.

Lu Tianhong, He Huahui: *Local Government and People's Representatives*, Beijing: Qunzhong Press, 1985.

Luo Haocai, Wu Xieying: *The Constitution and Political System of a Capitalist Country*, Beijing: Peking University Press, 1983.

Macao Law Journal, Issues 1–4.

Mao Zedong: *Ten Major Relationships, Selected Works of Mao Zedong*, Beijing: Peop'e's Publishing House, 1956.

Masaji Chiba: *Asian Indigenous Law: in Interaction with Received Law*. London: KP1, 1986.

Matsumura Kio, Sun Xin (Translate): *Local Self-government*, Beijing: The Economic Daily Press, 1989.

Mi Jian: *Legislations of Macao*, Macao: Macao Foundation, 1994.

Michael C Davis: *Constitutional Confrontation in Hong Kong*. Hong Kong: The Macmillan Press Ltd., 1989.

Ming K. Chan, David J. Clark: "The Hong Kong Basic Law: Blueprint for "Stability and Prosperity" under Chinese Sovereignty?" *The China Journal (Volume 28)*, 1991.

Norman Miners: *The Government and Politics of Hong Kong*. Hong Kong: Oxford University Press, 1991.

Norton-Kyshe, James William: *The History and the Laws and Courts of Kong Kong from the Earlies Period to 1898*. Vetch and Lee, 1971.

One Country Two Systems Research Institute: *Hong Kong in Transition 1992*, Hong Kong: Joint Publishing (H.K.), 1993.

Penlington, Valerie Ann: *Law In Hong Kong: An Introduction*. Hong Kong: Federal Publications Ltd., 1993.

People's Daily Overseas Edition: *Basic Law—A Creative Masterpiece*, Beijing: People's Daily Press, 1991.

Peter Duff & etc: *Juries: a Hong Kong Perspective*. Hong Kong: Hong Kong University Press, 1992.

Peter Wesley-Smith ed: *Hong Kong's Basic Law: Problems and Prospects*. Hong Kong: Hong Kong University, Faculty of Law, 1990.

Peter Wesley-Smith ed: *Hong Kong's Transition: Problems and Prospects*, Hong Kong University Faculty of Law, 1993.

Peter Wesley-Smith, Albert H Y Chen: *The Basic Law and Hong Kong's Future*. Hong Kong: Butterworths, 1988.

Peter Wesley-Smith: *An Introduction to the Hong Kong Legal System*. Hong Kong: Oxford University Press, 1993.

Peter Wesley-Smith: *Constitutional & Administrative Law in Hong Kong*. Hong Kong: China & Hong Kong Studies Ltd., 1988.

Peter Wesley-Smith: *The Sources of Hong Kong Law*. Hong Kong: Hong Kong University Press, 1994.

Pu Xingzu: *Contemporary Chinese Political System*, Shanghai: Shanghai People's Publishing House, 1990.

Qian Duansheng: *Selected Academic Works of Qian Duansheng*, Beijing: Beijing Normal University Publishing Group, 1991.

Qian Mu: *Gains and Losses in Dynastic China*, Taipei: Dongda Book, 1990.

Qian Qizhi: *A New Theory of Institutional Reform*, Beijing: Labor and Personnel Publishing House, 1988.

Raymond Wacks: *China, Hong Kong and 1997, Essays in Legal History*. Hong Kong: Hong Kong University Press, 1993.

Raymond Wacks: *Civil Liberties in Hong Kong*. Hong Kong: Oxford University Press, 1988.

Raymond Wacks: *The Future of the Law in Hong Kong*. Hong Kong: Oxford University Press, 1989.

Raymond Wacks: *The Law in Hong Kong 1969–1989*. Hong Kong: Oxford University Press, 1989.

Rholdes, R. A. W.: *Control and Power in Central-Local Government Relations*. Westmead: Gower, 1982.

Rong Chuan: *Basic Law—The Future of Hong Kong* (Papers), Hong Kong: Hong Kong Jinling Book Publishing Co., 1986.

Samuel P. Huntington, Wang Guanhua (Translate): *Political Order in Changing Societies*, Beijing: Joint Publishing, 1989.

Sang Yucheng, Zhou Luogeng: *A Sign of Reform Moving Forward—The Establishment of a Political System Commensurate with Economic Development*, Shanghai: Shanghai People's Publishing House, 1994.

Shen Baoxiang: *Special Administrative Regions and the Path of Socialism with Chinese Characteristics*, Beijing: Party School of the Central Committe of CPC Publishing House, 1993.

Shen Lepin: *Hong Kong's Future and the Basic Law*, Hong Kong Publishing Group LTD, 1994.

Sheng Xinmin: *Comparison of Legal Systems Across the Taiwan Straits—Constitution*, Xiamen: Xiamen University Press, 1993.

Shi Jun'an, Rong Chuan: *Basic Law* (Papers), Hong Kong: Hong Kong Jinling Book Publishing Co., 1984.

Shi Liang: *Discourse on Hong Kong's Politics*, Hong Kong: Joint Publishing (H.K.), 1988.

Shi Weimin: *Unification*, Beijing: Joint Publishing, 1994.

Sun Shu: *Taiwan Political System*, Nanjing: Nanjing University Press, 1993.

Ta Shi: *The 700-year History of Swiss Confederation*, Beijing: China International Broadcasting Press, 1990.

Tan Jian, Yang Baikui: *Research on the Reform of Government Management System*, Beijing: Spring and Autumn Publishing House, 1987.

The Central Institute of Socialism: *One Country, Two Systems—Selected and Compiled Theoretical and Practical Literature*, Beijing: Bibliography Press, 1987.

The Compilation Group of *Research on Local Authority: Study of Local Government*, Beijing: Qunzhong Press, 1986.

The editorial department of the *Outlook Weekly* Overseas Edition: *"One Country, Two Systems" and the Reunification of the Motherland*, Beijing: Xinhua Publishing House, 1988.

The teaching and research section of constitution & the reference room in the Department of Law, Peking University: *Selected Constitutional Documents* (Vol. 1–5), Beijing: Peking University Press, 1982.

Valerie A.Penlington, Li Jiming (Translate): *Hong Kong's Legal, Constitutional and Judicial Systems*, Hong Kong: The Commercial Press (Hong Kong) Co., 1992.

Wan Wenguo: *The Theory and Practice of Local People's Congresses*, Wuhan: Wuhan Press, 1990.

Wang Zhonghan: *History of Chinese Nation*, Beijing: China Social Sciences Press, 1994.

Wang Shuwen: *Decade of Democratic Constitutionalism*, Beijing: Red Flag Press, 1993.

Wang Shuwen: *A Guide to the Basic Law of the Hong Kong Special Administrative Region*, Beijing: CPC Central Committee Party School Press, 1990.

Wang Tieya: *International Law*, Beijing: Law Press, 1981.

Wang Wenxiang: *Manuals of Hong Kong and Macao*, Beijing: China Prospect Publishing House, 1991.

Wang Xiliang: *The History of the People's Republic of China*, Xi'an: Shaanxi Normal University Publishing House, 1990.

Wang Xing: *On the Construction of Local State Power Organs*, Guangxi: Guangxi Normal University Press, 1990.

Wei Liqun: *Reasonable Division of Central and Local Economic Management Authority*, Beijing: Economic Work Newsletter, Issue 13, 1994.

Wenwei Publish: *The Emergence of the Basic Law*, Hong Kong: Wenwei Publishing, 1990.

William McGurn: *Basic Law, Basic Questions*. Hong Kong: Review Publishing Co. Ltd., 1988.

World Affairs Press: *The Reunification and Rise of Germany*, Beijing: World Affairs Press, 1992.

Wright, Deil: *Understanding Intergovernmental Relations*. Mass: Duxbury Press, 1978.

Wu Jialin: *Constitutional Law*, Beijing: Qunzhong Press, 1983.

Xia Dongyuan: *Self-Strengthening Movement History*, Shanghai: East China Normal University Press, 1992.

Xiao Weiyun: *Hong Kong's Basic Legal System and the Great Practice of "One Country, Two Systems,"* Shenzhen: Haitian Press, 1993.

Xiao Weiyun: *One Country, Two Systems and the Basic Law of the Macao Special Administrative Region*, Beijing: Peking University Press, 1993.

Xiao Weiyun: *"One Country, Two Systems" and Hong Kong's Basic Legal System*, Beijing: Peking University Press, 1990.

Xin Xiangyang: *Princes of the Big States*, Beijing: China social Sciences Publishing House, 1995.

Xin Xiangyang, etc.: The Differences Between the North and the South—*Will China Break Up*, Beijing: China Social Press, 1995.

Xin Xiangyang, Ni Jianzhong, etc.: On Balance—*China in Balance*, Beijing: China Society Press, 1995.

Xu Chongde: *A Course on the Basic Laws of Hong Kong and Macao*, Beijing: China Renmin University Press, 1994.

Xu Chongde: *The Constitution and Democratic Governance*. Beijing: China Procuratorate Press, 1993.

Xu Chongde: *The Chinese Constitution*, Beijing: China Renmin University Press, 1989.

Xu Kesi: *Hong Kong: Unique Political Structure*, Beijing: China Renmin University Press, 1994.

Yan Jianguo, Liang Yuxia: *A Comprehensive Legal Counsel of the Latest Foreign Involving Taiwan, Hong Kong and Macao*, Beijing: Communication University of China Press, 1992.

Yang Jianxin: *"One Country, Two Systems" and the Future of Taiwan*. Beijing: Sino-culture Press, 1989.

Yang Jinghui, Li Xiangqin: *Comparison of the Basic Laws of Hong Kong and Macao*, Beijing: Peking University Press, 1997.

Yang Qi: *Introduction to Hong Kong*, Hong Kong: Joint Publishing (H.K.), 1993.

Yang Yunzhong: *Macao and Macao's Basic Law*. Macao: Macao Foundation, 1994.

Yang Yunzhong: *Macao and Modern Economic Growth*. Macao: Macao Economic Association, 1992.

Yao Donghua, Ouyang Boquan: *English and Chinese Legal Vocabulary*, Hong Kong: The Commercial Press (Hong Kong), 1992.

Yash Ghai: *Hong Kong's Constitutional Order—The Resumption of Chinese Sovereignty and the Basic Law, Second Edition*. Hong Kong: Hong Kong University Press, 1999.

Yu Shengwu, Liu Cunkuan: *Hong Kong in the 19th Century*, Beijing: Zhonghua Book Company, 1994.

Yue Linzhang: *Contemporary Western Political Trends*, Xi'an: Shaanxi People's Education Press, 1988.

Zhang Erju: *Theory and Practice of Regional Ethnic Autonomy in China*, Beijing: China Social Sciences Press, 1988.

Zhang Guofu: *A Brief History of the Legal System of the Republic of China*, Beijing: Peking University Press, 1986.

Zhang Qixiong: *Negotiations on Jurisdiction over Mongolian Sovereignty 1911–1916*, Institute of Modern History, Academia Sinica, 1995.

Zhang Tianlun: *The Evolution of Chinese Institutions*, Beijing: China Economic Publishing House, 1988.

Zhang Wenxian: *Politics and Rule of Law—Theoretical Consideration of China's Political System Reform and Legal System Construction*, Jilin: Jilin University Press, 1994.

Zhang Ye: *Introduction and Comparison of Capitalist Countries' Political System*, Beijing: Tourism Education Press, 1989.

Zhang Zengqiang: *Hong Kong's Rule of Law*, Guangzhou: Jinan University Press, 1993.

Zhao Baoxu: *An Introduction to Politics*, Beijing: Peking University Press, 1982.

Zheng Yongnian, Wu Guoguang: *On Central-Local Relations: an Axis Issue in China's Institutional Transformation*, Hong Kong: Oxford University Press, 1995.

Zhong Shiyuan: *Process of Hong Kong's Political Transition*, Hong Kong: The Chinese University Press, 2001.

Zhou Yizhi: Hong Kong and the *"One Country, Two System" Policy*, Beijing: China Social Sciences Press, 1988.

Zi Mu, etc.: *Conception of Democracy*, Beijing: Guangming Daily Press, 1989.

Zou Yongxian: *History of the State Theory*, Fuzhou: Fujian People's Publishing House, 1987.

Main Websites:

NPC news: http://zgrdxw.peopledaily.com.cn/

Ministry of Foreign Affairs of the People's Republic of China: http://www.fmprc.gov.cn/chn/index.html

The Supreme People's Court of the People's Republic of China: http://www.court.gov.cn/

The Supreme People's Procuratorate of the People's Republic of China: http://www.spp.gov.cn/

People's Daily website of laws and regulations: http://www.people.com.cn/zixun/flfgk/index.html

The Government of Hong Kong Special Administrative Region Beijing Office: http://www.info.gov.hk/bjo/

Hong Kong Judiciary: http://www.info.gov.hk/jud/

British Consulate-General Hong Kong: http://www.britishconsulate.org.hk/

Consulate General of the United States in Hong Kong and Macao: http://www.usconsulate.org.hk/

Us and Hong Kong: http://www.usconsulate.org.hk/ushk/

Macao Special Administrative Region Government: http://www.macau.gov.mo/

Us and Macau: http://www.usconsulate.org.hk/usmo/

Huaxia: http://www.huaxia369.com/

Basic Information about the United States: http://www.usinfo.state.gov/usa/infousa/

Bureau of International Information Program: http://usinfo.state.gov/regional/ea/mgck/homepage.htm

Index

A

Acting on one's free will, 384

Administrative regions, 4, 5, 7, 19, 31, 34, 39, 45, 47, 50, 52, 54, 62, 72, 74, 78, 81, 83, 86, 91, 96–99, 101–104, 106, 107, 110–114, 126–128, 136, 139, 164, 177, 181, 185, 186, 207, 219, 223, 224, 228, 244, 268, 331, 355

Alliance of workers and peasants, 2

"Alliance with Russia," "cooperation with the Communist Party," and "assistance to the workers and peasants", 71

American Civil War, 104

Anfu shisi, 35

Anwei shisi, 35

Articles of Confederation, 8

Autonomous localities, 12, 96, 186, 187

Autonomous prefectures, 102, 186, 202

Autonomous regions, 4, 45, 51, 52, 73, 95, 102, 105, 159, 160, 163, 164, 186, 200–202, 211, 215, 216, 219, 221–223, 229, 246, 253, 254, 275, 327, 333, 336–338, 346, 348, 349, 357, 375, 378, 383

B

Beiyang [Northern Warlords] Government, 40

"Bigger central and smaller local" administration, 107

Big government and small society, 399

Birthright order theory, 391

Bourgeois revolution, 40

Boxer wars, The, 37

British Commonwealth of Nations, 24

Bureaucratic systems, 25

Buzheng shisi (administrative secretariats), 35

C

Caifangshi, 31

Capitalist democracy, 1, 2

Case Laws, 280, 358

Central and local authorities, 3, 40–43, 48, 50, 53, 54, 107, 108, 133, 134, 137, 352

Centralization of power, 26

Centralized system, 11, 27, 41

Central government, 6, 9, 12, 15–20, 27, 29, 31, 34, 36, 40, 41, 44, 47, 50–52, 54, 57, 78, 83, 89, 92, 98, 102–107, 110–112, 114–119, 121, 124, 127, 132, 133, 135–140, 158–161, 163, 166, 167, 169, 171, 172, 178, 179, 182, 194, 196, 201, 204, 205, 217, 223, 225, 228, 229, 238, 241, 246, 250, 252–255, 260, 270, 275, 277, 284, 285, 291, 327, 333, 336–338, 343, 346, 349, 356, 357, 368, 375, 380, 382, 385, 386, 392

Central Military Commission, 106, 143, 169–171, 211, 219, 231, 238, 277, 326, 329, 338, 346

Central People's Government, 44, 45, 47, 51, 55, 56, 75, 105, 121–123, 126, 127, 143, 146, 147, 149, 157–159, 161, 162, 164, 165, 167, 169, 171, 172, 174, 182, 184, 185, 192, 194–196, 203, 205, 208, 211, 214–219, 221–226, 236–238, 240–243, 270, 279, 284, 329, 361, 367, 375

Central Plains, 26, 33, 38, 39, 385

Central/SAR relations, 112–114, 119, 120, 123–128, 130, 132, 139, 154–157, 211, 221, 225, 231, 234, 236, 238, 240, 241,

© Foreign Language Teaching and Research Publishing Co., Ltd and Springer Nature Singapore Pte Ltd. 2019
Z. Wang, *Relationship Between the Chinese Central Authorities and Regional Governments of Hong Kong and Macao: A Legal Perspective*, China Academic Library, https://doi.org/10.1007/978-981-13-2322-5

243–247, 257, 261, 272, 275, 279, 292, 297, 300, 319–321, 335, 352, 356, 357, 368, 382–384
Central Worker-Peasant Democratic Government of the Chinese Soviet Republic, The, 44
Chengxuan, 35
chengxuan (civil administrative) department, a tixingancha (judicial and prosecution) department, and a duzhihuishi (military command) division, The, 35
Chiang Kai-shek, 42, 43, 62, 65, 72
Chief Executive Election Ordinance, 162
China's Constitution in 1982, 403
Chinese Academy of Social Sciences, The, 213
Chinese Communist Party, 43, 44, 56, 74, 76, 94, 98, 200
Chinese Federalist Republic, 41
Chinese-foreign mutual protections, 37
Chinese Nationalist Party (Kuomintang), 41
Chinese World Empire, 386–388
Class domination, 5
Class oppression, 5
Closed-door policy, 193
Common Law system, 121, 155, 191, 278, 280, 282, 315, 320, 321, 346, 349, 350, 369, 374, 378
Common Program, The, 44, 75
Commonwealth of Independent States, 20
Confederal system, 7, 8, 12, 14, 15, 49
Confederal theorem, 73
Confucianism, 68
Congressional electoral districts, 9
Constitution, 1–4, 6, 8–13, 15, 16, 18, 19, 21, 40, 42, 43, 47, 49–54, 60, 68, 69, 72, 75, 81, 86, 89–101, 103–105, 107, 119, 120, 123, 134, 135, 137, 139, 143, 145, 146, 148, 151, 154, 155, 157, 159, 160, 163, 164, 166, 169, 173–175, 186, 187, 190, 197, 200, 201, 207, 212, 215, 219, 231, 232, 234, 236–238, 244, 246, 247, 258, 267, 273, 275, 277–283, 286, 287, 296, 297, 320, 321, 323, 324, 326–347, 349–357, 363, 367, 371, 372, 374–382, 389–391
Constitutional courts, 281, 321, 349, 350, 354, 373, 378, 382
Constitutionality examination, 328, 329, 332, 338, 339, 344, 347, 358, 360, 362, 363, 366, 368, 369, 374, 375, 378, 381–384
Constitutional law, 1, 3, 4, 12, 16, 19–21, 26, 27, 49, 50, 66, 83, 85, 86, 94, 108–110, 144, 154, 340, 350, 368, 370

Constitutional (public law) systems, 322
Constitutional Violations, 149
Constitution of the Republic of China, 43, 281
Continental Law systems, 192, 349, 350, 374
Convention of Beijing, The, 58
CPC Central Committee, 45, 47, 97, 143, 182, 191, 200, 205–207, 213, 214, 239, 241, 247, 253, 254
Criminal Jurisdiction, 299, 301, 303, 304
Cross-Strait relations, 86, 225, 227
Cultural Revolution, The, 48, 76, 116, 239
Customs General Administration, The, 212

D

Dachen (minister's office), 36
Dao, 30, 31, 61
Democratic centralism, 50
Democratic dictatorship, 2, 90
Democratic federalist state, 39
Democratic governance, 1, 154, 155
Democratic Progressive Party, The, 62, 112
Democratic system, 1, 2, 374
Democrat state, 11
Deng Xiaoping, 40, 48, 56, 65, 70, 73, 74, 78, 80–83, 85, 107, 109, 111, 112, 123–125, 127, 223
Derived powers, 6
Detailed rules of implementation, 283, 321
Directly administered municipalities, 4, 50–52, 102, 105, 107, 159, 186, 202, 211, 215, 216, 219, 221–223, 229
Divide-and-rule, 38
Divisions of power, 6, 52, 390
Dr. Sun Yat-sen, 40, 71
Dual leadership system, 51, 216, 217
Duhufu, 31, 32
Dutong (commander-in-chief's office), 36
Du zhi, 31

E

Eastern Jin period, 57
Eight-Power Allied Forces, 37
Electoral districts, 10, 203
Electoral system, 94
Elitist revolutions, 39
Emergence state, 162, 163, 165
Enfeoffment system, 27, 29
Equalism, 41, 43
Equity law, 365
Estatuto Orgânico de Macao, 166, 172
Ethnic minority autonomous regions, 4
Ethnic minority's local self-governance, 95
Exploitation classes, 5

Printed by Printforce, the Netherlands